The Spirit of Classical Canon Law

The Spirit of the Laws

Alan Watson, General Editor

The *Spirit of the Laws* series illuminates the nature of legal systems throughout the world. Titles in the series are concerned less with the rules of the law and more with the relationships of the laws in each system with religion and moral perspectives; the degree of complexity and abstraction; classifications; attitudes to possible sources of law; authority; and values enshrined in law. Topics covered in the series include Roman law, Chinese law, biblical law, Talmudic law, canon law, common law, Hindu law, customary law, Japanese law, and international law.

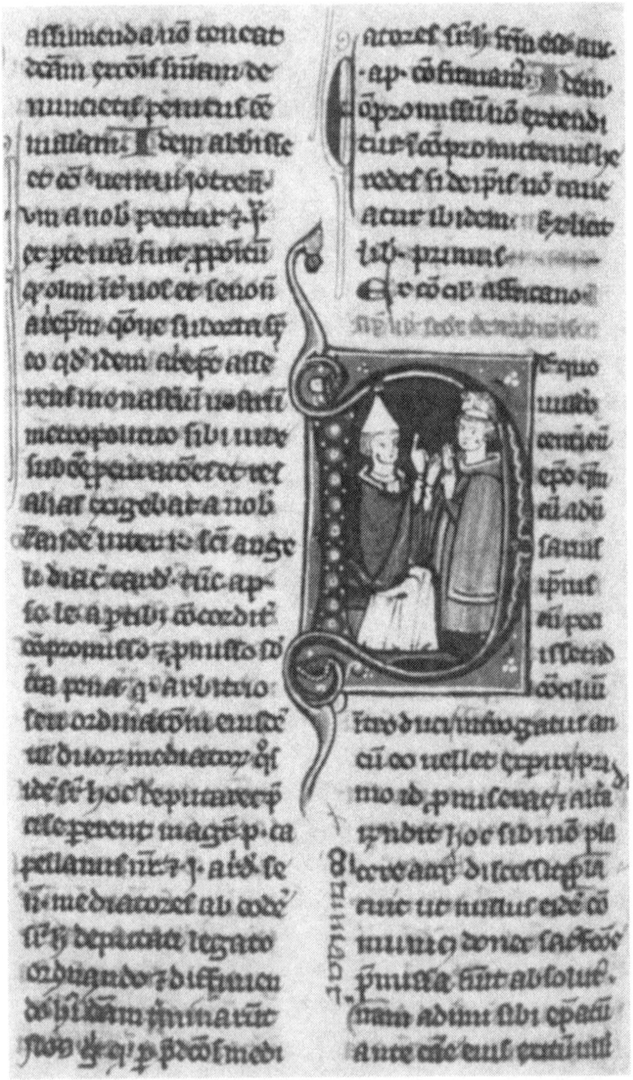

THE SPIRIT OF
CLASSICAL
CANON LAW

R. H. Helmholz

The University of Georgia Press
Athens & London

Paperback edition, 2010
© 1996 by the University of Georgia Press
Athens, Georgia 30602
www.ugapress.org
All rights reserved
Designed by Walton Harris
Set in 9.5/14 Trump by Books International

Printed digitally in the United States of America

The Library of Congress has cataloged the hardcover
edition of this book as follows:

Helmholz, R. H.
The spirit of classical canon law / R.H. Helmholz.
xiv, 514 p. ; 24 cm. — (Spirit of the laws)
Includes bibliographical references (p. [483]–490) and indexes.
ISBN 0-8203-1821-3 (alk. paper)
1. Canon law—History. 2. Canon law—Sources. I. Title.
II. Series: Spirit of the laws (Athens, Ga.)
LAW 1996
262.9—dc20   95-46621

Paperback ISBN-13: 978-0-8203-3463-9
          ISBN-10: 0-8203-3463-4

British Library Cataloging-in-Publication Data available

Frontispiece: Manuscript written in Northern France, ca. 1275 (no foliation). Beginning of book two of the Gregorian Decretals, with gloss. University of California School of Law, Berkeley, Robbins MS. 100.

CONTENTS

ABBREVIATIONS

MEDIEVAL LEGAL TEXTS

Dist. 1 c. 1   *Decretum Gratiani,* Distinctio 1, canon 1

C. 1 q. 1 c. 1   ———, Causa 1, quaestio 1, canon 1

De pen.   ———, De penitentia

De cons.   ———, De consecratione

X 1.1.1   *Decretales Gregorii IX,* book 1, tit. 1, cap. 1

Sext. 1.1.1   *Liber sextus,* book 1, tit. 1, cap. 1

Clem. 1.1.1   *Constitutiones Clementis V,* book 1, tit. 1, cap. 1

Extravag. 1.1.1   *Extravagantes communes,* book 1, tit. 1, cap. 1

d.a.   dictum ante (in *Decretum*)

d.p.   dictum post (in *Decretum*)

gl. ord.   *glossa ordinaria* (to texts of *Corpus iuris canonici*)

s.v.   *sub verbo* (reference to *glossa ordinaria* or other commentary on a legal text)

Dig. 1.1.1   *Digestum Justiniani,* book 1, tit. 1, lex 1

Cod. 1.1.1   *Codex Justiniani,* book 1, tit. 1, lex 1

Inst. 1.1.1   *Institutiones Justiniani,* book 1, tit. 1, lex 1

Nov.   *Novellae* (in *Corpus iuris civilis*)

OTHERS

BMCL   *Bulletin of Medieval Canon Law* (Berkeley, 1971–)

Coing, Handbuch	*Handbuch der Quellen und Literatur der neueren Europäischen Privatrenchtsgeschichte*, ed. Helmut Coing, vol. 1, *Mittelalter* (1100–1500), and vol. 2, *Neuere Zeit* (1500–1800) (Munich, 1973–76)
DD.	*Domini* (used to refer to common opinion of the jurists)
D.D.C.	*Dictionnaire de droit canonique*, 7 vols. (Paris, 1935–65)
Decrees	*Decrees of the Ecumenical Councils*, 2 vols., trans. and ed. Norman P. Tanner et al. (Washington, D.C. 1990)
Herde, Audientia	Peter Herde, *Audientia Litterarum Contradictarum: Untersuchungen über päpstlichen Justizbriefe und die päpstliche Delegationsgerichtsbarkeit vom 13. bis zum Beginn des 16. Jahrhunderts* (Tübingen, 1970)
Hinschius, Kirchenrecht	Paul Hinschius, *Die Kirchenrecht der Katholiken und Protestanten in Deutschland*, 6 vols. (Berlin, 1869–97; reprint, Graz, 1959)
MGH	Monumenta Germaniae Historica (Hannover and Berlin, 1826–)
PL	J. P. Migne, *Patrologia latina*, 221 vols. (Paris, 1844–64)
RHD	*Revue historique de droit français et étranger*
RIDC	*Rivista internazionale di diritto comune*
TRG	*Tijdschrift voor Rechtsgeschiedenis*
T.U.I.	*Tractatus universi iuris*
ZRG	*Zeitschrift der Savigny-Stiftung für Rechtsgeschichte*

PREFACE

When Alan Watson first asked me to undertake a book on the history of the law of the church in a series to be called "The Spirit of the Laws," the prospect brought me no immediate pleasure. The series, he told me, was meant to illuminate the basic nature of the legal systems covered, including the roles that moral, social, and religious values played within each. The series was further designed to explore the attitudes toward authority and the formal legal techniques of the practitioners within the systems to be covered. I hesitated. Not that the project itself seemed like a bad idea. It seemed like a good idea. The church's law has played an important part in the overall development of Western law, and even today it remains in use. It affects the lives of men and women. Indeed, it even provides the source of a career.

Knowing this, I nonetheless hesitated. I doubted my ability to generalize about a large subject like the canon law or even to write meaningfully about it as a whole. My prior work had concentrated on one or another discrete area of the law. The character of that area had more or less dictated the approach that was appropriate, making things relatively easy for me. This would obviously be something quite different. I doubted that it would be possible for me to carry out the task he described, and to the extent I could make the attempt, the prospect of filling a book with what might amount to no more than a series of vacuous generalities about the law of the church filled me with a kind of dread.

As I considered the prospect, however, this negative reaction disappeared. I hope this was the result of more than a desire to say yes to Alan Watson. It occurred to me that it might be possible to choose a number of subjects covered by the classical canon law and work through at least their most salient features. If the parts chosen were diverse enough and if they could be taken from representative areas of the law, the more general nature of the canonical system might emerge from their cumulation. Some overall conclusions about the canon law might become apparent. In other words, the choice of several suitable areas from the canonical system might uncover enough about the nature of the larger subject to make the project worthwhile. At any rate, that is what I thought. The small number of general works about the canon law written in English further emboldened me. I agreed to the proposal.

Whether or not the effort has succeeded in any measure I must leave to others to decide. But I must not omit to thank the people and institutions that have made working on it a pleasure. The happy occasion of receiving a Research Prize from the Alexander von Humboldt Stiftung enabled me to devote eight months in Germany working on the project during 1992 and 1993. The good offices of Professor Knut Wolfgang Nörr made it possible for me to spend those months in the Law Seminar at the University of Tübingen, where the bulk of the research on the book was done. Professor Laurent Mayali, director of the Robbins Collection at the University of California, Berkeley, was equally kind in allowing me to make use of the splendid resources of the best collection of works on the *ius commune* in North America. It is there that I did most of the checking and much of the investigation of the postmedieval history of my subject. Financial support from Robbins also helped me along, and I am grateful for it. Finally, thanks to Professor Michael Stolleis and the generosity of the Thyssen Foundation, I was able to spend a (too brief) period at the Max-Planck-Institut für Rechtsgeschichte in Frankfurt am Main working on three of the book's chapters. These opportunities and support, together with those afforded by the University of Chicago and in particular the Jerome S. Weiss Faculty Research Fund, have meant that I have never wanted for either financial support or a pleasant venue in completing this project. I am grateful and conscious of the several debts I have incurred.

Several other colleagues and friends have agreed to read chapters of this book and have helped me with specific criticism. Al Alschuler,

Michael McConnell, Kenneth Pennington, Peter Stein, John Witte, Alan Watson, and Gero Dolezalek stand out in my memory. I have also found myself writing about themes already dealt with by Professor Peter Landau of the University of Munich, and I have benefited both from reading his work and from discussing the subjects with him. Most important has been the help of my friend Knut Nörr. He has provided assistance of more than a material kind; his suggestions and guidance lie behind more of what is found in these pages than I could acknowledge without embarrassment.

A word about the method of research that lies behind this book and also the consequent limitations in it. I have selected fourteen different subjects, drawing at least one from what I conceived to be the most significant areas of the canon law. For example, it seemed obvious that a general book on the canon law should deal with the governance of the church, the sacraments, and legal sanctions. For the first of these, I took the law of election of bishops; for the second, the sacrament of baptism; for the third, the law of excommunication. I made similar choices in the other significant areas of the law. Procedural aspects of the law were especially prominent among my subjects. Not only were they important in themselves and influential in Western legal development generally, but they turned out to constitute a particularly good way of getting at the approach to law characteristic of the canonical system.

The book deals with the classical canon law, that is, the law of the church developed between the twelfth and fourteenth centuries. It covers Roman law only incidentally and other systems of the medieval law even less. I have tried to describe enough of the former to convey some idea of its lasting importance in the canon law, but my command of its intricacies is too weak to do it full justice. The bulk of each chapter thus describes the law found in the *Corpus iuris canonici* and then its treatment and enlargement at the hands of the jurists who commented upon it. In each case I have followed the subject into the literature of the sixteenth and seventeenth centuries, noting changes and consistencies where they occurred and checking my reading of the earlier commentators against the more systematic treatments characteristic of this later period. In general, however, I have not tried to cover the modern canon law. That is a separate subject and quite beyond my competence. In some cases, where modern developments shed light on the nature of the earlier canonical system, I have mentioned them briefly. But this is a book about history.

Although it will quickly become obvious to anyone who takes up and reads almost any chapter of this book, it is proper to acknowledge at the outset that in the course of the research, I sometimes formed opinions about some of the more controversial questions dealt with in the canon law. I fear it would be more accurate to say that they came into contact with my prejudices. Whichever it is, I have not altogether resisted the temptation to express these opinions or prejudices. I have tried in every instance, however, to separate my own views from the historical evidence and also to make the difference apparent.

I make no claims to originality for the book. I have not uncovered new manuscript material. I have not hit upon a new way of understanding the subject's history. Indeed, what follows could be done by any legal historian with an ability to make use of the resources of the *ius commune*. Moreover, I have not tried either to find exceptional legal ideas among the medieval jurists or to explore the rich byways of modern canonical scholarship. My goal has been to discover and describe the main features of the classical canon law. Finding and explaining the *communis opinio* among the commentators has been my goal. Readers who have an interest in the canon law but no detailed familiarity with it are the audience I have kept in my mind. It may be, therefore, that the book will not tell specialists in the history of the canon law anything they did not already know. But I do not believe this will be true, even among most specialists. I have myself learned so much from writing it that I have reason to hope that it will inform both kinds of readers.

1 Introduction: Sources and Literature of the Canon Law

The creation of the classical canon law was a signal event in the growth of the Western legal tradition. The imagination of its framers, the breadth of its coverage, the sophistication of its jurisprudence, the boldness of its claims, and the fecundity of its influence must attract the attention, if not the unstinted admiration, of all those who interest themselves in the history of our law's development. The reach of the classical canon law was exceedingly wide. From its inception in the mid-twelfth century, it was a pan-European legal system. The canon law was taught in virtually all European universities, granted coercive jurisdiction over all Latin Christians, and applied in practice before tribunals throughout western Europe.

The canon law merits our attention, moreover, because its coverage was not confined to ecclesiastical subjects straitly defined. The canon law dealt with worship, tithes, and regulation of the clergy, to be sure. However, it also dealt with much more. It reached subjects as diverse as theft, wills and succession to property, and sale of goods. Given this expansive coverage, it was natural that the canon law should interact with, and exert an influence upon, the development of secular systems of law. Many of its rules survived the Middle Ages and have been taken into modern law, even into modern English and American law.[1] The canon law also lasted for a very long time. Large parts of it were in force in England well into the nineteenth century; indeed, as a legal system it is not wholly without importance today. Courts of the Catholic Church in many parts of the world administer a modernized form of a law with deep roots in the past.

This book seeks to describe the character of the classical canon law. Its aspiration is to uncover the basic nature of this law by examining a series of representative examples. Consistent with this approach, the sources of the law cannot claim pride of place or even any considerable share of the reader's attention. Substantive law must. It is therefore appropriate that the book's opening chapter, which differs from the rest in being devoted to the law's sources, should attempt only to set the scene for what comes afterward and to do so in as brief a compass as is compatible with being understood. This chapter's aim is accordingly modest: to make it easier for readers to follow the discussion in the rest of the book by describing the most important institutions of the canon law.

Some background information about the sources of the canon law is undoubtedly desirable.[2] It may indeed be essential in a general treatment written for English-speaking readers.[3] Despite their historical significance, the institutions of the canon law are not generally familiar to educated men and women in English-speaking lands. This is true even among many readers who have a working understanding of English and American legal history. Because the canon law has been an indirect rather than an immediate source for our laws, most of us have not needed to know much about it. Therefore few have attended to it. Readers who do not fall under this generalization, and who do in fact have a familiarity with the basic sources of the canon law, may do as well to set this chapter aside.

THE ORIGINS OF A SYSTEM OF CANON LAW

For other readers, it will be helpful to begin by placing the classical canon law into its historical context. The formation of the classical law of the church formed one part of the movement Charles Homer Haskins described as the "Renaissance of the Twelfth Century."[4] The same progressive currents of thought, expanding and systematizing human knowledge, that produced scholastic theology and the European universities also produced the canon law. It would be something of a stretch to connect the formulation of the canon law directly with the revival of European economic and social life that also occurred during this period.[5] It would be an even greater leap to draw causal connections between it and the beginnings of Romanesque and Gothic art. Nonetheless, it was the same era that witnessed them all.

Of course it is of equal importance that the eleven centuries of the church's history that had gone before the twelfth-century Renaissance had not been without law. The *canones* were distinguished from the *leges* from the earliest times after the establishment of Christianity.[6] The affairs of the church have rarely been without controversy, and this oft lamented but hardy reality of ecclesiastical life has long seemed to require legal rules. Although convoked primarily to deal with great doctrinal issues, the ecumenical councils promulgated canons that were undeniably "legal" in some sense. Their *canones* were meant to regulate the government of the church and to prescribe habits of life appropriate for the clergy and all Christian people.

To appreciate the need that was perceived for specifically Christian laws from an early time, one has only to take brief note of some of the decrees of the early councils—for example, the decree of the Council of Nicaea (325) on the treatment to be accorded to persons who had been excommunicated,[7] or that of the Council of Chalcedon (451) dealing with the obligation of clerics to air their grievances before their bishop instead of before a secular tribunal.[8] Both these subjects will figure in this book. It will show that these conciliar decrees ended up as parts of quite complex areas of legal practice. The developed law was to go far beyond its modest conciliar inheritance. But that complexity had roots in the past that extended well back into the decisions and enactments of the early history of the church.

Gathering the conciliar decrees together and placing them alongside other authoritative sources of the church's law in order to make up formal collections of the law also has a history that antedates the twelfth century.[9] To cite but one example, the most famous ruler of the early Middle Ages, Charlemagne (d. 814), had required a copy of the canonical collection by Dionysius Exiguus so that it could be circulated and put to use in the churches in his realm.[10] What practical effect it had, if it had any, we cannot now discover, but there were many other canonical collections made and circulated, before and after the reign of Charles the Great. A number of them were quite impressive, and some became important in the eventual formulation of the classical canon law.[11] The pace of compiling canons itself also quickened with the stirrings of the Gregorian reform movement in the eleventh century. The names of the great compilers, Burchard of Worms and Ivo of Chartres, for example, are still known and admired by historians of the canon law. Though eclipsed by the coming of the classical law in the twelfth century, these collections were not without effect upon it. They are worthy of study in their own right.[12]

Even so—even recognizing that the classical canon law had antecedents—it nonetheless remains the fact that only in the second millennium of the church's existence did a body of canon law properly speaking come into existence. Historians rightly contrast the *ius novum* of the era with the *ius antiquum* that preceded it. Haskins had some reason to speak of the "confusion and contradiction in the authorities" of the church's law inherited by the century of his Renaissance.[13] The gap that separates the classical canon law as it emerged in the thirteenth century from the earlier medieval collections is not a chasm. But it cannot not be crossed with a single stride.[14]

Historians who specialize in the subject identify at least three fundamental ways in which the classical canon law differed in significant degree from what had gone before. First, it was more comprehensive in its coverage. Many of the earlier canonical collections were partial in the range of subjects they touched upon and sometimes (apparently) quite random in the order in which they arranged the canons they did include. The classical canon law was neither. Its aim was to regulate the whole life of the church, and its purpose was to place the authoritative texts in usable form, arranging them around basic subject matter categories. In both these aims it largely succeeded. Though not a code in the modern sense, the *Corpus iuris* that contains the classical canon law nevertheless impresses by the amplitude of its coverage and also (once one has the hang of it) by the ease with which it can be used.

Second, the classical canon law was founded upon an analytical approach to authoritative texts. It incorporated, if indeed it did not depend upon, the same kind of systematic analysis that we associate with Peter Abelard and the rise of scholasticism. Texts were taken, organized, and dissected to arrive at a synthesis. Together with theology, the canon law embraced the dialectical method as the primary method of organizing and furthering knowledge. It thus came to be taught in a separate faculty in most of the European universities, where it was regularly subjected to the process of distinction and harmonization characteristic of the medieval schools. The classical canonists thus put the texts inherited from the past into an organized form, and they sought to resolve inconsistencies between them. We shall see many examples of this technique. It had not been a regular feature of the earlier canonical collections or of the attention paid to them before the twelfth century.

Third, the scope of the classical canon law's application was geographically much wider than had been that of previous canonical collections. Although the decrees of the councils were meant to govern the entire church, this cannot be said of all the canonical collections before the appearance of Gratian's *Decretum* in the middle years of the twelfth century. At least they had not done so in fact. With the *Decretum*, however, one reaches a turning point. The popularity and applicability of the *Decretum* are attested throughout the Latin Church within a few decades of its appearance. Connected with the rise of the papacy as the mainspring of government in the church, the wide geographical recognition of this collection and the other parts of the *Corpus iuris canonici* that followed remains one of the most salient features of the classical canon law. It was a pan-European system of law.

One further basic point should be made about the twelfth-century development, though it is not so much a distinction from the earlier canons as it is the establishment of a principle implicit in them. The canon law stood on its own as a body of law and as an independent discipline. It had an existence separate and distinct from both theology and Roman law, even though it overlapped with both in its coverage and sources. The canonists, for example, made constant use of Roman law, but they did not feel themselves bound by its rules. Equally, the canonists dealt with many of the same problems as did the medieval theologians, but they brought a slightly different perspective to them and always felt free to formulate their own answers to specific problems.

The existence of separate canon law faculties within the medieval universities is one sign of this canonical independence that is clear to modern observers. It must also have been so at the time. The stated assumption among the canonists of the primacy of the canon law in cases of conflict with Roman and other secular laws provides a second indication of the independence of the church's law. But perhaps most important in this respect was the ability to create law by new enactment, as well as by the interpretation of old texts. Unlike Roman law (and to some extent theology itself), the canon law was not a closed body of texts in 1100. Authoritative statements of the law and conscious creation of new laws, both by conciliar decrees and through the issuance of the decisions by the popes contained in letters known as papal decretals, stood as a signal and also a guarantee of its ability to deal with law as an independent actor. It enabled the canon law to respond directly to new problems. These papal decisions were communicated to the schools and became in due course an ordinary part of the instruction provided in the canon law faculties. They were also put into practice in the courts of the church, though not without other influences running from the schools and local customs. In some measure, this is what made possible the "progressive" nature of the medieval canon law. Again, in the pages that follow will appear many instances in which the canon law was determined by papal decisions and the scholastic commentaries on them.

THE *CORPUS IURIS CANONICI*

Historical treatments of the English common law customarily begin either with the organization of the royal courts or with the writ system. For the canon law, a similar approach would be all but unthinkable. One must begin with books. Specifically, one must begin with the books of what came to be called the *Corpus iuris canonici*.[15] The texts collected in them were the foundation of the canon law. Indeed, these books came into existence before the church had an organized system of public courts or anything analogous to the English system of "forms of action" by which litigation could be initiated and governed. The courts were to be built around them, rather than the other way around.

The *Decretum Gratiani*

The starting point is Gratian's *Concordantia discordantium cano-num*, known familiarly as the *Decretum*. This "Concordance of discordant canons" constituted the first part of this corpus. Unfortunately, virtually everything about it, save its authority and importance, seems to be either disputed or unknown. Very little can be said with assurance about Gratian himself, although long tradition identified him as a Camaldolese monk who taught in Bologna during the twelfth century.[16] The date of the composition and first appearance of the *Decretum* is also uncertain, although it has long been customary, and it is certainly not seriously wrong, to assign it to the year 1140. The process by which it assumed the form in which it was used during the Middle Ages has likewise remained open to question. It appears that the text as it left Gratian's hand was "enriched" by subsequent writers and that this "enrichment" occurred early enough and to such an extent that Gratian's original text is beyond recovering. Many texts, known as *paleae*, were added to the *Decretum*, and it is also probable that the Roman law authorities found in it were later additions to the original text.[17]

For readers who wish to learn about these disputed questions, there is an abundant and impressive scholarly literature.[18] For present purposes, however, most of these interesting and difficult speculations must be set to one side. The aim here is to understand something of the canon law as it existed in its classical form. For that purpose it is essential only that the basic nature of the *Decretum*, as it was known and used by generations of canonists, be understood. In this, one should start by recognizing that the *Decretum* was, above all, the result of collecting and organizing a mass of authorities from the past. Canons of church councils, scriptural passages, excerpts from writings of the church fathers, decisions of popes, and parts of Roman law were included. It appears that Gratian rarely had recourse to original sources in bringing these together. He took virtually all his texts from prior canonical collections. Not all of his attributions were correct, it seems, though this scarcely mattered at the time. In all, something like thirty-eight hundred individual texts were included in the *Decretum*.

What made Gratian's *Decretum* the success it very quickly became was not, however, the large number of the texts he amassed. His fame rested on what he did with them. He organized the texts around discrete topics or questions, and he analyzed them in order to harmonize them where they seemed to conflict. He thereby brought "harmony to dissonance."[19] This was something that prior canonical collections had not done, even those that had grouped the authorities they collected under subject matter headings in a more regular fashion than Gratian did. Gratian's hand was that of a master, raising the difficulties, distinguishing the cases, stating the results, and offering a further citation or two in support of the wisdom and the authority of his conclusions.

To take an illustrative if slightly simpler example than most, Gratian asked whether all accusations against alleged criminals had to be made in writing.[20] On this subject, the *Decretum* contained four texts stating the affirmative. One of them, a statement ascribed to an early pope, held that it was necessary. "Accusers should not be received without a writing and in the absence of the accused."[21] There followed, however, one contrary authority from another pope. Gratian introduced this statement: "But Pope Stephan seems to write to the contrary, saying, 'The accusation of no man is to be received by a writing, but rather by his own voice.'" In other words, the first four canons seemed actually to require a writing, the fifth to reject it.

This "disharmony" stated, Gratian then resolved the seeming contradiction, putting his solution in what is called a *dictum post*. He interpreted Pope Stephan's statement to mean only that written accusations by the absent were being prohibited in it. The pope's reason for disapproving written accusations, in other words, had been to keep them from being made at a distance by someone who was absent and thus outside the control of the judge. It had not dealt at all with the case of the procedure to be used when the accuser was present. When he was there in person, Gratian concluded that the canons must be understood as meaning that the accuser must both read the accusation aloud and present it in writing to the judge. This is what the first four canons, rightly understood, had meant. Thus the apparently contrary authorities were not contrary to each other at all, and a rule of legal practice had been stated. Accusations should be made in written form. In the course of time, the church's law of criminal procedure would turn out to be a good deal more complicated than this simple example suggests. Exceptions were recognized, requirements were elaborated, and alternatives were developed. As an example of Gratian at work, however, the example is not misleading.

The *Decretum* as we have it is divided into three parts, the first of which consists of 101 *Distinctiones*. The first twenty deal with the sources of law. The rest take up various subjects related to ordination, the life of the clerical order, and organization of the church. *Distinctio* 78, for example, is made up of five canons stating the age required for ordination as a priest (thirty years unless necessity dictated, in which case twenty-five might suffice). Not all followed the method of presenting conflicting authorities and solving the conflicts; *Distinctio* 78 did not, for instance. But a great many (like that involving written accusations) did.

The second part of the *Decretum* does follow the dialectical method more rigorously. It consists of thirty-six *Causae*, each divided into separate *quaestiones*. In each *Causa* Gratian put forth a hypothetical set of facts, from which he derived several questions. For instance, *Causa* 28 posits this situation: a married infidel converted to the Christian faith. His wife left him out of hatred for the Christianity he had embraced, and he married another woman. She died, he was ordained, and he was later elected a bishop. The questions raised by this situation were: (1) Is there true marriage among *infideles*? (2) Is it lawful to marry another after one party becomes a Christian? and (3) Is the man who does marry in these circumstances to be reckoned bigamous and hence unfit for the episcopacy?[22]

The questions treated in the *Decretum* did not cover every area the medieval canon law was ultimately to encompass, but Gratian cast his net widely. He covered a great deal of what would become the law of the church, and it is unusual to find a discussion in later books that makes no reference to the *Decretum*. Gratian also pursued his

dialectical course energetically. This second part devoted to *Causae*
contained but one pause. A section, really a short treatise on penitential discipline called "De penitentia," was placed within *Causa* 34;
it reverted to the form of *Distinctiones* found in the first part of the
Decretum. Otherwise the *Causae* and attendant questions continued
methodically.

The final part of the *Decretum*, the shortest of the three, is called
"De consecratione." It was arranged into five separate *Distinctiones*,
which took up various aspects of the church's sacramental life and
worship. For instance, the ancient rule about when the laity should
receive the Eucharist is found therein.[23] This final section contains
a good deal of material we would classify as sacramental theology
rather than law; it stands as a reminder that Gratian was not simply
writing a textbook about law as it was to be applied in legal tribunals,
and also as a demonstration that the canonists did not draw a line
between the spheres of law and theology in the same way or in quite
the same place a modern lawyer would. We shall be reminded of these
things again at several places in what follows.

Gratian's *Decretum* was not an official publication or statement of
law by the church. It was a private effort, neither sponsored nor officially sanctioned by the papacy or any other office of the church. Nevertheless it quickly assumed an authoritative status, one that was
recognized generally throughout the Western Church. The *Decretum*
eclipsed earlier canonical collections virtually at once. It was known
and referred to throughout Europe at least by the last third of the
twelfth century. It also lasted. The *Decretum* retained an authoritative status in the legal system of the Catholic Church up to the present
century. This is true even though many of the legal rules found in it,
most famously in the law of marriage, were to be changed or quickly
shunted to one side by the subsequent march of the canon law.

The Gregorian Decretals

The papal decretal, mentioned briefly above, was the chief means
whereby that march was advanced, the other being decisions of
church councils such as the Third Lateran Council of 1179 and Pope

Innocent III's famous Fourth Lateran council of 1215. Gratian's work had left many questions open. Its coverage was partial and even sometimes regarded as mistaken in substantive ways. The papal decretals filled the gaps and corrected the mistakes; they also restated the principles when (as normally was the case) Gratian's work simply needed amplification and affirmation. These decisions of popes, rather than other textbooks or synodal decrees, were the basic building blocks by which the canon law after Gratian was constructed.

Most decretals were answers to specific questions that had been put to the popes. Borrowed originally from imperial practice, the decretal letter was a rescript, a written answer to a query from an official or private person that was meant to deal with a specific problem. It was not therefore "legislative" in a modern sense but rather a statement of law elicited by an inquiry. Some of the decretals came by way of an appeal to the papacy in a litigated case. The decretal letter was then normally embodied in instructions to local judges delegated by the pope to hear and decide the particular case. Others were raised by a bishop uncertain about a difficult point of law or administrative problem. In a few instances—not so much in the twelfth century but with greater frequency in the thirteenth—the decretals took the form of unsolicited rulings establishing a particular point of law. Increasing judicial authority exercised by the papacy was one of the most salient developments in church life during the twelfth century. Nowhere did it have more far reaching effect than in the canon law enunciated by these decretal letters.

From the time they were dispatched, papal decretals were saved and collected by those who received them and by those who were interested in what they contained. No other source furnished a more up-to-date statement of the law, and it was natural that copies should be made and then brought together. This collecting was—indeed, it had to be—a continuing process, so great was the output of decretals flowing from the papal chancery, particularly during the pontificates of Alexander III (1159–81) and Innocent III (1198–1216).[24] Eventually five of these collections emerged as the most important and reliable; they are known as the *Quinque compilationes antiquae*.[25] However, much as happened to the older canonical collections with the advent of

Gratian's *Decretum*, the disparate collections were rendered largely obsolete by the work of one man, Raymond of Peñafort. His efforts were contained in a book called the *Liber extra*, or as it is more commonly known today, simply "the Decretals."

At least as early as 1230, Raymond had been commissioned by Pope Gregory IX to bring the essential law of the decretals together into a single work. The multiplicity and inconsistency of the existing private collections made such a definitive, official collection highly desirable. Gregory IX also gave his editor a relatively free hand in carrying out his work.[26] Raymond made good use of it. He followed the general model of the earlier *Compilationes* but edited the decretals at his disposal to conform to the pattern of a true law book. Superfluous information was pruned away, doubts and contradictions in existing decretals were eliminated for the sake of consistency, phrases and words were altered in the interest of coherence, and decretals were divided up and parceled out to different titles according to the subjects contained in them. Raymond seems also, and I suppose quite unexceptionally, to have given a little extra weighting to his own opinions in reshaping the language of the decretals included in his work.[27]

The texts collected in Raymond's *Decretales* normally stated the essential facts behind the decretal and also the law applicable to those facts.[28] In a few cases, the events that had given rise to the decretal letter were suppressed in favor of a simple statement of the law, but for the most part the reader can discover enough about the facts to understand what events had given rise to the papal decision. The texts were thus not legislation in the sense of laws enacted by a deliberative body, but neither were they identical to what we would call "leading cases." Raymond's editing went too far for that. The Decretals also incorporated many recent conciliar decrees (twenty-seven from the Third Lateran Council, sixty-eight from the Fourth) as well as papal decretals more strictly defined.[29] The result is not a code in the nineteenth-century sense. It is, however, a more orderly and complete statement of the canon law than its predecessor.

In 1234, Raymond's work had been completed. He presented it to its patron, a scene memorialized by many illuminations found in early copies, and it was made "official" when the pope sent it to the University of Bologna to be incorporated into the ordinary teaching of the canon law. That Gregory IX chose this method of promulgation rather than any more general pronouncement to the bishops or officials of the church as a whole is testimony, among other things, to what a leading scholar of the subject has described as "that give-and-take between the universities and the papacy which later centuries unfortunately did not know how to maintain."[30] It underlined the importance of the law professor within the *ius commune*.

Raymond's great effort was known in the Middle Ages as the *Liber extra* in order to define it as an addition and complement to the *Decretum*.[31] It is still normal to abbreviate it in conformity with the original usage. The Decretals were normally abbreviated as "Ext." in medieval practice, and today the custom remains of citing this work by using the single letter "X"—this for the sake of brevity and continuity. In a modern edition the Decretals are slightly smaller than the *Decretum* despite their wider substantive coverage. They occupy less than two-thirds of the space required to print Gratian's work. The two thousand or so chapters found in Raymond's collection are divided into five separate books, each of which is itself divided internally into separate titles. These titles are in turn divided into a number of chapters. It is common among modern scholars to refer to the texts in the Decretals by number, starting from the book and working to the chapter. "X 4.1.7" thus refers to the seventh chapter of the first title in the Decretal's fourth book.

In earlier centuries, this same chapter would have been cited by its incipit—that is, by the first words of its text (*Ex litteris*), together with an abbreviated notation to show that it came from book 4's title, "De sponsalibus et matrimoniis." Numbers were occasionally used, but sparingly. Edward Gibbon later sneered at the "absurd and incomprehensible mode of quotation" of the jurists, and it does seem a little ungainly at first sight.[32] But in fact the method was (and remains) workable with the aid of an alphabetical list and a little practice. Given the absence of the printing press during the Middle Ages, and the absence of uniform standard editions of legal works even afterward, this apparently absurd system would have been much preferable to a modern system of page citation. Citation to page numbers in the treatises was then, and still is, almost worthless.

The first book of the Decretals dealt with the constitution and organization of the church, the second with jurisdictional and procedural rules, the third with the clergy, the sacraments, and ecclesiastical obligations, the fourth with marriage, divorce, and domestic relations, and the fifth with the penal law of the church. This same general order has been followed in arranging the chapters of this book. It served the canonists well enough, and no good reason occurs to me for inventing something else.

The *Liber sextus* and Later Collections

Lawmaking in the medieval church did not cease with the compilation of the *Liber extra*. Councils met and issued canons. Popes decided cases and issued decretals. These were in turn placed into collections. Only at the end of the thirteenth century, however, were the additions formally incorporated into the existing canon law. Pope Boniface VIII charged a commission to bring together the significant texts and enactments that had appeared since 1234. They were called, then and now, the *Liber sextus*, or "Sext." for short, meaning that it was a sixth book to be added to the five of Raymond's compilation. In reality, however, the name is not strictly accurate, since the contents of the Sext. followed the same general pattern adopted in the Decretals. It was divided into five books, and into separate titles and chapters within each book, largely reproducing the order and the substantive coverage of the Gregorian Decretals. The length of each section depended upon need—that is, how much change and how much legislation there had been. The Sext.'s title on marriage, for example, is brief; those dealing with episcopal elections and sentences of excommunication are long.

Similar, though smaller, compilations followed in due course, three of which came to be placed at the end of medieval and later copies of the *Corpus iuris canonici*. The first was the so-called Clementines, planned by Pope Clement V to incorporate the decrees of the Council of Vienne (1311–12) but actually published during the reign of his successor, John XXII, in 1317. Following that came two private collections of what are called *Extravagantes*, first twenty from Pope John XXII and then the later *Extravagantes communes*.[33] Thus the corpus of the classical canon law had been substantially completed by the first half of the fourteenth century and fully completed by the end of the Middle Ages. It remained the basic law for the Catholic Church until 1917.

The *Glossa Ordinaria*

It is an arguable question whether a description of the glosses to these texts belongs here with the sources or would better be dealt with in the section on canonical literature that follows. Analytically a stronger argument can probably be made for the latter. The *glossa ordinaria* is of a piece with much of the canonical literature. In explaining, reconciling, and commenting upon the texts of the *Corpus iuris canonici*, the earliest canonical literature is virtually indistinguishable from the gloss, except in its being presented separately from the texts. I have nevertheless placed description of the *glossa ordinaria* here. This is by way of stressing its invariable connection with the texts during the period of the law's formation. The texts were never read without the gloss. They were always used together. The frontispiece of this volume well illustrates the close association, and from this habit came the famous, if slightly exaggerated, maxim to the effect that the courts would accept an argument only if it could be found in the gloss: "Quod non agnoscit glossa non agnoscit curia."[34]

In its rudiments, a gloss is simply a marginal or interlinear note giving the correct meaning of a word or phrase in the text. From there it was but a step to stating and discussing the meaning of the text itself. It is an easy sort of exercise for a teacher or student to follow, useful for learning the law and capable of expansion and contraction as the need arises. By the late twelfth century, glossing already had a considerable history and had taken on a stable though not invariable form. A typical gloss set forth an abbreviated version of the facts that had given rise to the decretal and the issues it raised, stated clearly the legal principles the text contained, dealt with difficult words or concepts in the text, solved apparent contradictions or inconsistencies between the text and other parts of the law, raised variant interpretations and open questions, and referred the reader to other treatments of the same subject in the corpus of the law.

This method is adaptable to any text-based body of knowledge. In the Middle Ages glossing was the characteristic way of presenting and studying the ancient Roman law and most famously the Bible itself. The strengths of the method are certain, but it is also open to criticism. It was to become the subject of ridicule and distaste to some during the Renaissance of the fifteenth and sixteenth centuries. The gloss can come between the reader and the text itself, so that the gloss becomes all one looks at. That this intervention sometimes happened with the canon law cannot be denied. The *glossa ordinaria* became a filter through which the texts were invariably understood. The best of the later canonists were always able to go beyond the gloss, seeing more in the texts than the gloss stated and sometimes suggesting quite different understandings of the texts. But the centrality of the gloss to ordinary reading in courts and schools is undeniable.

Glossing the canonical texts began almost immediately after their inclusion in a collection. For purposes of understanding the law of the church, it is important only to remember that a gloss for each of the parts of the *Corpus* described above quickly achieved a standard form, distilled by an editor from what had already existed and what he himself added. For this reason one speaks of the "ordinary" gloss to each part. That for the *Decretum* was put together early in the thirteenth century by Joannes Teutonicus, with additions by Bartholomeus Brixiensis. The *glossa ordinaria* to the Gregorian Decretals was completed by Bernard of Parma by the 1260s,[35] and that for the *Liber sextus* was done by Joannes Andreae early in the fourteenth century. Specialists are required to know something about these men and their habits of work, but in truth their names scarcely matter for most of us. The essential fact is their existence and the product of their collective efforts.

One cannot speak of the works of these glossators as original in the modern sense. Their works were the product of the schools. Some were identified by the glossator's initials, it is true. But many were anonymous, and for later canonists the original source of a particular gloss only rarely made a difference. Moreover, like Gratian's work, the *glossa ordinaria* was in no sense a commissioned or official work. It was simply "received" as authoritative by the canonists. No one challenged the placement of the gloss alongside the texts, though it is also important to remember in addition that the gloss never had the force and the power to engender new interpretations that the texts themselves did.

THE ROMAN LAW

This is a book about the canon law rather than European legal history more generally. However, a treatment of the canon law would be altogether incomplete were it to take no notice at all of the Roman law. The *Corpus iuris civilis*, compiled at the instigation of the Emperor Justinian in the sixth century, played an important part in the development of the classical canon law. The church had lived according the Roman law during the early Middle Ages—hence the aphorism *Ecclesia vivit lege Romana*, a phrase meant to contrast the situation of the universal church with the particular and customary legal regimes of the peoples of western Europe.[36] From this past, if not simply because of the merit of Roman law itself, rules taken from the civil law worked their way into the canonical collections. They were part of the inheritance of the classical canon law. In many particulars, therefore, the canonists saw no need to deviate from the Roman law, no need to formulate a new set of rules. And they did not. Of the subjects in this book, probably the law of prescription best illustrates this facet of civilian influence on the canon law. A great deal of the Roman law on the subject was taken whole into the church's law. As the commentators expressed it, much of the Roman law was "canonized."

The formulation of the classical canon law in the twelfth and thirteenth centuries did not call a halt to civilian influence. In 1200 the Roman law and the juristic science that went with the texts were both older and more legally sophisticated than anything the church had produced. The stirrings of legal science in the late eleventh and twelfth centuries had centered upon the recovered Roman law. Gratian's *Decretum* did mark a decided advance in the systematic analysis of the law of the church. But when compared with the contemporary work of the Bologna civilians, few would deny that it cut a poor figure. On this account, the canonists were led by the civilians. Or, perhaps better said, they moved forward together. The canonists "caught up." All of the methods and many of the texts of the civil law were influential in the formation and the elaboration of the canon law. Of the subjects treated in this book, only in the canon law of excommunication did Roman law *not* play a substantial part in the way the canon law developed, and even within it procedural rules drawn from civilian sources played a part. The law of baptism, to take an example where one would not expect much but religious law to have played a part, can actually be shown to have been marked at several points by the hand of Roman law jurisprudence.

There was one other factor: rivalry. A respectable argument can be made that the canon law defined itself as fully as it did precisely to separate itself from the Roman law.[37] Although it is true to say—perhaps even to stress—that the *Corpus iuris civilis* was the work of a Christian emperor and that in the Codex and Novels it contained much law relating specifically to the clergy and to the church, it is also true that the assumptions and the goals of the church's law were not identical to those found in Roman jurisprudence. This was particularly apparent after the accomplishments of the Gregorian reform movement had made themselves felt during the eleventh and twelfth centuries. The canonists would not have denied that the *Corpus iuris civilis* held a place of honor in God's overall plan for mankind. They would have stressed the juristic excellence of many of its parts. But they would also have stressed its incompleteness, its need to be augmented and corrected by the law of the church. Where there was conflict between Roman law and the dictates of the Christian religion, the latter was to control. Establishing that principle required a work to rival the Justinianic compilations, and in some sense that is exactly what the *Corpus iuris canonici* was. It is no accident that the first title of the Decretals is identical to that of the *Codex Justinianus:* "De

Summa Trinitate et Fide Catholica." It is probably not an accident that many of the assertions of papal authority found within commentaries on the canonical texts sound very much like claims modeled upon the imperium of the Roman emperor.

Coming to the Roman law itself, one need here only take note of the basics. The *Corpus iuris civilis* consists of four parts: the Institutes, the Digest, the Codex, and the Novels. The first is a school-book, useful in setting forth the framework of the law but soon gone beyond by the serious student. In fact it was not much cited by the medieval commentators. The second, also called the Pandects, is the great edited compilation that was made from the works of the Roman jurists who flourished from the time of the late Republic to the mid-third century. Its rediscovery in the latter part of the eleventh century and its gradual absorption into the habits of mind of the medieval schools were the crucial factors in the revival of juristic science.[38] The third is a collection of imperial constitutions stating the law, taken from the second century A.D. to the time of the publication of the *Corpus* in the 530s. The fourth continued the collection for the imperial decrees issued after that date. This last naturally played a rather larger part in the medieval canon law than it does in most modern accounts of the Roman law system because of its treatment of questions relevant to the church.

Virtually all of these texts were cited and used in the writings of the canonists. No cleavage that could be called fundamental existed between the canonists and the civilians. True, there were barriers, real and apparent, between the professors of the two laws. The universities mostly placed the two in separate faculties, each devoted to expounding its own *corpus iuris*. The two laws also differed on many points of substance, large and small. Treatises of considerable length were written on the subject of the differences between them.[39] Even so, there was more convergence than divergence.[40] Many of the canonists had degrees in both laws, and the civilians were required to know something of the canon law. The *Decretum* itself stated that the civil law was to be used where it did not contradict the canons.[41] When one left the academy for the courts, the distinction between them had even less significance.

Over the course of the Middle Ages, there emerged from this convergence a law common to all university-trained jurists. For many purposes, the Roman law was in effect "fused" with the canon law.[42] By the sixteenth century it could be said that "the canon law and the civil law [were] so connected, that the one [could] scarcely be understood without the other."[43] The law of *restitutio in integrum*, to be discussed in Chapter 4, furnishes an obvious example. The canon law of restitution depended for its origins upon the existence of the Roman law and drew upon it constantly thereafter. But the two laws on the subject were not identical. The canonists were not bound by the civilian precedents, though they had no desire to cast themselves adrift from them.

The *ius commune* is the name usually given to this great repository of European law to which the combination of these two laws gave rise. The term means simply "the common law," but the Latin form has been retained in modern usage, a particularly good habit given the need for English-speaking countries to distinguish it from the English common law. The *ius commune* long dominated European legal education. This was so even in the English universities. It stood above the rules of the different courts, the particular lands, and even the individual legislative bodies among which European jurisdictions were divided. The *ius commune* was used to provide legal rules when no local statute or custom provided otherwise. It was used also as a way of interpreting statutes or customs that did provide otherwise. There was a medieval rule of thumb that statutes or customs in derogation of the *ius commune* were to be interpreted strictly, and they were to be harmonized with the *ius commune* if at all possible. The *ius commune* was influential even where it was not immediately authoritative.

THE BIBLE

Many historical accounts of the medieval canon law make very slight room for the Christian Scriptures. Perhaps the working assumption is that the Bible belongs to the world of the spirit, the law to the world of the flesh. Or perhaps the omission is explained by the undeniable fact that the canon law made relatively little use of the rules in the Bible that readers immediately recognize as legal, most characteristically those found in some of the books of the Old Testament. Or it may be that some modern specialists have wished to stress that the canon law was a forward-looking legal system, rather than the enactment of archaic religious rules, and have therefore had reason to ascribe little importance to what contribution the Bible did make. One can understand good reasons for concentrating on other sources of the canon law.

I think this understandable omission to be a mistake all the same. It is true that in the process by which the church's law was formed, the Bible was not often treated as directly stating legal rules to be applied in practice. The church did not reenact the Book of Deuteronomy. However, much of the canon law was shaped indirectly by the Bible. Passages from Scripture appear in many conciliar decrees and papal decretals. Biblical examples were used to justify a rule adopted or a decision taken. These decrees were taken in turn into the *Corpus iuris canonici.* These canonists, together with all Christians in the Middle Ages, regarded the Scriptures as the source of Christian life.[44] Their consciousness was soaked with the lessons and the outlook of the Latin Bible.[45] In the Scriptures were found principles that could not be put aside as simply inconvenient. These principles provided guidance and support for the canonists' work. The commentators made frequent reference to the Scriptures.

Of course it is undeniable that recognition of the Bible's importance in law did not become for the canonists an invitation to make free use of the Scriptures in the service of either law or religion. They understood the Bible as it had been handed down to them and as it was interpreted by the clerical interpreters of their day. Their use of the biblical texts does not always correspond with a "common sense" reading. Still less does it harmonize with modern scriptural exegesis. Few readers today would take Jesus' admonition (Matt. 22:21) to render unto Caesar the things that are Caesar's and unto God the things that are God's as an endorsement for ecclesiastical taxation.[46] The canonists accepted that as a permissible reading of his words. Thus was the Bible "filtered" through the schools. But this undeniable fact, true indeed of all medieval thought, does not necessarily render inconsequential the consistent use the canonists did make of the Bible. It simply affected the conclusions they drew.

One must certainly admit that some of the uses the canonists made of Scripture came to no more than the production of "proof texts"—simple, fanciful, or far-fetched—to buttress conclusions reached for other reasons or to support rationales drawn from other sources. But not all of it was. Important areas of the canon law, that relating to jurisdiction or baptism for instance, were grounded upon what is stated in the Bible better than anywhere else. At least so it seems to me. Readers of the chapters that follow may, I hope, judge for themselves. Throughout these pages I have sought always to include enough representative material, showing how the canonists employed the Scriptures, to allow readers to make their own assessment.

LEGAL LITERATURE

So far this introduction has dealt with the basic sources of the canon law. It remains to say something about the body of juristic commentary that accompanied the sources. The canon law would not be the canon law without that commentary. It shows how the law was taught in the medieval schools. It provided an essential means by which the law itself was moved forward, and it provides the modern student with an understanding of the inner nature of canonistic thought.

The size and form of this literature both repel and attract. It is sophisticated legal literature and impressive on that account. No one who confronts it can easily deny the great learning of the canonists. But it is not always easy for the outsider to make sense of what they wrote. The jerky style of argument, the innumerable citations to unfamiliar sources, and the abundance of incomprehensible abbreviations can be off-putting. I have known potential historians who have given up in disgust or despair. Particularly for students who know the sources of the English common law, it can also be forbidding by its very bulk. The learned works spawned by the *ius commune* before

1500 number in the hundreds; the number from the English common
law look paltry by comparison. By 1600 the situation, at least in numbers, would have been little changed. No one today could read more
than a small fraction of the literature of the mature *ius commune*.

Fortunately, it is not necessary to do so. This legal world gave rise
to a *communis opinio* on most questions of law.[47] It was a relatively
small and scholastic world, in the sense that the *ius commune* was
dominated by law professors, not by judges as was true in England.[48]
Therefore, their work took the form of treatise and scholarly commentary, rather than widely scattered or unprinted judicial opinions.
It was well arranged for the most part, since it normally followed the
order of the texts where its particular subject did not dictate something else. The professors (and former professors) in the *ius commune*
never made a large group at any one time during the Middle Ages.
They knew one another's work and referred to it constantly. In that
discussion, room was often made for criticism and disagreement. One
opinion might become "more common" than another. Commentators might deviate from the *communis opinio* if they had good reason to do so. However, there came to be a widely shared understanding among these men about most matters, and modern readers
can seek it out.

In time large, indeed huge, treatises were put together to collect the
common opinions of the jurists.[49] The *Tractatus universi iuris*, a
double folio set of seventeen volumes published in the sixteenth century, is the best-known such collection of basic works on the *ius commune*. There were several others. Dictionaries and *repertoria* of the
law had been compiled from the thirteenth century, and the tradition
was carried forward and augmented.[50] The alphabetical listings in
these works contained the best, or at any rate the most widely accepted, treatments of particular legal questions, and they made it possible for lawyers to find what they needed without great difficulty.
Some of these indexlike works amounted to treatises in their own
right.[51]

That contemporary method of research can be replicated today. Indeed, it lies behind most of what is in this book. These guides and the
indexes that accompany the treatises render the literature of the *ius*

commune accessible, even if no student can hope to investigate all that has been written on a particular topic. The student can dip into what F. W. Maitland once described as the *oceanus iuris* of European law without being drowned by it. He must learn some of the abbreviations without doubt, but there were even guides to abbreviations compiled from the fifteenth century that can be consulted for practical assistance.[52] Patience and some practice are all that are required.

It is an immense body of literature all the same. It contains many surprises (most of them pleasant) even for the experienced student. The description in this introductory chapter deals only with its principal forms. Nothing is said, for instance, of the *quaestiones disputatae* or the *dissensiones dominorum*, matters of dispute between the *doctores* (as the jurists were normally called). Nor have I made much room for the *repetitiones*, the *margaritae*, the *brocardica*, the *flores*, the *notabilia*, or the other collections thrown off by instruction in the law faculties of European universities.[53] It is worth knowing, however, that these varieties, and much more, are there to be explored.

Decretists and Decretalists

The starting point for the medieval canonists, the "model" as we might say today, was the gloss. Much of the earliest canonical literature was very much like a gloss, and this text-hugging form did not die out quickly. It is probably not unjust to say that the commentaries devoted immediately to the texts of the *Corpus iuris canonici* still claim pride of place as the characteristic form of canonical literature. Certainly they are the best known. Some examples of this genre are known as *lecturae*, or "readings," which is an indication of the closeness with which the work follows and explicates the canons themselves. The *Lectura* on the Gregorian Decretals by Henricus de Segusio (d. 1271), usually called Hostiensis, is perhaps the best-known example.[54] It follows the Decretals exactly, and indeed it can scarcely be used unless the reader has the text in front of him, or at least clearly in mind. The work of Pope Innocent IV (d. 1254), commonly known as his *Apparatus* to the Decretals, and the multivolume work of Joannes Andreae (d. 1348), known as his *Novella commentaria*, have much the same character.

This feature requires a certain caution or reserve in using the works of the canonists. Their principal task was to comment upon the texts and to understand the meaning of what was in the texts. It was not to develop their own ideas. The rhetorical tradition, with its greater admiration for a well-formed argument than for a particular substantive conclusion, also lay behind their characteristic approach to legal questions. Thus one finds different opinions expressed on the same topic within the writing of a single author—variant readings, if you like, of the same text.[55] At times, this habit extended even to a certain playfulness in the examination of the potentialities of the texts.[56] This does not mean that they were not "serious"—only that they were lawyers. They did certainly sometimes reach their own conclusions about particular problems, and they were quite capable of stating them without ambiguity. But it remains true that simply because a particular commentator expressed an opinion on a subject does not necessarily mean that he held it.

It is common to refer to the early canonists either as "decretists" or "decretalists," depending on whether they commented upon Gratian's *Decretum* or the Gregorian Decretals. One of the earliest among the former is called Paucapalea. His work is worth singling out because it was written between 1140 and 1148 and illustrates by its early date how immediately the text of the *Decretum* was accepted in the schools and subjected to scholastic commentary. The most famous of the decretists, however, is Huguccio (d. 1210), master at Bologna and later bishop of Ferrara. His influential work unfortunately remains in manuscript even today.[57] Two later decretists frequently referred to in this study are Guido de Baysio (d. 1313) and Johannes de Torquemada (d. 1468), uncle of the more famous Inquisitor.

The number of decretalists is legion; it makes a larger group than the decretists. Besides the three commentators just mentioned, most prominent in this book will be Antonius de Butrio (d. 1408), Petrus de Ancharano (d. 1416), and Nicholaus de Tudeschis, called Panormitanus (d. 1445 or 1453). Baldus de Ubaldis (d. 1400), better known for his commentaries on Roman law, is another famous name.[58] There were certainly differences between the views of these men, and the careers of several of them are interesting in their own right. But at least for purposes of this book, what is most significant about their work is the common tradition in which they stood. Explaining the texts of the *Corpus iuris canonici* was their common task. These texts always set limits to what they could do, and those limits allow us to consider them together. It was from their work, together with that of the great civilians, that the *communis opinio* of the *ius commune* emerged.

Besides these commentaries, but together in a class with them, are the *summae*, summaries of the law that similarly conformed to the order of titles in the Decretals. This form proved most suitable for works dealing with the church's penitential forum and for guides to pastoral legal practice designed for the use of parochial clergy.[59] However, there were many dealing with the general jurisprudence of the church. That from the pen of Hostiensis called the *Summa aurea* is the best known of these. More compact than his *Lectura*, it followed the order of the Decretals just as the *Lectura* did. However, it was not like a gloss. Instead, it summarized the law under each title of the several books of the Decretals. For example, the treatment in the *Summa* of the title on legal presumptions (X 2.23.1–16) took up three main questions and dealt with each systematically. They were: What is the nature of a presumption? What are the different kinds of presumptions? and, What are the legal effects of a presumption? The actual title in the Decretals, by contrast, had sixteen separate chapters, which were not arranged analytically. The *Lectura* necessarily followed them in order, explaining and commenting on each chapter separately.

Ordines iudiciarii and Procedural Works

One of the earliest forms of more specialized literature within the tradition of the *ius commune* was that devoted to procedure. *Ordines iudiciarii* were of the most immediate utility for the practice of law, for as their name itself suggests, they provided guidance about the steps to be taken in the conduct of litigation and sometimes models of the documents to be used.[60] From an early date, many of these *ordines* dealt with both canonical and civilian procedure. They were augmented by treatments of specialized aspects of court procedure, some obviously meant to be used by advocates and proctors. Most of the procedural works were designed for use in the courts of both church and state and are thus a particularly immediate example of the links that bound the Roman and canon laws together in the *ius commune*. Several modern editions of representative *ordines* have been printed.[61] It is undeniable that none of them makes particularly entertaining reading, but examining one or more of them does make it easier to appreciate how lawsuits went forward than one can see solely from examining the *Corpus iuris canonici*.[62] Their utility to the lawyers of the first generations of practicing jurists is also not hard to imagine.[63]

The early *ordines* led to the compilation of ever lengthier treatises on the procedure of the *ius commune*. The most elephantine example from the thirteenth century is the *Speculum iudiciale* of William Durantis.[64] It was a compilation of the work of others more than it was a product of original thought. Originality was not a virtue particularly prized by medieval lawyers. It has its limits today. Durantis pushed this rule of thumb hard, it must be admitted, perhaps beyond its natural boundary. A not inconsiderable part of the *Speculum iudiciale* was taken verbatim from other works. But his treatise was enormously popular during the Middle Ages, and it met an obvious need. Not long ago it was reprinted in two very large folio volumes.[65]

The life of Durantis is also illustrative of the sort of spectacular success that could crown, or at any rate follow, a career devoted to the academic side of the *ius commune*. A native of Provence, Durantis learned and then taught canon law at several Italian universities. Thereafter he served successively as *auditor generalis* of the apostolic palace, a papal governor in the Romagna, and bishop of Mende. All the while he managed to accumulate a considerable collection of other, revenue-producing benefices. He refused the archiepiscopal see of Ravenna in 1294 and died in 1296. The story of his career can be duplicated for many other commentators. Studying, teaching, and writing about the law was a means of rising in the world.[66]

Production of procedural literature continued throughout the medieval period and into the early modern era. In common with several

other parts of the law, it became both more abundant and more specialized with the coming of the sixteenth century. One finds more works
on the procedure of particular tribunals, such as that by Octavianus
Vestrius (d. 1573) on procedure at the Roman court.[67] The manuals
written for the Inquisition, such as the early example by Nicholas Eymericus (d. 1399),[68] probably should be classed among these specialized treatises.[69] One also finds more detailed treatises on special
aspects of procedure, such as that by Sebastianus Vantius (d. 1570) on
the law relating to the nullity of judicial sentences.[70] And of course one
continues to find many general treatises on the procedural law of the
ius commune, both in the civil forum and in the criminal.[71]

Treatises and Monographs

The history of treatises devoted to individual areas of the law approx-
imates that of the *ordines iudiciarii*. They began to appear almost
from the time the classical canon law was being formulated. Bernard
of Pavia wrote a *summa* dealing with the law of marriage during the
1170s, as did Tancred of Benevento writing on the same subject during the second decade of the next century.[72] Treatises on specialized
subjects continued to be written throughout the later Middle Ages.
They ranged from subjects as great as the disputes over church government that animated the conciliar movement to pedestrian subjects such as the law of tithes.[73] Their variety was great. Their growth
was luxuriant.

In reputation, most of the specialized treatises of the later medieval
period now seem pretty much overshadowed by the great commentaries on the books of the *Corpus iuris canonici* that were compiled at
the same time. This may not be wholly due to the low esteem in
which the period has been held among most historians of the law.
Some of the works one describes as monographic were minor exercises, and a few were actually portions devoted to a single subject
taken from a more general commentary.[74] The *Tractatus universi
iuris*, the already mentioned compendium of existing works compiled
during the sixteenth century to state the body of the *ius commune*,

incorporated several examples of this sort of "quasi treatise" extracted from a longer work.

Another kind of "quasi treatise" quite characteristic of the *ius commune*, though perhaps it was more appendage than treatise in form, was the addition of new material to an existing work. Sometimes taking the form of a gloss, sometimes the form of an addition to the text inserted at the end of each section, these additions were called *apostillae*, or *additiones*, or *suppletiones*.[75] Many canonists (and civilians) wrote them. They thought it no shame simply to supplement what others had written. And some of these efforts became famous. The *additiones* to the *Speculum iudiciale* of William Durantis written by Joannes Andreae and Baldus are probably the best-known example of the genre. And although modern historians have not paid a great deal of attention to them, so far do they seem from "original works" in the accepted sense, it is nonetheless clear that there is much to be learned from them.[76]

The writing of legal treatises of all kinds expanded exponentially during the years after printing them became feasible. Their extent is bewildering, and long bibliographical works eventually came to be written in order to help lawyers find their way through the forest of learned works to the exact information they required. It is not easy to convey the size of the forest. I hold in my hand a modern reprint of the *Bibliothecae iuridicae* compiled by Martin Lipenius (d. 1692). Not always complete or accurate, it nevertheless provides a glimpse of the reality. Under the heading "Excommunication," for example, Lipenius listed no fewer than thirty separate treatises written during the sixteenth and seventeenth centuries that were devoted exclusively to that subject. This does not count the more general works that also dealt with the subject. Nor does it begin to count the works on the closely related topic "Censures" to which Lipenius makes a cross-reference under that heading. When one follows the reference and looks at "Censures," forty-two other works are there to be found. This pattern is the norm. There are few legal topics within the *ius commune* about which no specialized treatise was ever written. For most subjects one has a very considerable choice.

Decisiones and Consilia

It is sometimes said that whereas English common law grew from the cumulation of case law, Continental law was formed from authoritative text and academic commentary. There is a good deal of truth to the statement, certainly as to the canon law. However, the generalization should not be extended to imply that there was no such thing as case law within the traditions of the *ius commune*. Actual litigation spawned something like collections of case law in at least two principal forms. The first, apparently the older, is the *consilium*. In its essential features, a *consilium* was the answer given by a learned jurist to a question, usually from a current case, put by the judge or requested by a party.[77] In most situations, we do not know the extent to which the jurist's opinion was binding upon the judge, but it stands to reason that it was not easily disregarded when requested, and *consilia* were sometimes acknowledged expressly by the judge's sentence. When the *consilium* was prepared for one of the parties to litigation, it rather resembled what would be called an "opinion of counsel" in English legal parlance. These were obviously less authoritative, but they are not without value for our understanding of how the *ius commune* could be applied to the facts of concrete cases.

Some of the resulting *consilia* proved to be quite elaborate. They contain real displays of learning, as well as applications of the law to practical problems. The *consilia* of many successful jurists were therefore collected together and published. Indices were added to make them accessible. The resulting literature is large. It has, perhaps because of its apparent immediacy to living problems, also attracted the particular attention of modern historians. Useful bibliographies of the *consilia* have been compiled in recent years,[78] and successful studies of individual examples of the genre have been undertaken.[79]

The second and related form is the *decisio*. A *decisio* differed from a *consilium* in that it came from a jurist who had taken a direct part in the litigation. Normally a *decisio* was put together by the judge or *auditor* involved in the case.[80] The two forms were alike, however, in applying the law to a particular set of facts, one that actually occurred. Indeed, many collections of *decisiones* read very much like collections of *consilia* in form and range.[81] In no case were they sentences of a court, as their name might seem to imply; canonical sentences normally contained no authorities or specific reasons for the judge's decision. *Decisiones* did. They thus contained abbreviated accounts of the facts and the legal questions involved in a case, put together with the arguments, the relevant authorities, and the solution reached by the court. Some of them became quite well known; the treatment of the law of blasphemy found in a *decisio* of Nicholaus Boerius (d. 1539), for instance, became a standard authority on that subject, much cited by other commentators. Other *decisiones* remained more obscure; their contents are only today being brought into the light.

The earliest reporting of *decisiones* did not take place in the courts of the church. It grew from the practice of lay tribunals—perhaps from the French *parlements*,[82] or even, it has been plausibly suggested, from the traditions of the English common law.[83] Whatever the source, from the fourteenth century the habit passed into the ecclesiastical forum. The *decisiones* of the papal court, called the Rota Romana, began to be collected. These reports turn out to deal preponderantly with procedural and beneficial matters, but they were influential in many particulars. Many volumes followed. *Decisiones* from other local courts were also compiled, and both ecclesiastical and temporal courts are represented in the resulting literature. A collection from the archiepiscopal see of Toulouse in what is now southern France was a particularly influential example of this form of literature.[84] Much remains to be done in exploring this special and intriguing body of literature from the *ius commune*.

CONCLUSION

It has been my experience that the best way to become familiar with canonical sources and the accompanying literature is to set out to discover the law on a particular subject—to learn by doing. Reading about the *fontes* without a specific interest has too often meant (for me at least) that the information does not stick for very long. This experience has colored my view of how the subjects in this volume should be presented. Much of what has been described briefly in this introduction will be illustrated, expanded, and repeated in dealing with the particular aspects of the classical canon law covered in the pages that follow. I hope that these discussions will convey something of the vastness and the interest inherent in the subject.

2 Governance of the Church: The Law of Episcopal Elections

What once was called the Investiture Contest is today more generally regarded as one part of a larger movement. The larger movement is now known as the period of Gregorian reform, the change being made to stress the vital importance of ideas associated with Pope Gregory VII (d. 1085).[1] It has also been called the "Papal Revolution" by historians, partly to deemphasize Gregory's personal role in the development of the canon law[2] and partly to emphasize the fundamental nature of the changes that a movement led by the papacy brought to Western society and government.[3]

Overall, this change in terminology has probably been a useful correction. The church's struggle to put an end to the practice by which kings conferred the insignia of episcopal office upon newly chosen bishops was undeniably part of a much wider and more fundamental change in the ways Western society was governed.[4] For purposes of introducing this chapter, however, the older term might usefully be held in mind.[5] It focuses attention on a question of greatest moment to the reformers: the need to prohibit laymen from taking a decisive part, indeed anything but a supernumerary part, in choosing the men who would rule the church. Lay investiture, by which the symbols of episcopal office were handed to the new bishop by a layman, was not *necessarily* affected by the way the bishop had been chosen. But to the Gregorian reformers, the ceremony represented in a particularly dramatic way the exercise of that lay power over the church they most wanted to eradicate.

Modern historians have argued at length about how far the *ultimate* purposes of the Gregorian reformers were meant to extend. I think it is fair to say that these historians have reached no unassailable conclusion on the subject. Some hold to the view that the desires of the reformers went no further than purification of the church; others believe that the reformers envisioned a thoroughgoing reordering of all society. However, all have perforce agreed about the existence and immediacy of the goal that is the subject of this chapter: securing the canonical election of bishops and freeing it from lay control. "Ecclesiastical liberty," the watchword of the reform movement, was a slogan invoked repeatedly in the effort to secure this immediate goal.[6] If the church was to be purified, this much at least had to be achieved.

The effort was more than a simple struggle for power between church and state. From the point of the view of the reformers, few things mattered more than placing the best men in positions of leadership. The exclusion of simony, the suppression of clerical marriage, the improvement in the quality of the clergy—none of these things could be achieved without effective leadership. Bishops beholden to princes for their offices were unlikely to be fearless in pursuing these goals. Moreover, the reformers argued that if purification of the church was to be accomplished, bishoprics could not be left vacant for extended periods, as had too often happened when the decision about the successor rested in lay hands. Rulers enjoyed some of the episcopal revenues in the meantime, and this tempted them to leave the bishop's flock without a shepherd. And finally, the reformers recoiled from the process by which bishops were chosen becoming the subject of public discord. The history of disputes over who should be chosen bishop was filled with examples of acrimonious divisions between partisans of this or that candidate. This unseemly squabbling was something reformers in the church were determined to eliminate if they could, to minimize if they could not.

It was in the classical canon law that these reforms took definitive shape. The law of episcopal elections that was developed was also new law for the most part. Though ancient building blocks were used, the edifice eventually constructed would have looked quite unfamiliar to earlier Christians. This is not an area of the law, as are several of those to be treated in this book, where the *Corpus iuris canonici* simply enshrined, elaborated, and made binding rules that had been inherited from the earliest days of the church's history. In dealing with episcopal elections, we can therefore watch from a particularly good vantage point the ways in which the canon law came into existence. Elections make a good place to start.

HISTORICAL ANTECEDENTS

The best attested and perhaps also the oldest rule of the church held that the choice of bishops should be made *per clerum et populum* (Dist. 63 c. 13).[7] It was, and remains, far from clear what this venerable formula, requiring some combination of assent from the clergy and people, actually meant in the earliest days. The church fathers did not write to satisfy an audience of Philadelphia lawyers, and it may be that they regarded the real choice as belonging to God, the voice of the clergy and people being simply the way in which God's selection was ordinarily made manifest.[8] The fathers also thought, it seems, in terms of a collective, unanimous expression of opinion by a corporate body of Christians, not a choice made by individual electors.[9] They may have expected that a minority would give way. That manner of thinking did not lend itself to the most exact of procedural rules. Whatever the right answer may be, there has long been scholarly controversy about the respective roles accorded to the opinions of the neighboring bishops, the clergy of the diocese, monastic leaders, and the people to be governed by the man elected.[10] And there is ample reason for uncertainty.[11]

It does seem certain, however, that in most of the early evidence clear room was made for the voice of "the people" in the selection of bishops. Consent of the laity, or something very much like it, appeared as a component of choosing bishops in the letters of St. Cyprian (d. 258), and it was explicitly recognized in the letters of the fifth-century popes. Thus Celestine I (d. 432) to the bishops of Gaul: "No bishop is to be given to the unwilling," or Leo I (d. 461) to the province of Vienne: "Let him who is to rule over all be elected by all."[12] At a Roman synod in 1080, Pope Gregory VII himself endorsed the rule that the selection should be made by the clergy and people.[13] Appearance of the formulaic "election by the clergy and people" in an appropriate canon in the *Decretum* (Dist. 63 c. 13) was entirely in line with the church's traditions.

When Pope Gregory and Gratian endorsed the formula *per clerum et populum*, however, their purpose was not to exalt the will of the people. Their purpose was to exclude the will of the prince.[14] Paying fuller attention to the language Gregory used makes their purpose evident. According to his synod's decree, the clergy and people were to elect "without any secular desire, fear or favor." But how, it may be asked, could "the people" possibly act without being influenced by "any secular desire"? That would seem to be a contradiction in terms. In fact, it did not look that way at the time. The incongruity is only apparent. The explanation is that the right to choose bishops for the church had, at least in the West, very largely fallen into the hands of princes—whether emperors, kings, dukes, or counts.[15] The canon law would take the position that for this purpose at least princes were mere laymen, and it was this "secular desire" that Gregory's synodal decree condemned. Election *per clerum et populum* could be contrasted without inconsistency with the system dominated by secular powers—the one that existed. By that system, kings and princes had been deciding who would serve as bishops within their lands.

Lay investiture was thus one part of a more pervasive system of royal control of the church. Royal nomination of bishops was the linchpin. It was vital to them. Kings depended upon the loyalty of their bishops for more than spiritual counsel, and they were loath to surrender the very rights that maintained that loyalty. Both long-established custom and several express recognitions in canonical sources encouraged them in clinging to that right. A decree of the Council of Toledo, for example, had authorized the consecration of "whomever the royal power shall select" (Dist. 63 c. 25). It was against this custom that Gregory VII and the reformers set their face. In doing so, they contrasted the ancient and canonical election *per clerum et populum* with the sad reality of what they saw around them. To them, the comparison showed a perversion in the law of the church. They used the ancient formulation as a stick to beat the proponents of what they regarded as a perversion of right order in society.

GRATIAN'S *DECRETUM*

Gratian devoted considerable attention to canonical elections, and it was natural that he should have. Elections raised one of the great ecclesiastical issues of his time. The subject is found in four of his *Distinctiones* and in parts of two of his *Causae*. Gratian's treatment of the questions involved is also quite characteristic of his approach, both in its strengths and (at least as we see them today) in its weaknesses. The *Decretum* did not create a satisfactory law governing episcopal elections, but it did state important principles. And it did bring a harmony of sorts to what look to have been hopelessly dissonant authorities.

The Necessity of Election

Quite apart from the question of who should take part in the decision, it could not have been altogether obvious that the process of selecting a bishop should take the form of an election at all. Though election was mentioned in ancient sources and supported after a fashion by biblical example (Acts 6:5), the canons taken together prescribed no certain method, and if one stood by customary right, the choice of bishops would be made by one man—the king. Many canons of the church also seemed to approve this power of choice in the lay ruler. It could even be said that the method of royal nomination had evident advantages besides its claim to long usage. It might be regarded as a legitimate way of curbing factionalism in a clerical population anxious for promotion, and it might serve also as a means of avoiding the unseemly strife of popular contests that was so roundly and repeatedly condemned in the canons (e.g., Dist. 63 c. 11).

Even setting royal nomination aside as unacceptable because of its incompatibility with Gregorian principles, the question still existed. Majority rule was far from being a reflexive answer to difficult problems of choice in the twelfth century, and several methods other than election were mentioned, or at least implied, in the *Decretum*. Some texts supported choosing "the best" candidate (e.g., Dist. 63 c. 19), though this raised the obvious difficulty of knowing how that person was to be identified.[16] It was also thinkable to give preference to the senior cleric of the diocese. There was a certain prestige accompanying the earliest ordination (C. 35 q. 6 c. 1), and it was not beyond the realm of possibility that seniority should carry the day here.[17] Alternatively, the metropolitan or the neighboring bishops might make the choice. Presumably they would be disinterested, and authority in the canons (e.g., Dist. 35 c. 35) could be marshaled to support their claims. Some form of election was perhaps the most commonly attested method of choice, but it was far from being the sole possibility.

The method that occurs most immediately to modern readers—appointment by the papacy—apparently did not arise as a possibility for Gratian. By the end of the next century, it would be strenuously maintained that in the earliest times, all bishops had been named by the bishops of Rome.[18] But this seems not to have been Gratian's assumption. The "descending theme" of papal government, by which all power was regarded as flowing from the top in the church's governance, is not what one sees here.[19] Election "from below" rather than an appointment "from above" would have to be the "theme" if one were required to characterize the Decretum's treatment of this subject. Nor is there any incongruity in this. The canonists of the classical period perceived no difficulty or inconsistency with papal authority in the situation. As a matter of practice, the popes had not ordinarily taken any role in episcopal elections, and as noted above, the canonists found endorsement for the principle of electing the leaders of the church within the pages of the Bible itself (Acts 6:5).

In fact, for this period the suggestion of direct choice by the papacy is slightly anachronistic. In 1140, papal power was still primarily exercised in the pope's role as supreme judge.[20] Its normal sphere within the law came in settling disputes. Its great advantage lay in the ability it claimed to give a final decision or statement of the law, one from which no appeal could be taken. In matters of routine administration of the church, the papacy took no direct part outside its own patrimony. The famous Dictatus papae (1075) made no claim, for instance, that papal rights were involved in the ordinary choice of bishops. Moreover, the practical problems in direct papal oversight of choice of bishops would have been very great. In 1140, no procedure or papal bureaucracy existed that would have been capable of selecting men in far-off sees whenever an incumbent died.

Gratian said nothing like this, of course. He took up this question of how bishops were to be chosen in a context different from either political theory or administrative convenience. He put the following case (C. 8 q. 1): By a last will and testament made as he was approaching death, a certain bishop instituted his successor. The old bishop made his selection in much the same way a testator instituted an heir as his legal successor under the civil law. The *Causa* turned out to raise other questions, since the same man was also subsequently elected bishop and since a subsequent and possibly simoniacal oath to the electors was also involved. But the first and most obvious *quaestio* raised was whether it was lawful for a bishop to institute his successor. If it was, the later election would have been superfluous.

The *Decretum*'s treatment began with several authorities in favor of allowing the practice.[21] A letter of Pope Zacharias (d. 752) had allowed the archbishop of Mainz to name his successor (C. 7 q. 1 c. 17). A decree attributed to Pope Symmachus (d. 514) had called for an election if the sudden death of the Roman pontiff prevented deliberation about the succession, suggesting *a contrario sensu* that a "premortem" choice would be lawful where no such special circumstances existed (Dist. 79 c. 10). Finally, a long ecclesiastical tradition, believed by many and cited with apparent approbation in a papal letter, held that St. Peter had himself named Clement his successor as bishop of Rome (C. 8 q. 1 cc. 1–2).

Having set out texts permitting a positive answer to the question posed, Gratian turned to authorities on the other side. The first, from a fourth-century church council, held directly: "It is not permitted to a bishop to constitute another as his successor, even if he is reaching the end of his life" (C. 8 q. 1 c. 4). The canons that followed reiterated this rule in much the same direct fashion. They also provided a reason that the choice of bishops should on principle be kept separate from the succession to a predecessor's estate. It was only natural that a man should choose his inheritors from among his relations and friends. That was the normal pattern of testation. So very likely would most bishops do in choosing their successors. But this should not happen. In governance of the church, ties of blood must take a back seat to merit and zeal.

The example of Moses, who had spoken with God face to face, was adduced to show that choices should not be the product of preference for kin and tribe (C. 8 q. 1 c. 6). Moses had been given a special power to choose his successor. He had, however, not done what was natural. He had picked someone from outside his own tribe (Num. 27:18–22). The wisdom of Moses provided a lesson for the canon law. Canonical procedure should minimize the likelihood that familial influence would come into play. Moreover, testamentary succession in whatever form might easily exclude the deliberation that was desirable in the choice of a bishop (c. 3). The great object of whatever form was selected was to choose the best-qualified person, and at least some discussion seemed necessary to achieve that end. Gratian therefore concluded that testamentary institution was unlawful.[22]

The authorities that seemed at first sight to permit the practice were distinguished in several ways, both by Gratian and in the commentary offered by the *glossa ordinaria*. They were read as having approved only deliberation, not decision, about the choice of a new bishop. It was said that the true constitutive act in every instance had been a later election, not the prior deliberation. Alternately, the contrary authorities were said to rest, like the right Moses had held, upon a special privilege given for a special reason. And, in the case of the designation of his successor by St. Peter, they were said to prove the reverse of what they seemed to say. Clement had not actually been the second pope but instead the third or the fourth. Seeing that it would be a pernicious example if he were to sit upon the Chair of St. Peter by direct designation, Clement had renounced the right. Popes Linus and Cletus had therefore followed in direct succession to St. Peter. Only when they had died had Clement taken charge of the apostolic see, and then it had happened by virtue of an election.[23] This was the example that was thought to have been followed invariably since that ancient event. Its rationale remained as applicable in 1140 as it had been in earlier days. Where a bishop became too old or infirm to act, the case could be dealt with by appointment of a coadjutor

(C. 7 q. 1 c. 17).[24] But that special situation should not be allowed to become the church's rule.

A subject neatly skirted by this account of the earliest papal succession raised the intriguing question of whether a pope could, if he wished, name his own successor. Clement's example suggested that the pope should not. But would the church have been bound to accept Clement as pope had he not chosen the path of renunciation and patience? Did the papal plenitude of power extend that far? Gratian did not himself confront the question; but it was raised in the *glossa* and answered in the negative.[25] That seems also to have been the answer favored by most commentators.[26] What had been solemnly ordained for the good of the church was not to be tampered with (C. 25 q. 1 c. 3). The long-established tradition of papal elections showed the wisdom of the rule. It was said that the only pope legitimately chosen through nomination of his predecessor had been St. Peter himself. The contemporary establishment of the right of election as belonging to the cardinals of the Roman Church (1059) and the election decree of 1179 (X 1.6.6) set the seal on this result.

This much was accomplished by Gratian within only the first seven canons and two *dicta post*. The entire *quaestio* contained twenty-four canons; the rest dealt with a miscellaneous group of subjects surrounding episcopal elections. They show how far Gratian was from writing a modern legal treatise. He had much to say about the qualities requisite in a bishop. Few of them could be reduced to a legal rule enforced in a law court. But several of them were useful as guides to conduct. For example, it was commanded in the Old Testament that a man should marry the wife of his brother who had died childless. If he refused, the woman was to remove one of his shoes and spit in his face for this refusal "to build up his brother's house" (Deut. 25:9). That rule was not accepted by the church. Indeed, it was rejected. The canon law ultimately held that such a marriage would be unlawful, requiring special papal dispensation. For Gratian, however, this text was useful in a different way. It stood as a reminder of the duty a worthy man was under to assume the duties of the episcopate if he was elected to it (c. 8). When a bishop died, a suitable spouse had to be found for the see, and when one had been found, that man could not refuse the duty without shame. He would not be compelled to take it up, any more than the brother in Deuteronomy was actually compelled to marry his brother's wife. But the better course for him was to prefer the utility of the many to his own convenience. For Gratian, that was the lesson taught by this biblical example.

Exclusion of the Laity

In *Distinctiones* 62 and 63, Gratian confronted the question of the laity's part in episcopal elections. From what has been said already, readers may suppose that the outcome was foreordained. Perhaps it was. The Gregorian reformers' desire to free the church from secular influence may well have made any other answer impossible. However, Gratian did not suppress the inconvenient authorities. He both distinguished them and made something useful out of them. From the conflicting authorities, he drew an affirmative set of principles for episcopal elections.[27]

Gratian began discussion in *Distinctio* 62, not as he would in *Causa* 8 with contrary authorities eventually to be distinguished away, but instead with three statements of basic principles, all of which purported to be taken from decretal letters. First, no one was to be held as bishop of a diocese unless he had been chosen by the clergy, consented to by the people, and consecrated by the bishops of the province. Second, the people were always to be led by the clergy (*Docendus est populus non sequendus*) so that they could be brought to understand and consent to the clergy's choice. Third, no man should be consecrated bishop unless there had first been a canonical election.

In the next *Distinctio* Gratian added thirty-six canons and several *dicta* in which these principles were amplified and clarified. He began in the same positive way. The first eight canons condemned the baleful influence of the crowd (*turba*) upon episcopal elections (e.g., Dist. 63 c. 6). Then in canon 9, Gratian turned to several canons that appeared to say the opposite: most notably that election was to be conducted "by the clergy and people." But what did this mean? And how was it to be brought into conformity with the texts that had come before? Gratian harmonized them by exploiting the ambiguity. The word "and" did not necessarily require that the role of each group be identical. The formula required that both take some part, but the language was compatible with limiting the role of the laity to one in which they consented to the choice of the clergy and acclaimed the newly elected bishop (Dist. 63 c. 12). Furthermore, the texts stating that no bishop was to be given to the unwilling did not actually require that the laity be given an equal voice, or even any voice at all. They were dealt with by supposing that they applied when unwillingness among the laity had stemmed from a proper canonical objection.[28]

Despite being diminished, the laity's role was not altogether eliminated. The ancient formula "clergy and people" set limits. It required that the laity be given *some* role, even if only that of giving their ritual consent after the election.[29] Moreover, the laity's role was a positive one in another sense. Episcopal elections were not to become the preserve of factions among the clergy, and they were to be kept free from secular influence.[30] Publicity in the process was therefore valuable. Perhaps it was even essential. By it, the best man might be selected (C. 8 q. 1 c. 15), dissension avoided (Dist. 63 c. 28), and the worthiness of the man elected openly proclaimed (d.p. Dist. 63 c. 25). The presence of the laity served these functions. A cynic might be tempted to say (Gratian did not) that the laity's right to consent kept the clergy honest.

Dealing with the pretended rights of the prince presented a more difficult problem than dealing with those of the crowd. Although several canons stated a principle that would clearly exclude the prince's taking any part (e.g., Dist. 63 c. 3, 4), several others actually seemed to permit the prince to make the choice of bishops directly. Indeed, some of the latter apparently confined the clergy's role to consenting and consecrating the person chosen for them by the prince (e.g., cc. 16, 17, 21, 23). How were these canons to be understood? The answer was found in the concept of a privilege, a subject to be examined in more detail in Chapter 12. In each case where the canon spoke of lay selection, it was contended, the prince had been granted the right of episcopal nomination for some special reason, the most pressing of which was the danger of heresy. To avoid the choice of a heretical bishop, extreme measures might be necessary, even intervention by the king or emperor. The canons permitting royal nomination of bishops might all be understood in this way. If so, once the danger of heresy or dissension had passed, so too would the princes' right of selecting bishops.[31] *Cessante ratione cessat dispensatio* (C. 1 q. 7 c. 7).

Furthermore, it was maintained that as a matter of simple logic, if the princes had always exercised a right to select bishops by virtue of a privilege granted by the church, it followed that the right must originally have existed in the church. Otherwise the privilege itself would have been invalid. And if the privilege's validity ceased for whatever reason, it also followed that the right granted must then revert to the grantor. Gratian concluded that exactly this had taken place. Any privilege may be lost by renunciation or abuse. The emperors had both renounced (Dist. 63 c. 33) and abused (d.p. Dist. 63 c. 28) their privileges. Hence the control over episcopal elections had reverted to the control of the church by ordinary process of law.

Gratian also saw a second, more positive value in the canons that had spoken approvingly of intervention by the princes. The occasions described in the canons had allowed the princes to show themselves the "obedient sons of the church" by repelling heretics from the episcopacy and by quelling disorder within the church.[32] Seeming to show lay power being exercised *over* the church, therefore, more fully understood the canons actually showed the reverse. The emperor had simply been obeying the dictates of the church when he exercised electoral rights granted by virtue of a privilege.[33] An agent may not impeach the title of his principal. The example of lay intervention had been meant to demonstrate the merits of obedience to the church by the prince.

The force of this argument, at least for Gratian, was more than merely logical, more than simple application of assumptions drawn from the law of privileges. A biblical example supported it. God had commanded Moses to make a brass serpent and set it up on a pole, so that by looking upon it the people might be saved from the death that followed the bites of the vipers then plaguing Israel (Num. 21:8–9). In the course of time, however, the people of Israel began to worship the brass serpent, and God eventually required Hezekiah to break it into pieces (4 Kings 18:4). So had it happened with the power of lay rulers over episcopal elections (d.p. Dist. 63 c. 28). What once God had allowed for the good of the church had been turned into a source of harm to the church. Because of the wickedness of the lay rulers, the power given to them to combat heresy had itself become a source of heresy, the simoniacal heresy. Their power must therefore be broken into as many pieces as the Bible's brass serpent had been.

A modern critic, probably not much impressed by this biblical argument, would probably conclude that in this analysis Gratian was treating the texts at his disposal as "historically contingent." He could even be described as "manipulating" them. It would be difficult to dissent categorically from this characterization, although one might wish to moderate it. The conclusion presumes a greater freedom in analyzing texts than was characteristic of the canon law. But whatever the best modern judgment of Gratian's technique may be, it was unquestionably one of the common ways in which he and other canonists were able to reconcile conflicting and inconvenient texts. Canons that appeared to contradict a canonical rule could be regarded as resting upon particular, historical circumstance. They had there- fore to give way when the circumstances changed.[34] On the subject of elections, the method served to preserve the force of the canons that excluded *all* the laity from episcopal elections. These canons were treated as stating a long-standing and principled rule of church government. Those canons that permitted it were treated as the product of exceptional circumstance.

Form of the Election

Gratian's *Decretum* had much less to say about the details of episcopal elections than about the principles that underlay them. It was left to the Decretals to fix upon the details of the canonical system. However, the *Decretum* did say a little: first, that there must be an election. There must be a coming together of those who were to make the decision, not merely the individual expression of opinion by each of the electors.[35] The first canon in *Distinctio* 63 defined the three

requisite elements of episcopal election; it must be "common, consonant, and canonical." The first requirement meant that if the electors
had done no more than to agree separately on a particular individual,
there would have been no election. To avoid faction, "private conven-
ticles" were also prohibited.[36] This was a form of the same rule applied in papal elections (Dist. 79 c. 1), and that precedent may have
been carried over here.

Second, at the very end of *Distinctio* 63 (c. 35), Gratian touched upon
the question of how the group of the clergy to make the election was itself to be determined. The treatment is short, perhaps because of a lack
of authority on the subject. The origins of the church's practice have
equally remained a little uncertain to modern historians.[37] There was
uncertainty and disagreement even at the time.[38] However, the basic
rule finally arrived at was fairly simple. In the absence of custom, prescription, or privilege to the contrary, the right to elect a bishop belonged to the cathedral chapter. Typically, this would have consisted of
the dean and the cathedral canons. Where a collegiate body was involved, as it was in many cathedrals, it seemed self-evident that the
body itself should make a collegial decision (X 1.6.1). The example of
papal elections, confined to the College of Cardinals by Alexander III
(1179),[39] may also have influenced the outcome in favor of having a restricted number of electors. Canon 28 of the Third Lateran Council,
from which Gratian took his canon 35, also envisioned the initial decision being made by the men who held the canons' stalls within the
bishop's cathedral church.[40] Whatever the reason, election by the
cathedral chapter became the rule. It was softened only to admit the
possibility that a customary right could be more generally shared, provided always that the custom did not include the laity.[41]

THE DECRETALS AND THE *LIBER SEXTUS*

The *Decretum* may be regarded as having settled several matters of
principle. The procedures by which episcopal elections would actually take place remained to be determined. It was an urgent need. Disputes abounded. In this circumstance, as a modern student has noted,

the law that was needed "seems to have developed with unusual rapidity."[42] In papal decretals and canons of the several councils held between 1140 and 1300, the basic rules were formulated. Eight (at least) separate areas of electoral law were covered and clarified in the 107 chapters of the titles "De electione" in the Decretals and in the *Liber sextus*. The achievements were to

1. restate the principles laid out in the *Decretum* and make specific rules to give them effect;
2. state the personal qualifications to be required of all candidates for episcopal election;
3. determine the necessary qualifications of the electors;
4. fix the permissible procedures to be used in all elections;
5. provide for failures to elect and for uncanonical elections, including penalties to be imposed on those who did not comply with the rules;
6. safeguard the ability to appeal to the papal court in disputed elections and set workable limits to the abuse of appeals;
7. clarify the role of the metropolitan (typically the archbishop) and the other bishops of the province in confirming the election;
8. establish the powers and duties of men who had been elected but not yet consecrated as bishops.

Formulation of workable rules for these areas, many of which were sure to be the scene of heated disputes in actual cases, was an ambitious though necessary task. It presented thorny practical difficulties, and the procedures that emerged turned out not to work in entire harmony with one another. Anomalies and difficulties were left. But it may be fairly said that respectable rules were evolved and that most of the detailed rules were developed on the basis of the principles enunciated in the *Decretum*. Of the eight areas, it seems right to leave aside only the last item. It dealt with a slightly different question than the subject of this chapter.[43] But any halfway adequate coverage of the subject of elections requires that the import of the others be stated and clarified with an example or two.

First was implementation of the principle of ecclesiastical liberty, so clearly stated in the *Decretum*. The electors must have free choice and their choice must not be subject to any interference by laymen. This required closing several "loopholes." Most of these involved rights of the laity based upon custom. They must have been quite widespread. They were struck down as illegitimate in every instance. For example, a decretal of Pope Celestine III (d. 1198) condemned a "perverse custom" by which the cathedral chapter presented two candidates to the prince, leaving it up to him to choose between the two (X 1.6.14). Similarly, electors could not validly create a custom by agreeing among themselves to leave their choice to a layman (X 1.6.51). Indeed, the distrust of lay influence was carried to the point of creating a presumption against the suitability of a candidate who had originally been suggested to the electors by a letter from the people of the diocese (X 1.6.2). That would open the door to abuses. "No one is to be elected through the clamor of the people" ran the canonical tag,[44] and in the law of the Decretals this came to mean their entire exclusion from elections. The door was shut. Later developments left it only slightly ajar.[45]

The second area related to the personal characteristics of the men qualified to be elected.[46] Some of these chapters were designed to preserve the good order of the church. For example, a monk could not be elected bishop without the consent of his religious superior (Sext. 1.6.27). The abbot of an exempt monastic house could not be elected to an episcopal see without the agreement of the pope or his special legate (Sext. 1.6.36). Other chapters stated traditional rules or merely reiterated the requirements for admission to all holy orders. Thus, a man must be of legitimate birth and at least thirty years old to be consecrated bishop (X 1.6.7). He must not be of servile condition, the subject to be taken up in Chapter 3, and he must not be currently excommunicate. He must not be a simoniac, a public usurer, or a spendthrift.[47] "Sufficient learning" was a requirement (X 1.6.17), though the *glossa ordinaria* and later commentary softened this by reading the standard as one of simple reasonability.[48] He must not be, at least in one formulation, likely to be "an enemy to hospitality" as a bishop.[49] In all, if fully implemented, the range of disqualifications would have eliminated a large number of potential candidates.

The third, dealing with the qualifications of the electors, proved surprisingly difficult in practical terms. Although laymen could not participate by making a claim to prescription or long-standing custom, clerics outside the cathedral chapter could (X 1.6.55). Indeed, it was possible to speak in terms of "quasi possession" of the right to participate in an election (X 1.6.24).[50] Electors, however qualified, had the right to be summoned to take part in the election if they were within the province. In the absence of that summons, the election itself was invalid (X 1.6.35–36). Electors could validly participate if they were bound by a sentence of minor excommunication, but not if by major excommunication (X 1.6.39).

Some of the rules adopted under this heading seem almost to have been designed to open elections to further dispute, such as the one that if an elector knowingly voted for an unworthy candidate, he himself would be disqualified from taking part in the election (X 1.6.25). The same exclusionary rule was applied if an elector made his choice "through abuse of the secular power" (X 1.6.43). "Freedom" of election in the canonical sense did not imply uncontrolled freedom to do whatever the elector wished. It was the type of freedom, of which we shall see several examples, to act freely in accord with the law, the well-being of the church, and the health of one's soul. If used wrongfully, the *ius eligendi* would be lost. That disputes were the inevitable consequence of this way of thinking seemed less important than securing the church's well-being.

The fourth area, regulation of the forms of election, has attracted the most attention among modern commentators, perhaps because of the strong element of strangeness within it that is nonetheless coupled with a certain anticipation of modern practices. There were three permissible forms, established by the decree *Quia propter* of the Fourth Lateran Council (X 1.6.42) and clarified by several following decretals (e.g., Sext. 1.6.43). Other forms, such as election by lot, were prohibited (X 5.21.3). Indeed, exact compliance with the terms of the three was required under penalty of invalidity.[51] Nor could one permissible method be substituted for the other once the choice had been made (X 1.6.58).

The first method, apparently the most frequently used, was by "scrutiny." In it, three tellers were chosen from among members of the chapter. They investigated the vote of each elector, interrogating him singly and secretly. They then tallied the votes and published the result in writing, declaring elected the candidate favored by the "greater and more discerning part" (*maior et sanior pars*) of the electors. A second method was the "way of compromise." It required that the electors unanimously agree in advance to cede their rights to *compromissarii*. These men then made the choice for the electors. A third, election "by inspiration," occurred whenever the electors all fixed upon a single candidate "as if by inspiration." Inspiration had been the source of some wonderful choices in the church's history—St. Ambrose of Milan for one, perhaps even Pope Gregory VII. Room was left for it in the canon law of elections as a way in which God's will could be manifested.[52] Where the Spirit of God was at work, there was freedom from formal rule (2 Cor. 3:17),[53] though even here later scholastic commentators managed in time to hit upon a subcategory of "election by quasi inspiration."[54]

The fifth area of the law covered in the Decretals dealt with faulty, incomplete, or nonexistent elections. Here is a sample of the many rules adopted. If the chapter failed to act within three months, the right to choose the bishop "lapsed" and devolved upon the metropolitan (X 1.6.41). If the chapter acted, but acted improperly in an election that was *ipso iure* invalid, it could not elect again until the first election had been formally quashed by its superior, in practice usually the pope (X 1.6.29). If the electors knowingly refused to follow the prescribed form of election, the right of choice passed to the apostolic see (Sext. 1.6.18). Electors who chose a candidate because of "the abuse of secular power" were deprived of the right to vote and suspended from their benefices for three years (X 1.6.43). No conditional, alternate, or uncertain votes were permitted; if attempted, the tellers were to disregard them (Sext. 1.6.2). The conjunction of these rules shows the law of episcopal elections becoming something of a minefield.[55] Stepping carefully was required if the possibility of invalidity was to be avoided.

The sixth area of coverage dealt with appeals. It contained two important but discordant goals. One was to secure the right of all interested parties to appeal to the papal court. The other was to discourage abuse of that right. For example, electors refusing to defer to an appeal were held to have lost their right to proceed to election whatever the fate of the appeal (X 1.6.10).[56] That encouraged appeals. On the other hand, if the party that appealed to the apostolic see because of an alleged defect in the candidate elected failed to prove the alleged defect, he was to be condemned to pay all the other party's expenses and deprived of his ecclesiastical benefices for three years (Sext. 1.6.1). That discouraged appeals.

This attitude toward appeals—intelligible if slightly schizophrenic—was not peculiar to disputed episcopal elections; it ran throughout the canonical system. However, it was particularly noteworthy here because of the far-reaching results to which it led. A disputed episcopal election was a *maior causa* under the canon law, one normally reserved for decision by the pope (Sext. 1.6.10). The strong suggestion from other sources in the historical record is that a great many of these disputes ended up with bishops being named in Rome after initial discord and subsequent appeal. The law on the subject shows one reason why this happened. The attempt to curtail appeals met with quite modest success.

Finally, the role of the neighboring bishops was tackled at least incidentally in several of the decretals. Although normally excluded from the election itself, these bishops retained real functions in examining the qualities of the man elected and of course also in consecrating him as a bishop. Confirmation extended both to the qualities of the candidate (X 1.6.3) and to the election itself (X 1.6.44). Mostly this function was exercised during the requisite confirmation of the episcopal election. In the *Decretum* it was carried out by the metropolitan and his suffragans in the case of bishops (Dist. 62 c. 1) and by all the bishops of the province where the metropolitan's election was at issue (Dist. 66 c. 1). Under Decretal law, the former retained its validity (X 1.6.32) and was exercised in fact,[57] but there was also some movement in the direction of putting this power, together with the power of confirming all metropolitans, directly into the hands of the pope (X 1.6.18, 28).

TWO SPECIAL LEGAL PROBLEMS

It has already been said that the law of episcopal elections was neither simple nor entirely harmonious internally. The observation is by no means original. The same point was being made already by writers in the thirteenth century.[58] Perhaps not incidentally, this aspect of the law attracted the first canonical monograph dealing with a subject other than procedure or marriage: the *Summa de electione* by Bernard of Pavia (d. 1213).[59] Here we take up two of these areas, both of which illustrate something of the inner character of the canon law.

The *Maior et Sanior Pars*

The method of election called "scrutiny" under the canon law, the most frequently employed of the three possible methods of episcopal election, was also the most like an election in the modern sense. The votes of the electors were taken and counted. Electors were expected to form their own opinion, and the law attempted to make sure that they enjoyed freedom from constraint in making up their minds. It is even possible to speak in terms of a "right" inhering in the voters, the *ius eligendi*.[60] However, readers will recall that under the canonical formula adopted by the Fourth Lateran Council in 1215, the majority of individual votes did not necessarily prevail. The decision was to be made by the *maior et sanior pars*, roughly speaking "the greater and more discerning part," of the electors. It is not immediately obvious, however, what these words mean.[61] Was any sort of effective qualification being placed on majority rule by the word *sanior*?

There was. A sophisticated twentieth-century commentator has spoken of a "hatred of the pure law of numbers" that lay behind the church's rule in episcopal elections.[62] Here it is evident. Unanimity had long been the goal. By the choice of all, the best candidate would be known. A choice arrived at by nothing more than the counting of votes had little or no textual authority to recommend it, and it did not seem instinctively right to the fathers of the classical canon law. Hence the provision for the *sanior pars*. But exactly what did the term mean in practice? Assume for the sake of simplicity that there were only two parties among the electors. There were four questions raised by the requirement in contested elections:

1. How to determine which side was *maior*?
2. How to determine which side was *sanior*?
3. Which side to prefer when the two were different? and,
4. Who should decide disputed cases?

The first of these questions seems to be just a matter of numbers, and it probably was the easiest of the first three. But even it was not necessarily simple. There might be questions about eligibility, since the *ius eligendi* could be held by custom. Not all electors might be present, and there might be questions in consequence about whether or not an absent elector had been legitimately summoned. Electors could lose the right to vote, and hence to be counted, if they were excommunicated or *irregularis* or voted for an unworthy candidate. The canonists saw the problem created. They discussed the possibility that by the process of eliminating ineligible voters the chapter's right to elect might conceivably come to rest in a single member. So the counting itself might be the subject of dispute.

Assuming this question was answered satisfactorily, as a practical matter the next question was whether the majority party was also the more discerning party. This was determined both by examining the choice it had made (i.e., comparing the two candidates elected) and by examining the qualities of the electors themselves. The formula for doing this was as venerable as it was lacking in precise content. One looked to the authority and the merits of the men involved (Dist. 63 c. 36).[63] Or, stated in the full canonical formula, one compared authority with authority, zeal with zeal, and merit with merit (X 1.6.55).[64] What did these mean? If one looks further at the explications of them found in the writings of the canonists, the definitions that are forthcoming will seem question-begging to most readers.[65] "Zeal" according to Hostiensis, "consisted of an affection of the spirit, namely whether one is moved by carnal or by spiritual desires, and [also] whether one is moved by bribery, entreaty and fear, rather than by the living font of charity."[66] Panormitanus described the quantity of each quality required simply as that degree most appropriate for the office involved.[67] A modern student summed up the results of his own inquiry into the historical meaning of "merit" by saying that it consisted of "wisdom, experience, authority, piety, education, firmness, zeal, equity, sweetness, etc."[68] Readers may find these definitions exasperating. But admitting the principle that a majority should not always prevail, what more precise definition was possible? Readers may well be able to recall that they themselves have sat in assemblies where the criteria for choice were no more capable of satisfactory definition.

Third was the question of what to do when the *maior pars* was not also the *sanior pars*. About this question there was a diversity of opinion among the canonists. No one answer was compelled by the texts. One possible opinion was that the *sanior pars* should prevail; authority and merit should always be preferred to pure number.[69] A second was that it would depend on in just how great a degree the number and the merit of the candidates exceeded each other, the extent necessary being left "for the determination of a good judge."[70] A third, seemingly the "more probable," held that the phrase must be understood *copulative*.[71] That meant that neither candidate would have been elected unless he had received the vote of both the *maior* and the *sanior pars*.[72]

Two factors tempered the uncertainty inherent in these answers to this problem. First, if one of the candidates was incapable or unworthy of election, then it would not matter if he had been chosen by the *sanior pars*. He would be disqualified in any case. In fact, his unworthiness would itself tend to show that his *pars* was not the *sanior pars*. Second, the Council of Lyons of 1274, perhaps borrowing from the rules regulating papal elections, established that where there was a two-thirds majority for one candidate, the others could not impugn the majority's authority, except in the case where the majority's vote had been an absolute nullity (Sext. 1.6.9). The movement of opinion, it seems, was toward putting more faith in majorities. By the sixteenth century counting was in the ascendant. This happened legally by strengthening the presumption that the *maior pars* was also the *sanior pars*.[73] The two-thirds requirement itself disappeared from most discussions of the presumption; the existence of a "supermajority" was no longer necessary to create it. By this time, however, such questions of calculating which side had won had become a matter of theory in most episcopal elections.[74] The elections had themselves become obsolete.

Fourth was the question of who decided these matters when they were the subject of dispute. At least this had a relatively straightforward answer. In the first instance the task was undertaken by someone nominated by the chapter itself.[75] Then if the dispute persisted, the decision devolved upon the same person who had the power of confirmation.[76] This would be the metropolitan or archbishop in the normal case, although as noted above, the power to confirm episcopal elections came increasingly into the hands of the apostolic see during the thirteenth century.

Postulatio and the Apostolic See

Episcopal elections had become infrequent by the sixteenth century. The system described here had ceased to prevail in practice. The choice of most bishops had been taken into the hands of the papacy. Before this happened, however, and even under the classical canon law, there were signs pointing in that direction. The role of the papacy in the classical law of episcopal elections deserves a separate word and example. It had indeed never been absent, though the pope played no direct part in episcopal elections under the classical canon law. The popes had, however, played a leading role in the reformation of the episcopacy from the start of the Gregorian reforms. This was significant for several reasons. During the first years of the reform, it had been the leadership of the popes that had caused the deposition of numerous bishops in the West, usually on the grounds of the simony by which the bishops were said to have acquired episcopal office. Papal decretals and councils convoked by the popes were also responsible for the elaboration of the law on the subject. Furthermore, the possibility of "lapse" could cause elections eventually to fall into the hands of the papacy. And of course the possibility of appeal of the many disputed elections to which the uncertainties of the law led had led also to papal intervention in many of them. In fact the popes had long exercised a crucial if indirect influence on them, this quite apart from the assertion of the papacy's duty to superintend the government of the whole church.[77]

These generalities do not exhaust the subject. There were also more direct forms of papal intervention in the process, all of which became sources of the centralization in the choice of bishops and some of which are quite revealing of the special position of the pope in the canon law. One of these was "postulation." It was important enough to be accorded a separate title in the Gregorian Decretals (X 1.5.1–6). The word *postulare* in Roman law referred to the right to make one's claim before the praetor; not everyone was given that right (Dig. 3.1.1). In the context of canonical elections, however, postulation referred to a request from the electors to their superior asking that a certain person, ordinarily ineligible for episcopal office by reason of a canonical defect, be chosen as their bishop nonetheless.[78]

The basic idea behind postulation was very old, having its roots in the tradition that bishops should be chosen from among the qualified priests of the city where the bishopric was located. The man to be elected should be of the church to be served and no stranger (Dist. 61 c. 12). He should be "tested in the faith" and no neophyte (Dist. 61 c. 6). He should also have ascended through the regular orders of the clerical army and be no layman (Dist. 61 c. 4). So held the ancient canons. The idea of the church as a "household" of faith centered around the bishop's *cathedra* was very much in evidence in some of these ancient pronouncements included in the *Decretum*.

What, however, if there was no suitable candidate in the household? Or what if a particular layman excelled all others in virtue and learning? The history of the Christian church had produced many famous examples where laymen had been chosen as bishops despite the violation of these norms. Gratian named three: St. Nicholas, St. Ambrose, and St. Severus (d.p. Dist. 61 c. 8). How were their cases to be harmonized with the rules? The reason for the prohibition of the consecration of laymen, Gratian explained, was that the life of the layman was ordinarily lacking in the virtues necessary in a bishop. Where that reason was absent, where a layman in fact stood above the others in faith, humility, and learning, it seemed that the rule itself might give way. *Cessante causa cessare debet et effectus.*[79] So had it been in the three historical examples cited by Gratian.

This deviation from the ordinary rule was not a matter of right, however, either on the part of the electors or the candidate they chose. There were obvious dangers that the exceptional case might become the norm, and it was therefore held that the elector's choice of a layman was not to be treated as an election even though it might have followed electoral form. It was rather a petition to the appropriate superior asking that the particular man be consecrated as the city's bishop (Dist. 61 c. 10–11). The choice lay with the superior. Hence the distinction: the person was to be "postulated" rather than elected. The same rule applied when the candidate chosen came from a different diocese (Dist. 71 c. 5), and particularly in cases where he was already the bishop of another diocese (d.a. Dist. 61 c. 11).

The more general principle drawn from these exceptional situations was that in them the superior exercised a power to dispense from the canons that dealt with the elector's qualifications. By accepting the postulation the superior was exercising exactly that power. He was removing the impediment to an otherwise uncanonical choice as bishop. The superior was not himself obliged to do so; the greater utility of the church might require that he reject the candidate (X 1.5.3). The canon law underlined the discretionary nature of the process by making express provision that the person enjoyed no right to the office from the fact that he had been duly postulated, not even the *ius ad rem* held by elected candidates.[80]

As the classical canon law developed, the superior charged with this decision to dispense from the canons was in most cases the pope himself.[81] Here it is important to note that whereas the *Dictatus papae* had not asserted any papal right to intervene in elections, it did assert that only the papacy had the right to effect the translation of a bishop from one see to another. If electors wished to choose a bishop from another see, therefore, they had to resort to postulation and the apostolic see. This turned out to be consequential, and not untypical of the ways in which the canon law came to put ordinary administration into the hands of the papacy. The powers of the metropolitans were circumscribed, and the defects from which the popes could dispense were enlarged or at any rate stated with as great an amplitude as could be made consistent with the authorities.[82] By the thirteenth century the power of accepting a postulated candidate had come largely, though still not entirely, to rest within the possession of the Roman pontiffs.

Just as the Decretals clarified the law of elections, so they did in dealing with the rules about postulation. For example, the rule that a bishop chosen for another dignity was to move only by *postulatio*, not by election, was restated in the Decretals (X 1.5.6). The relationship between *postulatio* and *electio* where two persons were chosen by different groups was in some measure clarified (X 1.6.23, 40). The defects for which postulation was possible (e.g., illegitimacy) were distinguished from those for which it was not (e.g., criminality) (X 1.5.1). The language and forms appropriate for *postulatio* were set out for the guidance of electors (Sext. 1.5.1). In all, postulation came to be a method of choice similar to election in that it originated with the electors but also distinct from election in that the ultimate decision in most cases came to belong to the apostolic see.

CONCLUSION

The drift of the law shown by the institution of *postulatio* proved to be the way of the future. As a modern student of the subject once described the fate of the system of episcopal elections of the classical canon law, "It is hardly an exaggeration to say that [it] was scarcely defined before it was obsolete."[83] Chiefly by the process of reserving particular sees to itself, the papacy extended its immediate control over the bishoprics of the West during the course of the thirteenth century. Innocent IV prohibited episcopal elections in Germany without his special permission. Boniface VIII took a similar step for France.[84] In such reserved sees, the "papal provision" of new bishops became the normal way of filling vacant sees. It formed part of what another modern writer has described as "vigorous practical centralization."[85]

Whether "vigorous practical centralization" of the choice of bishops was a good thing or a bad thing has long been a subject of contention. The question antedates the Protestant Reformation. The English Parliament legislated against the papal practice several times during the fourteenth century,[86] but statutes did not prevent the English kings from complying with the system of provisions and even turning it to their own benefit.[87] Critics have said that the motives behind the change were venal, that the popes brought down the system of elections because they profited from the provisions only they could make. Supporters have said that the motives were benevolent, that only the papacy could adequately take account of the interests of the church as a whole and sufficiently counterbalance local interest and corruption.[88]

A mere lawyer must not enter these lists. But it is certainly within the scope of his competence to say that much already found in the classical canon law of elections pointed toward centralization. The complexity of the law of elections, the ease with which mistakes could be made, the guarantee of appeal to the apostolic see, and the existence of postulation must have made more direct papal control seem less than a dramatic transformation of practice in the law of episcopal elections. It was what might reasonably have been expected.

The long-term importance of the law of canonical elections did not lie, therefore, in its vitality as an ecclesiastical institution in selecting the episcopate. It has been retained in modified form for some lesser offices within the Catholic Church, kept up as a matter of form in the Church of England, and occasionally brought back to life in ecclesiastical practices today. Its real historical importance, however, lay in its influence on other kinds of elections. The system of episcopal elections sketched here was drawn upon to shape the practice of secular elections in the course of the later Middle Ages. Unsatisfactory as the law of elections may have been in some particulars, the church did at least have a law on the subject. This was something not found in the civil law. It was only natural, therefore, that the canon law together with the commentaries on it should serve as a source of some of the secular rules on the same subject.[89] From the election of the medieval emperor to the election of masters of Cambridge colleges, reference was made to the canonical law of elections.[90] It gave guidance. It provided authority. This is a pattern of development that has been repeated more than once in the course of the history of our law.

3 Qualifications of the Clergy: Ordination of the Unfree

Perhaps the most salient objective of the Gregorian reform movement introduced in the previous chapter was to improve the morals, the status, and the education of the clergy. Closely allied with that objective was a second: to secure the independence of the clerical order from the control and perhaps even the influence of lay men and women. The reformers regarded the two as interconnected. In their view, any lasting improvement in the state of the clergy required both that the church impose high standards upon entrants to its ranks and that the clerical order be liberated from all domination by lay society. Whether this objective was ever achieved in any real measure is, of course, a separate question. Opinions differ.[1] The reality and intensity of the aspiration is beyond doubting.

In its strictest form, this call for separation between the church and the world led to the growth in the number and prestige of monastic orders; they were made up of men and women truly set apart from society. It did not stop there. The reformers' aspirations had important implications for the secular clergy, whose great responsibility was the cure of souls. One reason that clerical marriage came to be forbidden by the Latin Church, instead of simply being frowned upon, was that clerics with wives easily became entangled by worldly responsibilities.[2] One reason that simony, the buying and selling of church offices, became a scandal to the reformers, instead of being simply a disciplinary problem, was that simony treated a spiritual good as a purely temporal commodity. In addition, simony risked making the clerical buyer beholden to the layman from whom he had purchased his advancement. *Libertas ecclesiae*, the same watchword that was so much used in the development of the law of episcopal elections, thus encompassed not only improving the learning and manners of the parish clergy. It also required securing the independence of the lowliest curate from the contaminating influence of the laity.

The previous chapter examined one of the important consequences of the conjunction of these twin objectives, the exclusion of the laity from episcopal elections and the attempt to regularize the procedures by which the elections were conducted. This chapter deals with a different but equally vital aspect: securing a satisfactory clerical order. According to the lights of the reforming party, the regeneration of the church itself could not occur unless the clergy were qualified to lead, both in their life and in their learning. The clergy had therefore to be freed from the entangling secular ties that had long plagued their sacred calling and had kept them from fulfilling the role that God had assigned to their order. Laymen had been excluded from episcopal elections for that reason. It seemed just as crucial that the clerics who took part in them, and indeed in all the church's activities in the world, be more than merely tonsured laymen.

As we have seen and will see again—even in dealing with subjects as apparently far removed from the immediate concerns of the reformers as the canonical *restitutio in integrum*—the classical canon law was shaped by the goals and assumptions of the Gregorian ideals.[3] Indeed, it is not far off the mark to say that the canon law became the means by which the aspirations of the reformers were translated into enforceable rules. Any treatment of the medieval canon law must therefore attempt to provide some understanding of the law surrounding the qualifications and the privileges of the clergy, and it must also come to grips with the ways in which these rules were interpreted by the canonists. Here this attempt to treat these essentials has been put within the context of a specific example. The question is: Who should be ordained?

GENERAL QUALIFICATIONS

The starting point was provided by the apostle Paul, who had set out a series of injunctions to be applied to the holders of episcopal office (1 Tim. 3 and Titus 1). Among other qualifications, St. Paul required that a bishop be vigilant, sober, and apt to teach. He was to be blameless of life, no striker of persons, and no great lover of wine. A bishop was not to be greedy or covetous but rather holy, just, and temperate. Paul was speaking specifically about bishops, but following the lead of St. Augustine and St. Ambrose, the classical canon law extended the reach of these desirable qualities to all clerics to be ordained, not just to those who received the highest orders.[4] Paul's injunctions were taken almost word for word into the canon law (d.p. Dist. 25 c. 3; X 1.6.7).

These injunctions were not treated as pious but toothless platitudes by the canonists. If the blind led the blind, both would fall into the pit. So said the Bible (Matt. 15:14). So said the canon law (Dist. 38 c. 5). The canonists were determined that this should not happen. They therefore devoted their considerable energies to elucidating the reasons for the Pauline injunctions, to exploring the ways in which they were to be understood, and to spelling out the means by which they could be made effective. Hostiensis, for example, divided St. Paul's monitions into fourteen separate *regulae* that could be applied in determining a man's fitness for ordination.[5] The evident intent was that they be made available for practical application at the time of ordination. Those same questions would be relevant again at the time when the person was later to be promoted to offices and benefices in the church.[6] Treatises from later centuries went even further along this road of elaboration.[7]

Elaboration was not wholly without practical effect. The process of careful investigation before ordination envisioned in these treatises did not prove to be a dead letter. The canon law spelled it out with some care, and contemporaries took heed of it. Before a man could be ordained, he was obliged to submit himself to a formal inquiry, or scrutiny, conducted by the ordaining bishop or one of his officers. At this canonical examination, detailed inquiry was to be made into the sufficiency of the candidate's life and learning (X 1.12.1), and it was an inquiry he was bound to satisfy.[8] We know that these preordination examinations took place at least from the second decade of the thirteenth century.[9] Complaints from contemporaries about their inadequacy as guarantees of clerical quality tell us this much. The law contained in these *regulae* was not without effect even after ordination. If a cleric committed an offense against the canon law, he would often find that he had rendered himself *irregularis* and be suspended on that account from the exercise of his ministry, at least until the appropriate official could restore him to his full clerical status.

The difficulties of enforcing these rules as fully as was desirable in the conditions of medieval life were no doubt intractable. The same complaints that show the existence of preordination examinations also suggest that the results, in terms of success in securing an adequate supply of educated men for the church, were far from perfect.[10] Benefices were poor. Schools were lacking. Suitable men did not step forward. So at least it seemed at the time. Such lamentations and complaints are of course hard to evaluate accurately. As with many questions about practical implementation of the canon law in earlier centuries, it is dangerous to generalize on the basis of statements from men who hoped desperately for something better.[11] Perhaps it is just as important to note that attempts were made to put St. Paul's precepts into action as it is to lament that they were not perfectly accomplished.

The qualities of learning and sobriety formulated by St. Paul and discussed by the canonists were not all objective disqualifications from ordination. That is, they were not formal impediments that rendered an ordination invalid. Many of them were simply qualities that bishops were to look for in choosing whom to ordain. Discretion about the weight to be attached to them was left to the bishop involved. However, the canon law also contained a series of specific prohibitions that did amount to legal impediments to holy orders. Many of these had nothing to do with the moral character of the ordinand himself. They had to do with what the law called "defects" in his person, and no one thought that most of them grew from any fault of or sin by the candidate for ordination. Probably the most famous of these was that which prevented a person of illegitimate birth from being ordained unless he could secure papal dispensation (X 1.17.1–18). There were several others. For example, an epileptic could not be ordained, at least if he was commonly subject to more than isolated fits (C. 23 q. 4 c. 47). The canon law also required that an ordinand have an "undeformed" body (X 1.20.1–7). A blind man or a man without a nose could not be ordained without special dispensation. Canonical bigamy—that is, having married more than once, as after the death of one's first wife—was also a canonical impediment to receipt of, or promotion within, holy orders (X 1.21.1–7).

A large body of learning, collected under a heading called canonical *irregularitas*, was developed to give life to these impediments to ordination. The term, which in its origins meant simply a condition contrary to the *regula* of the church,[12] was more fully defined in the scholastic age as a "vice or defect by which one is prohibited from receiving holy orders or from ministering [while] in them."[13] *Irregularitas* became a test and a means of enforcing these, as well as many other, canonical requirements.[14] Some of the learning seems distinctly strange today, but its purpose is still discernible enough: to carry out the Gregorian reformers' aim of guaranteeing the independence and the quality of the clergy. The consequence, it was thought, would secure for the clerical order a status that was congruent with its high calling. Those linked purposes are evident in the rule that is the subject of this chapter: the canonical prohibition against the ordination of the unfree.

BASIC RULES AND PRINCIPLES

The basic principle, from which the canon law did not deviate until the most recent of times, was laid down by the first canon in *Distinctio* 54 of Gratian's *Decretum*.[15] In it, Pope Leo I (d. 461) stated that no bishop should presume to promote to an office in the church a man subject to the power of any other person, except where the bishop had first obtained the consent of that person. The pope reasoned that every man who was to be ordained must be free from obligations that might impede his service in the militia of Christ. He must not be called away from the tents of the Lord. A secular impediment growing from the retention of physical rights over him by his master would do exactly that. The next canon in the *Decretum*, from an early Spanish church council, stated the rule more succinctly: "No persons of servile condition may be promoted to holy orders unless they first secure legitimate freedom from their lord" (Dist. 54 c. 2). To make sure this procedure would be observed, the council ordered that the charter of manumission securing the ordinand's freedom be read out publicly prior to his ordination. The publicity stemming from this reading was intended to notify all persons who had an interest in the matter, presumably to allow them to voice objections to the ordination in something like the same way one could object to a marriage at the reading of the banns.[16] It became an accepted part of the classical canon law.

The rule nevertheless left questions unanswered. For example, were all unfree candidates for ordination covered by this prohibition or only some? There were several different kinds of servile status in medieval law.[17] A considerable range of rights in the persons and property of men and women could be held by their masters. The possibilities ranged from virtual chattel slavery to a servile status that admitted only minor burdens and restrictions on the unfree person's freedom of movement. Some men were undoubtedly more unfree than others, and one might suppose that distinctions between various kinds of slavery would have been drawn by the canonists, to whom drawing distinctions was second nature. They did so, for example, in interpreting the canonical prohibitions against ownership of Christian slaves by Jews and Moslems (X 5.6.2).

However, the law as to ordination of the unfree did not work itself out in quite the same way. This canonical impediment was applied to all the unfree, even to those who were subject to less than the full demands of chattel slavery (Dist. 54 c. 7). For purposes of suitability for ordination, no distinction was drawn between *servus*, *villanus*, and *nativus*, nor between *adscripticius* and *colonus*.[18] Thus, although the Middle Ages witnessed an important and liberalizing transformation from slavery to serfdom,[19] and although the Roman law left room for distinguishing between varying degrees of unfreedom in some circumstances,[20] the classical canon law treated all degrees of unfreedom alike. These distinctions made little difference to the canon law of holy orders, except for the situation in which an obligation that had once been servile had been commuted into a simple monetary payment. Only in that case could ordination go ahead without the lord's permission. Otherwise, the medieval serf, still subject in some measure to the corporal demands of his master even if no longer to the absolute and arbitrary power of chattel slavery, was treated for these purposes as if he had remained the *servus* of Roman law.[21]

Reasons of substance were given for this conclusion. It was something more than a mechanical application of the Roman law maxim that all men were either free or slave (*aut liber aut servus*), though it may be true that it exercised some hold on their imaginations,[22] and it is certainly accurate to say that Roman law precedents were used to support it[23] and that the civil law contained limitations on the ordination of the unfree similar to those of the canon law (Cod. 1.3.36.1). However, fresh reasons of substance were given for the rule. The principle of the church's *libertas* seemed to be at stake. Principle, not social snobbery, stood behind the requirement that no distinctions between grades of servile status be made. All unfree men were disqualified, because all unfree men would in some way be deflected from spiritual service by the fulfillment of their obligations to a secular master. The exact extent of that secular service was not the issue. Still less was the relative unfairness of the varying degrees of servitude in any way relevant. The reason for the canon law's position was that the unfree might be called to obey commands of their masters that were inconsistent with the needs and commands of the church. The protection of the clerical order in the independence of its calling was what mattered.

The principle also worked the other way around. It favored all former *servi* without distinction. All men who had been emancipated were treated equally with men born in freedom. Servitude was not a perpetual impediment. Roman law distinctions between freedmen and those born to liberty were not taken to imply any canonical limitation on the right of masters to manumit or on the rights of those manumitted to be ordained if they were otherwise qualified. Slavery was thus not an indelible stain, incapable of being erased entirely, as it had been in Roman law. The canon law was not "prejudiced" against the persons who happened to be of lowly and servile condition. There are undoubtedly comments scattered among the writings of the canonists that can be read to suggest approval of the institution of slavery. There are undoubtedly remarks disparaging the customs and habits of life characteristic of unfree men and women.[24] But every canonist admitted that slaves of all sorts and conditions were fully capable of receiving holy orders, provided only that they had first been emancipated.

This was the answer given to the objection made against these rules: that the law of the church should draw no distinctions based on purely personal status. The objection seems forceful and obvious. St. Paul had said that "in Christ there is neither free nor slave" (Gal. 3:28). The medieval church never understood these words as requiring social equality, much less as abolishing all social orders. But the apostle's statement had consequences. Under the canon law, for example, slaves were given a right to choose their burial site equivalent to that enjoyed by free men and women.[25] At the very least, Paul's statement of equality of persons meant that the Christian sacraments must be open to all. For baptism and Holy Communion, this conclusion seemed to follow as a matter of course. Marriage provided an even better example. Almost complete rights to marry were also opened to men and women of servile condition, despite Roman law rules to the contrary.[26] Ordination was a sacrament just as surely as marriage was. Should not this same reasoning obtain?

It did obtain in one sense. As persons, slaves were fully capable of ordination. But in another sense, the reasoning did not. The canon law accepted slavery as a part of human society.[27] It did not take St. Paul's injunction as a charter of freedom for the individual. According to the men who interpreted them, Paul's words must not become the means whereby slaves could shuck off their obligations. To read them in that sense would invade the rights of their masters. Following this principle, under the canon law a slave could not invoke the right of sanctuary allowed to ordinary criminals. If he sought to secure his freedom by taking refuge in a church, he was to be returned to his master (X 3.49.6). Nor were Paul's words read so as to do injury to the estate of the church. To permit this to happen, the canonists reasoned, would be "to make the pretext of piety the cause of impiety."[28] At other points Paul had been equally clear that the existence of slavery was not incompatible with Christianity (e.g., Titus 2:9; 1 Tim. 6:1). Medieval writers sometimes went so far as to ascribe a general utility to the republic to the institution,[29] and Western law long admitted various devices for depriving people of their liberty.[30] If the legitimacy of the rights of the masters over their slaves was thus to be admitted, the only sensible position for the canon law—and indeed the only way to harmonize the various biblical texts—was to forbid the ordination of slaves in the first place. That is what happened.

Joannes Andreae's *Lectura* on the Gregorian Decretals contains a particularly revealing exposition of this theme, although it is also one that is admittedly a little hard to grasp (much less accept) today.[31] Joannes was attempting to reconcile the canonical texts stressing the dignity necessary in the clerical order with those stating that the law should be no respecter of persons. On the one hand, he wrote, "baseness (*vilitas*) is incompatible with clerical honor." On the other hand, it was equally to be recognized that suitable men were to be ordained "no matter what their origins" might be. In such matters, the church must admit no distinctions of person. Thus there seemed to be a contradiction. These texts and the principles contained in them seemed almost to be at war with each other.[32]

The existence of any such basic opposition in the law would have seemed very unlikely to a canonist like Joannes. He would have thought that there must be a way to bring them into harmony. A possible avenue of reconciliation would have been to treat one as related to spiritual, the other to temporal, consequences. Joannes, however, did not take that route. He admitted that slavery was a form of worldly *vilitas*. That seems indeed to have been the universally held view in the Middle Ages.[33] However, he did reason that such baseness would only be truly incurred if a person, once validly ordained, were required to return to the base obligations of servitude. The man's current servile obligations, not his servile origin, was what would have redounded to the shame of the clerical order. Therefore it seemed right to Joannes, as to the canonists more generally, to prevent this from happening in the only way feasible, by refusing to ordain the man in the first place. As would be said by later canonists, although the church does not care about servile *origins*, it must concern itself with the present *fact* of servility, because that status would bring shame to the clergy when the master came to exercise his rights.[34]

In this view of the matter, there was no inconsistency in these texts. The canon law must simply, and above all, avoid the situation in which a man legitimately ordained could be forced to submit to obligations that were the badge of servitude.[35] Could he be called directly from the altar to perform menial service to the secular lord? That would have been unseemly. Or suppose he had become a bishop? Then it would have been unthinkable. Thorstein Veblen once described priestly vestments as showing, "in accentuated form, all the features that [are] evidence of a servile status."[36] He had a legitimate point to make. But Veblen was no canonist; he meant his description of servility in a special sense. The early canonists all stressed the incompatibility. Hostiensis, for example, wrote that "greater sadness would fall upon the church if a man were recalled to servitude than happiness would accrue to the church by his initial reception."[37] To avoid this unhappiness, and also what Hostiensis described as the "vituperation" that would be visited upon the whole clerical order from this shameful but likely event, it seemed preferable to eliminate the dilemma at its source, forbidding the ordination of the unfree altogether. As the contemporary French jurist Beaumanoir (d. 1296) was to put it, clerical orders and servility were two *"choses contraires."*[38] The canonists' argument was not controversial.

WRONGFUL ORDINATIONS

The canon law faced a particular dilemma where a man had actually been ordained without the consent of his master. Such ordinations were forbidden, as we have just seen. But they happened. The slave might have escaped, seeking ordination in order to seal his status as a free man as well as to enlist in the militia of Christ. Or there might even have been a bona fide dispute over the ordinand's status, one in which it became clear that he was in fact a slave only after the ordination had actually taken place. It even could happen that a headstrong or kindhearted bishop might ordain a slave over the express objection of the master. For such instances, there had to be a legal rule. Since the canon law could not admit the compatibility of servitude with holy orders, the question in all such situations was whether the ordination would be treated as invalid and the person returned to his prior servile state, or whether receipt of holy orders would effect automatic emancipation of the former *servus*. The canon law treated many actions as prohibited, but it admitted that if they were done de facto they would nonetheless be valid. The canonical response to the problem of wrongful ordinations was therefore not beyond dispute.

In this situation, the canon law adopted a solution that it would not be wholly misleading to describe as a compromise, although it was not so called (or so regarded) at the time. A compromise would have been the product of weighing opposing interests. The canonists themselves did not regard themselves as having the right to strike such a balance and thereby set a policy for the church. Their first task was to understand and reconcile the authoritative texts handed down from the past. It would have been all but inconceivable for them to have asserted that social conditions or moral ideas of their day had rendered inapplicable the ancient canons allowing and even approving the institution of slavery, thereby allowing them to forge a new rule by weighing competing social policies. Where dramatic changes occurred, as they did, for instance, in the law of marriage, they normally occurred by authoritative pronouncements in legislative form. Or at the very least, support for change from within the ancient texts themselves existed to make change possible. Neither possibility presented itself in this corner of the law.

This said, the canon law on this point looks like something of a compromise all the same. To appreciate this, one need only take the rules in the *Decretum* dealing with the ordination of slaves who had not been emancipated by their masters. These rules long remained in place. The Gregorian Decretals simply added and clarified a few points.[39] Here is what they said. If the ordination had taken place with the knowledge of the master, a distinction was made. The result depended upon whether the master had objected or not. If he had not, the *servus* was manumitted automatically. If the master had objected, however, the *servus* was to be returned to the master and the ordination treated as ineffective. Once returned, the man illegally ordained did not lose all clerical properties. He had "received the character" of holy orders, as the canonists said,[40] and was still bound by the vows consistent with servitude (e.g., continence) that he had taken. But he reassumed the badges of servility, becoming again subject to the will of his master.

In what must have been the more usual case, where the master had not known of the event at the time of ordination, the result depended on a number of distinctions. In the simple case, where minor orders had first been given, the master ordinarily had a year to object, a period that was extended to three years in the case of monastic profession. These were the periods prescribed in the Roman law texts, and presumably the church saw no reason to change them.[41] Where the master made timely objection, the man was to be returned to his control. If he failed to object within that time, however, the master was held to have consented by implication. There was an inevitable dispute over whether the year ran from the date of ordination or the date when the master knew (or should have known) of it, the better opinion apparently being the latter.[42]

Even with that qualification, the period seems short. It favored the interests of the slave and perhaps also those of the church. In sketching the law of canonical prescription in Chapter 7, we shall discover that the normal limitations period for the recovery of property was either thirty or forty years. Hence the comparatively short period adopted here is particularly noteworthy. No doubt its easy adoption from Roman law is a tribute to the closeness of the competing canonical principles in this case and also to the law's *favor libertatis*.

There was one important exception to these rules. The master's right to reclaim the slave was not available in a case where the slave had been ordained to the major orders of priest and deacon, and the Decretals later extended the exception to the order of subdeacon (X 1.18.7). The canon law held that the holy orders in effect trumped the prior servile condition, assertedly because of a greater quality residing in them than in the three lesser orders of acolyte, lector, and exorcist. It might seem that this exception would have swallowed the rule. But it was not so at the time. If the ordaining bishop followed the canonical rules about the conferment of orders, this exception would have been infrequently invoked. The minor orders were not the hurried act of one day. They were not simply the inevitable prelude to priesthood that they have largely become in modern conditions. This meant that by the time the former slave had reached the point of receiving major orders, the year for objection would have gone by in any event. Where it did somehow happen that the major orders had been conferred, however, the law held that the recipient retained the character of clerical liberty essential for exercise of major orders. This was so even within the year ordinarily allowed to the master to object.

When this happened, however, the rights of the master were not at an end. Compensation was owed to him, because he had been deprived of his rights by an action that was contrary to law.[43] If the bishop had known of the servile condition, he and the person who had offered the man for ordination were bound by the canons to restore two slaves of equivalent value to the former master (Dist. 54 c. 19). If the bishop had been ignorant, the new priest was himself bound to surrender his *peculium* to the former master, and if he had no *peculium* to give, he was bound to provide future spiritual services to the master. If he refused to provide those services, he was to be degraded and returned to his former master, a penalty for what the law called his "ingratitude" (X 1.18.4). The canons could not admit that men ordained as priests or deacons, or even subdeacons, should be returned to servitude. But neither were the canons to become the means of confiscating the legitimate rights of their masters.

The canon law's attitude toward this subject comes into particular focus if one contrasts it with the subject of marriage of the unfree. As just noted, the canon law held that slaves could validly marry. Unlike ordination, however, marriage did not alter the fact of slavery. A married slave was still a slave. The same conclusion followed where a slave was baptized. He remained subject to his master under ordinary conditions. Suppose, however, that conditions were not ordinary and that the two came into conflict in marriage, as well they might. Suppose, for example, the master demanded the slave's services in a fashion that made it difficult or impossible for the slave to "pay the marital debt" to his wife. Here the canonists distinguished. If the master had consented to the marriage, the duty to the spouse should be preferred, because the master must be presumed to have tacitly consented to the accessory (the marital debt) at the same time he had expressly consented to the principal (the marriage). On the other hand, if the master had not consented to the marriage, his rights prevailed. "Prior in time, prior in right," it was held, and the master's rights would ordinarily have come first.

However, this last situation was itself subject to a further distinction. If service to the master raised the reasonable probability of adultery by the other spouse, then the reverse was true. The marital debt came first. The master could not demand services that conflicted with the demands of the morality. But if on the other hand no adultery was to be feared, then the master's rights prevailed. The *salus animarum* of the people involved was the factor that determined this strange outcome. Compared with it, the "compromise" solution involving the ordination of the unfree who were not married must seem almost straightforward from a modern perspective. But the protection of the independence of the clergy, involved in one but not the other, again made the difference.

LEGAL DIFFICULTIES IN THE RULES

For all its logical focus on protection of the clerical order, the rules about ordination of the unfree that had been arrived at by the canon law left some loose ends, quite apart from the question of whether the temporal courts would respect the church's law on this point.[44] There were several matters within the canon law itself, matters to be attended to and rationalized by the canonists as best they could. Here we will look at three illustrative difficulties.[45]

The Slave's Conscience

The first, and perhaps the most revealing, difficulty was created by the conjunction of the limitations period just discussed and the requirements of the forum of conscience. A slave who knowingly received ordination without his master's consent had violated what the church regarded as a legitimate interest, the master's rights over his person. The slave had therefore committed an illegal act. Even if it was too late for the master to reclaim him, and even if compensation had been paid, this would not necessarily erase the former slave's guilt. If he took the canons seriously, it is not beyond imagining that he might feel slight pangs of conscience himself.

Moreover, in some circumstances it could happen that the master would not have been found at all, so that no compensation could be paid. The *servus* might have escaped and been ordained without anyone but himself being the wiser. Synodal decrees of the early thirteenth century show that this had happened in England.[46] Thus arose a potential conflict between the exterior results of the law and the interior claims of conscience—or, better said, a quite real conflict. The penitential literature spoke of the *servus* in these circumstances as a thief of his own body.[47] Even if there was no master to object (or to pay), it did not follow that the slave had no problem to address.

The solution adopted, at least under the English decrees, called for the former slave to seek consultation with his bishop, and presumably his absolution after making suitable satisfaction to the master if the master could be found and presumably also some other form of penance.[48] The impediment of servile condition was not subject to dispensation in the way, for example, the impediment of illegitimacy was under the canon law. In these circumstances, however, something very similar to an episcopal dispensation was required by the disjunction between the two parts of the canon law. The former slave who celebrated the sacraments without absolution was a free man. There was no doubt about that. But he was also *irregularis*.[49] The synodal enactments stated that he might not continue to celebrate or distribute the sacraments without danger to his conscience. Therefore episcopal discipline came into play. Occasional entries from the registers of English bishops during the later Middle Ages show that the solution contained in the synodal decrees was also the fact.[50] It was not supposed, even in practice, that no moral dilemma existed. Still less was it supposed that the incompatibility between slavery and natural law rendered the slave's act blameless.

Slaves Compared with Chattels

A second difficulty with which the canonists had to contend grew out of the rule that the master had only one year in which to reclaim a *servus* ordained without his consent. The difficulty was that this rule appeared to be, and indeed was, inconsistent with the rule applied to inanimate objects. If a stolen chattel was consecrated to the use of the church, the canon law held that the owner who discovered its whereabouts was not entitled to get it back, no matter how quickly he acted. Mitigating circumstances did not change this result. The owner would normally be entitled to compensation for the stolen chattel, but the chattel itself remained the property of the church. Its consecrated status rendered the church its owner beyond recall (C. 14 q. 6 c. 2). With unfree persons, however, the opposite result obtained.

Did this distinction make any sense? To some it seemed an incongruous outcome, as indeed it must seem today. It gave the owner greater rights over persons than he had over inanimate objects. Two explanations for the anomaly were proffered.[51] First, conscious fraud on someone's part, usually the slave involved, was normally present in the wrongful ordination. As a rational person, the slave had made a choice and could fairly be required to take the consequences.[52] This was not true with stolen chattels. The cleric who consecrated the stolen chattel would ordinarily be akin to a bona fide purchaser or an innocent donee. And of course no guilt could attach to the consecrated chattel itself. Hence a greater penalty (forfeiture) might appropriately be applied in the case of an ordained *servus* than in that of a stolen chattel.

The other half of the explanation was that ordination touched the interior nature of the person ordained, whereas consecration of a chattel—say a chalice—touched only the chattel's exterior. This made a difference because with a chalice the exterior *was* the thing. The canonists reasoned that if the owner were allowed to reclaim the chalice, he would necessarily be laying hands on the consecrated part, the exterior. It would be just the reverse, however, where the master reclaimed a slave. He would not be laying hands on what the church had consecrated to itself in ordaining him, the man's internal and spiritual part. The master would be laying hands only on the man's exterior, that is, the unconsecrated part. Hence there would be no sacrilege involved in allowing the master to reclaim his rights in the second case, whereas in the former case there would be. Strange as it seems, the canonists were not at all self-conscious about this ingenious and absurd distinction.

The Problem of Simony

The canonists had more difficulty in dealing with a third problem. Readers will recall that in several circumstances compensation had to be paid to masters whose slaves had been wrongfully ordained. The problem that arose was to explain why it was not simony to pay this compensation to the master. To compensate the master seemed very much like paying a sum of money, or its equivalent in goods, in order to effect the slave's ordination. To pay for the conferring of a sacrament was the very definition of the sin of simony. This appeared to be very close to what was happening when compensation was paid to a master deprived of his slave's services. Indeed, it appeared to be identical.

Yet the payment could not be simony. The canons clearly permitted compensation to be paid to the master. In fact they required it. And it would have been quite inconceivable to have supposed that these ancient canons and these recent decretals had expressly commanded commission of the very sin the Gregorian reformers regarded as the root of so many of the evils that assailed the church of their day. A solution had to be found.

The solution arrived at depended upon distinguishing the principal from the secondary purpose of the transaction.[53] The principal aim of the compensation paid to the master was said to be to compensate him for his loss, that is, the services of the man freed. Only incidentally was the man's ordination a consequence of the payment. It was perfectly lawful, for example, to purchase a slave in order to set him free. What happened to him afterward could not render the initial transaction suspect. It was only an incidental by-product. With only a little straining, this reasoning might be said to apply to the ordination of the unfree.

Moreover, the same approach had proved quite acceptable in other areas of the canon law. For instance, it would be ridiculous to suppose that if a man purchased a piece of land in order to build a church on it, the transaction could be treated as simoniacal simply because of the way the land was to be used after the sale. The money was being paid for the land, not for the sacraments to be performed in the church to be built on the land. That the purpose of the purchase had been clear from the start would not change the result. So, it could be said, it should be in the case of the ordination of the unfree. The ordination was only the incidental consequence of an otherwise lawful act.

This technique was called upon to distinguish away a text from the *Decretum* (C. 1 q. 2 c. 2) that appeared to contradict the rule. It condemned as simoniacal a transaction directly related to securing an ecclesiastical office. The text grew out of a request from one group of monks to another, asking for them to provide a particular man as abbot to rule over them. The monks who received the request, however, "not wishing to do this gratis, since [the man] was useful to them," agreed to send him only on condition that they receive compensation for their loss. The canon in the *Decretum* roundly condemned this agreement. The transaction amounted to trafficking in spiritual things.

It was impossible to deny the general similarity of this condemned agreement with what occurred when any master was compensated for having lost the advantage of his *servus*. The master had surrendered a slave, who would henceforth render only spiritual services, and he had received money in exchange. So had the monks done by receiving compensation after releasing one of their number to serve as abbot elsewhere. However, said the canonists, similarity is not identity. Clearly some conditions involving money could legally be placed in agreements that touched the sacraments—marriage contracts for one.[54] Moreover, in the case of the ordained slave, the condition was being placed upon the manumission, not upon the act of ordination itself. No payment for spiritual services, such as existed in the case from the *Decretum* where the payment was made directly for the spiritual service, existed in the case of ordination. The connection was not quite as immediate. A text from the Decretals provided support for this distinction (X 1.18.6).

Distinctions based upon very fine reading of texts were, as we shall repeatedly see, the habitual recourse of the medieval canonists when they were confronted with a hard problem. Not all of the distinctions they drew seem entirely convincing, and perhaps this is one of them. Even if readers may think so, however, it is equally impossible to deny that the reason underlying the payment made to the slave's former master was not really the same thing as the payment being made in the monastic case. Movement out of slavery is not the same thing as the monastic trade of man for money. However similar in their formal terms the two transactions were, compensating the master for the loss of his *servus* was not like the sin of the man who tried to "make a deal" for a spiritual good.

The canonists needed a formal way of describing this difference, one that could be supported from existing texts and analogies drawn from them. They rarely rested their position upon nothing more than what we would today describe as "policy analysis." Had this approach been suggested to them as a possible source of law, they would probably have found it quite intellectually unsatisfying. Among other things, it would be a method quite incapable of reconciling the authorities. They found solutions that grew out of distinctions such as that between payments coupled with manumission and those coupled with ordination preferable by far.

THE CHURCH AS SLAVE OWNER

The law permitting the ordination of slaves with the consent of their masters raised several special problems where other interests of the church came into play. At points where it intersected with other parts of the canon law, substantive choices had to be made. Without much doubt the problem that was the most difficult and that is in some ways the most revealing of the spirit of the canon law itself was caused by the ownership of slaves by churches. Surprisingly, it was not any embarrassment about the existence of ecclesiastical owner-ship that caused the problem. It was the incongruity between the manumission of slaves and the canonical rules against the alienation of church property.

No one can estimate accurately how large a servile population sub-ject to ecclesiastical institutions existed during the Middle Ages. The estimates that have been attempted vary wildly, and discussion of the question has not been without acrimony.[55] However, it is beyond doubting that the church did exercise rights of dominion over men and women of servile condition throughout the Middle Ages. A medi-eval precedent book from the English diocese of Rochester in fact en-visions an abbess as having to respond to a "criminal" prosecution brought against her for having manumitted one of her abbey's *servi* without having followed canonical norms.[56]

It is equally certain that this created a legal problem because, al-though Christian doctrine regarded the manumission of slaves as a pious act—something to be encouraged in laymen and clerics alike—this encouragement extended only to the manumitting party's own property rights. And clerics did not *own* the property of their churches. The canon law actually forbade manumission when the property (the slaves) belonged to the church. This was so because in most circum-stances the alienation of ecclesiastical property without equivalent recompense was directly contrary to the law of the church. The church's patrimony must be kept intact. The *servi* of a church were part of that patrimony. It must not be subjected to diminution through the actions of the individuals who happened to hold spiritual office at any particular time. If a particular bishop were to manumit his church's slaves, exactly that would have happened—hence the canoni-cal rule that such an act of manumission could be undone by the bishop's successor. The person once manumitted could be recalled to servitude of the church (X 3.13.4). Because the canon law required that persons ordained be free, it appeared to make ordaining a *servus* owned by a church a logical impossibility.

In this dilemma, making payment to the slave-owning church for the act of manumission that led to ordination would not ordinarily have provided a way out. It would have been all but impossible to pay for the slave to be ordained in these circumstances. Who would make the payment? By definition any goods possessed by the slave belonged to the slave's master, the church.[57] The slave himself therefore could not pay. He owned nothing. The individual church could not itself logically pay itself the value of the slave in order to permit the slave to be ordained. If it did so, the transaction would leave it poorer, because it would have lost the value of the slave's services and have received nothing tangible in return. That would violate the canonical rules against alienating church property. Thus there was rarely anyone in a position to pay, unless someone would undertake it as an act of charity. If a bishop or abbot were to emancipate his church's *servus* for purposes of ordination, therefore, the compensation to the church would have to come from his personal property or from a pious stranger. Otherwise, said an ancient canon that was included in the Decretals, it would have been "an act of impiety" for a prelate to do damage to his church by the act of manumission (X 3.13.4). In the absence of special circumstances, therefore, emancipation of persons of servile condition on monastic and episcopal estates would have been a rarity. The canon law itself created the obstacle.

It also overcame the obstacle. In this instance, the obstacle was not overcome by creating a special exemption simply allowing churches to do what otherwise was prohibited. That could have been done. It was done, for example, in permitting alienation of a church's goods in order to redeem captives (C. 12 q. 2 c. 14–15) or to feed pilgrims and the poor (C. 16 q. 1 c. 68).[58] There, the duty imposed upon the clergy outweighed the need to protect the church's material needs. Spending the church's patrimony was clearly permitted in allowing a bishop to use his see's wealth to erect a new church. There, the obvious spiritual needs to be served by the new church made it entirely appropriate that a special exception should be created (X 3.48.6). In meeting the problem caused by the ordination of the unfree, however, no such special exception was made. The canon law met the problem in a different way. It permitted instead the retention of services by the master where the master was an ecclesiastical institution. By permitting this, it could plausibly be claimed that the church manumitting its slave had suffered no loss overall on the transaction. Hence the manumission did not violate the canons against alienation of church property.

This permission to retain services in manumitted slaves was, however, an exception to another rule of the canon law, and to this extent manumission was marked out as a special case. Apart from one special kind of services, the canon law admitted no conditions in the manumission of a slave owned by a layman.[59] *Plenaria libertas* was required before the ordination could go forward. It was needed, the canonists said, "lest slaves should be made of the clergy" (Dist. 54 c. 5). Where it was a church or monastic house that owned the slave, however, the rule was otherwise. It was possible to condition a slave's manumission on the continuation of some of the badges of servitude: the inability to move from one place to another, the incapacity to sue or give evidence against the former owner, the necessity of leaving all property to the church at death, and the requirement that the freedman undertake the necessary business of the church he was ordained to serve.[60]

Such continuing badges of servitude were not added automatically to all ecclesiastical manumissions. Rights of lordship specifically had to be reserved in the charter of manumission if they were to be effective. But if they had been reserved, and if the cleric thereafter refused to fulfill one of the duties reserved, as, for example, by attempting to transfer to another church or monastic house, the canon law held that he was to be returned to his prior servile status (C. 12 q. 2 c. 35 and X 1.18.3). It was a penalty for what the law called "ingratitude" on the part of the freedman. It also offered a way out of the logical obstacle caused by the prohibition against alienation of a church's property.

There is some suggestion in the sources that this rule was recognized as one that had been adopted, at least in part, simply to favor the interests of the church.[61] This would not be the only such instance in the canon law. Perhaps the disparity between it and the situation of lay slave owners, who could retain no servile rights, was too stark for any other conclusion to be drawn. However, a simple desire to favor the church's interest cannot have been the single source of the rule. It was the logical, and practical, dilemma created by the rules about alienation of church property that made it necessary to find a solution. If slaves owned by a church or monastic house were to be manumitted at all—something clearly desirable and possible under the canons—an avenue within the other rules of the canons had to be found. It would not have seemed possible simply to waive the rules for slaves who sought ordination. The *favor libertatis* and the desire to encourage pious acts of manumission did not extend that far. They did not overcome a rule that was based upon a clear mandate in the canon law designed to secure a qualified and independent clerical order. In fact, the only real alternative to the solution the canon law embraced would have been to prohibit entirely the ordination of a *servus* owned by a church.[62] To have reached that hard conclusion would have been inconsistent with the demands of Christian charity.

CONTINUITY OF THE RULES

The rules of the classical canon law relating to the ordination of slaves proved to be remarkably durable. This is not an area of the law in which the conscientious searcher must follow the subject into the early modern period, noting strains within the law and changes to it. The ordination of the unfree did not become an area of scholarly controversy of which so many are found in the *ius commune*,[63] and it seems not to have been specially treated by the huge body of monographic literature produced during the sixteenth and seventeenth centuries. The great controversies about the rights and wrongs of slavery that followed the discovery of the New World seem to have had little impact in this corner of the canon law.

The subject did continue to find a place in canonical commentaries. If one looks, for instance, at the treatment of the subject in the work of Manuel Gonzalez Tellez, a Spanish canonist who taught at the University of Salamanca during the mid-1600s, one finds something very much like what one had earlier found in the pages of Gratian, Hostiensis, and Panormitanus. Perhaps there was in the Spaniard's writing a greater consciousness of arguments that slavery was a moral evil and contrary to some canonical and biblical precepts. But the conclusion was the same, and when this writer took up the question of the ordination of the unfree, he dealt with these arguments more as difficulties than as morally persuasive statements. They represented objections to be overcome, or at least to be explained away.[64] Thus he treated the canonical texts referring to slaves who had been ordained as all having had reference to cases in which the slave's master had consented. The sacraments of the church were to be open to all, he wrote, but the principle was not meant to open the paths of confiscating property rights or to become the means whereby the *ordo clericalis* would be subjected to shame. No man can serve two masters, and a man who takes up the clerical yoke must be free from subordination to an earthly master, in order that he may truly serve his heavenly master. It all has a familiar ring.

There was one development of potential significance. Opinion among later canonists took the position that servile status was an impediment that, like illegitimate birth, could be removed by papal dispensation. This opinion depended upon ingenious reasoning. Because the disqualification of slaves was an ecclesiastical rule, and because there was a decretal (X 1.18.2) specifically *denying* bishops the power to dispense from that rule, some canonists concluded that it must logically follow that the pope *did* hold that power. That is, the formal disqualification of bishops must imply the opposite: that the pope was not disqualified. Thus a path to freer ordination of the unfree was opened up by an argument *a contrario sensu*.[65] Papal dispensation in cases of illegitimate birth was frequent in practice; this idea offered the possibility that the same development might take place for servile status.

In fact, the path was not followed. We are told that in practice this part of the papal power of dispensation was "not easily, and scarcely ever, used."[66] A part of the reason must surely have been a lack of demand. Even some of the later commentators, who dutifully repeated the traditional rules, added that they were mostly moot in contemporary circumstance.[67] Although slavery existed even into the nineteenth century in parts of Europe,[68] it was a dying institution and it rarely involved Christian slaves, at least Christian slaves who sought to be ordained.

The other reason for this unwillingness to use this dispensing power was the same as that which long hindered the overall progress of the antislavery movement: exercise of the power would have interfered with the established rights of the owners of slaves. Indeed, it would have eliminated those rights. Dispensation from the "irregularity" of illegitimate birth again provides an instructive counterexample. Dispensation in that situation caused no material loss to a third person. Hence it could occur without objection. With unfree persons it could not. Until the question of individual rights could be isolated, until it could be separated from the larger question of the protection of property rights more generally, the step was hard to take. Only when this greater step was taken could slavery be treated as an independent moral problem, calling for special and more purposefully humane treatment of persons in the law.

CONCLUSION

Growing out of the great reform movement of the eleventh and twelfth centuries, and perhaps even from the constitution of the church itself, the spiritual ideals upon which the classical canon law was based included securing the independence of the clergy from demands that might prove inconsistent with full exercise of the church's ministry. The logic inherent in these ideals kept the church from ordaining unfree men. Such men were by definition subject to the control of others. Protection of property rights, including property rights held by churches themselves, long stood as a powerful impediment to alteration in this law. The church would not interfere with the institution of slavery directly, and its own insistence upon Gregorian ideals kept it from doing so indirectly.

The leaders of the medieval church did not approve of slavery in the sense that its bishops were encouraged to impose it or to promote its extension. In several ways the canon law actually discouraged perpetuation of the institution. For instance, the church took advantage of its jurisdiction over morals to embrace the rule that a master's attempt to prostitute one of his female slaves constituted an "abuse of right" and thereby effected her automatic manumission.[69] Some jurists were willing to move further in that direction.[70] There were rules in the canon law limiting some of the harsher effects of the institution of slavery.

However, it cannot be maintained that the sights of the men who guided the church were ever set fixedly upon the freeing of slaves. Securing freedom for enslaved men and women was not encouraged by the ancient texts. It was not a goal to which other interests could readily be sacrificed. The canonists' sights were fixed elsewhere, in particular upon the creation of a respected, worthy, and independent clerical order. The canon law fully embodied that attitude in its treatment of the question of ordaining the unfree. The result of attempting to balance these values turned out to include the creation of a complex body of law. That law attempted to reconcile the rights of the owners of slaves with the protection of the church's interests, creating in the process the somewhat untidy legal regime we have surveyed.

There is just a little more to report. Unlike the system of canonical election of bishops described in the previous chapter, the rule against ordination of the unfree lasted an uncommonly long time. The rule was repeated by commentators on the law of the church during the era of the Enlightenment, and it continued to be stated as good law well into modern times.[71] There is no substantial body of evidence of a desire to change the rules about ordination during the period when slavery itself came under worldwide attack. The prohibition against ordaining the unfree actually appeared unchanged in the Catholic Church's 1917 code.[72]

When one first comes upon this twentieth-century prohibition, seeing it does come as a bit of a shock. By then, the rule must have had little relevance to the ordinary life of the church. But there it is, all the same. When one has worked carefully through the history of the prohibition, however, the long life of this prohibition cannot come as a complete surprise. The rule existed from the earliest times of the church's history. Its adoption within the classical canon law grew out of one of the great movements for reform of the church, a movement aimed at securing the independence of the clerical order from lay control. The principles of that movement were not easily discarded. When one looks at the matter that way, and perhaps from all sides, it may actually be a greater surprise to find—as one does—that in the Catholic Church's latest revision of the Code of Canon Law, the prohibition against the ordination of the unfree has disappeared.

4 Remedies and Canonical Procedure: The Canonical *Restitutio in Integrum*

The law of procedure has been one of the more durable and influential parts of the canon law. Growing up as part of the medieval *ius commune*, the rules used to regulate litigation in the ecclesiastical courts have left an imprint on several systems of modern law. This is particularly true on the European continent. But it is not true only there. Even in England and the countries that have taken over the English common law, lands where the courts began with procedures and institutions in many ways quite unlike those of the canonical system, there has been selective and perhaps entirely unconscious influence from the procedural law worked out for the *ius commune*. Sometimes via the Court of Chancery, sometimes directly via absorption of remedies first offered in ecclesiastical tribunals, sometimes via the influence of learned judges and leaders at the bar, borrowing from the *ius commune* has left a mark on our law. It has been plausibly suggested, for example, that several parts of the common law of evidence were indirect imports from the *ius commune*.[1]

In the first millennium of the church's existence, there was little that would have led an observer to predict this promising future. Pervasive canonical influence on secular procedural law would have been the last thing a disinterested observer would have envisioned. Even the growth of anything like a distinctive canonical law of procedure might well have seemed unlikely. Without an organized system of public courts, the church needed no elaborate system of civil or criminal procedure for its purposes. The classification of the church's law into something resembling separate "forms of action," the product of a mature canonical science, would then certainly have been unnecessary and might actually have been unthinkable. Synods, not regularly scheduled courts, provided the proper venue for settling quarrels. The bishop and his *familia*, not professional lawyers, took the lead. And what procedural rules were needed for the settling of property disputes, the conduct of monastic elections, the disciplining of the recalcitrant, and the other such occasions came mostly from a Roman law inheritance. That inheritance would be augmented only by the customary practices, spiritual principles, and local variations that arose out of the special needs of the Christian community— hence the common saying *Ecclesia vivit lege Romana*. Indeed, some thoughtful men would probably have regarded the development by the church of a comprehensive procedural law of its own as antithetical to the tenets of the Christian religion. That would have raised an evident danger. Churchmen, some of them saints, warned against it.[2] It would thrust the church into the business of dealing with litigation that was worldly, complicated, and routine.

Exactly that occurred. The process was a by-product of the classical age of the canon law that is the subject of this volume. Canonical procedure began with the meager ecclesiastical inheritance of the early Middle Ages and with the more plentiful storehouses of the Roman law by which the church was said to live. However, as it emerged into the *ius commune*, it turned into an organized and sophisticated system, one that looked different in many respects from that inherited from the Roman law. A large number of the rules, principles, terms, and forms of the Roman law were retained by the medieval church. But, as with the law of episcopal elections, in reality a large part of its procedural law was a new creation.

Of this development there are spectacular examples, many of them clustered in the criminal law, the product of the church's fierce desire to combat religious dissent.[3] However, there is no more instructive example than the less emotive subject of this chapter: the remedy called *restitutio in integrum*. An ancestor of the modern law of restitution, the phrase was commonly translated as "restoration to a prior condition" (*in pristinum statum repositio*) by the early writers.[4] It was a judicial remedy, to be accomplished by an order issuing from a court or judge of competent jurisdiction. The order issued upon a showing that the complainant had met the several requirements to be described below.

The Roman law pedigree of this remedy was thought to be impeccable by the medieval canonists,[5] and they made connections with the civil law throughout the process of the remedy's incorporation within the canon law. They followed many of the civil law rules exactly. But the procedures adopted were also changed and enlarged at the hands of the same canon lawyers. Their suppositions about the purpose of the law and (very likely) the influence of practice in the tribunals where the *ius commune* governed gave a life of its own to what had been a classical institution. It is not too much to speak of its transformation. Restitution became a legal remedy at once more pervasive and more problematic than it had been in Roman law. The story of how this occurred reveals something about the nature of the classical canon law.

THE ROMAN LAW *RESTITUTIO*

As its name implies, the civil law *restitutio in integrum* restored the person who secured it to a legal position he had held before an event or a transaction that had caused harm to him or his interests.[6] It could extend to both the person's status and his possessions. The remedy, granted by the praetor as part of his imperium, was awarded to petitioners who had suffered a loss through an inequitable but otherwise valid transaction. Its application required that the petitioner have labored under some kind of legal disability at the time of the event or transaction. Captivity, minority, or absence on government service, for example, provided occasions for the remedy's invocation. A soldier returning from the wars might thus seek to recover property that had been alienated in his name during his absence. Restitution might equally be invoked because a petitioner had been under duress when he had entered into a particular transaction and had been the loser thereby. The legal essentials were the otherwise valid transaction, the substantial loss, and the disability.

Restitutio was an extraordinary remedy in Roman law, dependent originally upon exercise of the praetor's discretion. In time it became available more generally, as a *beneficium* or privilege granted by the law, but it never became what we would call an ordinary action at law. It could not be sought where another legal remedy was available. Moreover, *restitutio* was ordinarily granted only after a thorough investigation and evaluation of the facts. Restraint was the order of the day, and it never became a matter of right.[7] For instance, the initial investigation had to show that the petitioner had suffered a loss of some considerable size before restitution would be awarded to him. This was not a remedy, like the action of trespass in English law, where the size of the loss suffered and the circumstances attendant to it were irrelevant except for the question of damages.

The nature of the relief granted by *restitutio in integrum* also depended upon the circumstances of the individual case. Besides requiring judicial discretion in the initial grant of the remedy, the Roman law held that restitution was to be made only insofar as circumstances allowed. It might happen, for instance, that the property had passed into the hands of a bona fide purchaser, so that it would have been inequitable to restore the property itself to the petitioner. If the subsequent purchaser had been a party to the first transaction, however, and therefore lacked the requisite bona fides, the reverse obtained.[8] Equities like these could easily determine whether the remedy would be granted.

Several procedural limitations existed in the Roman law's remedy, and most of them were formally incorporated within the canon law. The foremost was the equivalent of a statute of limitations. The person harmed was required to seek the remedy within a year after the disability had been removed—for example, within a year after his release from captivity or from the time the duress ended. Originally, this year was not a calendar year but rather the *annus utilis*, a full period of 365 days. This standard of calculation excluded periods when the petitioner had been prevented from taking action, typically because absence on business or a legal holiday prevented him from asserting his legal rights. In practice the *annus utilis* might thus extend to a much longer period than a year—so much so that Emperor Justinian provided that four calendar years would thenceforth constitute the limitations period for all such petitions.[9]

Whatever strictness existed in applying even this longer limitations period was mitigated in fact under the developed *ius commune*. Much as happens today, when courts apply statutes of limitations by starting the period only from the moment the party had a realistic chance to sue, usually the moment when the event came to his attention, the canon law did not look simply to the existence of the injury. Until the petitioner's ignorance of the existence of his cause of action was lifted, the limitations period ordinarily did not start. The *ius commune* took over this approach. Any other must have seemed mechanical and unfair.[10]

The characteristic petitioner for *restitutio in integrum* in the Roman system was the minor, the child above the age of fourteen but under twenty-five whose interests had been materially injured by a transaction entered into during his minority. Upon reaching majority, the child was given the privilege of setting aside those transactions that had been to his disadvantage. Thereby he could be restored to the place or possessions he would otherwise have enjoyed. So, where he had disposed of his property for an inadequate price, upon coming of age the child would have the right to claim it back if he repaid the purchase price. If there had been a contract that worked to his disadvantage, he might similarly secure its recision. The procedure could be used whether or not he had acted with the advice of a guardian (*curator*).

It was necessary, of course, to show that the minor had been made worse off by the transaction; this procedure was not meant to become a license to undo any transaction that turned out not to be to his liking. If it had, no one would have dealt with minors. But the remedy did not require that any actual fraud or overreaching against the child be shown. In fact, it was assumed that the transaction had been formally valid. *Restitutio* was thus a powerful weapon against transactions that otherwise had been entirely lawful. Like the modern law of restitution, its outer perimeters were not absolutely fixed. There was some support in the texts for allowing *restitutio in integrum* to be invoked whenever the interests of justice demanded, but there was also some support for restraining the procedure's scope to situations in which the injury was substantial and other avenues of redress closed. The Roman law inheritance thus had some boundaries that were established but also some that were not.[11] It contained seeds capable of growth, if they were tended and nurtured.

RESTITUTIO IN THE CANON LAW

A remedy as flexible as *restitutio in integrum*, and one so attuned to undoing harm to the weak and disempowered, must have seemed a natural candidate for inclusion in a system of religious law. Its apparently impeccable Roman law pedigree made it all the more attractive to the men who formulated the medieval canon law. In the "internal forum" of the confessional, the principle of restitution would play a natural and pivotal role. Where restitution of ill-gotten gains was possible, it was required. No penitent was to be absolved who had not restored a thing wrongfully taken or left an injury unrepaired. The real question in the "external forum" of the church's courts would have been whether restitution would turn out to be the same remedy as had existed in the texts of the *Corpus iuris civilis* or whether the medieval jurists would take the principle that lay behind the *restitutio in integrum* and give it a procedural life of its own.

Something like a combination of these two possibilities was realized. From the perspective of the early twelfth century, however, this would scarcely have been predictable. The possibility of *restitutio in integrum* existing as a specifically canonical procedure, to be granted as a matter of course in the church's tribunals, must then have seemed quite impossible. The *Decretum* does contain several mentions of *restitutio*, but only in general terms. Gratian appears to have regarded it as a moral principle, justifying the restoration of a person's rights whenever justice demanded it. He did not treat it as a specifically judicial remedy. That he was familiar with the *restitutio in integrum* is evident.[12] But the *Decretum* neither gave it any special prominence within ecclesiastical jurisdiction nor spoke of it as a legal remedy available to a particular class of litigants.

At several points Gratian used the term itself in a way a strict Roman lawyer might have found imprecise. For example, a bishop removed from his see by force was entitled to seek *restitutio* before the hearing of criminal charges against him, even though the charges, if later proved, would disqualify him from continuing to hold the see (C. 3 q. 1 c. 6). He also used the term *restitutio* in speaking of a woman being restored to her family in a dispute over the validity of her marriage. Here "restitution" was being granted, according to the canons, in order to guarantee the integrity of the hearing of her case (C. 33 q. 2 c. 4). No exact connection with the legal remedy of the Roman law seems to have been in Gratian's mind.

This is not to disparage Gratian's abilities. In fact, to praise them on this account would be fairer. He made creative use of the idea that lay behind the *restitutio in integrum*. In this way he may well have opened up precisely that development of the remedy that would become explicit in the Decretals. For instance, he justified the important and controversial rule that a canonical judgment could not be absolutely final, "because a sentence even of the Roman see can always be changed for the better" (d.a. C. 35 q. 9 c. 3), in part by citation of the Roman law's *restitutio in integrum*.[13] That restitution against *infamia* might be granted under the canon law was made clear by another of Gratian's texts (C. 2 q. 3 c. 8 § 8). In these situations, restitution of one sort or another was mentioned in the *Decretum* and mentioned with approbation. The underlying principle was endorsed and applied. But it was far from clear whether introduction into the canon law of a precise legal remedy, based upon the civil law and subject to rules and restrictions inherited from the Roman law, was what the canonical texts Gratian adduced had in mind. Indeed, it seems likely that it was not.[14]

The "Canonization" of *Restitutio*

The uncertainty in this situation did not outlast the Gregorian Decretals. Building here, as in so much else, on the historical developments that shaped the canon law—the accelerating and sophisticated study of the Roman law, the movements toward creating a working legal system within the church, and the experience derived from litigation during the hundred years that separated the two basic collections of the classical canon law—the church "canonized" and expanded the *restitutio in integrum*. The Decretals contained a separate title devoted to it within the first book (X 1.41.1–10). They also contained a long title dealing with a related subject—restitution against forcible taking (spoliation)—in the second book (X 2.13.1–19). The remedy was further extended to include application within the law of marriage, ultimately giving rise to the action of restitution of conjugal rights (X 1.13.13–14). The *Liber sextus* and the Clementines followed suit by including titles on the subject (Sext. 1.21.1–2; Clem. 1.11.1).

The placement of the title in the Decretals followed that found in the Digest of the Roman law. Raymond of Peñaforte put it directly after his treatment of the legal effects of coercion.[15] In the opinion of the commentators, the placement signaled something important about the direction in which the canonical *restitutio in integrum* would move—that is, toward expansion. Where a person has entered into a transaction under duress, most legal systems permit that person to undo the effects of the transaction once the duress has been removed. Simple justice requires it. And in most cases it is unnecessary to inquire very closely into the nature of the transaction itself. Nor does the law require that separate rules be put into place for different kinds of coerced transactions. The principle that one should not be made the worse by what he or she has been forced to do is ample and clear enough to provide a workable general rule. Special cases in which coercion is justified (as, for example, with many transactions involving prisoners) can be dealt with as exceptions to the rule.

The first chapter of Title 41 treated the canon law's rules about coercion as one particular kind of *restitutio in integrum*. Having dealt with the former, the *glossa ordinaria* stated, it was proper to move to the general principle that underlay it, one that permitted the procedure to be used broadly.[16] And in a way, this is exactly what *restitutio in integrum* proved to be in the canon law, a principle that allowed any party unjustly disadvantaged by an otherwise legal transaction or procedure to undo its effects. A coerced transaction was simply one example of this moral principle. The extension of the principle behind the civilian procedure, so that it became a means of attacking all forms of judicial orders, even preliminary ones, and of introducing new evidence into cases even after their conclusion, ensured that *restitutio in integrum* would take on a lively existence of its own in the canon law. It would eventually reach the point where (at least as some of the canonists saw it) *restitutio* might be used to restore a person bound by a sentence of *infamia* given in a temporal court,[17] one of those indirect attacks on secular jurisdiction that will be examined in more detail in Chapters 5 and 13 of this book.

The important first step was to give express canonical sanction to the Roman law procedure. Several papal decretals accomplished this. For instance, a decretal of Pope Gregory IX approved an emancipated child's extended use of *restitutio in integrum* against the actions of the child's own father (X 1.41.8). The father had disposed of the minor's maternal inheritance for less than its true value, and Gregory permitted the child to reclaim his inheritance, despite the minor's having given formal consent at the time of the inheritance's initial disposition. That he had been emancipated by his father at that time should make no difference, the pope ruled, because all things considered, the minor had been substantially disadvantaged by the transaction and he had not been an adult when he had given consent.

On the other hand, the canon law of the Decretals also established a limitation. Acting in parallel fashion with secular legislation of the same time, the canon law embraced the limitation that the remedy could not be used to undo transactions entered into under oath.[18] If the minor were of sufficient age to appreciate the nature of his act, his sworn renunciation of the *restitutio* or the addition of an oath to his promise rendered the promise fully enforceable in law. The sanctity of oaths under the medieval law, a subject to be explored more fully in Chapter 6, in effect prevailed against the law's indulgence toward minors. There were circumstances, chiefly in cases of fraud, coercion, or lack of consent, in which the minor could first be absolved from the oath and then invoke *restitutio in integrum*.[19] But the rule in the *ius commune* was that the oath prevented its invocation in the first instance.

The Church as a Minor

More striking, and also approving of the canon law's adoption and extension of the Roman remedy, was the title's first decretal. In it, Pope
Alexander III authorized use of *restitutio in integrum* on behalf of a
church (X 1.41.1).[20] The matter came up in the context of alienation of
church property, in fact in a subject examined in the preceding chapter in connection with the manumission of slaves. The canonical rule
forbade clerics to give away their church's patrimony (X 3.13.5–6).
Here the same principle came into play. Where a prelate's alienation,
even though valid in formal terms, had materially injured the
church's interests, the decretal held that the church could later invoke this extraordinary remedy to undo the transaction's effects. By
repaying the purchase price plus the buyer's legitimate expenses, the
church could recover the property alienated. Alternatively the church
had the option of recovering the difference between the price originally paid for the property and its true value. The decretal, coupled
with two later decretals inserted into the *Liber sextus* (Sext. 1.21.1–2),
thus seemed to entitle individual churches to the status of perpetual
minority. It allowed them always to seek restitution where they had
suffered losses in transactions whenever these had been to their detriment.

At first sight, claiming for itself the privileged status of minority
will probably strike modern observers as an extravagant act of self-
interest on the part of the medieval church. The benefit of an extraordinary legal remedy made available to minors and a few other
unfortunates in Roman law was here being put into the hands of a
powerful and rich institution. The church held a virtual monopoly on
learning in many parts of western Europe, and it enjoyed an exalted
social position in every part. Was it not an arrogant and perverse action for such an institution to claim for itself the benefits of *restitutio
in integrum*? When one finds, as one does, that the exception for
sworn contracts of minors just mentioned did not apply to restrict the
rights of the church to seek restitution,[21] the claim seems clearly one
in which the church was brazenly looking out for itself.

It may be that this is true. We could not put a percentage figure on the amount of self-interest in the decision. Doubtless there was some. The canonists themselves described the situation as justified by a *favor ecclesiae*.[22] However, the decretals permitting churches to use *restitutio in integrum* were not quite so perverse as they appear initially. A child's legal problem is not simply that he is likely to be unsophisticated and apt to do foolish things. It is also that other people, guardians or even parents, may act for him or give him advice without being themselves being affected by the action. The problem inheres in the situation. Minors may act indiscreetly, and even if they receive advice from guardians, that advice may be tainted by the indifference or self-interest of a guardian. Hence permitting restitution after the minor had reached the age of majority makes sense.

Churches were in a not wholly dissimilar position. At the very least, the canon law confronted a real problem in this situation. Pastors were akin to guardians of infants in that they were given temporary charge of property belonging to another.[23] These pastors, be they bishops, abbots, or incumbents of the meanest parish churches, had to have the authority to act for their churches. Otherwise nothing could have been done. But they did not *own* the property they administered. In such a situation, it might easily happen that they would be tempted to put their own interests, or maybe the interests of their families, ahead of their church's long-term advantage, just a child or a child's guardian might. They might alienate some of the church's property for less than its true worth, perhaps even for nothing, and there might be no one in a position effectively to prevent it. It was out of just such a situation that Alexander III's decretal arose. All that the decretal did was to authorize the pastor's successor to take the illegally alienated property back and to use *restitutio in integrum* to accomplish this goal.[24] In this sense, a church's situation was very similar to that of any minor.[25] Both had the same right as petitioners to undo an ill-considered transaction.

Procedural Defects and *Restitutio*

Besides expanding the scope of who could use *restitutio in integrum*, the *ius commune* made the remedy available as a means of curing

procedural faults in litigation. It seized upon texts from the Digest
that envisioned the possibility of this use (e.g., Dig. 4.4.36) and exploited them.[26] *Restitutio in integrum* became a procedure available
wherever litigation had resulted in a harmful and incorrect order or
sentence, at least where the order had been made without fault of the
part of the petitioner and some disability, even that of ignorance, on
his part could be discovered.

An interesting and, as it turned out, typical case under the canon
law was presented by the title's second decretal (X 1.41.2). It arose out
of a dispute over the right to elect an abbot to rule over a monastic
house. The house's lawyer, a proctor, had negligently failed to produce the papal privileges that would have shown that the house was
exempt from episcopal jurisdiction and subject to the Roman see
alone. As a consequence, the decision of judges delegate was given in
the bishop's favor and against the right to self-government claimed by
the monastic house. The bishop was therefore allowed a decisive
voice in the election, contrary to the rights granted in the privilege.
Pope Innocent III, however, directed that the proctor's failure to produce the vital evidence should not redound to the detriment of the
monastic house or to that of the papacy. To allow this would permit
the proctor's fault to thwart justice. In consequence, *restitutio in integrum* should be granted to the house, in effect annulling the earlier
sentence. The conjunction of right on the house's side and substantial
harm caused by a formally valid act of the judge opened the door to
restitutio.

The stricter among the commentators objected that this could not
be considered a true *restitutio in integrum.* No transaction of a person
under a disability was being undone.[27] All that was being offered was
the chance to introduce proofs one party's proctor had negligently
failed to produce during the first hearing. The procedure sat uneasily
within the classical Roman scheme of things. However, the *communis opinio* among the medieval commentators defended the step.[28] In
fact, if not perhaps in strict theory, a prior transaction was being undone. A sentence that had led to the conferral of an office was being
challenged. An event or transaction by which one group of men had
failed to receive what was due to them would be justly set aside if the
omitted proof being offered turned out to warrant it. If any extension

to the Roman law of *restitutio in integrum* was made thereby, the principle that justice should be done on the basis of a fuller knowledge of the facts than the first hearing had produced fully justified the extension.[29]

Other decretals in this title dealt with different aspects of this same underlying principle. Restitution was made available in a divorce dispute, open to a woman seeking to undo a sentence given against her, when she had been tricked into missing the day assigned for hearing her case (X 1.41.4). It could be made available to all parties, not just a church, who sought the admission of new depositions of witnesses and new muniments, even after the term for their production had been formally foreclosed (X 1.41.7). And it was available to suspend execution of a sentence, even where the canonical limitation on time for lodging an appeal had passed (X 1.41.6). The procedure that emerged from the Gregorian Decretals, in other words, had something like a look of potentially unlimited scope. Where justice demanded, where there had been real injury, and where a petitioner could allege a good reason for having failed to produce evidence the first time round, *restitutio in integrum* might provide the means of relitigating a claim.

The procedural limitations placed upon invocation of *restitutio in integrum* in the canon law turned out not to be terribly strict, though the canonists always stressed that the procedure should not be allowed to become an instrument of fraud. The canonists were alive to the potentialities for abuse, and they sought to guard against them. *Restitutio* had been an exceptional remedy in Roman law, and in theory it remained an exceptional remedy in the canon law. It was not a right, though the commentators sometimes seemed to move in the direction of treating it like one. *Restitutio* was not, for instance, to be invoked in all cases of harm. There must have been *magnum detrimentum*.[30] At any rate there must be more than a trifling harm,[31] although what amounted to a sufficient detriment to warrant the remedy's granting was in the end left to the judge's discretion. Nor could restitution be sought where another, adequate remedy was available. However, this too was subject to significant qualification. For minors and churches, if *restitutio* proved more advantageous than the ordinary remedy, it could be chosen instead. In other words, the extraordinary nature of *restitutio*, instead of limiting its use, actually extended its use in practice.

The "extraordinary" nature of the *restitutio in integrum* turned out to have ironic consequences. The coming together of this rule with the attempts to curtail the endless appeals that were the bane of canonical procedure actually turned out to make the situation worse.[32] This happened because a negative conclusion was also drawn from the rule. It was held that wherever an appeal was not available, *restitutio* was (X 1.41.4). This conclusion, logical enough in itself, nevertheless made it very difficult to restrain appeals except in the most formal sense. *Restitutio* against a sentence became available where the right to appeal had been specifically forbidden in a papal rescript of delegation or when the time permitted for bringing an appeal had gone by, the argument being that *restitutio* was a remedy different in kind from an appeal and not to be withheld except where it had been expressly forbidden.[33] This sort of reasoning was taken to the point of saying that where a sentence had gone against a party, if the party had then not appealed but sought *restitutio in integrum* instead, he could seek restitution of the original right to appeal even after a decision had been made to deny him the right to restitution in the principal suit.[34] In other words, instead of limiting the availability of the right to appeal, the extraordinary nature of *restitutio* served to extend it.

This aspect of the remedy offered an additional possibility for revision of sentences, even those rendered by the papal court. In theory a decision of the Roman see was final. No appeal was allowed. The inviolability of papal sentences had been a tenet of Gregory VII's *Dictatus papae*, it enshrined an important principle of the movement of church reform, and it was a recurring theme in commentaries on the canon law.[35] However, from the principles just outlined an apparently contradictory conclusion followed. If the law forbade appeals, it must by implication allow *restitutio*. Why should this not apply to papal sentences as well as to sentences given by lesser judges? In the event, it did. So Pope Innocent III held in a decretal overturning actions that had been taken by one of his predecessors (X 1.41.5). As the canonists understood the situation, "even the sentence of a pope, if obtained through deception, may be exchanged for a better one."[36] *Restitutio in integrum* was a means by which this occurred.

RESTITUTIO IN THE HANDS OF THE CANONISTS

This remedial procedure, taken up and expanded by the Gregorian Decretals from the protean remedy of classical Roman law, was much commented upon by the canonists. Several treatises on the subject were produced in time. No legislation regulating it in any important sense was enacted before the very end of the Middle Ages,[37] so that it is within the pages of the medieval commentaries, by both canonists and civilians, that the nature of the medieval *restitutio in integrum* must be discovered. It was clear from the outset that the remedy would not be confined by the restraint characteristic of the Roman tradition. The question was how far it would move in the other direction.

Modern readers might expect the medieval commentators to have dealt with this question by taking questions of policy—whether, for example, it was sensible to allow churches to invoke *restitutio in integrum*, or whether it was permissible and desirable to give the procedure the extensive scope it enjoyed in medieval practice. There was some "policy-centered" discussion in the commentaries,[38] but more often one finds questions of legal detail discussed. For instance, could the right to seek *restitutio* be transmitted to an heir? Could it be alienated inter vivos? Could creditors of the person entitled to seek *restitutio* require him to do so?[39] These were the common inheritance of the *ius commune* and dealt with by canonist and civilian alike. *Restitutio in integrum* spawned a number of technical problems— puzzles one might almost call some of them—and it was to these that the jurists devoted most of their attention.

To illustrate the approach the commentators on the *ius commune* took toward the remedy, it is sufficient to take up four of the problems treated as of special importance or at least interest to them: (1) the application of *restitutio* to judicial proceedings prior to sentence; (2) the attempt to explain the nature of canonical rights that the Decretals stated could be recovered by *restitutio in integrum* but that fit uncomfortably into the procedure's Roman law inheritance; (3) the problematical relation between *restitutio in integrum* and ordinary rules of canonical prescription; and (4) the difficulties caused by the established legal doctrine that *restitutio in integrum*, as an extraordinary legal remedy, should be granted only where no ordinary procedure was available.

Preliminary Judicial Decrees and Orders

The first example is the question of whether *restitutio* should be granted in cases of preliminary judicial decisions and interlocutory orders. The alternative was to limit it to definitive sentences. The question was much discussed, and indirectly it raised issues involving the policy behind the remedy. Against granting *restitutio*, three arguments were made. First, preliminary orders normally caused minimal harm. Second, specific support for allowing it was both absent from the texts and denied by some of the most prominent early commentators. And third, the effects of an incorrect interlocutory order might always be corrected later in the same trial by the judge.[40] In other words, according to the accepted view the scope of the remedy should be limited to situations in which it was necessary to prevent injustice, and a preliminary order was therefore not a good candidate.

The *communis opinio*, however, was to the contrary. There was no blanket prohibition. Assuming that existence of substantial harm and a disability could be shown, this view allowed the application of the remedy even to preliminary decrees.[41] The reason given was that preliminary decrees might well do substantial harm as a matter of fact. Since substantial harm was always required in any event before *restitutio* was granted, that requirement was thought to provide a sufficient safeguard against excessive use of the remedy. For example, if one party sought to recuse the judge and the request was denied, it would be a denial of justice categorically to refuse *restitutio* in all such cases, even though the denial was not a final determination of the merits of the case. Refusal of the request to a judge to recuse himself could undoubtedly cause real harm. The canon law itself repeatedly said that it was "a heavy burden to litigate before a suspect judge."[42] If the party could meet the remedy's other requirements, therefore, he could have recourse to *restitutio* against a judge's interlocutory decree refusing to disqualify himself.

A whole series of similar possibilities presented themselves to the commentators. Suppose a minor in a criminal case was induced to make a confession by fraud. Could the minor seek *restitutio in integrum* short of final sentence because of the disadvantage that would likely ensue from the passage of time? Or suppose a party to litigation failed to challenge a witness because of ignorance amounting to a disability. Could the party take advantage of *restitutio* in order to make that challenge later during the same case? The *communis opinio* of the commentators held that these attempts were not barred.[43] Hence, if the other requirements of *restitutio in integrum* were met, the first defendant could have his confession revoked and the second party could challenge admission of the testimony of the witness. It could become a tool for opening up all kinds of procedures and arguments in litigation that would otherwise have been closed.

Subject Matter Open to *Restitutio*

Although *restitutio in integrum* was sometimes invoked to recover a person's legal status in the classical Roman law, as in the case of a man unjustly condemned of a crime and therefore deprived of his status in civil society, normally it was a remedy designed to undo disadvantageous contracts and to recover property alienated to the detriment of a minor (or other disadvantaged person). The idea was to recover a *res* or to restore a claimant's status. From the start, as we have already seen, it seemed clear that the canon law would exploit the opportunities for expansion found in some of the texts in the *Corpus iuris civilis*. The *Decretum* had used the term *restitutio* broadly, and one of the first of the Gregorian Decretals had allowed the procedure's use to challenge the results of a monastic election. Other decretals allowed its use simply as a means of reversing judicial actions taken in ignorance of relevant evidence. It also became clear that restitution, or something very similar to it, could be used to recover conjugal rights.[44] Was there a stopping point? Could the procedure be used to cure *any* injustice and to undo *any* human action? Would *any* failure not the product of supine negligence count as a disability?

The decretalists struggled with this question. It was as real to them as it is to us. To whom the remedy belonged and exactly what wrongs it could be made to encompass were staple parts of their discussion. Joannes Andreae, for example, began his treatment of the decretal relating to the abbatial election with the apparent inconsistency: properly speaking no restitution of a thing was involved but instead the recision of a judicial sentence.[45] Hence it might seem that this decretal was careless in describing the procedure being used as *restitutio in integrum*. However, Joannes answered, fully understood this was not so. The monks had the power to elect their abbot, and under the papal privileges enjoyed by their house, they could exercise it without episcopal interference. This was a real *ius*, a right amounting to something like an asset in their hands, and the judge's sentence had deprived them of it. It was possible to lose possession of a right, just as one might lose possession of a thing. The theory was that the party injured by the sentence was recovering a right or status he had enjoyed before the unjust sentence had been promulgated. Fully understood in legal terms, therefore, the situation appropriately called for *restitutio*.

Taking this step was to treat an incorporeal right (to elect) as in some sense a *res*. It "objectified" the right. This was an important development in the law, both because it enlarged the scope of thought about the nature of rights generally and because it facilitated the use of this extraordinary remedy in the courts of the church. No explicit formulation or discussion of the idea behind the development appears in the decretals themselves. In them, *restitutio in integrum* appears simply as a means of undoing an injustice. Nor did Joannes Andreae work through the larger implications of the expansive reach of the canonical remedy. It is difficult to believe that they played no role in the decision, although they were not the primary focus of his discussion. What is clear is that his treatment was part of a larger movement that had the effect of expanding the reach of the civilian remedies.[46]

There were limits to the procedure's use in the ecclesiastical forum, as there had been in Roman law. One was that *restitutio in integrum* could not be used to secure execution of a penalty.[47] The best example in the canon law was the sentence of excommunication. Suppose X had been rightly excommunicated at the suit of Y. Later X managed to secure his own absolution, even though he was not legally entitled to do so. Y could not bring *restitutio* to have the sentence of excommunication against X restored. Such sentences were given "to the detriment of the adversary," not "in favor of the petitioner."[48] Therefore, a petitioner had no right to seek restitution of the original sentence of excommunication even where his adversary had wrongfully managed to have the sentence of excommunication lifted. The petitioner's sole remedy was by way of appeal from the sentence of absolution that had remitted the original excommunication.

A second limitation was that *restitutio in integrum* could not be used to undo a monastic profession or a marriage. A person who had taken monastic vows while a minor could not take advantage of this procedure to seek restoration to a lay status. The canonists said that in such cases there could have been no real deceit of the minor. In any case entry into religion was an objective benefit to the minor involved, even if he himself ignorantly believed the reverse was true.[49] Hence, the minor's only remedy lay in undermining the initial validity of the profession or in seeking a dispensation. The same conclusion was reached about attempts to undo a marriage. If a young man, under the age of twenty-five, had been induced to marry "a toothless old woman," for example, no *restitutio in integrum* to recover his prior single state would be made available. The remedy was denied even though he might plausibly claim that the "transaction" of marriage had worked to his detriment.[50] To allow this, the canonists said, would undermine indirectly the canonical freedom to marry, which we shall examine in more detail in Chapter 9.

These cases were treated as canonical counterparts to the civil law's rule that manumission of a slave could not be challenged by *restitutio in integrum* (Dig. 4.3.7). An assumption about the value of the underlying transaction (e.g., manumission, marriage, or monastic profession) meant that granting *restitutio in integrum* to undo it would not be wholly consonant with doing justice. The principal difference between the two systems was that they made slightly different assumptions about what the doing of justice required.

The Relation of *Restitutio* to Canonical Prescription

A puzzle dealt with by all the canonists derived from the necessity of fitting *restitutio in integrum* into the canonical scheme of prescription. The fit was not obvious. As we shall see in Chapter 7, prescriptive rights could be claimed against a church, and in such cases the ordinary limitations period for recovering any right under the canon law was forty years. But if churches enjoyed a state of perpetual minority, as the Decretals expressly said they did, how could prescription ever be possible against them? If a church never came of age, by definition it would be impossible for it to ever reach an age when restitution would not be available. Since the canons showed that prescription was possible, that way of stating the matter was obviously incorrect. But why?

Indeed, the potential for incorrectness was even greater. Following the reasoning of the decretal might mean that a person who had received the church's property by an otherwise valid sale would be worse off than a thief who had actually stolen the same property.[51] This was so because *restitutio in integrum* was available only when the transaction harming a minor or a church had been formally lawful. A thief's possession was not lawful in any sense. Therefore, this argument went, the thief without lawful title, or at least a purchaser from him, could conceivably gain title by prescription.[52] The lawful alienee of church property, on the other hand, did have presumptively lawful title. It was just that the property was subject to *restitutio in integrum*, provided that the procedure was sought within the limitations period. However, if the church was *always* a minor, the right to seek restitution could *never* be barred against this alienee. There would be no limitations period to start. Such an outcome seemed unacceptable in any event. The contrast between it and the case of the thief made it seem absurd.[53]

Not only absurd—apparent absurdity might have been explained or distinguished away. But the result would also have been contrary to the express statements found in the *Corpus iuris canonici*. The canon lawyers could not have taken that position easily. A solution had to be found, and a variety of possible solutions were proposed.[54] All of them built upon qualifying the parallel between the church and a minor.[55] The canonists distinguished by imputing to the church a notional age at the time of the injurious transaction it was seeking to undo. Thereby a shorter period than the ordinary prescriptive period was allowed for seeking this extraordinary procedure. This avoided any possible inconsistency, because it left the ordinary law of prescription unaffected. It simply said that, if a church wished to seek restitution, it must do so within a shorter time than would otherwise be available to it. Under this approach, although the church remained a perpetual minor in a general sense, for any individual transaction, it was to be assigned an age.

What was the age? One early school put it at zero, so that a church would in effect have twenty-nine years to bring *restitutio in integrum* in order to come within the four-year limitations period allowed for invoking the remedy after removal of the disability (Cod. 2.52.7). Another put it at fourteen. A third, and eventually the majority view, put the age at twenty-five, so that a church would ordinarily have four continuous years if it sought to take advantage of this extraordinary remedy. This view had the added merit of symmetry with a decisive decree of Pope Clement V promulgated in the Council of Vienne (Clem. 1.11.1). It gave churches four continuous years from the time of injury to seek restitution where no impediment to bringing suit had existed at the time of injury.

Where there *was* an actual impediment, this four-year period could be extended, and these exceptions would prove large enough to cover the situation in which the particular pastor who had acted to his church's detriment remained in office. Since he neither could nor would contradict his own act, his continuing incumbency was treated as the equivalent of a disability.[56] Hence a new incumbent of a church would ordinarily have four years to act after the date of his predecessor's death or resignation.

It cannot be claimed that this solution, sensible as it may have been, provided an absolutely fixed term or that it solved all the problems that would be encountered. There were further exceptions. The canonists held that where the *laesio* to the church had been *enormissima* the four-year period might be extended. The same held true where fraud or deceit had been practiced against the church by the person against whom restitution was sought.[57] Practice at the Rota Romana had apparently allowed these extensions many times.[58] The canonists were reluctant to call a halt to the availability of *restitutio* where doing substantial justice was made possible by allowing it. Thus, although they "solved" the problem of the awkward fit between canonical prescription and *restitutio in integrum*, uncertainties remained. Most of them permitted extension of the remedy.

Duplication of Remedies

A final puzzle commonly treated by the medieval canonists will be the most familiar to students of English legal history. It is the problem of duplication of remedies. In English law, the rise of the action of assumpsit as a means of enforcing contractual obligations occurred at the cost of the action of debt.[59] Before this development could occur, however, the common lawyers had to overcome the argument that where the older writ of debt lay, assumpsit did not. It was settled law in England that a new form of action must not duplicate a long-established writ, and since this was apparently happening when assumpsit was brought on a promise to pay money, a way first had to be found to explain away the problem that the same underlying facts would give rise to either form of action.

The canonists faced a very similar problem in discussing the possible reach of *restitutio in integrum*. The remedy seemed to overlap in many situations with pleas of nullity, not to speak of appeals and petitions for equitable relief. Because it was an extraordinary remedy, *restitutio* was available only where no other appropriate legal remedy existed. Where a prior transaction or judicial sentence could be challenged as a nullity (and there were many grounds for nullity of a sentence under the canon law),[60] in theory restitution would be neither necessary nor permissible. For instance, if the transaction being challenged had been an illegal contract, strictly speaking *restitutio in integrum* could not be sought.[61] Because the contract itself would have been void, there would be no need for a special remedy, and restitution would not be available. Similarly, if a judicial sentence had been rendered by a judge without jurisdiction, *restitutio in integrum* would have been equally inappropriate, because the sentence would itself have been a nullity.[62] The proper way to proceed was to seek a formal declaration of that nullity, not to seek restitution of the thing or a status lost by the void sentence.

The difficulty for the canonists was that this separation was not being observed. In the decretals themselves, it was obvious that *restitutio in integrum* was sometimes being demanded (and offered) where another remedy was also available.[63] Practice went further down this road. The canonists told their readers that litigants were actually demanding *both* restitution and some other remedy. Litigants were "cumulating" petitions, seemingly claiming that prior sentences, events, or transactions were at once nullities and proper subjects for restitution. This should have been impossible. But it was happening. How could this state of affairs be understood? And defended?

At least three answers were given to these objections. The first, well enunciated by Innocent IV, rested upon what one must admire as a realistic view of litigation. It often happens, he wrote, that a person harmed will be unsure of all the facts when he initiates his action,[64] and it would be unfair to such a person to require him to make a final choice of remedies before he had become fully informed of the facts. Therefore, the law rightly permitted him to include cumulative prayers for relief in the same petition, requiring only that he make the final choice of remedies at some later point. As long as the plaintiff was honestly uncertain, the extraordinary nature of *restitutio in integrum* should not be a weapon to be turned against him.

The second answer depended upon an expanded notion of validity. Many invalid acts may later become valid, either by ratification or through the running of the prescriptive period. Suppose, for example, a bishop alienated his church's patrimony without the consent of the cathedral chapter.[65] That action was formally invalid under the canon law, and it would therefore have appeared that the alienation should not be a candidate for *restitutio in integrum*. However, it *was* a candidate. The Decretals so held. The reasoning given was that the alienation "was not wholly void," because the chapter might later ratify the alienation.[66]

A third possible answer was based upon a characteristic policy of liberality under the canon law. It was said that this sort of duplication "may be permitted by the liberality of the canon law, for the canon law proceeds with greater benevolence than the civil."[67] This attitude was even carried to the extent of allowing *restitutio* wherever it would prove "more useful" than an ordinary proceeding.[68] To say that this attitude and the extensions that went with it did not violate the rule against duplication of remedies would be in a certain sense to make light of the rule itself, though the canonists never drew that conclusion. They were content to retain the rule and permit the exceptions that virtually swallowed it. Of course this was not an outcome unique to the canon law. The English common law action of assumpsit also triumphed at length over the action of debt.

The law of marriage provides an additional and instructive example of the canonists' attitude on this score. In theory, it might have been said that restitution should never be available in disputes relating to marriage, since in the canon law sentences in matrimonial causes were never res judicata. If sentences, lacking finality, could always be attacked in the ordinary course of law, it must follow logically that *restitutio in integrum* should never be available. It would never be needed. However, again restitution *was* available. The texts showed this to be so.[69] Restitution of conjugal rights was a familiar canonical action. The canonists had only to explain why. They did so by distinguishing marriage from other institutions, and they looked at the apparent anomaly as part of the law's *favor matrimonii*.[70] That is, as part of its concern for the *salus animarum* of the persons involved, the canons treated marriage law as not subject to the strict rules of civilian procedure. In it, as in many areas of the law where the soul's health of the parties could plausibly be put at risk, strict rules might appropriately be abandoned, or at least set to one side for the moment. Consequently, restitution could be admitted into the law of marriage without doing violence to the application of the ordinary canonical rule against duplication of remedies.

RESTITUTIO IN THE COURTS

So far, this chapter has dealt with the legal issues raised by the acceptance of *restitutio in integrum* into the church's legal system. It has tried to show that this procedure, spurred by the canon law's desire to secure justice for those to whom it had been denied, took on a more expansive scope in the canon law than it had had in the classical Roman system. It has sought to indicate how the canonists discerned an important principle within the institution they inherited from the Roman law and applied that principle to make their system respond fully to claims of right. If rules of evidence or the mechanics of litigation had worked to obscure the truth and to frustrate the securing of justice, this exceptional procedure could be called into play. For this reason *restitutio in integrum* was not limited to minors, individual churches, or even persons laboring under physical disabilities. Anyone might be deprived of justice without being personally at fault. Ignorance of one's legal remedies might be reason enough to permit restitution. If this much has been established, it remains only to add a word about how the resulting system worked in practice.

There is not a great deal of evidence on the subject. But there is some. And what there is suggests two things: first, that *restitutio in integrum* was not used with enormous frequency in practice, and second, that the primary use made of it was procedural, either to prevent the giving of a sentence by seeking restitution against an interlocutory order or decree, or to overturn a sentence on the ground that fresh evidence had come to light or that some procedural irregularity had occurred. The remedy was not much employed to void the transactions of minors or to recover church property, as one might have expected from simply looking at the Roman and canon laws. Rather, in practice it became a means of introducing new arguments and new evidence into litigation. So at least it appears in the precedent books and the records of the English ecclesiastical courts.[71] So it appears when it has been mentioned in studies of ecclesiastical courts in other parts of Europe.[72] And so it appears in an excellent study of the related doctrine of *res iudicata* in the canon law written by Richard Puza.[73]

Puza's conclusion was that *restitutio in integrum* in effect prevented the sentences of the church's judgments from achieving finality. He found it being invoked with some regularity in the *decisiones* of the Rota Romana, particularly from the sixteenth century forward.[74] He concluded that the principle of *res iudicata* could scarcely exist as anything but a theoretical possibility as long as restitution was being welcomed to the extent it was in these *decisiones*. There is evidence to confirm this conclusion from the influential *Decisiones capellae Tholosanae* as well; *restitutio in integrum* was allowed to a minor after three definitive sentences had been given against him. The grounds: the existence of evidence that had been omitted in the prior decisions.[75]

So long as restitution was made available, the finality of sentences was ordinarily beyond the reach of the canonical system. The search for perfect justice can lead to judicial paralysis. Here, in Puza's presentation, a good historical example is found. Since *restitutio* could be used to introduce new evidence and to challenge past procedures, and since new evidence was easily discovered and past procedures easily faulted, litigation was subject to endless reopening in the canonical system. This was the "dark side" of the expansion of the benevolent principle the canonists discovered in the Roman law's *restitutio in integrum*.

The medieval canonists were not blind to this danger. Their writings in fact provide unintended testimony that tells in favor of Puza's conclusion, for what he described they wished to avoid. At several points they sought to restrain the reach of *restitutio in integrum*, precisely in order to keep it from becoming a means of delay and fraud. For instance, they held that there had to be real new evidence before the procedure was admitted. It was not enough that there had been a simple failure to prove a particular allegation in litigation. Something fresh in the way of evidence must have come to light. Similarly, the range of occasions that could give rise to restitution was not unlimited. An actual and substantial loss suffered by a particular church or minor had to be shown,[76] and *restitutio* could not be sought simply because a particular transaction had turned out badly for a church or a minor. That is, there had to have been an existing unfairness at the time of the original transaction.[77] The canon law was not meant to be incompatible with expectations that became settled at some point.

The question remains whether or not the canon law achieved a reasonable balance. At this remove, it is impossible to be certain where the balance should have been struck. The evidence is equivocal enough to make it difficult even to say exactly where it *was* struck during earlier centuries. Certainly, there is some support for supposing that the canon law went overboard in allowing matters to be relitigated.[78] Puza's conclusions suggest that this was so in the jurisprudence of the Roman Rota. Contemporary critics sometimes made the same point. One even hears *restitutio in integrum* described as "an abusive fomenter of perpetual litigation" by an early observer.[79] On the other hand, there is some evidence that points in the other direction. It suggests that in ordinary cases at least, the *restitutio in integrum* was not as much abused or even invoked as often as it might have been.[80] And there can be little doubt that the problem is inherently difficult. As long as actors in a legal system aspire to do justice, they will confront some form of the same problem. We have not solved it.

It should also be said, as Puza did in fact say, that the canon law contained an effective means of curbing some of the abuses of *restitutio in integrum* and that adoption of that means is increasingly evident in the Rotal decisions of the eighteenth century. It lay in the law of proof. Perhaps the civilians and the temporal courts had been leading the way.[81] The requirement that *laesio* to the petitioner had to be alleged and proved before a judge would listen to his prayer for restitution had long existed as a possibility for curbing the excesses of litigation. It meant that a petitioner might have to make a prima facie showing that he would ultimately prevail before *restitutio* would be allowed. By the eighteenth century, Puza found in investigating the evidence from the *decisiones* of the Rota Romana, the possibility for reducing the length and complexity of litigation was regularly being exploited. Moreover, for a petitioner's prayer for relief to succeed, the Rota began to enforce a standard under which the petitioner was required to show the injustice of the harmful transaction by proofs that were "clearer than light." Finally, a customary rule developed that forbade a judge from granting restitution against his own sentence. Unlike the situation in earlier centuries, only a competent, superior court could grant this extraordinary remedy.[82] These developments must have worked in tandem to curb some of the system's worst excesses.

CONCLUSION

To conclude from this development that these or some other means of curbing excesses in the use of *restitutio in integrum* should have been seized upon earlier, during the age when the classical canon law came into being, would be to say more than the canonists would themselves have allowed. Perhaps it would be to say too much. If put to a choice between justice and finality of judgment, the canonists would have chosen justice, admitting the almost inevitable disadvantages and inconveniences that accompanied that choice.[83] Their development of a canonical *restitutio in integrum*, growing out of the inheritance of classical Roman law but extending beyond it, demonstrates the strength of their preference for doing justice.

Were they wrong to have made that choice? Given their assumptions, it would take a more confident observer than I am to assert that they were. By way of comparison (but no more), one might think for just a moment of a modern parallel: capital punishment in the United States. It has been very hard for American courts to close the door to the introduction of new evidence in such cases. A convicted prisoner may be exonerated if introduction of new evidence, or even the consideration of a new argument, is permitted. He or she will surely be executed if his or her application is refused. The result is a kind of paralysis. Seemingly endless litigation has been the result. This modern parallel is imperfect no doubt. There are evident dissimilarities. But it does show in a particularly clear way how difficult legal systems can find it to countenance sentences that may turn out to have been unjust.

5 Principles of Ecclesiastical Jurisdiction: The Protection of *Miserabiles Personae* and Jurisdiction *ex Defectu Justitiae*

The canon law asserted a limited jurisdiction over the affairs of the world. Many canonists thought that the law of the church could without embarrassment have extended its reach further than it did. But unlike some systems of religious law that seek to regulate all aspects of human life, the canon law never claimed more than a partial competence over the lives of the men and women who were subject to it. Growing up alongside the sophisticated and venerable system of Roman law, and following the words of Jesus—that some things belonged to Caesar, some to God (Luke 20:25)—the canon law undertook from the start to fix upon jurisdictional principles that would accord with the church's spiritual mission in the world.

The result that issued from this understanding of its mission in the world was twofold: first, a claim to exclusive personal jurisdiction over the clergy; and second, an assertion of a subject matter jurisdiction over some selected and quite disparate areas of substantive law. The first embraced virtually all aspects of the life of the clerical order. The second depended, at least in some measure, upon the classification of matters according to religious principles. The canonists regarded some matters as inherently spiritual in nature and hence as falling within the church's exclusive and natural jurisdiction.[1] The law of marriage and divorce and questions of religious doctrine are evident examples. Other matters were regarded as decidedly secular and outside the competence of ecclesiastical tribunals. Crimes such as murder or arson, both of them commonly punished directly by death, provide examples of legal subjects that were left on principle to the secular courts.

Had the canon law stopped there, it might be possible to describe ecclesiastical jurisdiction fairly simply. One could work through the

practical implications of the division between the secular and spiritual spheres of life, though one would certainly come upon places
where there would be a dispute or an apparently arbitrary allocation
of jurisdiction to one side of the boundary line or the other. However,
to do this would be to describe only a part of the reality of ecclesiastical jurisdiction. The canon law did not in fact stop with these categories. In some sense the medieval church found it impossible to rest
within the limited jurisdiction it claimed in the first instance.[2] This
chapter deals with one example of that ambiguous and revealing attitude toward questions of jurisdictional competence.

The complexity of the subject of canonical jurisdiction becomes
evident the moment one begins to study almost any substantive area
of the law. Fewer areas of life were assigned to one side or the other
of the dividing line between secular and spiritual than might be
thought. Many more, perhaps most, heads of ecclesiastical jurisdiction came to the church from a mixture of sources not attributable directly either to spiritual principle or to the material interests of the
church. The result was a mottled picture. Many matters were regarded as being of "mixed forum" under the canon law. In them the
parties might choose either an ecclesiastical or a secular venue for air-
ing their complaints. Some cases of conflict might thus be determined simply by which court had acted first.[3]

This "mixed forum" existed even within the criminal law. Cases
involving sacrilege, even blasphemy as will be seen in Chapter 10,
were regarded as appropriate for either forum. Statutory enactment,
customary practice, or individual choice could dictate the court before which such crimes were tried. Moreover, the overall situation
was rendered more fluid because the church held both secular and
temporal power in some parts of Europe. In these areas, the canon law
might apply in any event.[4] There, all justice belonged to the church,
and it would have seemed inappropriate to have used any other law.
Finally, in some places the church held subject matter jurisdiction as
a matter of local custom. This was so, for instance, with jurisdiction
over last wills and testaments in England.

Of the many sorts of jurisdictional competence asserted by the
church, few better illustrate the inner nature of the canon law than

the subject of this chapter. It is the claim to exercise jurisdiction because of the special nature of the canon law and the special nature of the claim being heard. This was jurisdiction to protect the disadvantaged, *miserabiles personae* as they were termed. It lay somewhere between subject matter and personal jurisdiction. Also inevitably involved in the protection of the disadvantaged was the assertion of ecclesiastical jurisdiction *ex defectu justitiae*. That was the claim that the canon law should step in to do right in all matters, even purely secular matters, whenever it turned out that justice was unavailable in the temporal forum.

The basic notion, overriding the ordinary limitations of subject matter jurisdiction, was that certain classes of litigants needed and deserved special protection. The church had the responsibility to see to it that they received it. The previous chapter explored aspects of this attitude in discussing the rights of minors and others to secure *restitutio in integrum*. The canon law claimed the responsibility of assuring that they received their due. In its fuller juridical form, to be explored in this chapter, this same font of spiritual responsibility became a separate head of jurisdiction, allowing disadvantaged people both to invoke spiritual jurisdiction as plaintiffs and to decline secular jurisdiction as defendants if they could fit their status or their claim within one or another of the special categories opened up for them by the canon law.

THE BASIC PRINCIPLES

The relation of ecclesiastical jurisdiction to temporal law and the church's right to intervene in secular matters were the subject of two decretals of Pope Innocent III inserted side by side in the title "Of the Competent Forum" in the Decretals (X 2.2.10–11). They expressed older ideas, but with particular forcefulness and within a concrete legal context. Both involved an action of apparent self-denial by the church. They are examples of the phenomenon, by no means unique to the canon law, of laying claim to a greater jurisdiction by refusing to exercise it in a particular instance.

Authority for Jurisdiction *ex Defectu Justitiae*

In the second of these two decretals, here used to illustrate both, a question of inheritance had first been brought before papal judges delegate. A secular lord, a count, in whose lands the dispute arose, objected to the exercise of any jurisdiction by the church in such a case. He asserted (at least in the words of the papal chancery) that he would himself exhibit "the fullness of justice" to the litigants. He demanded that the matter be returned to his court. In response, Innocent issued a decretal an English lawyer might describe as akin to a writ of *supersedeas*. It stated that the ecclesiastical judges were to defer to the claim of the count if the facts were as stated in the decretal. The count's position prevailed.

However, the pope's response left an opening. The decretal specifically stated that the papal judges were to defer to the count's request because adequate justice was obtainable in the temporal forum. From this, the canonists drew the obvious conclusion *a contrario sensu*. That is, if justice was *not* available in the temporal forum, the church's judges were to retain jurisdiction and do justice themselves. So, as it was put somewhat bluntly in the *glossa ordinaria* to the decretal: "Note that because of the neglect of a secular judge, jurisdiction is transferred to an ecclesiastical judge."[5] The decretal's terms gave no guidance about exactly how the determination of whether or not justice was available in the temporal forum was to be made. The suggestion was that the papal judges' delegates were to decide the question themselves.

The canonical text found in the *Decretum* that was most frequently cited as precedent for this jurisdictional principle is instructive by its contrast with this decretal of Innocent III. The earlier text came from a ninth-century church council, and it directed bishops to urge, and in fact to warn, ministers of the temporal government to do full right by all those who stood in special need (C. 23 q. 5 c. 26). If the temporal ministers failed to respond after repeated warning, they were themselves to be excommunicated until they performed their office aright. The church was here undoubtedly asserting a claim to stand over and direct the temporal authorities. That much seems obvious. However, the earlier canon did not take the step envisioned by Innocent III's decretal. It did not offer a *substitute* system of justice. If the temporal authorities were neglectful in doing justice, they were subject to spiritual sanctions. But that was all. The notion of a separate and distinct spiritual jurisdiction was not mentioned, and indeed it was quite slow to work its way into the law of the church.[6] The possibility of spiritual jurisdiction in a positive sense, as an alternative forum for doing justice in a system of public courts, was what Innocent III's decretal seemed to offer, at least as his words were understood by the classical canonists. It was a large step. From this starting point was eventually to grow up a separate and controversial source of ecclesiastical jurisdiction.

Authority to Protect the Disadvantaged

The second and related possibility of intervention in temporal matters had to do with *miserabiles personae*. The plaintiff in the inheritance case that was the subject of Innocent III's decretal was a widow. No doubt she had expected a more sympathetic hearing from her bishop than she would have received before the justices of the count. And she would have had some reason for thinking she would receive it. Numerous canons might have encouraged her expectation. Although the church should not deny its aid to any person, it must succor widows and orphans above all (Dist. 87 c. 1). Defense of the weak, of pilgrims, children, and widows was the essence of doing justice (C. 23 q. 5 c. 23). All causes involving oppression of the poor called forth the special solicitude of the church (C. 24 q. 3 c. 21). Texts from the Bible were also available to be called into play in the extension of ecclesiastical protection to the disadvantaged. Thus: "Ye shall not afflict any widow or fatherless child" (Exod. 22:22). Or: "He [God] doth execute the judgment of the fatherless and widow" (Deut. 10:18). Or: The Lord acts by "bringing justice to the orphan and the downtrodden" (Ps. 9:18). The canonists cited these passages. They seemed to invite intervention in the widow's favor by the ministers of the church.

Pope Innocent's decretal nevertheless denied the widow's jurisdictional claim. That it was a widow who was suing was not enough in itself to confer a spiritual character on a claim that otherwise belonged to the temporal forum. However, here too an opening of sorts was left. At least the canonists perceived one. They distinguished "primary" from "secondary" jurisdiction over widows, asserting that this decretal had dealt only with the former. Although the temporal authorities clearly held the first, ordinary jurisdiction, the church held the second.[7] Just what these were was not made clear in the decretal, but it could happen that "secondary jurisdiction" would come to mean "supervisory jurisdiction." The potential for expansion was obvious. The canonists seemed almost to be taking back what the decretal had conceded to the count. It might be that he enjoyed his jurisdiction only so long as he acted in accord with justice as justice might be defined by the ecclesiastical authorities.

What did these claims mean when they came down to earth? That is the subject of this chapter, working through it as it related to widows and orphans. As a preliminary note, however, it deserves emphasis that the first function distinctions like that drawn between "primary" and "secondary" jurisdiction served was to allow the canonists to harmonize the confused collection of authorities on the point. Doing so absorbed a large part of their energies, and perhaps even a large part of their interest. It cannot be claimed that their writings show any special urgency they felt to advance a social policy favoring widows and children. But the canonists did need to bring the texts on the subject into internal harmony. In so doing, the canon law nonetheless achieved a good deal to create rules protecting widows and children, and at the very least it seems fair to think that the canonists knew what they were doing.

SPECIAL INTERESTS OF WIDOWS AND CHILDREN

Roman Law Precedents

The place to begin an examination of the rationale for this part of canonical jurisdiction is not in the canon law itself but rather in the Roman law on the subject. The *Corpus iuris civilis* and commentaries on it were cited repeatedly by the canonists, both as justification for their law on the subject and as informing the individual choices they made within it.[8] There are evident parallels here with the subject of the last chapter devoted to the *restitutio in integrum*. *Restitutio*, however, was not so much a special jurisdictional privilege conferred upon a special class of litigants as it was a procedural remedy, made available to anyone suffering under a legal disability. It did not provide the nearest model. Closer to the subject of this chapter is a privilege that was granted to all *miserabiles personae* by the emperor Constantine in A.D. 334.

By Constantine's privilege any widow or child who was *sui iuris* and below the age of majority had the right not to be drawn in litigation outside the province where she or he resided (Cod. 3.14.1). This immunity applied even at the highest level of courts. Baldus later explained that even though the court of the emperor was rightly regarded as the "general court of the whole world," by special grant of the emperor himself, *pupilli* and *viduae* could not be sued there without their consent.[9] Moreover, the rule did not work in reverse. It was only a benefit for the protected class. Fatherless children and widows could *invoke* imperial jurisdiction, even though they were not subject to it. They had the unfettered right to initiate litigation before the court of the emperor, just as did any other Roman citizen. The explanation for the special status, again given by Baldus, was that the emperor stood as the "special protector" of all such *miserabiles personae*. Appropriately for this position he had seen fit to make things easier for them.[10]

The canon law did not ape the provisions of this imperial decree. Its provisions relating to the special role of the emperor were not applied to ecclesiastical jurisdiction. To have done so might have been an impermissible limitation on the power of the "universal ordinary," that is, the pope. However, the decree was useful to the canonists all the same. They discerned a principle within the imperial decree: namely that widows, minors, and other *miserabiles personae* should be accorded special jurisdictional rights. They applied this principle mutatis mutandis within their own courts. The decree was thus treated as supporting the argument that children and widows rightly enjoyed a privileged status in the law. Exactly what the privilege entailed and how far it extended remained to be worked out. In fact it was always left slightly indefinite in scope. But the principle was there. In other words, what had originally been a privilege to decline a distant court's jurisdiction in the Roman law became a privilege to invoke a nearby court's jurisdiction in the canon law.

A second, separate legal strand from antiquity led to the same result. It was the venerable habit, recognized and authorized in the Roman law, of referring disputes between laymen to bishops for mediation and resolution. This was the so-called *episcopalis audiencia*.[11] There was biblical authority for settling disputes within the church rather than outside it (1 Cor. 6:1–3), and this was not forgotten when Christianity became the religion of the state. The Roman law's Codex contained a separate title on the subject (Cod. 1.4.1–33), and Emperor Justinian laid down several rules to confirm and regulate the practice (Nov. 83). The basic rule of the civil law was that episcopal jurisdiction had to be based upon the initial and mutual consent of the parties. But subject to this limitation, the bishop's sentences were to be regarded as on a par with those of the ordinary courts. Nor were bishops restricted to spiritual matters; any civil dispute could be brought before their *audiencia* if the parties agreed.

Legal Principles and the Canonists

The classical canonists regarded the precedents of the Roman law as the recognition of a legal principle rather than its source. The civilian limitations did not, therefore, bind them. For them, the imperial legislation was instead an express recognition by the highest temporal authority that the church might assume a civil jurisdiction under appropriate circumstances. What those appropriate circumstances were, the canonists held, was to be decided by the canon law itself. As we saw in looking at the decretal of Innocent III and the case of the disputed inheritance, the canon law did not claim universal competence over temporal matters, but it did claim the right to determine whether circumstances required, or at any rate permitted, the exercise of ecclesiastical jurisdiction. The underlying principle here was something like the same one the canonists invoked in discussing "invocation of the secular arm," the subject to be examined in Chapter 13. It was that the canon law held a superior jurisdictional position. Consequently it, rather than the civil law, determined the extent of its own jurisdiction.

In making that determination, many canonical texts suggested the existence of a special solicitude for widows and children. Some of these texts were taken note of above. Orphans and widows were treated as unfortunates for whom the church had a special protective responsibility. This meant, for instance, that they were to be given special protection against the ravages of warfare (C. 24 q. 3 c. 25).[12] Furthermore, although clerics were ordinarily forbidden to assume the burdens of acting in secular affairs, an exception was made for guardianship (cura and tutela) of minor children (Dist. 86 c. 26). In fact, clerics were required to assume this special responsibility under orders from their bishop.[13] Following this same rationale, the canon law held that an obligation to provide legal assistance without fee to disadvantaged persons unable to find it elsewhere rested with the clergy.[14]

This clerical solicitude for the earth's unfortunate was not based solely on texts generated by the medieval church. It came from, or at any rate was justified by, the use of biblical example. The canonists asserted that in fulfilling this duty to orphans and widows, the clergy were in fact imitating the angels of God. By Jacob's ladder angels had ascended and descended from Heaven (Gen. 28:12). On the strength of this biblical text, the canonists reasoned that since the angels could descend to the world without harm, the clergy might do the same. Mixing in secular affairs might not be wholly incompatible with clerical status. When there was reason enough, the angels themselves had descended.[15] The protection of miserabiles personae provided a good reason for clerics to make the descent, and the story of Jacob's ladder proved that it might be done without risking their soul's health.

As an aside, it is worth stating that the basis for the jurisdiction did not depend on sentimental thinking about children. The work of the canonists spent little time on the lovability of the children who would benefit from this jurisdiction involved in such thinking. In particular, the canon law never looked upon children as incapable of acting viciously. Nor did it assume they were the victims of circumstance when they did. "The life of minors and adolescents is uncertain," the canonists said, "because it is always prone to do wrong."[16] Children in the home were to obey their parents. Children in holy places were to be superintended by mature clergy (C. 12 q. 1 c. 1). Children under the direction of teachers were subject to correction, including corporal punishment, at the hands of these teachers (X 5.39.1). Children who committed crimes might be punished more leniently than adults because of their immaturity, but they were certainly to be punished. There was to be some protection of infants and widows under the canon law. However, the canonists insisted that it should not be the kind of idealistic protection that would easily turn into license.

The question was what these provisions would come to in fact. When one has exhausted these and similar early canonical statements dealing with the special protection of widows, children, and indeed of *miserabiles personae* of all sorts, it becomes quite apparent that nothing like an exact and separate heading of ecclesiastical jurisdiction in their favor had been created by the texts themselves. What authorization for the assertion of a coercive jurisdiction can be found in the *Decretum* is to be found in the later *glossa ordinaria* to it, and that was not very specific.[17] Even the Decretals were uncertain about exactly how far this supplementary form of ecclesiastical jurisdiction was to extend. Defense of the weak was stated to be a special interest of the church, but it was an interest shared with the temporal authorities (C. 23 q. 5 c. 23), and in some provisions it appeared to serve more as a more general admonition supporting favorable treatment than a source of ecclesiastical jurisdiction. Nor was it clear exactly what the protection of *miserabiles personae* should come to mean in practice. As in the law of episcopal elections and many other areas of the canon law, implementation of the principles was left for the canonists, working out the consequences of the principles stated in the *Decretum* and the general assertions of jurisdiction found in the Decretals.

IMPLEMENTATION OF SPIRITUAL JURISDICTION

Some of the basics of the subject of jurisdiction over *miserabiles personae* have already been outlined in discussing the case of the widow. Papal decretals and commentaries on them drew together the general principles inherited from the past and made them into an active spiritual jurisdiction. Once the church had established a network of regular courts, what had appeared as a statement of principle in the *Decretum* became a choice for litigants. The canonists claimed, for instance, that although ordinary spiritual jurisdiction did not extend to all causes of widows and other *miserabiles personae*, it did extend to causes "where it was a question of an injury or of violence done to them."[18] Many lawsuits do involve injury or violence, at least at the stage of the pleadings. Children or widows unable to protect themselves might thereby invoke ecclesiastical jurisdiction where they had suffered something qualifying as "oppression" at the hands of others. The canonists thus asserted a claim over what could come to be a considerable jurisdiction on the part of the ecclesiastical tribunals. It was not without a touch of realism that the *glossa ordinaria* to Innocent III's decretal concluded that "indirectly, by reason of sin, all causes belong to the church."[19] That the church ordinarily chose not to exercise this right in the world was a matter of prudence and of humility more than it was a question of necessity.

The church also asserted a criminal jurisdiction to protect the disadvantaged in these circumstances. An episcopal court might intervene of its own motion to protect the interests of *miserabiles personae*, rather than waiting for specific complaints by the disadvantaged persons themselves where the exigencies of life required it. Since many such persons would not in fact have complained, or even have been able to complain, the canon law's provisions in their favor would have been illusory without the addition of a criminal side.

Other decretals and the commentators added to this schema. They expanded the scope of special jurisdiction allowed to minors by drawing a distinction between petitory and possessory actions. *Miserabiles personae* were permitted to invoke ecclesiastical jurisdiction as a matter of right where only possessory rights were being litigated (X 2.2.15). For instance, even in a matter involving lands held by feudal tenure, spiritual jurisdiction might not be ousted where the question at issue in a particular case was one of spoliation or simple possessory rights in the land, rather than a question of ownership or inheritance. Readers familiar with the legal history of England will recognize here the parallel with the origins of the possessory writ of novel disseisin, recalling that this writ and its successors virtually superseded the petitory writ of right in litigation before the English royal courts.[20] Who was to say that something like the same thing might not eventually take hold in the canon law?

The rights of ecclesiastical jurisdiction with respect to the temporal courts were clearly asserted in some of the other decretals. The most famous claims to temporal authority of the medieval church were embodied in them, and some involved the rights of *miserabiles personae*. The decretal *Novit* (X 2.1.13) asserted the church's right to intervene in temporal matters "in order to decide concerning a sin." The much disputed decretal *Per venerabilem* (X 4.17.13) asserted the church's right to determine questions involving the legitimacy of a child's birth, even when the ultimate issue was the temporal one of determining the child's rights of inheritance. It claimed this, moreover, as an exclusive right that temporal courts were obliged to respect. What had been a sentiment—that the church should succor widows and orphans—thus was becoming an assertion that the church could exercise exclusive jurisdiction over their legal claims.

Pope Benedict XIV (d. 1758) was later to state the matter this way: "Lest the defense and protection [of *miserabiles personae*] be ineffective, it must be coupled with jurisdiction."[21] He was stating with particular clarity the logical conclusion drawn out of the earlier writings. In this sense he was merely summing up what the medieval canonists had said. It was nothing new. Nonetheless, taken all together this conclusion added up to a large claim to subject matter jurisdiction, and Benedict XIV was saying so with obvious clarity. Although the canon law began by denying itself temporal jurisdiction, a very large exception to that denial was opened up. Particularly would this be so if the category of *miserabiles personae* proved incapable of limitation to widows and orphans (as it in fact proved to be). Having absorbed its possibilities, one feels a kind of empathy with the kings of the time and with their advisers, who felt that their jurisdictional rights were being both threatened from the front and eaten away from the back by the several exceptions and open-ended interpretations of the canonists.

The canon law was not without difficulties of its own in dealing with the jurisdictional rules enunciated in the Decretals, quite apart from the need to fend off the inevitable complaints of secular officials. Many of the jurisdictional claims made in favor of *miserabiles personae* found in the texts seemed almost to have been the product of the moment, the result of a desire to protect vulnerable persons more than the result of a fully thought out jurisdictional scheme. It has rightly been said that the Decretals on the subject resemble "a mass of cases which had been resolved from day to day rather than a source of general principles."[22] There was a need for clear statement, and the canonists sought always to bring order to what they found. Here we look at two of the questions they dealt with: first, determining which children and widows qualified as *miserabiles personae*; and second, determining the exact conditions under which they could invoke spiritual jurisdiction *ex defectu justiciae*.

Who Qualified as a *Miserabilis Persona*?

One response to this question, that found often in the Roman law and its commentators, was to leave the definition of the term *miserabilis persona* purposefully vague. It treated the question as one of fact to be determined in the individual case. The text from the Codex upon which their jurisdictional privilege was grounded mentioned widows, *pupilli*,[23] the weak, and those suffering from a debilitating, long-term disease. But it seemed that this list had not been meant to be exclusive. How far did its underlying principles extend? The most famous civilian commentators of the Middle Ages added little to this text itself. Baldus de Ubaldis posed the question, Who is a *miserabilis persona*? But his answer was simply, "The text expresses some."[24] Bartolus, raising the same question, answers, "Briefly, I think this is to be left to the discretion of the judge."[25] Azo had described *miserabiles personae* as "all those whom nature moves us to pity."[26] Such open-ended answers (and perhaps they were the right answers) were by no means infrequent among the commentators on the *ius commune*. They are signals that we are not to expect too much by way of exact definition. And it is true that leaving difficult questions of this sort to the factual determination of judges remained a common way of resolving them in the *ius commune*.[27]

Many of the later civilians, however, were not content with simplicity or purposeful vagueness. It became possible, even common, for commentators to enumerate long strings of unfortunates who might make plausible claims to the status of *miserabiles personae*. The commentators of later centuries turned this into an exercise of industry and imagination. Thus the blind, cripples, captives, old people, newly baptized Jews, scholars, pilgrims, and foreign merchants subjected to local taxation were among those swept into the category by later writers.[28] Manumitted slaves, public penitents, and unmarried noblewomen without sufficient dowries could also be brought within it.[29] Discussion and elaboration of the class was to reach some ridiculous extremes. Speculation about whether or not a person "desperately in love" could qualify as a *miserabilis persona* filled a folio of one seventeenth-century treatise on the subject.[30] It was suggested in another that a sleeping person might qualify because of his special vulnerability at the time.[31] Parents with children and parents without children were both thought eligible, according to the way one viewed the matter.[32] Their "misery" may have stemmed from different sources, but the category could be made capacious enough for both through the industry and imagination of the civilians.

The early canonists were somewhat more forthcoming in definition than the medieval civilians and somewhat more restrained in elaboration than the later civilians. Innocent IV, the most cited commentator on the subject, listed several of those found in the list above: merchants, lepers, and pilgrims. Exposed children also fit. Under the same heading Innocent also asserted what became a kind of personal jurisdictional privilege for servants of the church. *Rustici* belonging to a particular church could thus come within the category of *miserabiles personae* under his view of the matter.[33] As with many questions within the *ius commune*, it is obvious that this one was capable of variant and extended answers, but it was not entirely open ended for the best of the canonists.

From the start, the canonists also dealt with the definitional question of whether the disadvantaged status was to be judged by the person or by actual condition. At first sight, the answer appears relatively simple: by actual condition. The locus classicus for the answer was a decretal of Pope Gregory IX (X 1.29.38). In it a widow, claiming to be poor, sought papal letters of justice to recover lands and chattels. Upon timely objection, the letters were revoked when it was discovered that she was no pauper but actually a rich noblewoman. Together with the decretal of Innocent III noted at the start of the chapter, this would seem to have ended the matter. Presumably the same principles would apply to the case of children and others who might claim this privileged status. If rich, the fatherless child would have to seek his rights before lay tribunals unless he could come within one or another of the other headings of ecclesiastical jurisdiction. He was not truly *miserabilis*.

There was lasting support for this position among the canonists. The *glossa ordinaria* to Gregory's decretal stated it squarely,[34] and there was a body of contemporary writing in support.[35] However, there was another position possible. This decretal left three openings for argument. First, it could be maintained that spiritual jurisdiction had been denied to the widow only because of the falsity in the letters of justice; that is, the case had been decided only because the plaintiff had falsely claimed to be something she was not, a pauper. Second, the decretal could be interpreted as stating that since this litigant was expressly denied the privileged status of *miserabilis persona* because she was a rich widow, had she been only a widow, she would necessarily have been a *miserabilis persona*. Finally, it could be asserted that since the decretal permitted ecclesiastical jurisdiction to "children, widows, and other *miserabiles personae*," the text was necessarily assuming that all widows and children were *miserabiles*. Had it been otherwise, the texts would necessarily have read "those children and widows who are *miserabiles personae*." From such arguments and distinctions the possibility arose that all children and widows, no matter how rich or powerful, could be brought within the category despite the apparently contrary holdings of the papal decretals.

The settled canon law went halfway down this road. It came to classify all fatherless children and widows as *miserabiles*, but it denied them the full privilege of invoking ecclesiastical jurisdiction unless they were also poor or otherwise pitiable in fact.[36] This sensible result was reached by subdividing the class of *miserabiles personae* between those who were pitiable only by virtue of their status—all widows and fatherless children might qualify for this—and those who were rendered yet more pitiable by the circumstances of their lives.[37] Poor widows and orphans, but not rich widows and orphans, qualified for this second group. As noted above, a few among the commentators pushed the category further, allowing all widows and orphans to invoke ecclesiastical jurisdiction as a matter of course.[38] But according to what remained the "more common opinion," only the conjunction of status as widow or *pupillus* and some form of poverty entitled the child or widow to invoke ecclesiastical jurisdiction without further justification.

What degree of poverty or pitifulness qualified a litigant for this privileged status? No exact text or amount appears ever to have been set under the *ius commune*.[39] However, three general matters were established: (1) Poverty was judged by the party's current means, that is, before the lawsuit. That one might become rich by securing a favorable sentence in the case was not a disqualification; (2) Poverty was judged on a sliding scale, according to one's status in society. Conceivably a queen, even one with substantial assets, might be found *miserabilis* if her current assets did not match her exalted station; and (3) Disposable income is what counted, not what we would call capital. The *miserabilis persona* was not counted rich if paying for the litigation required selling her patrimony. Apart from these three points, the question seems to have been left to the judge's discretion.

Jurisdiction *ex Defectu Justitiae*

Suppose the fatherless child was not poor and therefore not automatically entitled to invoke spiritual jurisdiction. This did not categorically rule out doing so, if the child could come within one or another of the several exceptions to the general rule that secular matters between secular persons must be tried in secular courts. The most prominent of these exceptions was without doubt that provided for cases of inadequacy in secular justice, ecclesiastical jurisdiction *ex defectu justiciae*.

The obvious question raised by this exception to ordinary jurisdictional principles lies in understanding exactly what "defect" meant in practice. On the one hand, the canon law could not hold itself satisfied with the simple existence of a temporal forum. That forum might not provide a remedy adequate for the widow or fatherless child. On the other hand, the canon law did not wish to go too far, dictating the procedures and the results in the temporal courts. It would not do for the church to say to the temporal magistrate, "Give shorter terms, or give judgment for the widow," and then intervene upon a pretense of failure of justice when the magistrate refused to alter his settled practice.[40] As with any "supervisory" jurisdiction, the hard problem was how to secure a reasonable standard of justice without second-guessing every decision.

It may be the delicacy and difficulty of this situation that caused the canonists to be more reticent about intervening here than they sometimes were. In some sense, they merely redefined the term "neglect," calling it "the malice or the idleness of a judge."[41] It seems clear, however, that more than a procedural error was required before a defect of secular justice could be found that would justify canonical intervention. Joannes Andreae wrote of three situations in which the requirements would ordinarily be met: (1) where there was no temporal judge at all; (2) where the temporal judge was subject to recusal as suspect; and (3) where the temporal judge adamantly refused to do justice.[42] He went on to remark that the church should intervene "only when the secular judge expressly denied justice or when this [denial] was otherwise notorious."[43]

Significantly, one of the few examples of neglect found in the Decretals involved the judges' refusal to take testimony from the witnesses who alone could establish a question involving *salus animarum*, the health of the souls of the parties in the case (X 1.31.6). In the minds of the canonists, that was just the sort of failing that cried out for action on the part of the spiritual courts. The normal expectation seems therefore to have been that ecclesiastical judges could exercise jurisdiction *ex defectu justiciae* only when there had been something approaching a breakdown in the doing of justice by the temporal courts, not where the temporal law simply reached a result the canonists thought was wrong.

A related problem was the question of exhaustion of remedies. Suppose the secular judge refused absolutely to do justice, so that this part of the claim was beyond dispute. Was the suppliant then required to appeal the denial or otherwise to seek aid from the secular judge's superiors before he could invoke ecclesiastical jurisdiction? All the canonists dealt with the problem, and it seems to have been a particularly difficult one for them.[44] No decretal supplied a clear answer. On the one hand, it was not their desire to interfere with the normal course of secular justice. That encouraged allowing the appeals to take their course. But on the other hand, it was their desire to secure justice for the person involved. That encouraged not burdening a person with repeated, expensive, and perhaps fruitless appeals for justice in a system where in the end justice would be denied. The one alternative was hard; the other was harder.[45]

In this situation, the canonists took refuge in distinction. At least that is what it looks to be. Some of the distinctions suggested in the commentaries were: (1) between states where the ruler recognized no political superior and those where he did; (2) between recourse to the pope and recourse to other ecclesiastical judges; (3) between situations where the imperial crown was vacant and where it was not; and

(4) between areas where custom permitted going to the church immediately and those where custom forbade it.[46] In each, the exhaustion of temporal remedies was required in the second situation but not in the first. However, the most common distinction found in the commentaries seems to have been none of these. It was taken instead from the related concept of *miserabiles personae*. The "more probable" answer seems to have been that only a *miserabilis persona* had the right to go immediately to the ecclesiastical forum and was not required to exhaust the remedies of secular justice. Others had to wait until the "defect" in temporal justice had been completed.[47]

This answer had the added merit of dealing with a troublesome puzzle: What rights did widows and orphans enjoy in this sphere that ordinary litigants did not? It was clear enough that *miserabiles personae* were entitled to a privileged position in the canon law. But it was also clear that *all* persons were entitled to seek out the ecclesiastical forum *ex defectu justiciae*. If the latter was so, what was so special about the position of widows and orphans? Here was a distinction that answered the question. Widows and orphans had a special right to invoke ecclesiastical jurisdiction at an early stage. This gave substance to the special character of the position of *miserabiles personae* before the law, because it meant that only they were not required to exhaust temporal remedies before applying to the church for assistance.

LEGAL PRACTICE AND *MISERABILES PERSONAE*

Readers who are more interested in what happened than in legal theory may wish to discover the extent to which the ideas sketched above were realized in practice. Some readers may well be impatient with the speculations and the distinctions of the canonists, preferring to discover whether any effective legal protection was in fact exercised on behalf of the indigent. They may also be curious to know whether the church succeeded in exercising the expansive claims to jurisdiction under these two heads. Jurisdiction to protect *miserabiles personae* clearly had the potential for unsettling secular justice and for upsetting secular rulers. This jurisdiction would allow the church to intervene in routine matters of the world, matters over which jurisdiction was everywhere claimed by emperors, kings, princes, and even municipalities in medieval Europe. The canonists themselves often pointed this out. Resistance was to be expected. What actually happened?

Before attempting an answer to the question on the basis of the research so far accomplished, there is one introductory remark to be made. When one thinks the matter through from a practical point of view, three possibilities appear to have been open to the church. First, intervention into temporal matters in favor of *miserabiles personae* could have been kept somewhat in reserve, mainly as a matter of theory and one not exercised in the ordinary course of things. It might be invoked only when there was a real breakdown of secular government, when the power of the papacy could be called upon without evoking strong reaction. Second, it might have been put into effect only where secular justice was systematically unavailable. No canonical remedy would be offered simply because individuals felt they had not been listened to in the secular courts. But where no secular remedy at all was provided for a class of legitimate claims, the church would provide one. Here the prince would have little (or at any rate less) reason to object, since the church would simply be opening up an avenue of justice that the prince himself did not wish to provide. This jurisdiction need last no longer than the temporal law continued to refuse a remedy for the wrong. Third, ecclesiastical justice might have been made available as a matter of course in individual cases. Any *miserabilis persona*, indeed any person, could invoke ecclesiastical jurisdiction whenever he or she could fit within one or more of the exceptions to jurisdictional rules provided in the first instance. This third possibility would evidently have been the most objectionable from the point of view of the temporal governors. It would also have been the most natural reading of the canon law.

The evidence suggests that all three of these possibilities occurred within the medieval church, although not everywhere and not all at the same time. Sometimes and in some places, no such jurisdiction would have been much in evidence had anyone thought to take a survey. But elsewhere it was more than theory. There was always a considerable geographical diversity in the jurisdiction actually exercised by the courts of the church. Jurisdiction over *miserabiles personae* makes an excellent illustration. None of the three cases below matches any one of the possibilities perfectly, but they match one of them closely enough to make an excursion into practice illuminating.

France

The first of these three possible ways of interpreting and implementing the church's supervisory power over lay justice would of course be the most difficult to discern. By definition the jurisdiction would normally have been left dormant. It would have come to the fore only in moments of crisis. Something like this situation might be said to have characterized France during the fourteenth century, although it must be admitted that the church attempted to assert its power over temporal government principally when its own interests were at stake, rather than specifically in favor of *miserabiles personae*.

Research into the contemporary records of the French ecclesiastical courts has revealed that no regular assertion of jurisdiction in favor of *miserabiles personae* was made in practice.[48] Nor was jurisdiction *ex defectu justiciae* made available in the tribunals of the church as a matter of course. In fact, the church was struggling with limited success to hold on to its exclusive personal jurisdiction over the clergy. What assertion of a supervisory jurisdiction over the government of the king that existed came only in a moment of crisis, when the church felt itself under threat. This happened most dramatically in the dispute between Pope Boniface VIII and King Philip IV at the start of the century. That dispute involved much more than a technical question of ecclesiastical jurisdiction. At bottom, however, it was about the same issue. In the decree *Unam sanctam*, the pope recalled to Philip, "If the earthly power errs, it shall be judged by the spiritual power" (Extravag. 1.8.1). The two sides were at issue over this fundamental question.

The outcome of this famous quarrel, however, cannot be described as a success for the church. Boniface died, and his successor found himself obliged to clarify the meaning of *Unam sanctam* in a direction more acceptable to the interests of the French monarchs (Extravag. 5.7.2). Perhaps Boniface had misjudged the realities of the situation. He had, however, *sought* to exercise the first of the three possibilities in a moment of crisis. He had tried to demonstrate a practical application of the principle that the church had the right to intervene whenever the temporal power had misused its authority. In this he was doing no more than asserting a right the canon law seemed to accord to him.

England

England's experience was something like the second of the three alternatives. No recourse to the courts of the church *ex defectu justitiae* was available to individual litigants in medieval England.[49] No one was permitted to seek a remedy in the courts of the church by alleging that the courts of the king had denied him justice or that he was *miserabilis* in fact. If any court came even close to offering that kind of remedy during the later Middle Ages, it was a royal tribunal, the Court of Chancery, not the consistory courts of the English bishops.

However, throughout the Middle Ages and into the post-Reformation period, the English ecclesiastical courts did offer legal protection for children in three situations in which the common law courts did not. The first was infanticide. Whereas the deliberate killing of infants was theoretically a crime under the common law, research into the subject has shown that in reality it was a crime rarely pursued.[50] In the courts of the church, the matter stood differently. Infanticide and abortion were treated as ecclesiastical offenses.[51] The second was guardianship. Although the common law had a law of guardianship over fatherless children, it was always incomplete. Not all children were covered, and not all guardians were legally obligated to act in the interest of their wards. In the courts of the church, efforts were made to take up part of this slack. Using a simplified form of the Roman law of *cura* and *tutela*, the courts provided guardians to protect the persons and property of infants as part of their probate jurisdiction.[52] The third was illegitimacy. Prior to 1571, the common law courts made no provision for the care or upbringing of illegitimate children. Such an infant was "a child of no one" (*filius nullius*) as far as the courts of the Crown were concerned. In the courts of the church, things stood differently. Fathers were routinely ordered to provide for the sustenance and support of illegitimate children they had caused to be brought into the world. The awards were not large, but they existed.[53]

It is obvious that the exercise of this sort of ecclesiastical jurisdiction was at best only a partial application of jurisdiction *ex defectu justiciae* discussed by the canonists. The English Church was simply filling gaps left by the common law, gaps that happened to concern the protection of children. One might well doubt whether this was directly related to the ideas sketched in this chapter, for the court records did not actually describe the children being protected as *miserabiles personae*. Nor did the officials of the spiritual courts require any showing of default of secular justice in particular cases, as the canon law specified. It may be thought of as the exercise of jurisdiction based upon local custom. On the other hand, the jurisdiction being exercised by the English courts did fit the canonical ideas in an important sense. It disappeared when the common law changed. For instance, once the common law began to enforce a support obligation against the fathers of illegitimate children, the church ceased to do so. This jurisdiction was provided only where there was a special need because of the perceived inadequacy of the common law.

Germany

It was in German-speaking lands that the fullest exercise of supplementary ecclesiastical jurisdiction seems to have been attempted.[54] Although the evidence is far from perfect, it appears that the officials of the spiritual courts in these territories regularly sought to protect *miserabiles personae* by allowing them to bring ordinary temporal claims before the spiritual courts. Efforts to secure ecclesiastical jurisdiction *ex defectu justiciae* were also at least fitfully made.[55] Such jurisdiction appears as part of much diocesan legislation, and there are individual instances of civil cases invoking this exceptional spiritual competence that we know were in fact brought before these courts. Whether it was fully effective in securing justice for those who would otherwise have been without remedy we cannot know. At the least, it appears that some men and women persisted in making ecclesiastical claims in attempts to secure their temporal rights through the jurisdiction of the church.

The best evidence on the subject comes from complaints and struggles that went on during the later Middle Ages. One can justifiably assume that the ecclesiastical courts must have been exercising this jurisdiction, because the temporal courts were actively and consistently seeking to prohibit them from doing so and in time seeking to take this contentious source of jurisdiction away from them entirely. The attempt to oust the church's jurisdiction over worldly matters has left loud and repeated evidence in the German historical record.[56] Obviously, this kind of negative evidence leaves much to be desired. It would be much better had we more studies based upon examination of the court records of the ecclesiastical forum. But at the very least, from what is known already we can say that the ideas of supplementary ecclesiastical jurisdiction discussed by the canonists had not been everywhere reduced to the realm of theory. They had enough bite to cause the temporal princes to object.

LATER DEVELOPMENTS

It will not have escaped the notice of readers that most of the reasons given for invoking ecclesiastical jurisdiction in secular matters were capable of being set on their heads. They could have been easily turned against the church. Stated differently, the reasons could have been framed to permit the courts of the state to assert a temporal jurisdiction over matters that were within the undoubted competence of the spiritual forum. If the church could bring a secular case within its courts because the secular courts had not done justice to one of the parties, might not the secular courts employ the same tactic and use it in an admittedly ecclesiastical matter because the ecclesiastical courts had failed to do justice to one of the parties? If the existence of violence against a widow would justify the church taking jurisdiction over a matter that would ordinarily be outside its competence, could not lay courts make something like the same claim in an ecclesiastical matter? Could not they (more plausibly) claim that violence could only be sufficiently dealt with in the temporal forum? Were this to happen, the church would be hoist with its own petard.

The canonists foresaw this possibility and sought to guarantee that it could not happen.[57] The texts and commentary on the law stated without equivocation that the sole remedy for any defect of justice in an ecclesiastical tribunal was appeal to the next higher authority and ultimately to the papacy itself. The remedy for defect of justice in a secular tribunal, on the other hand, was always to include invocation of ecclesiastical jurisdiction in appropriate circumstances, as we have seen. Although the canonists saw the analogy between the two situations, they did not admit their equality. To have admitted the possibility would have compromised the superiority of the spiritual over the temporal and undermined the liberty of the church.

Nevertheless, the possibility ultimately became the fact. During the later Middle Ages, temporal courts on the Continent began to exercise a supervisory jurisdiction over the courts of the church. They did so both by invoking the canonical principles described in this chapter and by building on customary and Roman law texts requiring the prince to do justice. The later treatises entitled "Of the Privileges of *Miserabiles Personae*" were for the most part written to assert the supervisory jurisdiction of the highest temporal courts, not that of the church. In them, the canonists' own arguments were turned against canonical jurisdiction. In Spain, the jurisdiction of the ecclesiastical courts was made subject to oversight by the royal courts, on the theory that the king had a responsibility to protect his subjects against "violence" at the hands of the ecclesiastics.[58] In France cases involving marriage were brought before lay tribunals, on the theory that only possessory rights or only questions of fact were being tried in them.[59] These were both rationales the canonists had developed to permit *miserabiles personae* to bring litigation in an ecclesiastical forum. Under this new way of seeing things, the rights of primary jurisdiction were being preserved to the church. But the evident reality was that spiritual jurisdiction was gradually being usurped by the courts of the king.

In both France and German-speaking lands, the idea of a jurisdiction *ex defectu justiciae* was also taken over by the lay tribunals and used against the immediate interests of the church.[60] Or better said, temporal jurisdiction was opened to litigants who claimed they had failed to receive justice at the hands of the spiritual courts.[61] The proponents of this development justified it, not by treating it as a matter of power politics or state building, but by saying that the prince had the ultimate responsibility for assuring the peace of his kingdom. Where the spiritual sword was used to the detriment of the republic, then the temporal sword must be wielded to fulfill the king's duty. From at least the late fourteenth century onward, many of the temporal powers were thus asserting a jurisdiction to intervene within the subject matter jurisdiction of the church whenever the church had misused its authority or failed to provide justice at all. It was the mirror image of canonical theory. Indeed, the very texts of the canon law that emphasized the importance of justice, the king's responsibility for securing it, and the necessity of cooperation between church and state were cited as precedents for ousting the jurisdiction of the church in particular cases.[62]

This jurisdictional disagreement was not settled by 1400. The changes in secular law and practice did not cause the church to abandon its claim to jurisdiction over *miserabiles personae* or its assertion of the right to intervene in temporal matters *ex defectu justiciae*. Some of the strongest hierocratic claims made by the church were in fact made in those years when these rights of the church were coming under the strongest attack.[63] The decrees of the Council of Trent affirmed the rights of jurisdiction.[64] Canonical handbooks from the sixteenth century described it as a source of spiritual jurisdiction.[65]

By 1700, however, developments in the world had reached a point where continued assertion of the church's claims must have been regarded as hopeless.[66] Pope Benedict XIV (d. 1758) remarked that it could no longer be expected that the temporal courts would respect even the established jurisdictional rights of the church.[67] He advised bishops against exercising any supervisory jurisdiction on behalf of the church, no matter how clearly it was set forth in the canons. Such exercise, in that great pontiff's judgment, would only encourage the tendency of the lay powers to reach even further into the affairs of the church. It was a lamentable situation. One had to make the best of it, he concluded, dealing with things as they actually stood, and so we must also take leave of it as an instructive but purely historical example of the nature of the classical canon law.

CONCLUSION

Looking back on the history of this subject, Catholic apologists in modern times have sometimes defended the hierocratic claims of the medieval church as resting not upon the essential nature of the church but upon the realities of medieval government. They portray what looks to modern critics very much like an unbridled willingness to interfere in temporal affairs as a proper response to the breakdown of all government except ecclesiastical government during the Middle Ages. They describe it as something that was only natural in the wake of the disappearance of the Roman Empire. Whether desired or not, the church "found herself, for several centuries, the sole guardian of the treasures of civilization."[68] In the circumstances it was natural that the church should assert a right to oversee temporal affairs. Jurisdiction over *miserabiles personae* and the exercise of jurisdiction in secular matters *ex defectu justitiae* were therefore simply instances where the church took this reluctant, temporary, and salutary step.

There may well be something to the argument. From a modern perspective, it appears to fit the idea behind the form of supplementary jurisdiction discussed in this chapter pretty well. The church claimed to intervene, in fact did intervene, only because special circumstances existed. The special solicitude for the poor and the powerless that was embodied in this jurisdiction also deserves full credit. No other government in the thirteenth century stood able and ready to take up their protection. The church did.

On the other hand, this modern and attractive argument would have astonished Pope Benedict XIV, as it would have astonished the medieval canonists. They did not regard the church's special jurisdiction over *miserabiles personae* or its claim to take action *ex defectu justitiae* as a response to the moment. To them, it was a permanent part of God's plan for the world. The church was always to stand over the state. Jurisdiction exercised by temporal authorities was always to be subject to correction and oversight by the representatives of God. The canonists would not have been cheered by this modern apology for the jurisdiction they had created.

If the partisan of the canon law were to take a longer view, however, something more positive could be said. Perhaps things would not look quite so black as they did to Pope Benedict. Spiritual jurisdiction over *miserabiles personae* and intervention in secular affairs *ex defectu justiciae* have not been abject failures, even if the Catholic Church has been obliged to give them up as sources of its own power. In a variety of circumstances and at a variety of times, the jurisdictional principles described in this chapter have actually been fruitful sources of legal development. This is so because the temporal lawyers have not restricted the uses they made of these ideas to simply purloining jurisdictional rights once enjoyed by the ecclesiastical courts. To the contrary, they have used them to assert the principle that higher courts have the responsibility to intervene to protect the weak and thereby to move toward establishment of a uniform system of justice in a society of splintered jurisdictions.

So we find these principles invoked in the service of the creation of uniform law by the Camera Imperialis in sixteenth-century Germany.[69] They were so used to bypass the courts of feudal lords in several parts of medieval Italy.[70] They became the means whereby long lists of special rights enjoyed by the poor were created in the *ius commune*.[71] One can find suggestions of the canonical principles in the creation of a uniform system of common law in medieval England.[72] Even

Presbyterian Scotland during the late sixteenth century witnessed a rule of jurisdiction *ex defectu justiciae* come into active play in the service of larger principle.[73]

It has been an achievement of the classical canon law to develop legal rules and techniques that have had a long-term and (mostly) beneficial impact on the Western legal tradition. Brian Tierney, taking the area of public and constitutional law, has shown how canonical ideas were fruitful in constructing the foundations of modern, secular political thought.[74] So it has been here. No doubt it is ironic that a principle of jurisdiction developed in the service of extending ecclesiastical jurisdiction served as an instrument in its demise. All the same, it does not seem wholly extravagant to conclude that the results vindicate the canon law's claim to a modern student's attention and perhaps even admiration. The result of the canonists' efforts in this corner of the law had an impact on the course of Western legal development far beyond what the canonists themselves envisioned or desired. Perhaps we are better judges of their success than they were.

6 Religious Principles and Practical Problems: The Canon Law of Oaths

A stranger who came to observe an ecclesiastical court in the Western Church during the later Middle Ages would have been struck, and very likely also surprised, by the frequency with which oaths were taken. It would have seemed to the outsider that they were being accorded a quite extraordinary importance. He would have noticed that both the parties and their lawyers were being required to take a formal oath at more than one stage in the proceedings. The witnesses would also have been formally sworn before their depositions were taken. In fact, the substantive issue in the case itself might have involved an oath. The suit might have been (as we would say) brought upon an oath. The plaintiff might have alleged that the defendant was liable to perform an obligation for him specifically because the defendant had taken an oath to do so. If the stranger was lucky, he might even have come upon a legal argument about the lawfulness of a particular oath. There might also have been a question raised about whether or not a particular oath had been taken freely or been instead the product of coercion. In some of the cases he observed, he would have seen the truth of facts in dispute being tested by the oath of one of the parties. And more likely than not, at the end of the litigation, some sort of oath, and sometimes more than a single oath, would again have been required of the parties to the proceedings. At least when compared with current judicial practice or even that of the medieval English common law courts, the canon law was an "oath-dominated" sort of justice. A modern author accurately describes the oath as "the institutional glue par excellence" of the way problems were dealt with in the medieval church.[1]

THE LAWFULNESS OF OATHS

Quite apart from any surprise he might have felt at the frequency with which oaths were employed, the observer might have wondered about an initial question: Was what he saw compatible with the Christian religion? This raised an old, much debated, and recurring question.[2] Could a Christian lawfully swear? The church fathers had wrestled with the problem, and Gratian took the question up in *Causa* 22, beginning with the texts from Scripture that appeared to settle the question in the negative. Jesus had said to his disciples, "I say unto you, Swear not at all" (Matt. 5:34), and he had said again, "Let your speech be, Yea, Yea, Nay, Nay; for whatsoever is more than this cometh from evil" (Matt. 5:37). This dominical command was echoed in the Epistle of James: "But above all things, brethren, do not willingly swear, neither by heaven, neither by the earth, neither by any other oath, but let your Yea be Yea and your Nay be Nay" (James 5:12). Christians were instructed to tell the truth simply, invoking no special name or thing and drawing no sophistical distinctions between the reliability of what they said with an oath and what they said without.

Despite the apparent clarity of these commands, the church did not conclude that oaths were unlawful—only that some oaths were. Theologians and canonists were at one on this point, though they sometimes differed slightly on the reasons given for the conclusion.[3] Andreas Gail (d. 1587) was later to sum up the canonical position as he observed it from the vantage point of the sixteenth century. His comment was made without irony: "Particularly by the canon law, every oath that can be kept without danger to [one's] eternal life is to be kept."[4] Gail's words may seem to turn the biblical commands on their head. They assumed the importance and ubiquity of the oath within the canonical tradition. Gail mentioned no incompatibility between oath and religious principle. Investigation will show that his statement sums up a considerable amount of legal development. Another sixteenth-century treatise, called "Privileges of Oaths," could list no fewer than 174 separate ways in which oaths held a special place in the canon law.[5] Gail's words thus provide an introduction to the canon law of oaths that is by no means misleading. But they do require some explaining.

Oaths in the *Decretum*

Gratian's *Decretum* makes a good place to start. After setting out the biblical commands against oaths (d.a. C. 22 q. 1 c. 1), Gratian followed with a series of canons and excerpts from the church fathers, all of which were intended to show that the biblical commands had not been meant to outlaw all oaths. As was so often true with such difficult questions, the sophisticated intelligence of St. Augustine stood much in evidence in the seventeen canons of Gratian's *quaestio* devoted to the subject.[6] In Augustine's view, the Bible itself made clear that some oaths were altogether consistent with the Christian religion (C. 22 q. 1 c. 16). Oaths were to be found, some of them uttered by saintly men, in both the Old Testament (e.g., Gen. 42:15; Jer. 4:2) and the New (e.g., Acts 2:30; Heb. 6:16). The Book of Deuteronomy even contained an injunction directing men and women to "fear the Lord . . . and to swear by his name" (Deut. 6:13). For Augustine, it was not lightly to be concluded that these oaths fell under the Lord's condemnation.

Gratian added other, similar authorities to those produced from St. Augustine's writing. Some simply reiterated the point that oaths were found too often in Scripture to be unlawful per se. A few of them were canons read *a contrario sensu*. In the latter, a condemnation of false oaths was said also to prove the converse: that true oaths were permitted to Christians (e.g., C. 22 q. 1 c. 13). The most famous such example was the Third Commandment (Exod. 20:7). That men were not to take the name of the Lord God in vain was thought to prove that it was legitimate to invoke the name of God in other circumstances, that is, when it was not being taken in vain.

Other canons in the *Decretum* asserted that oaths might not fall under the biblical proscriptions for another reason: they were justified by urgent necessity (C. 22 q. 1 c. 6). The standard example was the oath taken by an innocent man accused of a crime. Those who judged him, it was assumed, would believe his oath but not his simple affirmation of innocence. The Epistle of James (5:12) had spoken of oaths "willingly" taken (*nolite iurare*). It had specifically forbidden such oaths. The exculpatory oath of the man accused of a crime was not, it seemed, one of these being forbidden. Practical circumstances gave the man no real choice. The truth could be established no other way than by his oath. It was consequently regarded as having been taken only "out of necessity" or "because of the incredulity of others." This oath was to be distinguished on this account from oaths willingly sworn "for the sake of cupidity" or "for the love of swearing." A decretal of Innocent III was later to bring together and formalize the learning on the latter, and most important, point (X 2.24.26). In time, the long-established custom of using oaths within the church became strong enough so that it too could be adduced to prove their lawfulness.[7] If they had proved their necessity in practice for so long, with a history that went back to the Bible itself, one could not easily assume that they were wholly illicit. Gratian did not make exactly this argument, but he had opened the way to it.

In addition to these authorities, a canon taken from the writing of St. Augustine observed in particular that Jesus had not spoken of oaths as "evil." He had condemned oaths as "coming from evil." Augustine supposed that Jesus had chosen his words with care. He concluded that the dominical command condemned only oaths that had proceeded *from* an evil source. Not all oaths did proceed from an evil source, and therefore not all were thereby proscribed. An oath grounded in wrong or used for a nefarious purpose was contrary to the gospel. Herod's oath to Salome, by which he was induced to execute John the Baptist, was the familiar biblical example (Mark 6:22–27). It sprang from evil. However, the oath taken by an accused but innocent person was a quite different matter.[8] It did not.

Under this approach, swearing was by no means encouraged. Because Jesus had warned against them, oaths required careful scrutiny before being admitted to the life of the church. Like wine, they were to be used, but used with moderation.[9] Like medicine, they were not a good in themselves, but they could be good when used for purging an illness. Oaths were subject to abuse, and the biblical condemnations rightly warned against them because of the propensity toward evil that accompanied them. The likelihood of perjury was only the most obvious of these inherent and possible dangers. Irreverence toward God from casual invocation of his name was another. Oaths were therefore to be reserved for cases of necessity, or at least real utility.[10] They were never to be invoked indiscriminately.

The Classification of Oaths

In time the canonists reduced these perceptions to a system, in fact to a list. They divided the law into distinct heads under which oaths could be sworn. It was possible, for example, to enumerate seven separate lawful justifications for the imposition of an oath: (1) in default of other proof, (2) on behalf of the Christian faith, (3) to secure obedience to a superior, (4) for the sake of peace, (5) to secure indemnity to the church, (6) in order to be absolved from excommunication, and (7) to purge oneself of *infamia*. Some writers approached the question from the opposite direction, listing and describing those oaths that were not permitted.[11] Both approaches followed the principle that the use of oaths must be consistent with three requirements: truth, discretion, and justice.[12] Unless these qualities inhered in an oath, the oath would better be described as *perjurium*. The effect was to create a dividing line between those oaths that fell under the dominical prohibition and those that fell outside. It left, as we shall see, a quite large number on the side of legality.

The second qualification between serious kinds of oaths suggested in Gratian's *Decretum* and eventually put into systematic form was a result of the rule that some forms of oaths were unlawful, no matter what uses they were put to. Jesus had said that his followers were to swear "neither by heaven, nor by the earth, and neither by Jerusalem, [nor] by thy head" (Matt. 5:34–36). From this starting point two exceptions to the lawfulness of oaths were derived. First, it was morally impermissible to swear *per creaturas*, that is, by invoking the name of a thing, since this might divert the honor that was due to God alone (C. 22 q. 1 c. 7). Second, it was wrong to swear *per membra Dei*, that is, by invoking some particular part or property of God, since this might lead to blasphemy, irreverence, or (as we shall see in Chapter 10) even heretical belief about the nature of God (C. 22 q. 1 cc. 10, 16).

These two exceptions were themselves found to admit of exceptions, however. Had the first been taken literally, it would have prohibited virtually all oaths, because God had created all things. Such blanket coverage, therefore, could not be the meaning of the prohibition. Moreover, some of the biblical oaths appeared themselves to have violated a literal reading of the rule. Joseph had sworn "by the life of Pharaoh" (Gen. 42:15). His oath could scarcely have fit within those permitted by a rule restricting oaths to invocations of God, but it was equally clear to the canonists that Joseph's oath must have been lawful. A mediating principle had to be found to harmonize this material.

In addition, as noted above, an exception or an elaboration was required because some of the canons that condemned perjury were said to have shown the legality of oaths *a contrario sensu.* A canon condemning false oaths made "by the Cross" was read as proving that true oaths sworn "by the Cross" must be lawful (C. 22 q. 5 c. 2).[13] If this was so, however, an obvious problem arose. How could the conclusion be squared with the rule against invocation of God's creatures? It was clear beyond dispute that God had willed the Cross of Christ to be, apparently making it a thing or creature of God. Yet, the oath invoking it was lawful. Again, a mediating principle had to be found if this apparent anomaly was to be removed.

What was found turned out to be a web of casuistry. Since it clearly was permissible to invoke God in an oath, and since equally clearly it was permissible to invoke the Cross even though it had been created by God, the canonists reasoned that the Cross in this particular oath must have been meant only as something that reflected God's glory or his purpose in the world. On that account it might be invoked in an oath. The Cross was not, in other words, being invoked for its own sake but in a kind of representative capacity. The same would obviously hold true for the Scriptures. Even though created by God, the Scriptures might be invoked in an oath because they referred indirectly to God. They were not being invoked for themselves.

This argument was capable of major development. It could be thought applicable, for instance, to relics of the saints. As Rufinus described the taker of an oath on a relic, "Although he invokes these creations [of God], he does not swear by them, because he does not refer the oath to them, but to him to whom the relics are consecrated."[14] Joseph's oath "By Pharaoh" was similarly treated. Pharaoh had exercised dominion by the will of God, since all power came from God. Because the Gospels commanded Christians to honor the king, therefore, it must be true that Joseph had in reality been honoring God indirectly by invoking Pharaoh's name.[15] To this length the canonists went to harmonize the authorities and to legitimate the taking of oaths.

In fact, they went a bit further. What about an oath *per lunam* ("by the moon")? This may not have been a common oath in practice, but it was discussed by many of the canonists. In thinking it through, they came to the conclusion that its legality must depend upon the view of the moon the person taking the oath held at the time he swore. If he meant the moon in its own right, this would be unlawful, because it violated the rule against swearing *per creaturas*. If, however, he meant to invoke the virtue of God, who had created the moon and who sustained it, then the oath would pass muster.[16] "Sometimes a creature is invoked in that a vestige of divine truth shines in it."[17] That could apply to the moon.[18] Perhaps on this score they would thereby have distinguished Romeo's oath by "yonder blessed moon" from Juliet's invocation of the "inconstant moon."[19]

The solution based upon intention, though intelligible, could not be described as an advertisement for scholasticism. It coupled the difficulty of determining a speaker's subjective intent with the threat of eviscerating the rule entirely. Push it just a little further and the only oaths necessarily beyond the pale would be those that expressly invoked "false gods." Most canonists saw this danger and argued, as a matter of prudence, against such extreme oaths. They advised against anyone's using them, though they could not deny their likely legality.[20] The example of the oath *per lunam* therefore shows something of the possibilities attending the reconciliation of oaths with the scriptural prohibitions. The prudence that dictated not using such doubtful expressions shows the caution with which the canonists approached the everyday use of oaths.

OATHS IN ECCLESIASTICAL COURT PRACTICE

The legality of the oath being established as a matter of canonical principle, the relevant question became the extent to which oaths would be used in the canon law. Answering the question requires looking at both small and large aspects of the subject. It is convenient to begin with what most of us would regard as the smaller aspect: oaths in courtroom procedure. How much were they used?

The only possible answer to that question is that they were used at every turn.[21] The court-based oaths were many, so many that they came to be divided into different classes by the canonists, corresponding with their purpose in litigation. They were enjoined upon the participants, to be taken at the several stages of a case's hearing. If one examines these principal classes even briefly, the ubiquity of the oath stands out. It is entirely another matter to assume that the oaths automatically achieved the purposes for which they were adopted. One senses also that the initial caution that accompanied their acceptance into the canon law was not wholly without effect. Oaths were not used on every occasion where they might have been. But that still left a great deal of use.

Oaths of the Court Officials

Before their admission to practice before a court, the professionals involved in litigation, the judges, advocates, and proctors, were required to swear an oath to fulfill their duties faithfully. Advocates, for example, swore to serve their clients to the best of their ability and to abstain from all mendacious, unprofessional conduct.[22] They bound themselves not to delay litigation needlessly and not to act in cases they knew to be without merit. The exact wording of the oath seems to have been treated as a matter for local custom under the medieval canon law; variation in exact form was not regarded as compromising any principle so long as the substance was retained. The Second Council of Lyons (1274), which required that both advocates and proctors take such an oath, based upon a similar provision in Roman law (Cod. 3.1.14.4), and that they renew it annually,[23] spelled out no exact form for it. In England the contents of the oaths were prescribed by a series of provincial and diocesan synods,[24] and it is certain that they were taken in fact. At the papal court, the customary oaths of the various officials were also adopted and spelled out in full in the constitutions governing the papal chancery.[25]

How effective these formal oaths turned out to be in practice is one of those important questions to which trustworthy answers will always elude us. The oaths could be the source of disciplinary action, including even exclusion from office, since violating them constituted perjury.[26] The records of the ecclesiastical courts have likewise left some evidence that they had at least occasional effect on the conduct of litigation.[27] But the men who took them were lawyers, and it is (and was) natural to be suspicious of lawyers. In examining the place of oaths in the canon law, perhaps the most one can note is that these oaths were not regarded as simple formalities or the occasion simply for celebrating a lawyer's formal entry into the legal profession. They were meant to govern conduct.

Oaths *de Calumnia*

The faith in the efficacy of oaths held by the men who formulated the canon law is nowhere more apparent than in the importance they ascribed to the oath *de calumnia*. Canonists debated seriously whether the oath was owed *iure divino* or only *iure positivo*.[28] The Gregorian Decretals and the *Liber sextus* devoted a separate title to it, the only oath used in civil cases to merit separate treatment there (X 2.7.1–7 and Sext. 2.4.1–3). Taken originally from the Roman law (Cod. 2.58), the oath was essentially a sworn affirmation of litigants' faith in their cause. It meant swearing that they believed their cause was just, that their action was not the product of chicanery or malice, and that they would make no use of false proofs or unnecessary delays.[29] Both parties were required to undergo the oath, normally after the *litis contestatio*,[30] although proctors, the legal representatives of the parties in litigation, were at length permitted to swear the oath in the name of the party as well as their own (Sext. 2.4.3). If the plaintiff was unwilling or unable to swear the oath, his action failed and the defendant was dismissed by sentence. If the defendant was unwilling or unable to take this oath, he was to be taken *pro convicto*.[31]

The canon law hesitated before embracing this oath fully. It had not been required by earlier temporal enactments,[32] and two decretals of Pope Honorius II (d. 1130) limited the extent to which clerics could be compelled to take it. It was thought to impugn their veracity. In *causae spirituales* the oath was not to be imposed upon them (X 2.7.2). Nor were bishops permitted to take the oath without consulting the Roman pontiff (X 2.7.1). In this prohibition perhaps one sees something like a residual effect of the biblical warnings against oath taking.[33] In fact, however, the direction taken was toward greater use of the oath.[34] The first of these rules was "corrected," partially by a decretal of Pope Lucius III (X 2.7.5) and fully by a decretal of Pope Boniface VIII (Sext. 2.4.1). A most interesting "correction" it was. By the new rule all clergy were required to take the oath. Boniface stated that the rule was being changed because he had observed the frequency of chicanery in litigation and the utility of the oath in combating chicanery.

The second rule, requiring recourse by bishops to the Roman see before they took this oath, appears also to have fallen by the wayside. The *glossa ordinaria* reported succinctly: "It is not in use."[35] Characteristically, the canonists devised several ways of bringing practice into harmony with this decretal, as, for example, in supposing (sensibly although without textual support) that the decretal had been intended to apply only to bishoprics in the vicinity of Rome.[36] Again, at this remove it is virtually impossible to know what actual effect widespread employment of this oath had. There was a contemporary story that many litigants were pretending the oath required them to *commit* calumny rather than to *avoid* it.[37] But this was a joke.

Oaths *de Veritate Dicenda*

As its name implies, this oath required persons who took it to tell the truth. Although it could be put to the parties in addition to the oath *de calumnia*, its most frequent and important place in litigation was in the examination of witnesses. As in modern practice, witnesses swore to tell the truth prior to their examination, and at least if procedural manuals are accurate, they swore to a more detailed set of responsibilities than the normal oath requires today. The oath of witnesses included promises that they would speak truthfully for both sides, that they would add no falsehood to the truth, and that their testimony would not be motivated by fear, love, hate, or bribery.[38] Additions were possible in appropriate cases.[39] This oath was by no means regarded as a mere formality. It was a rule of the *ius commune* that unsworn statements could not constitute *plena probatio* or be the source of prejudice to third parties (X 2.20.51). Since there was no jury and since the judges evaluated the testimony according to these rules, this restriction was more than a test of a witness's veracity to be weighed as appropriate by the finder of fact. It kept the testimony from being considered at all.

The oath *de veritate dicenda* has a slightly sinister reputation in English and American histories. It is the canonical name for what is known to students of constitutional history as the *ex officio* oath. In the hands of the Court of High Commission, created by the Tudor and Stuart monarchs to enforce religious uniformity, the oath became a tool of despotism, used against opponents of king and church during the seventeenth century. It required defendants to agree, under penalties of contempt, to answer questions that would be put to them, and this before they knew what the charges against them were. Not without reason, defendants were reluctant to take it. Its subsequent repudiation and statutory prohibition have been one source of the modern privilege against self-incrimination, the right accorded to all persons accused of a crime not to be compelled to give evidence against themselves.[40]

Many of the questions about the extent, exact meaning, and desirability of the use of the oath in criminal cases that were debated in

English practice were also debated within the traditions of the *ius commune*. For instance, it was agreed that the oath should be administered to the defendant in a criminal case, but whether the defendant should be given the articles against him in advance of swearing was a matter of dispute. The better opinion was that they should always be delivered to the defendant, but as Julius Clarus (d. 1575) later admitted, the rule was "badly served in practice."[41] The primary protection for persons accused of crimes in the canonical tradition was that they could not be required to swear the oath unless something like a prima facie case against them had been made out. It was a maxim of the canon law that "no one [was] required to reveal his own shame,"[42] and this venerable maxim was interpreted by the jurists to mean that no one could be obliged to be the *source* of a criminal accusation against himself. They added, however, that if the proper groundwork against the person had already been laid—if there was independent and reliable reason for suspicion—then requiring the oath *de veritate dicenda* and subsequent answers did not contravene the prohibition.

Probatory and Supplementary Oaths

Where there was a partial failure of proof in litigation, particularly in cases of less than the greatest moment,[43] the canon law left open the possibility of making that failure whole by use of an oath. In a sense this was an exceptional use of the oath. The ordinary rule was that where the evidence introduced by the two parties was equal, the party with the burden of proof, normally the plaintiff, failed (X 2.19.3).[44] If on the other hand the plaintiff met this burden and the defendant did not, the plaintiff would be entitled to a sentence in his favor. No more in the way of an oath could be required of him (X 2.19.2). Canonists cited the biblical commands against oaths in support of this result.[45] It seems to have been a textbook case in which the oath was unnecessary and hence unlawful.

However, there was also an intermediate situation: where there was only partial proof or else simply a presumption of law in favor of the party with the burden of proof. Since the *ius commune* required two witnesses to make full proof, requiring that these witnesses be fully trustworthy and testify to the same underlying facts, cases of partial proof, normally called *semiplena probatio* or half proof, could easily occur. And since the *ius commune* indulged itself in presumptions galore, the possibilities of this intermediate situation arising were multiplied. The law was reluctant to base a sentence upon merely a presumption or half proof, but neither did it wish to disregard them entirely. They were not worth nothing.

Here the oath provided a solution. It was called a "suppletory" or "decisory" oath. It permitted a party who had furnished *semiplena probatio* to make up the rest of the case by swearing to its veracity. A party alleging prescriptive title to property who could not fully prove the good faith necessary for canonical prescription might thus make up the deficiency by swearing to it (C. 16 q. 3 c. 7). Taken originally from Roman law (Cod. 4.1.3) and a familiar part of many systems of religious law, this supplementary oath was fully "canonized" (X 2.24.36).

Normally, its authorization meant that when confronted by *semiplena probatio*, judges assigned an oath to either the plaintiff or the defendant. The choice of which party would swear lay ultimately in the judge's discretion, depending upon his assessment of the character of the parties before him and the circumstances of the case. This was not a situation that lent itself to resolution by fixed rule. Which party was more likely to know the truth of the matter at issue should weigh heavily in making this choice, according to the commentators.[46] The more substantial and trustworthy party was also to be preferred. In practice, it appears that the desires of the parties themselves were taken into account in the judge's choice. Following the civilian institution (Dig. 12.2.3), the canon law allowed a litigant to "defer the oath" to the other party if he chose.[47] This meant submitting one's case to a test within the control of one's opponent. It also meant casting the burden of proof, and the danger of perjury, onto that party. Whether the ensuing oath was best understood as a separate form of proof or only a way of confirming other evidence was a question that occupied the detailed attention of commentators.[48] But however understood and however evaluated, this oath played a regular role in canonical litigation. Parties themselves chose to rely upon it with some frequency, as they were fully authorized to do under the law.

Oaths of Compurgation

The practice of "deferring" the decisory oath was appropriate in civil cases. Much the same dilemma, however, existed in criminal matters and in a starker fashion. What should happen when there was some evidence to prove that a person was guilty of a crime but not enough to meet the law's strict requirements of proof? On the one hand, it seemed that the person should be acquitted. Particularly in criminal matters, where so much was at stake, proof should be "clearer than light" (Cod. 2.19.25). On the other hand, the canon law had a strong interest in the punishment of the wicked.[49] The spur summed up by the maxim that action should always be taken, "lest crimes should remain unpunished" (X 5.39.35), was taken seriously. It was to create the inquisitorial method of proceeding that characterized canonical criminal procedure.[50] The question in this context was whether criminals should be allowed to escape just punishment simply because of a failure of proof.

Even put in this one-sided way, to most people today the question answers itself. If guilt is not proved, the accused person should be released. That much is self-evident. This reaction was not, however, the reaction of the framers of the canon law. They chose an oath, called *purgatio canonica*, to deal with the problem of possible failure of proof, devoting a separate title in the Decretals to it (X 5.34.1–16). The procedure was old and relatively simple. The person publicly defamed of a crime was required to take a formal oath that he was innocent of the crime and to find a number of *compurgatores* willing to swear they believe his oath was true.[51] The accused swore to the truth; the compurgators swore to their belief in the accused's oath (X 5.34.5). The ancient canons contained rules for determining the numbers of compurgators that were required for specific crimes and persons (e.g., C 2. q. 5 c. 19), but it became the rule in the classical canon law that the number of compurgators required was "arbitrary." That meant that it was determined by the judge according to his view of the exigencies of the case. The compurgators were required to be familiar with the accused, to come from his vicinity, to be of good fame themselves, and to be "of the same order" if possible (e.g., clerics should serve as compurgators for clerics). If the accused produced compurgators who did not meet these requirements, the judge was entitled to refuse to admit them. This happened in fact.[52]

Although accusatory procedure, in which there was a specific accuser who conducted the prosecution and produced the evidence, was theoretically preferred in the canon law, inquisitory procedure using canonical purgation quickly became the ordinary way of dealing with most criminal matters. Herein lay a danger. It seems obvious to us, and it was in fact obvious to the canonists, that this resulting system contained the seeds of injustice. Men and women could be prosecuted, though no one had stepped forward to accuse them, and then required to assume the burden of showing they were innocent by taking this oath. If they were strangers or friendless, this might be hard. Although the procedure seems first to have been used for men about to assume episcopal office, and could be justified on the grounds that against such men there must be no taint of public scandal whatsoever, its spread throughout the church's tribunals and its use against quite ordinary men and women quickly took away this justification.

Two things can be said in its defense. First, the accused chose the compurgators and took the primary oath himself. If his conscience was clear, and if others trusted his word, he had a better than even chance of prevailing. The records of ecclesiastical courts in fact show men and women "passing" this judicial ordeal so frequently that some modern observers have dismissed it as a toothless farce.[53] Second, the procedure could not be initiated unless there was legitimate *infamia* against the person. This meant more than rumor or unsubstantiated belief. It had to be a serious belief held by the substantial members of the community. The opinions of one's enemies, or even beliefs that were traced to one's enemies, did not count. Under some formulations, only if public scandal would be generated by failing to clear the person's name would canonical purgation be required.

Oaths to Obey the Mandates of the Church

There is one additional kind of oath that calls for attention, the oath to obey the dictates of the church. It is true that there were many other oaths used from time to time in court practice—oaths of faithful administration by fiduciaries, oaths used in estimating the damages suffered by plaintiffs, oaths to prosecute appeals in a timely manner, oaths to report costs of litigation accurately. But the most revealing sort of oath used in regular practice was the sworn promise to obey the mandates of the court. It was the price of absolution. Where any party stood excommunicated, as he would be for deliberate nonappearance, for refusal to obey a sentence, or for having committed one of the many acts calling for ipso facto excommunication, it was customary practice to require him to take this oath.[54] Thus, if a man had been excommunicated for laying violent hands upon a cleric, a topic to be taken up in Chapter 14, he might be required to swear in some detail that he would never commit the offense in the future before he could be absolved for his present offense (X 5.39.10). If the reason for imposition of the sentence of excommunication had been the party's contumacy, the party might be required to take a simpler but broader oath: to obey the mandates of the judge.

The party who was the target of such mandates might not always know what their exact contents would include. Since excommunication was imposed only upon those who had deliberately refused to conform to the dictates of the canon law, it could be said in defense of the practice that this oath required no more than the law itself did. It could not lawfully require future conduct that was illegal or unjust.[55] If the future mandates of the judge were unlawful, they could be disregarded. The canonists were frank to state, however, that the oath's great utility lay in deterring a party who took it from breaking the oath. "By fear of the oath," they said, "he will the more greatly fear similar [conduct]."[56]

Its legality and utility being admitted, this oath did not raise much in the way of controversy among the commentators. There was a little. For instance, whether someone could take this oath by proctor was disputed. It may seem slightly absurd to suppose that one could.

Absolution required confession and contrition, and one cannot easily confess one's faults and promise amendment of life by proxy.[57] Opinion to this effect did exist, but the more common opinion was that if good cause was present, the oath to obey the mandates of the church might be taken by proxy.[58] Innocent IV had so held. It was the common practice at the Roman court. That buttressed the more common opinion.[59]

OATHS AS THE SOURCE OF OBLIGATIONS

Oaths were not only the means of carrying forward litigation within the church's jurisdiction. They were also a heading of jurisdiction itself. Under the canon law sworn promises were the source of an obligation.[60] These oaths were classified as "promissory," whereas the oaths used in court procedure (or most of them) were "assertatory" oaths, the legal difference being obvious from the names. The exact nature of the future promise was legally irrelevant in most cases. A few were excluded, at least according to the view of some canonists. Since an oath was defined as "the invocation of the divine name as a witness to the truth,"[61] promises made "by Jove" or "by Hercules" may not have given rise to what an English lawyer would call a "cause of action." But some quite indirect invocations of God did. "By my faith" was enough to constitute an invocation of God's name, according to the *communis opinio*.[62] All promises made with such invocations could be specifically enforced, and it was perjury to violate them.

In fifteenth-century England, jurisdiction over sworn promises (or contracts, as we would more realistically call them if we were obliged to describe the social function they served) came numerically to dominate litigation within the ecclesiastical tribunals.[63] Suits brought to enforce contracts made with an oath furnished by far the largest share of the litigation heard. Most were sworn promises to pay a debt, furnish services, or deliver goods. So far as I am aware, no study of jurisdictional practice has been conducted systematically enough for other lands to say whether this situation was unusual, but it is certain that in some parts of Europe the ecclesiastical courts also exercised an equivalent jurisdiction.[64]

That this should have occurred contains an element of incongruity. The medieval canonists were the first to break away from the formalism of the Roman law of obligations.[65] On the basis of the scriptural injunctions that Christians should speak the truth, making no distinction between oaths and simple promises, the canonists reasoned that since God took no account of a difference between our words and our oaths (C. 22 q. 5 c. 12), neither should the church. This opened up the argument that anyone might undertake an enforceable obligation by a simple promise, even though no *stipulatio* or other means of clothing a *nudum pactum* had intervened.[66] If this were applied in the judicial forum, it would have been the foundation of a general law of contracts.

However, this possibility did not quickly become the fact. The canonists held that although God might take no account of the difference between words and oaths, the church could not ignore it in its external forum. The regime opened up by their work, in which simple promises would be actionable, was limited to litigation between clerics, in which the church claimed personal jurisdiction in any case; to places where the church exercised temporal jurisdiction; and to the internal forum.[67] Elsewhere, the oath was what counted. Only if an oath had been added to the promise would the spiritual forum be generally available as a judicial means of enforcement (Sext. 2.2.3). The oath "clothed" the *nudum pactum*.[68] This is indeed exactly what happened in England, emphasized in practice by styling the ensuing litigation as *causae perjurii* in the court records. Contracts of all sorts, many of them debts of the most secular sort, were routinely brought before the ecclesiastical courts there during the later Middle Ages. The incongruous result was to replicate, in a slightly different form, the essential features of the Roman law *stipulatio*.

Whether this was a good idea or not was long a matter of dispute, first among the canonists themselves, then among critics of the church. Suppose a debtor had promised to pay a debt for ordinary goods and services and had added an oath to the promise. The church's claim was to jurisdiction over the oath, not the debt. The canonists held that the debt was "accessory" to the oath, and its enforcement was allowed to the church under the normal rule of the *ius commune* that for jurisdictional purposes the accessory follows the principal.[69] Because the ecclesiastical court had jurisdiction over the principal matter, the oath, it could exercise jurisdiction over the accessory matter, the money owed. Fair enough as a matter of logic, but it was hard to resist the conclusion that the argument allowed the tail to wag the dog. Realistically considered, the debt was the principal matter, the oath the accessory, and in time there came to be opinion among the canonists themselves that the disputes over such sworn contracts were not properly considered *causae spirituales* or even *causae spiritualibus annexae.* The canonical doctrine that the oath "assumes the nature" of the underlying transaction gained momentum.[70] Moreover, it seemed evident that the spread of this jurisdiction to encompass enforcement of debts of the pettiest kind was wholly at variance with the canon law's injunction that oaths should be used in moderation. In some ways it is surprising to find so many canonists defending it as long as they did.

The jurisdiction also raised the understandable ire of temporal lawyers. If canon lawyers recognized that the situation created a certain incongruity, the temporal lawyers regarded it as a decided affront. It permitted the church to remove ordinary contractual litigation from the temporal forum simply by characterizing it in a slightly different (and artificial) way. The temporal lawyers reacted, first, by attempting to confine the church's jurisdiction to properly spiritual contracts and, second, by adopting the canon law's rule in their own courts, to be used as a weapon against the church. The exact means by which the first was achieved seem to have varied from one land to another. However, in most parts the process was virtually complete by the sixteenth century. The church lost its jurisdiction over all oaths except those that involved matters otherwise within ecclesiastical jurisdiction, such as perjury by a witness in an ecclesiastical court. The second was achieved in the course of the sixteenth and seventeenth centuries by the process of opening the doors of European courts to the enforcement of *nuda pacta.*[71] As Matthaeus Wesenbecius (d. 1586) wrote, "Actions arose from any pact first according to the pontifical law . . . [and] today the same obtains in every forum."[72] The English common law took this step, or at least a step virtually identical in substance, by expanding the availability and scope of the existing "action on the case" called assumpsit.[73] This full story therefore provides an example—of which we see several in this volume—in which the secular law was indirectly influenced by the canon law at the same time it subjected the jurisdiction of the courts where canon law was applied to encroachments and attack.[74]

LICIT AND ILLICIT OATHS

The canon law announced that as a rule all persons were bound to observe their promises. The ecclesiastical courts enforced the principle when the promise was coupled with an oath. It by no means followed, however, that all sworn promises were to be treated alike. As in modern law, there were limits to the principle that a person could make any promise he wished and expect to have a court enforce it. There were also such limits about the binding character of oaths in the penitential forum. The world of the classical canon law was like ours in this respect, although of course the medieval rules for determining exactly which contracts ran afoul of the law's fundamental policies and assumptions were not always identical to those of the present day.

　　The principle against across-the-board enforceability of oaths was clearly stated in the texts. The titles on oaths in both the *Decretum* and the Decretals both began their treatment of this problem with canons stating that illicit oaths were not to be obeyed (C. 22 q. 4 c. 1; X 2.34.1). Herod's oath to Salome comes easily to mind, but the most quoted biblical text in support actually came from the twenty-fifth chapter of the first book of Samuel. David swore an oath to kill Nabal, the "impious and stupid man" who had railed against David's men. However, David yielded at length to the entreaties of Nabal's wife, Abigail. He returned his sword to its sheath and allowed Nabal to die a natural death. In St. Augustine's characterization of the incident, by electing the lesser evil (perjury) over the greater (murder), David won the favor of the Lord (C. 22 q. 4 c. 4). The biblical example proved, as the canonists saw it, that God's word itself demonstrated that not every oath was to be fulfilled.

The canonists took careful note, however, that St. Augustine had spoken carefully of the lesser of two evils. That David had made the correct choice did not mean he had committed no wrong. He had violated his oath, and this violation would subject him to punishment. This was also the result reached, or at any rate recommended, in the medieval church. Invoking God's name in an oath had such force that its violation could never be wholly praiseworthy. Those who did so would be punished by penalties appropriate for an act of perjury, even where they would not be compelled to fulfil an oath that would have led to worse results.[75]

Once it had been established that classifications had to be made between different oaths, the obvious question became: What made an oath illicit in the canon law? Several heads of illegality were recognized by the canon law. Not all of them were treated alike. Where some serious vices were present in an oath, there was no enforceable obligation at all, as has just been suggested. However, other sources of lesser evil were treated as leaving the oath enforceable, though making it illicit. Some fell in between, enforceable in the first instance but subject to limitations and a power of dispensation that rested in the church. Canonists did not develop a foolproof set of tests to tell which was which, but they provided enough examples and discussion so that cases on the subject could be handled with some assurance by courts and casuists.

Unenforceable Oaths

To begin with the worst, some oaths were unlawful by reason of the serious evil their performance would create and were not balanced by any consideration of the avoidance of a greater harm. An oath to kill an innocent person or to commit adultery were obvious examples (C. 22 q. 4 c. 23). David's oath to kill Nabal fell into this category. An oath to become a Muslim was treated similarly. A sworn promise by a husband or wife not to live together with the other was treated as contrary to the bond of marriage and the obligations of the Christian religion, except in the case where the spouses both made a vow of perpetual continence at the same time (X 2.24.24). These oaths were not enforceable.

An oath made "against the utility of the church" was likewise one not to be obeyed. The illustrative case in the Decretals was this. Electors in an episcopal election all swore an oath, the effect of which would have diminished the legitimate rights of the bishop elected. Then they elected one of their own number. The election was valid under the circumstances, but the oath was not (X 2.24.27). Oaths were not meant to be "chains of iniquity," and this seemed to be exactly that. Generalizing from this case, it was said that "an oath given to the detriment of the church was not to be observed."[76] It would thus always subject its maker to the penalties of perjury, but it would not survive judicial scrutiny to cause harm to the church itself. Oaths made by prelates not to reclaim alienated property of their churches seem to have been similarly treated under this same heading (X 2.24.2).[77]

There was also a class of oaths unenforceable not because of the evil they would cause but instead because of the incompetence of the promisor. The drunken oath is an interesting test case. It cannot have been a rare occurrence. Although there is no specific canon on the subject to be found in the *Corpus iuris canonici*, and only a little comment to be found outside it, the common opinion among the canonists seems to have been that these oaths were not binding if the party had been drunk enough to have lost control of his reason.[78] They were not, in other words, placed together in the category with oaths made under duress, examined briefly below, but rather with oaths made by lunatics and incompetents.[79] "Falser than vows made in wine," a pithy description of their worth taken from Shakespeare's *As You Like It*, sums up something like the canonical attitude toward them as well.[80]

Enforceable but Illicit Oaths

Apart from easy cases in which the oath directly contradicted the church's interests or its principles, there were many others in which the canon law sought to "strike a balance" between respecting the binding character of an oath and carrying out the goals of the law, one of which was that God's name should not be invoked without binding effect. This can be most easily appreciated by a brief description of seven cases in which an illicit oath was nonetheless to be observed under the canon law:

1. Oaths to pay usury. Although a simple promise to pay usury could not be enforced, an oath to the same effect could (X 2.24.20). Because this would lead to clear injustice, however, the canon law also held that in a separate action the debtor who had paid the obligation could recover the usurious part of the payment made in fulfilling the sworn promise. This was an ungainly result no doubt, but it was defended by the canonists as the only way to avoid derogating from the oath while at the same time upholding the canonical rules against usury.[81]

2. Oaths sworn *per creaturas*. Although the canon law held that oaths that invoked creatures instead of the Creator were illicit, they were nonetheless binding (X 2.24.26). This is a textbook example of the situation found with some frequency in the canon law—something that should not be done but, if done, was nevertheless binding.[82] The church did, however, subject the speaker of the oath to the public or private penance appropriate for those who had taken an illicit oath.

3. Coerced oaths. These were not ipso facto invalid. Although there was some dissent, the accepted rule came to be that if they could be fulfilled without endangering the health of the soul of the party coerced, their observance would be compelled (X 2.24.15).[83] The slightly disingenuous reason given for this, one inspired or at any rate supported by Roman law sources, was that "coerced willingness is still willingness."[84] Perhaps there was some not unreasonable concern that coercion might be too easily claimed in hard cases. However, coerced oaths were subject to the absolving power of the church, and it was the practice to allow persons to seek to be freed from their oaths if they could prove the requisite level of coercion.

4. Indiscreet oaths. One of the defining features of a licit oath was discretion (*iudicium*).[85] The canonical texts contained several examples of oaths lacking that quality, some of them renouncing valuable legal rights. The rule was that these oaths were nonetheless to be observed except in the case where observance would compromise the public interest or the soul's health of the person taking the oath. An example was the oath not to enter monastic life. Such an oath was regarded as foolish in the extreme by most of the canonists, but it was not thought to threaten the soul's health of the person within the meaning of the law, and however unwise it may have been, it was to be observed until a dispensation could be obtained (C. 22 q. 4 c. 23, d.p. § 4).

5. Contradictory oaths. The law on this point was not altogether harmonious. A great deal seems to have depended upon the substance of the matters promised at different times. In some cases, as an oath in a marriage contract after taking simple monastic vows, the later oath prevailed (Sext. 3.15.1). In others, as a sworn promise to forsake the monastic life after taking monastic vows, the earlier oath prevailed (X 2.24.13). The oath never to swear an oath created a particularly knotty problem.[86] In any case, the party who swore it clearly incurred the penalties of perjury for violating one oath or the other (X 2.24.11).

6. Oaths induced by mistake. If an oath had been made under a material mistake of fact, it could be described as lacking one of the requisite qualities of a licit oath: truth. However, under the canon law even this oath was to be obeyed, as long as the oath taker had been unaware of the mistake at the time and as long as the oath was otherwise lawful (X 2.24.18). The biblical example was the Israelites' observance of their oath to the deceitful Gibeonites (Josh. 9:15–20). It provided the canonists with an authoritative example in support of the virtue of fidelity to one's sworn word even under the most trying of circumstances (C. 22 q. 4 c. 23).

7. Oaths of minors. The force of an oath in medieval law is particularly well illustrated by the rule briefly mentioned in Chapter 4 that a minor could not invoke *restitutio in integrum* to avoid

transactions entered into during his minority if he had taken an oath not to do so or sworn to observe the obligation. Authorized by the constitution of Emperor Frederick II, *Sacramenta puberum*, the rule was taken into the canon law.[87] Where children had been old enough to appreciate the force of their action, they were not allowed to contravene their oaths. The medieval lawyers cautioned that children should be warned specifically on the point, lest they act unadvisedly to their own detriment. We saw how far the canonists were willing to extend the reach of the *restitutio in integrum*. However, it was not extended when it came up against the sworn promise not to invoke it.

Having worked through the list of some of the situations in which illicit oaths would be enforced, one is drawn back to the characterization of the canon law with which this chapter began: that from Andreas Gail, the German jurist of the sixteenth century. Readers may recall his conclusion that "particularly by the canon law, every oath that can be kept without danger to [one's] eternal life is to be kept."[88] His characterization seems entirely apt after a survey of the subject. It may be thought to understate the reality. In what we have just seen, even the category of oaths causing danger to the soul's health and unenforceable on that account seems to have been more narrowly interpreted than we might have suspected or wished.

Mitigation in the Binding Quality of Oaths

It might easily be concluded from this survey that the accumulation of situations in which oaths were to be obeyed despite their inconsistency with the good meant that the canon law could become a partner to wickedness or a promoter of unhappiness. Respect for the binding quality of an oath was carried too far, it would seem. Respect for oaths would stand in the way of attaining other clear goals of the canon law—discouraging usury, promoting monastic professions, or protecting children, for example. Although the requirement that the oath not risk the *salus animae* of the oath taker removed a significant number of cases from this regime, it still left quite a few enforceable but quite undesirable oaths, as the list above shows.

This negative conclusion would be incomplete, however, and perhaps even false. There were mitigating factors in the canon law, factors that had the effect of decreasing the number of sworn promises that had actually to be fulfilled as spoken. Again, a list of some of these is revealing of the interplay between the needs of practice and the principle of fulfilling oaths:

1. Relaxation by the promisee. Noted above was the ungainly system of dealing with oaths to pay usury. Although the oath itself was enforceable as an initial matter, the usury could be "reclaimed" afterward by the promisor in a separate suit. Actually, the system was a little more complicated still, and it provides a good example of the possibility of relaxation by the promisee. Under the canon law, the creditors could be proceeded against separately by the debtor and required to "relax" the oath to pay the usurious interest (X 2.24.1). In theory this should be a voluntary act on their part, but there was canonical opinion to the effect that, should they refuse, they could be excommunicated. Not all sworn promises could be released by the other party to a transaction—that would have been to license perjury.[89] But this particular oath, along with several others, could be.

2. Implied conditions. If an oath is sworn conditionally, it is binding only if the condition occurs, as in "I swear to pay you a hundred dollars if it rains tomorrow." Under some circumstances it is possible to suppose that the condition is implied rather than express, and the canon law made exactly that supposition. Thus, an oath to go to Spain was said to contain the implicit conditions "if I am living" and even "if it pleases God" (C. 22 q. 2 c. 5). A sworn promise to marry a woman was said to contain the implicit conditions "if she does not commit fornication" and even "if she does not become a leper" (X 2.24.25). An oath by judges to put sentences into execution within twenty-eight days was said to contain the implicit conditions "if it does not violate the rights of superior authority" and even "if it pleases the pope."[90]

Implicit conditions like these provided ways of interpreting sworn promises so as to avoid harm without contravening the principle that oaths should be obeyed. To take again the most famous example, Herod's oath to grant Salome's wish might have been understood to contain the implicit condition "if what you request is not immoderate."[91] Had Herod been able consult a canonist, he could have saved the life of John the Baptist without himself committing the crime of perjury. The dark side of this doctrine is, of course, that it lends itself to easy abuse. Unspoken conditions, the fruits of oversubtle casuistry, can vitiate too many promises. The canonists recognized the danger and warned against it.[92] It must be admitted nonetheless that the history of the church contains its share of examples in which the temptation to multiply unspoken conditions was not resisted.

3. Breach by the promisee. When a promise has been one part of a bargain between two people and the promisee refuses to carry out his side, should the promisor be bound to carry out his? The canon law adopted, and in fact seems actually to have introduced, the rule that a promisor had the right not to perform his undertaking under this circumstance.[93] The rule, summed up and widely known by the Latin phrase *fidem fragenti fides frangitur*, was applied to promises confirmed by oath (X 2.24.29). An alternate way of formulating the rule, also endorsed by the canon law, debarred a promisee who had not performed his part of the bargain from suing to enforce the other, amounting to something like an estoppel (C. 22 q. 4 c. 20).[94] As applied to commercial law, the approach to obligations made possible by applying this maxim was to have a long and controversial future, being taken up by the natural-law school and eventually also integrated into the modern civil law.[95]

4. Commutation of oaths. If a person has sworn to give one hundred dollars to charity, he can obviously give two hundred without committing perjury. The same result obtains if he gives no money at all but property worth two hundred dollars. So the canon law held that "no one breaks his promise who commutes it for a better one."[96] The example given in the Decretals was en-

tering religious life after having sworn to go on crusade to the Holy Land (X 2.24.3).[97] This was an improvement and hence no perjury. Obviously open to abuse, the common opinion interpreted the rule as holding that permission of one's appropriate superior was required before commutation of an oath could occur. But this "way out" was provided.

5. Absolution from oaths. The church asserted what might be described as a reserved power to dispense from the binding character of oaths.[98] Limited by the requirement of good cause, the power nonetheless tempered the capacity of the wide scope allowed to oaths causing indirect harm. The oath given under compulsion was the most frequent such case, at least if one judges by the Decretals (X 1.40.3; 2.24.2, 8, 14). The power of dispensation was also applied in some circumstances to a minor's oath not to invoke *restitutio in integrum*.[99] Readers familiar with English history will recall that King John was absolved of his oath to observe Magna Carta by taking advantage of this provision of the canon law. He had been coerced. Too ready recourse to this means of escaping an obligation was avoided in most cases by requiring that the party have recourse to his bishop before he could be absolved from the oath. Bishops were instructed to determine whether the coercion applied had been sufficient to sway the will of the "constant" man or woman before granting absolution from the allegedly coerced oath.[100]

CONCLUSION

It is not obvious that secure generalizations about the balance struck between illicitness, enforceability, and mitigation emerge from the evidence reviewed in this chapter. The author himself admits to doubts and vacillation. Was the system a realistic compromise between competing values, or was it simply an invitation to the excesses of casuistry? It is hard to know. Nor can it be easily determined, from a modern perspective, whether the elaborate system of oaths developed for ecclesiastical court practice made for real improvement in the honesty with which proceedings in those courts were conducted. What is clear beyond cavil is the importance and the ubiquity of the oath in the classical canon law. In this, the classical canon law shared with secular law, and indeed the societal assumptions of the day, a faith in the efficacy of oaths and a concern for the crime of perjury to a degree that seems all but incomprehensible today. Not that oaths have wholly disappeared from modern law. But their effect and importance is tepid by comparison. It is a weak imitation of what is found in the classical canon law.

It is also remarkable how intricate the canon law of oaths came to be. Besides their ubiquity, few clear themes other than this recurrent one rise to the surface. But rise it surely does. Perhaps only the principle of *salus animarum* and the concern for the good of church and society appeared often enough in discussion and decision on this subject to merit description as settled, recurring, and vital themes that tempered the binding quality of the canonical oath. Where fulfillment of a sworn promise jeopardized the soul's health of a promisor or the well-being of society's institutions, the oath was not to be observed.

Noting this concern for *salus animarum* is also another way of stressing what was given as one of the reasons for enforcing an oath in the first place: the promisor's own spiritual health would be imperiled by not fulfilling it. The oath taker had "invoked God as a witness to the truth." To make God a witness to falsehood would call a person's soul into question. In this emphasis on the soul's health, still visible after one has worked through the intricate law on the subject, one can perhaps detect an echo, though it is admittedly a little faint, of the scriptural admonitions against oaths with which this chapter began.

7 Economic and Property Rights: The Canon Law of Prescription

The medieval church was the holder of vast tracts of land and the owner of large streams of income. Or perhaps it would be slightly more accurate to say that medieval churches held such tracts and owned such streams. The concept of ownership of property by the church as a whole was foreign to normal ways of thinking during the Middle Ages. But no matter how one puts it, large quantities of property and economic power were in ecclesiastical hands. And in many forms. Even apart from direct ownership of real and personal property, the offices and benefices of the medieval church were fertile sources of income. They too were treated as property belonging (though in a kind of fiduciary capacity) to the men who held the offices and benefices.

Disputes about these rights in property and income were certain to arise. Rules against alienation of church property and the common belief among ecclesiastics that property belonged to the church's patrimony, if not indeed to the saint to whom it had been given, actually encouraged disputes. More than self-interest of the clergy was at stake. The clergy felt themselves under a legal and moral duty to preserve the rights of their churches, and they fulfilled that duty with dogged enthusiasm. Reading through almost any monastic chronicle, for instance, will show how tenacious monks could be in defending the rights of their house. Such tenacity was not regarded as at variance with clerical vows. Rather, it was seen as part of their fulfillment.

Conflicts over property rights arose in the widest sorts of contexts. To take an illustrative if small example that will be touched upon again later, the income of the rector of any church depended in part upon the geographical extent of his parish. To whom the people's tithes were paid was determined primarily by geography. Parish boundaries therefore had to be established. In an era without maps or adequate surveying techniques, geographical boundaries were subject to real uncertainty. It was sometimes quite impossible to determine the original boundaries of any parish, if indeed there had been boundaries fixed at the time the parish was set up. It was therefore necessary that the medieval canon law have rules for dealing with the disputes about the location of boundaries that were bound to occur.

Resolution of the disputes might, of course, have been left to the secular law, as is largely done in the United States today. The Roman law was available, and it supplied answers for many problems involving church lands and revenues. To have adopted these civilian rules as a matter of necessity would, however, have raised real problems. For great and ideological reasons, it would have been objectionable to have ceded this jurisdiction to the temporal forum. If disputes about property had been left to lay courts, for example, the principle of the *privilegium fori* that established the clergy's immunity from secular jurisdiction would have been breached. The result was that, although the classical canon law made constant use of the Roman law of property rights, the canon law always insisted on preserving some sphere for independent jurisdiction and independent legal rules in dealing with property disputes. No account of the classical canon law can ignore them entirely. Among the most illustrative examples of the way in which the problems were worked out is the subject of this chapter, the law of prescription.

THE PROBLEM FOR THE MEDIEVAL CHURCH

As is true with several of the aspects of the classical canon law surveyed here, the starting point must be a large question: Should the law admit the validity of claims to property or to office that are contrary to established property rights or legal rules when the claims are based on nothing more than long usage? Does the antiquity of an unlawful act serve to make an illegal act lawful? Unlike customary rights,[1] which normally arose out of the tacit consent of the people involved, prescriptive rights were initiated in circumstances in which one person's usage of property violated the right of someone else.[2] The usage would normally have been contrary to the desires of the person who originally possessed that right had he known about the usage.[3] It would have been a wrong. It was far from obvious, therefore, that prescription should be permitted at all within a system of religious law.

This is an old problem, one that continues to trouble the law even today. For a legal system expressly committed to promoting moral conduct, it was a particularly troublesome one. To admit such claims in some sense licenses the acquisition of title by theft. It may be said actually to encourage theft. As the medieval writers sometimes expressed the point, the long continuation of a sin cannot make the act less sinful. Indeed, it does the reverse. It augments the act's sinfulness.[4] Yet it was, and is, recognized that virtually every legal system in fact admits claims based upon no source of title save the passage of time—and this without hesitation or shame. Sophisticated observers rightly regard the law of prescription as standing "among the most important and most beneficial of legal institutions."[5]

During the period in which the classical canon law came into being, the underlying problem must have seemed particularly troublesome for those who formulated the church's law. Long-standing usages, many of them quite contrary to the stated rules, the material interests, and the most deeply held desires of the clerical order, existed in abundance. What the clergy regarded as unlawful usurpations of ecclesiastical property laymen regarded as established rights. From either perspective, they were undeniable facts of life.[6] Dislodging them would not be easy. Government itself was weak. Even had it been stronger, ascertainment of exactly what rights a church held would not always have been possible, since so many of the transactions upon which society depended were purely oral.[7] Keeping reliable records was the exception, not the norm, in the early Middle Ages. It seemed obvious, therefore, that if the nascent law of the church was to be brought effectively to bear upon the situation, as did indeed happen through the efforts of the canonists of the twelfth and thirteenth centuries, the law of prescription would inevitably come into play. And it did.

Acceptance left many choices all the same. The attitude taken toward prescription would influence the specific rules chosen. In the task of formulation, it would have been quite possible for the jurists to put the problem in terms we would recognize as instrumental legal policy. Had they taken that approach, they might have developed the consequences of assuming that the canon law should have given the narrowest reading possible to the possibility of prescriptive title. In purely economic terms, this would have made sense. The medieval church would probably have gained overall by the severe restriction of claims based on prescriptive right. Medieval chroniclers perceived the usurpation of the church's possessions by the laity to be a great endemic problem of their society. They were loud in condemning it. Even if one makes proper allowance for the pious exaggeration common among medieval monastic writers, one cannot think them wholly misguided.[8]

On the other hand, it would have been impossible for the canonists to create a legal system that sanctioned no prescriptive rights whatsoever. Not only would it have been a divergence from the Roman law in which so many of them had been trained. To have done so would have upset too many of the assumptions upon which society rested, and it would have been entirely impossible to enforce. A more realistic jurisprudence all but required the admission of some sorts of prescriptive right.

The argument would have been all the stronger because many of the church's rights themselves grew out of prescription. The example mentioned above relating to parish boundaries is but one example of many. Within the church's organizational structure many rights had become settled through long usage. Even as against the laity, to have embraced an abolitionist view of the subject would have threatened long-established rights, rights that everyone assumed to be legitimate. Perhaps the church would have gained overall thereby. But it is unlikely that the balance would actually have stood in its favor at the end of the day had the church abandoned all approval of claims to prescriptive right. In fact, the church would have given away all *its* rights and received only theoretical, unenforceable claims in return. From an instrumental point of view, it must have seemed that a more compromising policy was called for.

Whether this instrumental way of thinking affected the conclusions drawn by the canonists is a legitimate question. Certainly it was not the immediate way they approached the problem. Policy could not be an immediate source of law for them. One does occasionally find something like it in their writings, normally when they were called upon to discuss the reasons for and the consequences of the law. However, their initial approach was more formal. From Gratian right up through the writings of the later medieval commentators, the law of prescription was developed through reliance upon the texts found in the *Corpus iuris canonici* and the *Corpus iuris civilis*.[9] Out of these sources the commentators of the *ius commune* forged a law of prescription that turned out to be different from that found in any one of the sources. It was a system not without faults and absurdities. But it was a sophisticated and remarkably durable system nonetheless.

GRATIAN'S *DECRETUM*

The large question, confronted by Gratian at the outset, was the legitimacy of any kind of prescription. Gratian raised it in *Causa* 16 of the *Decretum*. Here is the case he put: A certain abbot had been in possession of a church without interruption or objection for forty years. He had taken its revenues and had nominated a monk to celebrate the church's services within it. However, the clergy of a nearby baptismal church were now objecting, claiming that the church in dispute was in fact a chapel within the precincts owned by their baptismal church. The right of nomination, they claimed, belonged to them because of that fact. Such dependent chapels were not at all unusual in the medieval church, and the *Causa* assumed that ultimate title rested with the baptismal church.

In the fashion characteristic of Gratian, the *Causa* posed several questions based upon it. The one treated in *Quaestio* 3 was "whether the rights of churches [were] to be taken away by prescription."[10]

Gratian's treatment thus placed the question of prescription's legitimacy into the context of a dispute between two competing churches, rather than in the more contentious context of a dispute involving lay usurpation of ecclesiastical rights.[11] The initial question did not, therefore, in any way raise the dispute to the level of disagreement between church and state. It did raise the more fundamental question of whether prescription had a place in a system of religious law.

Gratian began his analysis of *Quaestio* 3 with four texts from the earliest centuries of Christianity, each standing in favor of prescription: a canon from the Council of Chalcedon (451), a letter of Pope Gelasius (c. 494), and two canons from the Fourth Council of Toledo (633). All of them dealt with settling disputes over diocesan or parochial boundaries. They held that where these boundaries had remained unchanged and unchallenged for thirty years or more, they should not be challenged thereafter. These ancient canons were almost certainly following the outlines of the Roman law of prescription, perhaps self-consciously that of the Christian emperors contained in the Codex.[12]

For a modern student the prevalence of canons from Spanish councils is an especially notable feature of this part of the *Decretum*. Indeed, it is one of the most notable features of the whole *Causa*. The unsettled conditions in the Spanish church in consequence of the Muslim invasions and the reconquest must have rendered the problem of fixing boundaries particularly urgent, requiring immediate consideration of the relation between the Roman law of prescription and the dictates and aspirations of the Christian religion. Gratian said nothing about this. He fixed his attention on the texts themselves. Indeed, none of the texts employed by Gratian explicitly considered the question of policy or economic interest. They did not address the question of winners or losers, and it must appear that this was not Gratian's interest.

The subject of the reasons justifying prescription was taken up only in the *glossa ordinaria*, though not in terms of economic impact. The gloss explained that prescription was no part of natural law. Indeed, prescription was in one sense contrary to natural right, because one person was being made richer at the expense of another's right when-

ever it was allowed. The gloss suggested, on the contrary, that prescription had been introduced only "lest dominion of things be left
forever uncertain," citing texts from the Roman law as support and in
further explanation.[13]

This understanding of the place of prescription turned out to have
important results in the canon law. It meant that prescriptive claims
would not be favorites of the law.[14] Probably this is the attitude taken
by most systems of law. It was by the *ius commune*. Statutes allowing
prescription were always to be strictly construed. It may also be that
it was this grudging acceptance that caused the law of the church to
rely so heavily in practice on immemorial custom rather than prescription for the solution of practical problems of competing claims
between churches.[15]

The effect of this characterization of prescription as contrary to
natural equity must have had largely beneficial economic consequences for most medieval churches. Characteristically, however,
Gratian did not go into any of the consequences in this part of his
Causa 16. Instead, he continued along the same path, compiling and
distinguishing the authorities. He may have had consequences in the
back of his mind, it is true. But he did not mention them. The authorities he compiled had the effect of limiting the reach of the law of prescription, and along the lines suggested in the *glossa ordinaria*.

Limitations to Prescriptive Right

In the *Decretum* itself, several limitations to claims of prescriptive
right were introduced by Gratian's *dictum*. He began his treatment of
them by noting that there were some other canons that appeared to be
contrary to the rule of the four canons that had sanctioned prescription. The first of these authorities was a letter of the same Pope Gelasius dealing with the intrusion by one bishop into the spiritual rights
of the other, specifically the assertion of rights by the bishop of An-
cona over a church within a neighboring bishopric (C. 16 q. 3 c. 5).
The papal letter reproved the bishop's "temerity" and upheld the validity of what we would describe as the true title against the prescriptive claim. This appeared contrary to the first four canons. Gratian

distinguished it from the preceding four by limiting its holding to dioceses whose boundaries were "certain and distinct." In such cases, unlike the first four, prescription was not possible.

The *glossa ordinaria* also suggested that the rule applied in the papal letter was correct for acts of outright intrusion, thereby bringing it within the Roman law rule that kept prescription, at least in ordinary circumstances, from being asserted by those who had taken property by force.[16] One might therefore describe the papal letter as "being limited to its facts" by Gratian's treatment. At the very least, it was construed in such a way as not to contradict the first four canons directly and yet to leave the possibility of canonical prescription open.

One might note further that cases in which the property rights were objectively "certain and distinct" were exactly those in which a third party was least likely to be able to intervene without acting as an intruder. Where the boundaries were known and fixed, the reason for permitting prescription in the first place—to bring an end to uncertainty and strife—would have been entirely lacking. Gratian himself, however, did not draw this parallel from his text; it was enough for him to distinguish this letter of Pope Gelasius from the preceding four canons and to draw a conclusion from them. But thinking through the implications of his conclusion suggests its coherence with the goals of the law.

The next apparent dissonance came again from a letter of Pope Gelasius dealing with the subject of diocesan boundaries (c. 7). This letter disallowed the claim of prescription, and it might have been regarded simply as a restatement of the previous principle. However, in the *dictum* after the canon Gratian suggested that the decretal "might also be distinguished in another way."[17] That is, Gelasius's letter might be read as a statement that prescription was impossible where a possessor held property he was legally incapable of owning. One bishop cannot own rights that are essential to the episcopate of another. Neither may a cleric obtain the powers of a bishop by force of prescription.[18] Because they are legally distinct rights, not within the power of the possessor's office to hold, illegal possession of them must be treated as a pure act of usurpation. It could not be the source of legitimate title.

This is the law today.[19] It should nonetheless not be regarded as a simple truism. In fact, the principle had enormous consequences for the church. It meant, for example, that possession of tithes by laymen, even very long possession of tithes, would never ripen into legitimate ownership, since under the canon law, laymen could not legally own the right to collect tithes (X 2.26.7).[20] *Spiritualia* were hived off from *temporalia* for these purposes. A quarrel over boundaries between two bishops may seem an unlikely circumstance in which to find an enormously consequential rule stated. So we do find it, however. Not a word of the canon treated the desirable consequences as a reason for adopting the rule. It seems not to have been thought necessary that "social policies" be considered directly, though they might appropriately be used as illustration. It was entirely consistent with Gratian's normal approach to find the principle so drawn from one of the texts he selected.

Canons 13 and 14 follow, the one ascribed to a seventh-century church council, the other to a ninth-century papal letter. They also limited the availability of prescription by disqualifying possession where the "furor of hostility" or even the "fear of hostility" had prevailed. Under this formulation, the years when hostility had existed would not count toward the establishment of prescriptive right. Both canons came from lands where such hostility had been a fact of life: Spain and Germany. The principle they stated seemed self-evident and universal to Gratian. God himself would be subject to rebuke if possession maintained by force were to count toward establishing prescriptive right. Had not the Children of Israel been subject to Pharaoh's yoke during 430 years? Yet God had led them out of slavery (Exod. 12:40). God could not have been violating a legitimate right in so doing. It was not to be supposed that Pharaoh's kind of bondage, or anything resembling it, could be the source of legitimate prescriptive right. Legitimate prescriptive right could not arise out of pure force without contradicting biblical authority.

Starting from this principle, it would be contended that lands that had once been in Christian hands but had subsequently come under Muslim rule should be restored, no matter how long they had been withheld from their original Christian owners. If not restored voluntarily, they might lawfully be taken back by force. The result was the Crusades, or at least one of the several arguments justifying the Crusades.[21] Gratian himself, writing close to the height of the crusading fervor, said nothing about this possibility inherent in his text. Nor did the *glossa ordinaria* that accompanied the *Decretum*. Whether the canonists had the lands in the Middle East in their minds when they worked out this doctrine we cannot know.

Special Limitations

The *Decretum* envisioned several other situations in which prescriptive right was difficult or even impossible to establish. Some of these others will be familiar to readers. They exist in modern law as "legal disabilities" such as the minority of the holder of the property right against which prescription is being asserted.[22] Minority prevents the running of the statute of limitations today, and it prevented the start of prescription under the canon law. The rule was identical to that of the Roman law, if indeed it was not copied from the Roman law. Perhaps such a "disability" is a normal part of most legal systems, although the age of majority of course varies considerably from one to the other.

Other disabilities in the canon law, such as that disability allowed where the true holder had been excommunicated, seem distinctly more medieval, although the rationale for them was basically the same as in modern law. An excommunicate had no standing to sue.[23] Therefore, he could not have done anything about the interference with his rights, and it would have been unfair to have allowed the time to run against him. The gloss listed nine such disabilities, and more would be adduced by later commentators.[24] In the course of development within the *ius commune*, inroads would have to be made in the principle that disabilities tolled the prescriptive period in order to deal with cases of very long possession.[25] But that made a special case.

The final canon of this part of *Causa* 16 dealt with a different sort of problem: a claim of prescription against the Roman Church (C. 16 q. 3 c. 17). The facts that gave rise to the canon were largely suppressed, but enough was said to show that it dealt with a royal claim of prescription against the rights of the Roman Church.[26] The pope's letter asserted that only prescription of more than one hundred years should prevail against the Roman Church. This letter, although citing no specific legal texts, probably referred to an imperial decree allowing long prescriptive periods to religious institutions as a matter of pious humanity (Cod. 1.2.23). The Novels had preserved the rights of the Roman Church even while reducing the prescriptive period against the rights of churches to forty years (Nov. 131.6). This papal response was an effective way of dealing with an act by a king who himself claimed some of the power that the Roman law accorded to the ruler.

By implication at least, it was also something more. First, albeit in limited circumstances, it did subject the church's interests to prescriptive claims on behalf of the laity. Readers will recall that Gratian's *quaestio* had dealt with a dispute over prescriptive right between two churches. This canon endorsed the possibility that these rights could be asserted by the laity even against the highest authority in the church. Second, it raised the important question of the place of the civil law of prescription in matters pertaining to the church. This would turn out to be a complex problem for several reasons. Not least of these were the lively possibilities of future changes in the temporal law, particularly those that would be created by statutes authorizing prescription in special circumstances and also by the variegated sorts of disputes there could be pitting laymen and churchmen against each other. It was not obvious that one rule would fit all situations.

As to the first, it might have seemed tempting, at least as a matter of policy, for churchmen to claim all the privileges of the Roman fisc, against which prescriptive claims did not normally run. As Maitland once said, the medieval church was a state, and claims to sovereignty were made routinely on the church's behalf.[27] Why not claim this normal attribute of sovereignty? This would have protected the rights of the church against all contrary claims. Such an immunity to possessory claims might have been hard to vindicate in fact, but it might have seemed tempting to seek and valuable to assert. However, this final canon shows that such an immunity would not be asserted. The church would be content with the Roman law rules on this point.

Second, it was entirely characteristic of the canon law to adopt rules directly from the civil law, particularly when those rules worked in favor of the church's interest, as this one did. It was also characteristic of the canon law not to submit itself to automatic endorsement of these rules even while it borrowed them. The canons followed the civil law rule because it was reasonable in itself. The result, however, was not always the harmony one might expect. Very often it led to a complex and disputatious body of law. For example, how far did the term "Roman church" extend? Could it reach a monastic house that had been taken into the special protection of the apostolic see?[28] Or could the special status enjoyed by all churches be made to extend also to *miserabiles personae*?[29] And what prescriptive period applied to testamentary bequests made by laymen to churches? The canonists wished to have the last word on such questions. The temporal lawyers, not unnaturally, did not always see it that way. The canonists saw in this canon authority for their view. They followed the Roman law of prescription. However, for them it was a convenient source of law, not one they were bound to follow if a principle of canon law dictated a different result. This attitude, and the important consequences that followed from it, are manifest in the Decretals. If anything, it is even more evident in the writings of the medieval canonists.

THE GREGORIAN DECRETALS

The Decretals devoted a title of twenty chapters in its second book to the subject of prescriptive rights (X 2.26.1–20). These chapters accomplished several things. They restated and amplified rules found in the *Decretum*, drawing from them specific conclusions that Gratian's work had contained only in embryo. They dealt with some of the detailed problems of procedure and evidence that inevitably arose in canonical practice and that Gratian had left largely untouched. And they enacted a requirement of good faith for all prescription under the canon law, a requirement that turned out to have large implications for the European *ius commune*.

Except in correcting some of the inconsistencies and uncertainties in the earlier treatment, there was no serious break with the *Decretum* in Raymond of Peñafort's compilation. Only in setting the prescriptive period for the church can one detect any real discontinuity, and it might better be considered a clarification than a break. The Decretals did, however, bring the law of prescription into the context of a working legal system to a greater extent than the earlier work had. Gratian had been concerned with the basic question of whether prescription could be lawful at all. That principle established, it was necessary to care for some of the details.

Establishment of Working Rules

The Decretals repeated virtually all the limiting principles found in the *Decretum:* that the prescriptive period did not run in time of war; that only property the possessor could legitimately own could be acquired by prescription; and that force could not be the source of prescriptive title. The *Decretum* had been more textbook than statute book or case book, and it may have seemed useful or even necessary to state these in authoritative form. Certainly it must have seemed desirable to elaborate upon them in the many varied circumstances that arose in common practice. For example, the problem of interruption of the prescriptive period was dealt with in several decretals. Thus, it was established specifically that while an episcopal see was vacant, possession by a cleric of tithes belonging to the see did not count toward the forty-year prescriptive period (X 2.26.4). In the case of the papal see, it was stated definitely that periods of schism were similarly not to be counted as part of the hundred-year prescriptive period (X 2.26.14).

Likewise building upon the canons holding that in some situations prescription was not permitted at all, the Decretals specifically disallowed prescription for tithes (X 2.26.7), procurations owed to apostolic legates and nuncios (X 2.26.11), professions of canonical obedience owed to prelates (X 2.26.12), and rights of episcopal visitation (X 2.26.16). The underlying principle throughout was that spiritual rights should not be subject to prescription. They should never be determined by mere usage. There were enough such instances that, together with cases in which a disability interrupted prescription, they came to be encapsulated in a mnemonic device for use by students of the canon law.[30] Such devices are one measure of the importance this subject had in the medieval teaching of the church's laws, and in practical as well as theoretical terms, it is far from inconsequential that such a device existed here.

Necessarily raised in the Decretals were also several questions of interpretation. For instance, there was the awkward question of whether, prescription once begun, interruptions caused a new prescriptive period to begin or were simply to be subtracted from the total in determining whether enough years had passed. A decretal of Pope Innocent III, the architect of a good deal of the law in this title, made the assumption that subtraction was the proper measure to be used (X 2.26.25).[31] Although there was some authority on both sides of this question among the commentators, Innocent's opinion turns out also to have been the view taken by most. Later writers, for example, could speak of prescription "sleeping" while the condition that prevented suit being brought continued to exist.[32] Once it "awoke," the clock would begin ticking again.

Of the substantive details clarifying the scope of the law of prescription, perhaps the most important was that which fixed the applicable periods. Whereas most of the canons in the *Decretum* had either said nothing on the subject or had assumed a thirty-year prescriptive period, a decretal of Pope Alexander III stated that with respect to claims being made against the church, a forty-year period should prevail (X 2.26.4). This, as we have seen, was a statement drawn from the Roman law on the same subject. He made no overt change in this aspect of the law, but it cleared up the uncertainty in the *Decretum*, where the thirty-year prescriptive period of the civil law was assumed to apply in all suits against and among laymen.

This was not quite the end of the matter. There were other periods of limitation for different sorts of claims, and it was normal to treat all of them under the heading of prescription. Things became complicated enough in the provisions found elsewhere in the canonical texts that Hostiensis was able to list the stupefying number of fifty-five separate prescriptive periods allowed under the canon law.[33] However, most of these were straightforward statutes of limitation for initiating a lawsuit, and a few of them seem more feats of juristic imagination than rules we would consider authentic prescriptive periods.[34] It was Alexander III's decretal that contained the basic rule governing possession of most kinds of real and personal property. That decretal provided the workable base for computing the prescriptive period in most cases that arose under the church's legal system.

Pope Alexander's fundamental decretal seems legislative in character. Although the forty-year prescriptive period was drawn from Roman law,[35] and although the decretal in occasion and formal terms was simply a response to a question that had been put to him, it seems clear that the pope had meant to lay down a binding rule. He resolved contradictory authorities in the *Decretum*. The only reason for the ten-year extension given in the decretal was that "the Roman church [did] not admit a thirty-year prescription against the church." Separation of the clerical order from the laity and a privileged status for the former was, of course, one of the cardinal tenets of the Gregorian reform tradition,[36] and like much of the canon law that grew from that tradition, this decretal announced a rule discriminating in favor of material interests of the church. If they felt required to supply a substantive reason for this rule, commentators were content with saying blankly that ecclesiastical institutions were "favored" by the law.[37] Most, seeing no need for particular explanation at all, stated simply that Alexander III had corrected the canons found in Gratian's *Decretum*.[38]

The Requirement of Good Faith

A second feature of the Gregorian Decretals was clearly a legislative act, one meant to amend the inherited civil law. This was the establishment of a requirement of good faith for acquisition of property rights by prescription. The requirement in the canon law meant essentially what it does today: that the possessor must have acted honestly and without knowledge of the true state of the title. He must have thought that he was possessing what was rightfully his if he was to qualify as a bona fide possessor.[39] Although one might think that the requirement was implicit in parts of the *Decretum*, it appeared as an unstated assumption more than as a rule, and that only in limited circumstances. In fact, Gratian had seemingly assumed that good faith would *not* be present in some of the cases in which prescription was successfully established.[40] Two chapters in the Decretals changed this (X 2.26.5; X 2.26.20). They made bona fides an explicit requirement. The first was a papal letter of Alexander III;[41] the second the decree *Quoniam omne* of Innocent III's Fourth Lateran Council (1215).

Roman law had admitted the possibility that a mala fide possessor could acquire prescriptive title.[42] The canon law was consciously rejecting this part of its legal heritage. Echoing a phrase from St. Paul's Letter to the Romans (Rom. 14:23), to the effect that "whatsoever is not from faith, is sin," the Lateran Council decreed "that no prescription, whether civil or canonical, shall be valid without good faith."[43] Although there were undoubtedly commercial advantages to the requirement,[44] the moral underpinnings of the medieval canon law are the most readily apparent in this decree. The related requirement that the possessor have a *iustus titulus* to acquire prescriptive right, a requirement specifically incorporated into the canon law by Pope Boniface VIII in the *Liber sextus* (Sext. 2.13.1), sprang evidently from the same source.[45]

Although there were differences between the views taken by the medieval theologians and the canonists, the decision to require good faith stands as a reminder that the canon law had spiritual ends in view, even in a subject as apparently far removed from salvation as the law of prescription. *Salus animarum* was both a goal of the canon law and a reason for adopting several specific legal rules. To acquire property through a knowing wrong could not be done without sin.[46] It would have seemed quite wrong to the canonists had the canon law embraced a rule that threatened "to divide man from God."[47] At least the choice to have put aside the consideration would have required some elaborate explaining. Hence came the requirement of good faith.

FUNDAMENTAL PROBLEMS

Explanation of the law, together with explication of possible ways to deal with some of the problems that inhere naturally in the law of prescription, was the task of the canonists. Many such problems, large and small, existed. It was no exaggeration when a sixteenth-century commentator described the resulting law as "subtle and profound."[48] A modern observer might add the word "complex." Among the difficulties that had to be faced was arriving at a workable definition of what constituted good faith in specific circumstances. Others included questions that have continued to vex the law of prescription, such as fixing the nature of the possession that must underlie prescriptive rights, determining the rights of co-tenants among themselves, establishing the nature of control required to possess incorporeal rights within the law's meaning, and dealing with the variations caused by successive ownership.[49]

How the commentators of the *ius commune* attacked these problems is a subject worthy of study. However, most of the problems could be, and were in fact, worked out within the framework of existing Roman law. For example, when Hostiensis took up the question of what was meant by "continuity" in prescription, virtually all his answers came out of the civil law.[50] That it was in some circumstances possible to be absent and at the same time in possession of property, a perennial chestnut of the law of real property, could be explained from the texts of the *Corpus iuris civilis*.

In conceptual interest, the host of such problems and the complex law that accompanied them are now dwarfed by two questions more basic for understanding the classical canon law. Both of them presented real dilemmas for the commentators, and both were raised indirectly by the requirement of good faith.[51] First, what should the law hold about the common case in which the possessor acquired knowledge of the true state of the title *after* the prescriptive period had run? And second, how should it formulate the proper relationship between the long-established civilian rules and the canonical requirements? Both were new problems. Neither was fully answered either by Alexander III's decretal or by the formal enactment of the Fourth Lateran

Council. And both raised questions that caused the canonists to confront assumptions that were basic to their jurisprudence.

Prescription and Subsequent Knowledge

The first dilemma is easy to appreciate. If conscience provides the operative rule for determining prescriptive right, and if a person has knowledge of the true state of the title of the thing he has possessed, what does it matter how many years have gone by? Why does it make any difference when his mala fides began? He may not have known at the time his possession started. He may not have known while it continued. But *now* he does know. The property really belongs to someone else. Can he retain it without sin simply because the formal law appears to allow him to do so? It is far from obvious that he can, and there was respectable authority, particularly among contemporary theologians, holding that he could not.[52]

To have embraced these theologians' opinions would, however, have required the canonists to ignore some quite clear provisions of the Decretals, not to speak of the principal point made by Gratian's *Decretum*, namely that prescription was possible and ultimately consistent with the assumptions of the canon law. To have taken the negative position would also have reduced the place of successful prescription to a largely theoretical possibility, since actual disputes over prescriptive right normally arise only when the truth about the state of the title becomes known. If mala fides at a late point in time always defeated the prescriptive claim, there would have been very little room for successful prescription under the law. It was therefore necessary for the canonists to reconcile the formal canonical enactments allowing prescriptive title with the claims of conscience and the requirements of *salus animarum*.

They did this in two different, but not mutually inconsistent, ways. One was to distinguish. Joannes Andreae, for example, suggested making use of the quite reasonable distinction between taking and retaining.[53] It might reasonably be thought that where the possessor had not himself taken property but only held what someone else had taken, he should be treated more leniently than the possessor who had actually "usurped" it. This distinction would allow the former but not the latter to prevail when the truth became known after the prescriptive period. Other distinctions were also possible. Alanus Anglicus suggested that a distinction be drawn according to whether possession had been *ex causa lucrativa* or not.[54] Hostiensis mentioned the possibility of treating the question of bona fides as a question of fact, allowing the choice to be made by the possessor himself according to the actual dictates of his conscience.[55] The advantage of these distinctions—no small advantage in the eyes of the medieval jurists—was that they allowed the texts to be reconciled. Those texts that disallowed prescriptive title where knowledge had been acquired after the passage of forty years could be described as dealing with the situation where one side of the applicable distinction had been true. Those that allowed it could be described as dealing with the other.

The disadvantage of solving the problem through distinctions was that many of them, perhaps even most of them, seemed arbitrary. They were not being based upon any enactment or even any sensible rationale at all. They would have seemed intellectually unsatisfying. It could not be made wholly clear just why they were being suggested. Sometimes the law has to make do with such distinctions. The question of acquiring legal rights in property that belongs to someone else is inherently difficult. But most jurists seek a more elegant solution than that offered by these artificial distinctions. Certainly the medieval canonists did.

The solution most of them ultimately adopted depended not upon distinction but upon recognition of the power of the law and of the lawmaker. The canonists came to hold that the law itself created a wholly new title to the property. According to this way of seeing things, it was the law itself rather than any action by the possessor that extinguished the old title and created a new one.[56] The prescriptive owner's continued occupation of the property was the incidental result of his having following the law's dictates. His conscience at the end therefore played no part in this process, for he himself played only a secondary role in the transfer of title. Because the law was the primary agent, the possessor's title was complete.

Modern American writers on the subject of adverse possession have reached the same result, or at least something very similar to it. Most have written about it without consciousness of this episode of the subject's history.[57] They would probably be surprised to discover their own solution being worked out by the medieval canonists because of a conflict between the claims of conscience and the necessity of establishing prescriptive right. Some of the steps taken along the way to the solution would surely surprise them. But the ending place turns out to be pretty much identical in both contexts.

The canonists described the situation in this way: after completion of the prescriptive period, the possessor no longer held the property under the same title that had once belonged to the original owner. The *glossa ordinaria* put it bluntly: "The laws make this mine and that yours."[58] This of course meant that by definition, the possessor could not be holding in bad faith and in violation of the claims of conscience once the prescriptive period had passed. The prior owner had no more interest in the property than if he had parted with it by grant. There was nothing upon which claims of conscience could be founded. "The canons," it was concluded, "can give me a thing belonging to another, and I will be secure."[59] What no individual could do on his own the law could.

It should not be concluded from this account that the canonists regarded their solution as resting simply upon legislative fiat. There were good reasons for it. Ownership should not be left forever uncertain, and to upset a right established by prescription whenever its holder began to have mala fides would threaten to do just that.[60] As we say today, so said the canonists: at some point the law must put an end to the upset of lives and minds caused by uncertainty and litigation. It was entirely rational to accomplish this goal by sanctioning prescriptive right and embracing the notion that the law created a new title.[61]

The law was also fully justified in penalizing an owner who slept on his rights. If the opposite rule were to obtain, wrote Joannes Andreae, "the sin of neglect, which is contrary to the public good, would go unpunished."[62] In his view, prescription was therefore not contrary to the *ius naturae*, as it might seem to be at first sight and as many thought, because fully considered, no person was actually being enriched at the expense of another.[63] The original possessor had deserved the loss that occurred. If any real loss there was, it was *damnum absque injuria*.[64]

Conflicts between Jurisdictions

The second fundamental problem for the canonists lay in determining the relationship of the requirement of good faith to established Roman law, which, although requiring good faith for some purposes, contained no blanket requirement of continued good faith on the part of all possessors.[65] The problem existed because the Fourth Lateran Council's constitution stated in so many words that it applied to "prescription both canonical and civil."[66] Had it, in effect, therefore nullified the civil law? And if so, by what right? What justification did the canon law have for intervening in what would otherwise be a purely secular dispute over lands and chattels? As Baldus de Ubaldis phrased this commonly stated objection, "The pope cannot intrude himself into the affairs of laymen, since he is not a competent judge in their causes."[67]

Three different positions on this potentially divisive question were taken by the early canonists. One held that, rightly interpreted, the Lateran Council's decree did not reach prescription under the civil law at all. If so, the conflict was only apparent. A second held to a "hierocratic" view: that the conflict was real, that canon law had overruled the civil law, and that it was entirely within its rights in doing so. A third, best articulated by Joannes Andreae, held that there was a possible conflict between the two rules but that both positions were lawful and appropriate because of the disparate purposes of each legal system. The first and second of these are the easiest to describe. The third is harder to understand, but it is the more rewarding to consider, because it is revealing of the inner nature of the canon law.

The argument for the first position, that the decretals requiring good faith simply did not cover prescription under the Roman law, depended on a careful, perhaps creative, reading of *Quoniam omne*.[68] It held that the words *tam canonica quam civilia*, which seemed to require a conflict, might better be understood as referring simply to different kinds of causes coming before the courts of the church. Under the canon law, some matters were regarded as *spiritualia* (e.g., tithes), some as *temporalia* (e.g., ordinary rights in land). Under some circumstances either might become the subject of litigation in the ecclesiastical forum. The Lateran Council's decree might be read, therefore, as stating only that both of these would be judged by the good faith standard in that forum. If so, it would not prejudice the rules of the Roman law within its own forum. An alternate possibility was to say that the decree had been meant to apply to both civil and ecclesiastical pleas, as its wording implied, but only in those geographical areas (of which there were many) where the church held both spiritual and temporal jurisdiction. If this had been the meaning of the council's decree, again no conflict existed. The church had an undoubted right to legislate in such areas, and the Roman law could continue to apply unhindered in other places.

To modern tastes, such readings of *Quoniam omne* may seem purely formal, if not actually perverse. They were, however, quite normal within the *ius commune*. Indeed, it was possible to go further, asserting, for example, that the canonical decree had been meant to apply only in cases brought to penalize mala fide possessors. Consequently, it would have no application where the law's principal purpose was to penalize a record owner who had been negligent. Since that *was* the principal purpose of the civil law, the canon did not apply. In other words, since the purpose of a civil law in awarding land to the prescriptive possessor was to encourage record owners to be vigilant in protecting their rights, the question of good or bad faith of the prescriptive possessor would be entirely irrelevant. The possessor's gain would be only an indirect and incidental result of a positive achievement, taking the property from the slothful (former) owner.[69] Thus the Roman law of prescription did not conflict with the canonical decree.

The second possibility of answering the question about the relationship of *Quoniam omne* to Roman law was equally formal, although it led to the opposite result. It took the decree at face value, holding that the canon law had justifiably intervened by reason of the sin involved (ratione peccati) in order to correct the Roman law of prescription. The canon law held itself bound to respect the independence of the temporal law in ordinary circumstances,[70] but not where the temporal law would lead men into sin. The basic idea was to avert danger to the souls of the people involved. This might be the situation here. If a mala fide possessor risked eternal damnation by retaining property to which he had no right, then the canon law was correct in stepping in to overrule the temporal law's rule. Salvation was undeniably more important than temporal advantage, and the Roman law, some said, had lost sight of this. Medieval canonists habitually treated this sort of intervention as only "indirect." Like intervention ex defectu justiciae, it was said to imply no attack upon the independence of the temporal law, only an augmentation of it. It could therefore be said that the canon law was simply correcting an inherited part of the law of prescription in the exercise of this salutary principle.[71]

The obvious difficulty in this interpretation was that it proved too much. Since most litigation involves wrongdoing of some sort, if the principle was applied rigorously, it would risk putting all jurisdiction immediately into the hands of the church. Some of the canonists did not shrink before that possibility. Antonius de Butrio, for example, wrote that "it belongs to the Pope to annul all laws, constitutions, statutes and customs which foster sin."[72] In some parts of medieval Europe, the church courts in fact attempted to put the rule into practice, allowing it to be invoked in individual cases.[73]

The truth is, however, that application of jurisdiction ratione peccati went contrary to normal ways of thinking during the Middle Ages. Most people, canonists among them, assumed a "two swords" approach, under which church and state were bound to respect the legitimate exercise of the jurisdiction belonging to the other. As anything but an emergency measure, the actual exercise of ecclesiastical jurisdiction ratione peccati was quite unacceptable to most lawyers and temporal officials. The canonists were themselves aware of the dangers in pushing the hierocratic view too far. Some among them saw the need for a different approach to the dilemma.

The most sophisticated such approach to harmonizing the Roman and canon laws of prescription was written by Joannes Andreae, commenting on the *Regulae iuris* at the end of the *Liber sextus*.[74] Joannes did not approach the problem simply by asking which law should prevail. Instead he raised the possibility that on different levels both might be equally valid. This may seem unlikely, but in fact it followed from his way of putting the problem. Joannes began with the uncontroversial assertion that the law of prescription should stand in conformity with the law of nature and that such conformity furnished a test of its legitimacy. Was it possible, therefore, that both might be "in harmony with the equity of the law of nature," even while taking opposite positions on the requirement of good faith in prescription?[75]

It was. For the sake a greater good, Joannes noted, the law often permits consequences that it would not promote directly. It could, for example, legitimately require candidates for clerical office to answer questions about their past life that would be unlawful if asked of someone who was not a candidate. The ultimate good of protecting the clerical office from unworthy occupants rendered an intrusion, which would otherwise be unlawful, legitimate. Now the ultimate good of the Roman law was the preservation and enhancement of civil society. The civil law might therefore be acting in entire harmony with natural law if it adopted the rule of prescription best calculated to promote that good, even if the rule had incidental consequences that might be spiritually undesirable. Discouraging negligence by property owners and limiting the length of time during which quarrels and litigation could arise were proper ways of preserving right order within human society. "The public good," Joannes wrote, "is most seriously impeded by disputes that cannot readily be ended."[76] A rule of prescription framed to avoid that evil was thus entirely justified. It would not be wrong, still less would it be invalid, if the civil law left issues of conscience to one side. To Joannes, the relation between an adverse possessor and God neither was nor should have been of paramount importance to the civil law.

With the canon law, the situation was otherwise. The canon law's goal was to serve God's purposes in the world. Its rules must therefore comport with God's will and with the law of the gospel; its rules were to be fashioned "so that men may attain to glory."[77] If some compromises with this stern principle were unavoidable, at least the canon law must not endorse a rule that divided man from God. To do this would violate its great purpose. Its rule of prescription, if it were to stand in harmony with natural law, should therefore promote righteousness. The Roman law might simply promote peace. This difference required that the canon law concern itself with the inner man and adjust its rule according to the adverse possessor's bona fides.

This was not an "extrajudicial" appeal to religious sentiment. Had not Jesus, in teaching that the man who lusts after a woman has sinned in his heart, also said that he had come not to abolish the law but to fulfill it?[78] He must have meant that the law of the church must look to a person's intent. Because the goals of the two laws were different, it followed for Joannes that they were not incompatible, even though they adopted different standards for the acquisition of prescriptive title. Indeed, one could almost say that each had adopted the rule best suited for its inner nature.

CONCLUSION

The harmonization of Roman and canon law from the pen of Joannes Andreae was elegant and sophisticated. Perhaps it was too sophisticated for the realities of everyday litigation. The stubborn question remained: Which law of prescription would be applied by judges in the cases that came before them? Most of the time, judges need answers more than they need theories, even elegant and sophisticated theories. What happened in everyday court practice?

Joannes Andreae wrote during the first half of the fourteenth century, and for a time, it seems, his answer may well have described the realities of court practice. The temporal courts applied their rule; the ecclesiastical courts applied theirs.[79] Gradually, however, the canonical principle came to prevail. It became the rule of the *ius commune*. By the fifteenth century, it appears to have become the canonical rule about good faith that applied no matter which forum the plaintiff had chosen.[80] This change was not announced as the adoption of a new substantive policy but as one in which the Roman law rule had been "corrected" by the better-considered rule of the canon law.[81] This was in accord with the principle, endorsed by the canonists and many civilians, that where there was a conflict between the two, and where the canonical rule reached the better result, the latter should always be applied.

If one looks behind this "victory" in order to consider the question raised at the start of this chapter, the result gives only slightly less advantage to the church and to the canon law. The question, readers may remember, was whether the canon law should permit prescription at all. From the perspective of its consequences, allowing prescription probably hurt the material interests of most churches, and it certainly seemed to license the acquisition of title by theft. Yet permitting it could not be only a hard necessity. Prescription was permitted by the ancient canons and by the Roman law, and it was sanctioned by the papal decretals. The canonists of the formative age were obliged to develop a positive system of prescription.

All things considered, they did not do badly. When looked at in any detail, the canon law that was created was limited in such a way as to minimize the negative aspects of the doctrine. Prescription was not permitted in circumstances of forceful taking, it required good faith on the part of the party in possession, and it carved out a privileged position for churches. All this was achieved by making judicious use of the Roman law, the ancient canons, and one conciliar enactment from 1215. As in the creation of a canonical system of prescription as a whole, the canonists relied first of all upon formal rules, interpreting them in directions that were sometimes expansive and sometimes strict. They read these authorities according to their understanding of the inner nature of the canon law, as well as of the canon law's purposes in human society. The result was a system of considerable complexity. But it was not incompatible with some of the basic aims of the canon law, and its long life within the *ius commune* must stand as a tribute to more than simple force of habit.

8 The Christian Sacraments: The Canon Law of Baptism

Baptism is the first and perhaps also the greatest of the Christian sacraments. Jesus specifically commanded his followers to make disciples by baptizing (Matt. 28:19), and the church has sought to fulfill his command. This sacrament is the foundation and the point of entry for all the other sacraments (X 3.43.3).[1] According to settled Christian doctrine, baptism is both available to all and essential for all. It serves for the remission of sins (1 Cor. 6:11), and it allows the recipient to enter fully into the family of Christians (1 Cor. 12:13).

A common and doubtless derivative definition of baptism was given by one of the early decretalists, Geoffrey of Trani (d. 1245): Baptism is "an exterior washing accompanied by a certain form of words."[2] Obviously a very general sort of a definition, Geoffrey's words would seem to have stood much in need of elaboration. They did receive elaboration, and elaboration of a most extensive kind. It is the subject of this chapter. However, most canonists would have agreed that Geoffrey's definition succinctly and faithfully stated baptism's definition. As an initial formulation, it was a commonplace of the time and much repeated. Geoffrey's definition was virtually identical to that found in the *Sentences* of Peter Lombard[3] and to that given by most later canonists.[4] A definition very similar to it appeared at the outset of virtually every discussion in which the sacrament was taken up in medieval scholastic literature.[5]

About the accuracy of the definition or the centrality of baptism for Christian life there was little serious disagreement among medieval Christians. There was very little dissent to either until the Protestant Reformation. Even then, there was not much dispute. Although it became common form to impute error about the meaning of the sacrament to the writing of one's theological opponents, there was more noise than substance to most of the disputes. No basic disagreement with common assumptions about the sacrament became widespread until the rationalism of the eighteenth century challenged them.[6]

It was all but universally assumed among the learned, for instance, that infants who died without being baptized would not be saved.[7] Being without personal fault, unbaptized infants might not suffer the same torment that was the appropriate lot of adult sinners. They might either simply be denied the vision of God[8] or else be punished more leniently than would otherwise have been the case.[9] One could not be entirely sure which, and it was entirely permissible to hope for the best. Jesus, however, had declared that no man should enter the Kingdom of God except he be born of Water and the Spirit (John 3:5). In the eyes of the canonists, this declaration left no doubt about either the sacrament's central place in the life of the church or its necessity for human salvation. To them, the thief on the Cross who had died beside Jesus and been saved by his declaration of faith (Luke 23:43) made a special case.[10] The thief provided hope of salvation only when the impossibility of a person's actual baptism was coupled with the intensity of his desire to obtain it (X 3.43.2).[11] It was quite consistent with the canon law, as with medieval theology more generally, that unbaptized infants should be excluded from burial within consecrated ground.[12]

If there was consensus about the basic definition, it is also true that about a great many of the details involving the sacrament there was doubt and disagreement.[13] Perhaps there was a little more of the former than the latter. It is remarkable how often the canonists made reference to opposed, and often apparently quite permissible, opinions and practices in their discussions of this sacrament.[14] They left room for a variety of local customs in the rite's performance.[15] Should there, for instance, be triple or single immersion of the candidate? That could be left to choice or custom.[16] Some of this permissible diversity should be laid at the door of history. There had long been uncertainties surrounding the sacrament. There had also been change over time. A variety of rites and local customs,[17] a long history of conflicting theological views, a capacity to develop in important ways from the precedents of antiquity, and a tendency to generate new ideas and emotions have all marked baptism's historical course. Some but not all of these sources of uncertainty left their mark on the classical canon law.

THE CANON LAW'S INTEREST IN BAPTISM

One initial question. Why the concern? At first sight, it appears unlikely that the canon law would have taken any more than a passing interest in this subject. The sacrament of baptism comes more naturally within the bailiwick of theologians than of lawyers. Its basic nature had been fully explored during the controversies of the first centuries of the Christian era. And it is hard to envision just how baptism could have become a matter for litigation in the courts of the church. Consequently, it appears that there should have been little room, and even less necessity, for the lawyers of the church to enter very far into any of the doctrinal complexities that surrounded the subject.

For good or for ill, this is not the reality. Each of the reasons for excluding canonical treatment does contain an element of truth. The theologians did deal at length with the subject. Many of the essential questions about baptism had been answered. And certainly there never was any such thing as a *causa baptismi* that came regularly before the ecclesiastical courts of medieval Europe. Nevertheless, the subject was of obvious interest and importance to the canon law. Gratian devoted a very long *distinctio* to baptism (De cons. Dist. 4 cc. 1–156), and the subject occupied two separate titles in the third book of the Gregorian Decretals (X 3.42.1–6; X 3.43.1–3), as well as appearing incidentally at several other points in the canonical texts.[18] There was an answer to each of the plausible (modern) reasons for thinking that the canon lawyers would have left the subject alone.

First, the canonists would not have accepted the notion that they should avoid issues because theologians also wrote about them. The tasks of the canon law were different from those of theology, but the medieval canon lawyers believed that the law was an essential part of God's plan of salvation for mankind.[19] Law regulated human conduct and led men and women toward right action. Since God had ordained the sacrament of baptism as the public portal through which men and women must enter if they were to be saved, it followed that the canon law would very likely have something to say about the subject. That there would be "overlap" between the canon law and theology was only to be expected. The same sort of "overlap" was also found with several of the subjects treated in this book that were obviously within the canonists' realm—excommunication and blasphemy, for instance. In fact, there was a very substantial degree of agreement and duplication in medieval writings on the subject from the pens of canonists and theologians. But that did not mean to the canonists that they should step aside in favor of the theologians.

Second, although many settled principles about baptism had undoubtedly been inherited from Christian antiquity and were not subject to debate, a settled inheritance by no means precluded treatment of the subject by the jurists of the church. Originality was not a virtue they prized. One doubts that they recognized it at all. If they did, it was usually not a virtue. They were expected to state and to clarify the law, even where its principal features were firmly established. Moreover, it turned out that there were some new questions raised. Solutions to them had to be found. Everything about the sacrament was not in fact clear. And perhaps above all, there was a perceived need for the kind of systematic treatment at which the canonists excelled. The confusion in the authorities collected in the long *distinctio* on the subject in Gratian's *Decretum* was one measure of the need. The frequency with which Gratian turned to the subject was another.

Third, although baptism never provided a separate heading for litigation within ecclesiastical jurisdiction, it was not without effect on several severely practical matters that did come before the church's courts.[20] Jurisdictional questions are the most obvious examples.[21] Baptism was the very foundation for the church's jurisdiction over persons. St. Paul had himself refused pointedly to judge those outside the company of the faithful (1 Cor. 1:12). With few exceptions, therefore, only the baptized were subject to the reach of the ecclesiastical courts. Only they could be excommunicated. Only they could be prosecuted for heresy (to take only the most extreme case), because by definition persons who were not Christians could not commit the offense.[22] Much therefore might depend on the subject to which the canonists devoted the bulk of their attention—defining the validity of a person's baptism. The fate of the child of Jewish parents returning to them after being brought up as a Christian might well hang in the balance; it might be decided by exactly that question.[23] Far from being peripheral, therefore, baptism was a subject with which the classical canon law had to come to grips.

THE FORMAL VALIDITY OF BAPTISM

In common with the theologians, the canonists dealt with the origins and the effects of baptism, although of course neither from a historical perspective nor with the scholarly interest in early baptismal practices that is thought necessary today.[24] The necessity of the sacrament for salvation, the efficacy and desirability of infant baptism, and the relation between baptismal washing and original sin were all taken up in the *Decretum*. They were all at least mentioned, and sometimes discussed fully, by later canonists. These were never the principal concerns, however. The principal concern, and the most practical one, lay with the question of validity.[25] When was a baptism a baptism? It had been established in antiquity that the sacrament could not be repeated.[26] It had equally been established that the sacrament conferred an indelible character upon its recipient. Since baptism was both necessary for any person's salvation and the basis for the church's claim to whatever personal jurisdiction its courts exercised, it was of the most immediate importance to know whether it had occurred. This, as it turned out, was not always a simple matter to decide. To appreciate the difficulties, one may usefully divide the sacrament into its distinct elements, as the canonists themselves did.

The Season and the Ceremonies

It was the assumption of the Latin Church that the sacrament of baptism should be conferred twice a year, at Easter and Pentecost. This was the traditional rule, and Gratian began his treatment of the proper season for baptism by reaffirming it. He included two papal letters setting out this tradition and forbidding baptisms at other times in the church calendar (De cons. Dist. 4 cc. 11–12). Several reasons were advanced for the practice, some theological and some biblical. Easter, for instance, was regarded as an appropriate season because baptism "represented the death and resurrection" of Jesus. Pentecost was appropriate because the apostles had themselves baptized three thousand souls on that day (Acts 2:41).[27]

Why then, it was commonly asked, was the feast of the Epiphany not also a suitable season? Jesus himself had submitted to the baptism of John on that day (Mark 1:9–11), and there had long been respectable opinion in its favor, particularly in the East. Its rejection in the West was explained by a need to distinguish John's baptism from that of the church. John's had not served for the remission of sins.[28] The church's did. In this, Gratian's treatment of the proper season was simply restating the assumptions of the Latin Church; they were discussed in the Decretum both because the discussion served the positive role of giving directions to the parochial clergy and because it was conceivable that the question of the proper season might bear upon the question of validity.

In fact, it did not. Despite the strength of the arguments and authorities adduced in support of the two traditional seasons, the law of the church held that the validity of baptism was not affected by the time when it was conferred. It may even be said that the traditional dates were ultimately reduced to something like "sentimental favorites" for the rite. The apparently mandatory papal decretals on the subject were distinguished away by the canonists, interpreted as having referred only to "solemn baptism."[29] They were also matched by equally authoritative decretals authorizing an exception in case of necessity (De cons. Dist. 4 cc. 16–17). The reasoning behind this result seemed altogether compelling. Baptism was necessary for salvation. If a man, woman, or child was dying, it would have been an intolerable error to delay by waiting for the proper season.

In an age when the life of an infant was far from secure, it made sense to follow the same "emergency" procedure for all children. An

English provincial council in 1279, for example, restricted the ancient rule to infants born within eight days of Easter and Pentecost, and then only when their healthy condition permitted the sacrament to be deferred without risk.[30] Because infant baptism was the norm in medieval Europe, this became the ordinary rule for virtually all baptisms. There was some sentiment, echoed in the canons,[31] that for healthy adults it was right to follow the ancient rule as to season, at least in the absence of good reason to the contrary. But these were rare cases in the daily life of the medieval church. Otherwise, what had once been an exception became the rule.[32]

The other details surrounding the ritual of baptism were treated in much the same manner. There were rules that ought to be followed, but their observance did not affect the question of whether or not the recipient had been baptized. The question of validity was separated from that of legitimacy, although both were discussed. The ritual interrogation of the person to be baptized, for instance, was an undoubted part of the rite.[33] It should not be omitted. However, it made no difference to the sacrament's validity. The principle applied equally to many other aspects of the baptismal ceremony. An ancient canon prescribed abstinence from meat and wine for two weeks before baptism. Gratian included it in the *Decretum* (De cons. Dist. 4 c. 60), but the *glossa ordinaria* commented that it was merely "a counsel" without effect on the sacrament's validity. The same rule held, even for adults, as to the catechizing of converts to Christianity (id. c. 53). They should be adequately prepared for the reception of the sacrament, but the validity of their baptism did not depend on the preparation. The Council of Vienne (1312) required that baptism take place in the candidate's parish church.[34] If it was held elsewhere, however, although its minister might be subjected to formal canonical discipline, the sacrament's formal validity was once again not impaired.[35]

The Minister of the Sacrament

Was the validity of this sacrament in any way dependent on the identity, the character, or the state of mind of the person doing the baptizing? This had been the subject of one of the great controversies of the

early church: the dispute over the validity of baptisms (and ordinations) conferred by heretical clergy.[36] The practice of rebaptism had
been widespread, especially in North Africa. The practice was notably
defended by St. Cyprian (d. 258), with whom it has come to be indel-
ibly associated. Cyprian held that the sacraments could only be truly
conferred within the Catholic Church. This required rebaptism. This
position was stigmatized by its opponents as "subjectivist" in nature.
Against it stood the "objectivist" position, championed most forcefully by St. Augustine.[37] It held that baptism's validity in no way depended upon the purity of the minister's faith. To think so would be
to diminish God's power, rendering the grace conferred by the sacrament dependent upon the vagaries of human intention. According to
this view, it was not even essential that the minister of the sacrament
be a Christian of any stripe. A Turk or an atheist, properly instructed,
could baptize.[38]

The "objectivist" view prevailed in the ancient controversy. The
practice of rebaptizing the already baptized on account of the religious opinions of the minister at the first baptism was expressly
condemned by the church. It dropped out of accepted usage. Indeed,
under certain circumstances an imperial constitution actually prescribed the death penalty for knowingly rebaptizing (Cod. 1.6.2). The
canons of the church never went to that extreme, but they accepted
and implemented the substantive principle upon which it was premised. Clergy who offended against the law's prescription by rebaptizing were to be punished by automatically incurring canonical *irregularitas*.

By the twelfth century, this controversy was part of a distant past.
But it was also firmly established in the consciousness of theologians
and canonists. They made, indeed they stressed, the point that the
minister's unworthiness was irrelevant. They dealt with apparently
contrary authorities by scholastic distinction. Any of the older canons that called for rebaptism of persons baptized by heretics were interpreted as having had reference only to cases in which the proper
Trinitarian formula had not been used.[39] So long as the proper form
for baptism had been followed, the unworthiness of the minister in no
way impeded the validity of the sacrament (De cons. Dist. 4 c. 28).

In places this was actually a live issue, as the Greek Church had sometimes rebaptized men and women originally baptized within the Latin Church.[40] This was a clear violation of the ancient canons, as well as an implicit denial of the primacy of the Roman see. The subject was thought to merit extensive treatment in the *Decretum*. Gratian included something like twenty-five extracts from St. Augustine's writings on the issue in the *Decretum*, many more than were needed to establish the principle (De cons. Dist. 4 cc. 25–50). The point was taken up and affirmed by all the later canonists, who held uniformly that the "malice" of the minister did not affect the validity of the sacrament.

At this date in the West, one of the more pressing related areas for discussion of the subject would have been that raised by sacraments received at the hands of "simoniacal" priests, those who had purchased spiritual office in exchange for money. Heresy *simpliciter* was less in evidence than it had been at the time of the original controversy. But many among the reform party in Rome thought that simony could rightly be treated as a heresy, the *simoniaca haeresis*. However, although there was much concern about whether the laity might lawfully receive the sacraments at the hands of simoniacal priests, and some dispute about the validity of holy orders conferred by simoniacal bishops,[41] there seems to have been no doubt on this score about the validity of baptisms. The "objectivist" position held firm.

Under the canon law, the office of baptizing belonged to priests (De cons. Dist. 4 c. 19), not to the lower orders of the clergy or the laity. However, the same canon that stated this rule also contained an exception. Again announced for cases of necessity, where a delay might leave a dying person unbaptized and in danger of damnation, the canon allowed deacons to exercise the ministry of baptism. This exception was extended further by the following canons in the *Decretum*. The power to baptize was opened in cases of necessity to lay men and women. At least in theory, even Jews, Muslims, or persons of no religion whatsoever could baptize. The sacrament thus provided an exception to the general rule that a grant cannot be made by any person who does not possess a legitimate interest (*Nemo dat quod non habet*).[42] Here, to the contrary, an unbaptized person could confer a privileged status he did not himself possess.

The personal qualities of the minister were likewise quite irrelevant. Good and bad were treated the same for purposes of validity.[43] Anyone might validly baptize, so long as he or she meant to confer the sacrament. It might be said that this result was all but inevitable, that there was no available stopping point. Since it was established beyond doubt that heretics could validly baptize, all the others seemed to follow almost as a matter of simple logic. If baptism received at the hands of Judas Iscariot was a valid baptism, as the canons stated it would be (De cons. Dist. 4 c. 39), it is hard to think of who could be excluded. The situation illustrates a recurrent theme in the history of the canon law. A rule was announced: the sacrament must be conferred by priests. Except in cases of dire necessity, no one else must presume to baptize. However, if someone else did so presume, the baptism was not invalid. "Many things that should not be done," said the canonists, "are nevertheless valid if they are done." Baptism was one of many such examples.

If one searches for a modern equivalent, an unlawful arrest in a foreign country under modern American law comes to mind. The act is unlawful, but the person arrested may still be brought to trial. The unlawful act of arrest does not deprive the trial court of jurisdiction over the person of the accused.[44] If he is convicted, no one may challenge the conviction. Similarly, no one could challenge the validity of a baptism conferred by a layman, even if the layman were a bad man, there had been no emergency, and a clergyman had been present. The act would assuredly have been in violation of the canons. The layman might have acted unlawfully and thereby subjected himself to the penalties of ecclesiastical discipline. But it was God who baptized through his agency, and the result was not to be impeached.[45]

There were two exceptions, or perhaps three. First, no person could baptize himself (X 3.42.4).[46] The example of Jesus' baptism was invoked here, but rather differently than the way it was used in the question of whether Epiphany was an appropriate season for baptism. Here it supported a rule of invalidity. Since Jesus, who above all others had the right to baptize, had sought baptism at the hands of another person, it was right and indeed necessary that ordinary men and women should do the same.[47] Second, a person who could not speak could not baptize. As we shall see below, the baptismal formula had to be pronounced, and a person deprived of the ability to speak could not pronounce it.[48] Third, at least according to one opinion, baptism must not be parceled out between two or more agents.[49] That is, if one person uttered the baptismal formula and the other immersed the child, or if one said portion of the formula and the other the rest, there would be no true baptism. The possibility seemed to contradict the biblical injunction that there must be "One faith, one baptism" (Eph. 4:5) and also the church's belief in "one baptism" as expressed in the Nicene Creed.[50] It also raised the specter of rebaptism. Since neither the words nor the actions of the sacrament were of any effect without the other, the actions of each person in such a situation would amount to a simple nullity.[51] Except in these three quite unusual situations, however, the canon law would not question a baptism's efficacy by looking too closely at the quality of the hands administering it.

The inroads that were made in this principle came from a slightly different direction. A limited inquiry into the state of mind of the person administering the sacrament became permissible under the classical canon law in cases in which the intent of the minister had been seriously defective. Suprisingly, the biblical example was something of which all Christians approved: the baptism of John. He had not meant the same thing by his action that was understood as vital to the church's baptism. Hence those he baptized would properly present themselves at a baptismal font.

The questions that arose were difficult and controversial. These three hypothetical cases were commonly discussed by the canonists: (1) the minister who was drunk at the time of baptism; (2) the minister who intended his actions only as a joke; and (3) the minister who was wholly ignorant of the import of his words and actions. Since baptism required no solemnity and could be administered by any person, and because it could not be repeated, these hypothetical cases may not have been simply classroom exercises, although classroom exercises they most certainly were.[52]

At least as I read the commentary on these subjects, the more probable opinions about them were as follows. The first baptism was valid unless the minister was so drunk that he had lacked consciousness of what he was doing.[53] Partial, but not total, inebriation made no difference because the halfway drunk minister was capable of forming an intention to baptize. The second, the jesting baptism, raised a question even St. Augustine had found puzzling enough to leave to God's judgment. Under the canon law, the result depended on whether the jesting minister had intended to confer the sacrament.[54] If his intent had been simply to amuse, with no thought of the reality of the sacrament, this would not imprint the character of baptism. The third was valid if the minister had been instructed as to what the sacrament was, even though he had no faith in its efficacy.[55] If, however, what he said and did was wholly without meaning for him, simply a form of words, then the baptism would not be valid. In all these cases, the common thread lay in the presence or absence of the intent to baptize. It served as a prerequisite to validity. The minister must have intended to confer the sacrament. To this extent, even though it must have been a rare instance where one of these problems arose, the classical canon law admitted a more "subjectivist" view.

The Person Baptized

The most important questions involving the recipient of the sacrament were those dealing with unconscious and unwilling baptisms. They will be examined in more detail toward the end of this chapter. It is useful to say just a word here, however, about the basic requirements. In fact there were only a few that affected the validity of the sacrament.

First, no specific intent or understanding of the Christian faith on the part of the person baptized was required. Indeed, a person baptized only because of his or her own curiosity was still treated as validly baptized for purposes of the church's external forum. The canon law held that "the sacrament [was] complete despite a defect of faith."[56] Second, it was not necessary that the whole body be immersed or fully washed by the baptismal water, though there was some doubt about just how much of the body had to be reached by the water. The head was clearly enough and was always to be preferred. But if a lesser part of the body was touched, say only the shoulder or even the foot, the result was less sure among the commentators.[57] They were more certain, however, that the water must have reached the body itself to accomplish the candidate's baptism; it was not enough if the water touched only the person's clothing or (it seems) hair. Third, the person must be alive and have a soul capable of salvation. The dead could not be baptized. Neither could a "monster," even if it were born to a woman.[58] Fourth, it did not matter whether a child was known to or correctly named by the sacrament's minister. Problems were caused only when he got the sexes wrong, as by using a girl's name for a boy. There was respectable opinion that this mistake rendered the baptism invalid because of the minister's lack of intention to baptize the actual infant being presented.

The Element of Water

Water was necessary for baptism (X 3.42.5). Aquinas outlined the reasons,[59] laying them out in a treatment to which the canonists themselves made reference.[60] Water is almost everywhere abundant, it cleanses in a physical sense, it nurtures both seeds and animals, and words of Jesus specifically approved it as the foundation for entry into the Kingdom of God. The practice of bodily immersion in flowing waters, the immersion being repeated three times, had traditionally been the favored method. It continued to be admired and spoken of with approbation by the medieval canonists. Priests were directed to follow the ancient practice if they could.[61] However, the church and the canon law had long since moved away from what might look like a rigorist position with regard to this aspect of form. Single immersion was valid, and sprinkling with water upon the head was also sufficient to sustain the sacrament. As long as water was used externally, that was enough.[62] Similarly, although the water should be blessed first, the absence of this blessing did not affect the substance of the sacrament. For this result, the canonists found biblical precedent. Without such a "shortcut," it would not have been possible for

St. Peter to have baptized three thousand persons in a single day.[63] Since it was reported that he had done so (Acts 2:41), the abbreviated practice must be sufficient.[64]

Were we to enter fully into the subtleties that were raised by, or at any rate accompanied, the requirement of water, we should have to consider (among others) ice, spit, beer, tears, urine, milk, olive oil, snow, and sweat.[65] Perhaps this is not necessary. We may take just a peek. The canonists stressed that water was essential, and the law's preference was always for *aqua pura*. Did this rule out dirty water or seawater? It did not. Both were water. Philip had baptized the Ethiopian eunuch by the side of a road (Acts 8:38), and it might be necessary to baptize a child born at sea. What about broth in which meat had previously been cooked? Broth too passed muster, at least according to Antonius de Butrio.[66] However, most other "partway" liquids were ruled out even if they did incorporate some water.

What, then, if pure water was taken and mixed with some other liquid? Here the *communis opinio* among the canonists and theologians held that the result depended upon which element of the two predominated. If water was the predominant element in the mixture, the baptism was valid.[67] Otherwise it was not. This gave rise to a joke. A seminarian was asked by his bishop whether baptism using soup was valid. The alert young man replied, "I distinguish. If you mean the soup served in the episcopal palace, the baptism is invalid. But if you mean the soup served in the seminary, it is the reverse."[68]

The Trinitarian Formula

If we are to appreciate the canon law on this subject, it will be necessary to enter a little further into legal and verbal subtleties in dealing with the second necessary part of baptism, the words used by the sacrament's minister. The words occupied a large proportion of the canonists' attention. Jesus had commanded his disciples to baptize "in the name of the Father, and of the Son, and of the Holy Spirit" (Matt. 28:19). The prescribed form in Latin was for the minister of the sacrament to say, "Ego baptizo te in nomine patris et filii et spiritus sancti." These words could be uttered in any language. But they had to be uttered. Without words that contained the substance of the biblical formula, nothing would have been accomplished. The words *were* the sacrament. Although it was possible for the canonists to conceive of marriage being entered into without words having been spoken, or of blasphemy being committed through physical action alone, this was not so with baptism. The words were essential, just as the words of institution in the Eucharist were essential for that sacrament.

When exact words matter, as they very often do in the law, it can be difficult to disentangle form from substance. This is true today, and so it proved for the canonists. On the one hand, everyone agreed that no "magic words" were necessary to render the sacrament valid. Substance should control. On the other hand, everyone also agreed that if the substance of the Trinitarian formula was not included, the attempted baptism was invalid. And how was substance to be determined except by examining the words used? It is hard to see how else it could be done, even though the result left room for plenty of uncertainty. For instance, must the first words in the formula, "I baptize thee (Ego baptizo te)," be said? Yes, it seemed, they must. Otherwise the intent to baptize might not be present. Simply immersing someone "in the name of the Father . . ." would be consistent with an intention simply to bless.

The canonists examined each word of the formula. Even "Amen" was discussed.[69] "Ego" was disputed. Some said it was *de substantia* and must be used.[70] Probably the more common opinion, however, was that it was not necessary.[71] It might be understood in the verb *baptizo*, although this did not answer the question of using a vernacular such as English, where the personal pronoun is necessary to make sense of the verb. "Baptizo," however, was necessary. At least some form of it was. The third-person "Baptisat te Christus" might be substituted, but only if it was the general custom of the province to do so.[72] If the minister substituted another word entirely, such as "immerse (*mergo*)" or "bathe (*balneo*)," this was probably not a sufficient objective expression of the intent to baptize, even if the Trinitarian formula followed.[73]

"Te" was probably the most discussed of the three initial words of the baptismal formula. If no word to express the object of the verb *to baptize* was used at all, the baptism would be invalid, for it would be ambiguous who the object was. Spectators might imagine that the minister was baptizing his own hand, one canonist said.[74] What about the plural form of *you*, "vos"? Was that similarly ambiguous when only one person was being baptized? Some canonists apparently thought so, although the plural might be appropriate when a multitude was being baptized at the same moment. Others thought it might be excused even in the case of baptism of an individual if the candidate was a "great prince" who might take offense at the more informal "te."[75]

Whether the words that followed, expressing the Trinity, had to be stated with exactness raised the largest number of difficulties. It was accepted by all that the words must not admit of heresy in any sense. The church's stress on the importance of correctness in belief left a mark on baptism, as it did on so much else. The chief difficulty here was caused by the Bible. The Book of Acts twice describes baptism as being administered simply in the name of Jesus Christ, one of them being in response to a direct command of the apostle Peter (Acts 10:48, 19:5). These incidents appeared to sanction less than the full Trinitarian formula, now being stated as requisite for validity. The difficulty was compounded by the existence of two papal letters that seemed to point in the opposite directions. One called for baptism afresh where the full formula had been absent (De cons. Dist. 4 c. 30). The other forbade it (id. c. 24).

Reconciliation of these apparently inconsistent positions was possible, however. The mostly commonly stated means of reconciling them was to assume that the biblical version had been a special concession for the time of the apostles. It had been particularly appropriate at this early period of the church's existence because of the need to "amplify" the name of Jesus. With the passage of time and the establishment of the church, however, this urgent need subsided. The form could be set aside.[76] The church had the power to determine the correct form of the sacraments, according to the canonists' view, at least if the form chosen was drawn from the Scriptures.[77] This was the point here. The church had determined on the full Trinitarian formula, and it had the legitimate authority to do so. The end of it was that despite some disagreement about the result if the "short version" found in the Book of Acts was used in practice, more probably than not the baptism was invalid.[78] To have embraced the alternate view would have led to the odd but seemingly inescapable conclusion that baptism "in the name of Jesus" would be valid but baptism "in the name of the Father and of the Son" (i.e., without mentioning the Holy Spirit at all) would not.[79]

Perhaps the most challenging practical problems raised under this heading were caused by mistakes on the part of the minister of the sacrament. Some grew out of simple ignorance, some out of inadvertence, some out of foolishness, and some apparently out of a desire to experiment. What should be the result? Here are some examples. Words might be added, as by invoking the name of the Blessed Virgin Mary after the Trinitarian formula. These were treated by the canonists as surplusage and disregarded, much as happened in the Roman law of wills, here cited by the canonists as applicable or at least parallel to baptism. A more difficult problem occurred if the words used were not those of additional piety but instead the reverse, as by invoking the name of the Devil after the Holy Spirit.[80] It is hard to imagining this actually happening, at least unless the words had been intended as a parody of the Christian sacrament, in which case the intention of the minister might throw doubt on the result.

Suppose, however, the addition had been neutral in content and had come in the middle of the formula rather than at the end? Should that make a difference? Some pause had to be allowed, at least if it was not too long. Suppose one had to cough. But what if other substantive matter intervened? The canonists distinguished, and again made use of an analogy drawn from the law of wills. The Digest contained a text that required that a testament be a continuous act (Dig. 28.1.21.3). If, however, its making was interrupted only by a short pause or by an act related to the testament, its validity was not affected. This rule was taken over into baptism. The standard example given by the canonists used the opening words of the *Aeneid*. Thus, if the minister said, "Ego baptizo te in nomine patris arma virumque cano . . . et filii et spiritus sancti," the sacrament was of no effect.[81] However, if the inserted words had some relevance to the sacrament, then the baptism would have been validly conferred.

What if errors in the words were caused by ignorance of Latin? The textbook example, found in a decretal ascribed to Pope Zacharias (d. 752), dealt with the case of a priest who must have known only the barest essentials of the language of the church. He had performed the baptismal rite with the words, ". . . in nomine patria et filia et spiritus sancta" (more or less "in the name the country and the daughter and the wholly Spirit"). Were persons so baptized to be baptized again? The pope responded that if the fault was the result of simple ignorance, and the priest had not intended to introduce any error of faith, it would be unnecessary to repeat the rite (De cons. Dist. 4 c. 83).

One cannot but sympathize with this result. The *rigor iuris* might appropriately be relaxed in the canons in favor of the person baptized (C. 1 q. 7 c. 11). One could even think of legal arguments in its favor. The law of wills again supplied support for the canonists, if any were needed; the omission or change of a syllable does not affect the substance of a testamentary bequest if the testator's intent is clear (Dig. 40.4.54).[82] So here. The intent in the baptismal case had been clear. Ignorance alone had caused the mistake. Moreover, who could know how often there might have been some such small defect of form in country baptisms? Should their validity be thrown into doubt?

Nonetheless, there was a certain danger involved. The formalism and certainty of the law of baptism that were the law's achievement were undercut by this decretal. At least it opened that possibility. The decretal allowed the element of subjective intent to work its way into the canon law of baptism, and this to a greater extent than the cases of jocular or drunken baptisms examined already. The relevant question about validity would depend on whether the baptizing priest had intended to follow the form prescribed by the church, not whether he had spoken an objectively verifiable formula. And a means of distinguishing the two would have to be arrived at. Some quite unworkable distinctions were suggested to determine this inescapable question.[83]

Finally, there was something like the opposite situation, that of a minister who was too clever by half. Suppose, for example, a priest had baptized with words that were equivalent in meaning to the traditional formula but purposefully different from them. Here the canonists took the position that the result depended upon the substance of the words. Baptism "in the name of the Creator, the One who was Born, and the Sacred Flamen" would be a valid baptism because the words were equivalent to the invocation of the Trinity.[84] Just as with the opposite case of ignorance, if the clever minister had intended no theological error, his words sufficed if they were theologically correct. Baptism "in equivalent words" was certainly not encouraged, and there was ample room for doubt about its effect. But most of the medieval canonists held that such a baptism was valid if the words substituted were recognizably tied to the Trinitarian formula.

CONDITIONAL BAPTISM

When one totals up the uncertainties in the law of baptismal validity (of which the above has been only a sample), there can be little doubt that there were too many. The prohibition of rebaptism, a prohibition that could not have been repudiated or ignored, would have put people of good will in a difficult situation. Baptism was necessary for salvation, so it must be conferred. But it could work in exactly the opposite way, toward one's damnation, if it was knowingly repeated.[85] A priest in that situation might himself be punished for rebaptizing. One had, therefore, absolutely to know whether or not a person had been validly baptized. But this might not be easy. The subtle distinctions and the many arguable alternative readings in the law of baptism might well stand as an impediment to certainty.

Particularly was this so in the case of a man or woman who might, or might not, have been validly baptized as an infant. That person would have no recollection whatsoever of what had been said at the time. Hence there would be no way certainly to determine the question of validity. Legal presumptions might be used to answer some of the questions raised,[86] but would a sensible person wish to rest his or her salvation on a presumption? The question answers itself. Many problems that arose in the *ius commune* could reasonably be, and in fact were, left open to juristic speculation. But baptism could not be one of them.

The solution reached under the classical canon law, established in a decretal of Pope Alexander III, was baptism upon condition (X 3.42.2): "Si baptizatus es, non te baptizo; sed si nondum baptizatus es, ego te baptizo in nomine Patris . . ." [If thou art baptized, I do not baptize thee; but if thou art not yet baptized, I baptize thee in the name of the Father . . .]. This solution was not wholly without precedent. It is found, for example, among the capitularies of Charlemagne and of Louis the Pious collected in 827.[87] A Frankish council of 743 mentions it,[88] and a collection of statutes attributed to St. Boniface (d. 755) contains another example.[89] The practice seems not to have been particularly widespread, however.[90] There was no endorsement of it in Gratian's *Decretum*. One canon suggested that it was not considered an alternative (De cons. Dist. 4 c. 104); a *dictum* of Gratian suggested that it had been considered but thought unacceptable.[91] There was no indication that it had been resorted to in the controversy over rebaptism of the early church. One can certainly appreciate the reluctance to embrace it and even good reason for rejecting it. Peter Lombard and Peter the Chanter apparently did so.[92] Conditional baptism came close, perhaps too close, to allowing rebaptism. It avoided the undoubted prohibition against rebaptism by a fine distinction.

The problem remained, however—how to square the prohibition of rebaptism with the necessity of baptism. In the twelfth century, it might be said that the distinction involved in accepting conditional baptism was a sensible and perhaps even a brilliant way out of an otherwise almost insoluble pastoral difficulty. Sometimes distinctions must be fine in the law. This one seems also to have proved itself in practice. The later *Liber sextus* and the other canon law texts were able to omit any but the slightest treatment of baptism.[93] Still, doubts persist. Endorsing conditional baptism was a "legalistic" sort of solution, fully in character for the pope who had endorsed the distinction between words of consent *de praesenti* and words of consent *de futuro* as a sensible solution to the problem of distinguishing non-binding from binding contracts of marriage.

The solution has remained controversial to this day. The continuing problem has been to know how strong the doubt about the validity of the first baptism must be to warrant use of conditional baptism. The temptation has been to resort to it too readily. This is understandable enough in view of the necessity of baptism for salvation, the clerical suspicion of baptism conferred outside its sight and control, and the desire of persons converting to Catholicism to put their past behind them. It is nonetheless contrary to the ancient teachings of the church, and even to some more modern pronouncements. Repeated rulings from various parts of the Curia in Rome have stressed the importance of an investigation of the circumstances of the prior baptism and the need for "probable and prudent reasons" to suspect invalidity before moving to conditional baptism.[94] According to the official view, a conditional baptism premised upon a suspicion that the baptizing minister had not "intended what the church intends" must not become the canonical norm whenever a person converts to Catholicism. It would be "a strange abuse to renew under condition a baptism conferred by heretics who affirm that they had used the requisite matter and form, under pretext that one was ignorant about their intention."[95]

Yet something like this "strange abuse" became the rule in practice. In the sixteenth century, it was the normal course to rebaptize those who had received baptism at the hands of Calvinist ministers, the asserted ground being that these ministers had not intended their baptism to be a sacrament.[96] A decree of the Council of Trent lent the practice a kind of support.[97] A presumption came to stand in favor of using conditional baptism unless it could be shown that the prior baptism was intended as equivalent to a Catholic baptism, not always an easy thing to show. This attitude has lasted to our own century.[98] It is ironic that the modern practice re-creates in substance, even while it avoids in form, the "subjectivist" position of St. Cyprian. It is close to the very position St. Augustine, together with other adherents of an "objectivist" view, thought they had overcome many centuries before.

UNCONSCIOUS AND UNWILLING BAPTISM

Notable in what has been said so far is the scant attention that has been paid to the attitude or the character of the person baptized. Scarcely a word has been said about the question of the propriety of baptizing infants, who are wholly unconscious of the meaning of the action. Nothing has been said about the most notorious practice associated with medieval Christianity, the baptism of peoples conquered by military force. The reason for not having dealt with these problems is that they raised issues unrelated to questions of the formal elements of the rite. But these were real questions, and from a religious and social point of view, they were the more important questions. The canon law was not silent about them.

Two ideas underlay the law's treatment of the various problems posed. First, no one except persons who were willing should receive the sacrament of baptism (Dist. 45 c. 5). Second, the indelible character imparted by baptism did not depend on the faith of the person baptized (De cons. Dist. 4 c. 31). These ideas were at least potentially at odds, perhaps even at war, with each other. If the candidate's faith was irrelevant, was the way being opened for baptizing the unwilling? The two ideas called for some decisions to be made if they were to be brought into tolerable harmony. The "tension" inherent in them and the need for their harmonization came immediately to the fore in an important decretal of Pope Innocent III dealing with the efficacy of the baptism of infants (X 3.42.3).

The Baptism of Infants

In this decretal Innocent answered a challenge to the practice raised by unnamed heretics. These heretics had asserted, according to the pope, that the practice of baptizing small children was contrary to the biblical passage stating that charity was the necessary foundation for the remission of sins (James 5:20). Charity required consciousness of sin and a desire for amendment of life. Infants were necessarily unconscious of the circumstances and meaning of the rite, without the slightest understanding of Christian charity, and quite indifferent to amending their lives. They could not "repent and be baptized" (Acts 2:38). How then could their sins be washed away by baptism, the heretics were saying, without running afoul of the scriptural requirement?

Innocent did not rest his response to this challenge simply upon the antiquity of the practice of infant baptism or the magisterial authority of the church. In fact, he did not mention either. Rather, he combined scriptural exegesis with logic. There were two main points. First, Jesus had said that no man should enter the Kingdom of God unless he were made regenerate by Water and the Holy Spirit (John 3:5). If infants could not be baptized, they would be excluded from the Kingdom of God by these words. Did it make sense to think that God would ordain this fate for them? To assume so would have been to question the perfection of God's plan for mankind. Second, Innocent asserted that Christian baptism was the successor to Jewish circumcision. It "perfected" the Jewish rite and extended it to female as well as male. But circumcision was practiced among both adults and infants in Judaism. Could the more perfect rite be *less* widely available than the Jewish? That is, should baptism be restricted by age in a way the Jewish rite was not? Positive answers would not have been consistent with the Christian religion.

This position therefore fully accepted that infants could not possess the requisite belief in the Christian faith. Innocent did not assert that the parents' or sponsors' faith was imputed to the infants being baptized. Children neither consented to nor understood the meaning of the sacrament. However, the sacrament was nonetheless efficacious for the remission of their sin, the original sin that is the common inheritance of mankind. The biblical statements that seemed to link salvation with belief (e.g., Acts 16:31) were not so much ignored as they were distinguished. They were understood as having been meant to apply to adults, not to children.[99]

Unconscious Baptisms

If infants both could and should be baptized, did the same reasoning apply to adults who were unconscious of or uncaring about the mean-

ing of the action? The distinction used to deal with the biblical statements and taken to validate infant baptism suggested that the reverse
might be true for adults, that for them actual faith would be required.
But it did not logically require that conclusion, and there were strong
considerations pointing away from it. The problem arose most acutely
in the case of those who lacked the capacity to reason or believe, *furi-
osi* or *amentes* in the language of the day. But it also arose in a variety
of different situations in the canon law: for instance, baptism of the
sleeping, the scoffing, and the uninstructed.

As to the last of these, adults who desired baptism but had not yet
fully understood the religion into which they were being baptized, the
canon law held that they should first be instructed, if that was possible.[100] However, their baptism's validity would not be affected by
imperfections in the person's understanding. As to the next, those
who sought baptism but did so either in jest, as a matter of pure curiosity, or with a mental reservation positively disbelieving in the
Christian religion, the canon law allowed either of two positions,
both of which led to the same result. The first held that the baptism
was valid but that it would be ineffective to lead the person to salvation (De cons. Dist. 4 c. 42); the second held that the baptism was
invalid but that because of the rule precluding the church from inquiring into a person's secret thoughts (*de occultis non judicat ecclesia*) the church would nonetheless treat it as a valid baptism in the
external forum.[101] In neither situation would the baptism serve to promote the person's ultimate salvation, unless the person later turned
to God with sincerity of heart.[102] But the outward and visible results
would subject the person to the church's jurisdiction nonetheless. As
to the first problem, raised by those who were asleep or unconscious
at the time of baptism, the canon law again drew a distinction. Those
who had had an inclination toward baptism before falling asleep did
not need to be rebaptized. Their prior desire was enough to render the
baptism valid. The reverse, however, applied to those who had had no
such inclination. If they should desire to accept Christianity upon
awaking, they would need to be baptized afresh.

This leaves the insane, the *amentes*. The *communis opinio* among
the canonists also subdivided this group. Those who were perma-

nently insane from birth were treated like children; their baptism was valid and effective. This result was tempered by the admonition that if they were not baptized as infants, the better practice was to postpone their baptism until they were in danger of death.[103] The evident idea was that their willing baptism was to be preferred; they might later receive their sanity. The case of those who were permanently insane but enjoyed "lucid intervals" offered proof of the wisdom of this preference. If they had been baptized while insane, they were nevertheless to be rebaptized if they sought baptism during one of those intervals.[104] This possibility thus provided another reason for postponing the baptism of the insane until time of peril or imminent death.

Those who became insane during the course of their lifetime and remained so were treated something like the sleeping. Assuming they had not already been baptized, if they had a prior inclination to baptism, they would validly receive the sacramental character by being baptized. If they had an inclination against being baptized, they would not. In what one must assume was the normal case, where they had had no inclination one way or the other, they received a valid baptism. In that situation they would not be permitted to "reclaim" their unbaptized state if they regained their sanity. The power of the sacrament, in other words, was great enough to prevail over a vacillating or a nonexistent intention. It was great enough in fact in all situations except when the insane person baptized had a positive inclination not to be baptized.

Coerced Baptisms

The most perplexing and famous problem was undoubtedly that raised by baptisms forcibly imposed upon the persons being baptized. It was very far from presenting a purely scholastic problem. One thinks of the large-scale conversions of pagan peoples as a result of the Germanic *Drang nach Osten*[105] and of the many questionable practices involving the native peoples in the New World.[106] Were these mass baptisms canonical? Or were they "extralegal actions" the church came reluctantly to accept as in the long-term best interests of all parties? The answer turns out to be neither exactly the one nor the other. The canonists dealt with the problem at length.

First, it was a canonical principle that no person should be forced to embrace the Christian faith. The canonical texts, both old (C. 23 q. 5 c. 3) and more recent (X 5.6.9), stated this principle without equivocation. Christianity was committed to a regime of charity and peace. Its founder had specifically directed that the sword be put to one side (Matt. 28:56). Not only was this avowedly pacific regime accepted as an integral part of the canon law (Dist. 45 cc. 1–8), but the canonists also recognized that coerced baptisms ultimately would be unavailing to the person involved. Faith involves the will. Coerced or feigned belief would be of no effect before God, who knows our hearts. Both ancient text and simple logic thus led the canonists to the conclusion that the only candidates who should present themselves at the sacred font were willing candidates. Freedom of choice was an integral part of the canon law of baptism.

But what if forcible baptism took place? The second basic assumption of the classical canon law was that baptism's validity did not depend on the candidate's faith. Infant baptism proved this. So there was a problem. A choice had to be made, and the choice that was made entailed distinguishing between different kinds of force. Under the canon law, if the force was absolute, the person baptized did not receive the "character" of baptism. The baptism was a nullity. If the force was conditional, however, the opposite result obtained. The baptism was valid. It also could not be renounced. In theory at least, the person would be compelled to adhere to the Christian religion. To take a concrete example, if a person was tied up and baptized without being given any choice, the baptism was invalid. If, on the other hand, the same person was tied up, told that he would be untied if he willingly accepted baptism, and he agreed, then his baptism was valid. Any mental reservation he had would be irrelevant in the external forum. The canonists brought this result into harmony with the requirement of free will in baptism by supposing that "coerced volition is still volition."[107] For a person to choose one of two alternatives because the other was worse did not mean that he had not willed the one he had chosen.

I suppose that most observers today will greet this "solution" with skepticism, if not ridicule. Of course, it might be said that treaties between states are sometimes negotiated at the barrel of a gun, and few think them invalid on that account. But perhaps that precedent will not carry the day in a more personal subject like baptism. The canon law rule looks very much like a piece of "instrumental thinking" designed rather to advance the material interests of the church than to live up to the commands of the founder of the Christian religion. The contrast with the law of marriage, where such "conditional force" made a marriage voidable, suggests the additional vice of inconsistency in the medieval church's position on the effects of coercion. It would be wasted effort on my part, I am sure, to attempt to change any reader's mind on this score. The contrast between the result and the commands of the gospel as we understand them, not to speak of our common sense evaluation of what coercion is, seems just too great.

However, it does seem appropriate to recognize that, at least as far as the contemporary evidence shows, an "instrumental" approach is not the way the canonists approached the problem. They did not justify the result by its long-term good effects. They put the matter instead in terms of the objective effect of the sacrament.[108] The classical Roman law *stipulatio* was valid even when made under duress (Inst. 4.13.1). The formal validity was what counted.[109] And so it was with Christian baptism. The sacrament of baptism had been ordained by God as the formal and effective means of securing men's salvation. It was a fact. To subject the objective effect of that sacrament to the vagaries of the shifting desires of individuals was something to be avoided. What God had instituted was not to be made dependent upon individual whim.[110] Still less was it to be mocked by pretending that it had not occurred.

There is something to be said for this institutional way of thinking about a legal problem. We have already seen something of the unhappy results that may follow from requiring that the minister of the sacrament "intend" to baptize in the same way the church intends. For the classical canonists, an objective approach was much to be preferred. Not only did the ancient traditions of the church favor it; the canonists also thought that the order of the church would be put into danger if the efficacy of the sacraments was constantly thrown into doubt by inquiring whether or not the actors had possessed a specific intent (Dist. 27 c. 7). In the case of coerced baptisms, that meant putting a heavy onus on the person claiming that the baptism had been invalid because of coercion.[111] Baptism carried out in accord with the objective criteria on the law had a presumptive validity, and the presumption was a strong one. Only "absolute" coercion would overcome it. In the history of the subject, that must have been a rare event.

Today, it all looks more like cynical calculation. However, the easy modern judgment is not just to those who formulated the classical canon law. Their assumptions were not ours. The canonists did not accord the same centrality to individual preference that is common coin today. The freedom of individual choice was not their starting point. Freedom was an important value in the canon law, and it could have important legal consequences, as will be shown in some detail in Chapter 9. But it was not the invariable first point of reference. It was not the one value to which others were readily to be sacrificed. Unless we take this point seriously, we shall not understand how the canonists could stress the necessity for free will in baptism and at the same time accept baptism's validity where the will of the "candidate" had been less than perfectly free.

CONCLUSION

Readers who have persevered to this point must have asked the question posed—and answered after a fashion—at the start of this chapter. That is: Would not the canon law have been better off had it left most questions involving baptism to the theologians, or better still, to the judgment of God? Some of the fine distinctions and the far-fetched arguments found in the canonical commentaries on this subject are off-putting, if they are not actually absurd. They seem to put the centrality of baptism distinctly into the shade. What had all this casuistry to do with welcoming a new member into the family of

Christians? What, for that matter, is its connection with the remission of sins?

This may be the correct reaction. I will not maintain the contrary. Nonetheless, the issues dealt with by the classical canon law keep coming up. In our own day a question has arisen that would have awakened the interest and perhaps the indignation of the medieval canonists. Some persons, not excluding the clergy, desire to remove gender bias from the Christian religion wherever they can. They seek to avoid words like "the Father" in referring to God. A few have conducted the baptismal rite in accordance with this desire, conferring the sacrament "in the name of the Creator, the Redeemer, and the Comforter," or some variant of these designedly "sex-neutral" words.

Is this a permissible practice? Do these words make a valid baptism? Should such persons be baptized again? How is the validity of such efforts to be decided except by looking at the inherited law on the subject? This practice raises the same difficulty as that of "equivalent words" dealt with by the medieval canonists. Their solution, it will be recalled, was to look at the substance of the words and to uphold the baptism if the words used were substantially the same in meaning as the Trinitarian formula. It has been widely assumed among modern canonists that when baptism is conferred in such a "degendered" form, rebaptism is the proper course.[112] In this case, however, the traditional solution actually gives some comfort to the advocates of "sex-neutral" language.

Only *some* comfort, it should be said. The medieval canonists would have condemned the experiment. They would have been quick to point out the difference between validity and legitimacy. According to their view, "it is not licit to vary the form handed down by the church," no matter how the question of formed validity might be settled.[113] Particularly was this so where the form handed down was taken from the Bible. The medieval canonists did not always agree on the several (and hard) questions involving the proper baptismal formula. But I think they would have been unanimous on this one.

9 Monastic Vows and Marriage Contracts: Freedom of Choice in the Canon Law

Marriage and monastic vocations—living institutions today—were important sources of canonical jurisdiction throughout the Middle Ages. The classical canon law had much to say about both. In fact, it exercised a decisive and comparable influence over the development of these in some respects quite dissimilar institutions, and that influence has not wholly dissipated with the passage of eight hundred years. The tribunals of the Catholic Church today decide thousands of cases every year involving annulment of marriages, and the law applied in these cases has links with the past. The pressures of modern life have also caused questions of monastic vows and monastic life more generally to come under the scrutiny of contemporary canon law, although for reasons to be explored in this chapter, the solutions are customarily found outside the judicial forum.

Long-term influence persists in the law of marriage and divorce, even for men and women who profess no allegiance to the Roman Church and whose ideas about the marriage bond are almost wholly at variance with those of the era in which the classical canon law was born. The history of matrimonial law has been so strongly marked by the law of the church that some of its present-day features are scarcely intelligible without an acquaintance with the subject's past. This is particularly true for those who live in countries that have taken over the English common law. English law adhered to the classical canon law's definition of valid marriage as a contract entered into by words of present consent, even after the Catholic Church had itself abandoned it. Where English law deviated from the canon law of marriage, the steps were short and hesitant.[1] The legal links to the canonical past become obvious to anyone who takes more than a cursory look at the subject.

Certainly connections exist between the present and the past in the subject of this chapter: the role of freedom in contracting marriage and in entering monastic life. Connections are not only possible; they may be useful. The notion that selection of one's partner in marriage, as with a "life choice" such as entry into a religious order, should be the product of free choice has been and continues to be a foundational idea in Western culture. It was an idea that found early statement in the canon law, and this during an age when the proposition that young men and women should possess that freedom was far from a reflexive or unqualified assumption. If the modern notion of freedom in marriage turns out to be the product of long development and not exactly identical to the notion as expressed in the writing of the canonists, still the roots are there. Modern scholars have drawn connections back to these roots, illuminating both the history of marriage and of monastic vows.[2] Here the attempt will be to examine and understand the concept and place of freedom of choice in both institutions and then to test the two (as the canonists themselves did) by looking at the situations in which they came into potential conflict.

MONASTIC VOWS

That entry into the monastic life should be a free act in both a positive and negative sense was a clear and established principle of the canon law. Men and women should have the liberty to undertake the life of a monastic house if they wished. They should also have the liberty not to undertake that life if they preferred. The first chapter selected for the Gregorian Decretals title dealing with entry into religious life stated this both generally and unequivocally: "Let no one be tonsured, unless [he be] of legitimate age and acting of his own free will" (X 3.31.1). Similarly, the very first chapter of the title in the Gregorian Decretals dealing with transactions voidable because of coercion took up the situation of a woman who had allegedly taken the veil only under threat of death (X 1.40.1). The papal decretal held that she was free to leave the nunnery and to contract marriage if her vow had been the product of force and fear. Gratian's *Decretum* had stated this same principle: "Let no one be subjected to monastic discipline unwillingly" (C. 20 q. 3 c. 4). The contrast with the law involving ordinary oaths, examined in Chapter 6, is particularly notable here. Oaths taken under most forms of coercion were enforceable, though subject to relaxation and reformation under certain conditions (X 2.24.8, 15). Monastic vows were different. Although it was accepted as incontrovertible among the canonists that the monastic life was a spiritual good, perhaps the greatest of spiritual goods, the canonists regarded it as truly meritorious only if freely undertaken.[3]

The Requirement of Deliberation

The concern for unconstrained choice was also an operative principle in the creation of barriers to entering the religious life. Requiring that the monk or nun have reached the age of majority before assuming the monastic habit was one expression of the concern.[4] An examination, conducted privately by the bishop or his delegate, into the strength and sincerity of the desires of the aspirant to monastic life was another.[5] The canonists stressed the necessity for preparation. They found inspiration for this in the Bible itself. What man, wishing to build a tower, does not first count the cost so that he may know "whether he have sufficient to finish it?" (Luke 14:28). So, they said, must aspirants for the cloister count the cost of their choice.[6] Aspirants would be called upon, as we shall see, to finish what they had begun. Sufficient spiritual preparation and passage through obstacles of more than a purely formal character worked toward preserving the monastic aspirant's full freedom of choice.

Causa 17 of Gratian's *Decretum* contained a nice case in which this principle of freedom of choice came dramatically into play. "A certain priest, while gravely ill, vowed to become a monk and renounced his church and benefice." Later he recovered and changed his mind. The question was whether he should be compelled to fulfill the laudable intention he had undertaken while standing in anticipation of death, or whether he might instead retake his prior position in the world. Gratian used the *quaestio* to develop a distinction between a full monastic profession and lesser expressions of intent. He did not suggest that all acts induced by fear of death were invalid or even inherently suspect. He did not suggest that no person could be compelled to fulfill a vow taken while laboring under turbulence of mind. But he did take the position that *this* man would not be compelled to fulfill *this* vow. Even though he had formed a fixed intention to assume the monastic habit, expressed that intention openly, and taken concrete steps to cut his ties to the world, the priest had nonetheless not made a final choice. He was therefore free to return to his former station. "It is one thing to conceive a purpose in one's heart and to speak it with one's lips," Gratian wrote. "It is another thing to take upon one's person the full weight of a vow."[7] The priest involved in the case might have been guilty of sin in the sight of God. He had forsaken his expressed purpose to enter the better realm of the cloister. In the world, however, he would not be required to fulfill that vow.

Freedom of Choice

An affirmative sort of freedom, allowing all men and women to enter religious life, also found expression in the canonical texts and in the commentaries on them.[8] Slaves were capable of assuming monastic vows. So were minors of sufficient age, even children under *patria potestas* who were acting against their father's wishes. The same held for debtors, even those whose creditors insisted that they remain in the world to work off their debts. In each of these cases the canon law also recognized values other than the freedom of the individual. In each, the freedom to enter monastic life was limited in some way. The slave must seek the consent of his master; the son's absence must not leave his family destitute; the debtor must make a *cessio bonorum* in favor of his creditors. But if these legitimate interests were satisfied, the canon law held that no human law might stand between the willing aspirant and monastic life.

A second example, one that reveals the depth of the principle, again comes from the *Decretum*. A bishop refused to release a cleric subject to him who desired to enter a religious order (C. 19 q. 2). In support of his refusal, the bishop cited an ancient canon of the church holding that no one should accept (*suscipere*) a cleric against the will of his bishop (C. 19 q. 2 c. 1). Despite the canon's apparently mandatory nature, Gratian discovered a reason for requiring this bishop to give his permission: the ancient canon should be read as containing the implied exception: "unless he shall wish to pass to a higher life." The text was meant to restrain clergymen from leaving the jurisdiction of their bishops; it was designed to restrain wrongdoing and license. It was valid so far as it went. But it should not be extended further than its purpose dictated. There was another law, a private law written by the Holy Spirit on men's hearts. This man who desired to ascend to the higher monastic life was being led by this second law. It came from the Holy Spirit, and no bishop might presume to stand in its way. "Where the Spirit of God is, there is liberty," and "if you are led by the spirit of God, you do not remain under the law" (C. 19 q. 2 c. 2).[9] This principle of liberty was also at hand. Indeed, it was there to be uncovered in the Gospels themselves (e.g., Gal. 5:1–6), and the *Decretum* applied its reasoning in the cause of establishing the freedom to undertake a monastic profession.[10]

Limitations to Freedom of Choice

Of course there was another side, and any account of the canon law must take notice of it. This canonical freedom was the freedom to *choose* entry into monastic life. It was not the freedom to *leave* monastic life once the choice to enter had been made. The *glossa ordinaria* put this succinctly, "To make a vow is a matter of the will; to fulfill one is a matter of necessity."[11] We are not dealing with that sort of freedom, often assumed to be inherent in the concept of liberty and certainly more congenial today, which allows a person to change his mind and to put aside an obligation that has become irksome or a cause for regret. According to the canon law's rules, a monk who deserted his monastic house could be recalled to it.[12] He would be excommunicated, or worse, if he refused (X 3.31.15, 24). Pope Boniface VIII made putting aside a monastic habit cause for ipso facto excommunication (Sext. 3.24.2). A decretal of Pope Honorius III authorized "strict confinement" of any vagrant monk who first ignored the "medicinal" sanction of excommunication and remained obstinately in the world (X 5.9.5). Later canonical opinion even sanctioned condemning such vagrant monks to service in the galleys.[13]

This was not just clerical wishful thinking. In England, the abbot or prior of a religious house that a monk had deserted could bring a personal action in an ecclesiastical court to recall an apostate religious to the cloister.[14] If this failed, he also had the right to secure a royal writ *De apostata capiendo* in order to bring about the confinement envisioned in Honorius III's decretal. Under English common law, a writ was available as a matter of course to religious superiors, directing the sheriff to seize the person of an apostate monk. The sheriff restored the apostate physically to the hands of the abbot or his agent for suitable and presumably canonical treatment.[15] In making this writ available to the church, the English government was following the lead of the canon law itself. It was an example of cooperation between church and state to be examined more closely in Chapter 13. Nothing about the procedure was regarded as inimical to the principles of sound religion or the ends of good government.

It is worthy of note, and also revealing of the spirit of the canon law, that one special kind of freedom to take leave of a monastic house did exist. It was a freedom even fully professed monks and nuns had an unconstrained right to exercise. It was, however, a right only to move from a house of laxer to a house of stricter monastic observance (X 3.31.18). Such a move toward a more perfect and austere life was presumed to be the fruit of the Holy Spirit, and an exception was made to permit it. To sanction movement in the opposite direction—toward laxer observance of the monastic rule or toward no observance at all—was no part of a canonical notion of the workings of the Holy Spirit. Jesus himself had said that "no man, having put his hand to the plough, and looking back, is fit for the Kingdom of God" (Luke 9:62). For the canonists this text stood as a condemnation of monastic backsliding.[16] The Council of Trent expressly condemned allowing monks to yield to the temptation.[17]

Practical Problems

What, however, should happen if a professed monk could not bear the rigors of monastic life? What if cloistered life had become so difficult for him that he had become a burden to a particular monastic house and an annoyance to its inhabitants? The exigencies of daily life in such circumstances called out for a workable solution; in fact, the venerable monastic Rule of St. Benedict expressly envisioned that this sad situation would occur.[18] Separation—call it apostasy or call it something more pleasant—was bound to happen. When it did, what should the law's reaction be? There were choices. It was always possible to suppose that the vagrant or expelled monk was still bound by the monastic rule and that he could be recalled to this duty. Some long-lasting canonical authority stood in support of this view, and it carried concrete practical and not wholly impossible consequences along with it.[19] But this could never be a fully satisfactory solution, particularly if the errant monk's return was unthinkable as a practical matter and if he wished insofar as possible to conform his behavior to the church's law. Providing for the eventuality in some more realistic fashion became a matter of necessity.

This necessity made for a very painful choice nonetheless. The professed monk or nun had made a solemn vow to God to do that which was most pleasing in God's sight. The earliest decretalists were entirely logical in holding that no contrary desire and no earthly power, not even that of the apostolic see, could legitimately take away the effects of that vow.[20] A decretal of Innocent III in fact so stated and did so in uncompromising terms (X 3.35.6).[21] Even papal plenitude of power was not ample enough to make an exception. Where a monk had proved incorrigible, there was strong canonical opinion that the appropriate remedy was imprisonment and penance within the monastic house or, at worst, dismissal to another house of equivalent or stricter status, never dismissal into the world, where his vows might soon and easily be forgotten (X 3.31.24).[22]

In time, however, the common opinion among the canonists moved away from this rigorist position. Already in the thirteenth century, religious vows began to be treated as the creatures of positive law and therefore subject to the relaxing power of the church. The plenitude of papal power came to be more fully understood, or at any rate more fully exploited, in the interests of reaching a realistic solution. Perhaps Innocent III's decretal had meant only that papal power *should not* extend to dispensation from monastic vows, not that it *could not*.[23] Perhaps it really proved the existence of the dispensing power. Once this process had occurred, monastic vows could be read as containing an implied condition that would permit their relaxation by means of papal dispensation. That same fullness of power, residing in the papacy and meant to be exercised for the good of the whole church, could then provide for the formal dismissal even of those who had made solemn religious professions.[24]

An elaborate and somewhat disputatious system of jurisprudence dealing with the relaxation of monastic vows grew up to deal with it.[25] In it one finds development of legal possibilities that went with this fuller willingness to accept exclaustration. Monastic vows could be read as containing an unspoken limitation: "unless the church shall dispense." Alternatively, realists might conclude that "the pope [could] by the plenitude of his power turn a monk into a nonmonk."[26] Thus were the legal rules brought into conformity with the exigencies of monastic life. Ancient canonical enactments, to the effect that the monastic life was the highest good and not to be put aside, would long be repeated. But it began to be said among the canonists that the old canons had not necessarily meant that there were no *other* goods. Indeed, there were goods besides the monastic vocation that the church could also recognize and encourage.[27] It became gradually accepted that, where there was great and just cause, papal power was sufficient to grant the relaxation even of solemn monastic vows.[28] The power of forgiveness (2 Cor. 2:10) or absolution (Matt. 18:18) resided in the church, to be used for just such purposes. Today the process has become a matter of routine. The indult of exclaustration is a familiar part of monastic life.[29] It can be dealt with as an administrative matter, outside the judicial forum. Freedom of choice in leaving monastic life, first recognized grudgingly and only as a matter of necessity, came in time to be available, arguably as a matter of right, certainly as a matter of course.

MARRIAGE CONTRACTS

The law of marriage contained several parallels with the law that regulated the profession of monks and nuns. It also contained significant differences. One of the closest parallels is that being dealt with here, freedom in entering into a marriage. This was an oft stated principle of the law of the church, and it underlay several of the canonical rules regulating marriage practice. "Marriages should be free" (X 4.1.29). "No one is to be compelled to marry" (C. 31 q. 2 c. 1). Commentators echoed the theme. "Matrimony should be freely contracted."[30] "Marriage should be free from all coercion."[31] No canonist would have opposed these as statements of a general, and important, matter of canonical principle.

This principle brought concrete consequences in its train. For instance, just as in the case of monastic profession, a marriage contract entered into under compulsion did not bind the party who had been compelled to make it. Indeed, the standard was the same. If the force threatened had been sufficient to sway the will of a "constant man," the marriage could lawfully be disavowed once the party had escaped from the threat.[32] Consent to marriage must be unfeigned and unconstrained.[33] There was a rule of quite respectable pedigree within the traditions of the canon law, as there was in the Roman law,[34] declaring that "coerced consent is still consent."[35] Its application in the law of baptism was noted in Chapter 8. But this rule was not thought applicable to marriage. In marriage, "direct or spontaneous consent" was ever required.[36]

Many subsidiary rules that formed part of the canon law also worked to protect both the freedom to marry and the freedom not to marry. For instance, children were entitled to escape any marriage they had entered into below the age of puberty if they reclaimed against it once they reached that age. Parents were not forbidden to cause their children to contract such unions,[37] but they were prevented from making those marriages binding upon their children once the child had reached an age where he or she had a mind of his or her own. Similarly a clause in such a marriage contract requiring the payment of a penalty if the child did reclaim was found inconsistent with the requirement of freedom in marriage (X 4.1.29). The penalty need not be paid. The origins of the modern rule (or at least a parallel with it) to the effect that a condition in a bequest is void if it prohibits the legatee from marrying is found also in the *ius commune*.[38]

Informality and Freedom in Contracting Marriage

The most remarkable expression of the importance of freedom in marriage—and by far the most remarked upon by modern scholars—lay in the freedom allowed ordinary people to enter marriage. The canon law made contracting marriage simple, very simple. To do so required no license from church or state. It required no consent by parents on either side, nor any from a person's feudal lord. Even serfs or slaves were free to enter marriage without the consent of their masters.[39] Medieval marriage required neither public ceremony nor any sort of exchange of gifts. All that the canons required was the exchange of words of present consent between two persons otherwise competent to marry. Thus, if a man said to a woman, "I take thee N. as my lawful wife," and she answered with equivalent words, they were married. These words of present consent were enough to create a valid and binding union between them.

Strictly speaking, not even the presence of witnesses was required to make this exchange of words a binding union, although it would always have been difficult to prove that the words had been exchanged if there had been no one else in attendance to hear them. It was also unnecessary that the spoken words be followed by consummation. The marriage between Joseph and the Virgin Mary had been one of perpetual chastity, according to Catholic teaching. It was beyond doubting that this union had been a complete marriage. Consent alone must therefore have made the marriage in this central biblical example, and it was concluded that the result could not be otherwise with lesser, ordinary unions. Under the classical canon law, therefore, marriage became an act of the will in the fullest sense of the term.[40] All that it required was an open expression of present volition.

This regime was essentially the product of a choice made in the twelfth century. Though long bruited in the schools, it was established in a decretal of Pope Alexander III (X 4.4.3). Requiring no more than exchange of words of present consent was not a part of the legacy of Christian antiquity, and there were precedents in canonical traditions that would have authorized a slightly more restrictive system.[41] Gratian's *Decretum*, for example, had adopted an alternative. A possibility, therefore, is that the reason for adopting this remarkable regime was precisely to encourage freedom in the selection of marriage partners.[42] John Noonan once described the system, at least in canonical aspiration, as "a giant democracy in which everyone might marry anyone."[43] The law allowed young men and women to enter into marriages free from effective control exercised by their relatives or their lords. By omitting any requirement of consent, ceremony, or consummation, the law permitted young people to make decisions for themselves, and this occurred in a society where such free choice was by no means accepted as a matter of course.

The argument that this was a goal of the law has the merit of plausibility. The amplitude allowed to free choice in the canon law of marriage seems obvious. One might think of Shakespeare's Romeo and Juliet. The canon law on this subject seems almost to have been designed for their convenience. Had their marriage required banns or a public ceremony, to say nothing of parental consent, they would never have come together in any way but emotionally and (probably) physically. They were able to marry because of the canon law's rule that their consent alone constituted a true marriage.

It is a harder question, however, to know whether this sort of encouragement of matrimonial freedom was in fact the *purpose* of the canonical regime. About this question there has been legitimate doubt. There is little direct evidence to show that the men who formulated the canon law of marriage were consciously trying to promote freedom of action on the part of adolescents, and there is some to show that they also wished to discourage children from disobeying their parents. Unions like those of Romeo and Juliet were valid under the canon law, but they were treated as clandestine. Participants in them could be punished. It might reasonably be asserted, therefore, that a social policy of matrimonial freedom was not at all what the canonists had in mind.[44] At least it was not in the forefront of their minds. It is hard to dispute, however, that this was a result of the marriage law they created, and it is not illogical to think that they realized what they were doing.

Limitations to Freedom of Choice

Just as was the case with monastic vows, the canonical preference for freedom of choice in marriage did not extend to its dissolution. Once one had made the choice of a marriage partner, that act pretty much exhausted the possibilities. Christian marriage was indissoluble. Whether this was true of marriages between non-Christians was long the subject of debate among theologians and canonists.[45] It had not been true in Roman law, and everyone recognized that indissolubility was not a feature of marriages in the Old Testament. Obviously the institution of marriage could coexist with the possibility of divorce. However, this was not so with a Christian marriage. It symbolized the unbreakable union between Christ and the church, and its dissolution had been condemned in so many words by dominical statement (Matt. 19:9). Therefore, the canon law held that "the effect of marriage once contracted by the faithful, is dissolved by nothing except death, which loosens all things." Moreover, this marital union continued, "even if the other spouse becomes a heretic, goes blind, becomes a leper, or suffers any other kind of horror."[46] "Whither thou goest" was not only a poetic expression of love in the eyes of the canon law. It could be something like an affirmative duty.[47]

It has occasionally been suggested that the canonical impediments, particularly those relating to consanguinity and affinity, provided a "loophole" or "escape hatch" through which any seriously unhappily married man or woman could exit.[48] For example, the canon law prohibited all persons descended by blood from the same great-great grandfather to marry, and similar prohibitions obtained if one counted down from persons related by affinity, that is, by marriage. There were several other such far-reaching prohibitions, and if one of them could be discovered, the marriage in which the prohibition had been violated would be treated as having been void from its inception. The conclusion has seemed logically to follow that energetic genealogical research coupled with legal ingenuity would almost always have produced sufficient grounds for the annulment of a marriage.

The evidence of actual court practice so far uncovered, however, does not support this seemingly compelling conclusion.[49] Court records from the Middle Ages produce many fewer cases in which such divorces occurred than expected. Admittedly the historical record contains spectacular examples of divorce by the mighty on grounds of consanguinity and affinity, and no doubt collusive divorces must also have occasionally taken place at lower levels of society. But the records of ordinary practice suggest that it would be wrong to generalize on the basis of the spectacular case.[50] The dangers of "history by anecdote" are well illustrated by the history of the law of marriage. It appears that these impediments did not become a common, easy means of exit for the seriously unhappy or the cynical.

Judicial Separations

One must not leave the subject without taking account of the one "escape route" that did exist under the canon law. That was divorce *a mensa et thoro*, what we call a judicial separation. It did not break the marital bond. That is, it did not enable the parties to remarry. It did allow them to live apart and to do so in conscientious conformity with the law. The medieval law recognized three grounds for this sort of separation: adultery, heresy, or cruelty. If a woman could show that her husband had committed adultery or that he had been guilty of violence toward her, she could secure a judicial declaration permitting them to live apart. We do not yet know a great deal about the frequency with which men and women took advantage of this part of the canon law of marriage. But that it was used to some extent is clear enough, and when thinking about the place of freedom in the canon law, it is certainly important to note its existence. As was true in the case of apostate monks and nuns, some room for maneuver had to be left for partners to unhappy unions.[51] Separation without legal grounds the canon law did not admit, at least formally. But there are inevitable, practical limits to the church's treatment of marriage as a true and unbreakable union, and at this point some scope for freedom of escape was allowed.

One ought also to take note of the "escape route" that did *not* exist in the canon law. That is the route of dispensation. The possibilities parallel to the case of monastic vows seem obvious. The canon law moved toward mitigating the hardship caused by mistaken choice in monastic life by expanding the availability of dispensations from the vows that tied monks and nuns unwillingly to that life. One coming from outside the system might suppose that the same thing would very likely have occurred in the law of marriage. However, it did not. Dispensations played a part in the law of marriage—in dispensing from prohibited degrees of affinity and consanguinity, and (after considerable hesitation) in cases in which a marriage had not been consummated.[52] But a validly contracted though unhappy union could not be escaped through papal dispensation.[53]

When relaxation from the strict standards of the classical canon law came, as it has come with a vengeance in the twentieth century, that relaxation has occurred through an expanded notion of the nature of consent necessary to create an indissoluble marriage.[54] A sophisticated kind of emotional maturity is required before either spouse can enter into a union that will be treated as indissoluble under the present-day canon law of the Catholic Church. The marriage of Romeo and Juliet would probably have been subject to annulment, even had they been a little older and their parish priest been present. On the elegance and wisdom of this result opinions differ. It is no part of the purpose of this volume to enter into the dispute. It may be said, however, that for many a young couple today, a contemporary canonical treatise on the kind of maturity required to enter into a valid marriage would make for some very sobering reading.[55]

CONFLICTS BETWEEN MARRIAGE AND MONASTIC VOWS

All of the above may be accurate enough and show something of the canon law's approach to an important aspect of human life. It may even be illuminating about the canon law's place in the development of the Western ideal of freedom of choice. But in order to penetrate a little further into the canon law's interior, we ought also to look at cases of conflict—that is, to examine situations in which the two freedoms came into conflict with each other. Such situations are easy to envision and no harder to state: the married person who wishes to enter a religious order, and the member of a religious order who wishes to marry. Could either succeed? It may seem that the answer is obvious in both situations and that it must be in the negative. Neither could. But that obvious answer turns out not to be the absolutely correct answer in the canon law. At least it is not the full answer. The full answer is more interesting and also somewhat more revealing about the common assumptions and the directions to be taken by the men who framed the canon law.

Monastic Vows and Subsequent Marriage

Gratian put the following case in *Causa* 27: A certain man, after having made a vow of chastity, espoused a woman. This woman later renounced this union and joined herself in marriage with a second man. The first man then sought to get her back. Two legal questions arose. First, may those who have made a vow that excludes marriage nevertheless enter into marriage? Second, is it lawful for a person who is espoused to one person to leave that person and marry another? Again, it would seem that the answer to both these questions must be a negative answer under the Christian dispensation. However, in Gratian's hands (and in the classical canon law) the answers to these questions turned out to be far from obvious.

The first *quaestio* began with a series of authorities suggesting that the obvious, negative answer was also the correct answer. Any person who, having taken a vow of chastity, dared to render it a nullity by passing to secular nuptials was to be sequestered from the Christian communion and denied communication with the faithful (C. 27 q. 1 c. 1). If an adulterer was rightfully punished for sexual congress with another man or woman, how much more deserving of punishment was the person who violated a vow of chastity by entering into a contract of marriage? Such a person would have violated not simply an earthly vow but also a heavenly one made to Christ himself. Truly it was such a person that St. Paul had in mind when he spoke of those who were deserving of "damnation, because they have cast off their first faith" (1 Tim. 5:12). And again, if a husband naturally took up his sword upon finding his espoused in the arms of another man, how much more readily would Christ wield a spiritual sword if he found someone espoused to him languishing in the arms of another (C. 27 q. 1 c. 4)?

So Gratian continued through forty authorities. Some of them were of remarkable strictness. Any man who knowingly married a woman vowed to the religious life was to be deprived of the right ever to marry and to be condemned to lifelong penance (C. 27 q. 1 c. 13). Bishops who might be tempted to sanction marriages of monks and nuns out of human sympathy were themselves to be condemned (C. 27 q. 1 c. 2). Pope Gregory the Great had so written to the missionary bishop St. Boniface, citing the psalmist's praise for the man who "should wash his feet in the blood of the wicked." Over such a man would the righteous rejoice (Ps. 57:11). And so must a Christian bishop do if he were to merit a place in God's kingdom.

Readers coming fresh to the historical record sometimes wonder at the apparent pleasure medieval bishops took in the misfortunes of their enemies. Readers may react with amazement, even horror, at the vindictiveness with which supposedly saintly men carried out the task of chastisement. If so, it is right also to recall that they lived under the shadow of texts such as this one from the pen of Gregory the Great. They assumed that God would hold them responsible if they failed in the tasks appointed to them. Those tasks included scattering the wicked. Well might they exult in successful results. They were fulfilling the responsibility God had appointed to them. Some evils, of course, could not be rooted out. But where they could, the bishop must neither be ashamed to act nor blush at the result. He could in fact rejoice.

After canon 40, Gratian seemed to reverse directions. He did so, however, without endorsing the opposite and "laxist" position. He did so by distinguishing between different vows, beginning with three contrary authorities. The first was a long excerpt from St. Augustine's *De bono viduitatis* (C. 27 q. 1 c. 41). It extolled marriage as a service and solace to all people and as a remedy for their infirmity. Continence was to be preferred, but not every Christian could bear that state, and marriage was not to be despised because something else was better. Augustine took the argument further by distinguishing between marriages with Christ (monastic vows) and ordinary marriages. Reasoning that they were not necessarily identical in their effects, he concluded that the person who broke a monastic vow by marrying another did not thereby become an adulterer, as would have been true had the monastic vow constituted marriage in the normal sense of the word. Although that person sinned in breaking the vow, therefore, he did not enter into the subsequent earthly marriage invalidly, as would of course have been the case had he been a true adulterer. The other two canons reached the same conclusion in shorter space: that the marriage of the person who had taken a vow of continence was a wrong but that it was not invalid. The couple were not to be separated.

Had Gratian simply counted his authorities, he would have had to answer that the person who married after having taken a vow of chastity should be separated from his spouse. He did give that answer where the person had made a full monastic profession, but this was not his answer where the vow had stopped short of a solemn commitment. As in *Causa* 17, Gratian distinguished between cases in which the person involved had made a monastic profession and cases in which there had been only what the canon law would come to describe as a "simple" or "preliminary" vow. Something like the idea of a monastic novitiate was forecast in the distinction. Only where there had been a deliberate and formal handing over of a person's life to monastic profession would the monk or nun be compelled to return to the monastic life he or she had undertaken. If it was simply a question of a vow of chastity, the person would be admitted to penance and allowed to remain with the partner in human marriage.

Many of the authorities Gratian cited spoke of vows of chastity only in general terms. This was natural, since the life devoted to Christian chastity had been by no means confined to organized monasteries during the early Middle Ages and since professions within religious communities were not regularized to the extent they would later come to be. However, drawing a distinction was useful. If all the first forty authorities in the *Decretum* were read to refer to full monastic professions and the three that permitted the marriage to stand were read to refer to simple vows, then there was no contradiction between them. This was the path taken by Gratian and the canonists who commented on his texts. "If the persons have vowed simply, they are to be permitted to contract marriage, so that a greater evil [than breach of the vow] might be avoided."[56]

Thus the vow made to God became what the canon law would come to denominate a prohibitive rather than a diriment impediment. That meant that it was one that rendered a marriage unlawful and subjected the participants to canonical chastisement but did not render the marriage invalid. This decision was given formal expression by Pope Boniface VIII (Sext. 3.15.1). He added two requirements: the vow must be a profession to live according to a monastic rule, not simply a vow of chastity, and it must be taken within an order approved by the apostolic see. Practically speaking, then, it was entirely proper to seek to dissuade men and women who had made such simple vows from entering into a contract of marriage, but it was not permissible to excommunicate them if they persisted. Hostiensis suggested that if a cleric was asked whether such a marriage would be valid, he must say nothing at all. To assert its invalidity would be a lie, but to assert its validity would be an encouragement to sin.[57]

Was this a reasonable solution? It certainly contained some strange things, but overall it seems sensible enough, and medieval court records do show it being put into practice.[58] It preserved freedom of choice up to the point where a solemn monastic profession had occurred. There would be a time for repentance. Whether one admires

Gratian's artful reconciliation of authorities in reaching the result or finds it distasteful is perhaps besides the point. Entirely typical of his method, this method of reconciling texts is what allowed him to proceed. The modern reader will, of course, admire the solution more because it made sense in terms of the realities of monastic life than because it skillfully harmonized the authorities. Gratian facilitated the division of the beginning years of monastic profession into separate stages, in which the lifetime commitment became the final step of solemn profession and in which the preliminary or simple vows left open the possibility of a change of mind. Of course it would be going beyond the evidence, and perhaps quite wrong, to regard such a "policy approach" as the driving force behind Gratian's efforts. He wrote not a single word about policy as a reason for his solution, and he said little about its social consequences.

Marriage and Subsequent Monastic Vows

At least in what they committed to paper, few medieval canonists doubted that monastic life was a higher calling than married life. That opinion was common coin of the time. But did it follow that a married man or woman was free to choose that higher life? A monk or nun had the right freely to choose a stricter, and therefore higher, monastic order. Could married couples do the same? Around this question a considerable body of law grew up. Judging by the attention devoted to it in the Decretals, this must have been a more than purely a theoretical question in the early thirteenth century.[59] The call to the cloister was heard by more than a few men and women, and sometimes that call grew louder as they grew older. The example of Abelard and Héloïse also comes to mind.

The canon law's starting point we have already taken up. No one was free to leave a marriage once he or she had freely entered into it. Man and wife became one flesh, and that union was not to be severed.[60] Spouses did not have power over their own bodies; each had ceded that power to the other.[61] Even the limited remedy of separation *a mensa et thoro* was not available without good cause, and mutual consent was not regarded as a cause that was good enough. The evident and logical

conclusion about the question was that if a man entered a religious
order without his wife's consent, he could be compelled to return to
her (C. 27 q. 2 c. 21). This was stated expressly in the *Decretum* and in
the Decretals. The same result was reached even where the wife had
actually given her consent to his monastic profession. He was to be recalled from the monastery and returned to her (X 3.32.1). The answer
did not depend upon the departing spouse's sex. Where it was the
woman who had entered the religious order, the husband had the
power to "reclaim" her. For these purposes at least, the canon law
treated the rights of husband and wife as fully reciprocal.

There were two, or perhaps three, exceptions to this stern regime.
The first was opened for the case of the unconsummated marriage.
We have already examined the canon law's definition of marriage as
consisting solely in the exchange of words of present consent. That
definition was not, however, carried to the point where consummated
and unconsummated unions were treated alike for all purposes. Here
was one example where a distinction was drawn. If husband and wife
had not become "one flesh," then either was free to enter a monastic
order (X 3.32.2). No consent of the other partner was required; in fact,
that spouse was free to contract another marriage.

The second exception was opened for couples who had consummated their marriage when both wished to enter religious life. If they
both consented, and both abandoned the world for the cloister, the
canon law approved of their choice. This had to be a joint endeavor,
however. The consent of one spouse to allow the other to enter monastic life was not in itself enough. Each had separately to undertake the
religious profession or else to take a vow of personal chastity. And the
latter sufficed only in the case of an elderly spouse not in danger of
falling prey to incontinence. It was only where the spouse was *senex et
non suspectus* that a vow of chastity was sufficient to allow him or her
to live quietly at home (X 3.32.4). Each of these two qualities was essential for relaxation of the rule requiring mutual monastic professions. Both the *old* person who *was* suspect and likely to fall into sin
and the *young* person who *was not* suspect were disqualified from taking advantage of this "extension" to the exception. To make sure that
the requirements were met, episcopal consent was to be sought (C. 27

q. 2 c. 23),[62] although to precisely which part of the process it had to attach became a matter of dispute among the *doctores*.[63]

The third possibility, perhaps not so much an exception as an application of the principle of estoppel or of another part of the canon
law, occurred when one spouse committed adultery. In those circumstances, the innocent spouse was permitted to undertake monastic
vows, and the guilty spouse was not entitled to "reclaim" the innocent party. Since adultery was a cause for separation *a mensa et thoro*,
this result followed naturally enough. But what about the case in
which the monastic profession came first, and the spouse remaining
in the world in fact succumbed to sexual incontinence? Here the law
distinguished. If the adulterous spouse had given license for the
other's profession, he or she was to be compelled to enter a monastery
after having committed adultery (X 3.32.8). If, however, the adulterous spouse had not given the license, then he or she simply lost the
right to recall the innocent spouse back from the higher, monastic
calling.[64] This latter case was treated as if the adultery had come first;
it was something like *nunc pro tunc*.

Some Special Problems

So much for the rudiments of the law designed to deal with conflicts
between monastic vows and marriage. Admittedly these are only the
rudiments. There was more to the classical canon law on this subject,
and it is a source of legitimate wonder that so much law grew up
around this situation—so many limitations, subtleties, and controversies. We might assume that omissions in the law and further
conflicts between the two forms of life could best be dealt with by
leaving them to the discretion of the officials involved. This, however, was not the assumption of the classical canon law. Right from
the start, and increasingly as the law was subjected to greater systematic thought in the centuries after its formulation, the canonists assumed that legal solutions should be worked out. A small sample of
two such questions will illustrate something of what it was like. The
one comes from the writing of the canonists, the other from the Decretals themselves.

The first example was raised by this question: At what age did a person become *senex*, so that he or she could safely remain in the world when that person's spouse entered monastic life? Readers may recall that if either spouse was young or "in peril of incontinence," the canon law required him or her to enter a monastery before the other could lawfully take that step. But how old was *senex*? A simple question, it would seem. The legislator should establish a specific age. But this had not happened, and the question turned out to be anything but simple in the hands of the canonists who took it up during the sixteenth century. The texts of the canon law itself, and indeed the medieval commentators, had left the matter unresolved and in fact undiscussed. Thomas Sanchez, the great sixteenth-century Spanish writer on the law of marriage, regarded it as a *potissima difficultas*. He surveyed prior treatments and found "nothing among the older authorities discussing it."[65] That could not be a satisfactory situation.

There were, however, several possibilities for resolving it, and Sanchez canvassed them.[66] The easiest was to borrow the age from another area of the law; he suggested the age of sixty, at which men were normally excused from fasting. Another was to hit upon that age at which they commonly lost interest in sexual relations, a sensible choice in light of the question involved but difficult to determine as a matter of rule. A third was to treat it as a question of fact and allow the age to vary with the particular man or woman involved, since it was undeniable that not all persons grew old at the same rate. The evident difficulty with this sensible solution was that it could not be applied without an individual determination of fact. A fourth possibility, which avoided that particular problem, was to leave the matter to local custom. There was an additional question of whether the age should be the same for men and women. At the end of a discussion that could without exaggeration be described as exhaustive, Sanchez embraced the first of these four as the "more probable" opinion, though he admitted that it was "speculative." The truth is that there was no agreed-upon answer.

The second example of the complex character of the canon law on this subject was raised by this case: a man entered a monastery without his wife's consent. She "reclaimed" him from it and later died.

After her death, could the man be recalled to the monastery and required to fulfill the vows he had taken upon entering (X 3.32.3)? Another decretal raised the same question in a different setting: a woman entered monastic life believing her spouse to be dead. She was released from the cloister upon learning that he had not in fact died. Then he did die. At that point, could she be compelled to return to the monastic life she had once freely chosen (X 3.32.12)? The canonical answer to this dilemma was that the surviving spouse could not be compelled to return to the monastic life, but neither should the spouse remarry.

This was not a compromise designed to give something, but not too much, to the surviving spouse. The monastic vow of the surviving spouses could not be specifically enforced in these cases because, as we have seen, they had had no power to make it at the time they did. They might therefore be urged, but they could not be compelled, to fulfill the vow by returning to the monastery.[67] Remarriage was prohibited to them, however, because it was held that their monastic vows had not been wholly without effect. They had thereby put it out of their own power to "exact the matrimonial debt," as the canonists put it.[68] Although one spouse could not, by a vow of continence, prejudice the right of the other to exact this debt, he could undoubtedly do so as to his own right. No person may by his act diminish the property of another, but he is entirely free to give up his own. A vow of chastity was thus invalid in part and valid in part, and since the vow that required the surviving spouse to maintain his own chastity was the valid part, he could not lawfully remarry someone else.

In human terms, the conclusion reached at the end of this line of reasoning cannot be called an altogether happy one. The canonists went on to discuss what should happen if the surviving spouse *did* in fact remarry. On this point there were three possible opinions, but we shall not follow them any further.[69] Nor shall we follow the path of distinction and dispensation as a way out of this morass. Perhaps we have already followed them further than is profitable. Let us look back instead at the subject with which we began this chapter: the question of freedom in simple marriage contracts. There is a little more to be said about it.

REVERENTIAL FEAR

That little more concerns the potential for development that existed within the medieval canon law. It is important that this point be made, or in any event raised, because without it we will have an incomplete appreciation for the capacity for growth and change that has existed within the canon law. This is something like what Harold Berman has described as the "ongoing character" of the Western legal tradition.[70] It is a way of stressing the canon law's adaptability to changed circumstances and changed patterns of thought, all the while remaining connected with its past.

Although we have seen several examples in which strong statements of freedom of choice were qualified by other canonical principles and other rules of law, it remains true that the statements were there. Some of them did not have to await more recent times before they produced more sophisticated thought about the nature of consent and also results that would augment the freedom of choice for men and women in the world. One of the clearest examples is the concept of reverential fear.

The canonical standard for determining whether or not a marriage or a monastic profession could be undone because of coercion was whether or not the coercion applied had been sufficient to sway the will of a "constant" man or woman.[71] This was the same standard examined in connection with sworn contracts examined in Chapter 6. What exactly did it come to? Mostly the canonists left decision of the question to judicial discretion in actual cases. So many variables legitimately counted in determining whether or not the test of constancy had been met that although it was quite possible to list them, it was not possible to compress them into any very exact test. One matter that was much discussed was whether fear of one's parents should count as sufficient to meet the constancy test. What, for instance, should a court do when it could be shown that the child had consented to a marriage simply because of a desire to please his parents and that the child would not have agreed otherwise? The same problem could occur mutatis mutandis in a monastic profession.

Arguments that reverential fear met the constancy test were made. Roman law texts could be read as permitting recision of contracts or legacies made in such circumstances.[72] In them it seemed that reverential fear was being treated no differently than any other kind of fear.[73] Should not marriage or monastic vows, which by their nature required a more perfect freedom than temporal contracts, similarly be subject to recision?[74] This was suggested, for instance, by Petrus de Ancharano in taking up a man's marriage contract: "Because of its great force, reverential paternal fear, even though it does not tend to bodily torture or to death, is considered to have an equivalent effect upon a constant man."[75] Or similarly, Antonius de Butrio in dealing with a woman's monastic profession: "When it is an act that requires the utmost freedom, as in these spiritual matters, then the act is vitiated even where no blows have occurred beforehand."[76]

However, the more common opinion among the early canonists came to the opposite conclusion: that simple reverential fear, without something more in the way of physical compulsion or threat, was not an impediment to vows, whether matrimonial or monastic.[77] The textual argument was based on a decretal holding a child's marriage invalid if it had been induced by parental blows and threats (e.g., X 1.29.16). The canonists reasoned from the decretal a contrario sensu, as they did very often in interpreting papal decretals. They argued that because the decretal instructed the papal judge delegate to invalidate the union if the union had been the product of both fear and physical coercion by the parents, the reverse must also be true. It must equally follow that if there had not been physical coercion— that is, if there had been only reverential fear—then the judge was to treat the union as valid and binding.[78] Otherwise the judge would not have been instructed to determine both questions of fact.

A second argument tending toward the same conclusion was that children have a duty to obey their parents. Therefore simple direction by the parents could not satisfy a "constant man" test of coercion. The child's duty was not an absolute one, of course. No child could be excommunicated for refusing to follow the choice of a career or to accept a marriage partner his father had selected. But at the same time, parental authority was legitimate authority. The Ten Commandments required children to honor their father and mother. It would be a strange result, the canonists reasoned, if a monastic vow or a matrimonial contract could be avoided simply because a child had taken the Fifth Commandment seriously.[79] The constant man or woman might therefore have had just cause for following the wishes of his or her parents, even where he or she would not have made the same choice. It did not appear that such a legitimate kind of obedience could be the kind of force and fear being condemned by the canonical texts.

This widely shared opinion did not, however, entirely eliminate "reverential fear" from litigation or from further academic comment. Even while holding it insufficient for invalidity in ordinary cases, the canonists also held that it might be sufficient in unusual cases. Suppose the child was weak willed or terrified of the parent. Or suppose the father was cruel and accustomed to punish the child with stripes or blows whenever the child disobeyed him. Or suppose the reverence was accompanied by discussion, perhaps amounting to something akin to a threat, to cut off or diminish the child's inheritance. The canonists left room for invalidating monastic vows or marriage contracts entered into under such circumstances.

It was in dealing with the variety of cases that some of the more subtle treatments of the nature of consent occurred in the canonists' writings. By holding that marriages and monastic vows might be avoided where there was something more than simple "reverential fear," they were led to examine what was meant by free consent.[80] The conclusions they reached were not always those we would. It seems fair to say so, here and elsewhere. But the early commentators were talking about the essential nature of freedom of choice, and the concept of "reverential fear" was capable of considerable development.[81] The uncertain reach of several of the texts and the scholarly disagreement among the jurists, so common and so disquieting in many ways, left this subject open to speculation, disagreement, and growth.[82] And indeed it has grown beyond what the canonists themselves could have imagined.

CONCLUSION

The chapter began by asserting the existence of a large degree of continuity within the Western legal tradition in dealing with marriage and monastic vows. It suggested that the principle of freedom of choice provides an instructive example of such continuity. Between that beginning and these concluding words, we have seen several examples of the ways freedom of choice played a central role in both areas of the classical canon law, as it does in our own thinking about "life choices" like these. However, a fuller examination of the subject shows also that freedom of choice was not the sole value at work in the formation and elaboration of the classical canon law. Probably it could not even be called the primary value. When protection of the institutions of religious life and marriage came into conflict with a freedom of choice asserted by individuals, freedom of choice gave ground. Individual autonomy, said to be the mainspring of modern law,[83] was not the dominant force in the canon law. To the canon law and the canonists, it was essential that the desire for personal liberty not become the means of subverting right order either within the church or in society. The institutional, objective order of Christian life must be sustained. That goal, together with the theological assumptions of the canonists, called forth a different notion of freedom than our own.[84]

Much of the same can be said of concepts like "reverential fear." The classical canon law never allowed it to become a means of subverting the institution of parental authority. What the canonists did was to state a principle. That principle was capable of development. Indeed, the canonists developed it themselves. The notion of what it meant to give free assent to an obligation such as marriage or monastic life did not remain static in their hands, and the subject led them to examine consent given at a parent's command more carefully than they might have done without having to come to grips with the meaning of the principle. A good deal of this development is hard for us to appreciate, or even to see, encumbered as it is in the strings of citations and the hair-splitting distinctions characteristic of scholastic writing. But it is there. In this sense too, continuity exists between the classical canon law and the present state of thinking about the bonds of marriage and monastic vows. This is so even though the classical canonists might not have recognized, and most certainly would not have applauded, the matrimonial regimes that have become the norm in the late twentieth century.

10 Criminal Law of the Church: The Crime of Blasphemy

It was inevitable that the classical canon law should have concerned itself with crime, and it is only a little less surprising that this concern was by no means limited to ecclesiastical offenses. The medieval canonists regarded themselves as under a positive obligation to take cognizance over crimes most of us would consider distinctly secular. For this, they offered several reasons, in addition to what biblical authorization could be drawn from the words, spoken by Jesus, that stressed the need for fraternal correction within the church (Matt. 18:15–18).[1] Most immediately, crimes were also sins and therefore of immediate relevance in the church's internal forum, that is, in the realm of auricular confession. The medieval church's claim to exclusive jurisdiction over a huge clerical population also required laws defining and punishing misbehavior by its members. Moreover, some crimes, whether committed by layman or cleric, were of particular relevance to the church in the sense that they directly concerned religious belief and practice.

It is therefore not the least bit startling to find a full book of the Gregorian Decretals—the fifth—devoted almost entirely to the criminal law. It contained separate titles on forgery, heresy, homicide, arson, usury, adultery, theft, and sorcery, alongside several more strictly clerical offenses such as simony, apostasy, financial misconduct in office, and unlawful administration of the sacraments. The fifth book also included titles on criminal sanctions and criminal procedure. It was not a complete code of criminal law, but it had considerable breadth.

Criminal law was not only an obligatory subject for the canon lawyers. It held a particular interest for many of them. The number of treatises devoted to the subject in the *ius commune* is beyond counting. Again there was more than a single reason for this. Criminal law combined jurisprudential intricacy with immediately practical consequence. It called upon the canonists to take account of the opinions of contemporary theologians. It raised contentious questions of defining the proper division of competence between church and state. It required the canon law to develop a detailed system of criminal procedure, raising questions of legal due process, some of which have remained problematical, important, and controversial among thoughtful lawyers today. And the subject of crime brought the canonists face to face with the great dilemma of any organization that exercises a coercive, criminal jurisdiction: how to deter and punish crime while at the same time dealing justly with men and women who have behaved in ways that are seriously inimical to the interests of society.

Many of the canonists faced these questions outside the classroom as well as within. The formal law provided extensive treatment of most aspects of the subject, and the canonistic commentaries necessarily dealt with the texts. But ecclesiastical courts also, in fact, exercised criminal jurisdiction throughout Europe, though not everywhere with the identical jurisdictional competence. In their commentaries, the canonists recognized the relevance of this ordinary practice. They sometimes referred to actual cases with which they were familiar, in order to illustrate problems they faced. And they kept some of the realities of what the criminal law could accomplish in mind when it came to formulating answers to the problems raised by the canonical texts. In this area of the canon law at least, there was no great divide between theory and practice.

Of all these several and diffuse aspects of the canon law of crime, few provide any better example than the law of blasphemy. Its treatment by the medieval and early modern canonists draws together various strands of thought about criminal law as well as any other aspect of the criminal law. As a popular modern writer on such subjects has reminded us, blasphemy was in some sense "treason against God."[2] Its nature united the church's special interest in religious offenses with the common contemporary perception that blasphemy, at least if allowed to go unchecked, would inevitably cause actual and serious harm to society. The law of blasphemy, both in definition and nuances, also illustrates something of the legal complexity and the sophistication of the canon law.

The subject is even of inherent interest today.[3] To many modern men and women, blasphemy represents a kind of speech that is utterly without social value. It is inherently offensive to persons of religious sensibility. As such, blasphemy threatens to upset the good order of society and perhaps even the peace of the moment if it is uttered in an inappropriate context.[4] Others regard the prohibition of blasphemy as victimless, wrong headed, and perhaps even inherently silly. Prosecutions brought under this heading pose an obvious threat to civil liberties. To many, a law of blasphemy seems little more than an idle but potentially dangerous relic of a superstitious age.[5] It seems doubly worthwhile, therefore, to discover something about what the law of blasphemy was in its canonical form.

THE LEGITIMACY OF PUNISHING BLASPHEMY

Serious doubt about whether blasphemy should be treated as a crime seems not to have occurred to the men who formulated the canon law. For them, there was no shortage of convincing reasons for punishing blasphemers. An argument to the contrary—that God, the party directly injured, should have sole jurisdiction to punish the crime—was sometimes mentioned in the literature on the subject. But it was not much attended to, except sometimes as an additional punishment blasphemers could expect. Certainly it did not carry the day.[6] More often, the canonists made immediate reference to the canonical and Roman law texts that permitted—and indeed required—the punishment of all blasphemers. The authorities demanded that the crime be dealt with sternly. The texts said, for instance, that the seriousness of the offense ought to be judged by the status of the victim; the more exalted the person offended, the greater the offense. Using that test, blasphemy ranked easily among the greatest of crimes.[7]

Practical Consequences of Blasphemy

In some sense, this result was the result of the common assumption among our ancestors that blasphemy almost always had temporal consequences—disastrous consequences. It was the very opposite of a "victimless" crime. Blasphemy was a natural cause of famine, pestilence, and earthquake. There was impressive legal authority to that effect. It is so stated in an imperial constitution that found its way into one of the Roman Law Novels.[8] Blasphemy continued to be regarded as the cause of disasters in writings by commentators on the subject well into the sixteenth and seventeenth centuries.[9] To insult God was to risk God's wrath, and this was more than something to be feared in the world to come. The evil consequences of blasphemy would very likely be visited upon a wider group than the blasphemer alone. And it would happen soon. The medieval *glossa ordinaria* to the imperial constitution cited the fate of Sodom and Gomorrah as an all too probable example of the consequences to be visited upon societies that failed to prevent, or at least to punish, the crime.[10]

Pious tradition, long remembered and oft repeated in the course of legal commentaries, had it that Christ himself had spoken about the subject to King Robert I of France (d. 923). Christ had told the king expressly that he would never be able to establish peace in his kingdom until the crime of blasphemy had been extirpated.[11] Similarly, a German proverb ran, "When citizens of a land slander God, God punishes the land."[12] It was generally believed that God had caused an earthquake to strike the city of Rome in 1021 because Roman Jews had mocked the Cross.[13] This attitude was widely shared. While it was, blasphemy was bound to figure among those actions regarded as deserving of punishment. As a crime, it was dangerous and destructive to the sinews of human society in an immediate way.[14]

Biblical Authority

Apart from occasional references to these stories, to the imperial constitution, to the temporal consequences foretold therein, and to what they regarded as the lamentable ubiquity of blasphemy in their own day, the canonists themselves made less use of the justification from consequence than might be expected.[15] They did, however, fully explore the question of why it was appropriate that the canon law should punish the crime. The answer to the question of whether or not the canon law should exercise jurisdiction over the crime was not simply assumed. More often than not, the canonists looked to biblical examples as precedent and justification for enacting ecclesiastical laws against blasphemy. Here they found plenty to choose from. The Book of Leviticus, for instance: "He who blasphemes the name of the Lord shall be put to death: all the congregation shall stone him" (Lev. 24:16). Or the Second Book of Samuel: as punishment for having "given great occasion to the enemies of the Lord to blaspheme," King David's son was taken from him (12:14).

The most frequently cited of the biblical authorities in Gratian's *Decretum* was the example of King Nebuchadnezzar from the Book of Daniel. Readers will recall that Nebuchadnezzar had Shadrach, Meshach, and Abednego cast into a fiery furnace when they refused to fall down and worship the golden idol he had caused to be constructed. When the three emerged from the experience unharmed, Nebuchadnezzar was sufficiently impressed by the efficacy of their faith that he issued a decree punishing with death any person who spoke against their God (Dan. 3:29). St. Augustine had made use of this story as showing one man's repentance and amendment of life, approving in the course of his argument Nebuchadnezzar's decree against blasphemy as a commendable example of the fruits of repentance. In the hands of the canonists, the incident became an argument in favor of enacting and enforcing laws against blasphemy. Gratian employed extracts from Augustine's writing about Nebuchadnezzar for this purpose in no fewer than five places in the *Decretum*. This example, he thought, demonstrated that public laws, backed by severe punishments, were the proper response to the crime.[16]

As we have seen happen frequently, in the hands of the medieval canonists these biblical texts served as general statements of principle rather than as rules of positive law. No one contended that Nebuchadnezzar's decree remained in force. No one recommended that it should be reenacted. The texts demonstrated the crime's heinousness, but they were not treated as statutes prescribing the punishment to be imposed in medieval Europe. The result was that neither in canonical theory nor in the court practice of the day was the death penalty exacted for simple blasphemy, as might have been done had the canonists followed the Bible literally. A sixteenth-century Italian advocate wrote that the severest penalty he had ever heard of as being imposed for nonheretical blasphemy was a sentence to the galleys. Even this was quite rare; normally money fines or corporal punishments were used in practice.[17] Some of the latter were gruesome enough—perforation or amputation of the tongue for instance. Still, they were not the capital punishment ordered by Nebuchadnezzar's decree.

This apparent (to them) leniency does not mean that the medieval canonists regarded the severe biblical injunctions as irrelevant to their subject. By prescribing death, the texts proved the seriousness of the offense and provided more than ample reason for the sanctions that were actually imposed. The biblical example encouraged the jurists to describe blasphemy as "a great crime, [and] contrary to natural, divine, and human law."[18] The opinion that blasphemy was "a graver crime than homicide" was shared, or at any rate asserted, by more than a few of them.[19] When asked to explain why the Bible's apparent mandate was not being carried out, commentators were more apt to ascribe this to the lamentable "want of religion" in their own time than to any disproportion between capital punishment and the just deserts of a blasphemer. They found no fault in the mandate itself.[20] The problem, they said, was that if blasphemy were to be punished as it should have been, too few men would be left.[21] The canonists evidently did not think as we do: that it would have been unthinkable to visit such a punishment on one who had committed a "victimless" crime.

Roman Law Precedents

Roman law also provided the canonists with an argument in favor of punishment of blasphemy, quite apart from the imperial constitution noticed above. Not only did the crime exist in Roman law, but the ample storehouses of the civil law also contained a useful parallel text. The text forbade all reviling of the emperor and his companions (Cod. 9.8.5). For the canonists, this provided an a fortiori argument. If words spoken against the imperial majesty were rightly punished, then how much more surely, and how much more harshly, should words be punished when they had been spoken against the divine majesty?[22] Their common assumption—that the spiritual power was inherently greater than the temporal—made this answer obvious. It also opened up the possibility of dealing with blasphemy according to the expansive rules laid down for the Roman law lèse-majesté.[23] They could also be extended beyond God himself to cover God's companions, the saints. In time some commentators sought to extend it even to *res sacrae:* to chalices, Bibles, mass books, perhaps even to the surplices worn by the clergy.[24] Rules and analogies drawn from the civil law were taken over and applied to the canon law of blasphemy to facilitate this enlargement.

BLASPHEMY'S DEFINITION

Defining the offense of blasphemy long presented problems. To modern readers, it will probably appear axiomatic that if the act of blasphemy is to be brought within the criminal law and blasphemers punished, the crime must first be defined. It will seem equally self-evident that the definition must be sufficiently precise to pass the basic test of both modern and medieval criminal law: *nulla poena sine lege.*[25] No person should be punished in the absence of an established and ascertainable law, and that law must not leave the offense so vague that "men of common intelligence must guess at its meaning and differ as to its application."[26]

On the other hand, from the point of view of any lawgiver who is serious about punishing the crime, there are undeniable virtues to a certain degree of imprecision. "All definitions are dangerous," wrote the medieval jurists, and the crime of blasphemy furnishes a textbook example of what they had in mind. It is one of those things one recognizes readily enough when spoken, even without necessarily being able to define it exactly. Much may depend upon the speaker's intent, the accompanying circumstances, and even upon his tone of voice. Is he making a joke or railing against God? The words, if set down in isolation on the printed page, will not always give the right answer. Local custom may also play a determining role that is hard to factor into a precise definition. Particularly to those charged with administering the law, to define blasphemy simply as "reviling" or "vilifying" God and religion, as the English common law later was to do,[27] may seem preferable to any more exact kind of definition. It avoids quibbling, and it often yields a fairer result.

Early Canonical Definitions

Whatever may be the jurisprudentially preferable alternative, it was certainly true that the canonical texts inherited from the early Middle Ages were far from providing a precise and agreed-upon definition of blasphemy. There had always been a temptation to use the term in a loose sense, as meaning simply conduct or speech inimical to the Christian religion. The Bible itself encouraged this. St. Paul, for example, spoke of himself as a "blasphemer" (1 Tim. 1:13), apparently meaning no more than that he himself had once been a persecutor of Christians. Passages from the Old Testament used the term to refer generally to all insults or wrongs against God (Ezek. 20:27). There was also the startling reference in the Gospels for commentators to contend with. Jesus had said that although all manner of sins could in the end be forgiven, the sin of blasphemy against the Holy Spirit would not (Mark 3:29). What exactly had he meant? What did it mean to blaspheme against the Holy Spirit? The Gospels furnished no clear answer. The question has continued to puzzle Christian thinkers.

The *Decretum* contained little movement toward exact definition, and its compiler seems to have desired none. Gratian did not include any express treatment of the question, precluding any immediate narrowing of the issues. Indeed, the question does not seem to have occurred to him as requiring an answer, since he included texts that used the term *blasphemy* in quite disparate and confusing ways. One canon, for example, expressly equated simoniacs with blasphemers against the word of God (C. 1 q. 1 c. 21). Another purported to treat as blasphemy all intentional violations of the sacred canons (C. 25 q. 1 c. 5). A third used the term, as many of the church fathers had, in the sense of any Christian heresy (Dist. 15 c. 1 § 2). A fourth, one that turned out to be much used by later canonists, described as a blasphemer the man who had "sworn by the hairs or the head of God" (C. 22 q. 1 c. 10). It is evident from the most superficial perusal of the *Decretum*'s texts that nothing adequate for any kind of exact definition could have emerged from its pages.

The Gregorian Decretals and the succeeding canonical collections did not go much further. A title in the fifth book, "De maledicis," did take up the subject, but it contained only two chapters, neither of which directly confronted the problem of the crime's definition (X 5.26.1–2). Its primary contribution lay in its clear assertion that the church could exercise jurisdiction over the crime and in what looks like a certain extension of its coverage. The decretals in it stated the principle that blasphemers should be punished, claimed a right to do so for the ecclesiastical courts, and enlarged the category of punishable offenses to include blasphemy against the saints and the Virgin Mary, as well as that directed against God. The title's first chapter, a decretal of Pope Clement III, went further, stating that to speak insulting words of the papal office should also be punished—a decretal that cost the canonists some effort to explain. How, fully understood, could this decretal be said not to contradict the legal principle that no man should act as a judge in his own cause?[28] The pope seemed himself to be judging and condemning a man who had spoken ill of him.

Apart from these contributions, the Decretals seem simply to have assumed the existence of most of the substantive principles of the law of blasphemy. The second decretal in the fifth book's title simply laid out the jurisdictional principles stated above. There was little else in the classical texts of the canon law. The *Liber sextus* added little or nothing. It contained no title dealing with either blasphemy or cursing. Nor did the later Clementines or the later *Extravagantes*.

When one looks at the works of the thirteenth-century canonists, the same lack of concern for exact definition is found. In some ways this was inevitable. Their task was to comment upon the texts, and the texts did not raise the question. The contrast is great between their attitude here and their treatment of the law of baptism, where, as it appeared at length in Chapter 8, they devoted long and minute attention to the exact wording of the Trinitarian formula. Geoffrey of Trani, the *glossa ordinaria*, Hostiensis, and Innocent IV all dealt with blasphemy but without resolving, or even directly raising, the definitional question. They did take up some closely related points that were directly raised by the decretals themselves. Hostiensis, for example, wrote that the decretal rightly included saints in the group who might be the subject of blasphemy, because they were "companions of God." He dealt with the Roman law mentioned above that punished those who cursed both the emperor and the "companions of the emperor." The like principle applied in the canon law.[29] Hostiensis had nothing to say, however, about exactly what words such cursing had to include. The habit was general. A typical early confessor's manual defined blasphemy in a similarly general fashion; it occurred "whenever a person reproached God or his saints."[30]

Theological Definition

What attempts at more exact definition there were during the Middle Ages came first from the theologians. Their definition was commonly said to go back to St. Ambrose (d. 397) and was stated most famously and clearly by St. Thomas Aquinas. He began by defining blasphemy as any insult (*convicium*) against God,[31] going on to analyze this concept and concluding that the essence of such insult lay in the derogation from God's goodness. According to this way of seeing the matter, if a person attributed to God any characteristic that did not properly belong to God, that would be to derogate from his goodness. Hence it would be a blasphemous utterance. Similarly, if a speaker denied to God any characteristic that should be properly ascribed to God, that too would constitute blasphemy. Thus (though Aquinas did not give any examples) it would be blasphemous for a man to say that God was powerless or to assert that God would never discover the speaker's sins, because such a statement would deny to God one of his essential characteristics: omnipotence. Under this definition it would equally be blasphemous to deny the divinity of Jesus or to assert that the Devil was more powerful than the Holy Spirit. If read together with the "expansive" coverage of the Decretal law, this definition would also mean that for anyone openly to deny the qualities of sanctity to the Virgin Mary, or indeed to any of the saints, would also come within the realm of blasphemous utterance.

Later Protestant writers therefore fit into this tradition of more exact thought when they accused their Catholic opponents of blasphemy. By ascribing a plenitude of power to the occupants of the chair of St. Peter, they maintained, the Papists were ascribing to someone else a property rightly possessed by God alone.[32] Pamphlets entitled "The Blasphemies of the Popes and Their Sect" or the like were common enough in the age of religious controversy. They made and exaggerated the same point repeatedly: to say that the popes could dispense against all the precepts of the Old and New Testaments was to commit blasphemy precisely as blasphemy was defined by the greatest of the medieval theologians.[33] It was to derogate from the omnipotence of God. Similarly John Calvin was writing from within (or at least in accordance with) this tradition when he described it as blasphemous for King Henry VIII to have assumed the title of "Supreme Head" of the Church of England. According to the accepted definition, Henry was ascribing to himself a function that only God held. That was what blasphemy was.

The "theological" definition was not immediately or wholeheartedly embraced by the medieval jurists. It certainly was known to them.[34] A manual used in England in the fourteenth century and containing common canonical learning, for example, gave both the theological definition and the broader definitions found in the older canons.[35] However, the more precise, theological understanding did not become the basic test for most medieval canonists. Instead they normally contented themselves with repeating the less exact formulations found in the Decretum and the Decretals. If one follows the question into the works of Joannes Andreae, Antonius de Butrio, and Panormitanus, one finds little concern for exact definition, still less full acceptance of the theological meaning of the term. This seems surprising. These men were otherwise much concerned with defining terms. But so it is. Some of the canonical manuals designed for the Inquisition exhibit the same quality; in them the term *blasphemy* was defined only in a general way.[36] Indeed, many of the several conciliar and papal enactments of the first half of the sixteenth century, which established more specific penalties against blasphemy, were not much more precise.[37]

Later Developments

Fuller and more consistent attention to the question of blasphemy's legal definition, with the inevitably fine distinctions that would come with it, did begin to make its way into the law books during the sixteenth and seventeenth centuries. It appeared in some of the works of sophisticated casuistry that are common to this period.[38] For example, Prosper Farinacius (d. 1613), an advocate at the Roman court and influential writer on the criminal law of the church, repeated and approved the theological definition given above, and he sought to bring as many of the canonical texts within it as he could.[39] The results are clever, though not uniformly convincing. Farinacius explained that to swear "by the hairs of God" or "by the head of God" (an example found in the *Decretum* and the Roman law Novels)[40] might be considered blasphemous because the words implied that God had an actual head and that God was body rather than spirit. The words would therefore wrongly ascribe to God a corporal property he surely did not have and would fit within the technical definition of blasphemy. Similarly, Farinacius stated, if a man said that he would do something whether God tried to stop him or not, that would be blasphemy, because his words implied that some things on Earth were not under God's control. They could thus amount to a denial of the omnipotence of God.

Such efforts at definition and distinction were the habitual stuff of legal comment during the era that has been called a "Second Age of Scholasticism." As these examples suggest, the habit laid its heavy hand upon the law of blasphemy. Jacobus Menochius, for example, held that it would ordinarily be blasphemy for anyone to say that God could not stop him from committing a sin. As just noted, this assertion would deny God's omnipotence. However, he went on, it would *not* be blasphemy to say, "Whether or not it displeases God, I shall commit adultery."[41] The reason was that God would in fact be displeased by the speaker's adultery, and therefore the potentially adulterous speaker would have ascribed no quality to God that was contrary to God's true nature. Nor would he have asserted that God could not stop him if God so desired. He had merely said that God's likely displeasure would make no difference to him. Hence, carefully considered, the words were not blasphemous.

Along the same lines, according to Josephus Mascardus, it would not be blasphemy for a person in wrongful possession of another's goods to say mockingly, "If the Virgin Mary reproaches me, I will give them back." The Virgin Mary most certainly *would* reproach him for failing to restore stolen goods.[42] Therefore, his words did not deny to her any quality she possessed. They merely stated what the speaker intended to do. The literature of the period is filled with such hairsplitting distinctions. Were it necessary to pursue them, we should have to discuss (and learn to distinguish between) "conditional blasphemy," "comparative blasphemy," and "renunciatory blasphemy," among others.[43]

To explore this law fully would certainly be a tedious and probably also a fruitless effort. But these efforts at classification were not without effect. Litigation in European courts did, it seems, sometimes revolve around whether the words spoken had fit the exact definition of blasphemy.[44] Lawyers could argue in favor of clients who had uttered objectionable speech that even when God was spoken of with disrespect, "not all contumelious language is blasphemy."[45] One finds incidents that occurred on the other side of the world apparently based upon the distinctions drawn in the *ius commune*. In New Spain, where the laws prohibiting blasphemy had expressly been proclaimed in 1520 and 1524, one of the lieutenants of Hernán Cortés escaped any punishment for having said, "Damn God."[46] In colonial Delaware, Gabriel Jones was tried for blasphemy but acquitted for having said, "Cursed be my God for suffering me to be so old."[47] No specifically legal arguments survive from these incidents from the New World. They have puzzled the modern historians who have described them. Perhaps the puzzlement is justified and the results to be ascribed to local and special conditions. However, their outcomes are fully explicable if one assumes that the definitions of the mature *ius commune* were being applied.

In the literature of distinction and classification common to the period, the most important distinction worked out was that between heretical and nonheretical blasphemy, the latter normally being called *blasphemia simplex*. It was never true, as some modern writers have supposed,[48] that the two were ever regarded as identical. A Jew or a Turk, for instance, could commit blasphemy but not heresy. Even beyond this, the distinction was of the greatest immediate importance at the time because it determined whether the courts of the Inquisition had jurisdiction over particular utterances. The Inquisition could only deal with heresy, not ordinary crimes, and as these courts hit their stride in the sixteenth century, disputes over jurisdiction called forth a body of learned writing on the topic.

It had always been obvious that some, though not complete, overlap between the two crimes existed. At the same time, and particularly if one took an "open-ended" view of blasphemy's meaning as the medieval jurists did, for a man to revile God might be perfectly consistent with orthodox belief on his part. "May God be cursed" or "I despise all God's works" might be said by someone who is, strictly speaking, quite orthodox in belief.[49] It was therefore thought useful, and indeed necessary for delineating the scope of the Inquisition's jurisdiction, that jurists should attempt a clear distinction between the two.[50] Very likely, some of the expansive attempts to find theological error in merely scurrilous language, a clear feature of the writing of the period, owe something to the particular author's desire to expand the jurisdictional competence of the Inquisition. It is impossible to think that classifying a casual comment about an unhappy couple—that "God did not make that marriage"—as heretical blasphemy grew from anything other than a wish to sweep everything possible within the Inquisition's capacious nets.[51] Commentators asserted that these words derogated from divine omnipotence and goodness. God could not be the author of unhappiness. Hence they were theoretically blasphemous and subject to the Inquisition because they grew out of false belief. Even more aggrandizing in effect was the contemporary doctrine that all blasphemous statements raised a presumption of heretical belief on the part of the speaker.[52] It would justify the investigation, if not always the prosecution, of virtually all blasphemous offenses by the officials of the Inquisition.

Whatever the root cause may be, ingenious distinctions undoubtedly fill the literature of the period. Some of it provides a very good example of the scholastic method in full cry.[53] For example, it was asked whether it was blasphemous to swear "by the limbs of Christ." The words were disrespectful. But Christ did have limbs, and therefore the words did not quite fit the theological definition of blasphemy given above. Perhaps they were only an illicit form of oath. On the other hand, some of the texts in the *Decretum* appeared to treat such language as blasphemous and even as heretical. What to do? A tempting solution lay in distinguishing. The result was that if the speaker had meant "dishonest" parts of Christ's body, this would be blasphemous. However, if "honest parts" of Christ's body had been named or intended, then the expression would not be. To swear "per anum Christi" was blasphemous according to this understanding. To swear "per capud Christi" was not. "Per ventrem Christi" provided a good exam question.

The triumph of scholasticism made evident by these examples is not the whole story of the evolution of blasphemy's definition. Even some of the writers busiest in classifying the various forms of the crime could also repeat the traditional and more general definitions. They simply added the older formulations to their more systematic treatments of the crime. Moreover, it turns out that some writers on the *ius commune* continued to content themselves with a treatment that must have looked superficial and unsatisfactory to the more determined of the systematic thinkers. For instance, Julius Clarus, author of a much-used sixteenth-century work on criminal law, had only this to say about blasphemy's definition: "All insult, contumely, or cursing uttered against God or the saints is blasphemy."[54] Another defined the term simply as "speaking injurious words toward God."[55] A third attempted a reconciliation of the two approaches by saying the since God and the saints are good, any "speaking evil" of them would be to deny their proper characteristics to them.[56] In other words, during the sixteenth and seventeenth centuries there was both a concern for more precise definition of the offense and the continuation of the medieval habit of "open-ended" definition. The two existed alongside each other.

Given the state of the texts, it would have been difficult fully to eliminate the broader meaning of the term from the canon law. Too many authorities would have had to be disregarded or explained away. It may even be true that the canonists saw virtue in having both. For example, it seemed all but self-evident that a person who spit on the image of the Virgin Mary was somehow blaspheming. But it would have been difficult to integrate this conclusion into the theological definition given above. To have accepted a fully precise definition of the term risked putting some objectionable utterances out of the reach of the canon law of blasphemy.[57] Nothing was to be gained by adopting a definition exact enough to exclude these categories from the grasp of the courts of the church.

PRACTICAL AND JURISDICTIONAL QUESTIONS

Every aspect of the canon law of crime threw off organizational and practical problems. Many of them also raised problems of what one might call behavioral theory, and it was in the elaboration of criminal law that the canonists developed some of their most sophisticated approaches to crime and punishment. Here we deal with three questions raised: jurisdiction, punishment, and excuse.

Jurisdiction over Blasphemy

Blasphemy was regarded as a *crimen mixti fori* or *crimen communis fori* under the canon law.[58] That meant that either the spiritual or the temporal courts, or both, could lawfully exercise jurisdiction over it. In this respect, blasphemy was typical of many crimes that are now regarded as particularly religious in nature. In fact there were only a few crimes that the canon law regarded as reserved to the exclusive cognizance of the church. Adultery, for example, was regarded as belonging to either. Students of English history often assume the contrary, because custom in most parts of England allotted jurisdiction over adultery to the spiritual courts alone. But it would not have been a violation of the canon law had the temporal courts intruded themselves into the matter. This certainly happened on the Continent.

Blasphemy was much the same. In Italy, the secular courts commonly took cognizance over the crime. Local statutes prescribed a wide variety of punishments for it. German and French law likewise contained extensive enactments on blasphemy.[59] A modern writer has in fact described the crime of blasphemy as a "preoccupation" of the French kings during the sixteenth century.[60] The canonists mentioned such secular enactments in passing and for the most part without condemnation. Their principal concern was not that these statutes were illegitimate or unwarranted but rather that they should not become a means of ousting the church's concurrent jurisdiction over the crime.

The jurisdictional question under the canon law was actually a little more complicated still. Heresy, unlike common blasphemy, was taken to be a *crimen mere ecclesiasticum*,[61] that is, an offense reserved to the exclusive competence of the church. This had inevitable consequences for some forms of the crime, because much blasphemy involved heretical expression. It would have been a matter open to debate whether the lay courts could deal with such cases in the first instance, and the answer normally given was that they should not. The reason given for this rule was a substantive one: the church alone had the authority and the ability to define heresy. Hence the church alone could judge it.

One might suppose that the identical argument could have been sustained as to common blasphemy (and as to adultery and several other crimes for that matter). Since the church defined what blasphemy (or marriage) was, exclusive jurisdiction over its punishment might have been thought to follow from the premise. But except in the case of heretical blasphemy, the conclusion was not drawn in fact. Perhaps the fact that Jews and pagans could commit blasphemy but not heresy had an influence on the outcome.[62] Whatever the reason, in this instance the ability to define the crime did not dictate the jurisdictional rule. This was so even though ordinary blasphemy shared several procedural characteristics with heresy prosecutions; for instance, many witnesses who would otherwise have been excluded (e.g., participants, infamous persons) were admitted to testify in both because of the heinous nature of the offense.[63]

The canonical rule that encouraged this shared jurisdiction may have been attributable in part to the common medieval habit of ascribing the source of legal jurisdiction to customary practice. The widespread fear of the consequences of failure adequately to punish blasphemy may also have played some role. It is certain that the rule permitting shared jurisdiction described the reality. Temporal statutes penalizing blasphemy were enacted with some frequency in medieval and early modern Europe. They too seem to have assumed the competence of either forum.[64]

When it did come within the spiritual forum, common blasphemy was a crime ordinarily reserved to the bishop for punishment. In this it was typical of much of the church's criminal law. More serious offenses were to be kept for the determination of higher authorities. A division, however, was also drawn between public and private offenses. The former were to be dealt with by public courts, in this case that of the bishop. The latter could be dealt with privately, in this case by the speaker's parish priest in the confessional. In the case of blasphemy, the tendency ran toward treating many such utterances as belonging to the second category, except where the words also had been heretical. Much blasphemy would be treated as having been spoken privately (*occulte*). Hostiensis, for example, suggested that only blasphemy that could be fully proved in court and that had "scandalized" those who had heard it had to be remitted to the episcopal audience.[65] He seems to have regarded other blasphemous utterances as not having been made "publicly" in the technical sense of that word. Consequently they could be dealt with by the parish priest in the confessional.

Most commentators on the subject of blasphemy also dealt specifically with the possibility of double punishment for the crime, a subject to be examined in more detail in Chapter 11. Since the crime was triable in either a secular or a spiritual forum, an obvious question was whether the same offense could be tried either simultaneously or seriatim in both. Arguments could be made for several positions. One was to separate out clerics from laymen, determining the forum by the defendant's status.[66] This did not carry the day, however. It was overly restrictive and was apparently contradicted by too many of the canons. There was also some opinion that the law should be read as requiring an initial, and final, choice of forum, so that the system of *praeventio* would fix the proper court. If so, the first court to prosecute would oust any action in the other.

However, in this instance, the *communis opinio* came to hold that both temporal and spiritual authorities could punish the same offense. Gregory IX's decretal *Statuimus* gave a kind of authorization for double punishment, since it described the allotment of both spiritual and temporal punishment for the same crime. The decretal might possibly have been read as permitting the latter only when the former had failed. But it was not in fact normally so read. Hostiensis added that blasphemy offended the *genus clericorum* in a quite different way than it offended the *genus laicorum*.[67] Each jurisdiction had a legitimate interest to vindicate, the one worldly, the other spiritual. In the opinion of most canonists, therefore, blasphemy presented a proper offense for what was called the "accumulation" of penalties.[68]

Canonical Punishment of Blasphemers

The punishments for blasphemy or lèse-majesté found in the Roman law (death) and Book of Daniel (cutting the offender into pieces and making a dunghill of his house) were not taken into the classical canon law. In Gratian's *Decretum*, the sanction for the crime was stated only in general terms: excommunication for laypersons and degradation from holy orders for clerics (C. 22 q. 1 c. 10). Infliction of even these lesser sanctions must have seemed unworkable within the classical canonical system, for neither was adopted. Excommunication was coming to be used as a sanction for contumacy. It was imposed against persons in order to secure their obedience to the orders of the spiritual courts, not as a penalty against convicted criminals, and perhaps it seemed that automatic excommunication of blasphemers was inappropriate. Moreover, since degradation was regarded as too harsh a penalty to be extracted from clergy for a single instance of blasphemy, another remedy had to be found. Accordingly, the decretal letter *Statuimus*, issued by Pope Gregory IX, prescribed a detailed and elaborate public penance to be imposed upon those guilty of the crime (X 5.26.2). This decretal further specified that if the offender refused to comply with the penance, he was to be suspended from entry into the parish church, denied Christian burial, and subjected to a mandatory fine, which was to be imposed by the secular arm and which might run from five to forty *solidi* depending upon the offense and the offender's status.[69]

Like many of the decretals in the *Corpus iuris canonici*, this one was not treated as if it had been a statutory enactment. If it had been so regarded, it too would have required modification in any event. The exigencies of practice and the nature of the crime simply did not admit of the application of the penalty called for by a literal reading of the decretal's terms. For one thing, the penalty prescribed was regarded as entirely unsuitable for the clerical order. The canonists thought that for the clergy to perform public penance would have served to discredit the church as much as it would have led to amendment of life on the part of the offending cleric. That possibility should not be risked. Nor could it have been Gregory IX's intent, whatever the literal import of his decretal's words. Hence, all commentators assumed that the decretal would not apply in the case of blaspheming clerics.[70] The law thus fell back upon the infliction of "arbitrary" punishment, to be determined by the judge, for all clerics convicted of blasphemy.[71]

Even for laymen, treating all blasphemy alike according to the decretal's literal wording would not have been sensible. Not all blasphemy reflected the same degree of fault or the same kind of public consequence. The commentators therefore made considerable inroads in the seeming clarity of the sanctions prescribed in *Statuimus*. They treated it as stating valuable principles but not as a rule to be applied. One of these principles was that something less than capital punishment was appropriate for blasphemy. It became a justification for mitigating the harsh punishments found elsewhere in the law. In the end the important thing about the decretal was thus not so much the terms of the penalty it happened to contain but its assertion that commutation was appropriate. Commutation, in the form of public penance or monetary fine rather than death, was taken to be the appropriate remedy against blasphemers in the spiritual forum.[72]

In the end, as noted above, the actual punishment meted out to convicted blasphemers came to be left largely to the discretion of the judge involved or to the *stylus curiae* of the particular ecclesiastical court where the offense was tried. As one commentator summed up the situation in a blasphemy case, "The judge, in his discretion, can augment or lessen the penalties established in the laws, according to the nature of the facts and the persons."[73] Some canonists advised that it was best to deal with the variety of circumstance by imposing the "punishment that [was] the more greatly feared" by the offender.[74] But this solution was, of course, a counsel and nothing like a statutory requirement.

Circumstance, Intent, and Excuse

The medieval canonists were alive to the importance of circumstance in fixing the meaning of people's words. Deciding whether a particular utterance ought to be treated as serious blasphemy and dealing with the question of how speakers should be punished for that utterance were among their regular concerns. They were not content, as are many modern treatise writers on related subjects, to leave aside this aspect as one that by its nature cannot admit of adequate systematic legal treatment. It was in fact the canonists who first worked out many of the doctrines of degrees of guilt we still associate with the criminal law, though of course not only in connection with blasphemy.

The canonists allowed the importance of mitigating factors, but they tended toward minimizing the role that these should play in individual cases of blasphemy. They never admitted, for example, that there might be a complete excuse for blasphemy. They preferred instead to allow judges to lessen the punishment meted out according to judicial discretion where excusing factors existed. They spoke of "mercy" on the part of the judge rather than justification on the part of the blasphemer.[75] This same characteristic was what made itself evident in canonists' treatment of the decretal *Statuimus*. As such, it provides another example of the discretion commonly left to judges under the *ius commune*. However, it is equally important to note that judges were required under the law to mete out *some* punishment for the offense. In the eyes of the canonists, to have imposed no punishment at all would have been to license blasphemy and to invite the evil consequences that followed from it. Judges had an affirmative duty to punish blasphemers, though they should carry it out with circumspection.

The problem was particularly acute in dealing with the troublesome subject of customary blasphemous language. Suppose, as the canonists said was all too often the fact, a custom had grown up among the common people of using particular blasphemous words as a way simply of venting frustration, displeasure, or annoyance. Readers may recognize the possibility from their own experience. We often use words without thinking—certainly without considering fully what our words actually mean. As the medieval commentators themselves recognized, speaking such words implied no true blasphemous intent, in the sense of wishing to deny to God any attribute of divinity. Often they would not be meant (or understood) as showing any disrespect toward God at all. They would simply be words that people had grown used to saying when annoyed. Should such speakers nonetheless be punished when their words had been technically blasphemous?

This situation did not admit of an easy answer. There was some opinion to the effect that such words could not be counted as blasphemous at all. This was particularly true where the words were said by "rustics" who (we are told) habitually spoke without concern for exact meaning in what they were saying.[76] Thus the rustic who, in the course of a heated argument about what labor services he owed, had blurted out "God almighty could not make me do that work" might be excused the punishments of blasphemy, despite his words' clear denial of God's omnipotence.[77] A famous (and much criticized) *consilium* of Baldus suggested that language should always be evaluated by a standard derived from common usage (*secundum usum loquendi*) of the region. His view would treat much of language as merely scabrous talk rather than blasphemy.[78]

However, the *communis opinio* was against this seemingly sensible approach.[79] It threatened to license blasphemy by allowing the introduction of a *pessima consuetudo*. Indeed, such a custom would actually encourage repetition of the blasphemous words. This, one could only assume, would incur God's wrath. The normal response was therefore to hold that such customary words were indeed blasphemous and that the speakers should be subjected to discipline and appropriate penalities. But the discipline and penalties imposed should be more lenient than they would have been in the absence of the *consuetudo*.

For the first offense, some writers suggested that customary blasphemy might not be punished at all.[80] The underlying principle, embodied in the procedural law of the church and exemplified by God's admonition to Adam not to eat of the tree of knowledge (Gen. 2:17), was that there must be a warning before conduct could be treated as criminal. Normally, as in the case of theft or homicide, there was no real need for an express warning. Men knew that it was wrong to steal or kill. In all events, the law, which men are required to know, was quite clear on the subject. But in the case of customary curses or oaths, this was not always so. There was the problem of definition, and the offense included a mental element of intent to blaspheme, particularly where heretical blasphemy was involved. There was thus some real likelihood that mens rea would have been wholly absent from customary oaths or curses that verged on blasphemy. Once a specific warning had been given, however, as by a court or other authority taking action after a person's first offense, the situation changed. At that point a blasphemy repeated, even if customary in the vicinity, could quite properly be punished. Indeed, it *must* be punished. Otherwise the laws against blasphemy would be mocked.

This answer was worked out fully only during the sixteenth and seventeenth centuries. However, it had its roots in earlier treatment of the associated problem of drunken, careless, or angry utterances.[81] It seems obvious to us that these utterances ought not to bring the law's full force down upon the head of the speaker in the same way that a more deliberate statement should. So it seemed to the classical canonists. They said that the drunken or angry words should be punished but leniently. However, they did not reach this result simply by invoking human experience or a vague and general policy in favor of leniency in dealing with criminals. Their approach here, as in much else, was more formal. They looked for authority, and they found it in the texts of the canon law. They attached, for example, great importance to the word *praesumpserit* in the decretal *Statuimus*, which prohibited blasphemy. That decretal had dealt with a speaker who had *presumed* to blaspheme. That is, it could be said that the offender dealt with in the decretal had acted with deliberation. He had not spoken from weakness, inattention, or impaired understanding. Therefore, it could be maintained that the drunken, careless, or furious blasphemer had not fallen within this decretal's express terms. The Roman law had similarly held in the case of the parallel crime of treason: "A slip of the tongue should not readily bring punishment upon a man" (Dig. 48.4.7.3).

The canonists found additional support for this approach in a text from Gratian's *Decretum* called "Si quis iratus" (C. 2 q. 3 c. 5). It stated that where one man had, in the heat of anger, called another man a criminal, this was not to be taken as a true accusation. His words should be taken as an accusation only if later, after deliberation, he repeated them. The canonists applied the reasoning they saw underlying this canon to the case of blasphemy. If one man's accusation was not taken at face value because his mind had been disturbed by anger in the one case, his words should not be so taken in the other.

Drunkenness, although not specifically mentioned in the *Decretum*'s text, had the same sort of distorting effect on a speaker's meaning as anger did. Hence it could be brought within the same legal rule, and it was brought within by the canonists who discussed it.[82] "That was the whisky talking," we say, and the canon law was not so isolated from life that it did not recognize the truth in that expression. Particularly was this so when the person involved had retracted the blasphemous words once the drunkenness had passed.

These mitigating factors did not mean, in any event, that drunken or angry utterances were not to be punished at all.[83] They must not become licenses to blaspheme. The words spoken still constituted a punishable offense in legal theory, and they seem to have done so also in practice. Julius Clarus recorded that he had seen many men prosecuted under such circumstances, but he added that they never escaped punishment by pleading their own drunkenness.[84] The most the mitigating factors could do was to lessen the punishment appropriate to the blasphemer.[85]

In fact, the canonists took steps to narrow the scope of these potential excuses. For instance, some canonists held that slight drunkenness or slight anger would not qualify as a mitigating factor, because they would not truly have distorted the speaker's mind. Only if the speaker was so drunk or angry that he did not realize what he was doing would these factors come into play in mitigation of the offense. Moreover, depending on circumstances, it might even constitute an aggravating circumstance, as where a speaker with a propensity to blaspheme when drunk had intentionally become intoxicated.[86] The canonists were fully alive to the complexities of life that could affect the way the law should treat criminal defendants.

They also suggested looking to the underlying cause of the anger and drunkenness in assessing them as mitigating factors.[87] Some of the law that resulted took on the colors of scholasticism. For example, canonists wrote that only if the anger had arisen "out of a just cause" would it serve in mitigation. The speaker who became angry without a good reason would thus be treated for these purposes as if he had had no excuse at all. Moreover, it might also work in exactly the opposite direction. If a speaker was himself morally at fault in the anger, his fault might itself augment his guilt and hence the penance he should incur. Thus the commentators urged that it would make a difference when a card player uttered a blasphemy whether the card game he was playing was legal or not.[88] Similarly, to be intoxicated purposefully or shamefully only worked to increase the guilt of the blaspheming speaker. Intent obviously counted in the church's external forum. But it had a limited effect. Even where admitted, it was a mitigating factor only, and in the right circumstances it might actually augment the speaker's fault.

CONCLUSION

When regarded with even moderate attention, the writings of the canonists make it crystal clear that blasphemy was never an offense regarded as at the margins of the criminal law. Although it has become so in contemporary Western society, blasphemy was far from marginal for them. From first to last, they regarded it as a "horrible, impious and loathsome offense against the majesty of God."[89] They repeated the refrain—blasphemy was worse than homicide, theft, and arson—so often that one is bound to suppose they meant it. They came to adopt the position that although most criminals, even murderers, might claim sanctuary from arrest and punishment in a church, blasphemers could not.[90] To insult God and then seek refuge in his temple came to seem inconsistent and unacceptable forms of behavior.

This horror of blasphemy was, of course, widely shared outside canonical circles, and it did not disappear with the close of the Middle Ages. A modern writer on the subject has described its treatment in French legal practice of the sixteenth and seventeenth centuries in terms of a "collective psychosis."[91] There is some evidence from the law of the earlier period to suggest the possibility, if not the inevitability, of the outcome embodied in that slightly anachronistic description even from the law of the earlier period. This evidence consists not simply of the descriptions of the heinousness of the crime found in the *ius commune*. It consists also of the preference among the canonists for a broad definition of blasphemy, their endorsement of the rule that each blasphemous utterance constituted a distinct and separate offense, their ingenuity in construing language so as to constitute blasphemy, and their treatment of the detailed rules of culpability that governed this area of the law. Thus, although commission of the crime required an intent to blaspheme, intent could be presumed from the words themselves. Even drunken words counted as truly blasphemous, and in the opinion of the canonists they rightly subjected speakers to public punishment once sobriety had returned.

When the blasphemy contained heretical ideas or expressions, it could lead even to the severest of penalties. The entire legitimacy of punishing blasphemers—in fact, the danger of *not* punishing them—that was surveyed at the start of this chapter thus remained very much in the minds of the canonists as they discussed the problems raised by the need for definition and by variations in circumstance and intent. Biblical example, Roman law precedents, and social assumptions embodied in the statutes of many secular jurisdictions combined with texts from the *Corpus iuris canonici* to allow the canonists to create what can only be described as a strict law on this subject.

The canon law of blasphemy was meant to have what writers today commonly describe as "a chilling effect" on speech. It was designed to keep men and women from venturing too close to the line beyond which their words would risk incurring God's wrath. No doubt it did have something very much like that effect. But it is noteworthy that none of the commentators counted their efforts as a success as a result. To the contrary, they repeatedly lamented the prevalence and the evil consequence of the crime of blasphemy. Its extirpation seemed very far away. No progress was apparent. The principal complaint of the canonists at the time was not that the canon law of blasphemy had "chilled" the free discussion of ideas. Their complaint was quite the reverse: that the law had not proved "chilling" enough.

11 Criminal Procedure: The Law of Double Jeopardy

Many students of English legal history who have only a nodding sort of acquaintance with the canon law know that it contained a rule something like the modern prohibition against double jeopardy in criminal cases. The existence of the rule is known comparatively widely because a dispute about it provided the occasion of one of the most dramatic and famous collisions between church and state in the Middle Ages. This was the twelfth-century dispute over "criminous clerks" between King Henry II and the archbishop of Canterbury, Thomas Becket.[1] The story is particularly well known because in our own century it has provided the subject of T. S. Eliot's *Murder in the Cathedral* and also a successful play by Jean Anouilh.

The archbishop claimed that clerics could only be tried in a spiritual tribunal and that those who had been found guilty of a crime in that forum could not legitimately be brought afterward before the courts of the king. To do so would be putting them twice in jeopardy. This would, according to Becket, be contrary to the rules of the church and the commands of the gospel. The king argued that the archbishop's position would allow criminals to escape with the mildest of penalties. Even if ecclesiastical justice were trustworthy (which in the view of many it was not), the spiritual tribunals lacked the power adequately to punish "criminous clerks." The most that could happen there was that they would be stripped of their clerical office. To try them in the spiritual forum and then send them to the king's court for full punishment would be much the more sensible method. Properly understood, it would not be double jeopardy but instead simply an unobjectionable splitting of the trial from the punishment.

By his murder at the hands of the king's men, inside the walls of his own cathedral, Becket not only won the martyr's crown. The event also secured a victory for the archbishop's legal position, spawning the institution of benefit of clergy in English law. In the outcome commentators have seen the first open vindication of a prohibition against trying a person twice for the same offense.[2] The prohibition is particularly familiar because it won a place among the liberties guaranteed by the Constitution of the United States. The Fifth Amendment to the Constitution requires that no person shall "be subject for the same offense to be twice put in jeopardy of life or limb." As interpreted in American law, the guarantee extends to all crimes, not just those that impose physical sanctions. It provides a fundamental guarantee that individuals will not be harassed by multiple prosecutions for the same act.

Despite its fundamental place in the U.S. legal system, the history of the prohibition in the English common law is tangled, and the genesis of the constitutional prohibition is uncertain. There has been a tendency, even among historians, to treat the rule as simply axiomatic. It has been claimed, for instance, that it "hardly seems necessary to adduce reasons in its support."[3] Blackstone regarded it as a "universal maxim of the common law of England" and did not feel obliged to go much further.[4] Repeated decisions of the United States Supreme Court have declared simply that the right against double jeopardy is "deeply ingrained" in the "Anglo-American system of jurisprudence."[5]

When the time has come time to look further into the subject, commentators have found it difficult to penetrate much beyond these comfortable assumptions.[6] It may well be true that the arcane and apparently contradictory learning surrounding the pleas of *auterfois acquit* and *auterfois convict* in the common law expressed something like the sentiment that lay behind the constitutional prohibition. But the conclusion requires a stretch of the imagination. More recent investigation casts doubt on the antiquity and universality of the prohibition against double jeopardy in early English law. It has even been suggested that the principle was at some stage an import from the European *ius commune*.[7] English evidence can certainly be found to support such a suggestion[8]—all the more reason, it would seem, for examining the scope and meaning of the prohibition of double jeopardy as it existed in the classical canon law.

THE CANONICAL RULE

When one begins that examination, the law of the church appears to be a very likely candidate for whatever honor accrues to the prohibition's source. Or if it must, in the end, stand aside as the ultimate source in favor of Roman or even Greek law,[9] at least the canon law supplied a clear and early statement of the principle. Its statement is to be found in several canonical collections dating from the ninth century,[10] and the Gregorian Decretals contained the following chapter, taken from a canon of an earlier church council (X 5.1.6): "De his criminibus de quibus absolutus est accusatus non potest accusatio replicari" [An accusation cannot be repeated with respect to those crimes of which the accused has been absolved]. The *glossa ordinaria* commenting on this chapter also stated the principle with apparent clarity: "It is said here that if anyone is absolved of a crime of which he was accused, he should not again be accused of the same thing." The same sentiment was found stated in texts within the *Decretum*. Thus: "The Scripture holds, 'God does not punish twice in the same matter'" (Dist. 81 c. 12), and again, "Whether one is condemned or absolved, there can be no further action involving the same crime" (C. 2 q. 1 c. 14). Contemporary canonists made similar statements. Hostiensis, for example: "The delict of a man should not be brought into question more than once."[11] Or the influential proceduralist William Durantis: "Note particularly of those who are accused that they cannot be accused of the same crime by anyone if they are absolved."[12] If they were condemned, it was an a fortiori conclusion that they could not be again brought before court.[13] One punishment would have been enough.

The continuity and consequence of the rule within the canonical tradition is suggested by its regular inclusion in manuals of procedural law and practice from the later medieval period.[14] Prosper Farinacius, an advocate at the Roman court and influential writer on the criminal law of the church, summed up this learning: "A process cannot be initiated against a man who has otherwise been absolved of the same delict."[15] One of the other great sixteenth-century proceduralists of the *ius commune*, Julius Clarus, was stating the identical *com-*

munis opinio in writing that "the defendant in a criminal cause may plead that he was otherwise convicted or absolved of the same crime, for in this case no one may proceed further against him."[16]

The procedures that attached themselves to the rule turned out to be more complex than these statements seem to imply. Criminal defendants were not in the end given the blanket sort of protection the words suggest, although the reality of the basic principle within the canon law always remained real enough. The complexities surrounding the rule—the subject of this chapter—are also revealing about the inner nature of the canon law. Several of the canon law's twists and turns took on a rather different form than a modern lawyer naturally expects.

There is, however, one aspect of the general outline that will seem familiar to those who follow the subject of double jeopardy in modern American law. Indeed, the full meaning of the prohibition against double jeopardy in the canon law turns out to be not wholly dissimilar to the legal situation in the United States today. The constitutional prohibition seems clear enough on the surface. It is only when one penetrates beneath the surface that an intricate and (to many) troublesome body of law removes both that clarity and to some extent the constitutional protection afforded the criminal defendant.

BASIS FOR THE CANON LAW'S PROHIBITION

As was so often the case in the classical canon law, the commentators sought a justification for the principle of double jeopardy in the pages of the Bible. In this case, they found it in a maxim from St. Jerome's reading of a verse from the Book of Nahum (1:9): *Non enim judicat Deus bis in idipsum.*[17] God does not judge twice in the same matter. If this was so before God, it was reasoned, so should it be on earth. Although this passage may seem a very slender reed upon which to build a prohibition against double jeopardy in criminal cases, it was in fact so understood and so used in the twelfth century.[18] Citation to the passage figured more than once both in the canons of Gratian's *Decretum* (Dist. 81 c. 12; C. 13 q. 2 c. 30; C. 23 q. 5 c. 6; De pen. Dist.

3 c. 44) and in his own *dicta* upon them (d.p. De pen. Dist. 3 cc. 39, 42). It was buttressed by the example of the treatment of Abiathar the priest in the Book of Kings; Abiathar was "worthy of death" according to King Solomon, but because of his service and station he was returned "to his own fields" instead (3 Kings 2:26). Archbishop Thomas Becket and his supporters cited the passages seriously and repeatedly as providing a scriptural basis for their position,[19] and echoes of their efforts are found in the decretist literature of the day.[20]

The early canonists also discerned support for the prohibition against double jeopardy in several parts of the Roman law. They drew upon the civil law, and their discussion is matched by parallel development of a rule against double jeopardy among the medieval civilians. The treatments of the subject found in Baldus and Bartolus, for example, were relevant to many of the subjects taken up by the canonists.[21] The canonists cited their opinions frequently. For the most part these opinions were not much different from those of the canonists, although they diverged slightly when the special concerns of spiritual jurisdiction were involved. Apart from special areas, however, the work of the civilians was blended together with the canon law to create what we might call a *ius commune* of double jeopardy. It has led, and could be followed, into modern Continental law, where the principle is known as *Non bis in idem*.[22]

Even without the parallel development, it is obvious that the canonists found in the Roman law texts statements of fundamental principle that became important in the development of the canonical rule. Most direct was a decree of Emperor Honorius (Cod. 9.2.9): "Whoever is brought under accusation for a public crime cannot be brought by another for the same crime." There was also the clear statement of the rule in a work by the jurist Ulpian (Dig. 48.2.7.2): "The governor must not allow a man to be charged with the same offenses of which he has already been acquitted." The Digest also contained a number of different examples in which the jurists had applied the underlying principle to concrete situations. These too were found useful by the canonists. Thus, a defendant could not be sued twice for violation of a tomb, even though the first suit was brought by someone other than the person immediately entitled to bring the suit (Dig.

47.12.6). A loss to cargo at sea might be remedied by an action of theft against either the seaman who committed the offense or the master, but the one action would bar the other (Dig. 4.9.6.4). "We ought to be content with one [action]," the law said.[23] A further example was that in *actiones populares*, if more than one action was brought on the same ground, the defense of res judicata was regularly allowed (Dig. 47.23.3).

The canonists also found support for the principle in several canons and decretals, quite apart from the decree from the Council of Mainz quoted above. Innocent IV used the occasion of commenting on a decretal dealing with finality in compromised episcopal elections to state the broader rule. Where a sentence had been given in a criminal matter, the sentence bound all parties, even those who had taken no part in the first proceedings.[24] In discussing the import of a synodal decree that affirmed the rights of the bishop to investigate and punish crimes in his diocese and to do so by summoning laymen as legitimate participants, Hostiensis took note of an incidental benefit of the procedure. The accused would by this means the more readily be spared the possibility of two trials, one in the secular, the other in the spiritual forum. As an argument in favor of the result, Hostiensis proposed the same scriptural justification Gratian had: "The Lord will not judge twice in the same matter, nor is the delict of a person to be several times drawn into question."[25]

Statements like these, not compelled and only indirectly encouraged by the laws, canons, and decretals themselves, suggest that this prohibition against trying a person twice for the same offense was part of the normal habit of mind of the canonists and civilians of the classical period. This suggestion seems consistent also with the fuller treatment of the subject found in their works. This rule was not developed with the amplitude and care that one finds in its descendant in modern law. The medieval canonists sometimes "confused" it with the legal principle of res judicata. They were not always as careful to distinguish between acquittals and convictions as a modern writer would be, and they were less systematic in dealing with the subject than they were in some other areas of the law. They gave little attention, for example, to what has been called "the linchpin for all double jeopardy jurisprudence." That is the question of how far the proceeding must have gone for the prohibition to attach.[26] This said, however, it remains true that the rule was a fundamental part of the canon law. Clear acceptance of the rule was simply combined with a certain reluctance to explore its importance and scope as a means of protecting criminal defendants. The canonical rule of double jeopardy cannot be fairly described simply as "res judicata in clerical gray." The requirements of the church's interest in crime were thought special enough to give rise to a series of exceptions. They tell us something valuable about the canon law itself.

EXCEPTIONS TO THE RULE

Unlike most of the subjects examined in this book, the principle against trying a person twice claimed no special section within the canonical texts. Gratian did not treat it directly in any *quaestio* or distinction. The Gregorian Decretals contained no separate title devoted to it. The canon stating the principle is only one of twenty-seven chapters of the first title of the fifth book, which deals with criminal accusations. Nor did it have an identifiable "catchword" by which one can follow it with ease through the indexes of works on the *ius commune*. Yet the principle, or something very similar to it, appears with some frequency in the texts and works of the early commentators.

To one first coming to the texts, the rule against double jeopardy seems to have been a rule most conspicuous in canonical treatments when an exception to it was being stated. It seems almost to pop up from time to time in these circumstances. In treating a particular text, the canonists were given to saying something like, "Note this canon, one in which the same matter was twice raised against the accused," or "Here you have a case where diverse punishments are inflicted for the same offense."[27] Roughly the same method has been adopted in the treatment that follows. The question is: Where did the rule against double jeopardy *not* apply? When could a person in fact be subject to two distinct penalties for the same offense? Two relatively simple cases, both of which will probably appear obvious to modern readers, provide a starting point. Then there will be reason to move toward some of the more problematical exceptions.

Prior Excommunication

A canon in the *Decretum* (Dist. 81 c. 12) stated explicitly that a cleric guilty of crime was to be deposed but not deprived of communion. To do both, it declared, would violate the principle that God does not judge twice in the same matter. Despite this, the canon law came to allow a person both to be excommunicated and to be punished separately for the same offense. However, it directed that the sanctions should ordinarily be successive; the punishment would be one part of the means by which the sentence of excommunication was lifted.

Perhaps this result is best considered not so much an exception to the rule against double jeopardy as it is an application of the principle that excommunication was meant to be "medicinal" in nature, a subject to be more fully explored in Chapter 14. Excommunication was ordinarily imposed for contumacy, and it was meant to bring the person subject to it back within the Christian community. Hence it was not a punishment in the sense of the law of double jeopardy, and no defendant could object that he was being twice put in danger of punishment.

Once the problem is thought through, the result seems self-evident. It is important that it be stated nonetheless, because of the importance of the subject for understanding the assumptions under which the ecclesiastical courts worked. The sanction of excommunication was regarded as the most serious sanction at the disposal of the canon law, but in the eyes of the law a sentence of excommunication would not amount to a penalty for the crime itself but rather a sanction for the person's refusal to submit to the jurisdiction of the church and do penance for the crime. It could thus not be contended that the excommunicated person had ever been either condemned or absolved of commission of the crime itself.[28] It was because of this assumption that a person who had committed a crime and been excommunicated as a result could not complain about double jeopardy if he was later punished for the same crime. He had simply been excommunicated for refusal to conform his conduct with the law of the church. This was a case, of which we shall see several, in which a different purpose for a judicial action excluded application of the rule against double jeopardy.

Civil Proceedings

A second situation in which a difference in purpose led to the same result existed when the criminal matter arose within a civil context. It is a familiar exception to the law of double jeopardy today,[29] but it arose with more frequency under the canon law than it does in modern law, and it presented a more difficult problem than appears at first sight. The *exceptio criminis* was a normal part of ecclesiastical procedure; it meant challenging the right of a party to sue, or of a witness to testify, by objecting that he was guilty of a specific crime. The *exceptio* led to a judicial decision on the question, and that in turn raised the question of the decision's effect for the future. Similarly, before a cleric could be promoted or receive an ecclesiastical benefice, he was required to submit to an inquest as to his fitness for the office. One of the questions the inquest would be asked was whether the cleric had committed a crime. The same matter might even be raised later on, since the cleric's deposition from the benefice could be sought on the grounds that he had been made *irregularis* by committing a crime.

Would the determination of whether or not the individuals involved had committed the crime in this context exclude subsequent criminal prosecution for the same crime? In favor of an affirmative answer two things could be said: first, the criminal matter would be fully ventilated during the first proceedings, and second, being deprived of a valuable office or incurring *infamia* was in fact a punishment for the crime. The decision on the substantive question could not have been dismissed as so trivial or incidental as to preclude a claim of double jeopardy. If God did not judge twice in the same matter, should the ecclesiastical courts be allowed to do so by styling one case criminal, the other civil?

Despite the formal plausibility of this argument, the *communis opinio* was against it. The law held that the two proceedings were so separate in nature that it would not be a violation of the rule against repeated accusation to allow a second determination and a true criminal punishment. The principal end of the civil proceeding was to secure the removal of an unworthy person from ecclesiastical office or from acting as a plaintiff, not to punish him for his crime.[30] A papal decretal had drawn such a distinction in connection with simony, though not in precisely these circumstances (X 5.3.32).[31] And in terms of the underlying reason for the rule, it could be said that the crime would remain "insufficiently punished" if the criminal were allowed to rely upon the prohibition against double jeopardy in these circumstances.[32]

This exception was itself not without exceptions. Where the "civil" action had been brought *ad vindictam* rather than to recover damages or to restore a private interest, it did rule out further criminal proceedings.[33] The *actio iniuriarum* was the normal example given by the commentators. And the principal rule might also be invoked in one other circumstance: suppose X sued Y, raising a matter that could also be the subject of a criminal prosecution. If Y was absolved in this suit, X could not subsequently seek to commence a criminal proceeding against him.[34] It was something like an estoppel.

Defects in the Prior Proceedings

A further situation in which a plea of double jeopardy was excluded and a second proceeding permitted arose in cases in which the accuser in the first trial was a "prevaricator." That meant a sham accuser. To understand this exception, it is necessary to remember that under the *ius commune* there were three separate ways in which criminals could be brought to trial and punished. The first was the *accusatio*, in which an individual, usually a person who had suffered from the defendant's allegedly criminal acts, both initiated and conducted the prosecution. It differed from a civil action in that the accuser's intent was to subject the defendant to criminal penalties, not to recover damages. The other ways were *inquisitio* and *denunciatio*. The former was a criminal proceeding brought by and in the name of the judge. The latter was one based upon information that came to the judge's attention from an individual, but it was otherwise very much like the *inquisitio*. The denunciation was first supported by the individual's own oath and then carried forward by the judge.

The medieval jurists treated the *accusatio* as the standard form of prosecution. It was the oldest, and the form most often found in the texts. In fact, it had proved to be a clumsy method. Not only was it a generally inefficient way of combating crime, but the traditional *accusatio* required the accuser to submit himself to the same penalties, if he lost, to which a successful prosecution would have subjected the defendant. Although this penalty seems rarely to have been exacted in later medieval practice, its threat and the less efficient nature of the *accusatio* led to its being pretty much eclipsed in ordinary usage by the *inquisitio* as the Middle Ages went along. But it never went wholly out of use, and it was invariably treated first by the commentators.

Its continuing existence meant that it was possible for a criminal to take advantage of the rule against double trials by colluding with an accuser. For a price, the nominal accuser would first bring and then purposefully fail to prove the criminal charge. If this had happened, it would have seemed quite unfair to forbid a second prosecution brought by another person, and the Roman law so provided. A second *accusatio* could be brought either where the first absolution was the product of collusion or where a second accuser, having a personal interest in the matter, had been ignorant without fault of the existence of the first.[35] The canon law took over this rule. It was buttressed by adopting a presumption designed to overcome the difficult problem of proving actual collusion. Where the accused had been seen talking with the accuser in a familiar way, collusion would be presumed.[36]

This exception, once established, was capable of expansion. If this particular sort of defect in the first trial was enough to permit a second, it might equally be thought that other sorts of defects should also provide a similar exception. It might even be expected in the canon law. Errors in procedure in the first trial might be said to have prevented the court from arriving at the truth and thus to have justified another, better criminal prosecution. In the canonical *restitutio in integrum* examined in Chapter 4, something very much like this happened. Conceivably, it would even have been possible to interpret the canon forbidding a second *accusatio* (X 5.1.6) narrowly, so narrowly in fact that it would not have precluded a second *inquisitio*. That too might conceivably have been justified as part of the church's mission to punish crimes adequately.

However, this did not happen. For these purposes, the canon law treated the *inquisitio*, the *accusatio*, and the *denunciatio* as one. If the person was brought before a public court and tried by means of any one of them, he was protected against a subsequent action by means of any of the others.[37] It was concluded effectively that "the inquisition succeeds to the place of the accusation."[38] Similarly, the early canon law did not allow a second trial because of simple procedural error or failure of proof in the first instance,[39] although where defendant had secured his absolution by bribing the judge or the witnesses, a second trial could be held.[40]

The only real exception not connected with wrongdoing by the defendant or a nominal accuser commonly mentioned by the canonists of the classical era arose where the first case was dismissed because of what we would describe as a personal incapacity of the accuser.[41] For example, a person marked by *infamia* might not ordinarily bring a criminal accusation under the canon law. If the case was dismissed for that reason, then a second prosecution was not ruled out. The same held for dismissals for want of jurisdiction over the accused. As we would say, not having reached the merits, these proceedings did not count as double jeopardy.

It seems to be the case, however, that further inroads were made in the rule under the later *ius commune*. A distinction was drawn between absolution given for failure of proof and one rendered because the defendant's innocence had been established. There was authority in favor of restricting applicability of the rule against double jeopardy to the second case.[42] Even where the opposite rule obtained, the practice in some places when defendants were not convicted because of simple failure of proof was for sentences absolving the defendant to include a special clause: *rebus sic stantibus*.[43] The evident purpose was to avoid the prohibition against double jeopardy. Where new facts later came to light, facts that might allow a court to reach a different result, then a new criminal proceeding could in fact be commenced despite the normal applicability of the prohibition of double jeopardy, because of this proviso. If these rules became the normal practice, the canonical rule against double jeopardy must have been less important in practice than is suggested by its statement in the treatises. So far as I know, no one has examined the question. It would not have been the only occasion on which jurists have found a way around a rule ostensibly protecting criminal defendants.

Canonical Purgation

An ordinary way of "trying" a person publicly defamed on a crime in the medieval canon law was to require him to undergo canonical purgation. If sufficient *infamia* against him existed and he denied the crime of which he was defamed, he was required to swear an oath that he was innocent of the crime and also to find compurgators (or oath helpers in the parlance of the English common law) who could swear to their belief in his oath. Much has been written about this procedure in England, for it became the all but universal way of dealing with ecclesiastical offenses during the Middle Ages. We have already taken some notice of it in Chapter 6.

In the context of this chapter, it raises the question of whether or not successfully undergoing canonical purgation barred a subsequent criminal proceeding brought by the party injured. About this subject there was considerable division of opinion. On the one hand, there was a decretal that could be said to authorize the subsequent proceedings (X 5.34.8). It allowed a bishop to try a cleric by canonical purgation after the cleric had undergone the ordeal of cold water. The reasoning behind the papal ruling seems instead to have rested upon the Fourth Lateran Council's rejection of the ordeal as a proper means of proof. The bishop must not be kept from taking legitimate action by a procedure of doubtful validity.

On the other, the decretal was not exactly in point, and to allow indiscriminate ignoring of the results of compurgation whenever an accuser later appeared violated equitable principles and contradicted the assumptions discussed in the previous section. It went too far. Some canonists took positions one way or the other. Others offered distinctions.[44] Under one of the latter, the rule against double jeopardy would apply if the later accuser had been present or at least aware of the compurgation but not if he had been absent or ignorant. Another was that double jeopardy would apply but that the accuser could secure an equivalent conviction for perjury (i.e., the compurgation would have itself been the perjury). A third held that the result should depend on the bona fides of the accuser. If there came to be a *communis opinio* on the point, it has so far eluded me.

Settlement and Dispensation

A common habit of mind during the era when the canon law was born required the canonists to deal with the problem of what to do when the criminal charge was settled short of final sentence. People (but not the canonists) assumed that a party aggrieved by a theft, a physical injury, or even the killing of one of his kin might choose to settle, or in the language of the time, to compound with the criminal. The criminal paid a sum of money to the victim, and that settled the matter between them. Students of English legal history will be familiar with payment of the *wergeld* to settle disputes we would class under the law of crimes.

Something similar to this existed in the law of the church, where a bishop exercised a power of dispensation in a particular case. Allowing someone to breach the obligation incurred by an oath, a subject examined briefly in Chapter 6, would be one example in which this might happen. By "dispensing" against the oath, the bishop settled what might otherwise have been a criminal prosecution for perjury. Analytically, these two situations were much alike. Dispensations were not given in exchange for monetary payments, as secular compositions for crime were, but like them they involved a decision not to bring a criminal proceeding even though the law might authorize one. Moreover, they were made by the person who had the authority to bring the charge. Both raised the question of whether anyone else could subsequently raise the matter, or whether the excused criminal would instead have a valid defense to all further prosecution. It is not coincidental that both were commonly treated one after the other in the writings of the jurists.[45]

The canon law's answer to the two cases was not the same, however, and in this case the reason seems to have rested upon an important policy. The church set its face against private composition. The danger was that crimes against the church's law would go unpunished if compounding was given too wide a scope. Vindication of the law's purpose might be frustrated by private agreement. Therefore, it came to be the rule that a judge was perfectly free to initiate a criminal *inquisitio*, even after the injured party had settled his quarrel.[46] In fact, the judge was encouraged to do so, and others with an interest in prosecution of the crime might legitimately do the same.

This same reasoning did not apply to the dispensation, despite the analytical similarity between the two. If the crime was subject to episcopal dispensation and if the bishop had jurisdiction over the potential defendant, a dispensation would bar a subsequent criminal proceeding.[47] Since the bishop had the duty of enforcing the church's criminal law by virtue of his office, his dispensation would be a final determination of the case. It was in that situation, therefore, but not that of compounding by the aggrieved party that the canonical principle "Divine clemency does not permit that sins once dismissed shall be further avenged" (De pen. Dist. 4 c. 24) came into play.

The Penitential Forum

How far did the principle extend? The question was posed pointedly by the existence of the "internal forum." That was the normal canonical term for the penitential side the clergy's responsibility, the cure of souls. We associate it with private confession to a priest and the giving of absolution and a penance. The question can be put starkly. Did absolution in this forum serve to shield the penitent from subsequent prosecution in the church's external forum, that is, the consistory courts of bishops and archdeacons?

This was a separate question from the one to be taken up next: the relationship between results reached in spiritual and secular tribunals, although there were resemblances between the two problems. The medieval church possessed its own public courts. Criminal prosecutions were routinely undertaken in them. Many of the subjects of these prosecutions would also have come up within the internal forum. To take an example, the question might be whether public, ecclesiastical ex officio proceedings could be brought against a man or woman in the bishop's court for adultery or blasphemy after the man or woman had confessed the crime and received absolution in the penitential forum.

In some ways it seems logical that absolution should have barred later public prosecution, at least as far as the church went. The result might be different where secular courts were concerned; they might have their own laws. But as to the church, the priest was exercising a power conferred by Jesus upon the apostles, the power to loose men from their sins (John 20:23). In giving absolution, the priest was carrying out that grant of power and, it would seem, was thereby exercising in the fullest sense the church's hold upon the penitent. The priest said, "Ego te absolvo" [I absolve thee]. Did these words mean something other than what they said?

The short answer is that they did mean something else. The canon law drew a line between the internal forum and the external forum. Satisfaction in the one did not impede action in the other. In this respect it was actually preferable on the part of the criminal to have a dispensation.[48] Absolution in the confessional was no defense to a public prosecution. Even if one had been absolved by the pope himself, according to one seventeenth-century writer, the result would be no different.[49]

There seems to have been no direct ruling on the point, and there was some argument about its applicability in extreme cases. For example, suppose the criminal had been assigned a public penance in the internal forum. If he was subsequently prosecuted successfully in the external forum, the normal course would have been for him again to be assigned a public penance. That would amount to real duplication in remedies. Some of the canonists therefore argued that the prohibition against double punishment might apply in this situation.

However, even here, the *communis opinio* seems to have been to the contrary.[50]

The result was explained in several ways. The most prevalent way in the works of the medieval canonists was simply to point to the number of times it had happened. It was a common interpretative technique among the medieval jurists to draw out from a text a meaning that was implicit but not directly stated in the text. They applied this technique to the question of double punishment, pointing out several canons in the *Decretum* where the text seems to have made room for punishment in both the internal and the external forum (e.g., Dist. 48 c. 1; Dist. 50 c. 9; C. 1 q. 7 c. 2; C. 33 q. 2 c. 8).[51] For example, one text described a penitent priest as having been deposed from his office. The canonists concluded that the text must have been assuming that the penance had not prevented a public punishment; otherwise it would not make sense. The canonists drew that lesson from it. The Bible was also called into play and invoked in much the same way. It demonstrated the compatibility of forgiveness of a criminal by God with the criminal's further punishment. God had accepted and exalted David, even though David was a murderer and a fornicator. The early Christians remembered David as a "man after [God's] own heart" (Acts 13:22), no matter what his faults. Yet God's acceptance had not been complete. God had not allowed David to build the temple, because David had "shed much blood upon the earth" (1 Chron. 22:8). If God's forgiveness was compatible with additional punishment in that instance, the church might do likewise in its own tribunals.

This approach was entirely characteristic of the classical canonists. Today in the United States it would no doubt be regarded as a "purely formal approach" and criticized on that account. The approach lacks realistic analysis of what the rule would mean in practice. The closest the medieval canonists came to that "realist" way of thinking of analysis was to put the problem in terms of the interest being vindicated. In the penitential forum, God was being satisfied and the health of a person's soul being set right. That is one reason one was properly "convicted" without proof or other due process. In the exterior forum, however, it was otherwise. The interest of the res publica was being vindicated. That was one reason for the rule that only public crimes were to be dealt with there. Since different purposes were being served, there was no real duplication of remedies and no violation of the rule against double punishment.[52]

Another way of making essentially the same argument was to say that the public prosecution was undertaken *ad vindictam*, that is, in order to punish. The action in the penitential forum, on the other hand, was medicinal. It was curative in nature. Hence there was no overlap in purpose between the two. This analysis was suggested in the work of Innocent IV,[53] and it was more fully set out in that of Joannes Andreae.[54] To this extent it might be said that the canonists moved slightly away from a formal approach as time went on. Still, it hardly amounted to "realist jurisprudence," and the formal approach was still much in evidence in the fourteenth century when Joannes wrote. The more modern way of looking at this legal problem was not entirely absent from the *ius commune*, however, at least if one moves forward to the sixteenth century. Julius Clarus gave as the reason for excluding absolution in the penitential forum from consideration in the external: If the rule were otherwise, he wrote, "anyone could easily evade the punishment for a crime by getting absolution from his confessor. That would be ridiculous in the extreme."[55]

There were two more problems—conceptually harder ones. The first involved the subject we looked at in Chapter 8, the effects of baptism. If the canon law rightly permitted the church's courts to punish men and women who had violated the criminal law of the church and been absolved in the penitential forum, could the same be said in a case involving baptism? Would receiving baptism after having committed a crime prevent criminal prosecution in the church's external forum? The argument was most strikingly put in a famous decretal of Pope Innocent III (X 4.19.8) upholding the continuing validity of marriages contracted by pagans who subsequently became Christians: "Marriages are not dissolved by the sacrament of baptism. Crimes are." Although as a practical matter the question would have arisen much less frequently than that arising from penitence, perhaps that would have been all the more reason for giving effect to the washing away of sin accomplished in baptism. Nonetheless, the canon law reached the same

result here that it did in dealing with double jeopardy and the penitential forum. Baptism wiped away the candidate's sins before God. It did
not do so as to one's offenses against others.[56]

The second question, in many ways a more intriguing one, concerned the remitting of sins by a penitent. Suppose a person forgave
his enemy in the penitential forum—say by setting aside a long-
standing quarrel in favor of the Christian virtue of charity. Suppose
further that the quarrel was one that provided the penitent involved
with the right to accuse his enemy of a crime. Could that man leave
the confessional, then turn around and bring a criminal charge against
the person he had forgiven *in foro animae*? This would seem to make
a mockery of his forgiveness. But as it happened, he could.[57] Forgiveness in the penitential forum was thought to have removed the "ran-
cor of spirit" from the penitent's heart, but it did not remove the *ius
accusandi* that accrued on account of the crime.[58]

Probably this result was the only one the canon law could have accepted. To have allowed the plea of double jeopardy in these circumstances would have breached the line between the two forums and
probably also the seal of the confessional. The opposite result was not
expressly required by any canonical text, and in the view of the canonists, it would have subverted the public weal, confiscated a lawful
ius accusandi, and prevented a palpable wrong from being redressed.
Could a man steal another's possessions and pretend that he had done
no wrong when the person he had wronged fulfilled the Scripture's
commands to forgive him? Could the thief be forgiven *in foro animae*
and thereby bar his own punishment? To follow logic to that point
would have been to turn the gospel on its head.

The Temporal Forum

Jurisdictional rules kept many possible applications of the rule against
double jeopardy from occurring. The *privilegium fori*, for example, required clerics to be tried only before spiritual tribunals, so that in theory at least no problem of double punishment could arise. This was
the principle for which Thomas Becket fought. Nevertheless, under

the law of the church, many crimes were classified as "of mixed forum." Blasphemy, the subject of Chapter 10, was one of them, and there were many others. These crimes could be punished either in an ecclesiastical court or in a temporal court. The obvious question that arose, related to the subject of this chapter, was whether a criminal prosecution in one forum would bar a criminal prosecution in the other. The only slightly less obvious question was which of the two legal systems should have the upper hand in determining the matter. Duplication of jurisdiction was a question, as a later commentator was to note, "that ha[d] been much controverted among the *Doctores.*"[59] Readers will recognize a parallel in this to the problem of dual sovereignty, federal and state, that has bedeviled the modern American law of double jeopardy.

Unlike some of the other problems raised in this part of the canon law, this one appeared to be covered by a papal decretal. In the decretal that became the locus classicus for discussion of the subject, Pope Boniface VIII prohibited all manner of attacks and assaults against cardinals of the Roman Church and their *familiares*, adding a frightening list of penalties to be imposed upon all persons who in any way contravened its provisions or even contributed to their contravention (Sext. 5.9.5). For present purposes, the important feature of the decretal was that it specifically authorized temporal officials to apply temporal sanctions against the offenders for the same crimes. In fact, it required them to do so. If they failed to comply after due notice, they were themselves to be excommunicated. Thus in this situation the canon law seemed to envision that for "mixed" crimes each forum would subject the offender to its own penalties. Other decretals seemed incidentally to justify the same result (X 5.20.7; X 5.26.2).

There were at least three ways of understanding these decretals, all of which were fully consistent with a canonical understanding of the proper relationship between the "two swords."[60] First, it was said that the temporal courts were here simply being called upon to carry out the sentences of the ecclesiastical courts. This is the same canonical principle to be examined in Chapter 13. Pope Boniface's words were certainly compatible with the theory that secular authorities were required to respect the church's decrees and to lend physical support to them when necessary. Second, it might be said that the decretal was meant to be applied only *in atrocioribus*. That restricted its use to the most serious crimes. The extravagance of the decretal's language supported this understanding. Because of the horror of some crimes, it might be appropriate to make an exception to the prohibition of double jeopardy, and this would appear to have been one such situation.[61] Third, it might be said that the prohibition did not apply at all because the purpose of the two prosecutions would be categorically different. This was essentially a repetition in a new setting of the last subject treated. Proceedings in the ecclesiastical forum were medicinal in character; proceedings in the temporal forum were penal.[62] Hence it could be said that there was no real violation of the principle that God does not judge twice in the same cause.

Any of these three offered a way of salvaging the prohibition against double jeopardy. Where one of them could not apply, there the prohibition would, and the principle of *praeventio* would come into play to determine which jurisdiction's proceedings took priority.[63] The real danger apprehended by the canonists was something else: that the decretal might also be read as authorizing a breach in the canonical principle that required the temporal courts to respect the decisions of the ecclesiastical tribunals. It might be read as saying that the two systems were entirely separate. Each could then go its own way. This would mean that if a person was first acquitted in an ecclesiastical court, he could later be tried and convicted in a temporal court despite the early absolution. If convicted in the ecclesiastical court, he could be tried and punished again in the other forum. The canonists did not, therefore, read the decretal that way.

That is what happened all the same. The temporal courts in several parts of Europe came to accord no juridical force, or very little, to proceedings in the spiritual forum. In the sixteenth century, Julius Clarus justified this result by supposing that "ecclesiastical jurisdiction and spiritual jurisdiction [were] absolutely separate and distinct."[64] In a legal regime constructed from the combination of Roman and religious law, it may seem startling to come upon language as stark as these words of Julius Clarus. His statement might as easily have come from the pen of a modern American advocate of the strict separation of church and state as from a jurist of the *ius commune*, to whom the modern American doctrine would no doubt have appeared as mysterious as it would impious. But there it is.

Additional Exceptions

The seven or so situations just explored do not exhaust the canon law on the subject of double jeopardy. They were the main exceptions. But they were not the only ones a capable canonist could carve out. By canvassing the texts, it was possible, indeed customary, to discover twelve (or more) separate situations in which the prohibition against double jeopardy did not apply, or at least not fully apply.[65] Several of those now seem, at best, to have been variants of those stated above, and some of them seem more the product of juristic ingenuity than actual exceptions to a stated rule. When this is admitted, the canonists' treatment of the texts does nevertheless illustrate one way they were capable of broadening the scope of apparently restricted legal precedents. They did so to preserve the principle of the prohibition against double jeopardy without at the same time allowing it to become an impediment to effective criminal procedure.

THE CANONICAL RULE AND SUBJECTIVE RIGHT

Readers may have taken note of one thing that has been very much absent in what has been examined so far. That is the lack of any real discussion about the value most of us regard as animating the rule against double jeopardy: concern for the rights of the accused. Nowhere in the writings of the classical jurists does one come across expressions of concern about "callously subjecting an individual to successive retrials" such as one finds frequently in modern judicial opinions.[66] To all outward appearances the canonists simply did not look at the problems created by the prohibition against double jeopardy "from the standpoint of the individual who [was] being prosecuted."[67] And if they perceived any tension between the existence of dual sovereignties and the consequent possibility of the violation of human rights of the person subjected to successive prosecutions by each sovereign, as we clearly do today,[68] they did not say so.

Why was this? Attempting to answer that question sheds some valuable light on the interior of the canon law. It also takes observers into a subject of current scholarly debate: the origins of rights theories in Western legal thought. Briefly stated, the *status quaestionis* is the following. The emergence of theories of individual rights traditionally has been located in seventeenth-century England or in the European Enlightenment.[69] Locke and Rousseau are the great names. The view finds support in the words of a distinguished historian of the canon law, Walter Ullmann. As Ullmann saw it, the idea that individual men possessed "indigenous, autonomous and independent rights was a thesis for which we shall look in vain in the Middle Ages."[70] Indeed, for him the existence of any subjective rights would have been quite incompatible with the canon law's hierocratic, "descending" theory of government. Such rights could figure seriously in political thought only after an "unecclesiastical, liberal, modern spirit" had come to prevail.[71]

Contrary to this formulation stands the position—actually the newer one—that conceptions of natural and subjective rights actually had their origins in the Middle Ages. One strand of the "medievalist" position finds those origins in the nominalist tradition, specifically in the work of William of Ockham.[72] This view, in general, regards the notion of natural human rights with suspicion. A second strand of the "medievalists," vigorously disputing the conclusions of the first, finds the origins of conceptions of natural rights within the traditions of the *ius commune* itself.[73] According to this view, the canon law itself is the place where one should look for the origins of theories of human rights in Western legal thought.

A book about the spirit of the canon law is not the right place to enter very far into this contentious subject,[74] but the canon law of double jeopardy certainly raises it by way of example. Freedom from being prosecuted twice for the same crime is one of those essential legal rules that seem to grow out of a concern for protecting human rights. It is meant to protect the individual against the power of the state. In this sense, its existence within the canon law supports the second "medievalist" position. But on the other hand, as we have seen, the canonists discussed the subject without any real evocation of the kind of thinking we associate with subjective right. The subjective rights of the individual subject to possible double prosecution may have been there, but they were not brought to the surface.

Again, one must ask why this should be. And the answer, at least the full answer, must recognize that the question was not posed in exactly the way we would pose it today. The canon law did, in fact, contain a system of legal rights that an individual could exercise. A defendant in a criminal trial could object to double prosecution and cite canonical authority in his favor. Under the right set of circumstances, he would prevail. He could have the prosecution against him dismissed. However, the full answer must also recognize that this right was not then regarded as emanating from the individual but rather from an objective order of justice. The subjective right was only the "derivative" or the "likeness" or the "image" of an objective right.[75] In the canon law, the foundation was the objective right. The consequence was the existence of a subjective right that an individual could assert.[76]

It might be said either that this way of putting the matter amounts to simple quibbling and was without consequence or else that it is an unfortunate by-product of Germanic fascination with abstract thinking.[77] But this is not so. It had consequences. It is intelligible. In the classical canon law, the rule against double jeopardy was derived from the right ordering of society rather than from innate human rights. The canonists found it stated in the Bible, in the Roman law, and in the texts of the *Corpus iuris canonici;* as such it was a statement of how the criminal procedure was ordered according to God's plan for mankind. It was therefore not so much an end in itself as it was one part of the right ordering of society. We have seen a preference for objective ordering before—for instance, in the canon law of baptism, where the canon law refused to let the validity of the sacrament depend on the state of mind of the person being baptized. Here again that way of thinking about legal rights comes to the fore.

A concrete consequence of this understanding was the ease with which exceptions to the rule were formulated. The starting point for the canonists was an objective order. Where that right order would be jeopardized by a broad application of the rule against double prosecution, the rule gave way. In their understanding, the rule was a subsidiary part of the order of justice. As such, it could not have been meant to subvert that order. This would have happened, for example, had absolution in the penitential forum impeded prosecution in the public forum (and vice versa). Hence came the exception to the rule prohibiting double jeopardy that we explored above. Hence came also the exception for punishment in both the temporal and spiritual forum. This conclusion was not a mechanical application of a principle of double sovereignty. It was a recognition that each forum had a legitimate, but different, purpose in prosecuting those who had committed crimes. The prohibition against double jeopardy could not have been meant to stand in the way of the accomplishment of either. And it was not allowed to do so.

CONCLUSION

Two points arise by way of conclusion. The first has to do with a common characteristic of the rules of the canon law designed to protect the rights of parties to litigation. The second has to do with the utility of the history of such rules in dealing with current legal controversies.

The canonical rule against double jeopardy resembles several similar rules in the *ius commune*.[78] It was stated clearly and definitively enough, but it also contained so many exceptions and doubts, so many restrictions and limitations, that an impartial observer must wonder whether it can accurately be described as an operative rule of law. There does seem to be room for skepticism on this score. Certainly there were situations in which the rule applied. Certainly there were defendants who invoked it in practice.[79] The canonists took the rule seriously, always requiring a plausible justification before it could be set aside. But it turned out that there *were* many plausible justifications. One may legitimately ask, therefore, whether the rule provided an actual source of protection for persons accused of crimes in a way that would be thought sufficient to check the medieval equivalent of "overzealous prosecutors."

In the long run, it may even be that the early rule's lasting importance is to be found simply in the principle it laid down. Others might pick it up. They might make more of it than the canonists themselves had. If so, the canonical rule's legacy was greater than its actual significance within the *ius commune*—particularly if it is true, as some think it is, that the modern law on the subject had its origins in the *ius commune*. The history of the canonical rule would seem to be one such instance in which a rule, eaten away by exceptions in the juristic system that produced it, survived nonetheless to become a more comprehensive, effective, and human right.

The second point has to do with this outcome: the modern relevance of the rule's history. It has been the habit of American courts to look to the history of constitutional provisions for guidance in deciding difficult questions. For instance, in a landmark case of 1968 in the U.S. Supreme Court applying the constitutional guarantee against double jeopardy to proceedings in state courts, Justice Thurgood Marshall began his decision with a discussion of the history of the subject.[80] Marshall's opinion embodies what has been a frequent judicial response to hard cases.[81] Sometimes it has extended to the invocation of some very old history, not excluding history as old as that being described in this volume. It may even claim the authority of Justice Frankfurter's statement, borrowed for the occasion from O. W. Holmes: "Sometimes a page of history is worth a volume of logic."[82]

With the rule against double jeopardy, however, the invocation of history very likely has a more limited use than Frankfurter's attractive dictum suggests. Marshall was probably wise to look at the history only briefly and to draw nothing but the most general sort of conclusions from it. If it is true that the American constitutional provision was derived at some remove from the canon law, it is as important to remember the differences between the canonical rule and the modern provision as it is to note the connection between them. So different were the assumptions of the canonists from our own that looking to their opinions about double jeopardy can have only the most general sort of utility for us. It is no doubt interesting to note the connection, a quite common one as it turns out. Many of our liberties have roots that can be traced to the law of the church. It is another thing, however, to draw important conclusions from this history, at least any detailed conclusions that dictate the results in some of today's most intractable legal problems.

12 The Papacy in the Canon Law: The Law of Papal Privileges

The papacy stood at the center of the classical canon law. It was in the pages of the *Corpus iuris canonici* that some of the extraordinary claims to authority asserted by the medieval popes were most cogently expressed. The canon law's rules were themselves shaped, and in many cases determined, by the legislative and administrative powers of the Roman pontiff. And the courts of bishops and papal judges delegate, which sought to put into practice the dictates of the canon law, became one vehicle by which papal authority was made effective in parts of Europe far removed from the papal court. Prior chapters have given many an example of the exercise of papal plenitude of power. Papal authority made itself felt in virtually every corner of the canon law.

It is probably true that some modern writers have gone overboard in equating the medieval canon law with theme of the sovereignty of the papacy, thereby losing touch with the countervailing ideas and limiting factors found within the canon law itself and thereby also slightly obscuring the nature of the juristic science one finds in the writings of the medieval canonists. These modern writers have been wholly right, however, in drawing attention to the papacy's central role in many, perhaps even most, of the subjects treated by the classical canon law. That role was asserted in the canonical texts, reiterated in the commentaries, and realized in part within contemporary practice.

Prior chapters have taken up the papacy's role in leading the movement of Gregorian reform and in creating the legal rules that would carry out the program derived from it. This chapter offers a more direct look at another important aspect of the papacy's place in the canon law. It deals with the papal privilege, the grant of a special legal right by the apostolic see. The twelfth-century canonist Rufinus of

Bologna described privileges as one of the two principal ways in which the authority of the Roman Church was exalted in the world. The first came through exercise of the power to bind and loose men and women from their sins. The second came through exercise of this power of dispensation, "by which [the Roman Church could] endow churches with special privileges, establish new canons, and deprive other churches of the episcopal dignity."[1]

The authority of which Rufinus wrote was in effect the ability to stand outside the ordinary dictates of the law, to deviate from the normal rules that bound others. More than that, it was the ability to grant such a right to others, since the recipient of a papal privilege acquired a legal right that was contrary to, or at least existed outside, the dictates of the church's general law. Modern writers have echoed the substance of Rufinus's analysis,[2] and therein lies one source of the special interest of the papal privilege for working toward an understanding of the spirit of the canon law. It shows one way in which the powers of the papacy were conceived, and it illustrates one way in which those powers were exercised.

Both of these points deserve underscoring. First, papal privileges were frequent in practice and expansive in conception during the years when the canon law was being formulated. They were popular, much used both in Rome and on the fringes of Western Christendom. Their wide scope was assertive of the greatest claims to authority exercised by the medieval popes, and they occupied the respectful attention of commentators from the twelfth century forward.[3] Second, the subject illustrates some of the practical and theoretical limitations on the papacy's effective power. The medieval popes possessed no European bureaucracy. At the same time the popes were expressing sweeping claims to universal sovereignty over the government of the church and indirectly over the government of kings, they were in reality quite limited in their power to legislate and to enforce the legislation enacted. Outside the immediate environs of its own temporal authority, the papacy depended on others. The popes normally responded to requests and petitions from individuals and religious houses in issuing privileges. The growth of papal power was in a real sense dependent upon the demand for it. One will readily see both aspects in tracing the basic elements of the law of papal privileges.

Whatever the practical limitations and whatever the origins, it is certain that by adopting an expansive theory of the right to issue privileges, the canon law was asserting the pope's right to exempt individuals and groups of individuals from their normal duty to obey the law. This was a large claim. At the very least, it could become a large claim if it was often and expansively called upon in curial practice. Certainly this happened. It was also a potentially dangerous claim. Too widely dispersed, privileges can become subversive of the rule of law. One effort of this chapter will be to examine the extent to which this danger was recognized and avoided by the medieval canonists.

This is not, of course, a situation peculiar to the papacy or to the medieval canon law. Roman law contained a body of law on the subject, and the canonists drew on it. The existence of legal privileges is in fact a possibility for which most legal systems make room. It may even be a necessary part of all sophisticated systems of law, although not all systems give privileges that name. In modern law, the creation of a right in a particular group not to be subject to ordinary levels of income taxation, for example, as through special tax deductions or exemptions, is not regarded as unusual or necessarily subversive of the rule of law. The privilege, granted so generally to modern police, routinely to exceed the dictates of ordinary rules of law in the exercise of their duty is a right everyone accepts. These are modern analogies. Commentators do not find them at all strange, though they are often suspicious of their enlargement. Many observers wish to invoke, and some actually to implement, the maxim that grants in derogation of the law are to be strictly construed. Because they are concessions granted only for special and good reasons, such grants may require special justification, and many do not favor their extension without a persuasive reason. They remain lawful and routinely accepted nonetheless.

There was something of this unquestioned but limited kind of endorsement in the medieval canonists' treatment of this subject. Particularly when the rights of third parties intervened, as often happened, the canonists' habit was to allow the privileges but to read them narrowly. Their force was never interpreted away, however, and the scope and the inherent importance of the power to issue such privileges should not be allowed to drop from sight when examining the limitations. The canonist Rufinus was undoubtedly correct to stress that the right to grant privileges, as with dispensations generally, fully demonstrated the Roman Church's exalted status. The logical implications of this position led to some extreme and silly assertions—that a pope could square circles, turn black into white, transform a sinful action into a virtue. Such assertions are indeed to be found in the texts and commentaries of the classical canon law.[4] They are one part of its spirit—but only one part.

DEFINITIONS AND EXAMPLES

A privilege was defined in the canon law as "a special or private right (*ius*) allowed contrary to ordinary [law]."[5] Privileges were also sometimes described as "quasi-private laws" (Dist. 3 c. 3), or in Latin as *iura singularia*.[6] They conferred upon their recipients a legal right or status not enjoyed or exercisable by other persons or bodies.[7] The fully developed law of privileges would require that privileges *stricto sensu* be distinguished from statutes, dispensations, rescripts, apostolic graces, and the several other means of dispensing the special benefits that flowed from the plenitude of Petrine power.[8] However, most of these careful distinctions were the products of development over the course of time. At the origins of the classical canon law, some definitions were attempted. But these definitions were left more indistinct than they would be later on.

No one among the canonists challenged the lawfulness of privileges in principle. Indeed, the commentators had little doubt that such rights were authorized by divine as well as human law. In the First Book of Samuel, David had taken hallowed bread from the hand of Ahimelech the priest, even though under the law that bread was to be reserved for the priests (21:1–6). David had not incurred God's wrath thereby, and Jesus had spoken approvingly of David's example (Matt. 12:3–4). Moreover, Jesus had himself cleansed a leper "against the letter of the law" (Matt. 8:1–4). Since Jesus had also come to fulfill the law, this was thought to prove that there could be no fundamental incompatibility between the law and exceptions to it. These biblical examples showed that it was not just logical necessity—lawmaking power necessarily carries with it the power to make exceptions—that authorized the existence of privileges in the law. Scriptural authorization told in favor of the lawfulness in principle of permitting such special or private legal rights.[9]

The canonical definition of a privilege obviously had a broader scope than the exact subject of this chapter, privileges granted by the papacy, and in fact under the medieval canon law the ability to create a privilege was never confined to the Roman Church. Bishops, for example, could grant privileges in some circumstances, and secular rulers had the same right within their own sphere of authority. The rights of a privilege might even be acquired by prescription, the subject of Chapter 7 of this book. It was, however, the decided tendency of the classical canon law to concentrate the right to create privileges in the papacy, and it is this tendency that makes the subject of privileges a good vehicle for examining the role of the papacy in the canon law. In so doing, we are following the lead of the canonists themselves.[10]

Were we to follow their lead as far forward as it would take us, we should very soon find ourselves in a mass of confusing, and occasionally not quite sensible, distinctions between different classes of privileges. We should, for example, not only have to learn something about the difference between "real" and "personal" privileges and between "singular" and "communal" forms of "personal" privileges. We should have to master a complex system of classification and to think in terms of classes of distinct rights held by different classes of recipients. At the end of this chapter, we take a glance at the situation that was eventually reached. Here, however, there is no need to go that far. Writers on the modern law of the church have remarked on the unsatisfactory nature of the early thinking about exactly what a privilege was. According to these authors, the concept was not defined as clearly or as narrowly as it might have been,[11] and the proliferation of the several distinctions found in contemporary commentaries is one indication of the lack of adequate definition of which they complain. This commentary suggests beginning with the general definitions given above and postponing consideration of the developed law on the subject in the interests of discovering how the canon law on this subject grew.

GRATIAN'S *DECRETUM*

Gratian devoted *Causa* 25 of the *Decretum* to the subject of privileges, and in this instance, his treatment is extremely revealing of the spirit of the law of the church. The case he put was this: The Roman Church had granted the privileges of a baptismal church, including the right to take all tithes owed within the parish boundaries, to a particular parish church. The papacy had also granted a privilege to a monastic house, freeing the house from payment of tithes on its own lands. The monastic privilege was the later in time. By gift and by purchase, the monastic house then acquired lands within the boundaries of the parish church. Not surprisingly, the monks and the parochial clergy were at odds about whether tithes were due from these lands.[12] Two questions arose. First, did the parish church's privilege to take all tithes prevail against the ancient canons, which called for a fourfold division of tithes between the bishop, the parish clergy, the fabric of the church, and the poor? If this first privilege was invalid as contrary to the ancient canons, the other question was moot. If the parish church's privilege was valid, however, then a second question arose: Did the subsequent privilege granted to the monastery prevail against the prior privilege granted to the parish church? Was priority in time what counted, or was it something else?

Privileges and the Established Law of the Church

Gratian began with sixteen canons, most of which came from writings of the popes themselves and all of which suggested a negative answer to the first question. They read as if to say the parish church's privilege was invalid because it infringed the ancient canons

of the church. The very first (C. 25 q. 1 c. 1) was a letter attributed to
Pope Gelasius (c. 495) stating that when the universal church had
given assent to a conciliar decree, no one was more straitly bound to
secure that decree's observance than the first see of the church (i.e.,
Rome). A second canon (c. 5) equated violators of the sacred canons
with those who blasphemed against the Holy Spirit. The next (c. 6)
contained an explicit papal refusal to vary the plain terms of the ancient canons. It stated that some men had urged the pope to make
new laws and to remove the old, and the papal letter conceded that
such a power resided in the papacy. However, it went on to say that
this power must not be used to vary the law of the gospel or the decrees established by the fathers of the church. To the contrary, it asserted, the pope was bound to secure their observance, to defend them
even at the cost of his own blood. Were he to do otherwise, he would
become the source of error and confusion in the church, the very opposite of his duty. The occupant of the first see of the church is bound
above all others "to preserve the rule of true faith and to deviate in no
single wise from the constitutions of the Fathers" (C. 25 q. 1 c. 9).
From the congruence of these authorities, Gratian first drew out what
seemed to be the obvious conclusion (d.p. c. 16): "Privileges should
not be granted by the apostolic see."

Gratian then proceeded to treat the authorities he had himself adduced as objections and to answer them. It could not be true, he
began, that the *statuta* of the church constricted the powers of the
Roman Church. The Roman Church was the "heart and head" of all
churches. It was the organ of the church that God had designated as
possessing the power to establish *statuta*. The Roman Church exalted
its own power by obeying these decrees, for it was itself the source of
the decrees. To show this, Gratian invoked the example of Jesus, who
was obedient to the law but who was himself the source of the law.
Jesus had taught the scribes and the Pharisees "as one having authority, that is as *dominus* over the law" (Matt. 7:29). Yet Jesus also
stated that he had come to fulfill the law, not to destroy it, and he had
shown this to be true by his own voluntary obedience to the law. So
did the Roman pontiff. Gratian read the canons as showing that it was
expedient that the occupant of church's first seat should follow the

law. This was not because he could be obliged to do so but rather because the law itself would be exalted by his example.

The *glossa ordinaria* added to this analysis the telling example of the Roman law's *princeps*. It was clear from the Roman law texts (Dig. 1.3.31) that the emperor was *legibus solutus*. He was not subject to the law. Yet it was equally stated in the texts that the emperor should live according to the laws (Cod. 6.23.3).[13] No derogation of his authority would be involved in voluntary submission on his part. Indeed, it would increase the authority of the law if the emperor himself lent it his willing obedience. This voluntary acceptance would have the added and practical advantage of allowing lawyers to assume that the emperor would prefer the path of honesty to that of iniquity whenever a question involving his rights arose in litigation. His actions and his rights might be judged according to established legal rules. So things stood mutatis mutandis with the medieval popes. Indeed, the congruence was even greater, for the popes had the responsibility of fulfilling the law of God, not simply that of man. One may reasonably desire to follow the law of God because it is the law of God, even if one has a choice. In Gratian's view, this was exactly the situation of the Roman pontiff. The canons declaring his duty to obey the law, rightly interpreted, declared only the merits of his voluntary obedience.

Gratian found an additional reason within the canons themselves for concluding that the popes could not be considered bound by the ancient canons, as had been suggested by the first of the canons in the *Causa*. He held that "if we pay close attention to the decrees," we will see that they always contained a condition, implied or express, that they were subject to the authority of the Roman Church. "Unless the Roman Church decrees otherwise" could be considered an unspoken term of every ecclesiastical rule and every conciliar decree (d.p. C. 25 q. 1 c. 16 § 2). If this was so, no true contradiction could exist between the ancient canons of the church and the grant of a papal privilege making an exception to them. The canons, by their own (admittedly unstated) terms, were always to be read in light of the papacy's reserved power to create exceptions from them.

Finally, Gratian suggested a slightly more technical reason for excepting privileges of the apostolic see from the letter of the law: There could be no real contradiction between privileges and canons because privileges were never general laws but rather "private laws" reserved to specific grantees. The creation of a privilege, properly understood, could not involve invalidation of any of the ancient canons of the church. This was so because the grant of a papal privilege did not nullify them. The general law always remained intact after the grant of a privilege. A parish church's privilege, in other words, could not contradict the church's canons about tithes, because the canons remained valid after the privilege had been granted except insofar as it was necessary to give effect to the privilege's specific terms. That meant only the privilege's grantee. For others, the law remained intact. The apparent contradiction was thus illusory.

From these arguments, and at the end of a longish *dictum*, Gratian drew the evident conclusion about the first question raised by the quarrel between the monastic house and the parish church. By virtue of its papal privilege, the parish church should have the power to take all tithes, rather than being compelled to follow the ancient fourfold division. The papal privilege to the parish church was therefore fully warranted under the law. Gratian qualified this general conclusion, however. There were circumstances in which a privilege would not hold. The power reserved to the Roman pontiff to grant indulgences "outside the general decrees of the church" existed "for reasons of religion or necessity." It was not to be the source of tribulation. Gratian did not regard his solution as announcing that the papacy could exercise the powers of a despot. It was to be presumed that the apostolic see would act reasonably, and its acts were not wholly beyond scrutiny. The popes might not have acted with full knowledge of the facts. The power of dispensation was to be exercised carefully, in the interests of equity. Moreover, it was provisional. If there should occur a case of "the greatest need" on the part of the bishop, the fourfold division of tithes might be reinstated. Privileges contrary to the *ius commune* were thus permitted, but they did not become absolute rights. As Gratian put the point, a church's possessions were given to it only *temporaliter*. They were subject to higher necessity.

In this statement of the law, modern readers will no doubt see a contradiction, at least a potential contradiction. What would happen if the Roman pontiff should act expressly against the interests of the Christian religion? What if he should take the part of the despot? Gratian did not deal with the logical inconsistency; he did not identify the winner in the ultimate constitutional contest. Indeed, he assumed that the papacy would rule within the limits of justice, for that was its place in the church. He assumed papal observance of the law except where there was a sound reason for deviation. The time would come, however, when some men would suppose and openly assert that the papacy was, in fact, acting contrary to the commands of the gospel. The "spiritual" Franciscans saw something like this perversion of the papal power in the struggle over apostolic poverty in the fourteenth century. When that happened, one reason the struggle was both prolonged and bitter was that the canon law had also made Gratian's assumption.

Conflicts between Privileges

The second issue raised by Gratian's *quaestio* was that of priority in time. The baptismal church's privilege had been granted first. Did it prevail for that reason? Or was it the reverse? Did the subsequent privilege issued to the monastic house excepting it from the obligation to pay tithes on its lands and presumptively issued with knowledge of the prior grant take precedence? Gratian began with a papal letter stating that privileges, once granted, should remain forever inviolate (C. 25 q. 2 c. 1). There followed a series of authorities to like effect. Privileges granted to monasteries and churches by the holy fathers must not be overthrown or varied by any innovation or wickedness (C. 25 q. 2 c. 2). What had once been established rationally should on no account be disturbed (C. 25 q. 2 c. 9). It would be an injury to the authority of the papacy itself for one pope to infringe the wholesome privileges conferred by his predecessors (C. 25 q. 2 c. 11)—and to the same effect through twenty-one canons.

There was a possible limitation, however. Several of these canons contained wording describing the earlier privilege involved as having been given "for the benefit of the church," or as "reasonably granted," or as "made with the authority of the fathers." Gratian drew a negative statement of the principle from this language (d.p. C. 25 q. 2 c. 21), and it was buttressed explicitly in the *glossa ordinaria*.[14] If the first privilege had been obtained "by false suggestions," or "through deception," or by "suppression of the truth," then it would not carry with it the inviolability of a prior privilege. In other words, the contest between two privileges was not always to be decided by a simple test of priority in time. The circumstances under which the first had been granted had to be examined.

Gratian carried this limitation further in the second part of the *quaestio*. Privileges, though valid when granted, might be lost over the course of time. This could occur in various ways. Privileged status might be lost through misuse, as in the case of habitual abuse of the church's sacraments or where the privileged person fell into heresy (C. 25 q. 2 c. 24). It might be lost through cessation of the underlying reason for its grant, as in the case of a pilgrimage church after all pilgrimages to its shrine had ceased (d.p. c. 25). It might be lost through change of circumstance or necessity, as in the case where the greater utility of the church would be served by preferring the second to the original privilege (d.p. c. 25). Again, no mechanical test of validity was adopted. Under these rules, Gratian was obliged to leave his original case of the parish church and the monastic house open to further investigation of the circumstances.

The *Decretum* did state clearly, however, that the papacy had the right to determine these matters raised when the second privilege appeared to contradict the first. Popes might unite episcopal sees or vary their rights according to the needs of the church, notwithstanding any privileges that earlier bishops of those sees might somehow have acquired. As the *glossa ordinaria* summed the law on the point, "The privileges of churches are not to be understood as remaining inviolate in the sense that the apostolic see cannot derogate from them. They should rather be understood as remaining inviolate in the sense that no one without the authority of the pope may contravene them."[15] This question of authority to vary and interpret privileges was one that was to be taken up again in the Gregorian Decretals and stated in more emphatic terms. It created several problems for the canonists. But it also gave them opportunities to develop further the law of privileges.

PAPAL PRIVILEGES IN THE DECRETALS

The *Decretales Gregorii IX* contained a title in its fifth book called "Of Privileges and the Excesses of Those with Privileges" (X 5.33.1–32). The title gives a hint as to the nature of the disputes that must have arisen under this heading; the large number of the chapters in the title gives a further suggestion as to their frequency. The granting of papal privileges had accelerated in the eleventh and twelfth centuries. Petitioners from ancient institutions sought them out.[16] So did petitioners from new foundations. The erection of new monastic houses and the creation of new religious orders, many of them armed with papal charters and fortified with privileges of varying stripes, were facts of the time. Monastic exemptions from episcopal jurisdiction proliferated.[17] The military orders often enjoyed similar liberties.[18] Ensuing conflicts between overlapping privileges, such as the conflict Gratian himself had begun with, and questions involving interpretation of privileges granted in derogation of rights under the *ius commune* of the church were frequent occurrences in the life of the medieval church. The law developed in the *Decretum* had not solved questions of priority and conflict. Indeed, in a certain sense it had invited more. There had been every reason for resorting to the apostolic see in search of a way out of the ensuing tangles. Several of the canons found here bear the marks of use: "Daily alleged" (X 5.33.9); "Much alleged" (X 5.33.16); "A noteworthy case" (X 5.33.22). Similar comments would appear in the *Liber sextus*, the Clementines, and the *Extravagantes*. And the subject also arose in connection with several other areas of law contained in the *Corpus iuris canonici*.[19] With good reason papal formularies of justice took up the subject.[20]

The kinds of questions that were subject to decretal letters from the popes give a good idea of the problems raised and the answers given. For example, did a papal privilege to the effect that no bishop should presume to excommunicate a monk within a particular monastic house cover monks from the house who were serving parish churches appropriated to the monastery (X 5.33.21)? The answer was no. It covered only monks within the monastery itself: "Although his person is exempt, by reason of the nonexempt thing he possesses, he is subject [to the bishop]."[21] Or, did a papal privilege granting to a monastic house the right to retain tithes ordinarily due to the bishop also cover lands acquired subsequent to the date of the privilege (X 5.33.22)? The answer here was yes. It exempted the monks from paying tithes on newly acquired land, since "in privileges a word expressed generally and indefinitely should extend to future things."[22]

These examples could easily be multiplied, and the impression of complexity they give would not be wholly false. The principal goals of the diverse texts in the Decretals, however, can be stated. They boiled down to two. The first was establishing the authority and the inviolability of papal privileges. The second was restricting an injury to the rights of others and to the church's general law caused by expansive invocation of papal privileges. Both of these were worthy goals—at least they were intelligent goals. The difficulty was that, when applied to actual cases, they pulled in opposite directions. One finds in the *glossa ordinaria* statements to the effect that "the words of the privilege are not to be contravened"[23] and also statements nearby to the effect that "the intent rather than the words" of papal privileges should control their reach.[24] One even finds some apparently internally contradictory but blandly made statements: for example, that all privileges "are to be interpreted broadly and not to the detriment of third parties."[25] Later commentators would reproduce these remarks.[26] These may have been entirely accurate summaries of the texts collected in the Decretals, but taken together, they added up to an invitation to uncertainty and dispute. We shall see in due course the extent to which the canonists were able to reduce them to order and concord.

The Inviolability of Papal Privileges

The first goal was to ensure that papal privileges occupy a special, unchallenged place in the canon law. That they should be obeyed as a matter of course followed naturally from the papacy's place in the church. That they illustrated the powers inherent in the papal plenitude of power was likewise obvious. The Decretals contain some good illustrations of the idea. For instance, the famous decree *Super specula* (X 5.33.28), which prohibited the teaching of the civil law at the University of Paris, was treated as part of the law of privileges. The canonists assumed that the university was the creature of the papal right to grant privileges; it followed that the papacy had the right to interpret the privilege if need be. The existence of the decretal was taken to show that the right to create and govern universities lay with the papacy and also that grants exercising the right should be analyzed under the heading of the canon law of privileges.

The most far reaching of similar chapters in this title—at least the most aggressive—was the Fourth Lateran Council's canon touching the status of the church's ancient patriarchates (Constantinople, Alexandria, Antioch, and Jerusalem). It treated their status as having originated in and still remaining dependent upon the grant of a papal privilege (X 5.33.23). From a practical point of view, the Lateran Council's surprising decree would have had little effect. The split between the Latin Church and the Eastern churches rendered it of more theoretical than practical import. Nevertheless, the decree well illustrates the importance of the law of privileges in the overall governance of the church. It was the means for asserting the amplitude of papal power, and it provided the means for dealing with possibly inconvenient facts and authorities. We took note of this incidentally in Chapter 2, dealing with the law of elections. By treating the ancient canons that conceded rights to princes as resting on papal privileges, the canonists were able to bring them within the canon law. The rights of princes were subjected to the law of privileges, showing that their validity depended solely upon a grant by the church and allowing them to be disregarded under circumstances that permitted the abrogation of privileges. This was a vital juristic technique.[27]

A more immediately relevant and no less significant decretal than the Lateran Council's decree on the ancient patriarchates was one that appeared in the first title of book 2, otherwise devoted to the powers of judges. In it, Pope Innocent III, architect of much of the decretal law on this subject, stated: "When a dispute arises involving privileges of the apostolic see, we desire that they [the privileges] should be judged by no one but ourselves" (X 2.1.12). In other words, the principle that "the person who establishes the laws also interprets the laws" (Dig. 46.5.9) was to be applied to papal privileges and read in a further, negative sense. It was read as requiring that papal privileges be interpreted by the papal lawgiver and by no one else.

One readily sees the reason for this rule—a good reason. If it were open to bishops or their commissaries to sit in judgment on the validity of papal privileges, the rights and authority of the see of Peter might be opened to dispute, doubt, and even rejection. Inferiors would be standing in judgment on the deeds of their superior. That could not be. But there was a countervailing problem. If this decretal were applied literally, it would provide the means for undoing the ordinary course of justice. Every time a papal privilege was introduced into litigation, the case would come to an abrupt halt, delayed to await further consultation with the pope. That also could not be.

The canonists dealt with the dilemma by distinguishing. They created a number of exceptions. They left the rule intact but hived off situations in which it did not apply.[28] Their evident purpose was to reduce its potential for harm at the same time they preserved the principle stated by the decretal. Thus the restriction to papal judgment was said to apply only when the words of the privilege were unclear or doubtful, not when they were open and clear.[29] Otherwise any litigant could create a delay simply by introducing a papal privilege and suggesting that it be interpreted in Rome. The decretal's terms were also held not to apply when the privilege was raised "indirectly" in litigation. Only where it was "directly" put in issue were inferiors forbidden to take cognizance of it. And the rule did not apply where the pope himself had delegated the power to interpret a papal privilege to the judge, a situation most likely to occur, of course, where papal judges delegate were assigned to hear disputes appealed to the Roman Curia that were being returned for trial to the locality where the disputes had arisen. By these distinctions, the rule was domesticated. Insofar as possible, it was kept from interfering with justice.

By reading these exceptions into the rule, the canonists intended no slight to the principle of papal plenitude of power. That is clear from their treatment of a dilemma raised by the same decretal. It was this: If judging papal privileges was in any sense reserved to the Roman see, did not this mean that the popes would become the judges of their own acts, particularly where the privilege covered the rights of the Roman Church? Would they not thereby be violating a rule of natural justice that no one should be a judge in his own cause? That understanding of any decretal would ordinarily have been hard to accept, but here Innocent III's reservation of the power of interpretation to the apostolic see seemed actually to require it.

The canonists rejected this line of argument, though they regularly raised it. In the end, they held the rule reserving interpretation of papal acts to the popes to be warranted by the circumstances. This was so, first, because they maintained that the papacy held a special place within the church's law and, second, because they presumed that the pope would hear and decide any dispute over a privilege in accordance with the settled law.[30] They noted that Roman law had allowed the emperor to act as judge in his own cause. A fortiori the pope must be able to do so, since his powers were greater than those of the emperor. Moreover, since the pope could himself be judged by no man except when the pope fell into heresy, it was a logical necessity that he be able to judge his own acts. Otherwise, no one could. And, finally, they held that a papal privilege was rightly submitted to papal judgment "because it was not to be presumed that [the pope] would judge it otherwise than would God himself." Only as an act of prudence, therefore, should the Roman pontiff delegate the hearing of causes involving papal privileges to another judge. He could not be compelled to do so.

The amplitude of papal power exercised through privileges was recognized perhaps most spectacularly in the privileges that made exceptions to divine law. The most frequently cited such situation (surprisingly) had to do with tithes, the same subject Gratian had taken up in *Causa* 25. It was common ground among the medieval canonists that tithes were owed by divine law, not simply by a positive ordinance of the church. Nevertheless, the *communis opinio* held that as "general administrator and representative of God, the pope, [could] remit [tithes] in some cases."[31] By issuance of a privilege, a pope could permit clerics and even laymen to pay less than a full tenth, or even no tithes at all, where he judged that there was good reason for granting the exceptional right.

The larger question raised by this exercise of the plenitude of papal power was nonetheless controversial. The more probable opinion seems to have been that the pope could not have used this power to abolish tithes entirely, though he could make large inroads in their reach.[32] It would have seemed wrong, and probably also perverse, to have envisioned that sort of wholesale exercise of arbitrary power. The *plenitudo potestatis* could not have been extended as far, for example, as to allow dispensations against some divine laws—say, the law that commanded men and women "to have no other Gods before me" or to "honor thy father and mother." That much was clear. But this limit, and the uncertainty in the minds of the canonists about exactly when it applied, should not disguise the extent of the authority here being asserted and exercised by the apostolic see through the issuance of privileges. Tithing was a more frequent and contentious subject of litigation than was respect for one's parents.

Protection of the Ordinary Course of the Law

If establishing the inviolability and amplitude of papal privileges was one goal of the Decretals' title on the subject, protection of the law's ordinary course against overuse of papal privileges was another. It was at least as strong a goal. By definition, privileges created special rights. They stood outside, and sometimes contradicted, the general law of the church. Their reach, it seemed to all the canonists, should not be extended so far that it threatened to subvert the ordinary supremacy of the church's law. Some of the consequent working out of rules designed to avoid this danger occurred within the Gregorian Decretals themselves. Some of it was done by later commentators on the Decretals. Four aspects of this development can be singled out as especially noteworthy. Many of them would operate together to produce the same result in practice.

First, and already alluded to briefly, the scope of privileges should not be extended by implication. To the contrary, where privileges granted a right inconsistent with the ordinary law of the church—the ordinary situation—they were to be narrowly construed.[33] Several such cases appeared in the Gregorian Decretals. For instance, two military orders, the Hospitalers and Templars, had received papal privileges allowing them to build and maintain an oratory in their houses. The question addressed by Innocent III's decretal (X 5.33.10) was whether this privilege carried with it the right to have a church bell erected, to be rung as a call to prayer.[34] A bishop in whose diocese one of the military orders had erected a house with attached oratory objected to the plan. Probably he regarded it as an additional threat to episcopal jurisdiction, since these orders clearly were not immediately subject to his control. At any rate it would have made the oratory into something more like a public church. And the decretal held in the bishop's favor. The existing privilege was held not to carry the additional right to have the bell, and the members of the orders were ordered "to rest content with the right" as conferred by the privilege.[35] The *glossa ordinaria* added that even the right to have mass celebrated in such oratories was not to be assumed in the absence of express grant.[36] The word *oratoria* meant no more than exactly what it said.[37] This was typical of the readings given to terms used in papal privileges. Unless they specifically granted a right, they were read as standing in accord with the ordinary canon law.

Second, a line was drawn, or rather a distinction was created, between those privileges that involved injury to the rights of others and those that did not. Where there was a question of interpretation involved, privileges were always to be read so as not to diminish the rights of a third party, at least where the injury to the third part would be more than trifling. As Hostiensis put it, "Where it prejudices the right of another, [the privilege] is to reduced to the *ius commune* if it can be."[38] Thus, in the example just given, the Hospitalers' privilege was given a restrained reading precisely because rights of episcopal jurisdiction were involved. According to the preference, privileges to pay no tithes or to pay less than full tithes were ordinarily to be construed strictly because they always prejudiced the rights of another, the holder of the tithes (e.g., X 3.30.31).[39]

Two typical and contrasting examples make this point. A papal privilege was granted to clerics serving in chapels of the duke of Burgundy to be free from sentences of excommunication issued by the bishop of the diocese where the chapels were located. Because this diminished the bishop's rights, this privilege was read as not covering a ducal chapel established after the date of the privilege (X 3.33.16). However, a papal privilege conferred upon a monastic house to celebrate services quietly during an interdict, a time when all other church services were suspended, was interpreted more broadly (X 5.33.24). It was not given a restrictive reading precisely because no rights of others would be infringed by such celebrations. The canonists found the same approach being applied in the texts of the Roman law (e.g., Dig. 11.7.12) and cited them in confirmation of the good sense of their own efforts.[40]

Third, privileges did not necessarily effect a permanent change in legal rights or status under the law. Rights granted under a papal privilege could be revoked for cause by the papacy itself.[41] They could also be lost by prescription, renunciation, misuse, contrary act, or even nonuser by the grantee. There were thus several different possibilities by which a party might forfeit the benefits of a privilege. Hostiensis, summing up the common learning on the subject in the thirteenth century, was able to list nine different ways forfeiture or loss could occur.[42] Where one of them occurred, there was a reversion to the status quo ante, that is, to the general law of the church. This happened despite the existence of an otherwise valid and perpetual privilege.[43]

This result should not be regarded as having been inevitable. It might easily have been thought that a privilege granted by the papacy should be treated as an act or right of the papacy itself. If so, the privilege would have been much less vulnerable to loss. In the case of failure to make use of the privilege, for instance, a papal privilege would not have been subject to contrary prescription except in the unusual case of nonuser for a one-hundred-year period. This, however, was not the result reached in the classical law. A privilege was treated as a private right in most situations, subject to the ordinary rules of prescription described in Chapter 7, and fully subject to the possibility of return to the general law of the church. Thus, where Cistercian monks enjoyed a papal privilege not to pay tithes on lands they cultivated by their own labors, but had nonetheless paid those tithes for the prescriptive period,[44] the monks were held to have lost the benefit of the privilege (X 5.33.6). As the gloss stated, a legal right "reverts easily to its own nature."[45] So it was to happen with rights contrary to the common law of the church created by papal privileges.

Fourth, in situations of urgency, where the order or well-being of the church was at risk, the canon law allowed papal privileges to be over-ridden in favor of ordinary legal process. As the creature of the papacy, a privilege was subject to an implied reservation that the papacy might permit derogation from the rights granted in it if good cause existed, and this happened in fact. The best example is heresy. Where a papal privilege granted an exemption from ordinary episcopal jurisdiction to any individual, if that person was accused of heresy, he was subject to episcopal inquisition notwithstanding the privilege. So held a decretal of Pope Lucius III (X 5.7.9). This crime was regarded as so serious a breach of the church's law and heresy's extirpation so worthy a cause that the existence of a papal privilege could not have been meant to stand as an impediment to investigation of the question.

The canonists expanded on this notion of such exceptions "for good cause" in the interests of protecting the common order of the church. For example, in interpreting a privilege that expressly exempted a per-son from ordinary episcopal jurisdiction, Hostiensis was prepared to distinguish between "notorious" crimes that caused scandal to the faithful and "occult" crimes that did not.[46] He suggested that if an offender's action was the first, if it had risen to the level at which it had become a source of public discord, a bishop might punish him de-spite the privilege. If the crime had been private, however, the privi-lege prevailed and only the pope could punish.

Modern readers may regard this as an example of excessive freedom of interpretation. Should not the privilege have meant what it said? Did it not take away the force of a solemn papal act to subject it to im-plied and enervating exceptions such as this one? Perhaps so. But the canonists did not see things quite that way. They saw no slight to papal authority in this exception. It was rather a way of promoting the good order of the church, and had the papal privilege expressly said that it covered notorious crimes as well as occult crimes, Hostiensis would very likely have advocated its enforcement in both situations. But the canonists were loath to regard the exercise of papal power as if it had been intended to serve as an instrument of discord and lawlessness. The see of St. Peter was a force for building up the good order of the church, not for tearing it apart. Starting with that assumption, they found no artificiality in distinctions such as this one. They were embracing the result they believed, and with some reason, that occupants of the chair of St. Peter would themselves have chosen had they been fully informed about the uses to which their privileges were being put.

CREATION OF A SETTLED LAW OF PRIVILEGES

When one considers at leisure the interpretive principles that were adopted by the Decretals and expanded upon by the medieval canonists, one sees the settling hand of lawyers bringing order to a confused situation. Progress was made in the thirteenth century. Through the aid of the Roman law and the juristic skill of its commentators, principles were worked out that had the capacity to steady the uncertainty that had resulted from the proliferation of papal privileges during these years. Yet it was also obvious that much remained to be done, and it is no accident that a title *De privilegiis* figures in all the additions to the *Corpus iuris canonici* that followed the Gregorian Decretals.

The developed canon law of privileges was scholastic in the fullest sense of that word, although the principles covered so far cannot be said to have amounted to an organized *system*. Before that could exist, there had to be greater movement toward coherence and comprehension. Obvious gaps existed in the law relating to immediate problems faced by the medieval church, gaps that called out to be filled. Gratian had left the problem of overlapping and mutually contradictory grants unsettled, for example. How was it to be solved within a functioning legal system? Before leaving the subject, we ought to look at a few of these solutions, as well as examine briefly the system of law that eventually emerged.

The first step was to recognize that papal privileges were settling into common forms and to adopt rules that would allow these forms to

332 The Spirit of Classical Canon Law

be recognized and applied without dispute or unnecessary uncertainty. Terminology was one such problem. A good example is found in the Decretals. A rescript of Innocent III stated that a privilege taking its recipient "under apostolic protection" did not thereby exempt the recipient from episcopal jurisdiction (X 5.33.18). Monastic houses had long sought to bring themselves under the sheltering wing of the papacy. The term *protectio beati Petri* figured largely in many monastic documents. But what did St. Peter's "protection" actually mean? Here was the answer, noted in the *glossa ordinaria:* "Certainly very little . . . although perhaps the pope will intervene more quickly in granting letters in their favor when they are injured unjustly."[47] In this instance, clarification of the language frequently found in privileges resulted in diminishing their reach.[48]

One of the most important rules adopted covered cases we have looked at already: conflict between successive privileges. The object of the law was always to reconcile privileges if possible. But if their wording could not be reasonably brought into harmony, the rule adopted was this: If the later privilege made express mention of the prior privilege, it prevailed. If not—that is, if the later privilege was simply inconsistent with the earlier privilege—then the prior privilege controlled.[49] Thus, for example, if the second privilege contained a *non obstante* clause setting out and making a specific exception from the prior papal grant, the second would prevail. This solution was regarded as an application of the presumption that the pope would not be presumed to have intentionally diminished the right of any person. He *could* do so. But if he did, it must be by express words.

There were, of course, some exceptions to this solution,[50] and it was not always clear how specific the *non obstante* clause had to be for the second privilege to control. For instance, suppose the first privilege by express terms prohibited its infringement by any other privilege, and the second privilege was stated to take effect *non obstante* any prior privilege.[51] Which prevailed? That was a matter of dispute. The key was to discover the grantor's true intent.[52] But how was this to be done? No general rule could be given. Admitting the rough edges, however, the rule requiring express words solved many otherwise insoluble cases. This must be counted an improvement over the treatment accorded the matter in the *Decretum*. It provided a ready rule of thumb.

Much the same can be said of the difference between "narration" and "assertion" in papal privileges. Pope Boniface VIII, who took a lively interest in the whole subject of privileges, drew this distinction in a decretal that the *glossa ordinaria* described as "the best in the matter of interpretation" (Sext. 5.7.10). It came to this. Where a right or exemption was merely described in a papal act, no right was thereby created. "Assertive" or enacting words were required before any rights could be created. For many claimants to special rights outside or contrary to the law, there would have been a natural temptation to suppose that a papal document mentioning their asserted right should amount to a specific papal authorization of the right they claimed. The decretal attempted to cut off the argument by requiring a specific grant before a document could be recognized as an effective act of derogation from the general law.

In these and other changes, the canon law worked toward stability and regularity in the formulation of a more settled law of privileges. Yet none of it amounted to a complete system. In that direction, the early canonists took a few steps, but nothing like those that were eventually to come. The *Summa aurea* of Cardinal Hostiensis, for example, contained a section dividing privileges into several different classes.[53] He distinguished first between general and special privileges. A general privilege under the canon law was one granted to all persons or institutions that fit into a legal category. All consecrated churches thus enjoyed the privilege of sanctuary; all clerics enjoyed certain immunities from secular jurisdiction (the *privilegium fori*). No cleric needed to prove an individual or special grant. A special privilege, on the other hand, was one granted only to a specific individual or institution. The common example of this second kind we have seen repeatedly: the papal privilege granted to a monastic house permitting the house to exist in immediate subjection to the papacy rather than to the bishop of the diocese in which it was located.

It is true enough that at some point this distinction between general and special privileges breaks down. The same could be said of many other such distinctions.[54] What of the privileges granted to an entire monastic order like the Cistercians? And at what point did a general privilege become a law of the church? Hostiensis did not make these matters clear or even attempt to do so. He did not purport to assign all papal privileges to a particular class. Nor did he take up in a comprehensive and ordered fashion the consequences of several of the distinctions he drew. What he and the other decretalists did was to provide tools for further analysis. These tools were useful in deciding the questions that arose in the course of the life of the medieval church. But that many of the disputes ended in compromise, as they in fact seem to have ended in medieval practice,[55] was perhaps only to be expected. Fuller elaboration and regularization of the law of privileges was a later creation.

LATER DEVELOPMENTS

The canon law of privileges did not deviate in early modern times from the fundamental principles arrived at during the period of the law's formulation. There was real continuity, and it has lasted even up to the present day. However, two important developments in the law of privileges did begin, or at least increase in intensity, during the sixteenth and seventeenth centuries. These changes ran parallel to broader movements within the church. The first was a serious attempt to reduce the number of privileges outstanding. It was one part of the great movement of religious reform that occurred during the sixteenth and seventeenth centuries. The second was the attempt to formulate a more complete and systematic law of privileges. It was one example of the great drive forward in scholastic thought that took place during the same era.

The Restriction of Privileges

The Council of Trent was the setting for some of the most determined efforts to rein in the luxuriant growth of privileges that had occurred since the twelfth century, a growth that was said to constitute a "cause of disquiet" within the Latin Church.[56] One may recall the words of Rufinus of Bologna in the twelfth century, to the effect that the Roman see was exalted through their issuance.[57] This was true, but it had been more the result than the cause of their issuance. The initiative for issuing papal privileges virtually always came from the recipient. Privileges were sought from the papacy as protection from local threats or challenges,[58] and if there was any consistent papal policy involved in their granting, it was a financial rather than a theoretical one. It is not surprising, therefore, that no inconsistency was seen between the council's efforts to curtail the extent of papal privileges and its determined assertion of the primary of the Roman see. The assembled bishops and abbots did not regard restriction of papal privileges in favor of restoration of the *ius commune* as detracting from the authority of the papacy. They regarded it as a continuing and further application of one of the law's consistent themes: "Privileges are always to be kept in check."[59] It may be that the notion was pushed harder during the early modern period than it had been earlier.[60] But it was not a new theme.

Restraining the extent of privileges was at any rate what the Council of Trent attempted. For example, serious efforts were made to restrict privileges excepting the clergy from the obligation to reside in churches to which they were assigned.[61] It was also decreed that privileges should not be used to restrict the rights of a bishop to examine the competence of any person appointed to ecclesiastical benefices in his diocese.[62] Married clerics were commanded to serve in the churches to which they had been assigned and to wear proper clerical garb, "notwithstanding any privilege or custom, even immemorial, to the contrary."[63] There were several similar enactments, and a final constitution of Pope Pius IV, issued in 1565, specifically revoked all privileges contrary to the decrees of the council.[64] Of course, none of these restrictions abolished papal privileges. That would have been actually unwise. However, together with measures taken by succeeding popes, the decrees of the Council of Trent did trim their luxuriance.[65]

The Growth in System

The second notable development was growth in system. Two aspects of this development should be noted. From the efforts of canonists and civilians there issued a series of distinctions between various forms of privileges that could fairly be called elaborate in detail and comprehensive in intent. Some of these were traditional, useful, and widely discussed. The division of all privileges between "personal" and "real" was one such. Concrete consequences hinged on which class a particular privilege belonged to, whether or not it outlasted the life of the recipient being the most obvious (Sext. 5.12.7). The wisdom of some of the other scholastic efforts in the same direction is perhaps a little more debatable. Distinguishing privileges from other kinds of grants and documents issuing from the papal chancery was probably a useful effort, though it reached the point of artfulness. For instance, according to Petrus Rebuffus, "although speaking loosely all rescripts could be called privileges," if the matter was examined closely, it turned out that there were actually thirteen separate distinctions between rescripts and privileges.[66] Many of them, however, turned out to be without discernible consequence.

The movement toward system went much further. For instance, although the question continued (and continues) to be disputed, most commentators though it would be an advantage to place all privileges into one of three classes: privileges *contra ius, praeter ius,* and *secundum ius.* The first, those authorizing the exercise of a right otherwise contrary to the law, contained most of the privileges discussed above. The second encompassed privileges "beyond the law," that is, those by which rights were conveyed where the law was otherwise silent. The third, perhaps the hardest to understand, covered privileges granting rights already held by the recipient. A specific papal grant of episcopal rights to a bishop would be an example. It may be objected that only the first of these fit the definition of a true privilege. Exactly that objection was raised at the time.[67] However, the prestige of system, the love of distinction, and the desire for completeness won the day. The same author who rejected the threefold division went on to enunciate a series of eight additional distinctions that (he said) would better fit the realities. He listed them according to several classes of alternatives: affirmative/negative, absolute/conditional, remunerative/gratuitous, and so forth.[68]

Along with these systematizing efforts went the creation of an extensive literature on the subject. Most of it was organized not according to the privilege's grantor as it has been examined here but rather according to the privilege's recipient. The civil law provided the basic model, which was adapted by writers on the law of the church for their own purposes. This was, in fact, the more sensible way to arrange them, since privileges could accrue from diverse sources. Jurists devoted treatises to listing and examining the law of privileges of the various persons and entities within and without the church that enjoyed privileges of various kinds and stripes. Thus, among others, we find treatises devoted to the privileges of widows, of cardinals, of creditors, of students, and even of law professors.[69] Some of the subjects examined in this volume attracted authors willing to subject them to microscopic analysis as a privilege: the useful (and long) treatise "The Privileges of Oaths" by Seraphinus de Seraphinis is one example.[70] And as one would expect, treatises called "The Privileges of the Clergy" and "The Privileges of Churches," or some suitable variant of these phrases, were written in considerable numbers.[71]

CONCLUSION

At the end of the day, there remains a certain typicality, and perhaps also a slight irony, in the history of the development of the law of papal privileges. There are two points. First, exercise of the right to derogate from the law of the church was clearly a means by which the powers of the papacy were exalted, both in theory and in fact, during the years of the canon law's formation. This remained the reality well afterward and into modern times. However, even as it was being enlarged and elaborated by the jurists, the papacy's power to stand outside the law was also being brought within manageable limits. Assuming, reasonably enough, that the popes themselves wished to fulfill their duty to secure obedience to the church's law, the canonists restricted the possible effects of papal privileges. Privileges were not permitted to become an engine whereby the ordinary course of the canon law was overturned.

Second, it is undoubtedly correct, as several modern writers on the canon law have stressed, that the principles of the law of privileges have remained remarkably stable over the centuries. Much of the development described in this chapter consisted of working from the principles set forth in the *Decretum*, not their overthrow. The power of the apostolic see to stand outside the law was a consistent assumption of the medieval canonists. It did not disappear with the conciliar movement or with the passage of the following centuries. What was added was system and complexity. What changed was the extent to which the use of privileges was encouraged or restrained. Putting the whole together, it seems equally true to say that the law of privileges has remained stable and also reflected the great changes that have shaped the church's law.

13 Cooperation and Coercion in the Courts of Church and State: Invocation of the Secular Arm

Separation of church and clergy from the domination and perhaps even the influence of the laity was an avowed goal of the classical canon law. It has been a salient theme in several chapters of this book, episcopal elections and the ordination of the unfree being the most obvious examples. Yet in truth the matter was never simple, even in theory. It could not have been. It was just as evident in the twelfth century as it is in the twentieth that there could not have been anything like a perfect and utter separation of the church from the affairs and concerns of the world. Indeed, in the minds of the Gregorian reformers one of the reasons for establishing the church's independence from lay control was precisely so that the church might be at liberty to lead the laity. Any boundary that was created was certain to be crossed repeatedly. Any division that was made was certain to require an understanding of the relationship between the two spheres that would permit some interaction between them. This was (roughly speaking) the subject we call "church and state."

Two distinct conceptions of the proper relationship between church and state met and coexisted within the medieval canon law.[1] The first, often identified with Pope Gelasius (d. 496), held that temporal and spiritual authorities formed two distinct and independent powers (Dist. 96 c. 10). They were called the "two swords." Each was instituted by God. Each had its own sphere of competence. Neither had the right to intrude upon the other's sphere. Jesus himself had told his followers to "render unto Caesar those things that are Caesar's, and unto God those things that are God's" (Luke 20:25). He had disclaimed any attempt to establish an earthly kingdom (John 18:36) and had thereby laid out a path of humility for his followers.[2] As we saw in Chapter 5 in dealing with ecclesiastical jurisdiction, this attitude led to the initial assertion of only a limited jurisdiction over the laity by the courts of the church.

In the minds of the canonists, this division rested ultimately upon the conviction that in a Christian society, neither secular nor spiritual authorities should become puffed up with the pride that would almost inevitably come from possessing and wielding both a temporal and a spiritual sword. The "arms" appropriate to the clerical order were prayers and tears (C. 23 q. 8 c. 21). By contrast, the temporal authorities took up the material sword. For that very reason they were therefore forbidden to meddle in spiritual matters. Similarly the clerical order was bound to respect temporal government. God himself had blessed this division by retaining the Heavens but also "giving the Earth to the children of men" (Ps. 115:16). This dualist position did not mean anything as extreme as the modern American separation of church and state. It did mean that each was in some measure independent. To repeat a much-used medieval metaphor, neither was permitted to wield its scythe in the other's harvest.

The second conception is commonly associated today with the person and the papacy of Gregory VII, although in fact it was not articulated with any precision until after his death. This view did not reject the metaphor of "two swords," but it saw the relation between them rather differently. It built upon the principle, which would have been assented to by virtually all people of the time, that the spiritual side of life was inherently superior to the earthly. It also depended upon the principle, about which there would have been only slightly more disagreement, that the church represented the spiritual, the temporal government the earthly (Dist. 96 c. 11). In the striking metaphor popular at the time, the church was the sun, the state the moon. As the moon shone only by reflecting the light of the sun, so the *regnum* stood with respect to the *sacerdotium*.[3]

If one began from this starting point, it followed that the ecclesiastical authority must almost always prevail over the temporal whenever a choice had to be made between the two. This "Gregorian" position was avowedly hierocratic. It held that temporal rulers enjoyed no authority directly from God. Rather, they received their authority intermediately through the church. Temporal power was legitimate. In their proper sphere, the rulers of the world were to be obeyed. But their rights to compel obedience were derivative and not unconditional. If misused so as to become the occasion for sin, temporal power was subject to supervision and correction by the church.

The theoretical underpinnings of the view should not be lost from sight. It is too easy to regard this as a simple quest for power. From the beginning Christians had taken the view that the spirit was superior to the flesh, and from this premise, concrete and logical conclusions were drawn in the wake of the Gregorian reform. It was asserted that the recognized principle of spiritual primacy should control people's lives and indeed that it should be applied to the organization of Christian society as a whole. If this was correct, the priority of the spiritual realm would not stand simply as a counsel that people should give their allegiance to God rather than man. It would mean that the governors of the world would stand subject to the direction of the higher, spiritual power.

This hierocratic theory was buttressed by biblical authority, just as the Gelasian was. Canonists asserted that God had delegated all power to the church through the action of Jesus. Jesus had promised to give to St. Peter the power to bind and loose in heaven and earth (Matt. 16:19). Secular rights were not excluded from this plenary grant. St. Peter had in turn transmitted that power to his successors, the bishops of Rome. They held it. The popes did not actually exercise this temporal authority. That would have been inconsistent with the path of Christian humility. Rather, they delegated it to the rulers of the world. These rulers then exercised the power received by papal grant. Their authority was not on that account to be despised. The canon law did not justify routine meddling by ecclesiastics in affairs of state, and the temporal ruler's subjects were specifically enjoined to obey him. However, if the king strayed too far from the rightful exercise of his office, particularly if he showed himself hostile to the laws of God and his duty to the church, he might render himself subject to correction by the spiritual powers. Papal approval and coronation of the emperor thus symbolized the right order of society, furnishing the most vivid expression of the power reserved in the church's leader; at the same time it also hallowed secular rule. Hence the descriptive term *hierocratic*.

The Gelasian view had been largely endorsed by the clerical order during the early Middle Ages. It was faithful to their understanding of the biblical texts, and it was favorable to the church's interests when compared with the contemporary alternative to it. That alternative would have been the system inherited from antiquity, the Roman law that treated the clergy as fully subject to imperial laws, even if it often made special provision for their interests and status. The Roman law Codex and Novels contained much legislation regulating the clergy, and not all of it respected a basic division between the spiritual and the secular sides of life. It was against that background that the Gelasian "two swords" position was initiated. Pope Gelasius had meant to prevent the emperor from usurping authority that belonged, according to clerical lights, to the sacerdotal power alone.[4]

By the time the classical canon law was being formulated in the twelfth century, however, the Gelasian position had become distinctly the weaker alternative from the vantage point of high fliers within the church. It was not dead, of course. It had tradition and currency within the canon law itself; it retained its hold within the society of literate laymen;[5] and it continued to be useful for many purposes to the canonists themselves.[6] But the rise of theocratic ways of thinking about affairs of church and state had put a different complexion on the whole subject. The older view's dominance was being undermined by new papal decretals, by current events, and by the development of systematic canonistic thought. The more "modern" position was the view that the emperor, and by extension all secular rulers, occupied a position subordinate to that of the rulers of the church. It was asserted, for example, that any bishop could excommunicate any king whose faults were manifest[7] and that it must follow as a matter of logical deduction that all kings held their positions subject to oversight by the priestly power. Only the latter was derived immediately from God.

This conclusion did not mean, it should again be emphasized, that even the most advanced among the canonists had abandoned the idea that society was a unity or that the secular government had a distinct and legitimate part in the government of that society. The united *societas Christiana* continued to play a pivotal role in their thought and indeed in the thought of all Christian thinkers.[8] Each partner, *regnum* and *sacerdotium*, had a role to play in the regulation of society and the promotion of God's kingdom. What distinguished the hierocratic position from the earlier Gelasian position was its insistence on the dominant position of the church in the world. If things went wrong, it was for the priesthood to direct, for the laity to follow those directions. Those restrictions that did exist in what the church could do in fulfilling its role were imposed by the limitations of prudence.

It is certainly true that a good deal of contemporary writing about the subject from clerical pens amounted to theoretical froth. Some of it bore little relation to legal consequence, much less to any legal consequence that could be implemented. The temptation therefore is to write it off as clerical fantasy. But it very often happens that abstract theories turn out to have real-world consequences, and so it proved with this aspect of canonical thought. Indeed, it had several consequences. None is more illustrative of the spirit of the canon law than the subject of this chapter, the question of the extent to which temporal courts were bound to respect and, when necessary, actually to enforce the sentences of ecclesiastical courts.[9] Were the rulers of the world required to wield the secular sword at the bidding of the church?

The more exact legal question was whether the canon law required a temporal ruler and his courts to obey the decisions of an ecclesiastical court. A subsidiary but inevitable question was whether, if one of the parties to the ecclesiastical suit refused to obey the spiritual court's sentence, the church could call upon the temporal courts to impose temporal sanctions in order to secure the party's obedience to its sentence. Once the church had created a system of effective law, and particularly once it had erected a system of public courts throughout Europe in the thirteenth century, this problem was bound to arise. Working out a solution to it inevitably called both of these theories of government into play. In one sense, it pitted the Gelasian against the Gregorian theories of right order in society. In another sense it also opened up the possibility of allowing them to be combined.

A PRELIMINARY QUESTION

There was, however, one preliminary question—an important one: whether the canon law ought to have anything whatsoever to do with temporal law and temporal sanctions. Temporal sanctions meant money penalties at the very least and very often corporal sanctions as well. Given the assumptions of the time, the latter inevitably included capital punishment. If called upon by the church, the courts of kings and counts would first threaten, and then apply, real force against those who deviated from the laws of the church or refused to comply with the decisions of ecclesiastical tribunals. Were such worldly sanctions consistent with the Christian religion?

Biblical and Patristic Sources

Arguments based upon the most respectable authority suggested that temporal sanctions were not to be employed by the spiritual powers. Much Christian doctrine tended to prove that the church should confine itself to the higher realm of the spirit. Gratian's *Decretum* invoked several biblical texts to make this point.[10] There were counsels of patience before evil: "Resist not evil; but whosoever shall smite thee on thy right cheek, turn to him the other also" (Matt. 5:39). There were statements that God, not man, should punish sin: "Vengeance is mine, saith the Lord. I will repay" (Rom. 12:19). And there were explicit renunciations of the use of force: Jesus said to Peter when Peter sought to defend him before his crucifixion, "Put up thy sword; for all they that take the sword shall perish with the sword" (Matt. 26:52). Quite apart from the question of whether the church could actually require the temporal courts to do its bidding, therefore, stood a preliminary question, an obstacle as it must have seemed to some: How to understand these and similar biblical texts that appeared to disqualify the spiritual order from all use of force?

Of course the obstacle *was* overcome. Indeed, the successful effort to overcome it had not awaited the efforts of the classical canonists. Behind their efforts stood a long tradition of Christian thought and in particular the formidable intellect of St. Augustine. No one figured more prominently in Gratian's collection of authorities justifying the use of force against those who deviated from the church's law than did the famous bishop of Hippo. It was Augustine's view that the dominical counsels of patience had been intended to work upon the hearts of good men. They would serve to augment the number of such men. The counsels could not, however, reasonably have been intended to govern men's exterior actions in all situations; otherwise they would provide a license for wrongdoing (C. 23 q. 1 c. 2). Granting such a license to work iniquity could not have been part of God's plan for humanity. Something else must have been meant. For Augustine, God's ultimate vengeance stood as a reminder that the church would never be able to extirpate all evils in this world and that God would not leave sins unpunished. It had not been meant to keep the church from punishing evil where it could (C. 23 q. 4 c. 18).

Augustine's conclusions were taken into the canon law. A number of the canons reproduced them, and at points the canonists seem to have leaned heavily upon his understanding of the Scriptures. At least the canon law took his position as a normal reference point. For example, Augustine understood the admonition by Jesus to Peter just mentioned—that he put up his sword—as a warning against taking extrajudicial action to correct injustice, not as a prohibition against taking any action at all. When he read that the man who lived by the sword would also perish by the sword, Augustine believed that Christians must regard this as referring only to the sword being wielded without superior and legitimate authority (C. 23 q. 4 c. 36). So held the later canonists. When a criminal was executed, it was the law that executed the criminal, not the men who imposed the sentence or carried it out (C. 23 q. 4 c. 42). In the view of Augustine, there was no incompatibility between their actions and the gospel's commands. This position was fully incorporated within the canon law.

Modern commentators are sometimes inclined to regard this treatment, together with the distinctions that made it possible, as thin rationalizations for the medieval church's decision to resort to force against its enemies and therefore as something like a betrayal of the ideals of the Christian religion. Reading through Gratian's treatment of the subject gives reason for pause. The case for using force did not rest simply on ingenious and labored distinctions that explained away clear commands in the Gospels. Gratian provided varied, direct, and sophisticated arguments in favor of the legitimacy of secular sanctions. For one thing, forceful punishment for wrongdoing appears throughout the Old Testament. No division was admissible there that would wholly separate body from spirit in regulating human conduct. Had not Moses rightly put to death those who worshiped the golden calf (Exod. 32:27–29)? It seemed apparent to Gratian that the New Testament could not be said to forbid the use of force either (C. 23 q. 4 c. 44). The regime of law, necessarily including the application of physical punishment, was spoken of with approval at several points in the Gospels. Jesus himself had not reproved the soldier's profession.[11] The Bible, taken as a whole, seemed to invite distinctions, distinctions that would leave at least scope for forceful action. Temporal punishments were therefore legitimate under some conditions. If only the pacific sections of the Scriptures were attended to, it appeared, too much would be left out.

The *Decretum*, again from St. Augustine, took note that God himself sometimes made use of physical sanctions to lead men and women to the good. Of this, the most spectacular New Testament example was that of the apostle Paul.[12] Whereas the first disciples had been called by the spoken word, not so with Saul of Tarsus. God had cast him, forcefully and against Saul's will, onto the ground and had left him blinded (Acts 9:4–9). Now Paul was God's "chosen vessel." If this forceful action was the method God had chosen to convert the Apostle to the Gentiles away from his persecution of the church, could any sensible person think that force was altogether foreign to God's plan of salvation? To Gratian, as to many other medieval readers of the Scriptures, it seemed not.

By the lights of the men who formulated the canon law, the use of forceful punishment might be entirely consistent with God's benevolent care for mankind. This was apparent to them not simply from spectacular biblical examples like the conversion of St. Paul but also from the details of ordinary human life. The father who chastised his children, even with stripes, might be acting out of his love for them (C. 23 q. 1 c. 2). So might the church do in its paternal solicitude for its members (C. 23 q. 5 c. 10). Moreover, it was common coin among medieval thinkers that men and women might learn in the end to love the good by being obliged to shun the bad in the beginning. The image of humanity with which the canonists worked was not the hardened criminal, impervious to any inducement but the prospect of punishment. It was rather the person with capability for growth in both good and evil. Such a person might be usefully chastised, for (they said) it often happens that what a person first takes up under compulsion, he later embraces with joy.

The canonists added that such compulsion might actually be preferable to the person being punished. Fully informed, anyone would desire to suffer temporary punishment on earth if it meant the avoidance of much worse punishment in eternity (C. 23 q. 5 c. 6). It would thus be preferable to undergo any temporal punishment, even death, if temporary and earthly stripes would serve to avoid ultimate damnation. Criminals, were they but fully informed, would themselves desire it. Following this reasoning through to its logical conclusions was to lead the canonists to some horrifying results. From those results we cannot but recoil. But their reasoning does not lack cogency.

To have adopted the opposite view would, of course, have seemed infinitely worse to them. It meant that the church and its law stood powerless before the unrepentant sinner. The church was always made up of both good and evil men; to have read the biblical counsels of patience as though they required treating the two alike seemed the reverse of carrying out God's will. It would open a *via latissima* to evil men.[13] And what else could be done against the offender unmoved by spiritual sanctions? The church had been entrusted with the responsibility of leading men and women into the paths of righteousness. If the clergy to whom the authority had been committed failed to carry out that responsibility, at least where correction could effectively be applied, God would lay the blame upon them as well as upon the sinner.[14] That God would also punish the sinner furnished no legitimate excuse for neglect to do so on the part of the clergy. Just as we do not cease from prayer for sinners because God can cause their repentance, neither should we cease from their correction because God will cause them to be punished (C. 23 q. 4 c. 20).

All this did not mean that the canon law enthusiastically endorsed the use of temporal sanctions and that the biblical counsels against them were dead letters. The canonists limited their use in several ways: first, in forbidding the infliction of most kinds of physical punishment directly by the church; second, in requiring that spiritual means be applied *before* temporal sanctions could be sought; and third, in requiring that all punishments be applied with circumspection. Thus the *communis opinio* among the jurists held that although a bishop might lawfully keep a *familia armata* as part of his retinue, he could not make use of that *familia* to enforce the judgments of his courts, at least if the person subject to the judgment resisted the judgment in any way. Although the bishop might conceivably threaten the use of actual force, he could not actually employ it.[15] The "weapons" proper to the clerical order were spiritual in nature.

The *glossa ordinaria* summed up this circumspect but not altogether limp approach in taking up the sanction of capital punishment. The ultimate sanction of the criminal law was not contrary to the tenets of the canon law. However, spiritual courts were never to inflict it themselves. They might in some circumstances approve of its use by the temporal courts, even seek its application in those courts when the church's patience had been exhausted and the needs of society required stronger measures than the church had at its immediate disposal. However, the sanction might be sought only from a judge properly authorized to act; it could only be demanded for the sake of justice, never out of malice or a desire for vengeance; and it might be used only when no reasonable hope of amendment of life on the part of the criminal remained.[16]

Practical Applications

It may be objected, and not without color of reason, that these standards are too elastic to be meaningful in practice. They may have provided some good advice, but they permitted manipulation of the law by vindictive, arrogant, or frightened judges. The standards and monitions may be insufficiently concrete to have prevented ill-considered sentences and the most frightening punishments. The canon law's tendency ran toward giving judges a latitude in applying sanctions that was compatible with possible misuse. This characteristic quality is fully apparent here. Whether overall it worked for good or ill is one of the many tantalizing but difficult questions thrown off by the history of the canon law. Certainly there has been some of the latter.

The tendency toward widening judicial discretion can also be seen in an unemotive context in the canonists' treatment of the question of the use of monetary sanctions within the system of spiritual courts. The formal law of the medieval church was set out in *Licet iuxta apostolum* (X 5.37.3), a decretal letter of Pope Alexander III to the archbishop of Canterbury. The decretal apparently forbade the exaction of monetary penalties in the correction and punishment of spiritual crimes. Its point seemed clearly to be that there was an incompatibility between correction in the ecclesiastical forum and the exaction of money fines. A concern to raise money through law was the opposite of what law based upon the primacy of the world of the spirit enjoined.

However, the case had arisen in the first place because the archdeacon of Coventry was accused of having avariciously exacted such penalties, and this circumstance may have encouraged the canonists who interpreted the decretal to give it a restricted reading. It could, for instance, be understood to have applied only to archdeacons, who lacked the power to issue dispensations that only bishops held, and not to other judges.[17] Alternatively, it might have been meant to cover only pecuniary penalties that were paid to the judge himself, not those that were intended for pious uses, since the archdeacon involved had allegedly been taking the fines for his personal gain.[18] Further, the decretal might have been dealing only with those cases in which no monetary sanctions were provided for in the law, that is, where the question of penalty had been left open.[19] Any of these readings was possible. They would all allow exaction of money fines in all circumstances not expressly forbidden by the decretal.

The opinion that came to prevail was that the matter was best left to judicial discretion. The medieval gloss, for instance, held that a spiritual court had the power to apply that penalty "which [was] the more greatly feared."[20] That meant that monetary penalties could be used wherever other penalties had failed or were likely to fail. This interpretation became the accepted rule. The Council of Trent was later to carry it to a further conclusion, decreeing that money fines should be used in preference to spiritual sanctions, lest the latter fall into even greater disrepute among the laity than they had fallen already.[21] The obvious effect of these enactments and glosses was to render the prohibition in Alexander III's decretal ineffective except in the most limited of circumstances. Judicial discretion became the rule of the day, and it clearly encompassed the use, direct or indirect, of some temporal sanctions.[22] No canonist maintained that all temporal sanctions were open without restraints to the ecclesiastical courts, but there was to be no absolute prohibition against their taking a place in the church's legal system.

THE TWO SWORDS IN COOPERATION

The legitimacy of temporal punishment for canonical offenses having been established, the problem lay in defining the circumstances in which it would be used. This problem directly raised the subject of invocation of secular aid by and for the church. The canonists recognized that the spiritual courts of the church would not always be able to secure the willing obedience of those who appeared before them. As we have just seen, these courts could not normally invoke corporal sanctions, and they could never themselves issue a sentence of death. It might easily happen that stronger medicine would be required than spiritual sanctions and that the secular powers would have a monopoly on that medicine. Also lurking here was the "reverse problem" of deciding under what circumstances the church should respect and enforce the judgments of the courts of the state. This inevitably brings us back to the political theories with which this chapter began. It was the canonists' understanding of the proper relationship between the "two swords" that provided the normal way of thinking through the ensuing problems.

Gelasian Cooperation

Under the Gelasian view, the two jurisdictions were independent but mutually supportive. Where need existed, "each power [was] to be aided by the other."[23] This principle was recognized and clearly incorporated into the canon law by several of the texts in the Gregorian Decretals.[24] Against blasphemers, as we have already seen, Pope Gregory IX provided expressly that diocesan bishops should proceed "by coercion of temporal authority, if there be necessity for it" (X 5.26.2).[25] A chapter in the next title of the Decretals' book 5 authorized proceeding against suspended clerics who refused to desist from exercise of their office "by the judgment of the king, upon request of the church" (X 5.27.2). The most mundane matters, collection of tithes for instance, could lead under decretal law to the "invocation of the secular arm" and possibly even to the use of corporal punishment by that arm if no amendment of life, or at any rate no payment of one's tithes, was forthcoming.[26]

Invocations of temporal power on behalf of the church were not innovations of the twelfth and thirteenth centuries. They had a long history by the time the classical canon law was formulated. From at least the fourth century, episcopal synods and councils had called upon secular authorities to assist the church in executing its decisons.[27] Several ancient texts placed in the *Decretum* also endorsed the principle. One of them cited the example of the apostle Paul, who in Acts 23:17 was recorded as having called upon a Roman tribune when threatened with death (C. 23 q. 3. c. 2). Another, an extract from Isidore of Seville, held that the princes of the world had been given power within the church precisely so that they might support ecclesiastical discipline when the "sacerdotal word" proved unavailing (C. 23 q. 5 c. 20). A third, apparently taken from St. Jerome, described the essence of the royal office as the doing of justice (C. 23 q. 5 c. 23). This meant supporting the powerless where they had legitimate claims, and it was no great feat of the imagination to suppose that this was the situation in which the church could not enforce its judgments. Under the canon law, one source of legitimate respect owed to princes was that the prince was himself under a duty to come to the assistance of the church.

The canonists found recognition of something close to this ecclesiastical right to call upon the temporal power in the Roman law itself. An imperial decree, found in the Codex, ordered that when two men who had submitted a dispute between them to a bishop, they were to be compelled to observe the ensuing episcopal judgment. The decision was to be respected and enforced by imperial officials, "lest the episcopal judgment should be undone."[28] This law could have been read as stating simply that parties to litigation must abide by the ruling of a judge they themselves had chosen. Bartolus in fact did so read it.[29] For the canonists, however, the law of the Codex furnished valuable civilian confirmation of the principle that the temporal sword had been instituted so that it might come to the assistance of the spiritual.

Hierocratic Direction

Suppose, however, that the secular power did not wish to enforce the church's sentences. This might easily happen. Its own substantive law might be at variance with the canon law. Its officers might favor other interests. Refusal might even stem from quite good and legitimate reasons, as when an ecclesiastical sentence had been the product of malice or when a spiritual court had not complied with canonical procedure. The canonists were alive to the possibility; they did not assume that injustice could not occur in the spiritual forum.[30]

If for whatever reason there was a difference of opinion about the justice of a sentence pronounced in the spiritual forum, was the secular power nonetheless under a duty to do the church's bidding? In dealing with this extension of the problem, the hierocratic view of proper relations between church and state came directly into play. Assuming that the spiritual power had really delegated its temporal sword to the state, as the "Gregorian" theory held it to have done, the conclusion followed that the temporal judges had a duty simply to enforce the ecclesiastical court's judgment. They were agents. To them belonged nothing but "the pure and simple execution" of the decisions of the ecclesiastical tribunals.[31]

Joannes Andreae stated this uncompromising position with characteristic precision: "If the castigation of one condemned is officially requested of the king, he is to comply, and he is to be excommunicated
unless he does so." Further, "It is not for him [the king] to inquire
whether the sentence is just or not."[32] In fact, it would be at least a
technical violation of the legal prohibition against trying the same
matter twice, the subject examined in Chapter 11, if the king was to
inquire into the merits of the underlying cause. Subjects are often
bound to follow the dictates of their superiors, even when those dictates are mistaken, and that principle was thought entirely apposite
to requests by the church for the application of temporal sanctions.[33]

This was strong stuff. It would "scandalize" European kings and
their ministers, who had not the slightest wish to be regarded as pup-
pets in the hands of the bishops. The nomination and control of these
very bishops had been taken from them within living memory. The
conclusion also seemed directly contrary to the inherited Gelasian
tradition. Moreover, the kings might well recall that there were other,
competing views of the right relation between church and state than
the Gelasian and the Gregorian. The ruler's position in Roman law or
the thought of Marsilius of Padua offered more radical ways of resist-
ing the notion that the secular courts were required to serve as un-
questioning servants of the ecclesiastical. They were tempting. They
were possible. By the fourteenth century at the latest, some of them
were beginning to be exploited in practice, and the canonists were
quite aware of this unhappy development.[34]

There was some opinion within the canonical tradition itself that
would have allowed greater leeway to the temporal courts or that at
least tilted slightly away from the hierocratic position without actually disavowing it. Guido de Baysio raised, without endorsing, the
possibility that secular judges ought to be treated as the equals (pares)
of spiritual judges, allowing them greater discretion in executing the
judgments of the other forum.[35] Another possibility, mentioned by
Petrus de Ancharano, reasoned that since the decretal authorizing invocation of the secular arm spoke of "pleas that are of God," it might
follow that unjust pleas, which by definition could not be "of God,"
were not covered at all. Under canonical principles, the canon law

authorized only execution of just sentences, and this rule would be rendered meaningless if the secular judge could not examine the regularity of the spiritual court's action.[36] However, neither of these positions seems to have carried the day against the logic of the hierocratic position and the plain meaning of the the most recent decretal law on the subject.

The principal stumbling block to the hierocratic position on this subject, one to which the canonists were fully alive, was caught by an attempt at harmonization found in Petrus de Ancharano's statement. Although automatic execution of judgments followed logically enough from the Decretals, it meant converting that rule into an engine of possible injustice. The secular judge might be compelled to execute a sentence he knew to be wrong or procedurally invalid. Not only that, he might well be applying a physical punishment that had irreversible consequences. Could this be what he should do? Should the canon law excommunicate such a judge for following his conscience and doing what was clearly right? Many of the canonists recoiled from that conclusion.[37] Texts from the canon law commanded all men not to obey commands that were contrary to the word of God (C 11. q. 3 c. 92). That the command to do evil had come from a bishop, a judge, or a spiritual lord did not immunize it from comparison with the word of God.[38]

What might be called an "intermediate" position was offered in response to this dilemma. It seems to have had a larger following than either of the two just mentioned. This position was that the secular judge was not unconditionally obliged to enforce an unjust or invalid sentence. What he must not do, however, was to pass judgment against that sentence himself. He could not annul it. Neither could he ignore it. He would be obliged, therefore, to shun the person who had been excommunicated by the church, just as any other Christian would be. This might entail issuing an order exiling that person and condemning him for disobedience if he failed to obey the initial order of exile. However, it would not require the secular judge actually to execute the unjust sentence. He would not have had to pass on it one way or the other. He could thereby avoid imposing punitive physical sanctions on the unjustly treated defendant.

To describe this solution, Baldus de Ubaldis invoked the pleasant metaphor of two confederated cities, both of which had agreed to respect each other's proscriptions. Following the metaphor, he suggested that a secular judge need not actually enforce the erring ecclesiastical decree but should treat the person excommunicated in the same way one of these cities would treat a person who had been proscribed by the other. The judges of the former would order that person to leave its territory until he had returned to obedience and the good graces of the confederated city, but they would not be obliged by their treaty of confederation actually to execute the sentence of that city. So in this case. The temporal judge should do the same. "This," announced Baldus, "would not be execution [of the sentence], but instead a distinct proceeding."[39] It would involve the secular judge in no dilemma of conscience, and it would not be directly contrary to the canonical texts.

No definitive consensus on these variant positions was reached by the medieval canonists. In some ways it seems (to a modern reader) that the more they dealt with it, the more intractable it became.[40] But this is to some extent the fault of our expectations. The canonists' habit of commenting on individual decretals, raising the issues but not always taking a firm position one way or the other, can easily seem like confusion or imprecision to modern readers. And for many purposes, it was not necessary to reconcile them. They led to the same result. Nevertheless, it is beyond doubt that conflicting views about the "two swords" can be found in the works of the same jurists.

There were also many variants on this theme, variants that might call for slightly different forms of analysis. For example, the question of whether or not papal judges delegate could invoke the aid of the secular arm was a much debated question.[41] Not only did it involve the large theoretical question just described and the various permutations that accompanied it. An additional argument was that the *stylus curiae* of the papal court was routinely to add the words "invoking the aid of the secular arm if necessary" to rescripts of justice. Where they were omitted, it could therefore be said that the pope must have meant the power itself to be omitted. The argument on the other end was that papal judges delegate enjoyed a greater share of the papal plenitude of power than did ordinary bishops. Therefore, if bishops had the inherent right to require secular aid, a fortiori the delegated judges did too. About this question much dispute ensued.[42]

Ecclesiastical Cooperation with Temporal Sentences

The canonists were similarly exercised, although less ambiguous, on parts of the opposite situation: requests from the secular courts that an ecclesiastical judge excommunicate a person who had been proscribed or subjected to the secular ban.[43] There was no decretal specifically dealing with the question, but several texts from the *Decretum* stated the principle, consistent with Gelasian views, that the two powers should support each other in times of need.[44] From these, all canonists drew the conclusion that spiritual courts *could* lend their aid to the secular forum. To have permitted this aid would have followed equally from the Gelasian and the hierocratic view of relations between church and state.

Whether this kind of cooperation was to be made available as a matter of routine was, however, less obvious. Innocent IV's views on the subject are worth citing, since they are relatively straightforward and were influential in the sense that they were repeated regularly by succeeding canonists. He argued that in the ordinary case there should be equal cooperation. Each court system should come to the assistance of the other.[45] There were, however, two crucial differences. Whereas the secular judge could be compelled to lend his aid to the ecclesiastical, it did not work the other way around. Since the ecclesiastical judge wielded the superior sword, he could not lawfully be made the subject of a command. Supplication was the appropriate form of address. This result was required by the hierocratic understanding of the relation of church and state. Moreover, whereas in ordinary circumstances the secular judge must simply enforce the church's decree, the ecclesiastical court should always examine the merits of the underlying cause. There should be some sort of a hearing. As Hostiensis put it, "The ecclesiastical never excommunicates at the petition of the secular, except where reasonable cause exists and proper canonical process has been observed."[46]

These views and distinctions in turn led to problems of their own—as, for example, in determining whether the examination by the ecclesiastical tribunal amounted to a violation of the rule of res judicata. One need not go more than a step or two to appreciate the possible complexity of the problem. The essential for appreciating the way in which the canon law was put together, however, does not require traveling down the path at which we have just taken a look. The essential is to see how this large question was worked out within the context of what might be called a "creative tension" between competing theories of the "two swords." Each was found stated in the texts of the *Corpus iuris canonici.* The canonists made use of them both in the law relating to invocation of the secular arm, without feeling compelled to confront their fundamental incompatibility.

If a modern reader was obliged to pick the "majority view" on this question among the canonists, it would be the hierocratic view. Most canonists held that the temporal authorities were compelled to aid the spiritual courts and to execute their sentences if called upon to do so. They spoke of the "secular arm" for this reason. It had no will of its own. But despite this slight tip in the balance, the modern reader will also find much in the writing of the canonists to support the older Gelasian position. The two ideas, perhaps inconsistent at bottom, nevertheless coexisted in the canon law.

THE PRINCIPLES IN ACTION

A modern reader might be pardoned for thinking that the hierocratic system just described must have been more fantasy than fact. However, this would not be so. Canonical theory had immediate and practical consequences. The church made strenuous efforts to turn its ideas about the proper relation between its courts and those of lay princes into reality, and these efforts bore fruit in several parts of Europe. The resulting situation did not turn out to be everywhere identical, and in some places clerical agitation for the benefits of cooperation produced no results at all. In others, however, clerical efforts were crowned with success. Lay enforcement of clerical sentences appears in several of the German-speaking lands, for example. There, the rule was advanced that any person who had stood excommunicate for more than a year automatically fell under the emperor's ban as well.[47] In France, the results were less encouraging to the church. King Louis IX (d. 1270) refused to admit the practice on the grounds of the injustices to which it could lead, and it dropped out of use.[48]

It was probably in England that the system just described had its greatest impact. The canon law on this subject comes very close to describing what happened in fact. At least from the early thirteenth century, bishops and a few other ecclesiastical officials had the right under English common law to request "letters of caption" from the royal Chancery against any person who had remained excommunicate for more than forty days.[49] Upon receipt of the episcopal application, called a *significavit* in English legal parlance, the Chancery issued a writ to the sheriff, ordering him to imprison the offender until the latter made satisfaction and obtained absolution from the church. Securing release required that this process be reversed; that is, a similar request would be sent by the bishop to the Chancery, from which the order to release was then issued to the sheriff. The system of signification and caption was in regular use throughout the Middle Ages. It survived the Protestant Reformation, remained in regular use in the sixteenth and seventeenth centuries, and indeed lasted into the nineteenth.[50] It makes an ironic end to the story to find the system being used in Victorian times to imprison ritualist priests who defied their bishops ostensibly in the name of the freedom of the church.[51]

Under the English procedure writs of caption were issued *de cursu* by the Chancery, or in other words "as a matter of course." This was important to the litigants and also relevant to the subjects discussed by the canonists, because it meant that the royal officials normally undertook no investigation into the facts underlying the episcopal request for caption. In the medieval English system, it was enough that the request came from a bishop who had authority over the person excommunicated. What legal protection was offered to persons subject to this form of imprisonment came from within the canonical system. In fact, there was some such protection. Before the *significavit* was sent to the Chancery, defendants in the spiritual forum were regularly given a special term to appear before the judge of the ecclesiastical court who would make the request for caption. At that hearing they had the chance to show cause why the order should not be admitted.[52]

And if they appealed to a higher ecclesiastical court, this too would suspend the process for a time. Otherwise, however, the Chancery itself would not protect them. It would not seek to discover whether the ecclesiastical courts had acted properly or whether the sentence of excommunication itself was just. In other words, from a canonical perspective, the English government implemented the "hierocratic" view of right relations between courts of church and state.

Such an assertion, had it been made too loudly, would have angered the English kings and raised the hackles of the English common lawyers. They would have said that the system rested on immemorial English custom and upon a free decision of the king's government about what aid it should lend to the church, not on any coercive rule of the canon law. They could have pointed out that the royal courts did not actually punish anyone in response to a request for caption; they simply imprisoned the person until the offender agreed voluntarily to comply with the spiritual court's decree. They might also have challenged the speaker to produce an example of a royal judge's being excommunicated for failing to follow the church's invocation of the secular arm. That sanction was an established part of the canon law, and it was not being enforced or even threatened against them.

All that would have been fair enough. No evidence has surfaced so far to show any English judge or Chancery clerk being excommunicated for failing to do the bidding of the church in issuing the order for imprisonment. English ecclesiastical lawyers apparently left that contentious aspect of the canon law prudently unenforced. To have attempted enforcement to the letter of the Decretals might well have risked the system's collapse. It could also legitimately have been said that parts of the system were determined entirely by English customary law, not by the dictates of the canon law. An English common lawyer would not have regarded the details of the system of caption as a matter of his following any legal system but his own. But it is worth noting that the canonists themselves prescribed no exact form invocation of the secular arm would take. They were content to settle the outlines, leaving the details to be worked out according to local needs. If the outlines were respected, even with limitations and local variations such as existed in England, it would have seemed foolish for the canonists to complain that every jot and tittle of a hierocratic system was not firmly in place. They were not so foolish as that. They might indeed have cited the English customary system as an example of the Gelasian "two swords" acting in cooperation. And from a modern perspective, it could hardly be imagined that the English common law would itself have "invented" the system of caption without the lead of the canon law.

The situation in England would certainly have looked good to the hierocrats by comparison with the situation in some parts of Europe, even in the thirteenth century. The canonists did complain energetically about places where no respect whatsoever was being paid to the principle that lay power should come to the aid of the church. Of this, the best thirteenth-century example comes from the pen of Hostiensis. After describing a spiritual judge as "paralytic" without the aid of the secular and portraying the secular judge as "blind" without the leadership of the spiritual, Hostiensis lamented that the worst features of both had become the reality: "Today in many places, the blind lead the blind, for the spiritual neither instructs nor corrects, and the secular . . . takes occupation of ecclesiastical right."[53]

Hostiensis was pointing to a problem that, from the canonical perspective, would only get worse: a hierocratic system working the other way round.[54] By the later Middle Ages, the notion was abroad that the secular courts might call the ecclesiastical courts to account, determining whether they had properly exercised spiritual jurisdiction and even whether they had rightly treated the parties before them. The church might be confined within a "spiritual" sphere of action, one very straitly defined.[55] The ecclesiastical courts might be required to follow the dictates of the temporal forum. Instead of lending aid, the temporal rulers would in effect be treating the courts of the church as if they were the "spiritual arm" of the state.[56] That would be the hierocratic position turned on its head.

THE PUNISHMENT OF HERESY

The various strands of the canon law justifying the "invocation of the secular arm" came together in the question of how persons convicted of heresy were to be punished. It provided this part of the canon law on the subject with its severest test, its greatest triumph, and its most enduring shame. One must say a word about it. Applying either of the conceptions of the canon law, the secular courts would be called upon to aid the church in suppressing religious dissent. The only difference would lie in the theory underlying that aid and the possibility of disagreement between the two powers. Almost from the inception of the Christian era, Christians regarded heresy as a form of pestilence to be eradicated wherever possible. The temptation to call upon temporal rulers for help in its suppression had not been resisted in antiquity, and it was welcomed with enthusiasm during the Middle Ages. Some of St. Augustine's thought justifying the imposition of temporal punishment for spiritual offenses, dealt with at the start of this chapter, grew out of conflicts with the Donatists and involved invocation of the strongest secular measures to suppress dissent within the church.

The medieval church enacted several special provisions to combat heresy during the period of the formulation of the canon law. The principal such enactment of importance for this subject was a decretal of Pope Lucius III (1181–85): *Ad abolendum* (X 5.7.9). It contained five essential enactments, of which four are relevant here:

1. It defined heresy as belief contrary to that professed by the Roman Church and excommunicated all Christians whose beliefs did not conform to that definition.
2. It stated that all those who refused to abjure such beliefs were to be handed over to secular judges, who were to execute the ecclesiastical judgment by imposing "condign punishment" upon them.
3. It determined that if any person had once abjured, then later fallen back into heresy, he or she should be turned over at once to the secular arm for punishment, and this should occur quickly "without any hearing."
4. It required all persons in secular authority to swear to do all in their power to aid the church in combating heresy, excommunicating ipso facto those who refused or failed to act and placing their lands under interdict.

This papal ruling thus authorized invocation of the secular arm in all heresy cases, and it visited the heaviest canonical sanctions upon secular officials who might decline to execute the church's judgments. This was hierocratic theory put to the test. It might, of course, be said that *Ad abolendam* was merely making one concrete application of principles that underlay the canon law of cooperation between church and state. That would certainly be true. It drew those principles to their logical conclusion. However, it either went beyond or stated with much greater precision the canonical principles of the established canon law in at least three important ways.

First, although the decretal's terms left the question of the nature of the "condign punishment" undefined, and therefore formally to the determination of the secular power, in fact no one doubted that the punishment being referred to was death. The canonists fully understood that death by burning was being authorized by the papal decretal, and they approved this understanding of the law. On this score, it is not possible to convict them of hypocrisy, for they avowed the result.[57] Had not Jesus said (John 15:6): "If a man abide not in me, he is cast forth as a branch, and is withered; and men gather them, and cast them into the fire, and they are burned"? Who but a heretic could be meant by "a man not abiding in me"? Who was more worthy of this painful and exemplary form of death?[58] Glosses on *Ad abolendam* took the biblical passage and the papal decretal to state exactly that uncompromising position.

For this result, the canonists found support both in Roman law and in customary law. An imperial decree found in the Codex prescribed the *ultimum supplicium* as the proper fate of obstinate Manichaeans.[59] This clearly meant capital punishment.[60] Moreover, this understanding of the early decree was amply confirmed by "general custom" of the day, according to which all heretics were handed over to death by burning. Such a generally accepted custom, far from constituting an extralegal abuse, lent added strength to the canonists' interpretation of the term "condign punishment" used in the papal decretal. "Thus," concluded Hostiensis, "not only according to the law of the gospel, but also according to human [law] and general custom, this penalty is due to all heretics."[61]

Second, *Ad abolendam* formed one part of a series of canonical enactments restricting the legal rights of those suspected and convicted
of heresy. A denial of any right of audience or appeal to the relapsed
heretic was one such restriction. A second was extension of canonical
condemnation and punishment to "receivers, defenders, and promot-
ers" of all heretics, a rule evidently designed to discourage any cooperation with those suspected of religious dissent.[62] A third was the
rule that any person who refused to undergo an oath of purgation that
he or she was free from heretical belief should henceforth automatically be treated as a heretic.[63]

The canonists reconciled these rules with the Christian's assurance
that God did not desire the death of a sinner but rather that the sinner
should be converted and live, by saying that the assurance could not
have been meant to apply to an incorrigible man or woman who had
resisted God's express commands.[64] It applied to sinners who desired
actually to turn from their wickedness and follow those commands,
not to others. The assurance of God's patience was exhausted by allowing one recantation. To the canonists, as to the medieval church
in general, the threat of heresy seemed so perilous and so difficult that
extreme measures were required.

Finally, *Ad abolendam* raised the stakes in requiring the secular
courts to follow the spiritual court's direction. A specific oath to aid
the church's efforts to combat dissent was to be imposed on the appropriate lay powers by the decretal's terms. A consequence of failure to
fulfill that oath was excommunication and interdict. The Fourth Lateran Council and a decretal inserted in the *Liber sextus* added to this. If
the temporal lord, having been requested and warned by the bishop,
nonetheless disregarded the request for action against the condemned
heretic during the space of a year, his refusal was to be signified to the
pope, so that his vassals might be freed from the obedience they otherwise owed to him and so that his lands might be opened to occupancy
by other lords who would "preserve the faith in its purity."[65] No one
who reads these decretals can suppose that canonical theory about the
"two swords" was restricted to the realm of political theory. The temporal sword was to be wielded at the direction of the church in a way
that could undermine the legitimacy of temporal government.

It is quite possible, despite this, that one might legitimately regard *Ad abolendam* as a matter simply of canonical theory. This is not because no one took it seriously. Quite the reverse. It is because the results called for in these decretals were not only not actively resisted by the lay powers. They were embraced. Indeed, the extravagant denunciations of religious dissent that are found in the writings of the canon law were echoed by the secular authorities. They were all too willing to comply with most of the decretal's provisions. In England, the system of "signification" and caption examined above was supplemented by creation of the writ *de haeretico comburendo*.[66] It was issued as a matter of course upon episcopal request in order to consign heretics to the flames once they had been duly convicted in an ecclesiastical tribunal. The king's government, in other words, willingly assisted in the task of extirpating religious dissent. The same largely held true on the Continent.[67]

Historians of English law have sometimes insisted that acceptance of the system occurred only in the late fourteenth century and also that the common law judges always exercised control over its worst excesses through use of the writ of habeas corpus.[68] Their assessment has stressed that the common law set limits to the extent of ecclesiastical control. Historians of the English Church have insisted that in practice episcopal applications for the writ *de haeretico comburendo* were made only as a measure of last resort. Their assessment of the evidence has suggested that the medieval church's overall concern was not to destroy men and women but rather to save them. Though possibly quite oppressive in theory, the system was less so in fact.[69]

Both of these readings of the evidence may well be right. They rest on a thorough familiarity with the sources and upon the not wholly improbable assumption that medieval men would have applied the rules humanely. But the medieval canonists would have had some difficulty understanding the evident need these modern writers feel to apologize for the medieval system. Still less would they have tried to justify the system of cooperation to secure the imprisonment or execution of flagrant violators of the law of the church by saying that it was ineffective. The canonists were not embarrassed by any of what has just been described. They regarded it as an entirely proper application of the theory of cooperation between the temporal and the spiritual swords.

CONCLUSION

What the medieval canonists chiefly regretted was not that this system was repressive in theory or in fact. They lamented that in practice it was not being fully applied. They were realists in many respects. They knew that many, perhaps even most, of the contemporary secular powers had staked out their own independence from clerical governance. They saw well enough that, within many aspects of legal practice, lay princes were refusing automatically to allow application of temporal sanctions in response to ecclesiastical requests. The canonists remarked ruefully that temporal courts were taking cognizance of whether or not the ecclesiastical sentences had been just before they lent their aid.[70] Even heresy prosecutions depended upon the willing cooperation of those who wielded the temporal sword, not upon obedient application of the canonical penalties prescribed by *Ad abolendam*. Too often canonical theory was not being respected. It was only after the temporal courts had first determined the merits of the underlying case that the sentences of spiritual tribunals were being put into effect. That was obviously not the correct and automatic application role of the secular arm envisioned by the canon law.

It might fairly have been said, therefore, that by the thirteenth century it was becoming evident that the canon law dealing with invocation of the secular arm had won only a partial victory. It was put into practice, but not everywhere and not as a matter of right. Most of the temporal princes never accepted the hierocratic notion that lay behind it. The most they would concede was the Gelasian view of the "two swords," and to even that view they gave a different reading than most of the canonists did. In this instance, therefore, the canon lawyers, who pushed the hierocratic implications of the "two swords" the furthest, had to rest with an influence on European legal practice that was only practical and always incomplete.

14 Canonical Sanctions: The Law of Excommunication

Excommunication is a sentence of separation from the sacraments of the church, and in its strongest form, from the company of all Christian people.[1] The biblical locus classicus for it was found by the canonists either in Matt. 18:17 or in the fifth chapter of St. Paul's First Letter to the Corinthians. In the first, Jesus had directed that the sinning brother who would not hear the church's voice be treated "as a heathen and a publican." In the second, St. Paul had urged the Corinthians to "deliver to Satan" a man guilty of serious moral transgressions. The Christians at Corinth were directed "not to keep company" with such transgressors but rather to "put them away" from themselves, so that God himself might judge them. Exclusion of wrongdoers, often accompanied by some kind of ritual cursing, is a feature common to many religions, and Christianity practiced a form of it from the earliest days.

In examining the nature of the classical canon law, however, the best approach is not to deal with the relationship between excommunication and similar practices in other religions or even to examine it as part of the penitential practices of the early church. As revealing as these approaches might ultimately prove to be, understanding the nature of the classical canon law dictates a more restricted point of view. It requires looking at the ways excommunication came to be developed as a specifically judicial sanction. A judicial sanction is what one finds in most of the texts of the *Corpus iuris canonici* and also in the classical commentaries on these texts. Although there are discordant elements to be uncovered in some of these sources, elements that were inherited from the early period of the church's life and that fit awkwardly within the notion of a judicial sanction, it is the latter that the canonists kept to the fore. This chapter will deal with the early medieval inheritance, therefore, but principally as an introduction to the judicial sentence of excommunication central under the classical law.

According to the canon law, excommunication was a spiritual sanction administered by a court of competent jurisdiction and only after complying with the formalities of canonical due process. Strictly speaking, it was a form of censure. It must be kept distinct on that account from canonical remedies, such as the *restitutio in integrum* we looked at in Chapter 4, which were corrective procedures developed to do justice in a concrete setting. If one thinks, in a modern setting, of the difference between an order that a divorced father pay so much in child support and an order to imprison the father for failing to comply with the order, excommunication being akin to the latter, one can approximate this difference. It was a means to enforce the law's commands.

The sanction of excommunication must also be kept distinct from the various forms of penance commonly employed by the medieval church to effect the expiation of public sins. Excommunication was designed to enforce obedience to the lawful orders of the church, as by requiring that the sinner perform the duty or the public penance assigned to him. It might be a penalty, at least it might entail penalties, if it was disobeyed. But it was not a punishment strictly speaking. It did not require any specific act other than obedience to the church's law. Public penance, by contrast, was not a censure in the classical law of the church. Rather, it was one part of the process of restoring a person to full communion with the church and with other Christians. Although a person who had been excommunicated might have to perform a public penance as part of having the sentence of excommunication lifted, the juridical natures of the two were quite distinct.

EXCOMMUNICATION'S HISTORICAL REPUTATION

Few aspects of the classical canon law have attracted as much scholarly interest as excommunication. It is not hard to see why. One meets dramatic and controversial excommunications on virtually every page of the historical record. The subject has also seemed inherently interesting to historians. As a means of governing, its very strangeness to modern sensibilities attracts notice and curiosity. The subject can even be made sensational at points where it intersected with some of the most significant political questions of the time. In addition, there are several more technical aspects of the subject that have attracted the attention of scholars. The canon law of excommunication was complex and contained within it some inherently contradictory ideas.[2] The process by which it emerged as a legal sanction out of the vague and confused anathemas and the penitential practices of the early church is full of interest. The contrast between its assertedly spiritual nature and the temporal power and legal complexity it came to assume in the high Middle Ages has also made it a natural subject of interest for modern historians. Whatever a complete list of reasons might turn out to include, certainly it is evident that excommunication has long captured the imagination of some historians otherwise not much interested in the canon law.

Some of these modern writers essentially accept what might be called a "canonical" point of view. Indeed, they see even the sentences of excommunication launched against Christian rulers as the logical and correct result of the placement of the spiritual over the secular.[3] The sword of excommunication was the means of carrying out the church's mission in the world—one that did not except even the mighty from the judgments of God. St. Ambrose, as bishop of Milan, was said to have barred the emperor Theodosius from his church after the emperor had ordered a brutal massacre of the Thessalonians (390). This story, admittedly abstracted from other aspects of imperial relations with the church, came to stand for the vindication of a vital spiritual value. It was the very model for what should be expected from excommunication. That the church's mission was occasionally perverted to serve unworthy and earthly ends no one doubts; indeed, the canon law itself envisioned that exactly such misuse might occur. But by and large, it has seemed to many, excommunication has been exercised for essential and spiritual ends.

Some of the scholarly attention that has focused upon the subject has taken a quite different turn. It has belonged to what might be called the "Protestant alarmist" school, although this school is admittedly not much in fashion at the present time. Henry C. Lea began his study of the subject by describing its role in securing the power of the church over the laity. Its exercise, he wrote, was regarded as "plunging the rebellious into the pit of hell." The very threat of its use served to render the church's subjects "docile in this world."[4] Scholars who have taken this view have been repelled by the contrast between the elaborate law on the subject and the seemingly more straightforward law of the gospel. They have pointed to frequent examples of the misuse of excommunication for political or economic purposes as evidence of that basic disjunction. They have concluded that the sanction was effective much more often than it should have been, given the unworthy ends for which it was so often used.

More recent scholarly attention, to the contrary, has regarded the actual efficacy of excommunication with skepticism. This "school" has minimized the respect the sanction actually inspired among the laity and concluded that there was nothing to worry about after all. Rosalind Hill, for instance, concluded from her researches that already in the thirteenth century, excommunication had "degenerated from a tremendous spiritual sanction into a minor inconvenience."[5] Scholars have pointed to the same use of the sanction of excommunication for routine and trivialized purposes as the Protestant historians just mentioned, but they have drawn the opposite conclusion: namely, that the sanction was so frequent in practice that it could not have had the effects the canonists ascribed to it.

These are learned voices, and it will not be the purposes of this chapter to suggest, still less to prove, that they have been wrong. The book does not pretend to a viewpoint so dispassionate that it affords an accurate verdict on whether excommunication ever really served as an "effective instrument of social control" or whether its use has been a force for good or ill in Western society. Indeed, the historical record contains evidence to support both arguments. This chapter's more limited purpose is to examine the nature of the sanction as it was understood by the medieval and early modern canonists, together with tracing a few of the more important later developments in the law of excommunication. The chapter will also concentrate its principal attention on the question of when and under what circumstances excommunication could lawfully be imposed under the classical canon law rather than on the question of its legal (or practical) effects. In taking that approach, it is necessary to begin with the earlier history of the subject. That inheritance shaped the sanction's development in several ways.

THE EARLY MEDIEVAL INHERITANCE

The classical canon law affected the conception of excommunication so dramatically that one may without misleading draw a sharp contrast between the canonical sanction and the earlier and more "primitive" form of excommunication. The one was a legal sanction, the other a curse. That contrast is not one between black and white. Moreover, one can find examples of the older sort of excommunication throughout the later historical record, and as will be suggested at the end of this chapter, the sanction known as excommunication *latae sententiae* contained significant features from the older notion. Even so, the contrast exists and is particularly useful in understanding the development of the classical canon law. It is not incorrect to speak of a struggle between two different conceptions of excommunication during the period in which the classical canon law was born, a struggle from which a "judicialized" form of the sanction emerged as the victor, without, however, effecting the complete disappearance of its opponent. Some may think that the victory was achieved simply by papering over the confusing authorities inherited from the past with the habits of scholasticism. Others may regard the victory as a real triumph for the rule of law. Either way, it is useful to begin with the contrast.

The more "primitive" kind of excommunication—found frequently in the sources of the ninth through the eleventh centuries and indeed quite frequently well into the second half of the twelfth century—was not at all a judicial sanction. Commonly issued without prior citation or other formality, it was dependent for its efficacy upon the spiritual power of the person who issued it and the justice of his cause. This sort of excommunication was the anathema that appears at the end of many Anglo-Saxon charters.[6] It was the terrible curse of the early Irish saints[7] or the fearsome monastic maledictions of the ninth and tenth centuries.[8] Like the biblical curse of St. Peter against Ananias and Sapphira (Acts 5:1–10), it was a weapon to be unsheathed and wielded against the enemies of God. The effects of its rightful imposition were immediate, or if they were not immediate, they were seldom long delayed. And they were tangible. Ananias and Sapphira "fell down and gave up the ghost" directly after Peter's curse.

One particularly dramatic example of the inherited conception of what excommunication was appears in Galbert of Bruges's account of the dispute over the countship of Flanders. This dispute of the 1120s led to what Galbert described as the "War of Anathemas."[9] During this "war" priests on both sides of the quarrel fulminated a series of mutually contradictory sentences of excommunication against their opponents. Then they waited for results. At least according to Galbert's account, "In this interchange . . . the anathema of our priest prevailed." "It is marvelous," he reflected, "that a priest can cast a spell on God in such a way that, whether God wishes it or not, William will be thrown out of the countship."[10] "Fulmination" is certainly the right word to describe what happened. The requirements of judicial process did not come into the consciousness of the participants in the slightest. Indeed, in modern terms it would be quite absurd to speak in terms of a "sentence" of excommunication. There was no law in view. An excommunication's success was measured by its physical results. Modern readers commonly find this "War of Anathemas" either ridiculous or blasphemous (or both), as did the Bollandist fathers who suppressed it from their seventeenth-century edition of Galbert's work.[11] But the sort of ex parte excommunication involved in it is found in too many twelfth-century writings to be ignored as aberrations.

English sources from the twelfth century produce some dramatic accounts of such use of the sword of excommunication.[12] The *Magna vita* of St. Hugh, bishop of Lincoln from 1184, contains several examples. All are without the slightest sign of self-consciousness on the part of St. Hugh or his biographer that there was anything uncanonical about what he was doing. A barren couple pretended that the woman had given birth to a child in order to cheat a knight out of his inheritance.[13] Confronting the couple, but without anything like citation, hearing, or trial, St. Hugh excommunicated the man. The next day the man was found lifeless in bed, struck dead by the saint's anathema. On another occasion, St. Hugh rebuked a woman who had deserted her husband. She spat in the bishop's face. He excommunicated her at once, and three days later she too was discovered dead—"strangled by the devil," Hugh's biographer informs us.[14] Again, the saint's curse had done its work.

The direct excommunication involved in these examples is matched in the literature of Continental saints. On one occasion two monks from the house of St. Bernard of Clairvaux (d. 1153) came upon a brother cultivating a vineyard, an action they took to be incompatible with the monastic vocation. Unable to persuade the erring monk to desist by exhortation or shame, they proceeded to "excommunicate" the vineyard itself. In consequence, we are told, the vineyard shriveled and ceased to produce grapes until, after the death of the monk, the vineyard was finally absolved by St. Bernard.[15] A second Vita of St. Bernard recounts a similar use of excommunication by the saint himself. While dedicating a new monastic oratory, Bernard found that his discourse could scarcely be heard because of the din being made by "an incredible multitude of flies."[16] Unable to hit on any other remedy, he finally uttered an excommunication against them. The next morning the flies were found dead on the ground, victims of the saint's anathema.[17]

Alongside these bellicose examples, there existed a quite different conception of excommunication, one that also claimed historical precedents and one that became increasingly dominant over the course of the twelfth century. It regarded excommunication as a judicial sanction, normally reserved to bishops or their delegates, imposed as part of judicial process and inflicted only if procedural process had been observed. According to this tradition, a sentence of excommunication could not be pronounced by a person without proper judicial authority, no matter how saintly he might be. Moreover, the person excommunicated must be given proper warning, allowed to defend himself, and protected against abusive excommunications by a right of appeal to a higher court.

The roots of the principle were found in the crucial biblical example, specifically in the words of Jesus about fraternal correction in chapter 18 of Matthew. Only after refusing correction, Jesus had said, was the sinner to be treated as "a heathen and a publican" by the church (Matt. 18:17). A letter ascribed to St. Augustine (it appears wrongly) during the Middle Ages followed this by forbidding the excommunication of any person who had not first been found guilty by legitimate judicial process.[18] The argument was that because St. Paul said the person excommunicated had been "denominated" (*nominatur*) a sinner (1 Cor. 5:11), it followed that there must have been some judicial process against him (d.p. C. 11 q. 3 c. 21). In other words, "denomination" of the sinner meant more than the simple fact of his guilt. It meant that there had been a *finding* of his guilt.[19]

Conflict between these two understandings of excommunication and increasing insistence on subjecting excommunication to legal control were increasing features of church life in the twelfth century. Archbishop Thomas Becket, whose quarrel with Henry II provided the theme of Chapter 11, was one such offender against the emerging canonical rules. Gilbert Foliot, bishop of London and Becket's most implacable episcopal enemy, complained with some justification that the archbishop's habit had been "to condemn first, judge second."[20] Gerald of Wales (d. 1223), the vain and sharp-tongued critic whose opinions had been fortified by his experience in the Paris schools,[21] later took up this same theme, complaining that some bishops had been in the habit of issuing sentences of excommunication "with little discretion, and too frequently, without just reasons and warnings."[22] He spoke for the rising canonical tradition. By the first decades of the thirteenth century, it was clearly in the ascendant. Older and more informal habits, which left room for sudden and ex parte excommunications, issued without formal citation or judicial process of any sort, were coming to seem "both antique and antiquated" to men like Gerald.[23]

EXCOMMUNICATION IN THE
CORPUS IURIS CANONICI

Gerald's was the voice of the future. For the most part, his attitude is also that found in the *Corpus iuris canonici*. Its victory was signaled in a small but significant way by the canonical rule that the words "I curse you" were insufficient to excommunicate, even if spoken by one with legitimate authority to do so.[24] The law's forms had to be followed. The meaning had to be clear. It is important nonetheless to guard against the assumption that judicialized excommunication won an immediate, easy, and complete victory. It is important also to recognize that other and in some ways stronger values pushed the canonical conception of excommunication in directions modern readers will find unpalatable or at least unusual. The canon law developed against the background of older conceptions of excommunication, and the results were never wholly consistent with what Gerald desired. There were always loose ends, ambiguities, and contradictions. But the "mainstream" was with Gerald of Wales.

The complexity of the situation is evident in the very great attention that was paid to the subject in the canonical texts. Excommunication was one of the most fully treated subjects in the *Corpus iuris canonici*. In Gratian's *Decretum* the word *excommunicatio* or some derivative of it appeared 367 separate times.[25] All of the succeeding books contained sections dealing with excommunication, some of them quite lengthy. The Gregorian Decretals' title on the subject has sixty separate chapters. Twenty-four more were included in the *Liber sextus*. Such extensive treatment is itself a sign of the complexities of the subject.

The fully developed canon law came to divide excommunication into minor and major forms, the former requiring only the exclusion of the party from the sacraments, the latter from all contact with other Christians. It then further subdivided each of these.[26] Major excommunication contained a distinction between anathema and ordinary major excommunication, though not all canonists agreed on exactly what the dividing line actually divided. The better opinion seems to have been that there was no difference in substance, except as to the solemnity with which the sentence was promulgated. Excommunication was also only one part of a larger web of canonical sanctions; it was never the only censure at the disposal of the church. Canonists discovered that it was possible to elaborate seven separate sanctions within the canon law: interdicts, suspensions, and depositions from office, for example.[27]

When one sets such complications to one side, four principal themes, all of which raised difficult questions relating to excommunication, come to the forefront of the classical canon law and the commentaries by the medieval canonists. First, excommunication was the most serious sanction of the canon law and not to be invoked lightly. No weightier sentence lay at the disposal of ecclesiastical judges. Second, excommunication was a medicinal rather than a punitive sanction. Its purpose was to cure a spiritual disease, not to aggravate one, and this had consequences for the ways in which it was imposed. Third, unjust sentences of excommunication were conceivable, indeed likely. Provision had to be made for setting them right. Fourth, excommunication had the obvious potential for upsetting the order of civil society. The boundaries for determining when it should and when it should not have that effect were to be drawn with care.

Excommunication as *Maxima Poena*

The first point is the gravity of the sanction. Throughout the texts and the writings of the canonists one finds statements reflecting the seriousness both of incurring and of issuing a sentence of excommunication. The *Decretum* said that "no penalty in the church was greater" (C. 24 q. 3 c. 17). The *glossa ordinaria* to the Decretals called it "the eternal separation of death."[28] The fifteenth-century English canonist William Lyndwood styled the excommunicated person a "limb of the Devil."[29] There was no graver sanction than major excommunication.[30] That was a commonplace.

It had consequences. The primary among them was to hedge the imposition of excommunication round with procedural safeguards in order to keep it from being used unadvisedly.[31] If excommunication was the church's sternest sanction, it should not be imposed without circumspection. Thus ordinarily no person could be excommunicated except by a court with proper jurisdiction over that person. Only a person's judicial superior could excommunicate him in the external forum. Nor could one be lawfully excommunicated, except in special circumstances, without having been summoned by legitimate citation. There must have been a fair warning and an opportunity to respond.[32] Judges issuing a sentence of excommunication were also required to do so in writing. The person sentenced had the right to a copy of the sentence, and the sentence must express the cause of the excommunication.[33]

A particularly important example of the consequences that attended the seriousness of the sanction is the guarantee of protection for parties appealing a sentence of excommunication. More than the papal right to *decide* appeals was at stake. Appeals from sentences challenged as unjust were protected; the person sentenced must suffer no prejudice as long as he prosecuted his appeal with dispatch.[34] From this premise followed the extensive development of absolution *ad cautelam* (X 5.39.52).[35] It allowed the judge to whom an appeal had been taken provisionally to remit the sentence of excommunication while a hearing on the case proceeded. The procedure maintained the theoretical force of excommunication while in practice also protecting the litigant's right to a full and fair hearing.

This point is also connected with the view expressed by several canonists that only the contumacious were to be excommunicated. Only those who showed contempt for the courts or the law were to be punished, not those who had indicated signs of willingness to comply with the law.[36] Because excommunication was such a serious matter—cutting the excommunicate off from the fellowship of God and his neighbors—it was reserved for the offender against whom other means of correction had failed.[37] It was to be used with care (X 5.39.48).

The Medicinal Quality of Excommunication

The second principal feature of excommunication, one that was in some ways at odds with the first,[38] was that excommunication was meant for the restoration to spiritual health of the person subjected to it. It was not designed primarily to punish. The first decretal of the title on the subject in the *Liber sextus* began, "Because excommunication is medicinal and not mortal . . ." That was a recurring theme. Hostiensis was therefore building upon an established understanding of the sanction in asserting, "[E]xcommunication is medicine for the person excommunicated, not the right of any [other] person."[39] Its goal was that the person sentenced "should recognize his fault and turn toward God."[40]

It followed from this assumption that in litigation between parties no plaintiff had the unfettered right to insist that the defendant be declared excommunicate, even when the defendant was unquestionably liable to the plaintiff or otherwise in the wrong. Chapter 4 took note of this in dealing with the rule that *restitutio in integrum* could not be used to secure restoration of a sentence of excommunication. A more appealing example is the case of the poor man sued for a valid debt. If the poor man could not pay, he was not to be excommunicated for the failure, although he would be obliged to swear an oath to pay the debt when he returned to a prosperous state.[41] The creditor could not insist that the poor man be excommunicated for nonpayment because excommunication was medicinal, not punitive, and its imposition against a debtor too poor to pay would have served no restorative spiritual purpose.[42]

The attitude toward excommunication as medicinal had other legal consequences as well. The rule that a simple priest could absolve a dying person, despite reservation of the function to a bishop or even to the pope, was one.[43] The principle that no adverse consequences were to remain against the excommunicate after his absolution was another.[44] Perhaps the most striking manifestation of the view that the sanction was primarily medicinal was the permission given to judges to lift it if it failed to achieve its proper end. Joannes Andreae, for instance, noted that "the prelate, as a doctor, who sees that the medicine of excommunication, even if justly imposed, is not helpful but rather detrimental may discreetly remove it even during contumacy, if he sees that this will be useful to the health of the person excommunicated."[45] It was as if a modern injunction were to be lifted after a time if the person enjoined had refused to be guided by it.[46] Because a primary goal of the law was reconciliation between the sinner and God, use of the primary sanction of excommunication might appropriately be adjusted or even lifted to avoid frustrating that purpose.

There was bound to be some tension between this approach and the desire of the law to vindicate publicly the standards of the law and to avoid public scandal. But legal goals often come into competition in actual cases, and judges must make their choice of which is the more important. The canonists recognized the possible inconsistency, as shown by their attempts to distinguish those situations in which excommunication served as a *poena capitalis* from those in which its role was instead purely medicinal.[47] The attempt required balancing. In the end they concluded that excommunication would serve as a lasting punishment for the truly contumacious, for those who treated the sentence with contempt. For others, however, its medicinal purpose was paramount. The distinction is admittedly difficult from a modern juridical point of view. It is a good reminder that the canonists did not expect that excommunication should take effect exactly as a modern legal sanction does. Excommunication had the same purpose as a modern sentence: to do justice to the parties before the court. But in the medieval canon law it had an additional, and quite different, purpose as well.

The Problem of Unjust Excommunications

Also somewhat out of harmony with modern legal approaches was a third attitude of the classical canon law on the subject. The canonists recognized that excommunication did not represent a perfect determination of guilt or innocence and sought to provide for the eventuality. Unjust sentences were inevitable.[48] As Hostiensis put it, although the sentence is medicinal, it may well be that the judge is "an unskilled doctor."[49] And because the courts could only give judgment according to external proofs, incorrect judgments were bound to be made even by the most skilled judges. All canonists recognized this. Modern lawyers will of course admit the same. Who could deny it? The difference is that the canonists thought the subject worth discussing as more than an unfortunate fact of life. They dealt with it at length.

Their reaction to the problem took several forms. One was to attempt to secure the observance of canonical due process before excommunication was imposed. Another was an unwillingness to treat a sentence of excommunication, even if unjust, as of no force. The first of these has been discussed above. But the second is equally worth stressing. It is illuminating in its detail. Gratian's *Decretum* had taken up the point, one of the few places where the subject of excommunication was dealt with in any detail. In *Causa* 11, Gratian analyzed the reasons for which a sentence might possibly be unjust, dividing them into three separate kinds.[50] First, a sentence of excommunication might be unjust *ex animo*, as when the prelate issued it out of his own hatred, jealousy, or spite. Second, it might be unjust *ex ordine*, as when proper canonical procedure had not been followed but the sentence had been issued anyway. Third, it might be unjust *ex causa*, as when the reason for which the person was excommunicated did not exist.

Gratian and the canonists dealt with the possible permutations— for instance, a person might be deserving of excommunication for one serious fault but in fact be excommunicated for a quite different fault, of which he was not guilty. We might follow their speculations if it were profitable. But to do so would take us a considerable distance, and it is of more immediate significance to note that in all three cases, Gratian held that the unjust sentence was to be obeyed by the person sentenced. It was also to be respected by other persons. It was not a nullity. Even if the three sources of injustice were combined, as when a prelate excommunicated someone without due process, because of his hatred of the person, and without any just cause, neither the person excommunicated nor any other Christian was entitled to disregard the force of the sentence. The excommunicated person must first appeal and have the unjust sentence lifted.

This doctrine should not surprise us too much. We have essentially the same rule as to unjust court decisions. They are valid until vacated or reversed. However, the reach of the canonical rule and the reasons given for it were slightly different than our own. To have allowed anything other than the route of acceptance, appeal, and absolution, Gratian said, would have been to encourage human pride.[51] It would have encouraged individuals to set their opinions before those of the church. The canonists thus found virtue even in unjust sentences of excommunication. The keys of the church, wrote Antonius de Butrio, will be held in greater reverence where men augment the merit of obedience by obeying even a sentence known to be unjust.[52] Excommunication, whether just or unjust, was always to be feared.

However, there were limits. The first was a recognition of the restricted effect of such an unjust sentence and was properly the concern of the forum of conscience.[53] An unjust excommunication, though valid on earth, would not bind in heaven.[54] It might subject the person to mundane inconveniences, but excommunication was not an irreversible judgment. Thus the canonists could advise without hesitation that if it came to a choice between obedience to a sentence of excommunication that would involve danger to a person's soul and obedience to the law of one's conscience, one should choose the latter, patiently submitting to the earthly sentence.[55] Indeed, there was opinion that one would augment one's eternal merit by such submission.[56] In the end, as one canonist put it, "the unjust sentence binds the excommunicator, not the excommunicated."[57]

The canon law also provided several exceptions on earth.[58] One formulated in a decretal of Pope Innocent III held that when unjust sentences contained "intolerable error," they could be treated as automatically invalid (X 5.39.40). Suppose a bishop had expressly excommunicated X, "because X did not kill Y" or "because X refused to commit adultery with Z." Would the sentence against X be treated as valid? It did not seem possible to accept that it would. When the sentence was founded upon a cause that was plainly unlawful, impossible, or encouraging of moral turpitude, it could be treated as having been invalid *ab initio*.

From this opening followed some expansion. The direction taken after Gratian was toward enlarging the reasons for nullity. Sentences given without jurisdiction over the person were treated as invalid (X 3.29.3). So were excommunications issued against a party who had lodged an appeal before the sentence (X 2.28.16). A distinction was also drawn between errors in "essential elements of canonical due process" and errors in other procedural steps. It was held that when the procedural error had gone to the heart of procedural fairness, the sentence of excommunication was to be treated as invalid (Sext. 5.11.9).[59] It could even be maintained that when a sentence of excommunication would upset the good state of the church or lead to other evil and general consequences, the person need not obey it.[60]

Excommunication's Effects on Social Order

The fourth theme that ran throughout the canon law combined two contradictory possibilities. There was a recognition that the sanction could, and sometimes should, be used to undo the bonds of civil society. There was a disinclination among the canonists to allow it to go that far without strong justification. Where the effects of excommunication could lead to substantial harm to the church and to society, the canonists did not push toward the logical limits of the doctrine. In assessing how far to test these limits, they were, of course, insistent that the theoretical exclusion of the excommunicate from society not be turned to the person's practical advantage, as by claiming the invalidity of acts that turned out badly for him. However, they went further, refusing to deny some basic, favorable powers to the excommunicate. Thus, as we noted in Chapter 7, prescription did not run against him, since he could not sue to enforce his legal rights.[61] Moreover, although the law held that it was wrong for anyone to associate with an excommunicate, exceptions were carved out for family members and servants (C. 11 q. 3 c. 103).[62]

In much the same way, although a person excommunicated was subject to the loss of many of his civil rights, the canonists conceded to him a considerable number of retained rights by way of exception to the rule. He could, for example, enter into a binding contract of marriage even though the law said that he sinned by doing so.[63] Ordinary civil contracts entered into by an excommunicate were also valid under the canon law. They could be enforced against him even while the excommunication was in force, and he would be allowed to plead substantive defenses by way of exception in the ensuing litigation.[64]

The contract could also be enforced in favor of the excommunicate after the sentence had been lifted.[65] There was even support among the canonists for allowing an excommunicate to enforce a contract when he legitimately feared that irreparable harm would ensue from delay, as in the situation in which the debtor planned to flee before the creditor could obtain absolution.[66] Likewise, an excommunicated person could make a valid testamentary disposition of his property, according to the majority view of the canonists.[67] This was a subject of some dispute, for it accorded a considerable power to a person under the church's ban. But the opposite result would often have led to worse results, and the *communis opinio* recognized that fact.

On the other hand, the canon law of excommunication contained the means of dissolving the ties of civil government, and the canon law did not disavow them. Its most spectacular example—or at any rate its most spectacular success—involved Emperor Henry IV. Pope Gregory VII excommunicated him in 1076 and released his subjects from their allegiance to him. The juridical basis for this action, later stated in the *Decretum* (C. 15 q. 6 c. 4), was twofold: first, the claim that the pope had the power to loose men from their oaths and; second, the doctrine that association with an excommunicated person was forbidden. If the greatest of temporal lords could be excommunicated, and the canon law left no doubt that he could be, logic dictated that his subjects would not be obligated to obey him or even to associate with him.

The canonists clearly realized the potential import of this doctrine. They drew back slightly from its logical results, holding that the sentence of excommunication merely suspended the ties of fealty until the lord sought absolution and made restitution to the church. Still, they also held that the lord must take these steps in timely fashion. If he delayed too long, his vassals would eventually be freed from their ties to him (X 5.37.13). Securing recognition of the sacerdotal power to bind and loose seemed to them to make this result inescapable. Otherwise, the church itself might be mocked.

In practice this power to dissolve the bonds between ruler and subject was exercised with discretion, as the canonists themselves advocated. It normally required a special sentence dissolving those bonds in addition to that of excommunication.[68] But the spiritual power to excommunicate and then to depose kings, thereby inviting a breakdown in the order of society, was an accepted part of the classical canon law. It was exercised with moderate success against Emperor Frederick II in 1239 and 1245 and again, but with less success, against Queen Elizabeth I of England in 1570. If it might be justly concluded that the canonists "adopted a sensible, not a strictly logical, approach" to the extent to which excommunication should be used,[69] it should also be recognized that their notion of what was sensible was also a little different from our own.

EXCOMMUNICATION *Latae Sententiae*

If you push in on one side of a legal system, sometimes a bulge will appear on the other. So it was with excommunication. Submitting excommunication to the requirements of canonical due process and restricting its effects in practice did not cause the ex parte fulminations and anathemas characteristic of the period before the formulation of the *Corpus iuris canonici* to disappear entirely from view. It caused them to change their shape. They survived in a more "legalized" form: excommunication *latae sententiae*.[70] In some sense, a new name was put on an old practice, changing the practice in the process and bringing it within the law's control.

Nature of *Latae Sententiae* Excommunication

The essential feature of excommunication *latae sententiae* was that a person who committed certain defined acts incurred the sentence of excommunication automatically. In theory no judicial process was necessary. The sentence had already been issued. In effect, it could be said that a person sentenced himself by committing the act. The canonists normally expressed the difference by contrasting excommunication *ab homine* from excommunication *a lege*. The first was the judicial sanction described in the previous section of this chapter. The second was this one; it depended upon the doctrine that the law itself had sufficiently declared the excommunication of anyone committing a specific action and that those who committed the action had been sufficiently warned of the consequences by that law. This was the answer given to the obvious objection made against excommunication *latae sententiae*, that it violated the canon law's rules requiring monition and citation before anyone could be excommunicated.[71]

The best established example was heresy. A person who knowingly and openly espoused a belief the church had declared to be heretical could without too much exaggeration be said to have put himself outside the communion of the faithful. The anathemas of early councils could best be understood this way. They did not say that heretics might be subjected to excommunication if they could be convicted after a trial. They said that the heretics were already excommunicated. "If anyone holds this or that belief, let him be anathema," was the church fathers' refrain. It was oft repeated. The principle is brought into sharp relief by the law's treatment of the accused heretic who had died before any action could be taken against him. Such a person could scarcely be cited to appear before a tribunal of the church. But the received texts made it certain that he had died excommunicate (C. 24 q. 2 c. 6). From this the canonists reasoned that citation and trial could not be required in all cases.

The sheer volume of such ipso facto fulminations in the historical record must have eased the path for the development of *latae sententiae* excommunication, if indeed it was not required. Instead of setting the precedents aside as examples of a "prejudicialized" form of the sanction, the classical canonists treated them as belonging to this second and distinct form of excommunication. Thus they brought the unruly past of anathemas into a kind of harmony with evolving legal principles. The real difficulty was that once the procedure had been established, it was all too natural that the church authorities should apply it to anyone who, in their eyes, had done wrong.

Excommunication of Those Who Assaulted Clerics

The most prominent, frequent, and revealing example of *latae sententiae* excommunication in the classical canon law was that declared against those who "laid violent hands upon a cleric." Initially a product of the Second Lateran Council (1139),[72] the canon so stating was inserted into Gratian's *Decretum* (C. 17 q. 4 c. 29). Commonly known from its first words as *Si quis suadente*, it was also referred to as the *privilegium canonis* because it bestowed a special privilege upon the clerical order. It was one of those privileges, examined in Chapter 12, that was classified as a "real and general" privilege.

Si quis suadente contained two significant points: first, that anyone who laid violent hands upon a cleric or monk incurred ipso facto excommunication; and second, except when the offender was close to death, absolution was to be granted only when he appeared to seek it at the papal court. The canon formed one part of the great movement of contemporary church reform and aimed at separating the clerical order from the secular world. In the subject of Chapter 3, this aim was achieved, or at any rate attempted, by prohibiting the ordination of unfree men subject to the claims of masters over their servants. Here it was achieved by creating a privileged status for clerics, protecting them specially from attack and creating a difficult prerequisite for absolution. The contemporary importance of this canon is evident in the extensive treatment it received in the later canon law. Many papal decretals dealt with its interpretation, and *Si quis suadente* was the subject of quite extensive treatment and modification by the canonists. The subsequent evolution, and the consequent substantive scope of the canon, fall into four categories.

The first was the task of interpretation required by almost any legal text, at least any text formulated as broadly as *Si quis suadente*. That was the simple elucidation of its terms. For example, the text says "If any man." Does that include attacks on clerics by women? What about attacks made by an agent or a servant?[73] Or again, the text speaks of "hands." Does this cover attacks made with an assailant's feet or with a rock? Does it include the act of arson or throwing beer from a pitcher?[74] Or again, the text says "on a cleric." Does that permit a remedy for the cleric whose clothing has been torn but whose body has not been touched? Does it reach the case of a cleric without a tonsure and wearing secular clothing?[75]

These are familiar sorts of examples to anyone who has been through a legal education. They differ only in detail from one subject to another and from one generation to another. Perhaps it is as well to pass them by, noting simply that the canonists gave an expansive reading to the canon in treating them. All of the questions raised above were answered in favor of coverage, with the exception of the last, and even it was disputed. The difficult question of classifying imprisonment was also answered in favor of coverage. Where a cleric had been imprisoned without any direct use of force, the canonists held that this nevertheless constituted sufficient "violent hands" to call forth the sanctions of the canon.[76] In other words, although the canon provided a criminal penalty, it was not interpreted with the strictness of most criminal statutes.

In such interpretation, the canonists' efforts were directed at fulfilling the law's purpose. The spirit of the canon called for a wide sort of protection of the clerical order. Besides dictating that the normal preference for strict construction of penal statutes be set aside, the law's purpose meant that much would depend upon the intent with which the act had been performed. To seize a cleric in order to prevent him from falling into a hole should be treated differently than the same physical act done to keep him from entering a church.[77] It would have encouraged distortion of purpose and possibly evasion as well to have read the canon strictly. It might well have frustrated protection of the clerical order. To be true to its purpose, therefore, *Si quis suadente* required an expansive reading of its terms in the great majority of circumstances.[78]

A second kind of interpretation undertaken by the canonists, one that pushed slightly in the opposite direction, was the exclusion from the canon's coverage of cases in which the act of laying violent hands upon a cleric had been a justifiable act. These were cases in which principle of social order required exclusion: for instance, the act of a master disciplining his pupil. Although the pupil might be in holy orders, it would have been subversive of medieval ideas about the nature of the master-pupil relationship to have forbidden normal methods of discipline—hence this exclusion, reached by distinguishing violent from correcting hands.[79] Equally excluded, and under much the same sort of reasoning, were the chastising hands of a father upon his disobedient but ordained son and the restraining hands of a parish doorkeeper ejecting a clerical disturber of divine service.[80] Such situations fell outside *Si quis suadente* as a matter of principle. Official action taken against clerics acting unlawfully was also treated under this heading. Several such exclusions are found in papal decretals incorporated in the fifth book of the Decretals, and others were elaborated by the canonists themselves. Hostiensis, for example, was able to list twenty separate exceptions in which circumstances and social interests excluded application of *Si quis suadente*.[81]

In terms of practical importance, the most significant such exclusion was that of self-defense.[82] If a man was set upon by a cleric, the rule *vim vi repellere* was applied. The victim ought to be able to use at least enough force to defend himself and to repel the attacker. He must not use force in excess of what was necessary, but it would have been contrary to human nature and to good sense alike to have prohibited moderate force used in self-defense. So the canon law held, and evidence from ecclesiastical court practice shows that self-defense was in fact the most frequent defense to a prosecution brought under the canon.

A third kind of canonical development that followed on *Si quis suadente* was reduction in the number of cases in which recourse to the apostolic see was required for absolution. The canon itself contained one exception: when the offending party was in imminent peril of death. Subsequent canonistic development created many others. Unlike the situation of definitional coverage, in which the canonists gave the canon an expansive reading, here they restricted its scope, allowing local bishops or their *officiales* to absolve without reference to the Roman court in a multitude of situations.

One way in which the law reached this result was by enlarging the underlying rationale of the exception found in the text. The principle that excused the person facing his own death was used to excuse others who would find the trip impossible, hazardous, or even inconvenient. It was a principle capable of considerable expansion. Thus excused were women, children, and others not sui juris. So too were the indigent and those in danger from their enemies lying in wait along the way. Equally subject to local absolution, at least according to some canonists, were the opposite: those whose presence at home made them too important to spare. A nobleman or official whose presence local people counted on were examples commonly given.[83]

A further source of expansion in the cases not subject to the full sanction of *Si quis suadente* was invocation of the accepted notion that no one should take advantage of the law to cover his own wrong. No one should use the canon as an excuse to "get away." The two most common examples were the slave who wished to escape his master and the husband who wished to avoid the company of his wife.[84] If an oppressive master or a shrewish wife could be escaped simply by laying violent hands upon any convenient cleric, servants and husbands would be tempted to violate the law with ulterior motives. *Si quis suadente* might thus indirectly become an inducement for wrongful conduct, and this required that the necessity of recourse to the apostolic see be dropped in such situations.

Still another such exception was found in the restriction of the requirement to serious violence. Although no specific language in the canon justified this, a subsequent decretal drew a distinction between *levis* and *atrox iniuria*.[85] Only cases of the latter would call for the full sanction of recourse to the papal see. Others could be handled locally. Actions that would constitute only *levis iniuria* were treated as a matter of fact rather than of law and consequently left considerable room for judicial discretion.[86] The factors that tended in one direction or the other were the nature of the weapon, the place of the attack, the personal status of the parties, and of course the seriousness of the injury; these were common coin among the canonists.[87] It is difficult to generalize about their meaning in practice. But it is clear that the exclusion of the *levis iniuria* was a wide and important limitation in the canon's reach.

The result of these several exceptions was considerably to restrict the cases in which presentation at the papal court was necessary. It would be a fair summary to say that the trip was required only for a case in which there had been serious injury in a public place to a cleric known to be such at the time of the attack at the hands of a relatively well-to-do adult male, one who could make the trip without serious inconvenience to himself or to his neighbors and who was not using the canon as a way of evading his responsibilities. Such cases, it is easy to think, might well have been rare.[88]

A fourth development connected to the canon was the elaboration of subsidiary rules to ensure that its underlying purpose would be carried out. There were two principal rules. The first was that there could be no absolution without satisfaction to the injured party. *Non ualet penitencia sine satisfactione.*[89] The actual form such satisfaction should take depended on several variables; it might range from money damages to a simple public apology. However, satisfaction there must be. The canon was meant to protect individual clerics as well as to punish those who attacked the representatives of the church, and this rule was applied to *Si quis suadente* to effect that goal.

On the other hand, the church's interest stood paramount in the other rule or practice applied to the canon: an offense could not be compromised by the parties involved. Individual clerics could not renounce the privilege; nor could they remit a specific injury without the formal judgment of the church.[90] Thus, if the offender was reconciled with the cleric upon whom he had laid violent hands, nevertheless he remained excommunicate until he had satisfied the church, by submission to the mandates of the church and usually by the doing of public penance. Since *Si quis suadente* was meant to protect the clerical order as much as individual clerics, private agreements by the parties involved could not be permitted.[91] If they were condoned, the canon ran the danger of itself becoming merely a weapon in the hands of individual clerics with private grievances to settle. Although something like this may have happened in fact, it was not the law's purpose.

LATER DEVELOPMENTS

Many of the areas examined in this book—the law of privileges, for example—remained relatively stable over the centuries. Excommunication was not one of them. It underwent change and modification. One significant development in the subject just discussed was the multiplication of offenses for which *latae sententiae* excommunication was incurred. The medieval church did not resist the natural temptation to condemn the crime of the moment by visiting its severest sanction upon those who committed it. Thus men who feigned someone else's identity in order to obtain a benefice and who "offended" cardinals were declared to have fallen under the ban. Participants in duels, unlicensed removers of grain or vegetables from the papal states, "impugners" of the letters of still uncrowned popes—these miscreants along with many others were declared subject to ipso facto excommunication.[92] The vagueness of some of these offenses might have suggested hesitation before making the culprit's exclusion from Christian society automatic, but no such warning was given or heeded.

Something like the opposite also occurred, however—a restriction in the reach of *latae sententiae* excommunication. Perhaps this was in partial reaction against the multiplication of offenses.[93] In 1418 Pope Martin V restricted its full effects to those who had been declared excommunicate by a public sentence. An exception was made for those who had acted so notoriously and openly that "no tergiversation could hide" their guilt, but even this exception was narrowly interpreted and indeed gradually all but disappeared. A distinction was drawn between the *tolerati*, or those who were excommunicated but treated outwardly as if they were not, and the *vitandi*, those who were to be shunned by all Christians. The result was to "judicialize" excommunication *latae sententiae* in something like the same fashion that had happened earlier to ordinary excommunication. Accordingly offenders were cited, given the chance to defend themselves, and declared excommunicate by a judicial sentence only if they presented no valid defense. That is, for example, exactly what one discovers in the records of the English ecclesiastical courts from the later Middle Ages. Excommunicates *latae sententiae* were formally "denounced" as such by courts of competent jurisdiction. The difference between these two forms of excommunication had narrowed, almost but not quite to the point of disappearing.

Over the course of the later Middle Ages, criticism of overuse of excommunication, something that had never been wholly absent, seems to have grown.[94] Jean Gerson (d. 1429) declared that its use for trivial purposes had wrought confusion in the church and brought justified contempt upon it.[95] Probably this was to exaggerate, but in 1476 a French provincial estate complained that the judges had used excommunication so indiscriminately that "the greater part of the population was excommunicated."[96] In some measure, the situation was exactly what should have been expected. It was caused by the rule stated above: that excommunication was the regular sanction for contumacy. That meant that every person who failed to appear in the course of litigation or who refused to obey the sentence of a court with sufficient alacrity was subject to this sanction, in theory the most terrible the church could inflict. The inevitable result was to call forth a spiritual thunderbolt to deal with what might actually be a very trifling matter.

A good illustration of this occurred in England. Reference to it was made in Chapter 6. During the fifteenth century the English church courts exercised an extensive jurisdiction over sworn contracts. Many of the suits brought there were for quite small sums of money, often a few pennies, though in formal terms they were always brought for violation of an oath. If the defendant refused to appear or to pay after a sentence against him, he would in effect be excommunicated for those few pennies. Logically, the canonical position here was perfectly defensible. Contumacy, a deliberate refusal to submit to the jurisdiction of the church, was what was being punished. The underlying debt was entirely coincidental. But logic is not everything. It was too easy to think that the sword of excommunication was being unsheathed for purposes quite inconsistent with its medicinal character and quite at odds with the canonical theory that it was truly "handing over to Satan" a rebel against God and the church.

The English solution was to eliminate these cases from the jurisdiction of the church, a process that had been accomplished by 1520. The Council of Trent sought to do something about the general problem without going that far. Echoing the sentiments of Gerson, or at least enacting their substance, a conciliar decree limited routine use of the remedy. It emphasized the necessity of circumspection in its application. It also substituted a system of monetary fines in civil cases for indiscriminate use of excommunication.[97] However, it cannot be said that this decree remade the system of ecclesiastical sanctions. It was not meant to do so. Excommunication was, as stated in the decree itself, "the nerve of ecclesiastical discipline." It could scarcely be given up. *In coena Domini*, the famous bull with its lengthy list of those who had been excommunicated, continued to be read out yearly.[98]

Long before Trent, the canon law had in some sense "tamed" the sanction of excommunication by confining it to the judicial arena. The council carried that development further by restricting the occasions on which it would be imposed. In modern times, it has been virtually completed in its public form. A combination of desuetude and expansion of the group of *tolerati* among the excommunicates has "tamed" the sanction to the point of inertness. *In coena Domini* is read out no more. An estimate made in the middle years of the twentieth century put the total number of *vitiati* subject to the full penalties of excommunication within the Catholic Church at no more than a half a dozen.[99] This result would have amazed the medieval canonists and almost certainly also the medieval observers who regarded the sanction of excommunication as an inevitable consequence of the realities of ecclesiastical life and litigation.

CONCLUSION

Perhaps noting this reduction in numbers to something like a handful is an appropriate way to end this account of the development of the judicial sanction in the classical canon law. The history of excommunication must include some recognition of excommunication's excessive use during the heyday of the canon law. In some ways it seems fitting that the sanction has been reduced to a shadowy kind of existence today—possible certainly, but with nothing like the frequency or the fearsome results envisioned in the classical canon law.

It would seem too much to say, however, that excommunication has altogether disappeared and that it is gone forever. Exclusion from the sacraments and from Christian life has been a part of the church's rule for so long that it is hard to imagine the church entirely without it.[100] There is no doubt that to many people today, the deliberate shunning of one Christian by another seems to be a denial of charity.

But a review of the historical record of excommunication, with its many ups and downs and its many ins and out, must give anyone pause before accepting the finality of that judgment. In 1963 the Church of England attempted to put excommunication behind it, enacting a measure that substituted other, less threatening sanctions for the ancient anathemas.[101] In the opinion of the experts, however, the possibility of excommunication (albeit outside the measure) continues to reside within the power of the church.[102] The experts must be right. So long and so varied has been the subject's history that it takes a considerable stretch of the imagination to think of the church without some form of excommunication.

15 Conclusion: Common Themes and Observations

Quite disparate topics have been discussed in this book. Coverage has ranged from baptism to blasphemy and from the law of prescription to the law of freedom in monastic professions. It has dealt with the classical canon law of episcopal elections and with some of the practical and theoretical problems raised by the use of oaths in ecclesiastical courts. Have there been common themes in all this? Are there connecting links between the several chapters?

Given the nature of the sources and the common assumptions of the canonists, it would seem strange if there were not. It was the likelihood of such connections that emboldened me to undertake this work, and I think there have in fact been some. At least three continuing themes, somewhat different from the elements that are common to all legal systems, have recurred in the areas of the law examined in the foregoing pages. Not all of them have come equally to the fore in every area surveyed. But they have reappeared more than once, most several times. Moreover, three additional observations about the special nature of the canon law have been suggested by this survey of (I hope) representative topics from the classical law. In trying to say something about the spirit of the canon law, they seem to me to deserve specific mention by way of summary.

THREE THEMES

First and almost consistently evident of these themes has been the canon law's connection with the goals and the ideals of the Gregorian reform movement. Securing the independence of the clergy from secular control, implementing the superiority of the spiritual over the temporal, and building up the material strength of the church were conscious goals of the canonists. They shaped the law. From the rules relating to "invocation of the secular arm" to the principles animating the law of episcopal elections, these interrelated goals held a paramount place in the minds of those who formulated the law. They required particular rules. The canonical tag to the effect that "the people were to be led, not followed" was something the canonists put into practice at every turn. The ideals of the Gregorian reform movement were second nature to them, influencing their conclusions and never hidden from view. Nowhere is this more evident than in the law of elections, nowhere more dramatic than in the law of the ordination of slaves. The tenets of Gregorian reform meant that no laymen could take part in the former and that the canon law's customary *favor libertatis* was irrelevant in the latter.

Second, the concern for *salus animarum* emerges as an only slightly less pervasive theme in the development of the canon law. It was an animating legal principle at several of the points surveyed. The law of oaths, for example, was a product of the law's assumption that lawsuits were not simply contests over property but also tests in which the parties' souls might easily be endangered. From this assumption real consequences ensued. One sees them illustrated also in the law of marriage, restitution, baptism, and excommunication. This continuing concern for *salus animarum* emerges perhaps most strikingly in the law of prescription, but most strikingly there principally because of its unexpectedness. Even though ease of administration and consistency with Roman law would have suggested otherwise, the classical canon law on the subject of prescription was determined by a desire not to imperil the soul's health of the parties involved. The rules of law had to be shaped so that this danger was minimized, even if it could not be eliminated altogether.

Third, and to some extent in tension with the first, is the law's concern to secure full justice for the unfortunate and to establish a system capable of enforcing their rights. The jurisdiction over *miserabiles personae* is the best example, but in fact the medieval canon law can be described as "forward looking" in a number of ways. Its law of elections established principles that became important in the development of representative government. Its statement of the freedom in marriage moved the institution away from the rule of patriarchal control. Its jurisdictional rules attempted to secure justice for those who could not otherwise secure it. It would be, I think, an excess of cynicism to treat jurisdiction over *miserabiles personae* as simple aggrandizement on the part of the church. The same is true of the canonical *restitutio in integrum*. A concern that right be done, come what may, lay at the heart of the canon law. It was always tempered by a recognition that there were limits to what the church's tribunals could accomplish and also by the knowledge that the penitential forum was the appropriate place for dealing with many intractable human problems. But the desire to secure justice nevertheless animated large parts of the classical system.

This is not to imply that the canon law was unique. Many legal systems assess their success by a yardstick measuring the treatment of the unfortunate. Many legal systems take account of moral values. That similarity should not, however, cause us to overlook the extraordinary force they had in the canon law. It is well to note that at several points medieval ideas about the substantive content of doing justice diverged from our own. The preference given to the material interests of the church provides the obvious test; the canonists did not see them as inconsistent with right order or fairness. We may. But once one recognizes that inevitable divergence in assumptions, the canon law's creation of a system of right available for those persons most in need of it and its insistence on the importance of moral values in the law remain positive achievements.

THREE OBSERVATIONS

Three general observations about the canon law also seem appropriate in conclusion. None of the three could exactly be called a recurring theme within the classical canon law, but they were all undoubtedly characteristic of it. They reveal something important about the inner nature of the system.

The first observation is to take note of the lawyerly ability of the men who devoted their careers to the canon law. Whether one looks at their ability in mastering the relevant authorities, their proficiency in reasoning by analogy, their skill in analyzing precedents, their talent in drawing legal distinctions, or their energy in working through a large body of law, the canonists seem scarcely inferior to modern lawyers. In some ways they were probably better, for at least in the United States there is now a widespread distrust of traditional methods of legal reasoning and a widespread confidence that other methods offer more. Even leaving this American development aside, it is not clear that a simple comparison of analytical ability would put modern lawyers much ahead. If some of the distinctions the canonists drew seem forced and some of the categories they formulated seem artificial, and if the formalism of their approach to law is not quite congenial with our own, at the very least the modern observer can admire their skills as pure lawyers.

To this observation, one caveat is in order. The canonists belonged within a common tradition. They did not work in isolation or set out purposefully to create new theories of either law or government. They followed one another. They copied one another. This means that some part of the impression of their lawyerly ability grows out of their participation in an ongoing tradition. It is always hard to isolate the contribution of one particular canonist, and we may get a false impression of sophistication by looking at any one of them isolated from his fellows. This does not make the observation false, I think. It does require modern readers to recognize that working within the tradition of the *ius commune* imposed limits on what any one jurist could do.

Second, the canon law was ambitious in its goals, more so than is true of most legal systems with which we are familiar. Of the early English common law, Professor Milsom has written that its highest goal was to settle a quarrel. It aimed to provide a test of which party to a dispute had the greater right, but little in the way of substantive law emerged from the "ancient pattern of the law-suit."[1] The same observation could not be made about the medieval law of the church. From its inception, the classical canon law had ambitious goals. It provided

guidance to right conduct, as well as punishing evil conduct and settling disputes. Its purpose was to lead men to the good. For this, detailed rules of law were thought useful, appropriate, and even necessary. In the law of blasphemy, for instance, where the canonists hesitated to define blasphemy for fear of licensing it, the law's goal was
both to provide a warning against speaking ill of God and to punish
those who transgressed against that warning.

One sees this feature most clearly and repeatedly in a characteristic
feature of the canon law, of which we have seen several examples.
This was the separation of questions of the validity of a particular act
from questions of its lawfulness. In the law of oaths, baptism, marriage, and ordination, this distinction was drawn. The canon law provided rules for both, and the reason for this was that the canon law
was designed to guide Christians toward right conduct as well as to
establish an objective order with definite legal consequences applied
against those who broke the rules. Both guidance and sanctions were
required. The person who was subject to the canon law would wish to
know what the objective effect of his actions would be. He would also
wish to know what he *should* do. A part of the richness and complexity of the canon law results from the necessity of dealing with
(and coordinating) these two aspects of the law. The "bad man" theory of law associated with Justice O. W. Holmes works poorly in describing the medieval canon law.

Third, for all that there is to admire in the classical canon law, there
is much that one does not. Some of it repels. And how far removed
from us a good deal of it must seem! A system of law that regards all
courts of law as mechanical "executors" of decisions taken by the
clergy, or that prevents a baptized person from giving up outward belief in the Christian religion, or that regards requiring a priest to perform menial tasks as a greater scandal than human slavery, is not only
different from a regime we can wholeheartedly admire. It is a difficult
one to understand. Yet these features, and many more like them, were
undeniably endorsed by the classical canon law. They formed one
part of its spirit.

A few modern writers on the history of the canon law have left
these unpalatable features out. They have picked those elements that

accord with, and even anticipate, modern values and described them as lying at the heart of the canon law. For example, the rule that baptism should not be conferred upon the unwilling is mentioned; the rule that baptism was valid and permanent when chosen over the alternative of death is omitted.[2] Perhaps it is all too natural for people who have devoted any substantial part of their life's work to a subject to try to make that subject look as good as it can be made to look. I may have done the same myself in writing about freedom in marriage and monastic vows.

At any rate, it does seem certain that an adequate study of the classical canon law must take account of both the pleasant and the unpleasant found within it. Balanced presentation requires it. And there is an added advantage. Like most historical systems of law, one of the canon law's attractions is the leap of understanding required to study it. What one learns in attempting to come to grips with a legal system that has many similar features to our own but is nonetheless also quite different from our own provides a good reason for making the effort entailed.

NOTES

Chapter 1: Introduction

1 See, e.g., Kenneth Pennington, "Learned Law, Droit Savant, gelehrtes Recht: The Tyranny of a Concept," *RIDC* 5 (1994): 197–209.

2 For fuller introductions to the subject, the following recent works can be recommended: Péter Erdö, *Introductio in historiam scientiae canonicae* (Rome, 1990); Luciano Musselli, *Storia del diritto canonico* (Turin, 1992); Jean Gaudemet, *Les sources du droit canonique, VIIIe–XXe siècle* (Paris, 1993); idem, *Église et cité: Histoire du droit canonique* (Paris, 1994); Georg May and Anna Egler, *Einführung in die kirchenrechtliche Methode* (Regensburg, 1986); E. J. H. Schrage and H. Dondorp, *Utrumque ius, eine Einführung in das Studium der Quellen des mittelalterlichen gelehrten Rechts* (Berlin, 1992); Antonio Martínez Blanco, *Introducción al derecho canónico* (Barcelona, 1991). All contain abundant references to prior and more specialized scholarly work. For treatments putting the canon law into contemporary context, see Manlio Bellomo, *The Common Legal Past of Europe, 1000–1800* (Washington, D.C., 1995), and Ennio Cortese, *Il Rinascimento giuridico medievale* (Rome, 1992), 48–61.

3 For an excellent introduction to the medieval canon law in English, see James A. Brundage, *Medieval Canon Law* (London, 1995). For brief treatments of slightly earlier date, see R. C. Mortimer, *Western Canon Law* (London, 1953); E. W. Kemp, *Introduction to Canon Law in the Church of England* (London, 1957); Walter Ullmann, *Law and Politics in the Middle Ages* (Ithaca, N.Y., 1975), 119–59; and G. LeBras, "Canon Law," in *Legacy of the Middle Ages*, ed. C. G. Crump and E. F. Jacob (Oxford, 1926), 321–61.

4 Charles Homer Haskins, *The Renaissance of the Twelfth Century* (Cambridge, Mass., 1927). See also Stephan Kuttner, "The Revival of Jurisprudence," in *Renaissance and Renewal in the Twelfth Century*, ed. Robert Benson and Giles Constable (Cambridge, England, 1982), 299–323.

5 See the treatment by Georges Duby, "The Renaissance of the Twelfth Century: Audience and Patronage," in *Love and Marriage in the Middle Ages* (Chicago, 1994), 149–67.

6 Jean Gaudemet, *La formation du droit séculier et du droit de l'Église aux IVe et Ve siècles*, 2d ed. (Paris, 1979), 143–44.

7 *Decrees*, 1:8.

8 Ibid., 1:91.

9 The foundational work is Paul Fournier and Gabriel Le Bras, *Histoire des collections canoniques en Occident depuis les Fausses Décrétales jusqu'au Décret de Gratien* (Paris, 1931–32).

10 Bernhard Schimmelpfenning, *The Papacy* (Oxford, 1992), 99.

11 See Gérard Fransen, *Les collections canoniques* (Turnhout, Belgium, 1973), and Peter Landau, "Wandel und Kontinuität im kanonischen Recht bei Gratian," in *Sozialer Wandel im Mittelalter*, ed. Jürgen Miethke and Klaus Schreiner (Sigmaringen, Germany, 1994), 215–33.

12 There is an excellent review article, dealing with the quality and variety of the early canonical collections, written by Roger E. Reynolds, "Law, Canon: To Gratian," in *Dictionary of the Middle Ages* (New York, 1982–89) 7:395–412. For an example of the scholarly work possible on this subject, see Hartmut Hoffmann and Rudolf Pokorny, *Das Dekret des Bischofs Burchard von Worms*, MGH Hilfsmittel 12 (Munich, 1991).

13 Haskins, *Renaissance of the Twelfth Century*, 214. See also the forceful presentation of this theme by Harold J. Berman, *Law and Revolution* (Cambridge, Mass., 1983).

14 See, for example, the description of the sources of the canon law of marriage by F. W. Maitland in "Magistri Vacarii Summa de Matrimonio," *Law Quarterly Review* 13 (1897): 135: "A few brief texts in the Bible; a few passages in the works of the Fathers, some of which were but too mystical, while others were but too hortative; a few canons and decretals that were not very consistent with each other—these were the unsatisfactory materials out of which law was to be made."

15 The standard modern edition is *Corpus iuris canonici*, 2 vols., ed. A. Friedberg (Leipzig, 1879).

16 John T. Noonan Jr., "Gratian Slept Here: The Changing Identity of the Father of Systematic Study of the Canon Law," *Traditio* 35 (1979): 145–72.

17 Established by Adam Vetulani, "Gratien et le droit romain," *RHD* 24–25 (1945–47): 11–48.

18 There are several good treatments that also cite the more specialized studies; I have found particularly useful Gaudemet, *Les sources*, 102–19; Stephan Kuttner, "Research on Gratian: Acta et Agenda," in *Proceedings of the Seventh International Congress of Medieval Canon Law*, ed. Peter Linehan (Vatican City, 1988), 3–26; and Peter Landau, "Quellen und Bedeutung des Gratianischen Dekrets," *Studia et Documenta Historiae et*

Iuris 52 (1986): 218–35. There are two annual bibliographies of particular utility for this and most other questions involving the canon law: that in the *BMCL*, and that in the *RIDC*.

19 See Stephan Kuttner, "The Father of the Science of Canon Law, *Jurist* 1(1941): 2–19, and John F. McCarthy, *The Genius of Concord in Gratian's Decree* (Rome, 1964), 30–35.

20 C. 2 q. 8.

21 So put in the *glossa ordinaria* ad C. 2 q. 8 c. 1.

22 The anwers to these questions were: (1) Yes, but not a sacramental and therefore indissoluble marriage; (2) No, unless the non-Christian spouse refused to follow the Christian spouse; (3) Yes.

23 De cons. Dist. 2 c. 16. See Kuttner, "Revival of Jurisprudence," 299–323.

24 See Peter Landau, "Dekretalensammlungen des 12. und beginnenden 13. Jahrhunderts," *ZRG,* kan. Abt. 68 (1982): 453–61.

25 Edited and published under that title by Aemilius Friedberg (Leipzig, 1882; repr., Graz, 1956).

26 See the papal bull *Rex pacificus,* printed in Friedburg, *Corpus iuris canonici,* 2:1.

27 Steven Horwitz, "Reshaping a Decretal Chapter: *Tua nobis* and the Canonists," in *Law, Church, and Society: Essays in Honor of Stephan Kuttner,* ed. Kenneth Pennington and Robert Somerville (Philadelphia, 1977), 207–21.

28 Stephan Kuttner, "Raymond of Peñafort as Editor: The 'Decretales' and 'Constitutiones' of Gregory IX," *BMCL* 12 (1982): 65–80.

29 Gaudemet, *Les sources,* 127.

30 Kuttner, "Raymond of Peñafort," 66.

31 This took over the prior habit of referring to the law of papal decretals as outside (*extra*) the *Decretum Gratiani,* both in the schools and in legal practice.

32 Edward Gibbon, *Decline and Fall of the Roman Empire,* ch. 44 (Everyman ed., 1910), 4:374. It is well explained and illustrated in Brundage, *Medieval Canon Law,* 190–205.

33 For the history of these collections, see Jacqueline Tarrante, *Extravagantes Johannis XXII* (Vatican City, 1983), 1–27.

34 Quoted in O. F. Robinson, T. D. Ferguson, and W. M. Gordon, *An Introduction to European Legal History* (Abingdon, England, 1985), 98–99. For an example from practice, see Alexander Tartagnus, *Consiliorum,* VI, Cons. 139, no. 16: "in dubio ab opinione glossae . . . non sit recedendum in iudicando et consulendo." For recent research on the gloss, see Gero

Dolezalek, "Research on Manuscripts of the Corpus Iuris with Glosses Written during the Twelfth and Early Thirteenth Centuries: State of Affairs," in *El Dret comú i Catalunya* (Barcelona, 1991), 17–45.

35 See Stephan Kuttner and Beryl Smalley, "The 'Glossa Ordinaria' to the Gregorian Decretals," *English Historical Review* 60 (1945): 97–105, and Stephan Kuttner, "Notes on the Glossa Ordinaria of Bernard of Parma," *BMCL* 11(1981): 86–93.

36 So stated in the Lex Ribuaria (c. 741), found in c. 58, 1, in MGH Leges V, 185.

37 See Giulio Silano, "Of Sleep and Sleeplessness: The Papacy and Law, 1150–1300," in *The Religious Roles of the Papacy: Ideals and Realities*, ed. Christopher Ryan (Toronto, 1989), 343–61.

38 See Kuttner, "Revival of Jurisprudence," 300. A dissenting view, which lays more stress on the earlier work of Lombard jurists at Pavia, is Charles M. Radding, *The Origins of Medieval Jurisprudence: Pavia and Bologna, 850–1150* (New Haven, 1988).

39 See Martin Lipenius, *Bibliotheca realis iuridica*, 2 vols. (Leipzig, 1757; repr., Hildesheim, Germany, 1970) 1:260, under the heading "Collationes et differentiae iuris civilis et canonici."

40 E.g., Petrus de Ancharano, *Commentaria*, ad X 5.33.28, no 1: "Nota primo quod canones non respuunt leges, nam ipsas per reges et imperatores seculi Deus distribuit generi humano . . . et hoc intelligo leges canonibus famulari."

41 D.p. Dist. 10 c. 6.

42 See F. Merzbacher, "Die Parömie 'Legista sine canonibus parum valet, canonista sine legibus nihil,'" *Studia Gratiana* 13 (1967): 275–82.

43 Petrus Rebuffus, *Tractatus de nominationibus*, quaest. 5, no. 15, in T.U.I., vol. 15:2.

44 E.g., Hostiensis, *Lectura*, ad X 1.1.1, no. 15: "Ab initio tamen descenderunt canonicae sanctiones ex authoribus novi et veteris testamenti."

45 This also leaves out the important point of the large extent to which the Bible itself incorporated law; see J. Duncan M. Derrett, *Law and the New Testament* (London, 1974); Ullmann, *Law and Politics*, 43–47.

46 So stated by Joannes Paulus Lancellotus, *Institutiones iuris canonici*, lib. 2, tit. 21, gl. s.v. *nomine*.

47 See generally Helmut Coing, *Europäisches Privatrecht, 1500 bis 1800* (Munich, 1985), 124–26.

48 Many of these law professors also took active roles in the church and the world, most notably Sinibaldo Fieschi, who became Innocent IV. Rarely, however, were they simply the professional judges of the courts of the

church. Those judges themselves issued no opinions in the sense known to the modern common law world. There was thus no special precedential value to the outcome of particular cases and no body of judicial opinions available to dominate legal education.

49 For example, Antonius Gabrielius, *Communes conclusiones . . . in septem libros distributae* (Venice, 1593), sits in front of me; it is a large folio volume of 712 pages.

50 See the list in A. Van Hove, *Prolegomena ad Codicem iuris canonici* (Mechlin, Belgium, 1945), 486–88.

51 E.g., Albericus de Rosate, *Dictionarium iuris tam civilis quam canonici.*

52 See Van Hove, *Prolegomena,* 509–10. See also *Las abreviaturas en la enseñanza medieval y la transmisión del saber* (Barcelona, 1990).

53 The connection between this literature and university instruction is stressed and illustrated by Paul Ourliac and Henri Gilles, *Histoire du droit et des institutions de l'Église en occident, Tome XIII: La période post-classique* (Paris, 1971), 109–49.

54 Thanks largely to the work of Noël Didier, Hostiensis is one of the few canonists about whose career we know a fair amount of the details; see his articles listed in *Études historiques à la mémoire de Noël Didier* (Paris, 1960), 1b.

55 This may help explain, for example, some of the apparent "compound of irreconcilables" that have troubled and intrigued modern writers; see, for example, Michael Wilks, *The Problem of Sovereignty in the Later Middle Ages* (Cambridge, England, 1963), 538.

56 Peter Herde, "Ein Pamphlet der päpstlichen Kurie gegen Kaiser Friedrich II. von 1245/46 (Eger cui lenia)," *Deutsches Archiv für Erforschung des Mittelalters* 23 (1967): 468–538.

57 See, however, Wolfgang P. Müller, *Huguccio: The Life, Works, and Thought of a Twelfth-Century Jurist* (Washington, D.C., 1994).

58 See Joseph Canning, *The Political Thought of Baldus de Ubaldis* (Cambridge, England, 1987). Much useful information about the canonists is contained in Brundage, *Medieval Canon Law,* 56–59, 206–30.

59 Winfried Trusen, "Forum internum et gelehrtes Recht im Spätmittelalter," *ZRG,* kan. Abt. 57 (1971): 83–126. For more recent treatments of the subject, with its literature relating to the penitential forum, see Miriam Turrini, *La coscienza e le leggi: Morale e diritto nei testi per la confessione della prima Età moderna* (Bologna, 1991); Thomas T. Tentler, *Sin and Confession on the Eve of the Reformation* (Princeton, 1977), 28–53; and several articles collected in Leonard E. Boyle, *Pastoral Care, Clerical Education, and Canon Law, 1200–1400* (London, 1981).

60 See generally Linda Fowler-Magerl, *Ordo iudiciorum vel ordo iudiciarius: Begriff und Literaturgattung* (Frankfurt, 1984), and idem, *Ordines iudiciarii and libelli ordine iudiciorum: From the Middle of the Twelfth to the End of the Fifteenth Century* (Turnhout, Belgium, 1994).

61 See *Quellen zur Geschichte des Römisch-kanonischen Prozesses im Mittelalter*, 5 vols., ed. Ludwig Wahrmund (Aalen, Germany, 1905–31), and Pillius, Tancredus, Gratia, *Libri de iudiciorum ordine*, ed. F. C. Bergmann (Göttingen, 1842).

62 See the remarks by Jane E. Sayers, *Papal Judges Delegate in the Province of Canterbury, 1198–1254* (Oxford, 1971), 44–45. On the nature of the literature, see Knut Wolfgang Nörr, "Die Literatur zum gemeinen Zivilprozess," in Coing, *Handbuch* 1:383–97.

63 See André Gouron, "Zu den Ursprüngen des Strafrechts: Die ersten Strafrechtstraktate," in *Festschrift für Hans Thieme*, ed. Karl Kroeschell (Sigmaringen, Germany, 1986), 44.

64 J. F. von Schulte, *Die Geschichte der Quellen und Literatur des canonischen Rechts* (Stuttgart, 1875) 1:144–56.

65 A reprint of the Basel 1574 edition, printed in Aalen in 1975.

66 See Rudolf Weigand, "Frühe Kanonisten und ihre Karriere in der Kirche," *ZRG*, kan. Abt. 76 (1990): 135–55.

67 *In Romanae aulae actionem et iudiciorum mores introductio.* I have used an edition published in Venice in 1547.

68 *Directorium inquisitorum.* I have used an edition published in Rome in 1585.

69 Many of these works are listed in the bibliography of John Tedeschi, *The Prosecution of Heresy* (Binghamton, N.Y., 1991), 357–400.

70 *Tractatus de nullitatibus processuum ac sententiarium.* I have used an edition published in Venice in 1567.

71 In the civil forum, Petrus de Ferrariis, *Practica nova judicialis* (Lyons, 1556). In the criminal, I have frequently used, for instance, Julius Clarus, *Liber sententiarum receptarum* V § *Practica criminalis;* I have used an edition published in Venice in 1595.

72 Tancred, *Summa de sponsalibus et matrimonio*, ed. A. Wunderlich (Göttingen, 1841).

73 See the entry by Francis Oakley titled "Conciliar Theory," in *Dictionary of the Middle Ages*, 3:522–23, and, on tithes, von Schulte, *Quellen und Literatur des canonischen Rechts*, 1:289 (Treatise by Galvanus of Bologna).

74 See the many examples in the *T.U.I.*

75 Norbert Horn, "Die legistische Literatur der Kommentatoren und die Ausbreitung des gelehrten Rechts," in Coing, *Handbuch* 1:331–32.

76 See, e.g., Kenneth Pennington, "Johannes Andreae's Additiones to the Decretals of Gregory IX," *ZRG*, kan. Abt. 74 (1988): 328–47.

77 The standard work is Guido Rossi, *Consilium sapientis iudiciale* (Milan, 1958). In English, see Peter Riesenberg, "The *Consilia* Literature: A Prospectus," *Manuscripta* 6 (1962): 3–23, and introduction to *Consilia: A Bibliography of Holdings in the Library of Congress*, ed. Peter Pazzaglini and Catharine Hawks (Washington, D.C., 1990; hereafter cited as *Bibliography of Holdings*).

78 See *Bibliography of Holdings*; Heinrich Gehrke, *Die privatrechtliche Entscheidungsliteratur Deutschlands* (Frankfurt, 1974), 167–244; Guido Kisch, *Consilia: Eine Bibliographie der juristischen Konsiliensammlungen* (Basel, 1970); and Mario Ascheri, "Analecta manoscritta consiliare (1285–1354)," *BMCL* 15 (1985): 61–77.

79 Julius Kirshner, *Pursuing Honor While Avoiding Sin: The Monte delle Doti of Florence* (Milan, 1978); Mario Ascheri, "*Consilium sapientis*, perizia medica e *res iudicata*: Diritto di 'dottori' e istituzioni comunali," in *Proceedings of the Fifth International Congress of Medieval Canon Law*, ed. Stephan Kuttner and Kenneth Pennington (Vatican City, 1980), 533–79; Norman Zacour, *Jews and Saracens in the Consilia of Oldradus de Ponte* (Toronto, 1990).

80 See the discussion by G. Dolezalek, "Reports of the 'Rota' (14th–19th Centuries)," in *Judicial Records, Law Reports, and the Growth of Case Law*, ed. John H. Baker (Berlin, 1989), 69–99.

81 See Gero Dolezalek and Knut Wolfgang Nörr, "Die Rechtsprechungssammlungen der mittelalterlichen Rota," in Coing, *Handbuch*, 1:851–56.

82 Ibid., 1:851 n. 2.

83 J. H. Baker, "Dr. Thomas Fastolf and the History of Law Reporting," *Cambridge Law Journal* 45 (1986): 84–96.

84 *Decisiones capellae Tholosanae.* I have used an edition published in Venice in 1618.

Chapter 2: Governance of the Church

1 E.g., *La riforma gregoriana e l'Europa: Congresso internazionale, Salerno 10–25 maggio 1985* (Rome, 1991); H. E. J. Cowdrey, *The Cluniacs and the Gregorian Reform* (Oxford, 1970); H. Mordek, "Kanonistik und

Gregorianische Reform," in *Reich und Kirche vor dem Inverstiturstreit*, ed. Karl Schmid (Sigmaringen, Germany, 1985), 65–82.

2 Very few of Gregory VII's letters and decrees were incorporated into the *Corpus iuris canonici*. See John Gilchrist, "The Reception of Pope Gregory VII into the Canon Law (1073–1141)," *ZRG* kan. Abt. 59 (1973): 35–82, and Horst Fuhrmann, "Papst Gregor VII. und das Kirchenrecht," in *Studi Gregoriani* 13 (La Riforma Gregoriana e l'Europa, Congresso Internazionale, 1985) (1989): 123–40.

3 E.g., Harold J. Berman, *Law and Revolution* (Cambridge, Mass., 1983), 85–113; K. J. Leyser, "The Polemics of the Papal Revolution," in *Trends in Medieval Political Thought*, ed. Beryl Smalley (Oxford, 1965), 42–64.

4 One of the best and most influential works on this subject has been Gerd Tellenbach, *Church, State, and Christian Society at the Time of the Investiture Contest*, trans. R. F. Bennet (Oxford, 1940). See also his *The Church in Western Europe from the Tenth to the Early Twelfth Century*, trans. Timothy Reuter (Cambridge, England, 1993).

5 See Uta-Renate Blumenthal, *The Investiture Controversy* (Philadelphia, 1988), 90–91. The older term has not passed out of use. It is retained, for example, in the widely used and admired collection of sources by Brian Tierney, *The Crisis of Church and State, 1050–1300* (Englewood Cliffs, N.J., 1964).

6 See Brigitte Szabò-Bechstein, "'Libertas ecclesiae' vom 12. bis zur Mitte des 13. Jahrhunderts," in *Die Abendländische Freiheit vom 10. zum 14. Jahrhundert*, ed. Johannes Fried (Sigmaringen, Germany, 1991), 147–75. It includes a full range of citations to earlier work.

7 See, for example, the range of arguments and sources cited in Franciscus Hallier, *De sacris electionibus et ordinationibus*, sect. 1, c. 3 § 1.

8 See, for example, the apparent attitude of Origen, incorporated into the *Decretum* at C. 8 q. 1 c. 16. See also George Boas, *Vox populi: Essays in the History of an Idea* (Baltimore, 1969), 13–22.

9 See, for example, the opinion of St. Cyprian, quoted in Jean Gaudemet, "Unanimité et Majorité," in *Études historiques à la mémoire de Noël Didier* (Paris, 1960), 153–54; see also Alfred von Wretschko, "Die electio communis bei den kirchlichen Wahlen im Mittelalter," *Deutsche Zeitschrift für Kirchenrecht* 11(1902): 328.

10 See Paul Schmid, *Der Begriff der kanonischen Wahl in den Anfängen des Investiturstreits* (Stuttgart, 1926), and Hubert Müller, *Der Anteil der Laien an der Bischofswahl* (Amsterdam, 1977), 9–22.

11 See the summary of learning on the point, and contribution to it, in Stanley Chodorow, *Christian Political Theory and Church Politics in the Mid-Twelfth Century* (Berkeley, 1972), 199–210.

12 Quoted in Anscar Parsons, *Canonical Elections* (Washington, D.C., 1939), 23–24.

13 From the Lent synod of 1080, quoted in Colin Morris, *The Papal Monarchy* (Oxford, 1989), 118–19.

14 See Johannes Laudage, "Gregor VII. und die *Electio canonica*," *Studia Gregoriana* 14 (1985): 83–101, and F. Accrocca, "*Pastorem secundum Deum eligite:* La partecipazione del popolo all'elezione dei vescovi nell'epistolario di Gregorio VII," *Archivium historiae pontificiae* 28 (1990): 343–55.

15 Pierre Imbart de la Tour, *Les élections épiscopales dans l'Église de France du IXe au XIIe siècle* (Paris, 1890), 285–301; M. Brett, *The English Church under Henry I* (Oxford, 1975), 104–5; José Montserrat Torrents, *Las elecciones episcopales en la historia de la Iglesia* (Barcelona, 1972), 139–62.

16 See *gl. ord.* ad Dist. 63 c. 19, where this is more fully discussed.

17 See *gl. ord.* ad Dist. 63 c. 35 s.v. *nunc ergo quaerit*, where this test was mentioned as a way out if the normal methods failed.

18 *Gl. ord.* ad Sext. 1.6.18 s.v. *devolvetur:* "unde in principio ecclesiae solus Papa conferebat episcopatus." See more fully Joannes Bertachinus, *Tractatus de episcopis*, lib. 1, pt. 3, no. 1.

19 This is the great theme of many works by Walter Ullmann—for example, *Law and Politics in the Middle Ages* (Ithaca, N.Y., 1975), 136.

20 Giulio Silano, "Of Sleep and Sleeplessness: The Papacy and Law, 1150–1300," in *The Religious Roles of the Papacy: Ideals and Realities*, ed. Christopher Ryan (Toronto, 1989), 350–51; Hans Erich Feine, *Kirchliche Rechtsgeschichte: Die katholische Kirche*, 5th ed. (Cologne, 1972), 336–38.

21 The first two were incorporated by reference from elsewhere in the *Decretum*; see d.a. C. 8 q. 1 c. 1.

22 Later commentators added further reasons, some dealing with the problem caused by the church's belief that Jesus had chosen Peter as his successor, some going farther afield. The analogy of the marriage between a bishop and his see, for example, was said to prove the correctness of the rule, because no dying husband can choose his successor. See Joannes de Turrecremata, *Commentaria*, ad C. 8 q. 1, no. 1.

23 *Gl. ord.* ad C. 8 q. 1 c. 1 s.v. *aut ligandi*.

24 Joannes Bertachinus, *Tractatus de episcopis*, proem. no. 3.

25 *Gl. ord.* ad d.p. C. 8 q. 1 c. 7 s.v. *beatus:* "Sed nunquid adhuc Papa posset facere sibi successorem? Non quia hoc esset immutare statutum ecclesiae." Joannes Bertachinus, *Tractatus de episcopis*, lib. 1, pt. 3, no. 56, put the reason as "ne exemplum beati Petri trahendum est ad alios."

26 E.g., Petrus Maria Passerini, *Tractatus de electione canonica*, c. 1, nos. 4–8. It was said that Pope Boniface II had named his successor in 531 out of fear of the power of the Goths. However, once that power had subsided, Boniface had revoked the decree. See Diana Wood, "The Pope's Right to Elect His Successor: The Criterion of Sovereignty?" in *The Church and Sovereignty, c. 590–1918* (Oxford, 1991), 233–44.

27 See Müller, *Der Anteil der Laien*, 25–35. This book also contains a comprehensive collection of the opinions of later canonists on the subject.

28 *Gl. ord.* ad Dist. 61 c. 13 s.v. *nullus invitis.*

29 The classical law, it is true, whittled this down further by the doctrine that the laity would be understood as consenting if they did not object. See *gl. ord.* ad Dist. 62 c. 1 s.v. *nec a plebibus.* See discussion in Gulielmus de Mandagoto, *Tractatus de electione novorum prelatorum*, c. 35, allowing the announcement to be made after the canonical election had taken place.

30 See Petrus Maria Passserini, *Tractatus de electione canonica*, c. 8, no. 5: "nam laicos posse adesse in loco electionis ut iuvent defendant et protegant electores."

31 See *gl. ord.* ad Dist. 63 c. 23 s.v. *affici.*

32 D.p. Dist. 63 c. 27.

33 See DD. ad X 1.6.56.

34 See, for example, Joannes de Turrecremata, *Commentaria*, ad Dist. 63 c. 9, stating the church's power to revoke earlier rules "ex quo in detrimentum incipunt vergere et occasionem mali parere."

35 Eventually, these requirements of form took on a considerable complexity, regulating the religious solemnities surrounding the election in minute detail. See, for example, Petrus de Biaxio, *Directorium*, pt. 3, c. 38, no. 4, dealing with the rules enacted at the Council of Basel.

36 *Gl. ord.* ad Dist. 63 c. 1 s.v. *communem.*

37 E.g., Colin Morris, *The Papal Monarchy: The Western Church from 1050 to 1250* (Oxford, 1989), 224; Marcel Pacaut, *Louis VII et les élections épiscopales dans le royaume de France* (Paris, 1957), 47–50.

38 André Desprairies, *L'Élection des évêques par les chapitres au XIIIe siècle* (Paris, 1922), 1–14.

39 Ibid., 211.

40 *Decrees*, 1:203.
41 Hostiensis, *Summa aurea* I, tit. *De electionibus*, no. 5; see also X 2.12.3.
42 Parsons, *Canonical Elections*, 64.
43 It is also covered by a good book: Robert Benson, *The Bishop-Elect: A Study in Medieval Ecclesiastical Office* (Princeton, 1968).
44 *Gl. ord.* ad X 1.6.2 s.v. *populi:* "Nota quod ad clamorem populi nullus est eligendus." See also X 1.6.56.
45 See Petrus de Biaxio, *Directorium*, pt. 1, c. 5; the powers of the prince in elections eventually became partly incorporated into the law of force and fear, and this left some room for the prince to have a say. Perhaps he could exclude bishops suspect to him who might reveal the *arcana regni.* Perhaps there was a role for "reverential" influence on his part. See also Innocent IV, *Apparatus*, ad X 5.1.16, no. 8.
46 Hostiensis noted about the subject of persons who could be elected, "Anyone who is not prohibited. Many, however, are prohibited." *Summa aurea* I, tit. *De electionibus*, no. 9.
47 See Petrus Maria Passerini, *Tractatus de electione canonica*, c. 10, nos. 10–16; c. 25, nos. 444–520, for fuller coverage.
48 *Gl. ord.* ad id. s.v. *conveniens:* "Bene dixit conveniens, quia sufficit quod sit conveniens scientiae licet non sit eminens."
49 Joannes Bertachinus, *Tractatus de episcopis*, lib. 2, pt. 1, no. 77: "inimicus hospitalitatis."
50 This concept was needed because of the problem caused by the infrequency of episcopal elections (one could not really meet the requirement of continuity of possession necessary in prescription) and by the rule that incorporial rights were incapable of being effectively reduced to possession (*incorporalia non possidentur*) (see X 2.12.3).
51 See Petrus Maria Passerini, *Tractatus de electione canonica*, c. 10, no. 49, reviewing the question and stating this to be the *communis opinio.*
52 See Jean Gaudemet, *Les élections dans l'Église latine des origines au XVIe siècle* (Paris, 1979), 331–32, also providing an example, at 391, of the abuse of the process, in which Pope Sixtus IV suggested to the electors the name of a candidate who, the pope suggested, was to be chosen by divine inspiration.
53 Schmid, *Der Begriff der kanonischen Wahl*, 158: "Das alte Pauluswort war nicht nur ein Zitat, es war lebendige Anschauung der Zeit."
54 William Durantis, *Speculum iudiciale* IV, tit. *De elect.* § 3, no. 6, seemingly to deal with the situation in which there had been discussion about candidates before the convocation of electors.

55 See the long list of causes of invalidity, put into a mnemonic device, in Hostiensis, *Summa aurea* I, tit. *De elect.*, no. 28. See also Petrus de Bi- axio, *Directorium*, pt. 2, c. 35, no. 15: "Ex premissis habes sexaginta et tria requisita quo ad eligentes aut eligendos ex quibus poteris alia et per haec valebis multas impugnare electiones." But see Innocent IV, *Appara- tus*, ad X 1.6.28, no. 7, suggesting distinctions between canonical elec- tions, so that there might be a more relaxed standard *secundum ius naturale*.

56 Note, however, that there was a difficult distinction here. If the appeal was against the form of the election as uncanonical, an election held *non obstante*, the appeal might still be valid if it turned out that it was other- wise canonical (X 1.6.19). See, for example, the treatment of one con- fused case in Abbas antiquus, *Lectura*, ad X 1.6.10, no. 1.

57 J. E. Sayers, "The Medieval Care and Custody of the Archbishop of Canterbury's Archives," *Bulletin of the Institute of Historical Research* 39 (1966): 106.

58 So in the 1254 treatise written by Laurentius de Somercote, *Der Traktat des Laurentius de Somercote . . . über die Vornahme von Bischofswah- len*, ed. Alfred von Wretschko (Weimar, 1907), 27–28.

59 Published in a modern edition, ed. Laspeyres (Regensburg, 1860); see also J. F. von Schulte, *Die Geschichte der Quellen und Literatur des canon- ischen Rechts* (Stuttgart, 1875), 1:179, and Müller, *Der Anteil der Laien*, 78–84.

60 See Charles J. Reid Jr., "The Canonistic Contribution to the Western Rights Tradition: An Historical Inquiry," *Boston College Law Review* 33 (1991): 67–70.

61 There is a large literature on the subject of the origins and rise of ma- jority rule; see, for example, the discussion with reference to earlier lit- erature: Ferdinand Elsener, "Zur Geschichte des Majoritätsprinzips (Pars maior und Pars sanior), insbesondere nach schweizerischen Quellen," in *Studien zur Rezeption des gelehrten Rechts* (Sigmaringen, 1989), 17–51.

62 A. Esmein, "L'unanimité et la majorité dans les élections canoniques," in *Mélanges Fitting* (Montpellier, 1907), 375: "C'est la haine de la pure loi du nombre qui reparaît ici."

63 Taken from Pope Leo the Great.

64 *Gl. ord.* ad X 1.6.55 s.v. *ad zelum*; Bernard of Pavia, *Summa decretalium*, 315–16.

65 An opinion perhaps shared by Innocent IV, *Apparatus*, ad X 1.6.21, no. 1: "non possit certa regula dari."

66 *Summa aurea* I, tit. *De elect.*, no. 12: "Zelus consistit in affectione animi, scilicet utrum carnaliter moveatur quis vel spiritualiter, utrum moveatur prece, vel precio vel timore, vel ex fonte vivo charitatis."

67 *Commentaria*, ad X 1.6.7, no. 4.

68 L. Moulin, "Sanior et maior pars," *RHD*, 4th ser., 36 (1958): 504.

69 *Gl. ord.* ad X 1.6.57: "Nota quod non semper statur maiori numero, nisi numerus maior sit sanior. Item auctoritas praefertur numero."

70 Geoffrey of Trani, *Summa super titulis decretalium* I, tit. *De elect.*, no. 9.

71 For a fuller treatment, see Felinus Sandeus, *Commentaria*, ad X 1.2.2, nos. 21–38, where this is said to be the rule but subject to several *fallentiae* that were themselves subject to several *restringationes.*

72 Panormitanus, *Commentaria*, ad X 1.6.57, no. 13; Petrus de Biaxio, *Directorium*, pt. 3, c. 35.

73 According to the leading sixteenth-century writer on the subject in the *ius commune*, however, the presumption was not irrebuttable. See Jacobus Menochius, *De praesumptionibus*, lib. 6, praes. 85; see also Petrus Maria Passerini, *Tractatus de electione canonica*, c. 14, nos. 16–22, which also suggests a longer life for the older rule.

74 It was also obsolete in monastic elections, since the Council of Trent required them to be by secret ballot. That in effect rendered the possibility of discovering a *sanior pars* impossible.

75 See Petrus de Biaxio, *Directorium*, pt. 3, c. 31, no. 2.

76 *Gl. ord.* ad X 1.6.44 s.v. *examinet.*

77 See Gerhard Hartmann, *Der Bischof: Seine Wahl und Ernennung* (Graz, 1990), 25–29.

78 Later commentators discerned three basic differences between *electio* and the *collatio* that followed upon *postulatio:* (1) the latter was the act of a superior authority, the former of subjects; (2) the latter conferred *plenum ius*, the former required confirmation; and (3) once accepted, the person collated could not renounce office without permission of the superior. See Passerini, *Tractatus de electione canonica*, c. 1, no. 39.

79 *Gl. ord.* ad Dist. 61 c. 9.

80 See Harry Dondorp, "*Ius ad rem* als Recht, Einsetzung in ein Amt zu verlangen," *TRG* 59 (1991): 285–318, also containing notes to the abundant prior literature, and Peter Landau, "Zum Ursprung des 'ius ad rem' in der Kanonistik," in *Proceedings of the Third International Congress of Medieval Canon Law*, ed. Stephan Kuttner (Vatican City, 1971), 81–102.

81 For examples of the power's exercise, see Klaus Ganzer, *Papsttum und Bistumsbesetzungen in der Zeit von Gregor IX. bis Bonfaz VIII.* (Cologne, 1968), 102–5, 154–57, 212–13. See also Laurentius de Somercote, *Der Traklat,* admitting the possibility of other forms but forbearing to discuss them.

82 So covered were bishops of another diocese, illegitimates, cardinals, *bigami,* and *corpore vitiati;* see Petrus de Biaxio, *Directorium,* pt. 2, cc. 19–35.

83 Geoffrey Barraclough, "The Making of a Bishop in the Middle Ages," *Catholic Historical Review* 19 (1933): 284.

84 Ganzer, *Papsttum und Bistumsbesetzungen,* 181–224.

85 Parsons, *Canonical elections,* 63.

86 25 Edw. III, st. 4 (1351); 38 Edw. III, st. 2 c. 2 (1364). See also Frederic Cheyette, "Kings, Courts, Cures, and Sinecures: The Statute of Provisors and the Common Law," *Traditio* 19 (1963): 295–349.

87 Waldo E. L. Smith, *Episcopal Appointments and Patronage in the Reign of Edward II* (Chicago, 1938); R. N. Swanson, *Church and Society in Late Medieval England* (Oxford, 1989), 14.

88 E.g., Barraclough, "Making of a Bishop," 307.

89 See Gaudemet, "Unanimité et la majorité," 357–58.

90 On the former, see Peter Landau, "Einfluß des kanonischen Rechts auf die europäische Rechtskultur," in *Europäische Rechts- und Verfassungsgeschichte,* ed. Reiner Schulze (Berlin, 1991), 49. On the latter, see the case called "Electio praefecti collegii Christi," Borthwick Institute for Historical Research, York, Ms. Prec. Bk. 11, f. 21v (1606 case involving mastership of Christ's College and citing inter alia Panormitanus, Commentaria, ad X 1.6.6, no. 13.)

Chapter 3: Qualifications of the Clergy

1 Peter Marshall, *The Catholic Priesthood and the English Reformation* (Oxford, 1994), 138–41.

2 See X 3.3.5.

3 See generally Stanley Chodorow, *Christian Political Theory and Church Politics in the Mid-Twelfth Century* (Berkeley, 1972).

4 See Dist. 81 c. 1; Geoffrey of Trani, *Summa super titulis decretalium* I, tit. *De temp. ordi. et qualitate ord.,* no. 13.

5 E.g., Hostiensis, *Summa aurea* I, tit. *De temp. ordinationum et qualitate ordinandorum.*

6 E.g., Sext. 1.6.14 (dealing with collation to a parish church).

7 Martinus de Azpilcueta, *De regularibus*, Comm. 1, no. 7.

8 See a treatise devoted partly to the conduct of such examinations, Franciscus Hallier, *De sacris electionibus et ordinationibus*, sect. 2.

9 See the description in Robert E. Rodes Jr., *Ecclesiastical Administration in Medieval England: The Anglo-Saxons to the Reformation* (Notre Dame, 1977), 114–17.

10 C. R. Cheney, *From Becket to Langton: English Church Government, 1170–1213* (Manchester, 1956), 138–39; Philip H. Stump, *The Reforms of the Council of Constance (1414–1418)* (Leiden, 1994), 149–52.

11 For an example, see Petrus de Biaxio, *Directorium*, pt. 3, c. 49, a jeremiad about the failings of the clergy of the established church that, to outward appearance, might almost have been written by an English Puritan in 1630.

12 See, e.g., Dist. 48 c. 1.

13 See Nicolaus Plovius, *Tractatus de irregularitate*, Rubr.

14 E.g., Bartholomeus Ugolinus, *Tractatus de irregularitatibus* (254 pp.).

15 See Peter Landau, "Frei und Unfrei in der Kanonistik des 12. und 13. Jahrhunderts am Beispiel der Ordination der Unfreien," in *Die Abendländische Freiheit vom 10. zum 14. Jahrhundert*, ed. Johannes Fried (Sigmaringen, 1991), 177–96.

16 It was a disputed question whether the master's creditors had the right to object. See Marianus Socinus, *Tractatus de oblationibus*, lib. 2, no. 15: "quod dubium a maioribus nostris non memini tactum."

17 See generally Charles Verlinden, *L'esclavage dans l'Europe médiévale*, 2 vols. (Bruges, 1955). For contemporary recognition of the distinctions in England, see William Lyndwood, *Provinciale*, 172 s.v. *servilis conditionis*.

18 See *gl. ord.* ad Dist. 54 c. 7.

19 See William D. Phillips Jr., *Slavery from Roman Times to the Early Transatlantic Trade* (Minneapolis, 1985), 43.

20 Cod. 1.3.36(37).

21 See the instructive discussion, in a slightly different context, in Paul R. Hyams, *Kings, Lords, and Peasants in Medieval England: The Common Law of Villeinage in the Twelfth and Thirteenth Centuries* (Oxford, 1980), 3–16.

22 The continuing vitality of Roman law on the subject for jurists, not irrelevant for the subject of this chapter, is illustrated in Alan Watson, "Seventeenth-Century Jurists, Roman Law, and the Law of Slavery," *Chicago-Kent Law Review* 68 (1993): 1343–54.

23 These are well set out by Peter Landau, "Frei und Unfrei," 179–87.

24 E.g., Panormitanus, *Commentaria*, ad X 4.9.1, no. 2: "Nota secundo quod de iure canonico etiam servitus est approbata; immo quandoque per ius canonicum inducitur servitus, ut [X 5.6.6]."

25 Hostiensis, *Lectura*, ad X 3.28.7, no. 4.

26 See A. Esmein, *Le mariage en droit canonique* (Paris, 1891), 1:317–35, and Michel Legrain, "Les esclaves, le mariage et l'Église," *Revue de droit canonique* 38 (1988): 296–329.

27 See John Gilchrist, "The Medieval Canon Law on Unfree Persons: Gratian and the Decretist Doctrines, c. 1141–1234," *Studia Gratiana* 19 (1976): 271–301. See also the discussion in Alan Watson, *Slave Law in the Americas* (Athens, Ga., 1989): 115–24.

28 *Gl. ord.* ad Dist. 54 c. 12 s.v. *institutum:* "Id est, ne favore ecclesiae aliquid iniuste statuatur, quia praetextu pietatis non est facienda impietas."

29 St. Antoninus, *Tractatus de excommunicatione*, cap. 6, no. 10: "Ratio huius est clericalis dignitas et servilis utilitas."

30 David Eltis, "Europeans and the Rise and Fall of African Slavery in the Americas," *American Historical Review* 98 (1993): 1408–10; Watson, "Seventeenth-Century Jurists," 1343–54.

31 *Commentaria*, ad X 1.18.1.

32 He cited Dist. 54 c. 21, X 3.7.5, and X 3.5.37 as pivotal in this discussion.

33 Pierre Petot, "Serfs d'Eglise habilités à témoigner en justice," *Cahiers de civilisation médiévale, Xe–XII siècles* 3 (1960): 194.

34 See, e.g., Joannes Paulus Lancellotus, *Institutiones iuris canonici*, lib. 1, tit. 25 § 3, and *gloss* of Antonius Timoteus (Venice 1703 ed.) ad id. s.v. *insignere:* "De origine alia non servili non curatur, sed de servili statu bene curatur." It was a commonplace among the jurists.

35 E.g., Petrus de Ancharano, *Commentaria*, ad X 1.18.1, no. 1: "de nobilitate vero sanguinis non curamus, ut in contrario . . . esset enim vituperium cum ordinatus deduceretur in servitutem . . . et tangit hoc vituperium totum collegium clericale."

36 *The Theory of the Leisure Class* (New York, 1926), 182.

37 *Lectura*, ad X 1.18.1, no. 3.

38 Philippe de Beaumanoir, *Coutumes de Beauvaisis*, ed. A. Salmon (Paris, 1970), vol. 2, no. 1448.

39 D.p. Dist. 54 c. 8, and *gl. ord.* ad id. s.v. *caeterum si.*

40 Augustino Barbosa, *Collectanea doctorum*, ad X 1.18.1, no. 2: "characterem recepit . . . peccat tamen mortaliter."

41 Nov. 123.17; Nov. 5.2.

42 See Hostiensis, *Lectura*, ad X 1.18.2, no. 6, for discussion of the point.

43 For fuller, later exposition of these rules, see Marianus Socinus, *Tractatus de oblationibus*, lib. 11.

44 See Jean Gaudemet, *Église et cité: Histoire du droit canonique* (Paris, 1994), 480, on the French situation, in which the Parlement de Paris began to hear such cases in the second half of the fourteenth century.

45 Among others which would merit investigation was the question of where a dispute would be tried when the man ordained claimed to be free and a third party claimed the opposite. See Panormitanus, *Commentaria*, ad X 1.18.2, no. 2.

46 F. M. Powicke and C. R. Cheney, eds., *Councils and Synods with Other Documents Relating to the English Church* (Oxford, 1964), 1:25 (Canterbury 1213 x 14); 60 (Salisbury 1217 x 1219), 180 (Worcester 1225 x 1230).

47 See Robert of Flamborough, *Liber poenitentialis* 170. This went back to a controversial question in Roman law; see Cino da Pistoia, *Commentaria*, ad Cod. 6.1.1, nos. 13–14.

48 This suggests some hesitation in accepting Maitland's verdict that ordination was treated as one form of emancipation in England. See F. Pollock and F. M. Maitland, *History of English Law*, 2d ed. (Cambridge, England, 1899; reissued 1968) 1:429; see also Peter Landau, "Frei und Unfrei," 196, on the need for further work on the practical aspects of the subject.

49 Ugolinus, *Tractatus de irregularitatibus*, cap. 57 § 4.

50 Irene Churchill, *Canterbury Administration* (London, 1933), 1:322. See also Murner, *Die Pönitentiarie-Formularsammlung des Walter Murner von Strassburg*, nos. 721–25.

51 See *gl. ord.* ad Dist. 54 c. 10, s.v. *reddi.*

52 Marianus Socinus, *Tractatus de oblationibus*, libellus 11, no. 12: "quia cum servus sit res animata anima rationali delinquit permittendo se ordinari et ideo punitur in eo in quo delinquit quia revocatur in servitutem."

53 See *gl. ord.* ad Dist. 54 c. 12, s.v. *transactione.*

54 See Innocent IV, *Apparatus*, ad X 1.18.6, for the distinction noted here.

55 See the useful survey, with reference to past literature, by Rayford W. Logan, "The Attitude of the Church toward Slavery prior to 1500," *Journal of Negro History* 17 (1932): 466–80.

56 Kent Archives Office, Maidstone, MS. DRb O 10, f. 113v.

57 Rufinus of Bologna, *Summa decretorum*, ad Dist. 54 (p. 137).

58 See the summary of the exceptions in Hostiensis, *Summa aurea* III, tit. *De rebus ecclesiae alienandis vel non*, no. 3, listing five exceptional cases in which alienation was permitted under the canon law.

59 Dist. 54 c. 10; purely spiritual services could in some instances be retained, as by requiring the enfranchised cleric to serve as the enfranchising party's chaplain. See also *gl. ord.* ad X 1.18.4: "Nota in manumisso operas spirituales posse retineri." For an instructive treatment of the realities of French practice on this score, see William C. Jordan, *From Servitude to Freedom* (Philadelphia, 1986), 82–85.

60 For discussion, see Hostiensis, *Summa aurea* I, tit. *De servis non ordinandis*, no. 7.

61 Id., "quia summa ratio est, quae pro religione facit."

62 See Gratian's discussion in d.p. Dist. 54, c. 22.

63 See the treatment, virtually unaltered from earlier works, in Joannes Paulus Lancellotus, *Institutiones iuris canonici*, lib. I, tit. 25, §§ 2–4; Augustino Barbosa, *Iuris ecclesiastici universi libri tres*, lib. 1, cap. 33, nos. 130–34.

64 *Commentaria perpetua*, ad X 1.18.2.

65 See Franciscus Schmalzgrüber, *Jus ecclesiasticum universum*, lib. 1, tit. 18, no. 3, and Pirro Corrado, *Praxis dispensationum apostolicarum*, lib. 3, c. 8.

66 Schmalzgrüber, *Jus ecclesiasticum universum*, "Hoc tamen etsi verum sit, pontifex tamen hac sua potestate non facile et vix unquam utitur . . . quia tali dispensatione praejudicatur dominis."

67 E.g., Joseph de Gibalin, *De irregularitatibus et impedimentis canonicis*, cap. 3, quaest. 5, prop. 2: "omne prorsus servitus extincta est in Gallia."

68 See Charles Verlinden, *The Beginnings of Modern Colonization* (Ithaca, N.Y., 1970), 40.

69 See the discussion in Thomas Sanchez, *Consilia*, lib. 1, c. 1, dub. 9.

70 Nicholaus Rodriguez Fermosinus, *De officiis et sacris aecclesiae . . . libri* (Geneva, 1741), ad X 1.18.4, quaest. 1, nos. 32–35, enlarging the kinds of misconduct by the master that could lead to automatic freeing of the slave. See also the measured description in James A. Brundage, *Medieval Canon Law* (London, 1995), 14–15.

71 E.g., Anacletus Reiffenstuel, *Jus canonicum universum*, ad X 1.18.1, providing three reasons for the prohibition; Vitus Pichler, *Juris canonici summa seu compendium* (Vienna, 1764), 1:161–62.

72 *Codex iuris canonici*, c. 987 § 4, in *Canon Law: A Text and Commentary*, ed. T. L. Bouscaren (Milwaukee, 1966), 449.

Chapter 4: Remedies and Canonical Procedure

1 E.g., M. R. T. Macnair, "The Early Development of the Privilege against Self-Incrimination," *Oxford Journal of Legal Studies* 10 (1990): 67–84.

2 See *The Letters of John of Salisbury*, vol. 2, *The Later Letters (1163–1188)*, ed. W. Millor and C. N. L. Brooke (Oxford, 1979), no. 144 (1165).

3 Richard Fraher, "The Theoretical Justification for the New Criminal Law of the High Middle Ages: *Rei publicae interest, ne crimina remaneant impunita*," *Illinois Law Review* (1984): 577–95.

4 Sforza Oddi, *De restitutionibus*, pt. 1, quaest. 1, art. 1.

5 At least it was so regarded during the Middle Ages. See, however, the argument to the contrary for classical law: Berthold Kupisch, *In integrum restitutio und vindicatio utilis bei Eigentumsübertragungen im klassischen römischen Recht* (Berlin, 1974).

6 The subject is covered in all English handbooks on Roman law; the fullest and clearest are Henry J. Roby, *Roman Private Law* (Cambridge, England, 1902), 2:258–64, and W. W. Buckland, *Text-book of Roman Law from Augustus to Justinian*, 3d ed., rev. by Peter Stein (Cambridge, England, 1963), 719–24. For fuller treatment, see Max Kaser, *Das römische Zivilprozessrecht* (Munich, 1966), 330–38.

7 See Peter Stein, "'Equitable' Remedies for the Protection of Property," in *New Perpectives in the Roman Law of Property: Essays for Barry Nicholas*, ed. Peter Birks (Oxford, 1989), 191–92.

8 These limitations were for the most part taken into the *ius commune*. See, e.g., Kaspar Manz, *Tractatus de restitutione in integrum*, tit. 11, nos. 158–59.

9 Cod. 2.52.7. It was specifically adopted by the canon law in Sext. 1.21.1. See the fuller treatment in Sforza Oddi, *De restitutionibus*, pt. 1, quaest. 19, art. 3, nos. 19–20: "Hoc autem absurdum esset quod varietas locorum varietatem iuris induceret."

10 See, for example, the discussion and decision in Mattheus de Afflictis, *Decisiones sacri consilii Neapolitani*, decis. 329.

11 Max Kaser, *Restituere als Prozessgegenstand* (Munich, 1968), 192–93.

12 See Andrea Bettetini, La *"restitutio in integrum" processuale nel diritto canonico* (Padua, 1994).

13 See *gl. ord.* ad C. 35 q. 9 c. 4 s.v. *retractari possit*.

14 This is also the opinion of Thomas John Feeney, *Restitutio in Integrum: An Historical Synopsis and Commentary* (Washington, D. C., 1941), 21.

15 In the Digest they were placed in reverse order. See Dig. 4.1.1–2.

16 *Gl. ord.* ad X 1.41.1 *rubr.* "Supra visum est de quadam restitutione speciali, que scilicet datur occasione metus; sed quia quedam restitutio generalis per quam subvenitur ecclesiis et minoribus."

17 The question was disputed. See d.p. C. 2 q. 3 c. 7 and the treatment of the subject in Bettetini, *La "restitutio in integrum,"* 194–214; for the civil law on the subject, see Francesco Migliorino, *Fama e infamia: Problemi della società medievale nel pensiero giuridico nei secoli XII e XIII* (Catania, 1985).

18 By a constitution of Frederick II (*Sacramenta puberum*), placed in medieval copies of the Codex ad 2.28.2. It was recognized as a matter of course in the *ius commune;* see, e.g., Joannes Petrus Ferrarius, *Practica nova judicialis,* tit. *Forma libelli super restitutionis petitionis,* no. 1.

19 See Antonius Corneus, *Tractatus de absolutione forensi iuramenti,* pt. 1, quaest. 6, spelling out the complex developed law on this subject.

20 The Decretals did not use the express term, but it is clear that restitution is what the pope had in mind, for he stated that the church was to enjoy the privileges of a minor. The comparison is also found in civilian jurisprudence, for example, Cino da Pistoia, *Commentaria,* ad Cod. 1.2.10, no. 2.

21 Antonius Corneus, *Tractatus de absolutione forensi iuramenti,* pt. 1, quaest 6, no. 22: "in ecclesia non procedunt nam quando ecclesia contra contractum restitutionem petit, maius est suum privilegium quam minoris in hoc." See also Robertus Maranta, *Speculum aureum,* pt. 6, tit. *De appellatione,* no 88.

22 E.g., Sforza Oddi, *De restitutionibus,* pt. 2, quaest. 88, art. 2, no. 35: justifying one of the deviations from the Roman law, "quia non possunt iura civilia praeiudicare ecclesiasticae libertati." Or see Joannes Antonius de Sancto Georgio, *Additiones* to Joannes Andreae, *Commentaria,* ad Sext. 1.21.1, noting reproval of contrary authority, because "repugnat utilitati religionis et favore ecclesiarum."

23 The analogy was made at the time; see, e.g., William Durantis, *Speculum iudiciale,* lib. 2, tit. *de rest. in integrum* § 2, no. 22: "Isti enim funguntur vice tutorum vel curatorum."

24 For a later example, see Mario Antonino Maceraten, *Variae practicabilium rerum resolutiones,* lib. 1, res. 25.

25 E.g., Dominico Galesio, *Tractatus de restitutionibus in integrum,* cap. 1, no. 46: "minor enim et ecclesia quoad hoc pari passu ambulant."

26 Luciano Musselli, "La 'Restitutio in integrum contra sententiam': Riflessioni sull'evoluzione dell'istituto nel processo canonico," in *L'educazione giuridica VI: Modelli storici della procedura continentale* (Perugia, 1994), 2:221–53.

27 See Innocent IV, *Apparatus*, ad X 1.41.2.

28 E.g., Panormitanus, *Commentaria*, ad id. no. 8.

29 Sforza Oddi, *De restitutionibus*, pt. 2, quaest. 64, art. 8, no. 62, discussing the application to this question of introduction of evidence and justifying this use of restitution, "quia impossibile est quin is qui probare poterat et non probavit intentionem suam lesus sit."

30 Panormitanus, *Commentaria*, ad X 1.41.1.

31 E.g., Antonius de Amatis, *Decisiones rotae provinciae Marchiae* (Venice, 1610), dec. 77, nos. 16–24.

32 Bettetini, *La "restitutio in integrum,"* 190–95. On appeals under the *ius commune*, see Antonio Padoa Schioppa, *Richerche sull'appello nel diritto intermedio* (Milan, 1967), 2:70.

33 See Panormitanus, *Commentaria*, ad X 1.41.4.

34 See X 1.41.10 and DD. ad id.

35 See no. 18, in Brian Tierney, *The Crisis of Church and State, 1050–1300* (Englewood Cliffs, N.J., 1964), 50.

36 *Gl. ord.* ad X 1.41.5 s.v. *tum ex litteris:* "Nota quod sententia etiam pape quando per surreptionem lata fuit, debet in melius reformari."

37 See Feeney, *Restitutio in Integrum,* 39.

38 Others besides the examples given here were: Should the fruits of the chattel alienated also be restored to the petitioners? Before what judge should a petition be laid? and, Could it be used by a minor to recover an ecclesiastical benefice?

39 For a full discussion, see Kaspar Manz, *Tractatus de restitutione in integrum*, tit. 2, nos. 121–229.

40 Sforza Oddi, *De restitutionibus*, pt. 2, quaest. 68, art. 1, no. 68; see also Innocent IV, *Apparatus*, ad X 1.41.7, no. 7: "et ideo patet quod contra interlocutoriam vel denegationem restitutionis non datur restitutio."

41 Innocent IV, *Apparatus*, ad id., no. 2.

42 Sforza Oddi, *De restitutionibus*, pt. 2, quaest. 64, art. 6, no. 42: "Et facit fortis ratio, quia nimis grave et durum est coram iudice suspecto litigare."

43 All discussed in id., nos. 2, 6, 10. But cf. *Decisiones capellae Tholosanae*, quaest. 53, for some limitations.

44 X 2.13.13.

45 *Lectura*, ad X 1.41.2, no. 27: "improprie dicitur restitutio, quia per eam non fit restitutio rei, nam per ipsam rescinditur sententia contractus vel praescriptio."

46 Lucien Masmejan, *La protection possessoire en droit romano-canonique médiéval* (Montpellier, 1990), 118.

47 *Communes opiniones* (1571) s.v. *restitutio in integrum:* "cessat in executionibus poenarum."

48 *Lectura*, ad X 1.41.7, no. 8.

49 William Durantis, *Speculum iudiciale*, lib. 2, tit. *De restit. in integrum* § 3, no. 6.

50 Id., no. 5.

51 See id. § 4, no. 2.

52 This presumed the intervention of good faith, but that was possible in fact; see Chapter 7.

53 Sforza Oddi, *De restitutionibus*, pt. 1, quaest. 3, art. 16: "Primo quia ecclesia semper censetur minor . . . Sed hoc absurdum est, ut perpetuo possit ecclesia in integrum restitutionem petere."

54 See id. for description of these solutions.

55 Id., pt. 2, quaest. 88, art. 1, no. 37: "Intelligitur in iis in quibus possibile est ut fungi potest." Even more direct was Kaspar Manz, *Tractatus de restitutione in integrum*, tit. 3, no. 165, giving as the reason for the limitation on the principle that the church was entitled to minority, that otherwise the law allowing prescription would never take effect.

56 *Communes opiniones* (1571) s.v. *Restitutio in integrum:* "Nota secundo quod hoc quadriennium non currit per vitam prelati alienantis."

57 Didacus Covarruvias, *Variae resolutiones*, lib. 1, c. 3., no. 10.

58 See Franciscus Turzanus, *Communes opiniones* (Venice, 1569), no. 109, citing several *consilia* and examples from the *decisiones* of the Rota.

59 See generally A. W. B. Simpson, *History of the Common Law of Contract* (Oxford, 1975), 281–315.

60 See generally Sebastianus Vantius, *Tractatus de nullitatibus processuum ac sententiarum*, tit. 13, nos. 1–142, dealing with nullity *ex defectu processus*.

61 E.g., Hostiensis, *Lectura*, ad X 1.41.3, no. 8: "Non est ergo recurrendum ad extraordinarium auxilium ex quo ordinarium competit."

62 E.g., for the heads of nullity, see William Durantis, *Speculum iudiciale*, lib. 2, pt. 3, tit. *De sententia* § 8, no. 1: "Nulla autem dicitur sententia multis modis" (with a very long list of causes for nullity following).

63 E.g., X 1.41.2, use of the procedure called *imploratio officii iudicis* together with *restitutio in integrum*.

64 *Apparatus*, ad X 1.41.8, no. 1.

65 Guido Papa, *Decisiones*, quaest. 159, citing earlier canonical authorities.

66 Id., "non est omnino irrita."

67 See Panormitanus, *Commentaria*, ad X 1.41.4, no. 8: "Hoc puto procedere de iure canonico . . . de benignitate canonica, nam mitius proceditur de iure canonico quam civili."

68 Sforza Oddi, *De restitutionibus*, pt. 1, quaest. 17, art. 2, no. 33, saying of the rule against duplication: "ut non procedat quando utilius esset remedium extraordinarium quam ordinarium."

69 E.g., X 2.13.8.

70 Joannes Andreae, *Commentaria*, ad X 1.41.3, no. 16.

71 E.g., Ward c. Eland (Diocese of Bath and Wells, 1462–63), Somerset Record Office, Taunton, Act book D/D/Ca 1, pp. 225–27, in which the judge decided that the allegations about the materiality of injury and relevance of new evidence by the plaintiff's proctor (i.e., lawyer) were sufficient "ad proponendum materiam restitutionis in integrum," or Snow c. Wood (Diocese of Lichfield, 1465), Joint Record Office, Lichfield, Act book B/C/1/1, f. 9, in which the record stated that the judge "restituit dictum Thomam [the plaintiff] ad terminum tertii productionis [i.e., of witnesses]." See also a fifteenth-century formulary of ecclesiastical court practice, in which the procedure is mentioned only in a procedural sense: British Library, MS. Reg. 11 A XI, fols. 50–51v.

72 Anne Lefebvre-Teillard, *Les officialités à la veille du Concile de Trente* (Paris, 1973), 65.

73 Richard Puza, *Res iudicata* (Graz, 1973), on which much of what follows is based. Confirming evidence is also found in Juan Ignacio Bañares, "Función judicial y supremacía de la Signatura de Justicia en el siglo XVII," *Ius canonicum* 28 (1988): 339–43.

74 See also Octavianus Vestrius, *In Romanae aulae actionem*, lib. 8, c. 3.

75 *Decisiones capellae Tholosanae*, quaest. 54.

76 See Panormitanus, *Commentaria*, ad X 1.41.1, no. 9: "Prelatus non potest facere conditionem ecclesiae deteriorem in faciendo; secus in omittendo." But there was controversy on the extent of the exception; see Augustino Barbosa, *De officio et potestate episcopi*, pt. 3, alleg. 95.

77 Sforza Oddi, *De restitutionibus*, pt. 1, quaest. 4, art. 5, no. 29.

78 See, e.g., Robert Brentano, "Three Thirteenth-Century Italian Cases in Ecclesiastical Courts," in *Proceedings of the Second International*

Congress of Medieval Canon Law, ed. Stephan Kuttner and J. Joseph Ryan (Vatican City, 1965), 311–19, and J. C. Moore, "Papal Justice in France around the Time of Pope Innocent III," *Church History* 41(1972): 295–306.

79 E.g., Dominico Galesio, *Tractatus de restitutionibus in integrum*, cap. 1, nu. 75: "abusivum et perpetuarum litium fomentum."

80 R. H. Helmholz, *Marriage Litigation in Medieval England* (Cambridge, England, 1975), 114–17.

81 Joannes Petrus Surdus, *Decisiones*, dec. 4, nos. 7–15, outlines various probatory requirements that had to be met for the claim to be successful. The same impression—and it is no more—emerges from cases on *restitutio* in Stephanus Gratianus, *Decisiones rotae provinciae Marchiae*, decs. 172, 176.

82 See Feeney, *Restitutio in Integrum*, 36.

83 See, e.g., James Ross Sweeney, "Innocent III, Canon Law, and Papal Judges Delegate," in *Popes, Teachers, and Canon Law in the Middle Ages*, ed. J. R. Sweeney and Stanley Chodorow (Ithaca, N.Y., 1989), 50–51.

Chapter 5: Principles of Ecclesiastical Jurisdiction

1 They were called *causae spirituales* and *causae spiritualibus annexae* in canonical parlance. See Winfried Trusen, "Die gelehrte Gerichtsbarkeit der Kirche," in Coing, *Handbuch*, 1:485–86.

2 For instance, the church claimed the right to exercise jurisdiction over Jews and infidels under certain circumstances; see James Maldoon, *Popes, Lawyers, and Infidels* (Philadelphia, 1979), 9–12. See also the remarks by James A. Brundage, *Medieval Canon Law* (London, 1995), 70–72,

3 This is an oversimplification of a complicated area of law; see, e.g., Petrus Franciscus de Tonduti, *Tractatus de praeventione iudiciali*, pt. 2, cc. 22–29.

4 See, e.g., Petrus de Ancharano, *Commentaria*, ad X.2.2.10, no. 7: "ubi iudex ecclesiasticus habet temporalem iurisdictionem, secundum canones iudicat non secundum leges." See also Francesco Migliorino, *In terris ecclesiae: Frammenti di "ius proprium" nel Liber extra di Gregorio IX* (Rome, 1992).

5 Gl. ord. ad X 2.2.11: "Nota quod propter negligentiam iudicis secularis transfertur iurisdictio ad ecclesiasticum." For corresponding practice at the papal court, see Herde, *Audientia*, 1:208–12.

6 Martinien Van de Kerckhove, "La notion de juridiction chez les Déc-
rétistes et les premiers Décrétalistes (1140–1250)," *Études Franciscaines*
49 (1937): 420–40.

7 *Gl. ord.* ad X 2.2.11 s.v. *in iustitia:* "non pertinet principaliter ad ecclesiasticum iudicem, licet pertineat ad ecclesiam quantum ad protectionem."

8 For example, most of the terminology and definitions of minority were
drawn from the Roman law; see René Metz, "L'enfant dans le droit canonique médiéval," *Recueils de la Société Jean Bodin* 36 (1976): 11–18.

9 *Commentaria,* ad Cod. 3.14.1, no. 1: "curia generalis totius orbis."

10 Id., no. 2.

11 See generally Jean Gaudemet, *L'Église dans l'empire romain (IVe–Ve
siècles)* (Paris, 1958), 230–40, and Biondo Biondi, *Il diritto Romano cris-
tiano* (Milan, 1952), 1:445–61.

12 See Theodor Meron, *Henry's Wars and Shakespeare's Laws: Perspectives
on the Law of War in the Later Middle Ages* (Oxford, 1993), 91–96, and
Frederick Russell, *The Just War in the Middle Ages* (Cambridge, England, 1975), 70.

13 See *gl. ord.* ad Dist. 87 c. 2 s.v. *pupillis:* "Pupillo tu eris adiutor."

14 See James A. Brundage, "Widows as Disadvantaged Persons in Medieval
Canon Law," in *Upon My Husband's Death,* ed. Louise Mirrer (Ann
Arbor, Mich., 1992), 193–206.

15 Dist. 88 c. 1.

16 *Gl. ord.* ad C. 12 q. 1 c. 1 s.v. *Omnis aetas:* "In prima loquitur de impu-
beribus clericis et adolescentibus: quorum vita, quia semper ad malum
prona est."

17 E.g., *gl. ord.* ad C. 12 q. 1 c. 1 s.v. *pupilli:* "Pupilli, orphani, viduae, liberti,
miserabiles personae spectant ad iudicium ecclesiasticum."

18 Id., "et causa viduarum et aliarum miserabilium personarum spectat ad
ecclesiam ubi agitur de iniuria sive de violentia eis illata." See generally,
with reference to prior literature, Lucien Masmejan, *La protection possessoire en droit romano-canonique médiéval* (Montpellier, 1990), esp.
108–21.

19 *Gl. ord.* ad X 2.2.11: "et indirecte ratione peccati omnes causae pertinent
ad ecclesiam."

20 Donald Sutherland, *The Assize of Novel Disseisin* (Oxford, 1973).

21 Benedict XIV, *De synodo diocesana* (Ferrara, 1760), lib. 9, c. 9, nos. 9–10:
"Nam in primis tuitio et defensio, ne sit inefficax, debet esse conjuncta
cum jurisdictione."

22 *D.D.C.*, vol. 6, col. 255: "un recueil de cas qui avaient été résolus au jour le jour: on avait parfois de la peine à en dégager des principes généraux."

23 Note that the term *pupillus* confined the class of children to those who were both minors and not within the *patria potestas* of their father, thus excluding a large group of children within an existing family. The early canonists showed little inclination to penetrate within the family even indirectly to challenge paternal authority.

24 *Commentaria*, ad Cod. 3.14.1, no. 4: "Textus hic exprimit aliquas."

25 *Commentaria*, ad id., no. 5: "Breviter puto iudicis arbitrio relinquendum."

26 *Summa Codicis*, ad id., no. 6: "omnes ii quibus natura movemur ad miserandum propter fortunae iniuriam."

27 E.g., Sebastianus Medices, *De fortuitis casibus*, pt. 2, quaest. 4, no. 5; Guido Papa, *Decisiones*, dec. 566, no. 1.

28 E.g., Jacobus Menochius, *De arbitrariis iudicium quaestionibus*, nos. 13–23.

29 See the long lists in Dominicus Tuschus, *Practicarum conclusionum* V, lit. M, concl. 273.

30 Gabrielus Alvarez de Velasco, *De privilegiis pauperum*, pt. 2, quaest. 20: "cupidineo amore captus."

31 See annotation to Guido Papa, *Decisiones*, dec. 566.

32 Gabrielus Alvarez de Velasco, *De privilegiis pauperum*, pt. 2, quaest. 2, c. 26.

33 *Apparatus*, ad X 1.29.38; see also DD. ad id.

34 *Gl. ord.* ad id. s.v. *pauperem se dixisset*: "Et si pauper esset, adhuc coram iudice debet agere et sequi forum rei."

35 E.g., William Durantis, *Speculum iudiciale* II, tit. *de instrumentorum editione*, § 13 (*Nunc vero aliqua*), no. 62; Antonius de Butrio, *Commentaria*, ad X 1.29.38, no. 5: "Nota quarto quod sola viduitas vel miserabilitas personae laicum non submittit iurisdictioni ecclesiae nisi concurrat paupertas."

36 See Panormitanus, *Commentaria*, ad X 1.29.38, nos. 6–7; Prosper Fagnanus, *Commentaria*, ad id., nos. 60 ff.

37 That is *miserabiles habitu* and *miserabiles actu*.

38 See Didacus Covarruvias, *Practicarum quaestionum*, c. 6, nos. 1–3; Alexandro Sperelli, *Decisiones fori ecclesiastici*, dec. 156, no. 34 ff.

39 For what follows I have relied on Alexandro Sperelli, ad id., nos. 16–20 and citations given therein.

40 See discussion in Joannes Andreae, *Commentaria*, ad X 1.29.38, no. 3.

41 E.g., X 1.31.6.

42 *Commentaria*, ad X 1.29.38, no. 6.

43 Id., no. 3: "Sed tunc solum se intromittit quando secularis iudex expresse denegat iusticiam vel id alias est notorium."

44 See DD. ad X 2.2.10–11.

45 Petrus de Ancharano, *Commentaria*, ad X 2.2.11, no. 2: "durum enim primum et durius illum ultimum."

46 All four are put forward in Panormitanus, *Commentaria*, ad X 2.2.10, no. 9.

47 Joannes ab Imola, *Commentaria*, ad X 2.2.11, no. 2: "Et nota quod quando vidua vel miserabilis persona impetrat, sufficit quod proximus superior secularis sit negligens, licet alii superiores non requirantur." The locus classicus for the solution seems to have been Innocent IV, *Apparatus*, ad X 1.29.38, no. 2, suggesting that the privilege be allowed to the disadvantaged "ne diu pro iusticia laborent."

48 Anne Lefebvre-Teillard, *Les officialités à la veille du Concile de Trente* (Paris, 1973), 88–89.

49 I have found one invocation of jurisdiction specifically made *ex defectu justitiae*, but in the case it was alleged that another ecclesiastical court, not a secular court, had refused to provide justice; it is Lame c. Halle (York 1491), Borthwick Institute of Historical Research, DC.CP.1490/91.

50 Barbara A. Kellum, "Infanticide in England in the Later Middle Ages," *History of Childhood Quarterly* 1(1974): 371–75.

51 See R. H. Helmholz, in *Canon Law and the Law of England* (London, 1987), 157–68.

52 Ibid., 211–45.

53 Ibid., 169–86.

54 If more were known about the common activities of the ecclesiastical courts in Italy, this statement might well require amendment. See Winfried Trusen, "Die gelehrte Gerichtsbarkeit der Kirche," in Coing, *Handbuch*, 1:494.

55 Ibid.; Bernhard Diestelkamp, "Das *privilegium fori* des Klerus im Gericht des Deutschen Königs während des 13. Jahrhunderts," in *Festschrift für Hans Thieme*, ed. Karl Kroeschell (Sigmaringen, 1986), 109–25. See also Georg May, *Die geistliche Gerichtsbarkeit des Erzbischofs von Mainz im Thüringen des späten Mittelalters* (Leipzig, 1956),

428 Notes to Pages 139–142

138–44; Ingeborg Buchholz-Johanek, *Geistliche Richter und geistliches Gericht im spätmittelalterlichen Bistum Eichstätt* (Regensburg, 1988), 149–50; Jorg Müller-Volbehr, *Die geistlichen Gerichte in den Braunschweig-Wolfenbüttelschen Landen* (Göttingen, 1973), 14, 80; Nikolaus Hilling, *Die Offiziale der Bischöfe von Halberstadt im Mittelalter* (Stuttgart, 1911), 108–9.

56 In addition to the studies cited in the previous note, see Ludwig Kaas, *Die geistliche Gerichtsbarkeit der katholischen Kirche in Preussen in Vergangenheit und Gegenwart* (Stuttgart, 1915–16), 1–11.

57 X 2.1.17 ad DD. ad id.

58 See Francisco Salgado de Somoza, *Tractatus de regia potestate*, pt. 1, c. 1, prae. 1, no. 56.

59 See A. Esmein, *Le mariage en droit canonique* (Paris, 1891), 1:35–44. An instructive statement with an example is found in Guido Papa, *Decisiones*, quaest. 1, no. 1: "Sed contrarium dicendum videtur, quia quando agitur super possessorio vel quasi, etiam in spiritualibus vel beneficialibus causis, iudex laicus est iudex competens," citing treatises inter alia by Joannes Andreae, Innocent IV, Antonius de Butrio, and Franciscus de Zabarella in support.

60 The fundamental works are Eduard Eichmann, *Der recursus ab abusu nach deutschem Recht* (Breslau, 1903), esp. 24–33, and René-François Jahan, *Étude historique sur l'appel comme d'abus* (Paris, 1888).

61 Gabrielus Alvarez de Velasco, *De privilegiis pauperum*, quaest. 9, no. 3.

62 C. 23 q. 3 c. 10; C. 23 q. 5 c. 23; see, e.g., Francesco Ansaldi, *Tractatus de iurisdictione*, pt. 3, tit. 1, c. 21, nos. 73–77.

63 See J. F. von Schulte, *Die Geschichte der Quellen und Literatur des canonischen Rechts* (Stuttgart, 1875), 2:53–59.

64 Sess. 7, c. 14; Sess. 23, c. 1, *De Ref.* in Decrees 2:689, 744–46.

65 E.g., Joannes Paulus Lancellotus, *Institutiones iuris canonici*, lib. 3, tit. 1, *De iudiciis* § 3.

66 Joannes Maria Novario, *Praxis aurea*, priv. 92, no. 5, commenting nevertheless on the limitations of the church's ability to exercise this jurisdiction.

67 *De synodo diocesana*, lib. 9, c. 9, no. 12: "cum desperandum jam sit, ut potestas secularis intra constitutos sibi ab antiquo limites contineri patiatur, imprudenter ageret episcopus . . ."

68 Joseph Lecler, *The Two Sovereignties*, trans. Hugh Montgomery (London, 1952), 55.

69 Andreas Gail, *Practicarum observationum*, lib. 1, c. 1, no. 40. See also Ferdinand Elsener, "Der 'Arme Mann' (pauper) im Prozeßrecht der Grafen und Herzoge von Savoyen," in *Studien zur Rezeption des gelehrten Rechts* (Sigmaringen, 1989), 220–58.

70 Jacobus Menochius, *De arbitrariis iudicium quaestionibus*, lib. 2, cent. 1, c. 56, nos. 33–37.

71 See Joannes Maria Novario, *Praxis aurea*, priv. 62.

72 Joseph Biancalana, "For Want of Justice: Legal Reforms of Henry II," *Columbia Law Review* 88 (1988): 433–536.

73 Michael Graham, "The Civil Sword and the Scottish Kirk, 1560–1600," in *Later Calvinism: International Perspectives*, ed. W. Fred Graham (Kirksville, Mo., 1994), 239–41.

74 *Religion, Law, and the Growth of Constitutional Thought, 1150–1650* (Cambridge, England, 1982).

Chapter 6: Religious Principles and Practical Problems

1 Paolo Prodi, *Il sacramento del potere: Il giuramento politico nella storia costituzionale dell'Occidente* (Bologna, 1992), 161. See also Ulrike Marga Dahl-Keller, *Der Treueid der Bischöfe gegenüber dem Staat* (Berlin, 1994), 34–46.

2 For modern comments, essentially unfavorable to this aspect of practice in the medieval church, see Jean Gaudemet, "Le serment dans le droit canonique médiéval," in *Le serment*, ed. Raymond Verdier (Paris, 1991), 2:63–75, and André Vauchez, "Le refus du serment chez les hérétiques médiévaux," in Verdier, *Le serment*, 257–63.

3 See Thomas Aquinas, *Summa theologica*, 2a2ae, quaest. 89, art. 2.

4 *Practicarum observationum*, lib. 1, obs. 22: "Notum est, quod de jure praesertim canonico, omne juramentum servandum sit, quod absque dispendio salutis aeternae servari potest." He was repeating what Rota itself repeatedly held, e.g., *Rotae decisiones*, tit. *De rest. spoliato*, dec. 18 (401), no. 2.

5 Seraphinus de Seraphinis, *De privilegiis juramentorum*, contains that number.

6 Eight of the canons were ascribed to the bishop of Hippo.

7 Thomas Del Bene, *Tractatus de iuramento*, C. I, dub. 10, no. 5: "Secundo probatur ex consuetudine et usu ecclesiae, cuius authoritate saepe exigitur iuramentum."

8 See *gl. ord.* ad d.a. C. 22 q. 1 c. 1 s.v. *Quod iuramentum.*

9 See *Gl. ord.* ad X 2.24.26 s.v. *modico vino.*

10 *Gl. ord.* ad X 2.24.26 s.v. *necessitas:* "Sed haec necessitas includit etiam sub se utilitatem."

11 E.g., Hostiensis, *Summa aurea* II, tit. *De iureiurando,* no. 4.

12 See X 2.22.16 and DD. ad id.

13 See esp. *gl. ord.* ad id. s.v. *peierat.*

14 Rufinus of Bologna, *Summa decretorum,* 390: "Qui in hac forma iurat 'sic Deus me adiuvet et iste reliquie,' licet has creaturas nominet, non tamen per eas iurat, quia non ad eas refert iuramentum sed ad eum, cui iste reliquie sunt dicate."

15 See also C. 1 q. 7 c. 9, approving oaths invoking the name of the temporal ruler. For comparison, see Aquinas on Pharaoh's oath, *Summa theologica,* 2a2ae, quaest. 89, art. 6.

16 Rufinus of Bologna, *Summa decretorum,* 390. For fuller later treatment, see Thomas Del Bene, *Tractatus de iuramento,* C. I, dub. 1, no. 24.

17 Joannes de Selva, *Tractatus perutilis de iureiurando,* pt. 1 § *Quero quinto,* no. 3: "Aliquando invocatur creatura in testem inquantum relucet in ea divine veritatis vestigium."

18 But note the difficulties caused by C. 22 q. 5 c. 10, dealing with an oath *per lapidem.* Its apparent approval troubled the canonists.

19 *Romeo and Juliet,* I, ii, 107.

20 E.g., Raymond of Peñafort, *Summa de poenitentia* I, tit. *de iuramento* § 1: "hoc tamen non est in usu nec multum approbo" speaking of the oath *per salutem principis.*

21 For modern canon law and its historical background on this subject, see E. J. Moriarty, *Oaths in Ecclesiastical Courts* (Washington, D.C., 1937).

22 Apparently taken into the canon law from Cod. 3.1.14.4.

23 Canon 19, in *Decrees,* 1:324.

24 See the Legatine Council of London (1237), c. 29, and Legatine Council of London (1268), c. 26, in F. M. Powicke and C. R. Cheney, eds., *Councils and Synods with Other Documents Relating to the English Church* (Oxford, 1964), 2:258, 773.

25 Michael Tangl, *Die päpstlichen Kanzleiordnungen von 1200–1500* (Innsbruck, 1894), 33–52.

26 James A. Brundage, "The Bar of the Ely Consistory Court in the Fourteenth Century: Advocates, Proctors, and Others," *Journal of Ecclesiastical History* 43 (1992): 553.

27 See my "Ethical Standards for Advocates and Proctors in Theory and Practice," in *Canon Law and the Law of England* (London, 1987), 41–57.

28 See, e.g., Sigismundo Scaccia, *De iudiciis causarum*, lib. 2, c. 1, quaest. 15, nos. 221–22, listing authorities and leaning to the first position. The final position of the *ius commune* seems to have been that, if demanded, a failure to require the oath vitiated the process but that if neither party demanded it, the oath could be omitted. See *Decisiones novissimae S. R. Rotae*, Dec. 58 (28 February 1628).

29 Hostiensis, *Summa aurea* II, tit. *De iuramento calumniae*, no. 6: "Istud iuretur, quod lis sibi iusta videtur, scilicet actori in agendo, reo in defendendo." See also *gl. ord.* ad X 2.7.1 s.v. *calumniae iuramentum.*

30 Id., no. 4.

31 Id., no. 7. See also Thomas Del Bene, *Tractatus de iuramento*, C. I, dub. 7, no. 10.

32 "Leges Langobardorum. Leges Papienses Henrici II" (1002 x 1025), in MGH, Leges (Hannover, 1868), 4:584.

33 See Geoffrey of Trani, *Summa super titulis decrelalium*, ad X 2.7.1.

34 Its use seems to have fallen into desuetude in the seventeenth century; see Franciscus Schmalzgrüber, *Ius ecclesiasticum universum*, pt. 2, tit. 7, no. 5.

35 Ad X 2.7.1 s.v. *inconsulto:* "Istud difficile videtur, ut episcopus propter hoc debeat requirere Romanum pontificem, sed hoc non servatur."

36 I found two others also mentioned: (1) the existence of a general license by the papacy, and (2) a restriction of the decretal to bishoprics immediately subject to the papacy. See DD. ad id.

37 Sigismundo Scaccia, *De iudiciis causarum*, lib. 2, c. 1, quaest. 16, no. 125, with earlier references.

38 William Durantis, *Speculum iudiciale*, lib. 2, tit. *De teste* § 4 (*Sequitur de testium iuramento*), no. 1; the apparent source of these four was C. 11 q. 3 c. 78.

39 E.g., not to reveal the witness's own *dicta* to anyone connected with the litigation prior to publication of all the depositions.

40 The best-known work on the subject is Leonard Levy, *Origins of the Fifth Amendment*, 2d ed. (New York, 1986). This work is strong as a civil liberties perspective of the oath's history but deficient in historical understanding of the issues as they arose during the seventeenth century. See Charles M. Gray, "Prohibitions and the Privilege against Self-

Incrimination," in *Tudor Rule and Revolution: Essays for G. R. Elton from His American Friends*, ed. D. Guth and J. McKenna (Cambridge, England, 1982), 345–67; R. H. Helmholz, "Origins of the Privilege against Self-Incrimination: The Role of the European *Ius Commune*," *New York University Law Review* 65 (1990): 962–90; and John H. Langbein, "The Historical Origins of the Privilege against Self-Incrimination at Common Law," *Michigan Law Review* 92 (1994): 1047–85.

41 *Practica criminalis*, quaest. 45, no. 8.

42 Id., no. 9; Panormitanus, *Commentaria*, ad X 2.20.37, no. 13.

43 Seraphinus de Seraphinis, *De privilegiis iuramentorum*, priv. 33, no. 112: "Quod . . . non deferri iuramentum suppletorium procedit etiam in qualibet alia causa gravi."

44 Nonetheless, commentators held that where each party produced *semiplena probatio* (a case of partial proof), it was possible that the oath described here could be assigned to the defendant. See William Durantis, *Speculum iudiciale*, lib. 2, pt. 2, tit. *De iuramenti delatione*, no. 9.

45 Hostiensis, *Lectura*, ad X 2.19.2.

46 Thomas Del Bene, *Tractatus de iuramento*, C. 1, dub. 7, no. 7: "Ad iudicis prudentis arbitrium pertinet, ut consideratis causae et personarum circumstantiis, aliquando actori iuramentum deferat in probationis supplementum et litis decisionem." A fuller discussion of the complex law on this subject is contained in Seraphinus de Seraphinis, *De privilegiis iuramentorum*, priv. 33.

47 *Gl. ord.* ad X 2.24.36 s.v. *a te.*

48 See, e.g., Josephus Mascardus, *Conclusiones probationum*, lib. 1, quaest. 9, nos. 1–16.

49 Discussed, with appropriate conflicting authorities, in William Durantis, *Speculum iudiciale*, lib. 2, pt. 2, tit. *De iuramenti delatione*, no. 5.

50 See Richard M. Fraher, "The Theoretical Justification for the New Criminal Law of the High Middle Ages: 'Rei publicae interest, ne crimina remaneant impunita,'" *University of Illinois Law Review* (1984): 577–95.

51 Hostiensis, *Summa aurea* V, tit. *De purgatione canonica*, no. 3.

52 E.g., Guildhall Library, London, MS. 11448, fols. 88v–89, reporting cases from c. 1610.

53 F. Pollock and F. W. Maitland, *History of English Law before the Time of Edward I*, 2d ed. (Cambridge, England, 1968), 1:443.

54 Panormitanus ascribed its introduction to the "custom of the Church," adding that it had become part of the *ius commune* in the course of time. See *Commentaria*, ad X 5.39.15, nos. 4, 8.

55 *Gl. ord.* ad X 5.39.10 s.v. *debeat:* "non est astrictus nisi ad iustum mandatum."

56 *Gl. ord.* ad X 5.39.15 s.v. *ad cautelam:* "ubi post absolutionem timore iuramenti similia pertimescat."

57 Hostiensis, *Lectura,* ad id., no. 19: "unde sicut per procuratorem nemo potest peccata confiteri, immo praesentia requiritur confitentis . . . , sic dicendum est de excommunicati absolutione."

58 William Durantis, *Speculum iudiciale,* lib. 1, pt. 2, tit. *De procuratore* § 1, no. 6.

59 Panormitanus, *Commentaria,* ad X. 5.39.15, no. 7: "Item opponitur quod in curia Romana hoc servatur."

60 For a full treatment, with citation to existing literature, see Lothar Kolmer, *Promissorische Eide im Mittelalter* (Kallmünz, Germany, 1989).

61 *Summa theologica,* 2a2ae, quaest. 89, art. 1.

62 Panormitanus, *Commentaria,* ad X 2.24.10, no. 5. There was room for disagreement; see also the authorities cited and the discussion in Henricus Zoesius, *Commentarius,* lib. 2, tit. 24, nos. 15–19.

63 Brian Woodcock, *Medieval Ecclesiastical Courts in the Diocese of Canterbury* (Oxford, 1952), 89–92.

64 Anne Lefebvre-Teillard, *Les officialités à la veille du Concile de Trente* (Paris, 1973), 116; Ferdinand Elsener, "Die Exkommunikation als prozessuales Vollstreckungsmittel," in *Studien zur Rezeption des gelehrten Rechts* (Sigmaringen, 1989), 152–64.

65 See generally Jules Roussier, *Le fondement de l'obligation contractuelle dans le droit classique de l'Église* (Paris, 1933), esp. 46–94, and François Spies, *De l'observation des simples conventions en droit canonique* (Paris, 1928).

66 *Gl. ord.* ad C. 12 q. 2 c. 66 s.v. *promiserint:* "Videtur quod aliquis obligetur nudis verbis, licet non intercessit stipulatio." See also X 1.35.1 and DD. ad id.

67 Antonius de Butrio, *Commentaria,* ad X 1.35.1, no. 5.

68 Seraphinus de Seraphinis, *De privilegiis iuramentorum,* priv. 19, no. 3: "quod pactum nudum iuramento roboratum producit obligationem et actionem et consequenter ab illo vestiatur, est vera de iure canonico." See generally, on developments in the civil law, Jan Hallebeek, "Actio ex Iuramento: The Legal Enforcement of Oaths," *Ius commune* 17 (1990): 69–88.

69 E.g., Joannes Monachus, *Glossa aurea,* ad Sext. 2.2.3, nos. 5–6.

70 See the discussion and authorities in Antonius Gabrielius, *Communes conclusiones*, lib. 2, concl. 10.

71 See Klaus-Peter Nanz, *Die Entstehung des allgemeinen Vertragsbegriffs im 16. bis 18. Jahrhundert* (Munich, 1985); Robert Feenstra, "Pact and Contract in the Low Countries from the Sixteenth to the Eighteenth Century," in *Towards a General Law of Contract*, ed. John Barton (Berlin, 1990), 198–201.

72 *In Pandectas iuris civilis . . . commentarii olim Paratitla dicti* (Lyons, 1597), lib. 2, tit. 14, no. 10.

73 See generally A. W. B. Simpson, *History of the Common Law of Contract* (Oxford, 1975).

74 Reinhard Zimmermann, *The Law of Obligations* (Cape Town, 1990), 542–44.

75 See Kolmer, *Promissorische Eide*, 319–27.

76 *Gl. ord.* ad id. *rubr:* "Nota quod iuramentum in damnum ecclesiae datum non est servandum, nec obligat, sed potius periurium dicitur, et de hoc debet poenitentia imponi."

77 Another way of seeing this and reaching the same substantive result, however, held that the prelate was himself bound but that he could not prejudice the rights of his church. See X 2.24.19 and DD. ad id.

78 *Gl. ord.* ad C. 22 q. 4 c. 8 s.v. *quod ebrius.*

79 See, e.g., Hostiensis, *Summa aurea* I, tit. *De temp. ordinationum et qualitate ordinandorum*, no. 16.

80 *As You Like It*, III, v, 72–73.

81 It was also said in defense that the debtor had not committed a sin, or at any rate had committed only a lesser sin, by swearing to pay; the creditor, on the other hand, had committed the sin by requiring the usurious payment.

82 E.g., Hostiensis, *Summa aurea* III, tit. *De iureiurando*, No. 6 § *Per res:* "multa enim prohibentur, quae facta, tenent."

83 See generally Stephan Kuttner, *Kanonistische Schuldlehre von Gratian bis auf die Dekretalen Gregors IX* (Vatican City, 1935), 314–33.

84 Hostiensis, *Lectura*, ad X 2.24.8, no. 5: "nam et coacta voluntas voluntas est." See Dig. 4.2.21.5; C. 15 q. 1 c. 1. See also Rota Romana, *Decisiones novae*, tit. *De renunciatione*, dec. 5 (374), when an unsuccessful attempt was made to test the principle.

85 See X 2.24.26 and DD. ad id; Joannes de Selva, *Tractatus perutilis de iureiurando*, pt. 1, nos. 1–7.

86 See Seraphinus de Seraphinis, *Tractatus de privilegiis iuramentorum,* priv. 75.

87 Innocent IV, *Apparatus,* ad X 2.24.2, no. 2: "Et nota quod nulli contra iuramentum suum proprium datur restitutio in integrum sed absolutio tantum." See also Antonius Corneus, *Tractatus de absolutione forensi iuramenti,* pt. 1, quaest. 5.

88 *Practicarum observationum,* lib. 1, obs. 22.

89 See, e.g., Thomas Aquinas, *Summa theologica,* 2a2ae, Q. 88, art. 9; Antonius Corneus, *Tractatus de absolutione iuramenti,* pt. 1, quaest. 4, nos. 14–21; and esp. id., no. 7 "Deus recipit iuramentum ad illius hominis commodum et illo remittente, Deus etiam remittit."

90 *Gl. ord.* ad X 2.24.25.

91 Id., s.v. *conditio* for this and other implied conditions.

92 E.g., id., at end.

93 See Friedrich Merzbacher, "Die Regel 'Fidem frangenti fides frangitur' und ihre Anwendung," *ZRG,* kan. Abt. 99 (1982): 339–62.

94 See esp. *gl. ord.* ad id., s.v. *conqueritur.*

95 Zimmermann, *Law of Obligations,* 579.

96 *Gl. ord.* ad X 2.24.3, rubr. "Nota quod non frangit promissum vel propositum suum qui commutat illud in melius." See also Innocent IV, *Apparatus,* ad X 2.24.6, no. 2.

97 See James A. Brundage, *Medieval Canon Law and the Crusader* (Madison, 1969), 43.

98 See Ludwig Buisson, *Potestas und Caritas: Die päpstliche Gewalt im Spätmittelalter* (Cologne, 1958), 223–69.

99 See Antonius Corneus, *Tractatus de absolutione forensi iuramenti,* pt. 1, quaest. 6, nos. 7–16.

100 See Hostiensis, *Lectura,* ad X 1.40.3, no. 3.

Chapter 7: Economic and Property Rights

1 On this subject, there is now a very large collection of scholarship; see the recent treatments, with full bibliography: John Gilissen, *La coutume,* in Typologie des sources du moyen age occidental, A-III, I* (Turnhout, Belgium, 1982); John P. McIntyre, *Customary Law in the Corpus iuris canonici* (San Francisco, 1991). Suggestive and related to the subject of this book is Peter Stein, "The Civil Law Doctrine of Custom and the Growth of Case Law," in *Studi in memoria di Gino Gorla* (Milan, 1994,) 1:371–81.

2 There was, however, such a thing as "prescriptive custom" within the canon law; e.g., *gl. ord.* ad X 1.6.50 s.v. *iam prescripta* (dealing with the acquisition of rights to take part in canonical elections).

3 The *ius commune* developed six different distinctions between custom and prescription, holding, however, that they were not so fundamentally distinct that both could not be included in the same petition. See generally Joannes Franciscus Balbus, *Tractatus de praescriptionibus*, pt. 1 § 10, nos. 3–12.

4 *Gl. ord.* ad X 2.26.5: "Nota quod diuturnitas temporis peccatum non minuit sed auget."

5 Reinhard Zimmermann (echoing the verdict of Savigny) in "Extinctive Prescription in German Law," in *German National Reports in Civil Law Matters for the XIVth Congress of Comparative Law in Athens*, ed. Erick Jayme (Heidelberg, 1994), 153.

6 See David Herlihy, "Church Property on the European Continent, 701–1200," *Speculum* 36 (1961): 92–93.

7 M. T. Clanchy, *From Memory to Written Record: England, 1066–1307* (Cambridge, Mass., 1979), 3–4.

8 Montesquieu, *The Spirit of the Laws*, trans. and ed. Anne Cohler, Basia Miller, and Harold Stone (Cambridge, England, 1989) 684–87, pt. 6, bk. 31, cc. 9–10.

9 See generally Eltjo J. H. Schrage, *Utrumque Ius: Eine Einführung in das Studium der Quellen des mittelalterlichen gelehrten Rechts* (Berlin, 1992), 90–110.

10 "Tertio, an iura ecclesiarum prescriptione tollantur?" found in C. 16 q. 3, rubr.

11 This was not unrealistic; see, for example, the mid-twelfth-century case reported in *The Letters and Charters of Gilbert Foliot*, ed. Adrian Morey and C. N. L. Brooke (Cambridge, England, 1967), no. 66.

12 Cod. 7.39.7.

13 *Gl. ord.* ad C. 16 q. 3 c. 4 s.v. *legis:* "nam de iure naturali non sunt praescriptiones inductae; nam de iure naturali iniquum est aliquem ditari cum aliena iactura . . . sed ideo inventa est praescriptio, ne dominia rerum semper sint in incerto."

14 See, for example, the characteristic description in Dominicus Tuschus, *Practicarum conclusionum*, lit. P, concl. 70, no. 13: "iniquissimum remedium equitati contrarium."

15 This explanation of something that is very clear in the records of the English Church was suggested to me by reading Ludovicus Pontanus,

Consilia, cons. 368, nos. 11–14. He wrote that prescription should not be extended from one person to another (what we would call "tacking") because the prescriptive claim was "strictissimi iuris et odiosa."

16 *Gl. ord.* ad id. s.v. *invasa.*

17 D.p. C. 16 q. 3 c. 7: "Potest etiam aliter distingui."

18 *Gl. ord.* ad C. 16 q. 3 c. 11 s.v. *in ius proprium.*

19 In modern American law, the rule's primary importance lies in barring possessory claims to government property, but it also applies, for example, to title to wild animals or rights to marital status.

20 Tithes were very frequently in lay hands during the Middle Ages, particularly in France and Spain, so that this was both theoretically and practically a contentious point.

21 E.g., Innocent IV, *Apparatus,* ad X 3.34.8, no 7: "terram sanctam quam infideles illicite possident."

22 *Gl. ord.* ad C. 16 q. 3 c. 13 s.v. *post liminio:* "Alius est in pupillari aetate," citing a text from the Codex.

23 Id., "Item et tempore excommunicationis non currit praescriptio."

24 E.g., Dominicus Tuschus, *Practicarum conclusionum,* lit. P, concl. 75, nos. 1–82.

25 For an example, see *Decisiones capellae Tholosane,* quaest. 76.

26 See *gl. ord.* ad id.

27 The analogy is found in the civilians: Cino da Pistoia, *Commentaria,* ad Cod. 8.54.34 § Item: "Praeterea ecclesia et fiscus pariter ambulant."

28 See Joannes Franciscus Balbus, *Tractatus de praescriptionibus,* pt. 5 § 1, no. 19.

29 Id., no. 3.

30 It is given in the *glossa ordinaria* ad X 2.26.12 s.v. *non obstante,* toward the end.

31 The word used is *subducere:* "ut illo subducto."

32 E.g., Innocent IV, *Apparatus,* ad X 2.26.10, no. 1; Joannes Petrus Surdus, *Decisiones,* dec. 4, no. 1.

33 Hostiensis, *Summa aurea,* II, tit. *De praesumptionibus,* nos. 2–3.

34 Id.; for example, he lists the fact that under a text in the *Decretum* one became *immundus* for seven days after touching a cadaver. This seems a considerable stretch of the concept of prescription.

35 Cod. 7.39.2 (*praescriptio longissimi temporis*), on which see Dieter Nörr, *Die Entstehung der* longi temporis praescriptio (Cologne, 1969).

36 See Colin Morris, *The Papal Monarchy: The Western Church from 1050 to 1250* (Oxford, 1989), 316–20.

37 E.g., Rufinus von Bologna, *Summa,* 360 (speaking specifically about monasteries).

38 *Gl. ord.* ad C. 16 q. 3 c. 1 s.v. *triginta:* "Hodie non statur huic numero, extra de praescrip. de quarta."

39 See Joannes Franciscus Balbus, *Tractatus de praescriptionibus,* pt. 3 § 2, no. 1.

40 D.p. C. 16 q. 3 q. 15 § 1. Gratian omitted any mention of bona fides as a requirement where it would have been appropriate, and where he did seem to require bona fides, he spoke of its necessity at the start of the prescriptive period.

41 See Germain Lesage, "La nature du droit canonique d'après Alexandre III," in *Miscellanea Rolando Bandinelli Papa Alessandro III,* ed. Filippo Liotta (Siena, 1986), 323–35.

42 On the concept in Roman law, see Herbert Hausmaninger, *Die bona fides des Ersitzungsbesitzers im klassichen römischen Recht* (Vienna, 1964).

43 X 2.26.20; the phrase was: "Omne quod non est ex fide peccatum est." For background and assessment, see Angel de Mier Vélez, *La buena fe en la prescripción y en la costumbre hasta el siglo XV* (Pamplona, 1968), 52–74.

44 Rudolf Meyer, *Bona fides und lex mercatoria in der europäischen Rechtstradition* (Göttingen, 1994), 56–69.

45 It was generally defined as possession *iusta causa,* so that the requirement tended in practice to run together with the requirement of good faith. See Joannes Franciscus Balbus, *Tractatus de praescriptionibus,* pt. 3 § 1. The background is the subject of Jules Fauré, *Justa causa et bonne foi: Essai d'explication des singularités de l'usucaption pro emptore en droit romain classique* (Lausanne, 1936).

46 *Gl. ord.* ad X 2.26.20: "Quicunque facit contra conscientiam aedificat ad gehennam. Et ideo statuit concilium quod nulla valeat praescriptio absque bona fide."

47 So put by Joannes Andreae, *Commentaria,* ad Sext. 5.12.2, no. 20: speaking of acts "per quod posset a Deo deviare." See Knut Wolfgang Nörr, "Recht und Religion: Über drei Schnittstellen im Recht der mittelalterlichen Kirche," *ZRG,* kan. Abt. 79 (1993): 6–10, and idem, "Il contributo del diritto canonico al diritto privato europeo: Riflessioni dal punto di vista della identificazione del concetto di diritto," in *Diritto canonico e comparazione,* ed. R. Tertolino et al. (1992), 23–28.

48 See Joannes Franciscus Balbus, *Tractatus de praescriptionibus,* pt. 1, proem. "subtilis et profunda, ac in variis multifariis et prope infinitis iuris partibus diffusa."

49 See id. et seq. for fuller treatment of these and other issues.

50 *Summa aurea* II, tit. *De praescriptionibus*, nos. 5–6.

51 For some of the ramifications of the rule requiring good faith, see Thomas O. Martin, *Adverse Possession, Prescription, and Limitation of Actions: The Canonical "Praescriptio"* (Washington, D.C., 1944), 30–54.

52 This is usefully discussed by Hostiensis, *Summa aurea* II, tit. *de praescriptionibus*, no. 3. See also José Luis de los Mozos, "Del Aforismo 'Mala fides superveniens nocet' a la 'Bona fides' canonica," in *Estudios canónicos en homenaje al Profesor D. Lamberto de Echeverría* (Salamanca, 1988), 351–70.

53 See *Commentaria*, ad Sext. 5.12.2, nos. 33–38.

54 *Gl. ord.* ad X 2.26.5 s.v. *noverit.*

55 *Summa aurea* III, tit. *De praescriptionibus*, no. 3.

56 A. Van Hove, *De privilegiis*, in *Commentarium Lovaniense in Codicem iuris canonici* (Rome, 1939), 100–101.

57 See, e.g., Roger A. Cunningham, William B. Stoebuck, and Dale A. Whitman, *The Law of Property*, 2d. ed. (St. Paul, Minn. 1993), § 11.7. The subject does, however, also have old roots in the English common law. See James Barr Ames, "The Nature of Ownership," in *Lectures on Legal History* (Cambridge, Mass., 1913), 191–209.

58 *Gl. ord.* ad X 2.26.5 s.v. *noverit.*

59 Id.

60 *Gl. ord.* ad C. 16 q. 3 c. 4 s.v. *legis.*

61 Joannes Andreae, *Commentaria*, ad Sext. 5.12.2, no. 15.

62 Id., ad Sext. 5.12.2, no. 12.

63 For a long compilation of views on the subject, see Dominicus Tuschus, *Practicarum conclusionum*, lit. P, concl. 70.

64 Joannes Andreae, *Commentaria*, ad Sext. 5.12.2, no. 12.

65 For instance, *usucaptio* in Roman law required good faith only at the start of the period (Inst. 2.6).

66 See *gl. ord.* ad X 2.26.20 s.v. *quam civilis:* "quod nulla valeat praescriptio tam canonica quam civilis."

67 *Commentaria*, ad X 2.26.20, no. 2 : "Opp. quod papa non possit se intromittere de rebus laicorum cum sit iudex incompetens in causis eorum."

68 These arguments can be found in the *gl. ord.* ad X 2.26.20 s.v. *tam canonica.*

69 This argument is made by Bartolus de Saxoferrato, *Commentaria*, ad Dig. 41.3.4.26, no. 2: "Sed ego prescribo per tuam negligentiam, vel potius tu perdis quam ego praescribam."

70 See, e.g., A. M. Stickler, "Sacerdozio e regno nelle nuove ricerche attorno di secoli XII e XIII nei decretisti e decretalisti," in *Miscellanea historiae pontificiae* 18 (1954): 479–505. Hierocratic claims were, of course, also made by some canonists in favor of the rights of the papacy and the church: as that all jurisdiction had been placed into the papal hands and that princes exercised it only as his agents. See generally Michael Wilks, *The Problem of Sovereignty in the Later Middle Ages* (Cambridge, England, 1963).

71 E.g., Innocent IV, *Apparatus*, ad X 2.26.20: "Sed quid ad Papam de praescriptione inter laicos? Respondeo ratione peccati hoc statuit."

72 *Commentaria*, ad id., no. 3: "Nota ad Papam spectare ut casset omnes leges constitutiones statuta et consuetudines peccatum nutrientes."

73 See Eduard Eichmann, *Der recursus ab abusu nach deutschem Recht* (Breslau, 1903), 14–15; Jorg Müller-Volbert, *Die geistlichen Gerichte in den Braunschweig-Wolfenbüttelschen Landen* (Göttingen, 1973), 86.

74 *Commentaria*, ad Sext. 2.12.2.

75 Id., no. 19: "et concordat aequitati iuris naturae."

76 Id., no. 15: "quia bonum publicum maxime impeditur per lites quae non facile terminantur, et ideo illud legale ius quod imponit finem litibus talibus maxime congruit bono publico ac per consequens maxime concordat iuri naturali."

77 Id., no. 20: "Nam suus finis principalis est ordinare in Deum et in legem Evangelicam ut homo gloriam assequatur." And see more generally, with a host of examples, Pio Fedele, *Lo spirito del diritto canonico* (Padua, 1961), 812–993.

78 The reference is to Matt. 5:33 and 5:28.

79 See Baldus de Ubaldis, *Commentaria*, ad X 2.26.20, no. 6: "Quaero numquid haec decretalis servetur in foro seculari? Dicit Bernardus quod non et verum est quod de facto non servatur." See also Bartolus de Saxoferrato, *Commentaria*, ad Cod. 7.31.1, no. 2: "Item nota quod mala fides superveniens non interrumpit praescriptionem; secus de iure canonico."

80 Alexander Tartagnus, *Consiliorum*, vol. 4, cons. 99, no. 5: "Sed premissis non obstantibus contrarium puto de iure verius, quia de iure communi prescriptio etiam longissimi temporis xxx vel xl annorum hodie procedere non potest ubi prescribens est in mala fide." The authorities are collected in Dominicus Tuschus, *Practicarum conclusionum*, lit. P, concl. 71; see esp. nos. 27, 30–32.

81 Ludovicus Pontanus, *Consilia*, concl. 330, no. 71: "in hac materia ius cononicum corrigit ius civile quia agitur de peccato."

Chapter 8: The Christian Sacraments

1 Commonly expressed by saying that it was the door (*janua*) to the others; e.g., Bonifacius de Vitalinis, *Commentaria in Clementinas constitutiones* (Venice, 1574), tit. *De baptismo*, rubr. no. 3. For some of the possible implications of the subject, see Jean Gaudemet, "*Baptismus, ianua sacramentorum* (CJC, c. 849): Baptême et droits de l'homme," in his *La doctrine canonique médiévale* (Aldershot, England, 1994), no. 15.

2 *Summa super titulis decretalium* III, tit. *De baptismo*, no. 1: "Baptismus est exterior hominis ablutio cum certa forma verborum." The general acceptability of the definition did not prevent discussion of variant possibilities; see, e.g., Petrus de Ancharano, *Commentaria*, ad X 3.42.rubr. no. 1.

3 *Sententiarum libri quatuor*, lib. 4, dist. 3, c. 1: "ablutio corporis exterior, facta sub forma verborum prescripta." *PL*, vol. 192, col. 843.

4 E.g., Hostiensis, *Summa aurea* III, tit. *De baptismo et eius effectu*, no. 1.

5 E.g., Nicolaus Plovius, *Tractatus sacerdotalis de sacramentis*, pt. 1 c. 1, repeating this definition almost word for word. So in Martino Bonacina, *Tractatus de sacramentis*, disp. 2, quaest. 2, punct. 1, no. 11.

6 See, e.g., Hughes Oliphant Old, *The Shaping of the Reformed Baptismal Rite in the Sixteenth Century* (Grand Rapids, Mich., 1992), and G. W. Bromiley, *Baptism and the Anglican Reformers* (London, 1953), 133–47.

7 Hence the quite exceptional efforts commonly taken to detect enough signs of life in the infant to baptize him or her; see Jean Delumeau, *Le péché et la peur: La culpabilisation en Occident* (Paris, 1983), 303–14.

8 E.g., X 3.42.3 § 3. For a history of the theologians' treatment of the subject of the fate of unbaptized infants, see George J. Dyer, *Limbo: Unsettled Questions* (New York, 1964), 9–60.

9 De cons. Dist. 4 c. 3, and *gl. ord.* ad X 3.42.3 s.v. *carentia visionis*. Dyer's excellent book seems to me slightly to understate the predominance of the harsher Augustinian view of this subject during the thirteenth century, at least among the canonists.

10 Again St. Augustine; see De cons. Dist. 4 c. 34.

11 It also showed how infants might be saved even without faith. Two things were generally necessary: faith and baptism. Since the thief had been saved by only the former, so might infants, incapable of faith because of their years, be saved by only the latter. See De cons. Dist. 4 c. 34.

12 Jules Corblet, *Histoire dogmatique, liturgique et archéologique du sacrement de baptême* (Paris, 1881), 1:167.

13 For example, about the origin of the sacrament, Geoffrey of Trani proposed three different opinions. See *Summa super titulis decretalium* III, tit. *De baptismo*, no. 2.

14 Perhaps the best example is the *gl. ord.* ad Clem. 1.1.1 § 3, s.v. *hec est tertia pars* and s.v. *opiniones.*

15 E.g., Panormitanus, *Commentaria,* ad X 3.43.1, no. 3: "Dicit tamen Hostiensis tutum esse ut in verbis vel in factis observetur consuetudo loci."

16 So the custom of the church of Salamanca in Spain (1410); see Salamanca 8, "Liber synodalis de 1410," c. 16, in *Synodicon Hispanum,* ed. Antonio García y García (Madrid, 1987), 4:87–88.

17 See, e.g., Hermann Spital, *Der Taufritus in den deutschen Ritualien* (Münster, 1968).

18 E.g., X 5.9.1–6 (*De apostatis et reiterantibus baptisma*).

19 See, e.g., Hostiensis, *Lectura,* ad X 1.1.1, no. 15, for a discussion. See also Gabriel le Bras, "Théologie de droit romain dans l'oeuvre d'Henri de Suse," in *Études historique à la mémoire de Noël Didier* (Paris, 1960), 195–204; Jean Gaudemet, "Théologie et droit canonique: Les leçons de l'histoire," *Revue de droit canonique* 39 (1989): 9–12; and from a theologian's perspective, G. H. M. Posthumus Meyjes, "Exponents of Sovereignty: Canonists As Seen by Theologians in the Late Middle Ages," in *The Church and Sovereignty, c. 590–1918,* ed. Diana Wood (Oxford, 1981), 299–312.

20 See Carlos M. Corral Salvador, "Incorporación a la iglesia por el bautismo y sus consequencias jurídicas," *Revista española de derecho canónico* 19 (1964): 817–54; Donald Kelley, *The Human Measure* (Cambridge, Mass., 1990), 118–20. See also the thoughtful treatment in Gaudemet, "*Baptismus, ianua sacramentorum,*" and the insights, including the subject's importance for inheritance questions, in A. Lefebvre-Teillard, "*Infans conceptus:* Existence physique et existence juridique," *RHD* 72 (1994): 499–525.

21 Other examples: spiritual kinship arising from baptism that would be an impediment to subsequent marriage; the validity of holy orders, being dependent upon the cleric's prior baptism; the *irregularitas* incurred by any cleric guilty of rebaptism; the legality of burial in consecrated ground.

22 See, e.g., Caesar Carena, *Tractatus de officio sanctissimae inquisitionis,* pt. 1 § 6, no. 32, giving such a disputed case.

23 See Mattheus de Afflictis, *Decisiones,* no. 151. See also Aviad M. Kleinberg, "A Thirteenth-Century Struggle over Custody: The Case of Cath-

erine of Parc-aux-Dames," *BMCL* 20 (1990): 51–67; Kristine T. Utter-back, "*Conversi* Revert: Voluntary and Forced Return to Judaism in the Early Fourteenth Century," *Church History* 64 (1995): 16–28.

24 E.g., Peter Cramer, *Baptism and Change in the Early Middle Ages, c. 200–c. 1150* (Cambridge, England, 1993).

25 Hinschius, *Kirchenrecht*, 4:23–49.

26 This did not prevent discussion on the point; Henricus Bohic gave six reasons for the prohibition and discussed the merits of each. See his *Commentaria*, ad X 3.42.2, no. 6. He supposed, for example, that there could be no rebaptism because by baptism one became God's possession and that it would be contrary to the rules about acquisition of property found in Dig. 41.2.3.4 for the act to be repeated.

27 See *gl. ord.* ad De cons. Dist. 4 c. 13 for fuller statement.

28 *Gl. ord* ad id. c. 14 s.v. *Si quis.*

29 *Gl. ord.* ad id. c. 12: "hoc cap. intelligas de baptismo solemni." See gener-ally Walter J. Conway, *The Time and Place of Baptism* (Washington, D.C., 1954), 44–51.

30 Council of London (2), in F. M. Powicke and C. R. Cheney, eds., *Councils and Synods with Other Documents Relating to the English Church* (Ox-ford, 1964), pt. 2, 836.

31 De cons. Dist. 4 c. 17.

32 The process is traced in J. D. C. Fisher, *Christian Initiation: Baptism in the Medieval West* (London, 1965), 109–19.

33 For a useful and erudite look at one aspect, see Henry Ansgar Kelley, *The Devil at Baptism* (Ithaca, N.Y. 1985), esp. 112–18.

34 Inserted in Clem. 3.15.1.

35 *Gl. ord.* ad id. s.v. *presumant.*

36 The classic work on the latter, not without utility in understanding the former, is Louis Saltet, *Les réordinations: Études sur le sacrement de l'ordre* (Paris, 1907). There are also many parallels with the law relating to the consecration of churches; see Peter Landau, "Das Verbot der Wie-derholung einer Kirchweihe in der Geschichte des kanonischen Rechts," in *Studia in honorem eminentissimi Cardinalis Alphonsi M. Stickler*, ed. R. Castillo Lara (Rome, 1992), 225–40.

37 See J. Patout Burns, "Christ and the Holy Spirit in Augustine's Theology of Baptism," in *Augustine from Rhetor to Theologian*, ed. Joanne McWil-liam (Waterloo, Ont., 1992), 161–71.

38 Joannes Andreae, *Commentaria*, ad X 3.42.1, no. 3, gives this common example.

39 E.g., c. 19 of the Council of Nicaea (325), in the *Decretum:* C. 1 q. 1 c. 51.

40 See X 3.42.6.

41 John Gilchrist, "*Simoniaca Haeresis* and the Problem of Orders from Leo IX to Gratian," in *Proceedings of the Second International Congress of Medieval Canon Law*, ed. Stephan Kuttner and J. Joseph Ryan (Vatican City, 1965), 209–35.

42 X 4.20.6.

43 There was some discussion nonetheless about whether it was preferable to receive the sacrament at the hands of a more worthy minister and what advantages accrued to the recipient thereby. See Nicolaus Plovius, *Tractatus sacerdotalis de sacramentis*, pt. 1 c. 4, no. 2.

44 This is commonly known as the Ker-Frisbie doctrine, from its statement in two U.S. Supreme Court decisions, *Ker v. Illinois*, 119 U.S. 436 (1886) and *Frisbie v. Collins*, 342 U.S. 519 (1952).

45 See De cons. Dist. 4 c. 26 and *gl. ord.* ad id.

46 There was some contrary opinion, however. See DD. ad id.

47 Hostiensis, *Summa aurea* III, tit. *De baptismo*, no. 7 The person involved would presumably be saved by his belief and desire, however, because of the impossibility of securing baptism; Panormitanus, *Commentaria*, ad X 3.42.4, no. 1.

48 Antonius de Butrio, *Commentaria*, ad X 3.42.5, no. 3

49 A bewildering diversity of views on this subject is to be found in Joannes de Turrecremata, *Commentaria*, ad De cons. Dist. 4 c. 107, no. 3; he supposed a hard case in which there was an emergency and the only persons present happened to be someone without the power of speech and also someone with no arms.

50 *Gl. ord.* ad Clem 1.1.1 § 3 s.v. *confitendum*. See also the slightly confused account in Henricus Bohic, *Commentaria*, ad X 3.42.5, no. 14, drawing a distinction between the ordinary case in which each takes a part and the case in which each intends to do all.

51 Thomas Aquinas, *Summa theologica* 3a, quaest. 67, art. 6.

52 See the story of the furor caused by discussion of one such case in Antonius de Butrio, *Commentaria*, ad X 3.42.5, no. 4.

53 *Gl. ord.* ad De cons. Dist. 4 c. 26 s.v. *ebriosus*.

54 *Gl. ord.* ad De cons. Dist. 4 c. 31 s.v. *implorando*. There seems also to have been some authority the other way; see Joannes de Turrecremata, *Commentaria*, ad id., no. 9. See also C. 1 q. 1 c. 58 and commentary thereupon.

55 See Antonius de Butrio, *Commentaria*, ad X 3.42.1, no. 10.

56 E.g., Joannes de Turrecremata, *Commentaria*, ad De cons. Dist. 4 c. 1, no. 8: "Sacramentum baptismi est integrum cum defectu fidei."

57 The question, discussed by many canonists, was often raised by situations in which a child who died was baptized upon emerging from his mother's womb. See *gl. ord.* ad De cons. Dist. 4 c. 13 s.v. *trium millium;* Hostiensis, *Summa aurea* III, tit. *De baptismo*, no. 10; Panormitanus, *Commentaria*, ad X 3.42.4, no. 5; Martino Bonacina, *Tractatus de sacramentis*, disp. 2, quaest. 2, punct. 3, nos. 19–23.

58 See Nicolaus Plovius, *Tractatus sacerdotalis de sacramentis*, pt. 1c. 3, no. 5, for some discussion of this bizarre subject. Pope Pius V (d. 1621) authorized conditional baptism for monsters, however. There was actually a treatise written on the subject: Girolamo Fiorentini, *De hominibus dubiis sive abortivis baptizandis* (Augsburg, 1761). His discussion of the "monster case" is at disp. 2 § 6, no. 6.

59 *Summa theologica* 3a, quaest. 66, art. 3. It was held required in *Decisiones capellae Tholosanae*, quaest. 395.

60 Antonius de Butrio, *Commentaria*, ad X 3.42.5, no. 5 Other reasons were also possible—for example, Joannes Andreae, *Commentaria*, ad X 1.42.4, no. 4, where water was said to be suitable because it was the opposite of fire. Sin being equated with fire, water was suitable because it extinguished fire.

61 E.g., Thomas de Chobham, *Summa confessorum*, tit. *De confessario*, quaest. 3a, c. 2: "Providendum est sacerdotibus ut trinam faciant immersionem."

62 The question of the effect of drinking the baptismal water presented some problems, but the common assumption seems to have been that it would not be effective for baptism. See Panormitanus, *Commentaria*, ad X 3.42.*rubr.* at no. 1.

63 Hostiensis, *Lectura*, ad X 3.42.5, no. 5

64 The Bible records simply that that number was baptized; the canonists ascribed the action solely to St. Peter.

65 E.g., the requirement that the water be flowing, so that baptism in snow was ruled out. See Nicolaus Plovius, *Tractatus sacerdotalis de sacramentis*, pt. 1, c. 1.

66 *Commentaria*, ad id., no. 6: "Quid dices de . . . brodio, ubi sunt decoctae carnes?"

67 *Gl. ord.* ad De cons. Dist. 4 c. 34 s.v. *necessitatis;* Antonius de Butrio, *Commentaria*, ad X 3.42.5, no. 2.

68 Corblet, *Sacrement de baptême*, 1:220.

69 Joannes Andreae, *Commentaria*, ad X 3.42.1., no. 1, holding that it was not *de substantia*. See also *Summa Sylvestrina* s.v. *Baptismus* I, no. 3, ascribing it simply "de quarundam ecclesiarum more."

70 See Hostiensis, *Summa aurea* III, tit. *De baptismo*, no 7.

71 So stated as the *communis opinio* in Panormitanus, *Commentaria*, ad X 3.42.1, no. 5.

72 Antonius de Butrio, *Commentaria*, ad X 3.42.1, no. 4; Joannes Andreae, *Commentaria*, ad X 3.42.1. Panormitanus, *Commentaria*, ad id., no. 6, cited it as an example of a papal decree's not affecting those who had the opposite custom. This was apparently the custom among the Greeks.

73 See Joannes Andreae, *Commentaria*, ad X 3.42.4, no. 4; Petrus de Ancharano, *Commentaria*, ad X 3.42.1, no. 10; Dominicus Tuschus, *Practicarum conclusionum*, lit. B, concl. 24, no. 2.

74 See authorities cited in note 73 above.

75 Antonius de Butrio, *Commentaria*, ad X 3.42.1, n. 6.

76 See *gl. ord.* ad De cons. Dist. 4 c. 24 s.v. *Trinitatis*.

77 Innocent IV, *Apparatus*, ad X 3.42.2, no. 7.

78 See, e.g., Antonius de Butrio, *Commentaria*, ad X 3.42.1, making reference to Thomas Aquinas, *Summa theologica* 3a., quaest. 66, art. 6. The habit seems to have grown, if anything; see Martino Bonacina, *Tractatus de sacramentis*, disp. 2, quaest. 2, punct. 4, no. 7.

79 See *gl. ord.* ad De cons. Dist. 4 c. 83.

80 See *gl. ord.* ad id. c. 72 s.v. *evacuatur*.

81 See *gl. ord.* ad De cons. Dist. 4 c. 72 s.v. *evacuatur*.

82 So cited in *gl. ord.* ad id. s.v. *introducens*.

83 E.g., *Summa Sylvestrina* s.v. *Baptismus* I, no. 5, distinguishing between a mistake *ex industria* and one *ex ignorantia*.

84 *Gl. ord* ad De cons. Dist. 4 c. 82 s.v. *Trinitatis*: "Ego baptizo te in nomine genitoris et nati et sancti flaminis." The stated rule was that "sub nominibus synonymis bene potest fieri baptismus." For a fuller discussion, see Martino Bonacina, *Tractatus de sacramentis*, disp. 2, quaest. 2, punct. 4, no. 12, seemingly inclining to the negative view of most alterations.

85 See De cons. Dist. 4 c. 117. Even innocent rebaptism ordinarily barred the person from receiving holy orders.

86 Thus a child raised by Catholic parents in a Catholic country might be presumed to have been validly baptized (X 3.43.3), but the common rule recognized the uncertainty in other situations. It was that in doubt, no

person should be presumed baptized, according to Jacobus Menochius, *De presumptionibus*, lib. 6, praes. 14, no. 8.

87 *D.D.C.*, 2:129.

88 *PL*, vol. 79, col. 823.

89 Canon 28 (c. 745), in C. J. Hefele, *Histoire des conciles* (Paris, 1910), vol. 3, pt. 2, 932.

90 Compare the ninth-century capitulary, in *PL*, vol. 97, col. 850, whereby rebaptism *simpliciter* is ordered in case of doubt.

91 See also d.p. Dist. 68 c. 2, stating that in cases of doubt, rebaptism should be used. It would be only *ad cautelam salutis*, not a reiteration of the original baptism.

92 Corblet, *Sacrement de baptême*, 1:196.

93 Clem 3.15.1.

94 See Benedict XIV, *De synodo diocesano*, lib. 7, c. 6.

95 *D.D.C.*, 2:129.

96 Prosper Fagnanus, *Commentaria*, ad X 3.42.1. He disapproved of the practice, even while admitting its prevalence.

97 Sess. 7, c. 11, *De sacramentis*, in *Decrees*, 2:685.

98 See *New Catholic Encyclopedia* (1967), 2:66, acknowledging the ubiquity of the practice, "except when one is absolutely certain . . . that the baptism is not doubtful."

99 *Gl. ord.* ad X 3.42.3: "Qui crediderit et baptizatus fuerit, tota intelligitur de adultis, cum parvuli non possint credere, sed adulti."

100 See Hostiensis, *Summa aurea* III, tit. *De baptismo*, no. 9, telling the story of a Jew who came to him, telling him that he was in danger of death from his relatives, and was baptized under hurried circumstances.

101 Joannes Andreae, *Commentaria*, ad X 3.42.1, no. 3.

102 See also Dist. 27 c. 7; C. 1 q. 1 c. 35; *gl. ord.* ad X 3.42.3 s.v. *sed ficti.*

103 C. 26 q. 6 c. 7 and *gl. ord.* ad id.

104 Prosper Fagnanus, *Commentaria*, ad X 3.42.3, no. 66.

105 E.g., the mass thirteenth-century baptisms recounted in *The Chronicle of Henry of Livonia*, trans. James A. Brundage (Madison, 1961), 193–95.

106 See Sabine MacCormack, "Ubi Ecclesia? Perceptions of Medieval Europe in Spanish America," *Speculum* 69 (1994): 74–100.   .

107 E.g., Hostiensis, *Summa aurea* III, tit. *De baptismo*, no. 16: "Ratio quia character semel receptus amitti non potest quia quod factum est nequit non fieri." Balthasar Mongollon, *Tractatus de his quae vi metusve causa fiunt*, cap. 8, no. 2. The locus classicus for the result was C. 15 c. 1 q. 1.

108 E.g., Panormitanus, *Commentaria*, ad X 3.42.3 § Item quaeritur, no. 7: "Ratio, quia contra impressionem characteris, cum sit indelibilis, restitutio fieri non debet nec potest."

109 Reinhard Zimmermann, *The Law of Obligations* (Cape Town, 1990), 652–54.

110 See also the perceptive comments by MacCormack, "Ubi Ecclesia," 83–84.

111 Antonius de Butrio, *Commentaria*, ad X 3.42.3 § *Item queritur*, no. 3: "Nota quod repugnantia voluntatis in baptismi sacramento repellit characterem."

112 James C. Gurzynski, "How Variations in the Baptismal Formula Impact the Validity of Marriage," in *Roman Replies and CLSA Advisory Opinions* (Washington, D.C., 1992).

113 E.g., Panormitanus, *Commentaria*, ad X 3.42.1, no. 5: "Item non licet variare formam per ecclesiam traditam."

Chapter 9: Monastic Vows and Marriage Contracts

1 This is a principal theme, and is convincingly argued, in Eric Josef Carlson, *Marriage and the English Reformation* (Cambridge, Mass., 1994).

2 E.g., John T. Noonan Jr., "Power to Choose," *Viator* 4 (1973): 429; Charles Donahue Jr., "Canon Law on the Formation of Marriage and Social Practice in the Later Middle Ages," *Journal of Family History* (1983): 144–58; Michael M. Sheehan, "The European Family and Canon Law," *Continuity and Change* 6 (1991): 347–74.

3 See *gl. ord.* ad C. 20 q. 3 c. 4: "cum nullum bonum sit nisi voluntarium." See also Giles Constable, "Liberty and Free Choice in Monastic Thought and Life, Especially in the Eleventh and Twelfth Centuries," in *La notion de liberté au Moyen Age: Islam, Byzance, Occident*, ed. George Makdisi, D. Sourdel, and J. Sourdel-Thomine (Paris, 1985), 106–7.

4 This was fourteen for males, twelve for females, the same ages as one finds for the law of marriage. However, unlike marriage, it was held that no other factor could supply the defect ("malitia non supplet aetatem"). See *gl. ord.* ad Clem. 3.9.2 s.v. *aetate*. The Council of Trent raised the age to the end of the sixteenth year. See Sess. 25, c. 15, *De reg.* in *Decrees*, 2:781.

5 E.g., Petrus de Ancharano, *Commentaria*, ad X 1.40.1, no. 4: "Quinto nota quod examinatio voluntatis illius qui vult ad professionem recepi debet fieri in secreto per episcopum. In secreto enim magis libere quis exprimit voluntatem suam."

6 See Martinus de Azpilcueta, *De regularibus*, comm. 1, no. 7

7 D.p. C. 17 q. 1 c. 4. The canon is discussed in James A. Brundage, *Canon Law and the Crusaders* (Madison, 1969), 40–43.

8 The following is worked out, with appropriate references, in Martinus de Azpilcueta, *De regularibus*, comm. 1, no. 7.

9 The text, commentary, and implications are discussed in the context of episcopal decisions to enter monastic life without papal authorization in Kenneth Pennington, *Pope and Bishops* (Philadelphia, 1984), 103–10.

10 The authenticity of this canon has long been a subject of dispute; see the authorities cited in Stephan Kuttner, "A Forgotten Definition of Justice," in *History of Ideas and Doctrines of Canon Law in the Middle Ages* (Aldershot, England, 1992), V, n. 44, and with informative commentary on its treatment in contemporary canonistic literature, Peter Landau, *Officium und libertas christiana* (Munich, 1991), 64–96.

11 *Gl. ord.* ad X 3.34.6: "Nota quod vovere est voluntarium, sed adimplere est necessarium."

12 Albert Joseph Riesner, *Apostates and Fugitives from Religious Institutes* (Washington, D.C., 1942), sketches the relevant canon law on this subject, including tracing it up to more modern times.

13 Martinus de Azpilcueta, *De regularibus*, comm. 3, nos. 50–52.

14 See, for example, a form in a fifteenth-century precedent book now kept in the Kent Archives Office, Maidstone, MS. DRb O 10, f. 56v: "Querela in causa reductionis sive revocationis monialis ad claustrum."

15 See Anthony FitzHerbert, *Novel natura brevium* (London, 1534), 233–34. F. Donald Logan is currently conducting an investigation of this neglected subject.

16 *Gl. ord.* ad X 5.9.4 s.v. *retroire.*

17 Sess. 25, c. 19, *De reg.*, in *Decrees*, 2:782: "Nemo etiam regularis, cuiuscumque facultatis vigore, transferatur ad laxiorem religionem."

18 Reg. 28, in *Rule of Saint Benedict*, ed. J. McCann (London, 1952), 78–79.

19 Martinus de Azpilcueta, *De regularibus*, comm. 2, no. 33, to the effect that the principal monastic vows still bound. See also Leonardus Lessius, *De iustitia et iure*, lib. 2, cap. 41, dub. 14, nu. 115; Thomas Sanchez, *Opus morale*, lib. 6, c. 9, n. 27.

20 *Gl. ord.* ad X 3.31.8 s.v. *triduum.* The gloss adopted a slightly forced reading of a decretal in order to avoid reaching the conclusion that the pope had dispensed in such a case: "Sed haec solutio non valet, quia contra votum continentiae non admittitur dispensatio . . . ut nec summus pontifex valeat dispensare."

21 See also *gl. ord.* ad id. s.v. *abdicatio proprietatis:* "Et ita habes hic quod papa in multis praeter articulos fidei dispensare non potest."

22 More satisfactory and complete law on this subject did not come into being until the seventeenth century. See Charles Gerard O'Leary, *Religious Dismissed after Perpetual Profession* (Washington, D.C., 1943), 11–22. For discussion and some medieval examples, see Herde, *Audientia*, 1:375–83.

23 See the discussion in Kenneth Pennington, *The Prince and the Law, 1200–1600* (Berkeley, 1993), 68–73.

24 This was provided in general form under Pope Urban VIII (1623–44). See ibid., 23; P. Bastien, "De evolutione historico-iuridica processus dimissionis," *Jus pontificum* 11(1931): 24–25; and Brundage, *Canon Law and the Crusaders*, 36.

25 See, e.g., Prosper Fagnanus, *Commentaria,* ad X 3.31.24, stretching over several large folios.

26 Id. ad n. 11: "[P]apa secundum plenitudinem suae potestatis possit de monacho efficere non monachum."

27 See, e.g., Panormitanus, *Commentaria,* ad X 3.34.1, no. 8.

28 See, e.g., Leonardus Lessius, *De iustitia et iure,* lib. 2, cap. 40, dub. 17, nos. 114–19. The story is succinctly and well worked out in James M. Lowry, *Dispensation from Private Vows* (Washington, D.C., 1946), 34–53.

29 See Cyril Piontek, *De indulto exclaustrationis necnon saecularizationis* (Washington, D.C., 1925), and a fascinating study, including many actual cases: Gerardo Pastor, *Analisis de contenido en los casos de abandono de la vida religiosa* (Rome, 1974).

30 Hostiensis, *Summa aurea* I, tit. *De his quae vi metusve causa,* no. 6.

31 *Gl. ord.* ad X 4.1.29.

32 X 1.40.6; X 4.7.2.

33 For this and other examples of impediments stemming from lack of consent, see A. Esmein, *Le mariage en droit canonique* (Paris, 1891), 1:302–35, and Joseph Sangmeister, *Force and Fear as Precluding Matrimonial Consent* (Washington, D.C., 1932).

34 Dig. 4.2.21.5: "quia quamvis si liberum esset noluissem, tamen coactus volui."

35 C. 15 q. 1 c. 1. The question was whether the sins of those who were forced to commit them were still sins.

36 *Gl. ord.* ad C. 33 q. 5 c. 2 s.v. *licentiam:* "Secus est hic et in matrimonio ubi exigitur voluntas directa vel spontanea."

37 Note that a marriage contracted below the age of seven was treated as a nullity. The text refers to marriages contracted between the age of seven and fourteen (twelve for girls).

38 See *Decisiones capellae Tholosanae*, quaest. 292; Joannes Petrus Surdus, *Decisiones*, dec. 30, nos. 28–30, including fuller citation of authorities on the point. It was possible to fasten a more limited restraint on marriage, as to time and person, however.

39 See Michael M. Sheehan, "Theory and Practice: Marriage of the Unfree and the Poor in Medieval Society," *Mediaeval Studies* 50 (1988): 457–87.

40 See, e.g., Dyan Elliott, *Spiritual Marriage: Sexual Abstinence in Medieval Wedlock* (Princeton, 1993). There were, however, difficulties and possibilities for the full realization of this position inherent in the law of proofs and presumptions, well described in Jochen Otto, *Zwang zur Ehe: Andreas Alciat (1492–1550) und die klandestine Ehe* (Frankfurt, 1987).

41 Philip Lyndon Reynolds, *Marriage in the Western Church: The Christianization of Marriage during the Patristic and Early Medieval Periods* (Leiden, 1994), 315–27.

42 See Charles Donahue Jr., "The Policy of Alexander the Third's Consent Theory of Marriage," *Proceedings of the Fourth International Congress of Medieval Canon Law*, ed. Stephan Kuttner (Vatican City, 1976), 251–81.

43 Noonan, "Power to Choose," 429.

44 They seem also not to have raised systematic objection to the use of money penalties imposed by secular authorities for marrying someone outside the geographical control of the authorities. This is a subject, however, that calls for more investigation than it has received so far.

45 See, e.g., Thomas Sanchez, *De sancto matrimonii sacramento*, lib. 2, disput. 2–4, with many references to work of his predecessors.

46 Hostiensis, *Summa aurea* V, tit. *De matrimoniis*, no. 20.

47 See Hostiensis, *Lectura*, ad X 4.9.1, no. 11, discussing the problem created when a lord sold a slave to a master from a distant region.

48 E.g., Beatrice Gottlieb, *The Family in the Western World from the Black Death to the Industrial Age* (New York, 1993), 105, describing Henry VIII's attempts to secure an annulment from his marriage with Catherine of Aragon at the papal court as "the time-honored way."

49 Michael M. Sheehan, "The Formation and Stability of Marriage in Fourteenth-Century England: Evidence of an Ely Register," *Mediaeval Studies* 33 (1971): 228–63; Anne Lefebvre-Teillard, *Les officialités à la veille du Concile de Trente* (Paris, 1973), 154–79; Rudolf Weigand, *Liebe*

und Ehe im Mittelalter (Goldbach, Germany, 1993), 230–34; Ralph Houl-brooke, *Church Courts and the People during the English Reformation, 1520–1570* (Oxford, 1979), 74–75; R. H. Helmholz, *Marriage Litigation in Medieval England* (Cambridge, England, 1974), 77–87.

50 Generalizations based upon the ecclesiastical court records raise prob-lems of their own; see, e.g., Robert C. Palmer, "Contexts of Marriage in Medieval England: Evidence from the King's Court circa 1300," *Specu-lum* 59 (1984): 42–67.

51 For some good examples, see Andrew Finch, "*Repulsa uxore sua*: Marital Difficulties and Separation in the Later Middle Ages," *Continuity and Change* 8 (1993): 11–38.

52 For the latter, see Thomas Sanchez, *De sancto matrimonii sacramento*, lib. 2, disp. 15: "In hac quaestione satis confuse loquuntur DD. et vix est qui explicet quid sentiat." Establishment of the dispensatory power seems in this instance to have been a case in which hesitation among the learned was overcome by curial practice; see John T. Noonan Jr., *Power to Dissolve* (Cambridge, Mass., 1972), 129–36.

53 The extent of the canonical practice during the twelfth century, together with a gentle suggestion of present-day possibilities, is explored in Ru-dolf Weigand, "Unauflösichkeit der Ehe und Eheauflösung durch Päpste im 12. Jahrhundert," in *Liebe und Ehe im Mittelalter* (Goldbach, Ger-many, 1993), 157–77.

54 See the instructive exposition of the sophisticated kind of consent re-quired to contract an indissoluble marriage in modern Catholic practice: Peter J. Riga, "The Catholic View of Marriage in the New Code of Canon Law of 1983 and the Nullity of Marriage in Canon 1095," *Journal of Law and Religion* 9 (1992): 515–44, or J. Gressier, "L'incapacité d'assumer les obligations essentielles du mariage," *Revue de droit canonique* 44 (1994): 1–55.

55 E.g., Luis Gutierrez Martin, *La incapacidad para contraer matrimonio* (Salamanca, 1987).

56 *Gl. ord.* ad C. 27 q. 1 c. 42 s.v. *laqueum*.

57 *Summa aurea* III, tit. *De voto et voti redemptione*, no. 5. On practice in Spain, see Federico R. Aznar Gil, *La institución matrimonial en la His-pania cristiana bajomedieval (1215–1563)* (Salamanca, 1989), 117–19.

58 Ex officio c. Twisill (York 1516), Borthwick Institute of Historical Re-search, York, Act book D/C. AB.2, f. 172v. It was alleged against Eleanor Twisill that she had contracted marriage after making a vow of perpetual

chastity before a bishop. She admitted the allegations and was assigned a public penance, but her marriage was not declared a nullity.

59 No title devoted to it appears, however, in the later canonical collections.

60 See *gl. ord.* ad X 3.32.4 s.v. *constitutioni:* "quia cum vir et uxor postquam copulatione coniugii una caro effecti sunt, non potest alter ad religionem transire altero in seculo remanente."

61 See James A. Brundage, "Implied Consent to Intercourse," in *Consent and Coercion to Sex and Marriage in Ancient and Medieval Societies,* ed. Angeliki Laiou (Washington, D.C., 1993), 245–56.

62 See also Hostiensis, *Lectura,* ad X 3.32.4, no. 3: "Nam sine te, qui es episcopus, non possunt talia expediri. . . . Et episcopus non debet tolerare quod fiat in aliquo loco suae diocesis contra iura."

63 Thomas Sanchez, *De sancto matrimonii sacramento,* lib. 7, disp. 32, no. 3. He suggested three possibilities raised in the literature and examined the advantages of each.

64 X 3.32.16, dealing with license given under duress; the canonists treated the case of no license at all as similar.

65 *De sancto matrimonii sacramento,* lib. 7, disp. 32, no. 15: "Potissima tandem difficultas discutienda superest, an sit praescripta senectutis aetas. . . . Neminem ex antiquioribus hoc discutientem reperi."

66 Id., nos. 15–17.

67 See Panormitanus, *Commentaria,* ad X 3.32.3, no. 4, stating that new vows were required, "nam votum fuit nullum respectu ingressus monasterii, cum tunc non haberet consensum habilem ad se obligandum."

68 Based upon 1 Cor. 7:3–4 See Elizabeth M. Makowski, "The Conjugal Debt and Medieval Canon Law," *Journal of Medieval History* 3 (1977): 99–114; Pietro Vaccari, "La tradizione canonica del 'Debitum' coniugale e la posizione di Graziano," *Studia Gratiana* 1(1953): 535–47; John W. Baldwin, "Consent and the Marital Debt: Five Discourses in Northern France around 1200," in Laiou, *Consent and Coercion,* 257–70.

69 That the marriage was binding, that it was not binding, and that it was binding but that the husband could not exact the matrimonial debt. See *gl. ord.* ad X 3.32.3 s.v. *non exigere;* Leonardus Lessius, *De iustitia et iure,* lib. 2, cap. 40, dub. 15, no. 19.

70 See *Law and Revolution* (Cambridge, Mass., 1983), 9.

71 See above, text at notes 32–35.

72 Dig. 44.5.1.5–6.

73 See esp. *gl. ord.* ad id. s.v. *metu solo:* "Argumentum quod mulier quae rem suam vendidit vel hypothecavit, si renuntiavit metu vel reverentia, quod possit revocare." For a later example in the case of a legacy, see Mattheus de Afflictis, *Decisiones*, dec. 69, no. 4: "Unde sicut actus rescinditur stante metu reverentiali, vel metu verberum vel stantibus minis [citing Bartolus ad id.] actio non datur."

74 See Thomas Sanchez, *De sancto matrimonii sacramento*, lib. 4, disp. 6, no. 4.

75 *Commentaria*, ad X 4.2.11, no. 2.

76 *Commentaria*, ad X 1.29.16, no. 6: "Modo vos habetis hic casum, in quo etiam non praecedit verberatio, vitiatur actus, puta quando est actus que requirit omnimodam libertatem." He distinguished this case from marriage.

77 DD. ad X 4.2.1.

78 See *gl. ord.* ad X 1.40.6 s.v. *metu* and DD. at id.

79 See Thomas Sanchez, *De sancto matrimonii sacramento*, lib. 4, disp. 6, no. 5, and authorities collected therein.

80 See the remarks by Christopher Brooke, *The Medieval Idea of Marriage* (Oxford, 1989), 129–30.

81 Pio Ciprotti, "Jurisprudentia S. R. Rotae de metu reverentiali ex parentum iussu," *Apollinaris* 14 (1941): 84–88. See also the early authorities cited in Balthasar Mongollon, *Tractatus de his quae vi metusve causa fiunt*, cap. 4 § 1.

82 See Roch Knopke, *Reverential Fear in Matrimonial Cases in Asiastic Countries: Rota Cases* (Washington, D.C., 1949), 71–84.

83 Alexander McCall Smith, "Is Anything Left of Parental Rights?" in *Family Rights* (Edinburgh, 1990), 4.

84 See the remarks by Constable, "Liberty and Free Choice," 100–105.

Chapter 10: Criminal Law of the Church

1 See the treatment and literature cited in Wilhelm Rees, *Die Strafgewalt der Kirche* (Berlin, 1993), 140–46.

2 Leonard W. Levy, *Treason against God: A History of the Offense of Blasphemy* (New York, 1981); the equation is old; see Jodocus Damhouder, *Praxis rerum criminalium*, ch. 61, nos. 8–9. Professor Levy's latest treatment of the subject is *Blasphemy: Verbal Offense against the Sacred from Moses to Salman Rushdie* (New York, 1993).

3 The Salman Rushdie affair and the successful prosecution brought by Mary Whitehouse in England against *Gay News* (*Whitehouse v. Lemon* [1979] A.C. 617, 1 All E.R. 898) furnish two modern examples. See generally David Lawton, *Blasphemy* (London, 1993).

4 Louis B. Schwartz, "Morals Offenses and the Model Penal Code," *Columbia Law Review* 63 (1963): 672–73.

5 E.g., Levy, *Treason against God;* Nicolas Walter, *Blasphemy Ancient and Modern* (London, 1990).

6 Ludovicus Montaltus, *De reprobatione sententiae Pilati* § Blasphemia, no. 10: "ergo cum solus Deus offendatur solus Deus sit ultor."

7 E.g., Jodocus Damhouder, *Praxis rerum criminalium*, ch. 61, no. 1: "Gravissimum et omnium criminum maximum est crimen laesae maiestatis divinae." See also the conclusion of Richard C. Trexler, *Synodal Law in Florence and Fiesole, 1306–1518* (Vatican City, 1971), 128: "the prince of impieties."

8 Nov. 77.1.

9 E.g., Bonifacius de Vitalinis, *Tractatus de maleficiis*, tit. *De poena blasphemantium*, no. 1; Joannes Bernardus Diaz de Luco, *Practica criminalis canonica*, c. 103 § *Blasphemia*.

10 See Nov. 77.1 and *gl.* s.v. *et civitates*.

11 Cosmas Guymier, gloss to *Pragmatica sanctio* [of Charles VII (1438)], (Paris, 1503), proem. f. 9v: "et Roberto Francorum regi filio Hugonis Capet oranti pro pace in civitate Aurelianensi crucifixus respondit quod non haberet pacem in regno suo donec blasphemiae crimina notoria extirpasset." The story is repeated in Francesco Ansaldi, *Tractatus de iurisdictione*, pt. 4, tit. 9., c. 2, nos. 36–37.

12 Siegfried Leutenbauer, *Das Delikt der Gotteslästerung in der bayerischen Gesetzsgebung* (Cologne, 1984), xi: "Lästern Bürger eines Landes Gott, so straft Gott dieses Land."

13 Cited in Gerd Tellenbach, *The Church in Western Europe from the Tenth to the Early Twelfth Century*, trans. Timothy Reuter (Cambridge, England, 1993), 98.

14 See, e.g., Wilfried Hartmann, *Die Synoden der Karolingerzeit im Frankenreich und in Italien* (Paderborn, Germany, 1989), 463.

15 For an example, see the long and hysterical discussion of the crime's heinousness and its prevalence in Joannes Bernardus Diaz de Luco, *Practica criminalis canonica*, c. 103.

16 See Dist. 9 c. 1; C. 11 q. 3 c. 98; C. 23 q. 4 c. 22; C. 23 q. 4 c. 39; C. 23 q. 4 c. 41.

17 Prosper Farinacius, *Variarum quaestionum*, lib. 1, quaest. 20, no. 67.

18 Didacus Covarruvias, *Relectio ex rubrica de pactis*, lib. 6 c. Quamvis pactum, pt. 1 § 7, no. 27: "cum sit maximum crimen legi equidem naturali, divinae et humanae contrarium."

19 Ludovicus Gilhausen, *Arboris iudiciariae criminalis*, cap. 2, tit. 1, no. 20; see also lib. 1, c. 22, nos. 1–2, with collection of similar descriptions from the pens of other jurists.

20 Nicholaus Boerius, *Decisiones Burdegalenses*, dec. 301, no. 9: "ob defectum religionis." See also Josephus Mascardus, *Conclusiones probationum*, lib. 1, concl. 194, no. 1, giving examples from history and from the Bible of blasphemers punished by death.

21 Prosper Farinacius, *Variarum quaestionum*, lib. 1, quaest. 20, no. 64: "[S]i omnes blasphemi decapitarentur pauci superessent qui possent blasphemare."

22 *Gl. ord.* ad X 5.26.2 s.v. *blasphemiam:* "ergo multo fortius isti puniendi sunt et gravius."

23 As, for example, by allowing any person to bring a complaint. See Hostiensis, *Lectura*, ad id., no. 2.

24 Franciscus Bordoni, *Casuum de blasphemia*, cas. 28.

25 See Orio Giacchi, "Precedenti canonistici del principio 'Nullum crimen sine proevia lege poenali,'" in *Studi in onore di Francesco Scaduto* (Florence, 1936), 433–49. See also Hans-Ludwig Schreiber, *Gesetz und Richter* (Frankfurt, 1976), 17–28.

26 See 41 A.L.R.3d 514 (1972). The argument is put in a modern canonical context in J. A. Coriden, Thomas Green, and D. D. Heintschel, *The Code of Canon Law: A Text and Commentary* (New York, 1985), 921: "The practical relevance of this canon is somewhat questionable because of its lack of precision."

27 See G. D. Nokes, *History of the Crime of Blasphemy* (London, 1928), 81. This also seems to have been the medieval practice at least in some places on the Continent; see Jacques Chiffoleau, *Les justices du pape: Delinquance et criminalité dans la region d'Avignon au XIV siècle* (Paris, 1984), 204–5.

28 See *gl. ord.* ad X 5.26.1 s.v. *a temeritate* and DD. ad id. At least two solutions were offered: to draw a distinction between the pope's person and the office of the Roman Church, and to say that the crime would have gone unpunished otherwise, since the pope had no superior on earth who could judge his case.

29 *Summa aurea* V, tit. *De maledicis*, no. 4: "nec mirum si socii Dei privilegium gaudent, quia etiam socii Imperatoris, ut notat supra eodem § 1."

30 Robert of Flamborough, *Liber poenitentialis*, 181: "quando scilicet homo obloquitur Deo vel sanctis ejus."

31 *Summa theologica* 2a2ae, quaest. 13, art. 1.

32 Kenneth Pennington, *The Prince and the Law, 1200–1600* (Berkeley, 1993), 54–55.

33 E.g., Lambeth Palace Library, London, MS. 562: "Blasphemia paparum et suorum," fol. a: ascribing the view to the canonists that "papa potest dispensare de omnibus preceptis veteris et novi testamenti" and concluding that this was one of the many such blasphemies found in their commentaries.

34 E.g., *Summa Roselle*, f. 27v: "Blasphemia secundum Ambrosium est vel cum Deo attribuitur quod ei non convenit vel cum ab eo removetur quod ei convenit."

35 Ranulf Higden, "Speculum curatorum," lib. 2, tit. *De blasphemia* (University of Illinois, Champaign, MS. 251 H 53s), 165, defining the crime as "quando mala dicuntur de deo vel sanctis" but also mentioning Ambrose's definition.

36 E.g., Nicholaus Eymericus, *Directorium inquisitorum*, pt. 3, quaest. 41, nos. 1–2.

37 *D.D.C.*, vol. 2, s.v. *blasphème*, cols. 914–15.

38 E.g., Sylvestro de Prierias, *Summa Sylvestrina* § Blasphemia, no. 3: Angelus Carlettus, *Summa angelica* s.v. *Blasphemia*.

39 Taken from *Variarum quaestionum*, lib. 1, quaest. 20. To the same effect is Jodocus Damhouder, *Praxis rerum criminalium*, c. 61, no. 11.

40 C. 22 q. 1 c. 10 and Nov. 77.1

41 *De arbitrariis iudicum quaestionibus*, lib. 2, cent. 4, cas. 375, no. 11.

42 *Conclusiones probationum*, lib. 1, concl. 195, no. 8.

43 They are fully discussed and illustrated in Franciscus Bordoni, *Casuum de blasphemia*, cas. 20, 21, and 22.

44 Thomas Grammaticus, *Decisiones novissimae*, dec. 50, the question being whether the words "al despetto de Dio te delibero ammazzare" were blasphemous, subjecting their speaker to punishment by having his tongue perforated.

45 Id., "non ergo omnis contumelia est blasphemia."

46 Luis Weckmann, *La herencia medieval de México* (Mexico City, 1984), 369: "pese a Dios, e no creo en Dios."

47 Lawrence M. Friedman, *Crime and Punishment in American History* (New York, 1993), 32–33.

48 See Levy's *Treason against God*.

49 See Bartolus de Saxoferrato, *Consilia*, lib. 2, cons. 31–33.

50 E.g., Prosper Farinacius, *Variarum quaestionum*, lib. 1, quaest. 20, no. 29, divided heretical blasphemy into that *cum fide* and that *sine fide*.

51 Franciscus Bordoni, *Casuum de blasphemia*, cas. 87: "Dio non ha fatto questo Matrimonio . . . est haereticalis, quia derogat divinae omnipotentiae. Deus enim omnium verum est conditor."

52 Id., cas. 55.

53 See Nicholaus Boerius, *Decisiones Burdegalenses*, dec. 301, nos. 5–6.

54 *Liber sententiarum receptarum*, s.v. *Blasphemia*, no. 1: "Omne convitium, contumelia, vel maledictum, prolatum in Deum vel sanctos, est blasphemia," citing Bartolus ad Dig. 47.10.15. See also Joannes Baptista Zilletus, *Criminalium consiliorum*, lib. 1, cons. 48; Sylvestro Prierias, *Summa Sylvestrina* s.v. *Blasphemia*, no. 2.

55 Angelus de Gambilionibus, *De maleficiis tractatus* § *Verba iniuriosa*, no. 13.

56 Franciscus Bordoni, *Casuum de blasphemia*, cas. 1, no. 5. See also Egidius Bossius, *Tractatus varii*, tit. *De inquisitione*, nos. 129–31.

57 See Jacobus Menochius, *De arbitrariis iudicum quaestionibus*, lib. 2, cent. 4, cas. 376.

58 See the full treatment in Mario Antonino Maceraten, *Variae practicabilium*, lib. 3, res. 13, no. 1: "Primo, quia absolutissimum est in iure, crimen blasphemiae esse mixti fori." See also Petrus Franciscus Tonduti, *Tractatus de praeventione iudiciali*, pt. 2, cap. 27, no. 12.

59 See, e.g., Siegfried Leutenbauer, *Das Delict der Gotteslästerung*, and Jean Delumeau, *Injures et blasphèmes* (Paris, 1989).

60 Elisabeth Belmas, "La montée des blasphèmes à l'âge moderne du moyen âge au XVIIe siècle," in Delumeau, *Injures et blasphèmes*, 13. See also Olivier Christin, "Sur la condamnation du blasphème (XVIe–XVIIe siècles)," *Revue d'histoire de l'Église de France* 80 (1994): 43–64.

61 See, e.g., Julius Clarus, *Liber sententiarum receptarum* V § *Haeresis*, no. 4; Petrus Franciscus Tonduti, *Tractatus de praeventione iudiciali*, pt. 2, c. 28, nos. 6–7.

62 Apparently the distinction was followed in practice; see Michèle Escamilla-Colin, *Crimes et châtiments dans l'Espagne inquisitoriale* (Paris, 1992), 2:217, and Thomas Calderinus, *Consilia*, tit. *De iudeis*, cons. 1.

63 Francesco Ansaldi, *Tractatus de iurisdictione*, pt. 4, tit. 9, c. 1.

64 E.g., Rafael Gibert, "Blasfemia en el antiguo derecho español," in Estudios en honor de Alamiro de Ávila Martel, *Anales de la Universidad de Chile*, 5th ser., 20 (1989), 131–46.

65 *Lectura*, ad X 5.26.2, nos. 2–4.

66 So suggested as one possibility by Abbas antiquus, *Lectura*, ad X 5.26.2.

67 *Lectura*, ad X 5.26.2, no. 9.

68 Petrus de Ancharano, *Commentaria*, ad X 5.26.2, no. 6: "Nota . . . quod poena spiritualis non tollit poenam temporalem et est speciale secundum Phil. in odium criminis." Said also to stand as the *communis opinio* in Panormitanus, *Commentaria*, ad X 5.26.2, no. 4. But cf. Franciscus Bordoni, *Casuum de blasphemia*, cas. 8, nos. 6–8, apparently inclining to the view that *praeventio* ought to control.

69 See Hinschius, *Kirchenrecht*, 5:699–701.

70 See Hostiensis, *Lectura*, ad X 5.26.2, no. 1.

71 Panormitanus, *Commentaria*, ad X 5.26.2, no. 8.

72 See, e.g., Prosper Farinacius, *Variarum quaestionum*, lib. 1, quaest. 20, no. 62.

73 Mario Antonino Maceraten, *Variae practicabilium*, lib. 3, res. 12, no. 5.

74 *Gl. ord.* ad X 2.6.5 § 8 s. v. *timeri.*

75 Hostiensis, *Lectura*, ad X 5.26.1, no. 2: "Sed contra quia quod ex temeritate sive iracundiae calore fit, veniam meretur."

76 See the discussion in Prosper Farinacius, *Variarum quaestionum*, lib. 1, quaest. 20, nos. 52–53.

77 Caesar Carena, *Tractatus de officio inquisitionis*, pt. 2, tit. *De blasphemis* § 6, no. 30, gives this example.

78 *Consilia* III, cons. 476.

79 See, e.g., the collected opinions in Joannes Bertachinus, *Repertorium*, tit. *Blasphemia*, or Caesar Carena, *Tractatus de officio inquisitionis*, pt. 2, tit. *De blasphemis* § 10, nos. 56–57. See also the modern treatment: Bernard Durand, *Arbitraire du juge et consuetudo delinquendi: La doctine pénale en Europe du XVIe au XVIIIe siècle* (Montpellier, 1993), 135–38.

80 Thomas Sanchez, *Opus morale in Praecepta Decalogi*, lib. 2, c. 32, no. 45; Didacus Covarruvias, *Relectio* c. quamvis pactus, pt. 1 § 7, no. 9 (in *Opera omnia* [Lyons, 1568], 1:376). See also the authorities collected in Josephus Mascardus, *Conclusiones probationum*, concl. 194, nos. 9–11, holding that the custom should excuse from temporal but not divine punishment.

81 See Stephan Kuttner, *Kanonistische Schuldlehre von Gratian bis auf die Dekretalen Gregors IX* (Vatican City, 1935), 85–124.

82 For examples from practice, see Michèle Escamilla-Colin, *Crimes et châtiments*, 2:222–23.

83 See, e.g., Panormitanus, *Commentaria*, ad X 5.26.2, no. 6.

84 *Liber sententiarum receptarum*, quaest. 60, no. 9: "Vidi ego plerosque imputatos pro variis delicitis, non potuisseut praetextu ebrietatis impunitos evadere, et in specie Christophorus de Prinis pro blasphemia fuit affectus uno ictu funis publice, 5 Septembris 1559."

85 See, e.g., Ludovicus Gilhausen, *Arboris iudiciariae criminalis*, cap. 2, tit. 1, no. 6: "Hinc vulgo dici solet: Quod ebrietas excusat culpam a tanto sed non a toto."

86 Petrus Joannes Ancharano, *Iuris quaestionum*, lib. 2, quaest. 13, no. 6, with reference to other treatments.

87 See, e.g., Franciscus Bordini, *Casuum de blasphemia*, cas. 62, nos. 33–34, for fuller discussion.

88 Francescus Merlino, *Controversiarum forensium juris communis et regni Neapolitanti* (Naples, 1720), c. 97, no. 5.

89 Balthasar-Conrad Zahn, *Tractatus de mendaciis*, lib. 1, cap. 22, no. 1: "Tam horribile foedum ac nefandum est hoc mendacium contumeliosum in divinam maiestatem, ut nullus aliud crimen ei aequiparari possit." See also Francesco Giuseppe de Angelis, *Tractatus de confessionibus*, lib. 2, quaest. 69, no. 7, for a typical description.

90 Joannes Guttierrez, *Practicarum quaestionum*, lib. 3, quaest. 4, nos. 18–19, citing also Petrus Rebuffus and Covarruvias. The result seems not to have been the rule earlier, and it was controverted; see Petrus Gambacurta, *De immunitate ecclesiarum . . . commentariorum* (Lyons, 1622), lib. 4, cap. 9.

91 Elisabeth Belmas, "La montée des blasphèmes," 22.

Chapter 11: Criminal Procedure

1 For the legal issues involved in the quarrel, see Richard Fraher, "The Becket Dispute and Two Decretist Traditions," *Journal of Medieval History* 4 (1978): 347–68; this article corrects in several particulars the account found in Charles Duggan's work on the subject (note 20 below).

2 Frederick Pollock and F. W. Maitland, *History of English Law*, 2d ed. rev. (Cambridge, England, 1968), 1:448.

3 "Jurisdiction with Respect to Crime," in Supplement, *American Journal of International Law* 29 (1935): 603.

4 *Commentaries on the Laws of England*, 4:335.

5 E.g., *Green v. United States*, 355 U.S. 184, 187–88 (1957); *Benton v. Maryland*, 395 U.S. 784, 796 (1969); *U.S. v. Halper*, 490 U.S. 435, 440 (1989).

6 See Martin L. Friedland, *Double Jeopardy* (Oxford, 1969), 5–15.

7 See Note, "Double Jeopardy and Dual Sovereigns," *Indiana Law Journal* 35 (1960): 446–47; Stefan Riesenfeld, "Law-Making and Legislative Precedent in American Legal History," *Minnesota Law Review* 33 (1949): 117; and Max Radin, *Handbook of Anglo-American Legal History* (1936): 228. See also Jay A. Sigler, *Double Jeopardy* (Ithaca, N.Y., 1969), 3, where the author remarks, "Speculation on this point is difficult to resolve since much of Western law derives from a common fund of shared judicial concepts."

8 See Coke's use of a maxim drawn from the *ius commune* in *Hudson v. Lee*, 4 Co. Rep. 43a (K.B. 1589), and a remark that might have come from the pages of a canonical commentary in *Eyre of Kent 6 & Edward II, A.D. 1313–1314*, Selden Society 24 (1910), 76.

9 The other obvious candidate is the Roman law. It is by no means obvious that one must choose one or the other, given the nature of the medieval *ius commune*. See text below accompanying notes 21–23.

10 The textual history is admirably worked out by Peter Landau, "Ursprünge und Entwicklung des Verbotes doppelter Strafverfolgung wegen desselben Verbrechens in der Geschichte des kanonischen Rechts," *ZRG*, kan. Abt. 56 (1970): 124–56.

11 *Lectura*, ad X 5.1.6, no. 2: "quia de delicto unius hominis saepius quaeri non debet."

12 *Speculum iudiciale* III:1, tit. De abolitione et purgatione §1, no. 6: "Porro de accusatis nota, quod non possunt ab aliquo de eodem crimine accusari, si alias fuerint absoluti." See also id. I:2, tit. *De accusatore*, no. 3.

13 Petrus de Ancharano, *Commentaria*, ad X 5.1.6, no. 2; Egidius Bossius, *Tractatus varii* § *De sententiis*, no. 64: "*multo magis*" if the defendant was condemened.

14 E.g., *Summa Sylvestrina*, tit. De accusatione et accusato, no. 7.

15 *Variarum quaestionum*, tit. *De inquisitione*, I, 1 q. 4: "Inquisitio formari non potest contra illum qui alias de eodem delicto de quo inquiritur fuit absolutus."

16 *Liber sententiarum receptarum*, lib. 5, quaest. 57, no 1: "Alia est etiam defensio, quam reus in iudicio criminali proponere potest, quod scilicet alias de eodem crimine absolutus fuerit, aut etiam condemnatus, nam eo casu non potest ulterius contra eum procedi."

17 The text of the Bible reads: "Non consurget duplex tribulatio," or "Tribulation shall not rise up the second time." It is cited by Francesco Bordoni, *Casuum de blasphemia*, cas. 58, no. 23.

18 Its citation drops out of common usage among the later canonists, probably because the most important canon stating it (Dist. 81 c. 12) was superseded by later legislation. See *Summa Parisiensis* 65.

19 See *Materials for the History of Thomas Becket* (Rolls Series 67), 2:28; 3:281; 4:39, 96, 202; D. Whitelock, M. Brett, and C. N. L. Brooke, eds. *Councils and Synods with Other Documents Relating to the English Church*, vol. 1, *A.D. 871–1204* (Oxford, 1981), 851.

20 See the manuscript references given by Charles Duggan, "The Becket Dispute and the Criminous Clerks," *Bulletin of the Institute of Historical Research* 35 (1962): 18 n. 3. For fuller discussion of the contemporary references, see Landau, "Ursprünge," 138–52.

21 E.g., Bartolus de Saxoferrato, *Commentaria*, ad Dig. 4.2.7.2, no. 4, discussing the relationship between *accusatio* and *inquisitio*, citing Innocent IV on the subject and reaching the same conclusion as the canonists.

22 Alec Barbey, *De l'application internationale de la règle Non bis in idem en matière répressive* (Paris, 1930); Markus Mayer, *Ne-bis-in-idem-Wirkung europäischer Strafentscheidungen* (Frankfurt, 1992); Sebastian Cording, *Der Strafklageverbrauch bei Dauer- und Organisationsdelikten* (Berlin, 1993).

23 Id., "sed una [actione] contenti esse debebimus." The person who recovered against the master was required by this provision, then, to make over his cause of action against the seaman to the master.

24 *Apparatus*, ad X 1.6.32, no. 9: "Nota quod sentencia lata in causa inquisitionis vel denunciationis vel exceptionis praeiudicat aliis volentibus agere de eodem. Hic idem videmus circa crimina et circa populares actiones."

25 *Lectura*, ad X 1.31.1, nos. 12–13: "Prima autem expositio displicet, quia nec iudicabit dominus bis in idipsum, nec de delicto unius saepius est quaerendum."

26 See Wayne R. LaFave and Jerold H. Israel, *Criminal Procedure* (St. Paul, Minn.,1984), § 24.1(c).

27 E.g., *gl. ord.* ad C. 17 q. 4 c. 13 s.v. *et carceri*.

28 Antonius de Butrio, *Commentaria*, ad X 5.1.6, no. 6: "quia per hoc delictum non est punitum, et sic non potest dici condemnatus, nec absolutus."

29 See LaFave and Israel, *Criminal Procedure*, § 24.1(b).

30 Panormitanus, *Commentaria*, ad X 5.1.6, no. 4; Petrus de Ancharano, *Commentaria*, ad id., "non proponit ad eundem effectum et non obstante absolutione super exceptione poterit iterum accusari."

31 See esp. *gl. ord.* ad id. s.v. *taliter.*

32 Robertus Maranta, *Speculum aureum*, pt. 4, tit. *De inquisitione*, no. 90: "alius graviter criminosus puniretur sola poena iniuriarum et sic delictum semper remaneret insufficienter punitum."

33 E.g., Alexandro Sperelli, *Decisiones*, dec. 134, no. 20; it would not be a sufficient reason for a second proceeding that the penalty in the first had been lesser than that in the second. See DD. ad Dig. 47.10.7.1.

34 Petrus de Ancharano, *Commentaria*, ad X 5.1.6, no. 7. This was itself subject to the limitation that the result in the first case had been decided *super facto* rather than *super iure.*

35 See Cod. 9.2.9 and *gl. ord.* ad id. s.v. *non potest:* Egidius Bossius, *Tractatus varii* § *Si adversus rem iudicatam*, nos. 10–12.

36 Panormitanus, *Commentaria*, ad X 5.1.6, nos. 7–8.

37 Innocent IV, *Apparatus*, ad X 1.6.32, no. 9: "Nota quod sentencia lata in causa inquisitionis vel denunciationis vel exceptionis praeiudicat aliis volentibus agere de eodem."

38 William Durantis, *Speculum iudiciale*, lib. 3, pt. 1, tit. *De abolitione et purgatione canonica* § 1, no. 6 "cum inquisitio accusationi succedat."

39 *Gl. ord.* ad X 5.1.6 s.v. *replicari.*

40 Antonius de Butrio, *Commentaria*, ad X 5.1.6, no. 4

41 Hostiensis, *Lectura*, ad X 5.1.6, no. 3: "Forte et in tertio quando, scilicet reus non absolvitur sed accusatori silentium imponitur, ut indigno."

42 Egidius Bossius, *Tractatus varii*, tit. *De sententiis*, no. 77; Angelus de Gambilionibus, *De maleficiis tractatus* § *Et ad querelam Titii*, no. 90; Cino da Pistoia, *Commentaria*, ad Cod. 9.31.1, no. 3.

43 Julius Clarus, *Liber sententiarum receptarum* V, quaest. 57, no. 3.

44 See Petrus de Ancharano, *Commentaria*, ad X 5.34.8, no. 3, for exposition of the positions that follow. See also *gl. ord.* ad C. 2 q. 5 c. 6 s.v. *proprium.*

45 William Durantis, *Speculum iudiciale*, lib. 3, pt. 1, tit. *De abolitione et purgatione canonica* § 1, nos. 9–11.

46 Antonius de Butrio, *Commentaria*, ad X 5.1.6, no. 4. See also the intricate analysis in Robertus Maranta, *Speculum aureum*, pt. 6, tit. *De inquisitione*, nos. 55–67.

47 *Gl. ord.* ad id. s.v. *replicari.*

48 See Hostiensis, *Lectura,* ad X 5.1.6, no. 4: "Hoc intelligitur quando in foro contentioso absolutio facta fuit nam penitentialis accusationem non impedit."

49 Francesco Giuseppe de Angelis, *Tractatus de confessionibus,* lib. 2, quaest. 69, no. 4. This was qualified, however, by the ability of the pope to remit public prosecution if he did so expressly.

50 See DD. ad X 1.38.5.

51 All cited in *gl. ord.* ad C. 6 q. 1 c. 6.

52 See Panormitanus, *Commentaria,* ad X 5.1.6, no. 3: "nam pro delicto imponitur penitentia in foro animae ut satisfaciat Deo et animae . . . Item punitur in foro contentioso, seu iudiciali, quia laesit rem publicam."

53 *Apparatus,* ad X 5.34.11, no. 4.

54 *Commentaria,* ad Sext. 5.9.5, no. 8.

55 *Liber sententiarum receptarum* V, quaest. 57, no. 10: "alias enim quis de facili habita absolutione a confessore posse evadere penam delictorum quod esset valde ridiculum."

56 *Gl. ord.* ad X 4.19.8 s.v. *poterit obiicere.* There is a longer discussion reaching the same conclusion in Angelus de Gambilionibus, *De maleficiis tractatus* § *Et ad querelam Titii,* no. 91.

57 Of course, he might subject himself to additional penance in the internal forum.

58 So phrased in Robertus Maranta, *Speculum aureum,* pt. 6, tit. *De inquisitione,* no. 88.

59 Manuel Gonzalez Tellez, *Commentaria perpetua,* ad X 5.1.6, no. 9: "satis controversum esse inter DD."

60 They were collected in Augustino Barbosa, *Collectanea,* ad Sext. 5.9.5 (c. *Felicis*), nos. 36–43.

61 E.g., Francesco Bordoni, *Casuum de blasphemia,* cas. 58, no. 4, "Intellige quando per unam sufficienter punitur . . . aliter potest quis pluribus poenis castigari." See also C. 17 q. 4 c. 13 and X 2.1.4, canons that also suggested the same result.

62 This seems to have been the justification used in at least one case from English practice: Ponder c. Somer (London 1490), London Guildhall MS. 9065, fols. 70–71. The allegation was that the defendant had alleged that the plaintiff's wife had given birth to a child fathered by a friar. For this she had been presented as a scold and common defamer by the homage of a secular court and subsequently punished. Here the suit went ahead, apparently on the theory that the child's marriage prospects had been affected by the words.

63 See Petrus Franciscus de Tonduti, *Tractatus de praeventione iudiciali,* pt. 2, cc. 27–29, for more exhaustive treatment of the rule that the first court to exercise jurisdiction in such "mixed cases" prevailed.

64 *Liber sententiarum receptarum* V, quaest. 57, no. 11: "Nam iurisdictio ecclesiastica et secularis sunt prorsus separatae et distinctae."

65 Antonius de Butrio, *Commentaria,* ad X 5.1.6, nos. 4–6; Felinus Sandeus, *Commentaria,* ad id., nos. 2–10.

66 From Justice Felix Frankfurter, in *Brock v. North Carolina,* 344 U.S. 424, 499 (1953).

67 From Justice Hugo Black, in *Bartkus v. Illinois,* 359 U.S. 121, 155 (1959).

68 See, e.g., Harlan A. Harrison, "Federalism and Double Jeopardy: A Study in the Frustration of Human Rights," *University of Miami Law Review* 17 (1963): 306.

69 See, e.g., the review article, with bibliography, Burns H. Weston, "Human Rights," *Human Rights Quarterly* 6 (1984): 257–83.

70 Walter Ullmann, Historical introduction to Henry Charles Lea, *The Inquisition of the Middle Ages* (New York, 1969), 37.

71 Ibid., 50.

72 Michel Villey, *La formation de la pensée juridique moderne* (Paris, 1968).

73 See Brian Tierney, "Villey, Ockham, and the Origin of Individual Rights," in *The Weightier Matters of the Law: Essays on Law and Religion,* ed. John Witte Jr. and Frank S. Alexander (Atlanta, 1988), 1–31; Charles J. Reid Jr., "The Canonistic Contribution to the Western Rights Tradition: An Historical Inquiry," *Boston College Law Review* 33 (1991): 37–92. See also Kenneth Pennington, *The Prince and the Law, 1200–1600* (Berkeley, 1993), 119–64.

74 See generally Mordecai Roshwald, "The Concept of Human Rights," *Philosophy and Phenomenological Research* 19 (1958–59): 354–79.

75 Knut Wolfgang Nörr, "Zur Frage des subjektiven Rechts in der mitelalterlichen Rechtswissenschaft," in *Festschrift für Hermann Lange,* ed. Dieter Medicus et al. (Stuttgart, 1992), 199: "Viele erkennen das subjektive Recht an, aber nur als Abbild des objektiven Rechts." See also Jean Gaudemet, "Il diritto canonico nella storia della cultura giuridica Europea," in *Scienza giuridica et diritto canonico: Atti dei seminari internazionali di diritto canonico,* ed. Rinaldo Bertolino (Turin, 1991) 9.

76 W. Onclin, "Considerationes de iurium subiectivorum in ecclesia fundamento ac natura," *Ephemeres iuris canonici* 8 (1952): 10–11: "Funda-

mentum iuris subiectivi seu titulus dictae relationis est norma iuris objectivi."

77 Max Kaser, "Zum 'Ius'-Begriff der Römer," *Acta juridica 1977* 2 (1979): 63.

78 Another is the rule that is the ancestor of the modern privilege against self-incrimination: *Nemo tenetur prodere se ipsum*. See my "Origins of the Privilege against Self-Incrimination: The role of the European *Ius commune*," *New York University Law Review* 65 (1990): 962–90.

79 It was asserted, and apparently allowed, for example, in a late medieval case from the diocese of Hereford in England: Ex officio c. Gore (1518), Hereford Record Office, Act book O/27, p. 30. It was asserted in a case involving prosecution for fathering two illegitimate children in Ex officio c. Brian (York 1542), Borthwick Institute of Historical Research, York, Chanc.AB.2, f. 261v.

80 *Benton v. Maryland*, 395 U.S. 784, 795.

81 E.g., Justice Scalia, dissenting in *Grady v. Corbin*, 495 U.S. 508, 529-37, (1990).

82 *Ullmann v. United States*, 350 U.S. 422, 438 (1956). He was quoting Justice Holmes, in *New York Trust Co. v. Eisner*, 256 U.S. 345, 349 (1921).

Chapter 12: The Papacy in the Canon Law

1 *Summa decretorum*, 421–22.

2 E.g., Charles Augustine, *A Commentary on the New Code of Canon Law*, 6th ed. (St. Louis, Mo., 1931), 1:152.

3 See Richard Spence, "A Twelfth-Century Treatise on the Writing of Privileges," *BMCL* 12 (1982): 51–63.

4 See, e.g., Hostiensis, *Lectura*, ad X 2.1.12.

5 Hostiensis, *Summa aurea* V, tit. *De privilegiis*, no. 1. See also Hinschius, *Kirchenrecht* III, 805–08.

6 See generally A. Van Hove, *De privilegiis—De dispensationibus* (Mechlin, Belgium, 1939), 6–10.

7 Hostiensis, *Summa aurea* V, tit. *De privilegiis*, no. 2.

8 See, e.g., Edward G. Roelker, *Principles of Privilege According to the Code of Canon Law* (Washington, D.C., 1926), 20–22.

9 See the text and *gl. ord.* ad d.p. C. 25 q. 1 c. 6.

10 E.g., Hostiensis, *Summa aurea* V, tit. *De privilegiis*, no. 5.

11 See Charles Lefebvre, in *D.D.C.*, vol. 7, s.v. *privilege*; James A. Brundage, *Medieval Canon Law and the Crusader* (Madison, 1969), 140: "slow to crystallize."

12 See generally Giles Constable, *Monastic Tithes from Their Origins to the Twelfth Century* (Cambridge, England, 1964), 270–320.

13 *Gl. ord.* ad C. 25 q. 1 c. 1, s.v. *oportere.*

14 See esp. *gl. ord.* ad C. 25 q. 2 c. 16 and d.p.

15 *Gl. ord.* ad C. 25 q. 2, c. 25 s.v. *hostilitatis.*

16 See Gerd Tellenbach, *The Church in Western Europe from the Tenth to the Early Twelfth Century*, trans. Timothy Reuter (Cambridge, England, 1993), 68–69.

17 See David Knowles, "The Growth of Monastic Exemption," *Downside Review* 50 (1932): 201–31.

18 See, e.g., A. J. Forey, *The Templars in the Corona de Aragón* (London, 1973), 167–68.

19 E.g., tithes (X 3.30.3); monastic houses (X 3.35.3); or excommunication (X 5.39.50).

20 Herde, *Audientia*, 1:407–25.

21 *Gl. ord.* ad X 5.33.21 s.v. *permanentibus.*

22 *Gl. ord.* ad id. s.v. *sed futuri.* See also Petrus de Ancharano, *Commentaria*, ad id., no. 3: "Nota quod simplex dispositio porrigitur ad futura."

23 *Gl. ord.* ad X 5.23.7 s.v. *ex inspectione.*

24 *Gl. ord.* ad X 5.23.26 s.v. *sola verba.*

25 See, e.g., *gl. ord.* ad X 5.23.30.

26 E.g., Dominicus Tuschus, *Practicarum conclusionum*, lit. P, concl. 752, about whether special mention in the second privilege was necessary to prevail over the first: His answer is yes, but no if "the mind" of the grantor meant for the second to prevail despite the lack of specific mention.

27 See, e.g., John A. F. Thomson, *Popes and Princes, 1417–1517* (London, 1980), 152, referring to the canonical treatment of the exercise of rights of *spiritualia* by the kings of Hungary and England.

28 See, e.g., Hostiensis, *Lectura*, ad X 2.1.12, nos. 4–7.

29 E.g., Petrus de Ancharano, *Commentaria*, ad X 5.33.21, no. 2: "Secundo nota quod verba ambigua privilegii debent interpretari per Papam."

30 See, e.g., Antonius de Butrio, *Commentaria*, ad X 2.1.12, no. 9, for these arguments.

31 Panormitanus, *Commentaria*, ad X 3.30.24, no. 4: "Papa tanquam generalis administrator et vicarius Dei potest hanc commoditatem in aliquibus remittere et dispensare."

32 See Petrus de Ancharano, *Commentaria*, ad X 3.30.24, no. 10: "Potest ergo quosdem eximere et decimas debitas uni ecclesiae alteri dare et de his disponere prout placet dummodo dictum ius in toto non tollat."

33 It was a maxim of the *ius commune* that "privilegia semper restringenda sunt." See, e.g., Joannes Petrus Surdus, *Decisiones*, dec. 274, no. 8, dealing with the soldier's privilege to pay no more than half expenses in litigation and giving that privilege a restrictive meaning.

34 Bells could have further significance, however; see Robertus Maranta, *Speculum aureum*, pt. 6, tit. *De citatione*, nos. 113–14.

35 *Gl. ord.* ad X 5.30.24 s.v. *patentibus*.

36 Id., s.v. *Non licet*.

37 See also *gl. ord.* ad Sext. 5.7.4 s.v. *oratoria*. The term was, however, susceptible of several meanings: e.g., William Lyndwood, *Provinciale* 233, s.v. *oratoriis*.

38 *Summa aurea* V, tit. *De privilegiis*, no. 9. For a fuller list of authorities in support, see Dominicus Tuschus, *Practicarum conclusionum*, lit. P, concl. 729.

39 On the complex law involving the construction of privileges, see Hinschius, *Kirchenrecht*, 3:815–17. For an example, see note 50 below. To the same effect as the text is the dispute described in James A. Brundage, "A Twelfth Century Oxford Disputation Concerning the Privileges of the Knights Hospitallers," *Mediaeval Studies* 24 (1962): 153–60.

40 See, e.g., Ludwig Engel, *Tractatus de privilegiis et juribus monasteriorum ex jure commune deductus* (Salzburg, 1712), prin. 1, nos. 1–2, for a collection of authorities.

41 See Sext. 5.7.5 and *gl. ord.* ad id.

42 *Summa aurea* V, tit. *De privilegiis*, no. 10: "Qualiter amittitur? Multis modis."

43 See generally Henricus Zoesius, *Commentarius in jus canonicum universum*, tit. *De privilegiis*, nos. 29–42; for modern commentary, see Jeremiah Kelliher, *Loss of Privileges* (Washington, D.C., 1964).

44 The canon allowed a thirty-year period, but it was held that this had been "corrected" by X 5.33.16 to a forty-year period.

45 *Gl. ord.* ad X 3.33.6 s.v. *tempore*: "res de facili ad suam naturam revertitur."

46 *Summa aurea* V, tit. *De privilegiis*, no. 12 at end.

47 *Gl. ord.* ad X 5.33.9 s.v. *protectione*.

48 Thus, a privilege granting parish churches to a monastic house "*in proprios usus*" was held not to make the churches exempt from episcopal jurisdiction (X 5.33.19); the grant of property "*pleno iure*" similarly left it subject to episcopal jurisdiction (X 5.33.21). See Panormitanus, *Commentaria*, ad X 5.33.19.

49 See X 5.33.31 and DD. ad id.

50 For example, the situation was different if the second privilege had no meaning whatsoever unless it derogated from the first. That is, if the only way it could convey any rights at all was to take away from some other person's privilege, then the principle that privileges must be read as having *some* effect controlled. See Panormitanus, *Commentaria*, ad X 5.33.31, no. 1.

51 See the discussion in Thomas Sanchez, *Consilia*, lib. 6, c. 9, dub. 8.

52 Dominicus Tuschus, *Practicarum conclusionum*, lit. P, concl. 752, no. 7.

53 Lib. 5, tit. *De privilegiis*, no. 3: "Quot sunt species privilegiorum."

54 E.g., between perpetual and *ad tempus* grants; given the ways in which privileges could be lost, none was truly perpetual, and a temporary privilege could amount to no more than a dispensation and be no privilege at all.

55 See, e.g., Frederick Pollock and F. W. Maitland, *History of English Law*, 2d ed. (Cambridge, England, 1968), 1:157–58.

56 See Sess. 24, c. 11, *De Ref.*, in *Decrees*, 2:765.

57 See note 1 above.

58 Tellenbach, *Church in Western Europe*, 68–69.

59 E.g., Joannes Petrus Surdus, *Decisiones*, dec. 174, no. 8: "Privilegia semper restringenda sunt"; dec. 323, no. 1: "Privilegia non sunt multiplicanda."

60 *Decisiones Rotae Romanae*, dec. antiquae, tit. *De privilegiis*, dec. 1, no. 1 (235), holding that "in privilegiis concessis a Papa, maxime in privilegiis exceptis, debet esse subscriptio Cardinalium aliquorum."

61 Sess. 6, c. 2, *De Ref.*, in *Decrees*, 2:682.

62 Sess. 7, c. 13, *De Ref.*, in *Decrees*, 2:689.

63 Sess. 23, c. 6, *De Ref.*, in *Decrees*, 2:747.

64 *In principis apostolorum*, printed in *Canons and Decrees of the Council of Trent*, ed. H. J. Schroeder (St. Louis, Mo.,1941), 543–45.

65 See Van Hove, *De privilegiis*, 12.

66 Petrus Rebuffus, *Praxis beneficiorum*, tit. *Differentiae inter privilegium, rescriptum, et mandatum*, nos. 3–38.

67 Remigius Maschat á San Erasmo, *Cursus juris canonici*, tit. *De privilegiis*, no. 2.

68 Id., no. 3.

69 Bartholomeus Bersano, *Tractatus de viduis earumque privilegiis* (Lyons, 1699); Franciscus M. Brancaccio, *De privilegiis cardinalium in eorum cappellis dissertatio* (n.p., 1671); Petrus Vanderanus, *De privilegiis cre-*

ditorum commentarius (Antwerp, 1560); Jacobus Fr. Ludovicus, *Observationes de privilegiis studiosorum* (Magdeburg, 1705); Everhard van Bronkhorst, *Brevis tractatus de privilegiis studiosorum tam professorum quam doctorum* (Lyons, 1621).

70 Seraphinus de Seraphinis, *De privilegiis juramentorum tractatus amplissimus.*

71 E.g., Paulus Squillante, *Tractatus de privilegiis clericorum*, listing thirty separate *privilegia clericorum* under the canon law.

Chapter 13: Cooperation and Coercion in the Courts of Church and State

1 The scholarly literature on this subject is enormous and a trifle disputatious. For a flavor and abundant reference to other works, see John A. Watt, *The Theory of Papal Monarchy in the Thirteenth Century* (New York, 1965); Paolo Prodi, *The Papal Prince: One Body and Two Souls: The Papal Monarchy in Early Modern Europe* (Cambridge, England, 1987), 59–78; Jürgen Miethke and Arnold Bühler, *Kaiser und Papst im Konflikt: Zum Verhältnis von Staat und Kirche im späten Mittelalter* (Düsseldorf, 1988). Probably the most accessible introductory treatment in English is Brian Tierney, *The Crisis of Church and State, 1050-1300* (Englewood Cliffs, N.J., 1964).

2 Thus, whereas in the Old Testament the two swords had been united, after the new dispensation ushered in by the coming of Christ, the emperor was set over terrestrial affairs, the pope over celestial affairs, "ne propter duplicem potestatem homo superbiens rursum ad inferna demergatur." See *gl. ord.* ad Dist. 10 c. 8.

3 Hostiensis, *Summa aurea* IV, tit. *Qui filii sint legitimi*, no. 9.

4 E.g., Dist. 96 cc. 10, 12.

5 E.g., *Bracton on the Laws and Customs of England*, ed. Geoge Woodbine, trans. Samuel E. Thorne (Cambridge, Mass., 1977), 4:298 (f. 417b); see also Joseph Strayer, *Medieval Statecraft and the Perspectives of History* (Princeton, 1971), 323–25.

6 See, e.g., G. Catalano, *Impero, regni e sacerdozio nel pensiero di Uguccio da Pisa* (Milan, 1959). The approach of Alphonse Stickler to these questions has influenced my understanding; e.g., "Concerning the Political Theories of the Medieval Canonists," *Traditio* 7 (1949–51): 450–63.

7 See *gl. ord* ad Dist. 96 c. 10 s.v. *excommunicavit:* "Nota principem posse excommunicari etiam a quovis episcopo."

8 A classic formulation, still worth reading on this subject, is Otto Gierke, *Political Theories of the Middle Age*, trans. F. W. Maitland (Cambridge, England, 1900), 9–21. For a recent treatment, see Kenneth Pennington, "Pope Innocent III's Views on Church and State: A Gloss to Per venerabilem," in his *Popes, Canonists, and Texts, 1150–1550* (Aldershot, England, 1993), no. 4.

9 The point is made by Jacobus Antonius Marta, *Tractatus de iurisdictione*, pt. 1, c. 49, tit: *De impartitione brachii secularis*, taking the hierocratic position that there was "nullam iurisdictionem que non habet originem dependentiam et confirmationem ab ecclesia et a summo pontifice."

10 E.g., C. 23 q. 1.

11 E.g., Matt. 8:8.

12 See C. 23 q. 4 c. 43, where these conclusions are drawn by St. Augustine.

13 Francesco Ansaldi, *Tractatus de iurisdictione*, pt. 2, tit. 11, c. 16, nos. 18–23: "Quis monoculus etiam non vidit quod contra leges et canones via latissima pravis hominibus deliquendi apireretur."

14 C. 23 q. 4 c. 47.

15 Panormitanus, *Commentaria*, ad X 1.31.7, nos. 9–10. For later statement of this as the dominant opinion, with variant opinions, see Jacobus Menochius, *De iurisdictione*, lib. 3, c. 22.

16 Gloss at C. 23 q. 5 c. 1 s.v. *quod autem*.

17 *Gl. ord.* ad id. s.v. *poenam pecuniariam*.

18 Id.

19 Id.

20 *Gl. ord.* ad C. 23 q. 5 c. 35: "quod ecclesia potest infligere poenam pecuniariam quando magis illa timetur." See also the textual authority for the principle at X 2.6.5 § 8.

21 Sess. 25, c. 3, *De ref.* in *Decrees*, 2:785–86.

22 See also *gl. ord.* ad X 5.16.2 s.v. *castigatus*, for the same tendency with corporal sanctions.

23 *Gl. ord.* ad X 1.31.1 s.v. *publicum convocent auxilium*.

24 X 1.31.1; X 1.31.14; X 5.26.2.

25 See also the discussion accompanying nn. 3–7.

26 Petrus Rebuffus, *Tractatus de decimis*, quaest. ult., no. 18: "Immo si non possunt compelli per censuram ecclesiasticam imploratur brachium seculare licet sanguinis effusio immineat."

27 Maurice Morel, *L'excommunication et le pouvoir civil en France du droit canonique classique au commencement du XVe siècle* (Paris, 1926), 5–12.

28 Cod. 1.4.8.

29 *Commentaria*, ad id.

30 See Raffaele Balbi, *La sentenza ingiusta nel Decretum di Graziano* (Naples, 1990).

31 Panormitanus, *Commentaria*, ad X 1.31.1, no. 12: "pura et nuda executio ad eum pertinet ad requisitionem iudicis ecclesiastici."

32 *Commentaria*, ad id., no. 10.

33 See Baldus de Ubaldis, *Commentaria*, ad id., nos. 15–16.

34 For a summary, see Hans Erich Feine, *Kirchliche Rechtsgeschichte: Die katholische Kirche*, 5th ed. (Cologne, 1972), 453–59.

35 *Rosarium decretorum*, ad C. 23 q. 5 c. 26, no. 4: "de secularibus potestatibus, quae non sunt subditae imo pares."

36 *Commentaria*, ad X 1.31.1, nos. 4, 6–7. Both sides of the argument are put.

37 See, for example, Oldradus da Ponte, *Consilia*, no. 93, dealing with the conflicting claims of conscience and feudal homage on the part of a Spanish judge.

38 *Gl. ord.* ad C. 11 q. 3 c. 93 s.v. *Si dominus:* "Dicitur hic quod si dominus praecipiat ea quae bona sunt, ei est obediendum; si vero mala praecipiat, Deo coeli potius quam terreno est obediendum."

39 *Commentaria*, ad X 1.31.1, no. 11.

40 As by distinguishing between the way in which the request came to the secular judge, the effect of an intermediate appeal, and the extent to which he could inquire into the legality of the process before the ecclesiastical court. See Panormitanus, *Commentaria*, ad id.

41 Almost the entire treatment is devoted to the question in the only express treatment of this subject to be included in the *Tractatus universi iuris* (Venice 1584 ed.): Martinus de Fano, *Tractatus de brachio seu auxilio implorando*, nos. 3–16, in *T.U.I.*, vol. 11:2, fols. 409–10.

42 For characteristic discussion, see Joannes Andreae, *Commentaria*, ad X 1.29.7. A possible solution, also suggested here, was that the judge delegate could implore the aid of the ordinary, who would in turn invoke the secular arm, so that by a "*via indirecta*" the same result would be achieved.

43 The question was slightly different from the related one of the circumstances in which criminal jurisdiction ordinarily the province of secular courts could devolve on an ecclesiastical court in the first instance, on which see *gl. ord.* ad X 2.2.10 s.v. *vacante imperio.*

44 Dist. 10 cc. 7–8; Dist. 96 c. 6.

45 The precise understanding of this aid might differ, however, in order to save the theoretical point that the spiritual outranked the secular; see Jacobus Menochius, *De iurisdictione*, lib. 3, c. 23: "et rursus iudex ipse ecclesiasticus prestabit auxilium hoc, non obediendo iudici saeculari sed patrocinando."

46 *Lectura*, ad X 1.31.1, no. 8.

47 E.g., Othmar Hageneder, *Die geistliche Gerichtsbarkeit in Ober- und Niederösterreich von den Anfängen biz zum Beginn des 15. Jahrhunderts* (Graz, 1967), 182; Fritz Michel, *Zur Geschichte der geistlichen Gerichtsbarkeit und Verwaltung der Trierer Erzbishöfe im Mittelalter* (Trier, 1953), 72.

48 See the celebrated refusal of St. Louis, king of France, to follow the canon law on the grounds that it would violate his duty to God. See J. de Joinville, *Histoire de Saint Louis* (Paris, 1868), 241–42. And see generally Jean-Pierre Royer, *L'Église et le Royaume de France au XIVe siècle* (Paris, 1969), 228–61, including references to other literature found therein.

49 See F. Donald Logan, *Excommunication and the Secular Arm in Medieval England* (Toronto, 1968), upon which I have drawn for much of what follows. Also useful, and presented within a wider scope, is W. R. Jones, "Relations of the Two Jurisdictions: Conflict and Cooperation in England during the Thirteenth and Fourteenth Centuries," in *Studies in Medieval and Renaissance History*, ed. Willam M. Bowsky (Lincoln, Nebr., 1970), 142–57.

50 Dr. Logan (preceding note, at 157) suggested that the system had disappeared as a matter of practical consequence by the end of the sixteenth century. The basis of his conclusion was the end of Chancery files of significations. I believe that this decline reflected a change in the handling of the writs, which were no longer kept in Chancery files but made returnable.

51 Robert E. Rodes Jr., *Law and Modernization in the Church of England: Charles II to the Welfare State* (Notre Dame, 1991), 300–301.

52 See, e.g., the example in Brian Woodcock, *Medieval Ecclesiastical Courts in the Diocese of Canterbury* (Oxford, 1952), 96.

53 *Lectura*, ad X 1.31.1, no. 10.

54 Id.

55 See Alexander Dordett, *Der geistliche Charakter der kirchlichen Gerichtsbarkeit* (Vienna, 1954), 55–68.

56 That the royal judges in Spain must stand ready to correct oppression at the hands of the ecclesiastical courts, Francisco Salgado de Somoza,

Tractatus de regia protestate vi oppressorum appellantium, pt. 1, cap. 2, no. 46.

57 See, e.g., Alexander Murray, *Excommunication and Conscience in the Middle Ages* (London, 1991), 8.

58 E.g., Hostiensis, *Lectura*, ad X 5.7.9, no. 7.

59 Cod. 1.5.5.

60 Hostiensis, *Lectura*, ad X 5.7.9, no. 7, citing Dig. 48.19.21.

61 Id., no. 8.

62 X 5.7.13.

63 Id.

64 *Gl. ord.* ad X 5.7.9 s.v. *Audiencia.*

65 X 5.7.13; Sext. 5.2.18.

66 2 Hen. IV, c. 15 (1400–1401); 2 Hen. V, st. 1, c. 7 (1414).

67 See, e.g., Peter Diehl, "*Ad abolendam* (X 5.7.9) and imperial legislation against heresy," *BMCL* 19 (1989): 1–11.

68 James Fitzjames Stephen, *History of the Criminal Law of England* (London, 1883), 2:445–51.

69 E.g., R. N. Swanson, *Church and Society in Late Medieval England* (London, 1989), 338–43. See also, in a European context, Albert C. Shannon, *The Medieval Inquisition* (Collegeville, Minn.,1991), 132–37.

70 E.g., Gonzalvo Suarez de Paz, *Praxis ecclesiastica et secularis* (Madrid, 1760), tom. 2, proem. no. 7, to the effect that there was always a summary *cognitio de justificatione* before the "secular arm" would enforce the ecclesiastical sentence.

Chapter 14: Canonical Sanctions

1 Panormitanus, *Commentaria*, ad X 5.39.pr. no. 3: "[E]xcommunicatio est censura a canone vel iudice ecclesiastico prolata privans legitima communione sacramentorum et quandoque hominum."

2 Elizabeth Vodola, *Excommunication in the Middle Ages* (Berkeley, 1986), 2. There is a considerable body of modern scholarship devoted to the subject. Besides that by Vodola, I have made use of Angel Marzoa Rodriguez, *La censura de excomunion* (Pamplona, 1985); Francis E. Hyland, *Excommunication: Its Nature, Historical Development, and Effects* (Washington, D.C., 1928); Alexander Murray, *Excommunication and Conscience in the Middle Ages* (London, 1991); Josephus Zeliauskas, *De excommunicatione vitiata apud glossatores (1140–1350)* (Zurich, 1967); Eugene Vernay, *Le "Liber de excommunicatione" de*

Cardinal Berenger Frédol précédé d'une introduction historique sur l'excommunication et l'interdit en droit canonique (Paris, 1912).

3 E.g., Walter Ullmann, *The Growth of Papal Government in the Middle Ages*, 2d ed. (London, 1962), 299–303, distinguishing excommunication of rulers from their deposition.

4 *Studies in Church History* (Philadelphia, 1883), 235.

5 "The Theory and Practice of Excommunication in Medieval England," *History* 42 (1957): 11.

6 See, e.g., the charter of King Ethelred (d. 1006) in *English Historical Documents, c. 500–1042*, ed. Dorothy Whitelock (London, 1955), no. 123: "May Almighty God and his holy Mother and Ever-Virgin Mary . . . despise him in this life and destroy him, despised, in the future, world without end."

7 See the discussion and examples in *Vitae Sanctorum Hiberniae*, ed. Charles Plummer (Oxford, 1910), 1:clxxiii–clxxiv.

8 Lester K. Little, *Benedictine Maledictions* (Ithaca, N.Y., 1993).

9 *Histoire du meurtre de Charles le bon, comte de Flandre (1127–28) par Galbert de Bruges*, ed. Henri Pirenne (Paris, 1891).

10 Id., no. 113: "Et mirum est quod sacerdos ita Deum incantare possit ut, velit nolit Deus, Willelmus a comitatu ejiciatur."

11 See *The Murder of Charles the Good by Galbert of Bruges*, trans. James Bruce Ross (New York, 1960), x n. 5.

12 See those collected in Gerald of Wales, *Gemma ecclesiastica*, c. 53, translated as *The Jewel of the Church*, ed. J. Hagen (Leiden, 1979), 121–23.

13 *Magna vita sancti Hugonis*, ed. Decima Douie and Hugh Farmer (London, 1962), 20–25.

14 Ibid., 31–32. See generally Karl J. Leyser, "The Angevin Kings and the Holy Man," in *Saint Hugh of Lincoln*, ed. Henry Mayr-Harting (Oxford, 1987), 19.

15 Vita S. Bernardi auctore Joannis Eremitae, lib. 11, c. 10, in *PL*, vol. 185:1, col. 546: "Fratres tui excommunicaverunt eam, et deinceps fructuum non fecit."

16 Vita S. Bernardi auctore Guillelmi s. Theoderici, c. 11, no. 55, in *PL*, 185:1, col. 256. For a clear treatment of St. Bernard's attitude toward the canon law, see James A. Brundage, "St. Bernard and the Jurists," in *The Second Crusade and the Cistercians*, ed. M. Gervers (1992), 25.

17 Id., "Nullo igitur occurente remedio, dixit sanctus, 'Excommunico eas' et mane omnes pariter mortuas invenerunt."

18 *PL*, 39, col. 1547.

19 See d.p. C. 11 q. 3 c. 24; Vodola, *Excommunication*, 10–11.

20 *The Letters and Charters of Gilbert Foliot*, ed. Adrian Morey and C. N. L. Brooke (Cambridge, England, 1967), no. 167: "Ordo iudiciorum novus hic est, hucusque legibus et canonibus, ut sperabamus, incognitus: damnare primum, et de culpa postremo cognoscere." See also a similar characterization of the archbishop's actions in *The Letters of Arnulf of Lisieux*, ed. Frank Barlow, Camden Society, 3d ser., 61 (1939), no. 54a.

21 Robert Bartlett, *Gerald of Wales, 1146–1223* (Oxford, 1982), 29.

22 *Gemma ecclesiastica*, c. 53 (*Jewel* 122.)

23 *Giraldi Cambrensis Opera*, Rolls Series, vol. 21:1 (Epistolae), 227–28: "antiquo, sed et antiquato more."

24 Bartholomeus Ugolinus, *De censuris ecclesiasticis*, tit. *De excommunicatione maiore*, c. 28 § 1, no. 1, with citations: "per verbum illud Maledico excommunicationem non ferri."

25 Timothy Reuter and Gabriel Silagi, *Wortkonkordanz zum Decretum Gratiani* (Munich, 1990), 2:1716–24.

26 Hostiensis, *Summa aurea* V, tit. *De sententia excommunicationis*, no. 2. For the divisions and effects, see Hinschius, *Kirchenrecht*, 5:493–504.

27 See Stephanus de Avila, *De censuris ecclesiasticis*, pt. 1, dub. 5.

28 *Gl. ord.* ad Extrav. Johannis XXII: 14.5, s.v. *excludere debet a regno*.

29 William Lyndwood, *Provinciale* 264 s.v. *reconciliationis*.

30 See C. 24 q. 3 c. 17.

31 On this subject generally, see Clarence Gallagher, *Canon Law and the Christian Community* (Rome, 1978), 154–62.

32 *Gl. ord.* ad Sext. 5.11.3, s.v. *monitionem canonicam*: "Hoc est regulare in excommunicatione hominis, ut semper procedat monitio."

33 See generally Sext. 5.11.1 and especially *gl. ord.* ad id.

34 See Panormitanus, *Commentaria*, ad X 5.39.48, nos. 2–10.

35 See F. Donald Logan, *Excommunication and the Secular Arm in Medieval England*, (Toronto, 1968), 116–20. See also the similar rule in Franciscus Herculanus, *De attentatis*, cap. 21, no. 6.

36 E.g., Innocent IV, *Apparatus*, ad 5.39.6: "cum excommunicatio non cadat nisi in contumacem." Antonius de Butrio, *Commentaria*, ad X 5.39.21, no. 9: "Et ratio, quia sententia excommunicationis non ligat nisi ex contemptu." Angelus Carlettus, *Summa Angelica* s.v. *excommunicatio*, lib. 1, no. 22: "Quare debet quis excommunicari? Respondeo quod solum pro peccato mortali cui est annexa contumacia."

37 Hostiensis, *Lectura*, ad X 5.40.23, no. 8: "quia nemo excommunicatur nisi pro mortali et qui aliter corrigi non potest."

38 The tension between purposes of the sanctions at the disposal of the church, between punishing and restorative aims, seems to me not to have been resolved in the classical canon law. Perhaps this was the wisest course. See, in a slightly different context, discussion in Joseph Christ, *Dispensation from Vindicative Penalties* (Washington, D.C., 1943), 2–13.

39 *Lectura*, ad X 5.39.40, no. 5: "Est enim excommunicatio medicina excommunicati non ius alicuius."

40 St. Antoninus, *Tractatus de excommunicatione*, C. 76, no. 1: "Causa finalis est ut excommunicatus delictum suum recognoscat et ad deum redeat."

41 Hostiensis, *Lectura*, ad X 5.40.23, nos. 10–11: "Caveat quod satisfaciat cum pervenerit ad pinguiorem fortunam . . . et si non potest aliam cautionem prestare, iuret."

42 Panormitanus put this point generally in *Commentaria*, ad X 5.39.59, no. 3: "sed excommunicatio non est proprie pena sed animae medicina . . . unde eo ipso quod excommunicatus vult satisfacere obtineat absolutionem."

43 E.g., Panormitanus, *Commentaria*, ad X 5.39.19, no. 3: "in articulo mortis ubi etiam incendiarius absolvi potest a sacerdote."

44 E.g., Innocent IV, *Apparatus*, ad X 2.20.54, no. 5: "Exommunicatio non est culpa sed est medicina vel poenitentia . . . et ideo ea cessante non debet aliqua infamia remanere."

45 *Commentaria*, ad Sext. 5.11.1, no. 1: "quod prelatus medicus qui videt hanc medicinam excommunicationis etiam iuste latae non proficere sed officere illam discrete tollere potest etiam durante contumacia ex quo videt illius saluti sic expedire." See also the comments of Bartolus de Saxoferrato, *Commentaria*, ad Dig. 48.1.2, no. 7: "illa poena non imponitur perpetuo sed ut a delicto desitat et emendetur quod facit." See also the comment on its use in a modern setting: R. C. Mortimer, *Western Canon Law* (London, 1953), 88–89.

46 This was put bluntly by Felinus Sandeus, *Commentaria*, ad X 1.29.1, no. 16: "quod non debet imponi sententia excommunicationis quoties non timetur."

47 E.g., id., ad X 5.1.24 § licet autem, nos. 51–52; Philippus Decius, *Repertorium aureum*, ad X 1.5.1, no. 29.

48 E.g., Panormitanus, *Commentaria*, ad X 5.39.28, n. 2: "Secundo nota quod quandoque ecclesia errat ligando non ligandum vel absolvendo non absolvendum hoc enim ideo procedit quia ecclesia non potest iudicare de occultis sicut ipse deus." See also William Durantus, *Speculum iudiciale*, lib. 2, tit. *De positionibus*, nos. 42–43, distinguishing excommunication incurred *latae sententiae* by violation of a canon from that imposed by judges on this basis. See also Laurent Mayali, "Entre idéal de justice et faiblesse humaine: Le juge prévaricateur en droit savant," in *Justice et justiciables: Mélanges Henri Vidal* (Montpellier, 1994), 91–103.

49 *Lectura*, ad X 1.31.8, no. 13: "quia posset esse medicus imperitus."

50 See d.p. C. 11 q. 3 c. 65. This is well described and discussed by using the writings of the canonists in Zeliauskas, *De excommunicatione*, 166–206.

51 D.p. C. 11 q. 3 c. 77.

52 *Commentaria*, ad X 1.29.36, no. 40.

53 See Murray, *Excommunication and Conscience*, 33–43.

54 For Hostiensis's treatment, see *Lectura*, ad X 5.39.40, nos. 3–4.

55 E.g., Panormitanus, *Commentaria*, ad X 5.39.44, no. 3: "Tertio nota quod contra legem conscientie non est obediendum superiori etiam pape." See also Hostiensis, *Summa Aurea* IV, tit. *De clandestina deponsatione*, no. 3.

56 See Bartholomeus Ugolinus, *De censuris ecclesiasticis*, tit. *De excom. maiore*, cap. 9 § 9.

57 Antonius de Butrio, *Commentaria*, ad X 1.31.5, no. 8: "Et potius ligat iniuste excommunicantem quam excommunicatum."

58 The *glossa ordinaria* found twelve exceptions; see gl. ord. ad Sext. 5.11.10 s.v. *ad cautelam*.

59 An example of the former would be omitting any notice or citation to the party; of the latter one would be omitting the triple monition called for in the texts.

60 Panormitanus, *Commentaria*, ad X 5.39.44, no. 5. "nisi ex precepto pape vehementer presumatur statum ecclesie perturbare vel aliqua mala futura quia tunc non est sibi obediendum."

61 Bartholomeus Ugolinus, *De censuris ecclesiasticis*, tit. *De excom. maiore*, cap. 15, proem. no. 4.

62 See also Panormitanus, *Commentaria*, ad X 5.39.8, and Angelus Carlettus, *Summa Angelica*, s.v. *excommunicatio* § VIII, no. 6: "Item licite possum participare cum excommunicato pro salute animae meae et pro

utilitate temporali puta querendo ab eo consilium cum alios peritos habere non possum."

63 See William Lyndwood, *Provinciale*, 78 s.v. *actu legitimo*; Innocent IV, *Apparatus*, ad X 2.14.8, no. 2.

64 Philippus Decius, *Repertorium aureum*, ad X 2.1.7, no. 6.

65 Hostiensis, *Lectura*, ad X 2.14.8, no. 11: "Hic autem generaliter dicimus quod contractus initi cum excommunicato non solum ignoranter sed etiam scienter et excommunicatione durante tenerent." See also Panormitanus, *Commentaria*, ad X 5.39.34, no. 8, noting the existence of contrary opinion and commenting, "Et communiter moderniores tenet oppositum dicentes contractum validum."

66 Felinus Sandeus, *Commentaria*, ad X 2.25.5, no. 16: "ut si debitor suus fugitivus est quia audiretur super eius captura."

67 See Panormitanus, *Commentaria*, ad X 2.27.24, nos. 9–10; Felinus Sandeus, *Commentaria*, ad id., no. 1, where the question is described as "vetus querela." See also the discussion in Bartolus de Saxoferrato, *Commentaria*, ad Dig. 28.1.4, no. 8, concluding, "in antiqua glossa non determinabat, hodie in novella determinat quod possit facere testamentum."

68 This is well described in Vodola, *Excommunication*, 67–69.

69 As, for example, by the author of this book; see *Canon Law and the Law of England* (London, 1987), 110.

70 Peter Huizing, "The Earliest Development of Excommunication *latae sententiae* by Gratian and the Earliest Decretists," *Studia Gratiana* 3 (1955): 319: "In a certain sense it was the restoration of the primitive penal discipline."

71 See notes 32–34 above.

72 Canon 15, in *Decrees*, 1:200. See generally Herde, *Audientia*, 1:296–311, and literature cited therein at 297 n. 1.

73 See *gl. ord.* ad C. 17 q. 4 c. 29 s.v. *si quis*, and *gl. ord.* ad X 5.39.6 s.v. *auctoritate vel mandato*.

74 See *gl. ord.* ad C. 17 q. 4 c. 29 s.v. *manus*.

75 Hostiensis, *Summa aurea* V, tit. *De sent. excom.*, n. 10.

76 X 5.39.29.

77 E.g., Antonius de Butrio, *Commentaria*, ad X 5.39.29, n. 10: "In talibus voluntas et intentio est multum attendenda."

78 Apart from the case of the cleric acting as a layman, I have found no suggestion of the restriction, found in later canon law, to attacks intended specifically to impugn the clerical status of the victim, that is, violence "against a cleric as a cleric."

480 Notes to Pages 386–391

79 E.g., Panormitanus, *Commentaria*, ad X 5.39.10, no. 4: "Quid si moderate quis percutiat clericum sibi servientem causa correctionis? Doctores dicunt talem non esse excommunicatum quia non potest in hoc notari violentia."

80 X 5.39.16.

81 *Summa aurea* V, tit. *De sent. excom.*, no. 4.

82 X 5.39.3.

83 Hostiensis, *Summa aurea* V, tit. *De sent. excom.*, no. 4: "Duodecimus, in his qui nobiles et magnae potentiae sunt." And see generally Panormitanus, *Commentaria*, ad X 5.39.32, nos. 9–11.

84 X 5.39.37; and see Antonius de Butrio, *Commentaria*, ad id., no. 8.

85 X 5.39.17.

86 E.g., Panormitanus, *Commentaria*, ad id., no. 3: "Et quae dicatur iniuria levis, mediocris et quae enormis recurrendum est ad arbitrium iudicis."

87 See "Constitutio secundum quosdam facta . . . per archiepiscopos abbates et priores et per assensum totius cleri Anglie anno domini mcclx ad declarationem decreti Si quis suadente, viz. que lesio censetur leuis et que atrox, et de modo absoluendi," found in British Library, London, Harl. MS. 3705, Lambeth Palace Library, London, MS. 778, Durham U.L. Cosin MS. Vv, and Cambridge, Peterhouse MS. 51 ii. I am grateful for the first of these references (and for much else) to the late Professor C. R. Cheney.

88 The rule, however, was that the offender was obliged to undertake the trip *impedimento cessante*. Sext 5.11.22.

89 *Gl. ord.* ad X 5.39.7, s.v. *satisfaciant*.

90 See, e.g., Panormitanus, *Commentaria*, ad X 5.39.9, no. 4: "unde actionem competentem clerico non potest ecclesia remittere, sed competentem sibi; sic ita econtra."

91 X 5.39.15 § 3.

92 See Lucius Ferraris, *Prompta bibliotheca canonica* (Rome, 1785), 354–58. See also St. Antoninus, *Tractatus de excommunicatione*, listing seventy-six separate classes.

93 Hyland, *Excommunication*, 41–47.

94 See Paul Adam, *La vie paroissiale en France au XIVe siècle* (Paris, 1964), 179–83.

95 See the discussion and sources cited in D. Catherine Brown, *Pastor and Laity in the Theology of Jean Gerson* (Cambridge, England, 1987), 274 n. 88; Louis B. Pascoe, *Jean Gerson: Principles of Church Reform* (Leiden, 1973), 56–58.

96 Quoted in Vital Chomel, "Notes sur l'activité disciplinaire des officialités du diocèse de Grenoble (1418–1449)," in *Études historiques à la mémoire de Noël Didier* (Paris, 1960), 57.

97 Sess. 25, c. 3, *De ref.*, in *Decrees*, 2:785–86.

98 See Wilhelm Rees, *Die Strafgewalt der Kirche* (Berlin, 1993), 147–50.

99 *D.D.C.*, vol. 5, col. 619.

100 See, e.g., *Korean Presbyterian Church of Seattle Normalization Committee v. Lee*, 880 P.2d 565 (Wash. Div. App. 1 1994).

101 Ecclesiastical Jurisdiction Measure 1963, no. 49.

102 *Moore's Introduction to English Canon Law*, ed. T. Briden and Brian Hanson, 3d ed. (London, 1992), 85.

Chapter 15: Conclusion

1 See S. F. C. Milsom, "Law and Fact in Legal Development," in *Studies in the History of the Common Law* (London, 1985), 187.

2 E.g., Pier Giovanni Caron, "Non asperis sed blandis verbis ad fidem sunt aliqui provocandi," in *I diritti fondamentali della persona umana e la libertà religiosa* (Rome, 1985), 397.

BIBLIOGRAPHY OF EARLY
LAW BOOKS CITED

Listed below are the works from the *ius commune* that are cited more than once in the notes to this book. They have been given in short form in the notes themselves; reference to this list is therefore necessary to discover the full title and edition being cited. As a general practice, I have given the names of authors in their Latin form, with the exception of most post-1600 authors and in those cases where another name has established itself in normal scholarly usage. In this, I have been guided in most cases by the bibliographical work of Dr. Douglas J. Osler. Several editions of many of the books listed below were published. Sometimes, in fact, the identical work was published at different times and places under slightly different titles. In this list the version found on the title page of the edition I have myself used is given.

Abbas antiquus (d. 1296). *Lectura sive Apparatus ad decretales Gregorii IX.* Venice, 1588.

Afflictis, Mattheus de (d. 1523). *Decisiones sacri consilii Neapolitani.* Venice, 1604.

Albericus de Rosate. See Rosate.

Alvarez de Velasco, Gabrielus (fl. c. 1660). *De privilegiis pauperum et miserabilium personarum.* Lyons, 1663.

Ancharano, Petrus de (d. 1416). *Commentaria in libros decretalium.* Bologna, 1580.

Ancharano, Petrus Joannes (fl. c. 1580). *Iuris quaestionum libri tres.* Venice, 1580.

Andreae, Joannes (d. 1348). *In quinque decretalium libros novella commentaria.* Venice, 1581. Reprint, Turin, 1963.

———. *In sextum decretalium librum novella commentaria.* Reprint, Turin, 1966.

Angelis, Francesco Giuseppe de (d. 1692). *Tractatus de confessionibus maleficiorum.* Venice, 1716.

Angelus Aretinus. See Gambilionibus.

Ansaldi, Francesco (fl. 17th C.). *Tractatus de iurisdictione*. Lyons, 1643.

Antoninus, St. (d. 1459). *Tractatus de excommunicatione, suspensionibus, interdictis, irregularitatibus et penis*. In *T.U.I.*, vol. 16.

Aquinas, Thomas (d. c. 1274). *Summa theologica*. In *Opera omnia*, vol. 3. Parma, 1853. Reprint, New York, 1948.

Archidiaconus. See Baysio, Guido de.

Aretinus. See Gambilionibus.

Avila, Stephanus de (d. 1601). *De censuris ecclesiasticis tractatus*. Lyons, 1608.

Azo [of Bologna] (d. c. 1230). *Summa Azonis*. Basel, 1563.

Azpilcueta, Martinus de (d. 1586). *Opera omnia* (Rome, 1590).

Balbus, Joannes Franciscus (fl. 16th C.). *Tractatus de praescriptionibus*. Cologne, 1573.

Baldus de Ubaldis (d. 1400). *In decetalium volumen commentaria*. Venice, 1595. Reprint, Turin, 1971.

———. *Opera omnia*. Venice, 1577.

Barbosa, Augustino (d. 1649). *Collectanea doctorum tam veterum quam recentiorum in ius pontificium universum*. Lyons, 1656.

———. *Iuris ecclesiastici universi libri tres*. Lyons, 1634.

———. *Pastoralis solicitudinis sive de officio et potestate episcopi*. Lyons, 1649.

Bartholomeus Bersano (d. 1707). *Tractatus de viduis earumque privilegiis*. Lyons, 1699.

Bartolus de Saxoferrato (d. 1357). *Opera omnia*. Venice, 1570–71.

Baysio, Guido de (d. 1313). *Rosarium decretorum*. Lyons, 1549.

Benedict XIV, Pope (d. 1758). *De synodo diocesana*. Ferrara, 1760.

Bernard of Pavia (d. 1213). *Summa decretalium*. Edited by E. A. T. Laspeyres. Ratisbon, 1860.

Bertachinus, Joannes (d. 1497). *Repertorium . . . iuris utriusque*. Venice, 1590.

———. *Tractatus de episcopis*. In *T.U.I.*, vol. 2.

Biaxio, Petrus de [or Baysio] (fl. 2d half 16th C.). *Directorium conficiendarum electionum*. In *T.U.I.*, vol. 14.

Boerius, Nicholaus (d. 1539). *Decisiones Burdegalenses*. Geneva, 1620.

Bohic, Henricus (d. c. 1350). *In quinque decretalium libros commentaria*. Venice, 1576.

Bonacina, Martino (d. 1631). *Tractatus de sacramentis*. Brescia, 1623.

Bordoni, Franciscus (d. 1671). *Casuum de blasphemia*. In *Opus posthumum*. Parma, 1703.

Bossius, Egidius (d. 1546). *Tractatus varii qui omnem fere criminalem materiam . . . complectentur.* Venice, 1581.

Butrio, Antonius de (d. 1408). *Commentaria in libros decretalium.* Venice, 1578. Reprint, Turin, 1967.

Calderinus, Thomas (d. c. 1395). *Consilia seu responsa.* Venice, 1582.

Capella Tholosana. See *Decisiones capellae Tholosanae.*

Carena, Caesar (fl. c. 1645). *Tractatus de officio sanctissimae inquisitionis et modo procedendi in causis fidei.* Bologna, 1668.

Carlettus, Angelus [or Angelus de Carletto] (d. 1494 or 1495). *Summa Angelica de casibus conscientialibus.* Venice, 1569.

Chobham. See Thomas of Chobham.

Cino da Pistoia (d. 1336). *In codicem et aliquos titulos primi Pandectorum commentaria.* Frankfurt, 1578. Reprint, Turin, 1964.

Clarus, Julius (d. 1575). *Liber sententiarum receptarum V § Practica criminalis.* Venice, 1595.

Clavasio, Angelus de. See Carlettus.

Communes opiniones sive receptae iuris utriusque sentenciae. Lyons, 1571. (Various authors.)

Corneus, Antonius. *Tractatus de absolutione forensi iuramenti promissorii sive observationis.* Rome, 1606.

Corpus iuris canonici cum glossis. Venice, 1615.

Corpus iuris civilis cum glossis. Venice, 1606.

Corrado, Pirro (d. 1666). *Praxis dispensationum apostolicarum pro utroque foro.* Cologne, 1697.

Covarruvias y Leyva, Didacus (d. 1577). *Opera omnia.* Frankfurt, 1573.

Damhouder, Jodocus (d. 1581). *Praxis rerum criminalium.* Antwerp, 1601. Reprint, Aalen, 1978.

Decisiones capellae Tholosanae. Venice, 1618.

Decisiones Rotae Romanae. See Rota Romana.

Decius, Philippus (d. 1535). *Repertorium aureum ad omnes lecturas super Decretalibus.* Lyons, 1564.

Del Bene, Thomas (d. 1675). *Tractatus de iuramento.* Lyons 1669.

Diaz de Luco, Joannes Bernardus (d. 1556). *Practica criminalis canonica.* Lyons, 1554.

Dominicus de Sancto Geminiano (d. a. 1436). *Lectura super sexto libro decretalium.* N.p., 1502.

Durantis [or Durandus], William (d. 1296). *Speculum iudiciale.* Basel, 1574. Reprint, Aalen, 1975.

Eymericus, Nicholaus (d. 1399). *Directorium inquisitorum.* Rome, 1585.

Fagnanus, Prosper (d. 1678). *Commentaria in quinque libros decretalium.* Besançon, 1740.

Farinacius, Prosper (d. 1618). *Variarum quaestionum et communium opinionum criminalium liber.* Venice, 1589–93.

Ferrarius, Joannes Petrus (fl. c. 1400). *Practica nova judicialis.* Lyons, 1556.

Gabrielius, Antonius (d. 1555). *Communes conclusiones . . . in septem libros distributae.* Venice, 1593.

Gail, Andreas (d. 1587). *Practicarum observationum . . . libri duo.* Turin, 1595.

Galesio, Dominico (d. 1679). *Tractatus de restitutionibus in integrum concedendis vel denegandis.* Cologne, 1689.

Gambilionibus, Angelus de (d. a. 1451). *De maleficiis tractatus.* Venice, 1584.

Geoffrey of Trani (d. 1245). *Summa super titulis decretalium.* Lyons, 1519. Reprint, Aalen, 1992.

Gibalin, Joseph de (d. 1671). *De irregularitatibus et impedimentis canonicis.* Lyons, 1652.

Gilhausen, Ludovicus (d. 1642). *Arboris iudiciariae criminalis liber.* Cologne, 1642.

Grammaticus, Thomas (d. 1556). *Decisiones novissimae.* Venice, 1547.

Gratianus, Stephanus (fl. early 17th C.). *Decisiones rotae provinciae Marchiae.* Rome, 1619.

Guido Papa. See Papa.

Guttierrez, Joannes (d. 1618). *Practicarum quaestionum civilium super prima parte legum novae collectionis regiae Hispaniae.* Lyons, 1661.

Hallier, Franciscus (d. 1659). *De sacris electionibus et ordinationibus.* Paris, 1636.

Henricus de Segusio. See Hostiensis.

Herculanus, Franciscus (d. 1569). *De attentatis appellatione pendente tractatus.* Cologne, 1649.

Hostiensis (d. 1271). *In decretalium libros Lectura.* Venice, 1581. Reprint, Turin, 1965.

———. *Summa aurea.* Venice, 1574. Reprint, Turin, 1963.

Imola, Joannes ab (d. 1436). *In libros decretalium commentaria.* Venice, 1575.

Innocent IV, Pope (d. 1254). *Apparatus in quinque libros decretalium.* Frankfurt, 1570. Reprint, 1968.

Lancellotus, Joannes Paulus (d. 1590). *Institutiones iuris canonici.* Venice, 1703.

Lessius, Leonardus (d. 1623). *De iustitia et iure.* Lyons, 1654.

Lyndwood, William (d. 1446). *Provinciale (seu Constitutiones Angliae.* Oxford, 1679.

Maceraten, Mario Antonino (fl. c. 1600). *Variae practicabilium rerum resolutiones in tres libros digestae.* Pavia, 1606.

Mandagoto, Gulielmus de (d. 1321). *Tractatus de electione novorum prelatorum.* Cologne, 1573.

Manz, Kaspar (d. 1677). *Tractatus de restitutione in integrum.* Ingolstadt, 1662.

Maranta, Robertus (d. 1540). *Speculum aureum et lumen advocatorum praxis civilis.* Venice, 1605.

Marta, Jacobus Antonius (d. 1629). *Tractatus de jurisdictione per et inter judicem ecclesiasticum et saecularem exercenda.* Avignon, 1679.

Mascardus, Josephus (d. 1588). *Conclusiones probationum omnium quae in utroque foro quotidie versantur.* Frankfurt, 1593.

Maschat, Remigius [á San Erasmo] (d. 1747). *Cursus juris canonici.* N.p., 1735.

Medices, Sebastianus (fl. 16th C.). *De fortuitis casibus.* In *T.U.I.,* vol. 7.

Menochius, Jacobus (d. 1607). *De arbitrariis iudicum quaestionibus et causis libri duo.* Venice, 1590.

――――. *De iurisdictione: Imperio et potestate ecclesiastica et saeculari libri tres.* Lyons, 1695.

――――. *De praesumptionibus, coniecturis, signis, et indiciis commentariorum.* Venice, 1587.

Monachus, Joannes (d. 1313). *Glossa aurea . . . super sexto decretalium libro.* Paris, 1535. Reprint, Aalen, 1968.

Mongollon, Balthasar. *Tractatus de his quae vi metusve causa fiunt.* Seville, 1623.

Montaltus, Ludovicus. *De reprobatione sententiae Pilati.* In *T.U.I.,* vol. 8.

Murner, Walter. *Die Pönitentiarie-Formularsammlung des Walter Murner von Strassburg.* Edited by Matthäus Meyer. Freiburg, 1979.

Mynsinger, Joachim (d. 1588). *Singularium observationum iudicii imperialis camerae.* Turin, 1595.

Navarrus. See Azpilcueta.

Novario, Joannes Maria (fl. 17th C.). *Praxis aurea privilegium miserabilium personarum.* Naples, 1623.

Oddi, Sforza (d. 1611). *De restitutionibus in integrum tractatus.* Venice, 1591.

Oldradus da Ponte (d. 1335). *Consilia, quaestiones et allegationes.* Lyons, 1550.

Panormitanus (d. 1445 or 1453). *Commentaria super decretalium libros.* Venice, 1615.

Papa, Guido (d. 1487). *In augustissimo senatu Gratianopolitano Decisiones.* Geneva, 1667.

Passerini, Petrus Maria (fl. 17th C.). *Tractatus de electione canonica.* Cologne, 1661.

Paucapalea. *Summa über das Decretum Gratiani.* Edited by J. F. von Schulte. Giessen, 1890.

Plovius [or de Plowe], Nicolaus (fl. 15th C.). *Tractatus de irregularitate.* Paris, 1514.

――――. *Tractatus sacerdotalis de sacramentis.* In *T.U.I.,* vol. 14.

Pontanus, Ludovicus (d. 1439). *Consilia sive responsa.* Venice, 1581.

Prierias, Sylvestro (d. 1523). *Summa Sylvestrina.* Venice, 1584.

Raymond, St., of Peñafort (d. 1275). *Summa de poenitentia et matrimonio.* Rome, 1603. Reprint, Turin, 1969.

Rebuffus, Petrus (d. 1557). *Praxis beneficiorum.* Venice, 1563.

――――. *Tractatus de decimis.* Lyons, 1566.

――――. *Tractatus de nominationibus.* In *T.U.I.,* vol. 15:2.

Reiffenstuel, Anacletus (d. 1703). *Jus canonicum universum.* Rome, 1831.

Robert of Flamborough (d. c. 1224). *Liber poenitentialis.* Edited by J. J. Francis Firth Toronto, 1971.

Romanus. See Pontanus.

Rosate, Albericus de (d. 1354). *Dictionarium iuris tam civilis quam canonici.* Venice, 1573. Reprint, Turin, 1971.

Rota Romana. *Rotae Romanae auditorum Decisiones novae, antiquae et antiquiores.* Venice, 1570.

Rufinus of Bologna (d. 1191). *Summa decretorum.* Edited by Heinrich Singer. Paderborn, 1902.

Salgado de Somoza, Francisco (d. 1664). *Tractatus de regia potestate vi oppressorum appellantium a causis et iudicibus ecclesiasticis.* Lyons, 1647.

Sanchez, Thomas (d. 1610.) *Consilia seu opuscula moralia.* Parma, 1723.

――――. *Disputationum de sancto matrimonii sacramento libri sex.* Lyons, 1739.

――――. *Opus morale in Praecepta Decalogi.* Parma, 1723.

Sancto Geminiano. See Dominicus de Sancto Geminiano.

Sandeus, Felinus (d. 1503). *Commentaria ad quinque libros Decretalium.* Venice, 1574.

Sayrus [Sayres], Gregorius (d. 1602). *Thesaurus casuum conscientiae continens praxim exactissimam.* Venice, 1627.

Scaccia, Sigismundo (fl. 17th C.). *De iudiciis causarum civilium, criminalium et haereticalium.* Venice, 1663.

Schmalzgrüber, Franciscus (d. 1735). *Jus ecclesiasticum universum.* Rome, 1843.

Selva, Joannes de [or de Selve] (d. 1529). *Tractatus perutilis de iureiurando.* In *T.U.I.*, vol. 4.

Seraphinus de Seraphinis (fl. 16th C.). *De privilegiis juramentorum tractatus amplissimus.* Frankfurt, 1652.

Socinus, Marianus (d. 1467). *Tractatus de oblationibus.* In *T.U.I.*, vol. 15.

Somercote, Laurence de (fl. 1250). *Tractatus seu summa de electionibus episcoporum.* Edited by A. von Wretschke. Weimar, 1907.

Speculator. See Durantis.

Sperelli, Alexandro (d. 1672). *Decisiones fori ecclesiastici.* Venice, 1651.

Squillante, Paulus (fl. c. 1630). *Tractatus de privilegiis clericorum.* Naples, 1635.

Stephen of Tournai (d. 1203). *Die summa über das Decretum Gratiani.* Edited by J. F. von Schulte. Giessen, 1891. Reprint, Aalen, 1965.

Suarez de Paz, Gonzalvo (d. 1590). *Praxis ecclesiastica et secularis.* Madrid, 1760.

Summa Angelica. See Carlettus.

Summa Parisiensis on the Decretum of Gratian. Edited by Terence P. McLaughlin. Toronto, 1952.

Summa Roselle. See Trovamala.

Summa Sylvestrina. See Prierias.

Surdus, Joannes Petrus (fl. c. 1600). *Decisiones sacri Mantuani senatus.* Venice, 1615.

Tartagnus Alexander (d. 1477). *Consiliorum Alexandri volumen primumseptimum.* Venice, 1569.

Tellez, Manuel Gonzalez (d. 1649). *Commentaria perpetua in singulos textus quinque librorum Decretalium.* Lyons, 1715.

Thomas of Chobham (d. a. 1236). *Summa confessorum.* Edited by R. Broomfield. Louvain, 1968.

Tonduti, Petrus Franciscus de (fl. 17th C.). *Tractatus de praeventione iudiciali sue de contentione iurisdictionum.* Lyons, 1673.

Torquemada. See Turrecremata.

Tractatus universi iuris. Venice, 1549.

Trovamala, Baptista [de Salis] (d. a. 1494). *Summa Roselle.* Venice, 1516.

Tudeschis, Nicholaus de. See Panormitanus.

Turrecremata, Joannes de (d. 1468). *Super toto decreto commentaria.* Lyons, 1516.

Tuschus, Dominicus (d. 1620). *Practicarum conclusionum iuris in omni foro frequentiorum.* Rome, 1605–70.

Ubaldis, Baldus de. See Baldus.

Ugolinus, Bartholomeus (fl. c. 1600). *De censuris ecclesiasticis . . . tractatus.* Bologna, 1594.

———. *Tractatus de irregularitatibus.* Venice, 1601.

Vantius, Sebastianus (d. 1570). *Tractatus de nullitatibus processuum ac sententiarum.* Venice, 1567.

Vestrius, Octavianus (d. 1573). *In Romanae aulae actionem et iudiciorum mores introductio.* Venice, 1547.

Vitalinis, Bonifacius de (d. 1388). *Tractatus super maleficiis.* Venice, 1560.

Zahn, Balthasar-Conrad. *Tractatus de mendaciis.* Cologne, 1686.

Zilletus, Joannes Baptista (fl. 16th C.). *Criminalium consiliorum atque responsorum.* Venice, 1559.

Zoesius, Henricus (d. 1627). *Commentarius in jus canonicum universum.* Venice, 1757.

INDEX OF BIBLICAL CITATIONS

INDEX OF LEGAL CITATIONS

GENERAL INDEX

Hostiensis, 24, 26, 53, 63, 70, 188,
192, 246, 266, 274, 286, 289,
328–30, 333, 356, 360, 362, 377,
378
Hugh, bishop of Lincoln, 371–72
Huguccio, 25

Illegitimacy, 64, 75, 84–85, 138
Imprisonment: of excommunicates,
358–60; of monks, 234–35
Infamia, effects of, 94, 96, 292, 295,
296–97
Infanticide, 137
Infants. See Minority
Ingratitude, of children, 82
Inheritance: disputed, 96, 119, 372;
jurisdiction over, 117, 119–20
Innocent III, pope, 11, 99, 101,
118–20, 123, 126, 148, 189,
221–22, 235, 324–26, 328, 332, 380
Innocent IV, pope, 24, 58, 110, 129,
266, 289, 301, 356
Inquests, in canon law, 63–64, 292
Inquisition, 28, 270–71, 294–96, 330
Insanity, 223–24
Intention: importance of, in canon
law, 151, 191–92, 198, 210–11,
265, 277–82, 379, 386; irrelevance
of, in canon law, 206–7, 211, 227
Interdict, 329, 363, 375. See also
Censures
Interlocutory decrees, 103–4
Internal forum, 93, 164, 257, 266,
274, 298–302, 330
Investiture controversy, 33–34
Irregularitas, canonical, 53, 64–65,
75, 85, 292, 351
Italy, law of, 143, 273

Ius commune, European, 20, 288,
397; complexity of, 22–24, 129,
literature of, 23–24, 28–31, 257,
267–68, 336–37; uncertainties in,
130–31, 218–19, 269–70, 308–9.
See also Canonists; Civilians
Ius. See Rights
Ivo of Chartres, 4

Jacob's ladder, 124
Jews, 66, 129, 204, 208, 222, 260,
270, 273
John XXII, pope, 15
Jokes, 154, 213; status of, in canon
law, 210–11, 223, 264
Judges delegate, papal, 11, 79, 355
Judges: duties and powers of, 90–91,
152–53, 276, 348, 354, 376,
377–78; in own cause, 265–66,
325, 26; misconduct by, 132–33,
295; recusal of, 103–4, 132. See
also Sentences
Jurisdiction, canonical: basis of,
203–4, 265, 339–40; concurrent,
117, 303–4; conflicts of, with
secular, 194–98, 360; cooperation
of, with secular, 350–52, 364–65;
customary, 117, 137–38, 273,
359–60; episcopal, 3, 119, 123,
330, 352; nature of, 116–18, 120,
135–36, 340, 348, 376, 380; over
baptism, 203–4; over blasphemy,
272–75; principles of, 118–21;
secondary, 121, 132, 141;
superiority of, 123–24, 136,
341–42, 356, 368
Jurisdiction, imperial, 122–23. See
also Secular courts

The Spirit of the Laws

Alan Watson, General Editor

David J. Bederman, *The Spirit of International Law*
John Owen Haley, *The Spirit of Japanese Law*
Bernard G. Weiss, *The Spirit of Islamic Law*
Calum Carmichael, *The Spirit of Biblical Law*
R. H. Helmholz, *The Spirit of Classical Canon Law*
Geoffrey MacCormack, *The Spirit of Traditional Chinese Law*
Alan Watson, *The Spirit of Roman Law*

CPSIA information can be obtained at www.ICGtesting.com
Printed in the USA
LVOW061130211112

308226LV00004B/5/P